1942
THE YEAR THE WAR
CAME TO AUSTRALIA

Peter Grose began his working life as a journalist for the Sydney *Daily Mirror* before becoming the first London correspondent of *The Australian*. He switched from journalism to literary agency, setting up Curtis Brown Australia, then the first literary agency in Australia and now the biggest. After moving to the London office of Curtis Brown, where he continued as a literary agent, he joined the London publisher Martin Secker & Warburg as publishing director. In his 'retirement' he returned to his first love: writing. He is the author of three best-selling history books. He is also the proud holder of British, American and Australian private pilot's licences, and has flown all over Australia, Europe and the United States in single-engined aircraft. His most recent book is *Ten Rogues*. He lives in France.

1942

THE YEAR THE WAR CAME TO AUSTRALIA

The bombing of Darwin and the attack
on Sydney by the Japanese

PETER GROSE

ALLEN&UNWIN
SYDNEY • MELBOURNE • AUCKLAND • LONDON

This edition published in 2021

A Very Rude Awakening first published in 2007

An Awkward Truth first published in 2009

Copyright © in this collection Peter Grose 2021

Allen & Unwin
83 Alexander Street
Crows Nest NSW 2065
Australia
Phone: (61 2) 8425 0100
Email: info@allenandunwin.com
Web: www.allenandunwin.com

A catalogue record for this book is available from the National Library of Australia

ISBN 9 781 76106 664 1

Set in 10.5/16 pt Bembo by Midland Typesetters, Australia
Printed and bound in Australia by Griffin Press, part of Ovato

10 9 8 7 6 5 4 3 2 1

The paper in this book is FSC® certified. FSC® promotes environmentally responsible, socially beneficial and economically viable management of the world's forests.

AN
AWKWARD
TRUTH

*For Anouchka and Tamara, who can both write
their Dad under the table*

Bloody Darwin

This bloody town's a bloody cuss,
No bloody trams, no bloody bus,
And no one cares for bloody us,
Oh bloody, bloody Darwin.

The bloody roads are bloody bad,
The bloody folks are bloody mad,
They even say 'you bloody cad',
Oh bloody, bloody Darwin.

All bloody clouds and bloody rain,
All bloody stones, no bloody drains,
The Council's got no bloody brains,
Oh bloody, bloody Darwin.

And everything's so bloody dear,
A bloody bob for bloody beer,
And is it good? No bloody fear,
Oh bloody, bloody Darwin.

The bloody 'flicks' are bloody old,
The bloody seats are bloody cold,
And can't get in for bloody gold,
Oh bloody, bloody Darwin.

The bloody dances make me smile,
The bloody band is bloody vile,
They only cramp your bloody style,
Oh bloody, bloody Darwin.

No bloody sports, no bloody games,
No bloody fun with bloody dames,
Won't even give their bloody names,
Oh bloody, bloody Darwin.

Best bloody place is bloody bed,
With bloody ice on bloody head,
And then they say you're bloody dead,
Oh bloody, bloody Darwin.

—Anon.
(Soldiers' doggerel, circa 1941)

Contents

Introduction to
the 75th anniversary edition

The birth of Australia as a nation took place on 25 April 1915, so we are told, when Australian troops stormed ashore on the beaches of Gallipoli. For the first time, the mostly British settlers in Australia saw themselves as Australians, not as scattered British colonists in an inhospitable southern wilderness. If that is true, I would argue that Australia became an *independent* nation on 19 February 1942, when the Japanese bombed Darwin.

Consider the evidence. The first two years of the Second World War were fought exclusively in Europe, North Africa and the Middle East. Australia was then a British Dominion, part of the British Empire. When Britain and France declared war on Germany on 3 September 1939, the Australian prime minister, Robert Menzies (a lawyer), thought Australia was legally bound to join the war on Britain's side. Menzies' exact words, in a radio broadcast to the nation, were: 'Great Britain has declared war upon [Germany] and ... *as a result* [my emphasis], Australia is also at war.'

The Royal Australian Navy was simply merged into Britain's Royal Navy, under British command. In 1941 Menzies felt obliged to move to London for a few months, while he held long discussions with Churchill on the conduct of the war, and took part in some British War Cabinet meetings. In his absence, his political enemies plotted his downfall, and they lay in wait for his return. On 28 August 1941 Menzies was forced to resign. After a brief period of turmoil, on 3 October 1941 the opposition Labor Party was asked to form a government, with the untried John Curtin as the new prime minister.

Curtin saw things differently from the anglophile Menzies. Japan had entered the war on 7 December 1941, when it attacked the American Pacific Fleet at anchor in Pearl Harbor. Australia was now directly threatened. The war was no longer confined to Europe, North Africa and the Middle East; it had spread to the Pacific and Australia's doorstep. Less than three weeks after Pearl Harbor, Curtin stood Australian foreign policy on its head. In an article in the Melbourne *Herald* dated 27 December 1941, he wrote: 'The Australian government regards the Pacific struggle as primarily one in which the United States and Australia must have the fullest say in the direction of the democracies' fighting plan.' Then came the killer punch: 'Without any inhibitions of any kind, I make it quite clear that Australia looks to America, free of any pangs as to our traditional links or kinship with the United Kingdom.'

This produced a gasp of shock around Australia. In an editorial, the *Sydney Morning Herald* called the article 'deplorable' (while pinching its nose and reprinting it in full). Australia looks to America, not Britain? Free of any pangs? It sounded like madness. But Curtin's radical thinking was well vindicated seven weeks later, on 15 February 1942, when Britain's 'impregnable' Singapore base fell to the Japanese, opening a gateway to Australia. It was now clear that Britain couldn't or wouldn't—the difference was immaterial—defend Australia.

Four days later the Japanese struck directly. The same carrier force that had devastated Pearl Harbor now wreaked similar havoc on Darwin, dropping more bombs there than they had dropped on Pearl Harbor, and killing more civilians than they had killed at Pearl Harbor.

There could be only one conclusion: Curtin was right. Australia had to fight its own battles, form its own alliances, and look to its own interests. Independent Australia was born that day. The events in the pages that follow are too terrible to call for any celebration, but if Australians want to mark an anniversary of their independence as a nation, 19 February is the day to do it.

I would make one further point. I hope this book, and the television drama documentary *The Bombing of Darwin* that is based on it, have helped to change Australia's perception of events in Darwin on 19 February 1942. When I began researching this book, it quickly became apparent that there were two almost entirely unconnected stories of the Japanese air raid on Darwin. Paul Hasluck, then Australian Minister for Territories, encapsulated the first story—also the best known and the most widely believed—in a speech delivered in Darwin on 25 March 1955. Speaking to the Northern Territory Legislative Council while unveiling a plaque commemorating the civilians killed by bombs in the Darwin Post Office, Hasluck described 19 February as 'not an anniversary of national glory but one of national shame. Australians ran away because they did not know what else to do.'

However, my research led me to another story. Undoubtedly there was panic, incompetence, looting and desertion during and after the Darwin attack. But there was also a disciplined and dogged counter-attack from the Australian anti-aircraft gunners, and an exemplary display of heroism by a tiny handful of US Army Air Corps fighter pilots, blown out of the sky as they squared up to an overwhelmingly superior Japanese force. The doomed yet magnificent reply by the destroyer USS *Peary* as Japanese dive bombers swarmed around her in Darwin harbour, deserves a place in the legend books of American military history. The heroism of the Australian rescuers who braved burning oil, strafing aircraft and huge explosions to pull their comrades to safety is simply beyond praise.

In 1942 the Australian government had a commendable policy of sending only volunteers off to fight in wars overseas. Conscripts stayed behind, to defend the homeland. This led to a division of esteem. The conscripts were known as 'chockos', in other words chocolate soldiers liable to melt in the heat of battle. They were generally treated with contempt by the elite volunteers, and had to suffer inferior training, outdated weapons and poor status. The men who defended Darwin were largely 'chockos', which makes their heroic actions all the more commendable. The Australian Army has campaign medals aplenty for those who served in the Second World War in the Arctic, Africa, the Pacific, Burma, Italy, France and Germany. There is no campaign medal for those who fought in Australia, and no official recognition of their heroism and discipline.

This book has found its way into the hands of many readers. I like to think that it and its associated film have done something to correct that first perception of the Darwin story. The most frequent reaction I've had to the book and the film, either from friends or from readers and viewers, is: I never knew any of this happened. Australians have tended to treat the events in Darwin as a bit of an embarrassment, something best swept under the carpet. I sense this is changing, and Australians are now willing to face up to the worst because it is often balanced by the best. If this book and its film have played a part in that shift in attitudes, I'm delighted.

Peter Grose
December 2016

Chapter I

'Big flight of planes . . . Very high'

As the sun rose in an almost clear sky and the temperature climbed towards the regular Darwin seasonal average of 32°C, 19 February 1942 looked like an unseasonally good day. It was a Thursday and a normal working day. Nevertheless, the good weather meant there might be time after work to walk the dog, have an evening beer on the verandah or go to the open-air picture show. It would also be, if that was your fancy, a perfect day to go flying.

Like most tropical cities, Darwin has no real summer or winter. The seasons are divided into the Wet, between December and March, and the Dry, between May and September. January and February produce the heaviest rainfall, often in the form of violent tropical downpours. A single Darwin thunderstorm can produce 300 millimetres or more of rain and as many as 1600 lightning flashes in the space of two or three hours. The storms are so spectacular that the city today treats them as a tourist attraction, offering visitors and locals alike a *son et lumière* display to make up for the steamy humidity, ankle-deep water and flooded storm drains.

However, the Wet elected to take a day off on 19 February 1942. The sun rose over a few scattered white cumulus clouds and promised the tiny population of Darwin a pleasant morning. There was a sense of relief throughout the town that the evacuation of civilians, mostly women and children, had passed off relatively smoothly. The last batch of evacuees had left by plane the previous day. The two-month exodus reduced the civilian population from an original 5800 to about 2000. Of those who stayed behind, only 63 were women.

◆ ◆ ◆

The two large Tiwi Islands of Bathurst and Melville lie 80 kilometres north of Darwin. A quick glance at a map might lead a casual observer to believe they are a single island, but for the narrow and treacherous Aspley Strait which keeps them apart. Today they make a nice one- or two-day outing for visitors to Darwin looking for something else to do after the obligatory trip to Kakadu National Park. In particular, the art of the Tiwi Island Aborigines is distinctive and much sought after all over the world.

Abel Tasman first sighted the Tiwis in 1644, when he slipped past on his journey to Batavia. The British made a brief attempt in 1824 to establish a fort on Melville Island, but the Tiwi Islanders proved a tough and hostile bunch, and the fort was abandoned in 1828 after one spearing too many. There was no particular reason to settle the islands, and they remained largely untouched by Europeans until the early 20th century. In 1910 Francis Xavier Gsell set up the next European presence there in the form of a Mission of the Sacred Heart. It got off to a slow start. After 28 years Gsell had still not succeeded in converting a single Tiwi adult to Christianity. He fared better with the children, to the point where Tiwi Islanders today are almost all Catholics. Father (later Bishop) Gsell is best remembered for having 150 'wives'. This was not quite as sybaritic as it sounds: he disapproved of the Tiwis' polygamous habits and bought the wives himself to spare them from forced marriages to older men. He then sold them on to men of their own choosing. It was Christian mercy at its practical best.

In February 1942, Father John McGrath ran the Mission of the Sacred Heart at Nguiu. As well as his mission duties, Father McGrath operated as a volunteer coastwatcher. The mission was equipped with a radio transceiver linked to the Amalgamated Wireless of Australia (AWA) Darwin Coastal Station, call sign VID. These so-called aeradio stations were scattered all over Australia and operated by AWA under contract to the Australian Department of Civil Aviation. Civil aircraft used them for both ground-to-air communication and navigation. VID also acted as a voice communication station in contact with other radio transmitters as far away as Dili, in Portuguese Timor.

We can readily imagine a standard mission day for 19 February 1942, starting in the dry and sunny morning with prayer followed by breakfast, then school or work. The mission cared for 300 Tiwi Islanders, so any morning was busy. Work was well under way at 9.30 a.m., when the missionaries and the islanders were brought up short by a sight too disturbing to be ignored. Everybody downed tools to stare. Above them, and flying very high, was a huge formation of planes. They were heading south-east on a track that would take them towards Darwin.

Only 15 minutes earlier, well to the south and out of sight of the Bathurst Island mission, a group of ten American Army Air Corps P40 Kittyhawk fighters escorted by a B17 Flying Fortress bomber had taken off from Darwin's military airfield on their way to reinforce Java. However there were reports of bad weather at their first destination, Koepang, at the western end of Timor, so after less than 20 minutes in the air the Kittyhawks took the Darwin controller's advice and reluctantly turned back. Their return track would bring them well to the south of Bathurst Island and out of view of the mission.

The large formation over Bathurst Island was still highly visible, and Father McGrath switched straight to coastwatcher mode. An emergency radio frequency was kept permanently open and monitored at VID in Darwin, and the priest set off at a brisk pace to the mission's wireless room to call the Coastal Station. His radio set took an agonising time to warm up, but by 9.35 the valves were glowing and he was ready to transmit.

The mission's call sign was Eight SE. 'Eight SE to VID,' Father McGrath began. 'Big flight of planes passed over going south. Very high. Over.'

From VID the duty officer, Lou Curnock, replied: 'Eight SE from VID. Message received. Stand by.'

Father McGrath had no chance to stand by. At about that moment a Japanese aircraft screamed low over the mission on a strafing run, raking it with cannon and machine-gun fire on its way to destroying an American Beechcraft aircraft on the ground at the Bathurst Island airfield. Father McGrath abandoned the radio and raced to shelter. He had unwittingly taken part in a watershed moment in Australian history. For the first time since European settlement 154 years earlier, Australians were under attack on their own soil.

◆ ◆ ◆

Radio operating is a meticulous business, and Lou Curnock stuck by the rules. In his radio log sheet he recorded the time of Father McGrath's message—0935 local—and the readability. It came in as strength four, meaning 'readable but not perfect'. Strength five would be 'perfectly readable'. He recorded atmospherics as A3—'intermittent interference'. He then wrote down the text of the message and of his acknowledgement. His next entry is timed at 0937, two minutes later. 'Phoned R.A.A.F. Operations. 9.37 A [a.m.].'

The protocol was simple. Warning messages like this went first to RAAF Operations, located on the RAAF airfield just outside the town. It was the job of the RAAF duty officer who received the warning to raise the alarm by passing on the message to the RAAF section of Area Combined Headquarters, located at the same airfield. Next the Navy, then the Army, then the civilian air-raid wardens would be alerted, all by the RAAF.

In a situation like this, seconds count. People invariably need to go some distance to a slit trench or air-raid shelter. Fighter aircraft—had there been any—need to be given the order to scramble. Anti-aircraft gunners need to go to action stations and prepare their guns. Predictors who control the AA guns need to start looking for incoming aircraft, to establish fuse setting, height and bearing. With enough warning, ships in a harbour can start engines, cast off their moorings and prepare to take evasive action.

But at RAAF Operations there was uncertainty. The Army's AA gunners had already caused uproar two hours earlier. A group of RAAF Lockheed Hudson bombers had arrived from the north and failed to observe the established 'friendly' route inbound. They had also failed to provide proper light signal identification. Although the AA gunners were reasonably proficient at identifying Japanese aircraft, they had a legitimate worry that the Japanese might use captured Allied aircraft in a surprise attack. There was also, let it be said, some exasperation on the part of the gunners at the RAAF's persistent failure to use correct identification procedures. The Acting Gun Position Officer at Fannie Bay, Sergeant Laurie Huby, had had enough. He ordered a warning shot fired across the path of the inbound Hudsons. This led to indignation all round and a generally jumpy mood at RAAF Operations and at the AA batteries.

As well, RAAF Operations knew that the ten Kittyhawks were now on their way back to Darwin, on a reciprocal track to their westerly route to Timor. A glance at a map might have told them that the Kittyhawks' return track would be well to the south and out of sight of the Bathurst Island mission. But the possibility that the mission had seen the returning Kittyhawks could not be ruled out. Too many false alarms were bad for morale, so the decision to set off the sirens could not be taken lightly. While RAAF Operations pondered, the clocks kept ticking.

The Army maintained a series of observation posts strung out around Darwin. According to the military log: 'Post M4 reports six planes approaching from seawards flying at great height, unable identify at 0938 hours.' Post M4 had trouble getting the message through to the fixed defences. Twelve minutes later, at 0950, the message finally made it. At 0955 it reached the military barracks at Larrakeyah. The clocks kept ticking.

Lieutenant Commander James McManus was senior intelligence

officer at Navy Headquarters on The Esplanade, overlooking Port Darwin. He was chatting to the Naval Officer in Charge, Darwin, Captain Penry Thomas, when the direct-line phone rang. The signalman from RAAF Operations had a simple message: a large number of aircraft had been sighted over Bathurst Island. McManus and Thomas looked at their watches. It was 9.46. McManus spoke first. 'We have 12 minutes before they arrive.'[1]

It was the job of the RAAF to order the air-raid warning sirens to sound. In general, the first siren to go off would be at the airfield. After this, sirens spread around the town would be set off either after a message delivered by landline, or simply by troops and the air-raid wardens overhearing the airfield sirens and following suit. At this point the RAAF was by no means certain that the arriving aircraft were hostile, so no sirens sounded. However, the Navy had a separate warning system, consisting of an old foghorn mounted on the roof of Navy Headquarters. This appears to have sounded some time between 9.46 and 9.58 a.m., but it had limited range and in any case was not associated in the minds of the townspeople with an air raid. They had been told to listen for a series of air-raid siren blasts—four blasts of 30 seconds each, with five seconds in between. Nobody was going to leave their shop or desk and dive into a slit trench or air-raid shelter on the say-so of an old foghorn bleating faintly in the distance.

◆ ◆ ◆

Although the Pacific war was only ten weeks old, Captain Mitsuo Fuchida had already earned a formidable reputation. He had, after all, triggered that war by leading the Japanese aerial assault on Pearl Harbor in a Type 97 'Kate' bomber. Again flying a Kate, he now commanded a slightly larger force of 188 aircraft for the raid on Darwin. Fuchida knew what he was doing. He led his planes on a track that would take them to the north and east of the town, making them hard to see against the tropical morning sun. The huge formation tracked south-east, following the coast of Melville Island as far as Cape Gambier before crossing the narrow Clarence Strait separating Melville from the mainland. They

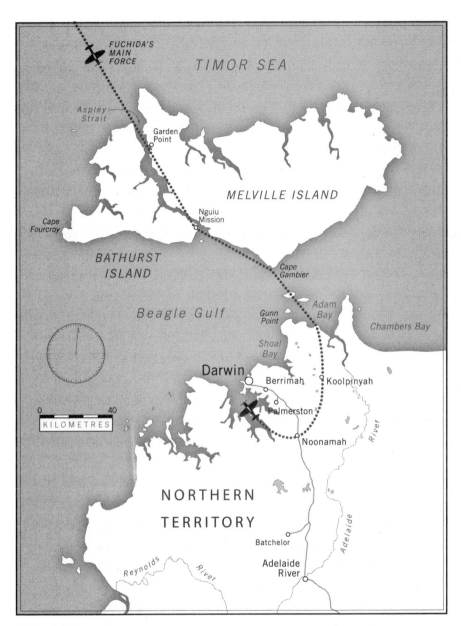

The route taken by the main attacking force of Japanese bombers. Note that the route produces a double benefit: as they cross the coast at Adam Bay, the attackers have the sun behind them when seen from Darwin; and the final line of attack is from the least likely direction, the south-east.

arrived over the Australian coast about 40 kilometres north-east of Darwin, somewhere around Adam Bay. They then followed a huge clockwise arc over Koolpinyah, to the east of Darwin, before swinging around south of the town, passing over Noonamah, then turning back somewhere around the East Arm of Port Darwin onto their final north-west heading, with the harbour, town and Larrakeyah military barracks directly ahead of them. Fuchida had judged correctly that nobody in Darwin would be expecting an attack from that direction.

In 1942 the telephone system in use in Darwin generally involved a kind of 'open line'. Anyone picking up a receiver would very likely overhear other conversations passing through the switchboard. The telephonist at the 14th Anti-Aircraft section based on Darwin Oval had been casually eavesdropping on the town chatter when he overheard an urgent voice say something about a 'dogfight' over the sea. This, as we shall see, was a reference to the first encounter between the returning Kittyhawks and the Japanese fighters. The telephonist did not wait for orders but sounded the alarm for his gunners, and the Oval's AA crews manned their guns.

By now the gunners could hear the roar of approaching aircraft. More sinisterly, the volume of noise from 188 Japanese aircraft pounding towards them was way beyond anything that could be generated by a flight of ten Kittyhawks. Clearly this was something different. The Gun Position Officer swung his Toc I (telescope identification) in the direction of the approaching planes, still half expecting to find Allied aircraft in his sights. The red spots on the wings told another story. He indicated a target, called a bearing, then yelled: 'This is not a false alarm. This is for real! This is for real!'

Out on Darwin wharf, No. 3 gang of dock labourers had opened the No. 1 hatch of the *Neptuna*, ready to start unloading the ship's cargo of explosives and depth charges. Before unloading began, they exercised their right to knock off for ten o'clock 'smoko'. They trooped off to a recreation shed on the wharf. As they did, they saw a huge wave of planes bearing down on them from the south-east. 'Yankee reinforcements at last,' one of the wharfies mocked.

Gunner Jack Mulholland remembers firing the first salvo from the Oval section's anti-aircraft guns before the air-raid sirens sounded, and well before the first bombs struck. The gunners' shells and the bombs crossed in mid-air. The first bombs detonated in the harbour, near the wharf, some time around 9.58 a.m. The same pattern of bombs swept on and caught the wharf itself. The last bomb of the stick detonated on the Oval and showered the gunners with flying rocks, stones, gravel and dirt. The roar of the first bombs merged nicely with the opening wail of the air-raid sirens.

Chapter 2

A very sinful people

Darwin has something of a history of being knocked flat. The most recent memory is of Cyclone Tracy, which struck on Christmas Eve 1974, killing 71 people and leaving the town devastated and in shock. Tracy was not the first. On 6 January 1897 a cyclone hit Darwin at the precise moment that the tide peaked in the harbour. It killed 15 people and wrecked 18 pearling luggers, three sampans and the government launch. The combination of high tide and howling wind pitched some of the wrecked boats a hundred metres or more onto the shore, giving the foreshores the appearance of a boat wrecker's yard. A local preacher proclaimed that it was 'a gentle reminder from Providence that we are a very sinful people'.

Cyclones struck again in 1917 and 1937, each time devastating the town and leaving behind more death and destruction. The local Larrakia Aboriginal people came up with an explanation much in keeping with the views of the 1897 preacher: white settlers had enraged Nungalinya, the Dreamtime ancestor responsible for earthquakes, storms and cyclones, and Nungalinya was taking his revenge. (Nungalinya can be seen to this day in the form of Old Man Rock, off Darwin's Casuarina Beach.)

Whether the destruction was the work of Providence or Nungalinya or merely bad luck, it all gave support to the view that Darwin was no place for the quiet life. From its birth until the mid-20th century, Darwin was a hard-drinking frontier town, a last outpost, perched precariously on the far and steamy fringes of the civilised world.

♦ ♦ ♦

Lieutenant John Lort Stokes first mapped the Darwin area in 1839. He happened to be a friend of the great naturalist Charles Darwin, and he named the place in his honour. The first Europeans, who began arriving in 1869, would have none of it. They were not about to live in a town named after the man who said they were descended from monkeys. They renamed it Palmerston, after a former British prime minister.

European settlement of the area gathered momentum with the construction of the overland telegraph line. As early as the middle of the 19th century an overland and undersea cable from London terminated on the island of Java, in the Dutch East Indies. Furious competition broke out between the Australian colonies of Victoria, Queensland and South Australia (which then included what is now the Northern Territory) to complete the Australian link. South Australia won. In 1862 John McDouall Stuart, at his sixth attempt, finally crossed the continent from Adelaide and Port Augusta in South Australia to the Northern Territory coast, and returned to tell the tale.[1] He reached the sea about 80 kilometres east of the present site of Darwin, at a place he named Chambers Bay. Stuart's expedition proved that a north–south telegraph route across Australia was feasible. In 1870, a year after the arrival of the first European settlers, work began at both ends of the telegraph line, the aim being to meet in the middle. A separate company set about laying a submarine cable from Java to Palmerston. Thirty-six thousand poles and 3200 kilometres of floods and hardship later, on 22 August 1872 the lines all met, linking Java to Palmerston and Palmerston to Adelaide in South Australia. Australia was now in instant contact with the rest of the world.

Palmerston became a critical link in the chain of communication between Britain's most distant colonies and London. That would hardly have been enough to attract settlers to the otherwise swampy and hostile tropical outpost. However, in 1865 gold was discovered in modest quantities at the Finniss River, just south of Palmerston, followed by further modest finds at nearby Tumbling Waters. Gold even found its way to the surface in the diggings from an overland telegraph post hole at Yam Creek. Rumours spread. Gold fever hit hard with the discovery in 1872 of the big Priscilla reef at Pine Creek. Miners poured in, especially Chinese, to the point where Chinese gold miners at Pine Creek outnumbered Europeans 15 to 1. Towns sprang up. The Northern Territory underwent its first boom.

The overland telegraph opened the rest of Australia's eyes to the possibilities of the empty north, and a new breed of settler began to arrive. Cattle station owners from South Australia sent their sons north to claim vast tracts of land around Alice Springs. Queensland's cattle barons looked west and snapped up the cattle country of the Top End, with Palmerston as the key town. By the turn of the 20th century a pearling industry was well established along the northern and western coasts of Australia. Palmerston/Darwin never quite matched Broome, in Western Australia, for the quality and quantity of its pearls, but it was a major player in the world pearling industry. Then, just before the outbreak of the First World War, the British company Vestey built a giant meat-works in Darwin. While it lasted, the Vestey works gave new importance to Port Darwin as a distribution centre for beef as well as minerals.

The biggest losers were the Aboriginal people. Although they managed to maintain their traditional lifestyle in large areas of the Territory and continued to outnumber the European population until well into the 20th century, too many were forced off their lands by the cattlemen and by the miners and mining companies, large and small, digging for gold, copper, silver and tin. Some Aboriginals found work as stockmen on the cattle stations. Others worked in the mines. Those who found employment with the new European businesses were ruthlessly exploited, usually working for little or no pay beyond rations. Women could sometimes find domestic work in the homesteads or towns, again for little or no pay. Aboriginal camps sprang up on the edges of settlements. A few Christian missions offered rudimentary schooling and health care, and sometimes rations to lure children into the classroom. In general, the Aboriginals were marginalised, victimised and even massacred.

Throughout the 19th and early 20th centuries, there was a widespread belief that white men could not handle hard manual work in the tropics. So, whatever the White Australia policy might have dictated elsewhere, there was no squeamishness about importing non-European labour into the Territory. Rich Chinese brought some 3000 Chinese indentured labourers to work on construction of the Darwin to Pine Creek railway. At the time there were only 400 Europeans in the whole Top End. During the wet season the Chinese employers switched their labour force to the search for alluvial gold. Chinese who had came to the territory as part of the gold hunt retreated to the towns as shopkeepers and businessmen. Darwin catered to their every need, including the establishment of gambling rooms and—so went the rumour—opium dens in Cavenagh Street, known as Chinatown. The Chinese were more tolerated than liked by the minority Europeans, but as long as they provided much-needed services they could stay.

The Japanese were essential for pearling. They had a near monopoly on the necessary diving skills. Japanese luggers and their crews made Darwin their base. Non-British Europeans arrived in Darwin to swell the mixed population: Greeks in particular poured in, followed by Italians. In Darwin today there is a small but touching monument in the smart Smith Street shopping mall celebrating the link between Darwin and the Greek island of Kalymnos. More people from Kalymnos live in Darwin than anywhere else except Kalymnos.

The wild atmosphere of the tropical north of Australia in its pioneering days is beautifully caught by A.B. 'Banjo' Paterson, creator of 'Waltzing Matilda'. Two incidents from his travel diary *Happy Dispatches* paint the picture. The first took place on Thursday Island, off the northern tip of Queensland, but it might as well have been written about Darwin. On 30 July 1901 Paterson recorded:

There are more nationalities here than there were at the Tower of Babel—every Caucasian nation, local blacks, kanakas [South Sea Island indentured labourers], Chinese, Japanese, Javanese, Malays, New Guinea boys. The local white police have to be very wide awake to nip any troubles in the bud; for, when the Orientals, especially the Malays, have any grievance to avenge, they go stark staring mad. So the police here act like American police—club them first and find out about the trouble afterwards. Nobody has any rights up here; the glorious doctrine of democracy does not run north of Rockhampton. A pearler engaged two men, a Malay and a kanaka, to work on his lugger, and gave them the usual advance of ten pounds. They made a plot to stow away on our ship and get away with the tenners. The Malay billiard-marker at the local hotel gave the plot away and the kanaka was captured and locked up. The Malay evaded capture till dark. Then he went to the hotel, called out the billiard-marker and opened fire on him with a revolver. The first bullet took the ground; the second hit a bystander; and the third broke some bottles on the bar. The billiard-marker ran upstairs chattering like an ape. The barmaid lay flat on the floor among the bottles. She said: 'I guessed he would have to fire low if he wanted to lay me out.' Then the Malay decamped, and up to the time we left he was at large in Thursday Island.

The journey continued to Darwin. Paterson resumed:

Off Port Darwin. One of these violent little interludes that occasionally enliven a tropical voyage was staged to-day. The chief steward had been allowed to bring his wife with him as far as Port Darwin on their honeymoon trip, and the lady had laid out all her best clothes on the bed, intending to stagger Port Darwin when she went ashore. A Malay deckhand, washing down the decks, let a full head of water go down a ventilator into the cabin, soaking the lady and her clothes and the chief steward's papers. The chief steward ran on deck and hit the Malay; then the Malay dropped the hose and charged straight at the steward with a *kris* in his hand. The steward ran for his life with the Malay after him, round the horse-stalls and up the alley-way like a rabbit. The steward darted through the door into his cabin, and while the Malay was fumbling with the lock the second engineer arrived, hit the Malay a couple of times, took his *kris* from him, and scragged him back to his work.

♦ ♦ ♦

Rather like the Wild West of America, the Northern Territory needed an urgent dose of law and order, not to mention managed development. The system of government put in place was, however, less than ideal and well short of democratic. The Northern Territory had been part of the colony of South Australia, but this proved to be a failure, particularly when it came to development. The cattle industry in the Top End never lived up to expectations. Vesteys closed the meat-works after a mere three years. The Northern Territory historian Bob Alford summed it up: 'For almost 50 years successive South Australian administrations had encouraged and supported all manner of projects to realise the economic potential of the Territory. None of these efforts met with success and by 1910 the public debt on the Northern Territory account was nearly £4 million. Moves by SA to transfer the NT to the new Commonwealth government began in earnest in 1905 in the hope of relieving the state of the ever-mounting liabilities of its dependency.'

In 1911 the South Australians finally got their way and passed control of the Northern Territory to the new Federal Government. Prime Minister Alfred Deakin put the best face he could on it by declaring: 'To me the question has been not so much commercial as national, first, second, third and last. Either we must accomplish the peopling of the Northern Territory or submit to its transfer to some other nation.' In other words, if something was not done fast to build up the Territory, some other nation—Russia? Japan? China?—would step into the gap. As part of the Territory's fresh start under Commonwealth rule, on

18 March 1911 the governor-general, the Earl of Dudley, renamed the town of Palmerston. Darwin it was to be, monkeys notwithstanding.

Deakin and his successors governed the Northern Territory like a subject colony, rather as they administered Papua and New Guinea. The Territorians elected a single member to the House of Representatives in Canberra. Otherwise they were spared the trouble of having to vote. Their sole representative was similarly spared: at first he could neither speak nor vote in Parliament. Canberra appointed an Administrator, based in Darwin, and he ruled on Canberra's behalf, under the direction of the Minister for Territories and without the benefit of popular support.

Not to be outdone, the population of Alice Springs asked if they could have their own separate Administrator. Instead they were given a District Officer. The phrase 'District Officer' conjures up an image of a mustachioed and pith-helmeted public servant in khaki shorts dispensing justice to the fuzzy-wuzzies from a tent somewhere in the bush. It was, of course, a bit more businesslike than that. But the job titles left the local population in no doubt that they were colonial subjects with little or no say in how they were governed. In the 1930s Darwin briefly had a Town Council, but this modest experiment in democratic local government quickly collapsed, and its powers were handed back to the Administrator. The man from Canberra would see to it all.

Brough Newell, a Darwin solicitor who later became Director of First Aid in Darwin's Air Raid Precautions unit, summed it up as follows: 'We have no Government. We have two taxing authorities. We pay the ordinary Commonwealth tax, Territorial income tax, stamp duty, and we also pay the Commonwealth government, the Municipal rates, and what is called the health rate. We have no Parliamentary representative and have not got a State Parliament to decide who is to carry the baby. No one carries it in Darwin.' Yet, incredibly, this remained the system of government in the Northern Territory until 1947, when the Federal Government in Canberra finally granted limited powers to a 13-man Legislative Council. Only six of the councillors were elected: the remaining seven, who included the Administrator, were appointed by

Canberra. The Northern Territory did not have a democratically elected Parliament until 1978, when a Legislative Assembly took over the administration of the Territory for the first time.

♦ ♦ ♦

As happens in every democracy, government appointees to prestigious jobs are usually politicians who have either passed their prime or need to be got out of the way. Aubrey Abbott, appointed Northern Territory Administrator on 29 March 1937 by the conservative Menzies government, could claim a bit of both. He came from a solid political background. His two uncles had been members of the New South Wales Legislative Assembly, while two of his cousins were elected to Federal Parliament. Abbott left school at 14 and went to work on cattle stations. In 1908, at the age of 22, he joined the New South Wales Police and remained with it until the outbreak of the First World War. He served with distinction in the Army. He fought at Gallipoli, where he was commissioned, then took part in the famous Australian Light Horse charge at Beersheba. He was wounded and promoted to Captain.

On his return to Australia, his Uncle William helped him to buy Echo Hills, a sheep and cattle station near Tamworth, New South Wales. He became active in the Graziers Association and politically active in the Country Party. In 1925 he was elected to Federal Parliament for the seat of Gwydir. In 1928 he joined the government as Minister for Home Affairs. The Northern Territory became part of his responsibilities. He lost the Gwydir seat in the 1929 election.

The Great Depression now struck, with its attendant social unrest. According to the *Australian Dictionary of National Biography*, Abbott appears to have responded by becoming an organiser for the New Guard, a loony right-wing paramilitary group that was as near as Australia ever came to Britain's Blackshirts or Mosleyites. His career on the right-wing fringe ended in 1931, when he recaptured the Gwydir seat. He remained in Parliament (but not in government) until his appointment as Administrator.

The government announced that appointment three weeks to the day after the deadly 1937 cyclone struck Darwin, causing one death and leaving a trail of devastation across the town. Winds gusting up to 158 kilometres an hour sent waves breaking over the cliffs on the port foreshore. Trashed buildings littered the landscape. His Honour's first task would be to supervise the rebuilding of the town.

Administrator Abbott controlled the police and public servants and all the usual trappings of colonial power. However, he was not the only authority in the Northern Territory. The Army, Navy and Air Force all answered to their own military hierarchies. There was a third significant force: workers were heavily unionised, and trade union leaders enjoyed a level of power and influence unimaginable today. Each was elected to office, so each could claim a democratic mandate not shared by the Administrator. There was only one newspaper in Darwin at the time, the *Northern Standard*, and it was owned and controlled by the powerful North Australian Workers' Union (NAWU). The *Standard* was a captivating mish-mash of local news and shameless left-wing propaganda. Every minor Russian military success was trumpeted as though it marked a turning point in the war, while no slight to a trade unionist was too trivial to escape the *Standard's* pitiless gaze. Within four months of his arrival in Darwin, Abbott had alienated both the NAWU and the *Northern Standard* by organising a group of civil servants as strikebreakers to intervene in an industrial dispute on the wharves. From then on, as far as the unions were concerned, he was the enemy.

Thus a picture emerges of Abbott as an old-fashioned right-winger with a strong leaning towards pastoralists and landowners. He regularly attended meetings of the executive committee of the Northern Territory Pastoral Lessees Association. While happily mixing with the 'elite' of Darwin society, he made little secret of his contempt for the rest, whom he regarded as riff-raff. His divisive personality and lack of rapport with most of those he administered would shortly cost both the Administrator and the town of Darwin dearly.

◆ ◆ ◆

The European war got under way on 3 September 1939. By 1941 roughly half of Australia's Army had embarked for foreign shores: two and a half infantry divisions faced Germans, Italians and Vichy French in the Middle East; a further division shipped off to Malaya, ready to defend Singapore. The Royal Australian Navy sent about half its strength to the Red Sea, Mediterranean and Atlantic to fight as part of Britain's Royal Navy. Australian airmen were assigned to British RAF squadrons in Europe, where they fought in the Battle of Britain. This was normal. Australians had never been forced to defend their own territory against foreign attack, and anyway there was no war near home to fight. They slipped seamlessly into their traditional role alongside Britain, and that meant shipping large quantities of men and military equipment to the other side of the world.

Although more than half of the RAAF's planes remained on Australian soil, that still left Australia pitifully short of any serious air defence. Even in April 1941, with the war 19 months old, the RAAF's best fighting strength at home consisted of 67 ineffectual Wirraway fighters and 60 Hudson bombers. As long as the war continued to be fought in the northern hemisphere, the RAAF's principal role was not to defend Australia but to take advantage of the more reliable flying conditions Australia offered to train pilots for the European war. This was the Empire Air Training Scheme (EATS), which relied on Canada, Australia, New Zealand and Rhodesia to maintain a steady flow of pilots to confront the Luftwaffe in Europe. EATS became Australia's key contribution to the air war.

◆　◆　◆

The citizens of Darwin were never in doubt that, if war did finally reach Australia, their town would be among the first to come under attack. Anyone who owned a school atlas could work that out. However they appear to have felt no obligation to do much about it. As early as September 1939, in the first month of the war, the Red Cross organised public lectures in Darwin on First Aid, Home Nursing, Air Raid Precautions (ARP), Anti-gas and Transport. Hardly anybody from the town turned up. As long as the war remained half a world away, what was the point?

Civil Defence, as its name implies, is usually a matter for the civilian administration and not a military responsibility. In June 1940 the Government Secretary, L.H.A. Giles, held a conference in his office. He invited the Chief Surveyor, a newly arrived public servant called Arthur Miller who administered land divisions throughout the Northern Territory, to take on extra duties as Chief Air Raid Warden. The Administration proved unable to deliver much by way of support for its new Civil Defence supremo. Miller wrote afterwards: 'Assistance was promised from many quarters but it was found later that little was forth-coming.' Things got worse rather than better. Darwin's citizens are not easily led at the best of times, and the division of the town into ten ARP groups under the control of a Senior Warden, with each group broken into sectors under control of a Sector Warden, produced zero result. By July 1940, Miller wrote: 'The whole organisation contained 75 per cent of Government officers and the public generally ignored its existence, at the same time holding its members up to ridicule. Volunteers for first aid squads were called for, also for fire fighting and demolition, but the response was negligible.' Two months later, in August 1940, Miller reported: 'A general appeal was issued for the con-struction of shelters by volunteer labour. Only two groups, Nos. 8 & 9, responded, but in a half-hearted manner. Several shelters were constructed at the workmen's camp at the R.A.A.F. aerodrome, and commencement was made on one at Parap where eight men turned up on a Saturday afternoon. Within three weeks this work was abandoned owing to lack of volunteers.'

By February 1941 the international situation had worsened. As we shall see in the next chapter, Japan looked increasingly likely to enter the war on the Axis side. If Japan declared war and struck south, the threat to Darwin from sea and air would be immense. Administrator Abbott asked Miller if the ARP organisation could be revived. Miller appears to have been more successful this time. First Aid classes were well attended; the Army, Navy and Air Force consulted with the ARP organisation to draw up Notices to Householders and Notices to Business Houses, setting out what was required of them in the event of an attack; and in May 1941 a trial blackout was held. The results, according to Miller, were 'excellent'.

At this point Miller felt the burden of two jobs was beyond him, and he recommended the appointment of a Permanent Officer in charge of ARP. He had his way. 'Mr Harrison, a draftsman in my office, was appointed to the position,' Miller wrote later. 'Working with the General Staff, an extensive programme was prepared wherein every phase of A.R.P. work was covered. This even provided for the evacuation of the female population and children, and the aged and infirm. Estimates of the requirements were prepared and forwarded. The latter covered the cost of equipment needed and the labour for certain shelters and aid posts.'

This burst of activity rapidly went the way of earlier schemes. Let Miller take up the story again:

From September [1941] onwards, apathy crept in again, and the number of wardens diminished to some extent. The attitude of the general public remained the same as ever, a laissez faire attitude mostly, and we were told that we were wasting our time, that nothing would ever happen.

Ten days before Japan declared war, a public meeting was called to take place at the Public School. This meeting was well advertised, but apart from the Wardens, only two members of the public turned up.

◆ ◆ ◆

It is ironic that communication in the form of the overland telegraph line was the making of Darwin, because communication now became its biggest headache. Until as recently as 4 February 2004 there was no railway line connecting Darwin to the rest of Australia. The main rail link from Adelaide in South Australia to the Northern Territory ended at Alice Springs, 1500 kilometres south of Darwin. This was the legendary Ghan train, a contraction of its original name, *The Afghan Express*. That, in turn, honoured the Afghan camel-train drivers who had earlier followed the same route north. Work on the Ghan railway began in 1878, but the line did not reach Alice Springs until 1929.

Another line ran from Darwin to Birdum, about 500 kilometres south, but it was both narrow gauge and poorly laid, so it could not carry much by way of heavy traffic. The local population, and later the soldiers who had the misfortune to travel on it, referred to the engine as 'Leaping Lena', and to the whole train as the 'Spirit of Protest'. Even Leaping Lena still left a yawning gap of 1000 kilometres of scrub and desert between Birdum and the railhead at Alice Springs.

Road transport could bridge the gap for an average of only eight months a year. Before war broke out, the road between Darwin and Alice Springs was little better than a dirt track. In the four months of the Wet it became a slippery, treacherous quagmire. In 1940, the states of Queensland, New South Wales and South Australia combined to resurface about 500 kilometres of the road with gravel, replacing the sand and mud. The first Army convoy made its way gingerly up the new road in March 1941. But despite the genuine efforts of the three states, in 1942 the road remained unreliable in the Wet. Without proper grounding and draining and a tarred surface, cars and trucks regularly bogged down on what the Territorians still call 'the track'.

The other land access to the Northern Territory was via the far-western railheads of Queensland, notably Cloncurry and Mt Isa. Stock routes linked cattle stations in the Northern Territory to western Queensland, but these were scarcely even tracks: they were suitable for men on horseback and for cattle on the hoof, but not for heavy trucks or even cars. In the Wet they were impassable. Until well into 1942 there was nothing linking Queensland and the Northern Territory that could decently be called a road. There were tracks through the cattle stations, but these were little more than pairs of haphazard wheel ruts dodging between the anthills. The Army found this unacceptable, and in March 1941 the government in Canberra approved construction of what is now known as the Barkly Highway, linking Camooweal in western

Queensland with Tennant Creek in the Northern Territory. Until this was built, and until the road from Darwin to Alice Springs was properly surfaced, no bulk goods or people could move reliably by road to or from Darwin for four months of the year, until the Wet ran its course.

The movement of supplies by air is a comparatively new phenomenon, largely forced on planners by the demands of the Second World War. The first serious air freighter was the Douglas DC3 whose maiden flight took place on 17 December 1935. The mass production of Dakotas did not really hit its stride until the United States entered the Second World War in late 1941. At the outbreak of war, civil aircraft in Australia were mostly light, designed to carry not much more than mail and a few passengers. The idea that a town the size of Darwin could be supplied by air would never have occurred to anybody.

That left sea transport. The only way bulk freight could reliably move into or out of Darwin all year round was by sea. So the harbour in Darwin was more than just a convenience: it was Darwin's only full-time lifeline to the outside world.

◆　◆　◆

If anyone had set out to design the worst possible port facility imaginable, they might easily have come up with the Darwin harbour of the first half of the 20th century.[2] Stokes Hill Wharf today is a slightly faded example of conspicuous consumption, overshadowed by the smart new Convention Centre nearby. At the end of the wharf is a collection of bars and fast-food cafés, plus an up-market seafood restaurant packed nightly with tourists and Darwin yuppies. The ships that tie up there now are often round-the-world luxury cruise liners full of well-heeled holidaymakers from Asia, Europe and the United States. The Convention Centre and wharf complex today reek of prosperity and all-purpose international good living. To put it mildly, it was not always like this.

Port Darwin has huge tides, so ships at the wharf regularly rise and fall by seven metres or more twice a day. That would have made life difficult enough, but the design of the wharf piled on more misery. The wharf itself had no cranes, so goods had to be unloaded using the ships' own derricks. These were usually lighter than a typical shore-based crane and therefore carried smaller loads in their slings. Lifting hundreds or even thousands of tons of freight in small lots from the hold of a ship bobbing up and down seven metres every 12 hours was no picnic. At low tide, when the ship dipped furthest from wharf level, the job was almost impossible. The shipboard derricks were often not tall enough to lift goods onto the wharf. The ships themselves invariably had no air conditioning in the hold, so the hard physical work of unloading in the tropical heat was both uncomfortable and exhausting.

The problems did not end there. The wharf itself was a triumph of bad design. The first Stokes Hill Wharf was built in 1885 and promptly eaten by termites. The second wharf, generally known as Town Wharf, was built on the same site in 1904 and remained Darwin's only wharf until the Japanese raid. It could take no more than two ships at a time, one berthed on the inside and one on the outside.

The design beggars belief. The railway line from Birdum in the south led ultimately to the wharf. Tracks ran along the wharf itself for about 100 metres. Then, for reasons known only to the original designer, the wharf turned a right angle, known as the 'Elbow'. On the elbow was a turntable operated by a steam-driven 'donkey engine'. A locomotive could shunt rail cars as far as the turntable but not beyond. The turn-table would accommodate only two cars at a time. Once they had been shunted into place, the donkey engine then spun the turntable through 90 degrees to line the carriages up with rail tracks running along the wharf right-angle's outer arm. The carriages were then dragged two at a time *by hand* a further 100 metres to put them alongside the ships being unloaded. A maximum of five carriages at any one time could be accommodated on the loading arm of the wharf. Once a carriage was loaded it would then be pushed, again by hand, back to the turntable. Because of the added weight, the wharf labourers could push the loaded carriages only one at a time. Once two loaded carriages had been dragged to the turntable, the donkey engine would spin them through 90 degrees to line up with the original track. A locomotive then dragged the loaded trucks back to land. It was unbelievably slow, inefficient and wasteful.[3] Given that the sea route was the only reliable year-round transport serving Darwin, the Darwin wharf was not, in the management-speak of the 21st century, 'fit for purpose'.

◆ ◆ ◆

One day someone will write an honest history of the role and behaviour of Australia's trade unions during the Second World War. There is not room for it in this book, nor would it be appropriate in what is simply an account of the Darwin air raid of 19 February 1942. Nevertheless there is a story to be told, and some of it would not make pretty reading. When John Curtin's Labor government came to power on 3 October 1941, taking over from the conservative Robert Menzies, the new prime minister might have reasonably expected a better level of cooperation from his comrades in the trade union movement. After all, he had been secretary of a small trade union himself, his only public office before becoming prime minister. He shrewdly chose the firebrand Sydney left-winger Eddie Ward as his Minister for Labour and National Service, and Eddie Ward set off to talk to the unions man to man. It didn't work. In vital industries like coal mining and the wharves, union militancy was the order of the day. Coal production actually fell under Eddie Ward's stewardship. The unions might once have seen Eddie Ward as one of their own, but when it came to a choice between facilitating the war effort or downing tools, they knew where their loyalties lay. They struck, and struck again.

In Darwin the working conditions for the wharfies, as Australians call their stevedores, were undoubtedly grim. As described above, the heat was intolerable and safety levels were lamentable. As well, the abysmal workings of the Darwin wharf made for poor morale in the workforce. That having been said, the wharfies were militant to a point where the troops and the townspeople saw them as something akin to saboteurs. Wharfies loved a good strike everywhere in Australia, but in Darwin they enjoyed it more than most. Scarcely a day went by without some sort of trouble on the wharves. It became a standing joke in the town. Whenever anything ran short, it could always be explained with the phrase: 'It's on the ship.' And why was it still on the ship? 'Blame the wharfies.'

♦ ♦ ♦

This, then, was the scene in Darwin when the Pacific War began. It was a town still being rebuilt after a devastating cyclone four years earlier. About 5800 people lived there in mostly ramshackle wooden houses lining mostly unpaved streets. For six months of the year it was uncomfortably hot and dry. For four months it was uncomfortably hot and wet. For the remaining two months it was a bit of both. Darwin was home to a mixed population of white Australians, Europeans, Chinese, Malays, Japanese, Timorese, Filipinos and Aboriginal Australians, some 'full bloods' and some of 'mixed blood', all of them convinced they had been forgotten and abandoned at the far edge of civilisation. The town was virtually cut off from the rest of Australia except via one of the most inefficient harbours in the world. It lived on cattle, mining, fish and pearls. It had no elected government, only an appointed Administrator who held its citizens in contempt. It was hardly going to present a united front in a crisis.

Chapter 3

Horribly strained relations

The Japanese fought on the allied side in the First World War but felt cheated of a proper reward for their part in the victory over Germany. In the postwar division of spoils they were granted a mandate over the former German colonies of the Marianas and the Caroline and Marshall Islands (which they had already captured in the course of the war). This may have troubled Australia, where it was seen as bringing the Japanese too close for comfort, but it was a meagre return for a substantial contribution to the war effort in the Pacific. Worse, although Japan now saw herself as a major power, she found herself once more forced into a corner by her erstwhile allies. The Washington Naval Treaty of 1922 and the London Naval Treaty of 1930 limited Japanese sea power to 60 per cent of the sea strength of the United States and of Britain. Japan had asked for 70 per cent.

The Japanese based their demands on a fairly simple calculation. Military orthodoxy at the time said that a navy needed to be able to field 150 per cent of the enemy's strength before it could be confident of mounting a successful attack. With Japan at 70 per cent of either country's strength, Britain or America would need one-and-a-half times that to be confident of success, or 105 per cent of what they had. At

70 per cent Japan would be safe from attack. At 60 per cent it would be exposed to (likely successful) attack by 90 per cent of either the British or American navies. So the 60 per cent ruling left Japan feeling vulnerable and deeply uneasy.

Japan's foreign policy never wavered throughout the first decades of the 20th century. The Japanese felt there should be an Asian nation among the great powers of the world, and they nominated themselves for the task. By the 1930s they were hinting at plans for a Greater East Asia Co-prosperity Sphere, though they did not formally announce the project until 1 August 1940. They had in mind that the United States, Britain, France, Holland and Portugal should gracefully abandon their Asian and Pacific possessions and allow them to pass into Japan's sphere of influence. They even offered to include Australia and New Zealand in the package. The five colonial powers concerned greeted this with less than acclamation, as did the Australians and New Zealanders. In an atmosphere of mounting acrimony, Japan withdrew from both the League of Nations and the two naval treaties, and began a furious program of warship and warplane building.

Although the government of Japan came to be dominated by the military, there were wide philosophical differences between the rival armed forces. The Japanese had already fought a war with Russia in 1904–05, ending in a clear if narrow win for Japan. The Japanese Army remained convinced that Russia was the logical enemy and based its plans on a return match. The Navy, on the other hand, saw the United States and its powerful Pacific Fleet as the most likely opponent and began planning accordingly. So the Army looked west for an enemy, while the Navy faced east.

In fairness, the Imperial Japanese Navy's plans in the beginning were entirely defensive. It expected the first attack to come from the United States, not the other way round. The Japanese fleet was designed to mount an effective defence in home waters. They accepted that Japan could not match the industrial output of the United States in terms of quantity. Instead they concentrated on quality. Their ships would have less range than the American ones but would be faster, better armed, and more suited to fighting in the stormy waters near home.

Japan opened the Co-prosperity Sphere account in 1931 by seizing Manchuria, which they renamed Manchukuo, setting up a puppet government there. This move was badly received by China, and the two countries began jostling and glowering at each other in a series of 'incidents'. Full-scale war broke out after one incident too many, on 7 July 1937. The Japanese had no capacity to conquer and subdue a country with seven times their population: their only hope was to overturn the weak and corrupt nationalist government of Chiang Kai-Shek's Kuomintang and put a puppet government of their own choosing in its place. As fighting continued, Japan managed to seize and hold some Chinese territory, but the war meandered along inconclusively. There was no shortage of death and destruction, merely a shortage of clear-cut results.

Japanese expansion increasingly worried the western powers, particularly those with something to lose. France then held the Indo-Chinese colonies of Laos, Cambodia and Vietnam, plus a scattering of Pacific islands. Britain had Hong Kong, Singapore, Malaya and Burma. The Dutch had the East Indies (now Indonesia). The Portuguese had East Timor. The United States controlled the Philippines, the Hawaiian Islands and their own scattering of small Pacific islands including Wake and Midway. All were targets for the Co-prosperity Sphere, and Japan was clearly on the move.

The United States led the anti-Japanese push. In January 1940 President Franklin Roosevelt ended his country's commercial treaty with Japan. In June of the same year he imposed limited sanctions, banning exports of aviation motor fuels and lubricants and No. 1 heavy melting iron and steel scrap. He also stepped up support for China.

The Japanese were unfazed. In September 1940 they signed a deal with Vichy France, still nominally in control of France's Indo-Chinese colonies, which allowed the Japanese to station a limited number of troops in Vietnam. They justified this by saying the troops were needed to block the supply route through Vietnam to China. Having been given an inch, the Japanese took a mile. Troops poured into Vietnam, using force against any who stood in their way, including their supposed Vichy partners. The French were powerless to stop them.

Next the Japanese had a stroke of luck. On 10 January 1941 the Thais, noting the ease with which Japan had pushed back the French in Vietnam, struck at the French colonies of Laos and Cambodia, quickly capturing most of Laos. The Japanese stepped in as mediators between the Thais and the Vichy French. The upshot was agreement with the French that Japan should 'station' troops in the whole of northern Indo-China. By July 1941 some 120,000 troops had moved in, brushing aside any resistance they encountered on the way. It might not have been called an invasion, but for most observers it was hard to spot the difference.

This proved too much for the western powers. Roosevelt decided he had to crack down hard. On 26 July 1941 the United States froze all Japanese assets, effectively imposing a complete ban on trade between the two countries. For good measure Roosevelt closed the Panama Canal to Japanese shipping. A week later he specifically banned all supply of oil to Japan. The British government and the Dutch government in exile followed suit. Japan was now between a rock and a hard place. Eighty per cent of Japan's oil came from the United States. It needed an alternative source, and fast. The most promising target looked like the Dutch East Indies, particularly Java, where oil flowed in abundance.

Suddenly the creation of the Greater East Asia Co-prosperity Sphere became not a vague dream of Japanese grandeur but a matter of life and death. The Japanese saw the problem, and the likely solution, quickly and clearly. Not long after the embargo was imposed, American code-breakers intercepted a cable from Japanese Foreign Minister Teijiro Toyoda to his ambassador to the United States, Kichisaburo Nomura. Toyoda wrote: 'Commercial and economic relations between Japan and third countries, led by England and the United States, are gradually becoming so horribly strained that we cannot endure it much longer. Consequently, our Empire, to save its very life, must take measures to secure the raw materials of the South Seas.'

◆　◆　◆

In the 1930s Japan was fortunate to have some of the most brilliant and clear-headed military thinkers anywhere in the world, as the Allies were shortly to find to their cost. In particular, Admiral Isoroku Yamamoto, Commander in Chief of the Combined Fleet, and Admiral Osami Nagano, the Chief of the Naval General Staff, were sophisticated and able men. Both had served as naval attachés in Washington, and both knew America's strengths well.

They were supported by able younger officers capable of radical thinking. While the early focus in the shipyards was on building super-battleships, others saw a different future for naval warfare. Mitsuo Fuchida, later to lead the air attacks on Pearl Harbor and Darwin, remembers a debate at the Japanese Naval College in the late 1930s, where he took the lead by arguing: 'We must abandon the idea that all we need to do is outbuild our rivals in warships. In the future, aircraft will be the decisive factor. Conventional naval armament based on surface strength has become largely ornamental.' The Imperial Japanese Navy came to the same radical conclusion. Japanese shipyards raced to produce aircraft carriers as well as battleships. However, the emphasis remained on quality: Japanese aircraft carriers needed to be the best.

Deep divisions remained, particularly between the Army and the Navy. Whatever the frustrations of the war with China, the Army was spoiling for a fight with Russia. The easy success of the invasions of Manchuria and Indo-China (let us abandon euphemisms about 'stationing' troops there) led the Army to believe the time was ripe for further expansion on the Asian mainland. The Navy was less sure. It saw the United States as the logical enemy. Yamamoto in particular had a healthy respect for America's industrial strength. He argued that Japan could not hope to win an extended war against the United States, and he remained opposed to war.

While these arguments raged, the Navy's backroom strategists began to develop a whole new concept for the use of sea power. As we have seen, the Navy's original strategy had been to prepare itself to defend the Japanese homeland. Until well into the 1930s it was a defensive force, not an attacking force. The new situation in 1941, when oil would have to be seized by one means or another, meant that the Japanese would have to go out looking for it. They would have to cross oceans to do it, and that meant the Navy would spearhead the attack.

Before 1941, a naval attack on a land target involved warships standing off the enemy coast to pound their objective with heavy guns. This inevitably meant the attacking ships would be easily seen by the enemy and met with shore-based guns and planes, not to mention enemy ships. The Japanese Navy had a new idea. What if, they asked, the naval force stayed hundreds of miles from the target, out of sight and out of range of shore guns and shore patrols, and used ship-launched bombers instead of the ships' guns to carry out the attack? The sheer suddenness of the strike would mean that, with luck, the attackers would have the advantage of surprise. Once the target had been rendered harmless by the planes, the Army and Navy surface ships could move in as required. The planners considered all the implications. The bombers would need fighter cover if they were to do their work effectively. Clearly a large carrier force would be needed, larger than any yet seen in any battle anywhere.

A new split opened up, this time between the Combined Fleet, led by Yamamoto, and the Naval General Staff, led by Nagano. Both men agreed that Japan needed to strike south to seize the oil wealth of the Dutch East Indies. Nagano argued for a conventional strategy: an immediate thrust south to capture the oilfields straight away. This opening action would take place thousands of kilometres from the United States Pacific Fleet, based at Pearl Harbor in the Hawaiian Islands. By the time the American fleet could mobilise and counter-attack, the oilfields would already be seized, and the Japanese Navy would be ready to turn and face the Americans. It had long prepared itself for exactly this fight and would be conducting it near to home. The Americans, on the other hand, would have long supply lines and difficult sea conditions, for which they were ill prepared.

Yamamoto proposed a bolder and more radical strategy. Use aircraft to knock out the US Pacific Fleet on the first day of the war, he argued. Then, at leisure, grab the southern oilfields and anything else Japan wanted, with no risk of interference from the Americans. This would involve an attack on Pearl Harbor itself, right in the enemy's heartland and thousands of kilometres from the Japanese homeland. The Japanese Navy would be undertaking a task for which it had not prepared. It, not the Americans, would have the problem of extended supply lines and unfamiliar waters. Nevertheless, Yamamoto could see no other way to fight the war successfully.

In February 1941 Yamamoto took his plan to Rear Admiral Takijiro Onishi, Chief of Staff of the 11th Air Fleet of the Imperial Japanese Navy. Onishi liked the idea but felt his Air Fleet could not undertake the job. His aircraft were land based, and could not possibly attack from his nearest airfield on the Marshall Islands, over 3000 kilometres from Pearl Harbor. However, Onishi had a better idea: he suggested that Yamamoto talk to Commander Minoru Genda of the 1st Air Fleet.

Genda was one of the most brilliant air tacticians in the Navy. He was something of a war hero himself: in his days as a fighter pilot in the war with China his dashing air unit had been known as 'the Genda Circus'. He was called back from the China front line and sent to London as Assistant Naval Attaché for Air, where he learned the latest aerial tactical thinking. He was the author of the policy of mass fighter cover for bombers, and he supported the then radical idea of a large carrier-based striking force. Genda seized on Yamamoto's plan. His 1st Air Fleet, based on the Navy's six large aircraft carriers *Zuikaku*, *Shokaku*, *Akagi*, *Kagi*, *Hiryu* and *Sôryu*, could do the job, he said.

Genda and Yamamoto now put the plan to the Naval General Staff. At first the General Staff stuck to their argument for an initial thrust south. They were supported by Vice Admiral Chuichi Nagumo, who would lead the 1st Air Fleet in the event of the Genda's and Yamamoto's plan going ahead. Carriers were vulnerable to even a very few bomb hits, they argued. The whole thing would need complete surprise to work. How could that be achieved when so many people and ships were involved? It was too risky.

The argument became heated. Yamamoto, who remained opposed to war anyway, was adamant that the only chance of success lay with an early defeat of the US Pacific Fleet. If war broke out, however much that might have been against Yamamoto's wishes, it would be up to him as Commander-in-Chief to bring it to a successful conclusion. He threatened to resign unless he had his way and was authorised to attack Pearl Harbor first. If Admiral Nagumo was half-hearted about the plan and did not want to lead the Carrier Striking Force to Pearl Harbor, then Yamamoto would be happy to take over and do the job himself.

Faced with this ultimatum, Nagumo and the General Staff relented. Postwar records show that the last barrier to Yamamoto's plan fell at a meeting between Yamamoto and Nagumo in Tokyo on 3 November 1941, only 35 days before Pearl Harbor. Now the old defensive strategies of the Imperial Japanese Navy were gone forever. The new philosophy could be reduced to a single word: 'Attack!'

◆ ◆ ◆

It was not enough for Japan simply to build more ships if it was to match the strength of the Allied navies. If aircraft were to take the place of battleships' guns in a naval offensive, then the Japanese Navy would need a whole new breed of warplanes to do the job. An analysis of the likely requirements led them to demand a mix of dive-bombers, conventional 'horizontal' bombers, torpedo bombers, and fighters to escort them, all capable of being folded into the tight hangar space of a ship, then launched with a full load of fuel and bombs from the perilously short runway of a carrier's flight deck. It was a supreme design challenge, and the Japanese rose eagerly to meet it.

A direct comparison tells how thoroughly they succeeded. The Japanese Zero fighter first flew in 1940.* It was a stocky, agile, brutish little aircraft, with a top speed of 300 knots and a ceiling of 33,000 feet. The single pilot had at his command two 20-mm cannons and two 7.7-mm machine guns, and the option of carrying either two 30-kg

---

* That is how it got its name. Japanese aircraft design numbers derive from the last two digits of the calendar year in which the type first took to the air. The Japanese calendar began in 660 BC, so the western world's 1940 was 2600 to the Japanese. The Mitsubishi A6M first flew in the year 2600, so it became a Type 00, hence Zero.

bombs or a single 60-kg bomb. Compare this with the Wirraway fighter, then the commonest fighter in service with the Royal Australian Air Force. The Wirraway had a top speed of 191 knots and a ceiling of 23,000 feet. Its only weapon was a pair of .303 (7.7-mm) light machine guns. The Zero could out-run, out-climb and out-gun the Australian fighter every time.

Japanese carrier-borne bombers were equally impressive. The Nakajima B5N, known to the Allies as the 'Kate',[1] could carry either an 800-kg torpedo or bomb or three 250-kg bombs. It had a top speed of 199 knots and a ceiling of 27,100 feet. The three-man crew consisted of a pilot, a navigator/bombardier and a radio operator/gunner. The gunner had two rear-facing 7.7-mm machine guns to discourage any pursuing fighters. The Aichi D3A 'Val' dive-bomber was lighter but faster. It had a top speed of 232 knots and a ceiling of 35,000 feet. It could carry one 250-kg bomb slung under the fuselage and two 30-kg bombs on racks under the wings. The two-man crew consisted of a pilot and a gunner. The gunner had two forward-facing 7.7-mm light machine guns, and a rear-facing 7.7-mm heavy machine gun. The forward-facing guns could be used for strafing, while the rear-facing heavy machine gun defended the Val against pursuers.

Yamamoto decreed that the Pearl Harbor attack had to meet three essential conditions: Japan's entire large carrier force should take part, with no large carriers kept in reserve; only the best crews and commanders should be selected; and total secrecy should be preserved. Sending the entire large carrier fleet and the best crews was the equivalent of betting the farm. If the attack worked and crippled the Americans, then Japan would be free to roam the Pacific and South-East Asia with little to challenge it. If it failed and the carrier force was lost, then on the first day of the war Japan would see its key strength and fighting capability destroyed. Even a large carrier could be taken out by just two or three bombs. If the Americans got a warning, or just got lucky, Japan could lose the war in a day.

♦　♦　♦

On 5 November 1941, two days after the fateful meeting between Yamamoto and Nagumo in Tokyo, the Japanese government decided that if the negotiations currently taking place in Washington had not produced an acceptable result by 30 November then Japan would go to war. Essentially, the Japanese wanted all sanctions against them lifted and all assets unfrozen, while still being allowed to hold on to their current conquests and continue their program of expansion. The Americans wanted them to cease all hostile operations, withdraw from their conquered territories and generally behave themselves. The two sides were miles apart, and the chances of a deal were slim.

As soon as he heard of the 30 November deadline, Yamamoto ordered the Combined Fleet to prepare. Two days later he set the date for the attack—8 December.*

On 22 November the Japanese Task Force assembled in Tankan Bay, in the Kurile Islands, an obscure port well to the north of Japanese population centres and out of sight of prying eyes. At 6 a.m. on 26 November the fleet sailed for Pearl Harbor.

Given the scale of the job ahead of him, it is no surprise that Yamamoto put together one of the mightiest fleets ever to sail into battle. In all, 31 ships set off for the rendezvous point at 42°N, 170°W, over 2000 kilometres north-west of Pearl Harbor. Here they would receive final orders. The fleet had four sections. The Striking Force consisted of six aircraft carriers and 353 attack aircraft. A Screening Force of two battleships, two heavy cruisers, one light cruiser and nine destroyers escorted them. An Advance Patrol Unit of three submarines made sure the way ahead was clear. A Support Unit of eight tankers tagged along with reserves of fuel for the return journey.

The Washington negotiations were still stalemated when 30 November came around. The Japanese government did not hesitate. On 1 December they ordered Yamamoto to take his country to war.

◆　◆　◆

---

*Because of the position of the International Date Line, 7 December in the Hawaiian Islands is 8 December in Japan.

At 12.50 a.m. on 7 December (Hawaiian time), Japanese intelligence radioed the fleet with alarming news. The American aircraft carriers were not in Pearl Harbor, nor were the heavy cruisers. They had put to sea. The Japanese had been expecting to find four carriers—*Yorktown*, *Hornet*, *Lexington* and *Enterprise*—all key targets.[2] Should the attack go ahead? Nagumo pondered, then decided. The same intelligence report told him 'a full count of battleships' and plenty of lesser targets were still in Pearl Harbor. There could be no turning back now. In the early hours of the morning of 7 December 1941, the Combined Fleet arrived at a point 320 kilometres north of the target, about an hour's flying time away. The carriers turned into the 20-knot north-easterly wind. At 6 a.m. the first plane took off.

Captain Fuchida's Kate bomber took the lead. As he climbed in the pre-dawn darkness, he had to pick his way through a dense cloud layer extending upwards from 5000 feet. At the prearranged height of 10,000 feet he was in clear air, and the formation assembled behind him. In all, 183 planes made up the first wave: 89 Kates, 51 Vals and 43 Zeroes. Fuchida's own flight consisted of 49 Kates, each carrying one 800-kg armour-piercing bomb. Below and to his right flew 40 more Kates, each armed with an 800-kg torpedo. To his left and a little above him the 51 Vals took up station, each with a single 250-kg high-explosive bomb. Above them all 43 Zeroes stood ready to deal with any challenge. In strict radio silence, the giant formation growled its way towards Pearl Harbor.

The port of Pearl Harbor and the city of Honolulu are both on the southern side of the Hawaiian island of Oahu. A high mountain range runs south-east across the centre of the island, with Honolulu and Pearl Harbor in a large coastal plain beyond the mountains. Fuchida's formation was approaching from the north, so they would have to cross the range before they could attack. Fuchida noted the time. He had been airborne one hour and 40 minutes. They were still flying over thick cloud, but they must be getting close to the target.

Now the cloud broke a little. Fuchida peered down. Suddenly one of the most famous lines of surf in the world appeared beneath his wings.

Fuchida recognised it as the north coast of Oahu. The formation crossed the shoreline not far from Waimea Bay. Fuchida could now see that the air above Pearl Harbor itself was clear of cloud. He swung his formation right, away from the target towards the western end of Oahu, while he studied Pearl Harbor through his binoculars. He counted eight battleships and large numbers of other warships, all calmly at anchor. Disappointingly, he saw no aircraft carriers.

What happened next is one of the iconic moments of Second World War history. Whole movies have taken it as their title, hundreds, even thousands, of writers have solemnly repeated it, and it is now an indelible part of the legend of Pearl Harbor. According to the legend, Fuchida broke radio silence by yelling into his microphone: 'Tora! Tora! Tora!' ('Tiger! Tiger! Tiger!'), the signal to begin the attack. So far I have found only one tiny dissenting voice from this otherwise unchallengeable narrative: Fuchida's own. If $135-million movies have to be re-shot and thousands of books and articles have to be withdrawn and rewritten as a consequence of what follows, all I can do is apologise for the inconvenience and press on with the story. In Fuchida's version, at 7.49 a.m. he ordered his radio operator to send the command: 'Attack!' The radio operator then tapped out in Morse code the prearranged signal: 'TO, TO, TO.'

The 51 Val dive-bombers now climbed and prepared to strike, while the Kate torpedo bombers dropped towards the packed lines of ships in Pearl Harbor. Fuchida's own group of bombers, armed with armour-piercing bombs, circled Barbers Point on the southern coast of Oahu and a few kilometres west of the target, waiting their turn. At 7.53 a.m. Fuchida sent a second radio message, this time to his aircraft carrier *Akagi*, saying: 'Surprise attack successful.'

The first bomb fell on Wheeler Field, a US Army Air Force base just north of Pearl Harbor, at about 7.55 a.m. Next the Vals attacked Hickam Field, near the entrance to Pearl Harbor, before moving on to the main naval base on Ford Island in mid-harbour. The torpedo bombers now joined the fray, concentrating on the battleships anchored in tightly packed rows along the eastern side of Ford Island. Fuchida watched as a series of white waterspouts in the harbour marked the sites of exploding torpedoes. A few American fighters scrambled in an attempt to offer some opposition. The Zeroes made short work of them. With no enemy aircraft to challenge them in the air, the Zeroes switched to strafing the airfields, wrecking any planes they could find on the ground.

Fuchida next led his own formation of Kates, carrying armour-piercing bombs, into the attack. By now the ships' anti-aircraft batteries had come to life, as had some of the land batteries, and Fuchida's wing did not have things all their own way. As he recalled later: 'Dark grey puffs burst all around. Suddenly my plane bounced as if struck by a club. When I looked back to see what had happened, the radio man said: "The fuselage is holed and the rudder wire damaged." We were fortunate that the plane was still under control.'

Despite his damaged aircraft and the furious barrage of anti-aircraft fire, Fuchida successfully released his bomb on his second attacking run, aiming for 'Battleship Row'. As soon as the bomb dropped clear, Fuchida lay on the cockpit floor of his aircraft and opened the vision panel to watch the result. Altogether he could see four bombs falling, and they grew smaller and smaller until he lost sight of them. Then he saw two small puffs of smoke on one of the ships. He guessed, probably correctly, that he had just hit the battleship USS *Maryland*.

The pounding from Fuchida's attack force lasted for nearly an hour. But the Imperial Japanese Navy was not finished with Pearl Harbor. A second wave of 170 attackers, led by Lieutenant Commander Shikegazu Shimazaki, had taken off from the carriers at 7.15 a.m., 75 minutes after Fuchida. At 8.54 a.m. Fuchida heard Shimazaki give them the order to attack. Shimazaki personally led a force of 54 Kates to devastate the airfields, while Lieutenant Commander Takashige Egusa led 80 Vals to mop up in the harbour. They were escorted by 36 Zeroes, but this was overkill: by now Japan had complete control of the skies over Oahu.

By 1 p.m. all surviving aircraft returned to the carriers. The Japanese had lost nine Zeroes, 15 Vals and five Kates, together with 55 aircrew, all to anti-aircraft guns on ships or ashore. Not a single US plane had successfully attacked a Japanese aircraft. Fuchida later described his force's losses as 'negligible'. The Americans lost three battleships sunk: *Arizona*, *California* and *West Virginia*; one battleship capsized, *Oklahoma*; one battleship heavily damaged, *Nevada*; three battleships damaged, *Maryland*, *Pennsylvania* and *Tennessee*; two light cruisers heavily damaged, *Helena* and *Raleigh*; one light cruiser damaged, *Honolulu*; three destroyers heavily damaged, *Cassin*, *Downes* and *Shaw*; one minelayer sunk, *Oglala*; one repair ship badly damaged, *Vestal*; one seaplane tender damaged, *Curtiss*; and one miscellaneous auxiliary vessel capsized, *Utah*. The death toll stood at 2335 military and 68 civilians.[3]

◆ ◆ ◆

There is now a fashion for saying Pearl Harbor was a disaster for the Japanese because it dragged an angry and vengeful United States into a war the Japanese could not hope to win. What is certainly true is that the attack fell far short of attaining its original objective. The returning Japanese pilots hopelessly overestimated the success of the raid. They thought they had crippled all eight battleships, as well as wreaking havoc on the rest of the fleet. While the damage and loss of life were dreadful, it was far from the knockout blow that Yamamoto set out to deliver. The US Pacific Fleet's aircraft carriers and heavy cruisers escaped entirely unscathed. So did an astonishing number of American ships in Pearl Harbor: five cruisers, 26 destroyers, nine submarines and 48 others. Even the damaged ships were not entirely lost. Many of them were quickly repaired and put back into service.

However, the Japanese concluded, with some justification, that the new naval tactic of using carrier-based bombers rather than heavy guns had proved itself and then some. If the right opportunity presented itself, it could certainly be used again. Yamamoto had bet the farm and got away with it.

Chapter 4

One suitcase, one small calico bag

The legend of Pearl Harbor endlessly requires that the Pacific War began with the first bomb falling on Wheeler Field, Oahu. Not so. The Pacific War began on 7 December 1941 Hawaiian time, all right, but not at Pearl Harbor and not even in the Hawaiian Islands. The first Japanese shots were fired not at Americans but at British and Indian troops in north-east Malaya. An amphibious landing force of the 25th Japanese Army poured ashore at Kota Bharu on the north-east coast of Malaya at about 12.45 a.m. on 8 December, 70 minutes before the first bomb hit Wheeler Field.

The Japanese attack was not confined to Malaya. They struck simultaneously on an audaciously huge front extending from Hong Kong in the north to Singapore in the south. Three hours after the landing at Kota Bharu, at 4 a.m. local time, Japanese bombs rained down on the supposedly impregnable British stronghold of Singapore, killing 61 people and injuring over 700. Next to bear the brunt of Japanese military wrath was Hong Kong. At 8 a.m. 36 Zeroes struck Kai Tak airfield, while three battalions of Japanese infantry supported by three brigades of mountain artillery swept across the Sham Chun River and poured into the colony, heading for Kowloon.

Pearl Harbor was bad enough. Next came one of the great fiascos of the Second World War. The Philippines, then an American colony, provided a home for the US Navy's Asiatic Fleet. Although the Asiatic Fleet boasted nothing like the bristling strength of the Pacific Fleet, it was nevertheless a significant force. Within 30 minutes of the first bomb falling on Pearl Harbor, American forces in the Philippines were informed that war had broken out. Herb Kriloff, Officer of the Deck on the seaplane tender USS *William B. Preston*, was anchored in Davao Gulf, off Mindanao in the southern Philippines. At about 3 a.m. the deck watch woke him to pass on a decoded message from the Commander-in-Chief, US Asiatic Fleet: 'Japan has commenced hostilities. Govern yourselves accordingly.' The *Willy B* went to battle stations, upped anchor and moved to a safer area.

Others were less zealous. The vain and vainglorious General Douglas MacArthur, commander of US forces in the Philippines, also received the warning at 3 a.m. He had just hosted a lavish party in his hotel, and his response was decisive: he chose to do nothing. At 5 a.m. Major General Lewis Brereton, commander of the Far East Air Force in the Philippines, put his crews on alert but needed MacArthur's permission to launch his aircraft against Japanese bases on their nearby colony Formosa (now Taiwan). MacArthur's Chief of Staff, Brigadier General Richard Sutherland, refused Brereton access to the general. Still nothing happened. At around dawn a group of six Japanese fighter aircraft and seven bombers attacked *Willy B* and her PBY Catalina aircraft riding at anchor nearby. A shooting war had now started in the Philippines, with US forces under direct attack. Still MacArthur did nothing.

Brereton next ordered some of his aircraft to take off and circle overhead rather than run the risk of being caught on the ground. MacArthur did nothing. At 9 a.m. Brereton again asked Sutherland for MacArthur's permission to attack Japanese targets. Sutherland again refused to put the request to the general. Nothing happened.

Finally, at 11 a.m., MacArthur agreed to a counter-attack. Brereton ordered all his planes back on the ground to rearm and refuel. That was when the Japanese struck. At 12.20 p.m., over nine hours after the first warning that war had broken out, a massive wave of some 500 aircraft swept in from Formosa and caught the Americans at their most defenceless. In the space of an hour, they destroyed half of MacArthur's Far East Air Force on the ground. The most important US power base in the Pacific region after Pearl Harbor was now incapable of defending itself successfully.

That same day the Japanese attacked American bases on Wake and Guam islands. With the notable exception of Wake Island, where the Japanese were initially beaten off, from Hong Kong to Malaya to Singapore to the Philippines to the Hawaiian Islands, the Japanese had overwhelmed Allied forces wherever they struck. Their rampaging Army and Navy could now turn their attention towards the real target of the Pacific War: the rich resources of the Dutch East Indies, particularly Java's oil and Malaya's rubber and tin. The whole eastern hemisphere seemingly lay at their feet. All in the space of a single day.

In Darwin, tension was high even before news arrived of Pearl Harbor. On Friday, 5 December, troops were due to sail south on leave aboard the *Zealandia*. They had already handed in their equipment and boarded the ship when all leave was suddenly cancelled. They stomped back to barracks in a foul temper. The town braced itself for a riot. If it came, it would not be the first: the boys were given to venting their frustrations on Darwin's pubs, cafés, shops and civilians whenever things went wrong. They would be bound to tear the town to pieces, smashing whatever shop windows were still intact, or so everyone thought. The riot happily failed to materialise, but the fear of it was symptomatic of tensions between the town's military and civilian populations.

Molly Walsh, a civilian typist working for the Army, recalled how she first heard that the Pacific War had begun. Her husband Jim came home for lunch and told her Pearl Harbor had been attacked and the Americans had been taken by surprise. That was all he knew. For the next 24 hours life in Darwin continued as normal. Then the pace quickened. 'For the next week there was colossal activity,' Molly remembers.

'Our men, ordinarily clerks and such, worked like slaves carting sand, filling sand bags, building gun emplacements and learning to be efficient members of Lewis gun crews. We were fed on atrocity stories, and laughingly devised a scheme of cyanide capsules for women, on the death before dishonour principle.'

Molly's boss, an Army major, asked her bluntly: 'Well, when are you going home?'

'Home? This is my home,' she told him, 'and as far as I know I'm not going anywhere.'

'You'll be evacuated,' the major replied. 'The women will all have to go, and soldiers' wives will be first. If you're sensible you won't wait for an evacuation order. You'll go straight to town and book a passage.'

✦ ✦ ✦

When war with Japan looked likely, Britain had Asian colonies to defend and expected to play a major role in any Asian and Pacific conflict. The key British contribution would be its naval base in Singapore. Britain, India, Australia and New Zealand concentrated on making Singapore impregnable—the so-called 'Singapore strategy'—pouring in resources that might with hindsight have been better deployed elsewhere. No need to worry about Darwin, ran the thinking; the Japanese will never get near it. Singapore will stop them. Late in 1941, Churchill ordered two of his newest and most formidable battleships, HMS *Prince of Wales* and HMS *Repulse,* to reinforce the British base. Land-based bombers from Rear Admiral Onishi's 11th Air Fleet sank them both on 10 December 1941, when the war was two days old. That same day the Japanese captured Guam from the Americans.

✦ ✦ ✦

The gallant cry 'women and children first' was, in Darwin's case, rather less chivalrous than it sounds. The women and children were certainly seen as vulnerable and in need of protection. But, more to the point, they drank and ate. The adults enjoyed a beer, smoked cigarettes, and drove cars that needed parts and petrol. Women and children required doctors and dentists and hospitals and schools and teachers and what were delicately referred to as sanitary services (Darwin had no sewerage system). All of this put pressure on the already stretched supply routes and on local resources. The war had just moved much closer to Darwin, and the ships might have to run a gauntlet of submarines to bring in essential supplies for a town with a population of almost 6000. The ships would need to be escorted and to travel in convoys. Even more crucially, they would need to make room for increasing quantities of military equipment. That left less capacity for civilian needs. The fewer non-military mouths to feed in Darwin the better. If that meant packing the women and children off south, so be it.

Edgar Harrison, the Permanent Officer in charge of Air Raid Precautions, drew up a plan for the evacuation. It took him months and involved cooperation with the Army, which would be charged with the task of actually moving the evacuees out. On 5 December 1941 he handed the plan over to the Darwin Defence Coordination Committee, consisting of the heads of the three services. They approved and passed the plan on to the Administrator, who also agreed. Three days later, the Pacific War began.

On 9 December, the day after the Japanese entered the war, the air-raid wardens met to discuss next steps. The evacuation of Darwin's civilians was at the top of the agenda. There is some debate over exactly what happened next. After the Darwin raid, the government appointed a Royal Commissioner, Charles Lowe, to investigate the circumstances surrounding the attack. The Administrator, Aubrey Abbott, gave both written and verbal evidence to the Lowe Commission. The Chief Warden, Arthur Miller, prepared a written report, which was taken in evidence by Lowe. The Permanent Officer, Edgar Harrison, and the Acting Government Secretary, G.V. Carrington, both gave contradictory verbal evidence to Lowe. Talking afterwards to the author Douglas Lockwood, both Abbott and Miller told a story that was often at variance with their evidence to Commissioner Lowe. This leaves the researcher with six different versions of what took place. Abbott's evidence to the Royal Commission does not match his version in

Lockwood's book *Australia Under Attack*. The same could be said of Miller. In the face of all these memory lapses, I have simply done my best to piece the story together in a way that makes most sense.

In his evidence to the Royal Commission, Edgar Harrison recalled that he attended a meeting with Administrator Abbott on 10 December at 10 a.m. Accompanying him were Arthur Miller, the Chief Air Raid Warden; Miller's Deputy, E.V. White; W.A. Hughes, Director of Demolitions; and Brough Newell, Director of First Aid. Abbott's account omits this meeting altogether, though he discussed with author Lockwood a meeting on 12 December with a slightly different cast list. My own view favours two meetings, on 10 and 12 December. Whatever the timing or number of meetings, the delegation told Abbott that the evacuation of women and children from Darwin should begin as soon as possible. Abbott promised to consult Canberra.

At 11 p.m. on Thursday 11 December, three days into the Pacific War, Darwin's air-raid sirens wailed in earnest for the first time. Revellers at a party in the smart New Darwin Hotel abandoned their glasses and headed for the shelters. Orderlies at the hospital carried patients down to the beach. The citizens of the town headed for open ground, as they had been briefed to do, and waited for the all-clear, which came through 90 minutes later. The next day Berlin Radio announced that Darwin had been wiped off the map. This turned out to be a little premature, though it caused some anxiety among short-wave listeners in other parts of Australia. Darwin had survived its first false alarm, and its citizens had a good laugh at the expense of the over-excitable Hun.

Nevertheless, all did not go smoothly. Someone had left a light burning in the ladies' underwear shop window at C.J. Cashman & Co. A passing soldier hurled a brick through the plate glass and shattered the light. Lights had been left on at the Soldiers' Hall: someone broke in and smashed the offending electrical fittings. At Young's Garage a light had been left burning on a battery charger: someone forced the door and put it out.

The following day, 12 December, the air-raid wardens were seriously jumpy. It was a Friday morning, and the four most senior wardens descended on Administrator Abbott's office again. Arthur Miller arrived with Edgar Harrison and two of his zone wardens, Eric Wilmott and W.J.E. White. They were in mutinous mood. They demanded two things: an evacuation of Darwin's civilians straight away, and an end to their ambiguous legal status as air-raid wardens. The military already had statutory powers under the National Security Act, but these powers were limited to enforcing a blackout and regulating road traffic. No one had taken the trouble to delegate power to the civilian air-raid wardens. As things stood, they could not enforce their orders. Statutory powers might require the declaration of a State of Emergency, which would in turn involve the Federal Government in Canberra and a gazetted notice under the National Security regulations.

Abbott resisted. His Honour argued that a declaration of a State of Emergency would cause unnecessary panic. The four wardens refused to accept this. They eventually persuaded Abbott to cable Prime Minister Curtin in Canberra and ask for a decision. Curtin sent an encrypted reply to Abbott on the afternoon of Friday 12 December. The War Cabinet had decided, Curtin wrote, to evacuate compulsorily all women and children from Darwin with the exception of nurses and the wives of missionaries. The first group of evacuees should leave the following Thursday on the *Zealandia*, which had just been used to bring troops to Darwin. His Honour had just six days to get the evacuation organised and under way.

♦ ♦ ♦

Darwin's defences came in for a lot of scrutiny at the Royal Commission. In particular, Commissioner Lowe spent a lot of time looking at 'gun density'. How many heavy anti-aircraft guns did Darwin need? The ideal answer seemed to be 36. But it was hardly negligent of the defences to deploy a smaller number. There weren't 36 heavy AA guns to spare in the whole of Australia.

Similarly, with fighter aircraft, Commissioner Lowe was told Darwin needed 250 front-line fighters to be effective against a bomber force of the size that struck on 19 February 1942. This was a pipe dream. The

RAAF didn't have 250 fighters to its name. Most of the few it had in Australia were spread thinly around the large cities in the south. Others were in Malaya and Timor. Still more were in the Western Desert, facing the Luftwaffe rather than the Imperial Japanese Navy. In 1942 the RAAF's only possible response to a call to station 250 fighters in Darwin could be to shake its collective head and say: I wish.

The Royal Australian Navy had built a boom net, the longest of its kind in the world, sealing off Port Darwin. The net gave the harbour some protection against submarine attack but not much else. There were heavy guns mounted around the foreshores and facing the sea, particularly at East Point. So a seaborne invader might have faced a tougher time than an attacker from the air. However, there were no fighting ships of any consequence permanently based in Darwin, for the simple reason that they were all needed elsewhere. The Army, Navy and Air Force all faced accusations of failure to provide adequate defences for Darwin. The hard truth is that in those desperate days there were no resources available, and all three services provided Darwin with as much as they felt they could spare at the time.

However, the defenders could reasonably face a different set of charges. The defence planners made elementary mistakes. Rather than keep important resources like hospitals and reinforcements away from the likely first line of attack, they piled everything into the front row. The civil hospital at Cullen Bay was right next to the Larrakeyah Army barracks.[1] Both were on the shore, about a kilometre from the harbour and town. They could expect to be caught up in the first wave of any attack. The new military hospital at Berrimah was further inland but barely 1500 metres from the runway threshold at the RAAF airfield. There could be no question of moving the wounded to safety at the rear, and no question of keeping troops in the barracks and back from the fight until they were needed.

The positioning of the new RAAF airfield just a few kilometres inland from the coast showed the same lack of foresight. Rather than place aircraft, hangars, fuel dumps, workshops and ammunition stores well back from the opening onslaught of any attack, the defence planners had put them in the most exposed area of all. To cap it all, the nerve centre of any coordinated response by Army, Navy and Air Force, known as Area Combined Headquarters, was part of the administration complex at the RAAF airfield. If the airfield came under attack, so would ACH.

✦ ✦ ✦

The Army rather than the RAAF provided Darwin's most potent defence against air attack. By late 1941 four sections of heavy anti-aircraft guns, each consisting of four QF 3.7-inch guns, stood at sites on the Oval in central Darwin, at Fannie Bay just north of the town centre, at Berrimah to the east of the town, and at McMillans, well outside the town to the north of the RAAF airfield. Each gun fired 28-pound (12.7-kg) shells, and each gun could launch between ten and 20 rounds a minute, depending on the skill of the gunners. They were serious weapons. The shells could reach a height of 29,500 feet (9000 metres) and had a maximum horizontal range of 11.7 miles (18.8 kilometres). However, as late as mid-February 1942, the sites were far from complete. The revetments—earthworks mounded up around the guns to protect the gunners—were still unfinished. The cables linking the guns to their command post still ran above the ground, making them a very likely first casualty of any direct hit. Nevertheless, the guns were in place and ready. In addition to the four sections of 3.7-inch guns, two 3-inch anti-aircraft guns were mounted at Elliott Point near the Quarantine Station, five kilometres south-east of the town centre.

Jack Mulholland, a gunner with the 14th Heavy Anti-Aircraft Battery, remembers the training he and his fellow soldiers received on the 3.7-inch guns. 'All the training was with dummy rounds against slow-moving targets. Even the Flying Doctor came in for our attention. He would be returning from one of his missions and as he flew over our site, he would cut his motor and yell out: "Don't shoot, you bastards." He had no worries because the one thing we did not do was waste ammunition in practice shoots. There were none.' Mulholland's unit arrived in Darwin at the end of 1940. By the time the Japanese arrived over

Darwin 14 months later, he and his comrades had fired just a single live round from their guns (a warning shot across the nose of a 'friendly' incoming plane that failed to observe the correct approach procedures). The deafening noise, heat, smoke, shouting and confusion of a full-blooded barrage would all have to be discovered in action on the day.

The big 3.7-inch AA guns, often referred to as HA (High-Angle) guns, were designed to tackle high-flying 'horizontal' bombers. They were less useful against low-level strafing fighters, dive-bombers or torpedo bombers. The height and bearing of a dive-bomber or any low-flying attacker are both changing rapidly all the time, and it is difficult for the heavy guns to track them. To meet this type of attack, the Army used a handful of Lewis machine guns. The 14th AA Battery had a group of about eight Lewis guns on top of the oil tanks at the harbour, for instance, and a single Lewis gun was assigned to each of the four AA sections to defend against strafing aircraft. The Lewis guns were largely useless. Each magazine held only 50 rounds of light .303 ammunition, so there was no chance of sustained, heavy fire. Darwin desperately needed the heavier punch of rapid-firing pom-poms, or Bofors guns, to repulse dive-bombers or strafing fighters. There were none.

A shortage of Lewis guns led to more problems. At Mulholland's battery, he recalls: 'It was necessary to share our Lewis gun with a searchlight unit. At dusk of an evening a truck would arrive, pick up the Lewis gun and take it to the searchlights for the unit's protection during the night.'

Improvisation was the order of the day. Mulholland again: 'The Lewis machine gun was originally an infantry weapon in the Great War. To adapt the gun to anti-aircraft defence, a length of sapling was embedded in the ground. On top of the sapling a piece of pipe allowed the gun to be mounted and the gun could be traversed through 360 degrees. Anti-aircraft mountings were not provided.' So a handful of First World War light machine guns mounted on bits of old pipe that spun around a sapling jammed in the ground provided Darwin's main protection against Japan's notoriously effective strafing fighters and dive-bombers.

◆　◆　◆

Ground-based anti-aircraft guns are one thing. The best defence against air attack comes not from the ground but from fighter planes, which can mix it with the bombers and challenge them in their own element. When the Pacific War broke out, Darwin was home to two RAAF squadrons. The brand new RAAF airfield north-east of the town played host to the Hudson bombers of 13 Squadron, while the Wirraway fighters of 12 Squadron were based at the smaller civil airfield at Parap.[2]

12 Squadron began its life at Laverton Air Base in Victoria, under the command of Squadron Leader, later Wing Commander, Charles 'Moth' Eaton. Eaton is one of the legendary characters of Australian aviation. Born in London, he flew with the Royal Flying Corps on the Western Front in the First World War. He crashed behind German lines, was taken prisoner, and repeatedly escaped, finally making it back to his own side in the last few days of the war. Eaton flew on the first regular passenger service between London and Paris, ferrying delegates to the Paris Peace Conference. After marrying, he moved to Australia and worked as an instructor for the RAAF, training some of Australia's best pilots. He was a stickler for discipline and he trained his pilots well. In September 1941, Wing Commander, later Air Marshal, Sir Frederick Scherger, took over from Eaton as Station Commander in Darwin.

12 Squadron was originally equipped with four Avro Anson and four Hawker Demon fighters. The Avro Anson was generally used as a trainer rather than a front-line fighter, while the Hawker Demon was a slow, under-armed two-seater 'fighter' adapted from a 1928 bomber design. Happily for 12 Squadron, the Ansons and Demons were replaced by Wirraways. As we have seen, the Wirraway was no match for any of its likely Japanese opponents, but it was an improvement on the Anson and the Demon. I have found it impossible to establish with any certainty how many Wirraways 12 Squadron had at its disposal either at the time the Pacific War broke out or when the first Japanese raid on Darwin took place, but the most likely number is 14, of which as many as nine were not in Darwin but dispersed to Batchelor airfield, 75 kilometres to the south. So if the Japanese arrived unexpectedly in the skies over Darwin, the town could not expect much protection from the RAAF.

Chapter 5

No place and no time for argument

Japanese troops poured into Thailand and down the Malay Peninsula, swatting British, Indian and Australian defenders aside. On 11 December they attacked the British colony of Burma and headed for the capital, Rangoon. On 18 December Hong Kong surrendered. Two of the returning aircraft carriers from the Japanese Pearl Harbor force detached themselves and diverted to join the attack on Wake Island, begun on 8 December. After a 15-day siege, Wake Island fell. The sheer speed and ruthlessness of the Japanese advance left the Allies reeling. They had hopelessly underestimated Japanese strength and military prowess. Now they knew better. Anyone with a map could see what was afoot. The Japanese were being denied oil and other essentials by the Allies. They clearly intended to bulldoze their way south and grab it for themselves.

As the pace of war quickened, Darwin found itself playing a major role as both a staging post and a maintenance base for aircraft. The Hudson bombers of 13 Squadron had moved north to the island of Ambon, in the Dutch East Indies. They were quickly followed by the Hudson bombers of the RAAF's 2 Squadron, who staged through Darwin on their way to Penfoie in Timor. However, the forward bases on Timor and in the Dutch East Indies had poor maintenance facilities, and the aircraft had to be rotated back to Darwin whenever they needed attention.

On 22 December 1941 General George C. Marshall, Chief of Staff of the US Army Air Corps, directed that Darwin be used as an American Army and Navy base. The Americans had previously been wary of Darwin after two of their four-engine B17 Flying Fortress bombers were damaged breaking through the unpaved surface of the new RAAF field's runway. They preferred to use the stronger (if narrower and shorter) runway to the south, at Batchelor. However, the Darwin strip was strong enough to handle the Air Corps' P40 Kittyhawk fighters as well as the lighter Hudson bombers of the RAAF, and a steady stream of aircraft swept into Darwin on their way to the Dutch East Indies to confront the Japanese advance.

The Curtiss P40 Kittyhawk was no slouch as a fighter aircraft. It had a maximum speed of 310 knots, which made it a whisker faster than the Japanese Zero. It was manoeuvrable and tough, and its six M2 Browning 50-mm guns gave it plenty of punch. It could not match the Zero at high altitude, but low down it could compete on something like equal terms, especially if it used its speed advantage. It was never quite as agile as the Zero, but it was more robust because it had armour protection for the pilot and self-sealing fuel tanks, which could survive a few bullet strikes. The Zero had no such shielding and tended to succumb to comparatively light damage. A skilful and experienced pilot in a Kittyhawk could expect to meet a Zero and survive. The problem was the almost total lack of Kittyhawk pilots who could be classified as skilful and experienced.[1]

The Kittyhawks were shipped in from the United States in kit form. Usually they were unloaded at either Brisbane or Townsville. They were then assembled and flown to the front line, using Darwin as a final refuelling point before beginning the perilous journey over water to Timor and Java. Outback airfields in Queensland, including Charleville, Winton and Cloncurry, and Daly Waters in the Northern Territory, suddenly found themselves vital links in the supply chain. Other aircraft flew to Darwin from bases in New South Wales and Victoria, staging through the same airfields.

The Kittyhawk pilots were pitifully inexperienced. All were unfamiliar with Australia and the special problems of Outback flying, particularly navigation. They began the multi-stage trip to Darwin armed with the barest of briefings. It was not an easy journey. One pilot recalled asking about finding his way. 'Simple,' he was told. 'Just follow the trail of crashed Kittyhawks.'[2]

◆ ◆ ◆

Inexperienced pilots from the United States were not the only problem. On 27 December 1941, Prime Minister Curtin published in the Melbourne *Herald* his famous declaration that Australia 'looks to America' (and, by implication, away from Britain) for protection in the face of the Japanese threat. This turned out to have unforeseen consequences. For one thing, the Americans sent black troops to Australia. When the first convoy arrived in Melbourne in January 1942, Australian Customs refused the desperately needed troops permission to land. The Australian Minister for the Army rapidly countermanded the order and referred the whole issue to the External Affairs Minister, Dr. H.V. Evatt. Evatt grumpily agreed that there was not much choice but to let in black troops if that's what the Americans sent. However, he thought the Americans might be persuaded to go a bit easy. He cabled his Minister in Washington, Dick Casey, on 21 January 1942 with 'guiding instructions on the subject of coloured troops'.

Under the heading MOST SECRET IMMEDIATE, Evatt wrote:

Whilst the Advisory War Council decided that the Australian reaction to the despatch of negro troops to Australia would not be favourable, the composition of the forces that the U.S.A. government might decide to despatch is a matter for that Government to determine.

If the U.S.A. Authorities find it necessary to include certain coloured labour units as a proportion of coloured troops to their forces it is not the desire of the Commonwealth Government to make any stipulation which might destroy the nature of the organisation of the Army formation.

Nevertheless it is assumed that the U.S.A. Authorities, being aware of our view, will have regard to Australian susceptibilities in the numbers they decide to despatch.

The Americans, quite rightly, took not a blind bit of notice.[3]

♦ ♦ ♦

With Darwin now a major supply base for the defence of the Dutch East Indies, the situation on the wharves became critical. The combination of the desperately inefficient wharf and the bloody-mindedness of the wharfies ensured that the harbour was a serious bottleneck blocking the flow of men and military equipment northwards to the fight. The Americans found it intolerable and decided something had to be done. When a convoy including the *Holbrook* arrived in Darwin on 5 January 1942, the wharfies saw something akin to a job for life arrayed invitingly before them. Unloading the *Holbrook* alone would be good for three weeks. The whole convoy might, with luck, take forever.

Colonel John Robenson, the US base commander in Darwin, had enough. Despite pleas from Administrator Abbott, he posted guards with machine guns along the wharf and told his own men to get on with unloading. The guards held back the fuming wharfies while the troops started unloading the ship. The political explosion is thought to have rumbled as far as Washington before a compromise was reached: the wharfies could work one small hold of the ship while the troops worked the other nine. Robenson had made his point: the convoy now unloaded at normal speed, using a mixture of troops and wharfies to do the job.

The situation on the wharves clearly could not go on. Eddie Ward, the Minister for Labour, had appealed to the Darwin wharfies on 11 December to speed up the job. It is only fair to acknowledge that the wharfies responded by increasing the length of their working day, but it was not enough. Ward flew to Darwin and negotiated a new deal: he would increase the workforce by 160 men brought in from other ports around Australia. They began arriving a few days later, on planes from the south, and were generally known as the 'Flying Wharfies'. The Darwin workforce accepted them grudgingly, and not without cause. Port Darwin was not exactly a workers' paradise, and the volunteers who arrived were not exactly the pick of the crop. No doubt the Darwin wharfies' motives in resisting the infusion of extra workers were entirely selfless, and the fact that the new arrivals meant less overtime pay for them never entered their heads.

The combination of Flying Wharfies, longer hours and the intervention of troops speeded work at the wharf a little, but the situation remained profoundly unsatisfactory. Large convoys took weeks to load and unload, and ships piled up in the harbour while the whole creaking system failed to deal with them. Meanwhile, they made an inviting target for the Japanese.

◆ ◆ ◆

The Northern Territory administration's first task, in the wake of the prime minister's cable directing them to evacuate Darwin's women and children, was to decide who should go and who should stay, and in what order those leaving Darwin should depart. The air-raid wardens had already drawn up a comprehensive survey of Darwin residents, dividing them into women and children, the elderly, essential workers and so on. Administrator Abbott was not satisfied. A month earlier, in November, he had asked Edgar Harrison, the Permanent Officer in charge of ARP, to conduct a census of the civilian population. By coincidence, the census was set for 12 December, the day of the air-raid wardens' confrontation with Abbott in his office. As the wardens all had other jobs, they could undertake census work only in their spare time in the evening. Abbott felt they would not be able to do the job quickly enough, and switched the task to the police.

In his nine-page report on 'Plans for Air Raid Precautions and Evacuation of Civilians, Darwin' (one of the exhibits at the Royal

Commission on the Darwin attack), Abbott wrote: 'The Police started upon this job [the census] on Sunday, 13th December and completed it on Monday, 14th. The Police Return gave the number of women and children as 1,066 women and 900-odd children.[4] Advice was received from the Army that 822 women and children could be embarked upon the "Zealandia" which was an Army transport and under Army control.'

On Sunday afternoon Harrison and other wardens were working on evacuation plans in their office. Harrison wanted to challenge some points, and rang the Administrator. Abbott now dropped his bombshell. This was no place and no time for argument, he told Harrison. The air-raid wardens' plans for the evacuation were scrapped. From now on His Honour would issue such instructions as he considered necessary. Administration of the evacuation would be taken over forthwith by the Acting Government Secretary, Mr Carrington. The wardens' plan had divided Darwin's population into women, children, the sick and so on, and had assigned priorities for evacuation. Carrington's plan, based on the police survey, simply divided the population by street. Darwin's evacuation priorities would be determined by address, not by need.

It is hard to like Charles Lydiard Aubrey Abbott. Most writers have tended to spring to his defence, believing that the Royal Commission treated him harshly. Yet, when his words are read all these years later, not the least of his misdemeanours is that he is often economical with the truth. In the report quoted above he sets out to create the impression that he was simply following orders sent peremptorily from Canberra. He makes no mention of any meeting with the air-raid wardens and no mention of scrapping their evacuation plan. He describes Curtin's telegram ordering the evacuation as though it arrived out of the blue, rather than in response to a request from him. He is quick to blame others. In the report quoted above, he wrote: 'I visited the A.R.P. headquarters and saw that matters were becoming chaotic. Whilst Mr Harrison, the Permanent Officer, had done a very good job in fixing up preliminary organisation in connection with evacuation, Army assistance and other matters, his temperament was such that he rapidly lost his head and I was overwhelmed by complaints from the public regarding his manner.' Harrison was an ex-Sergeant Major in the Army, so Abbott may have had a point there. Others certainly agreed that he was officious and excitable. Nevertheless, Abbott's report was hardly loyal to his staff, and in fact many of the public's complaints were directed not at Harrison but at Abbott himself. His Honour's minor carelessness also suggests an untidy mind: 14 December 1941 was a Sunday, not a Monday.

Curtin's telegram to Abbott did not give the ARP wardens anything like what they wanted. It did not include the promise of a declaration of a State of Emergency in Darwin, nor was any measure gazetted to give the wardens statutory powers. Furthermore, although the wardens were no longer in charge of the evacuation, it would nevertheless be their job to bluff the public into complying.

On Monday 15 December the Administrator issued 2500 printed notices to be delivered to every household in Darwin. The full text is reproduced in Appendix I. This first notice did not actually order the evacuation. It merely told everybody what to expect if the order came. Each evacuee could take personal belongings including a small calico bag containing hair and tooth brushes, a towel and toilet soap, and a suitcase of clothing weighing not more than 35 pounds. In addition each person could take two blankets, eating and drinking utensils, and a two-gallon (eight-litre) water bag per family.

No pets were allowed. 'Any pets owned by Evacuees should be destroyed before the Evacuation,' the notice declared. The order did not apply to the chooks. 'Domestic Poultry,' it continued, 'would be an Auxiliary Food Supply for those remaining in Darwin, and as such will not be destroyed under any circumstances.' So Darwin's chooks suddenly found themselves in the unusual position of being a better life insurance risk than its cats and dogs.

On the day the first notice was issued, Darwin residents packed the local school where they were told they would receive instructions and the latest information. There they learned that the evacuation would be overland, by road, though how this was to be achieved remained a mystery. They left the meeting little the wiser about anything.

The actual order to evacuate took the form of a notice published in the *Northern Standard* on Tuesday 16 December 1942. It betrayed no nervousness over the dubious legality of the evacuation order. Instead it told the citizens of Darwin that they had been ordered to leave by no less august a body than the War Cabinet, and pleaded with them to go willingly. The notice read:

COMMONWEALTH OF AUSTRALIA
NORTHERN TERRITORY ADMINISTRATION
PROCLAMATION
EVACUATION ORDER

CITIZENS OF DARWIN

The Federal War Cabinet has decided that women and children must be compulsorily evacuated from Darwin as soon as possible, except women required for essential services.

Arrangements have been completed and the first party will leave within the next 48 hours.

This party will include sick in hospital, expectant mothers, aged and infirm and women with young children.

You have all been issued with printed notices advising you what may be taken and this must be strictly adhered to. Personal effects must not exceed 35 lbs.

The staff dealing with evacuation is at the Native Affairs Branch in Mitchell Street and will be on duty day and night continuously.

The personnel who will make up the first party will be advised during the next few hours and it will be the duty of all citizens to comply at once with the instructions given by responsible authorities.

Remember what your Prime Minister, Mr Curtin, said recently. 'The time has gone by for argument. The instructions of the Federal Government must be carried out.'

The Federal Government has made all arrangements for the comfort and welfare of your families in the South.

Darwin citizens will greatly assist the war effort by cheerfully carrying out all requests. There will be hardship and sacrifice, but the war situation demands these, and I am sure Darwin will set the rest of Australia a magnificent example to follow.

(Sgd.) C.L.A. ABBOTT
Administrator of the Northern Territory

The first group of evacuees, 225 women and children, left Darwin on 19 December 1941 not by road but by sea, aboard the *Koolinda*. They could count themselves lucky, certainly luckier than the next batch of 530 evacuees, who left on 20 December aboard the *Zealandia*. Their trip was a nightmare. Some had been given only one hour's notice to leave their houses and board the ship. The journey began with the guards throwing overboard any bags weighing more than 35 pounds. *Zealandia* had been used for transporting troops to Darwin from the south and had not been cleaned for months. Food and water ran short. Toilet and washing facilities were a calamity. Some cabins designed for four people were occupied by 11 instead. The ship called in at Thursday Island and collected 200 Japanese internees, who were kept in the hold under armed guard. Chinese families were made to travel on the open deck rather than in cabins. The stories the evacuees sent home did nothing to improve morale in Darwin or boost confidence in the authorities' assurances about comfort and welfare. The *Adelaide News* got hold of the story and had its entire report blocked by the censors.

Others were more fortunate. The remaining women and children of Darwin might have waited another three weeks for the next ship if it had not been for a stroke of luck. The 12,000-ton American luxury passenger liner *President Grant* had been tied up in Manila harbour when the Japanese invasion of the Philippines looked likely. The captain received orders to sail for the nearest friendly port. Armed only with a chart torn out of a *National Geographic* magazine, he set off for Darwin and, against all the odds, made it there safely. On 23 December the *President Grant* left Darwin for Brisbane, carrying better charts and a further 222 evacuees. All but 20 were placed in first-class cabins, and the crew treated them royally, including giving everyone a small present on Christmas Day. There were 166 adults conveyed at full fare of £18 each, 38 half fares, three quarter fares and 15 infants travelling free. On 8 July 1942, almost seven months later, the Department of the Interior wrote to the ship's agents, Wills Gilchrist and Sanderson Pty Ltd, in Brisbane, to say that the government's long-overdue cheque for £3,343.10.0 was in the post.

There can be no doubt that the evacuation was chaotic. The neatly typed passenger lists, on file at the National Archive in Darwin, have been converted to a maze of arrows and scribblings and marginal notes, with endless revisions and crossings-out. Nobody seemed able to agree on who had sailed on which ship, or where they disembarked, or what happened to them afterwards. Short words tell long stories: 'missing', or 'plane', or, in one sad case, 'Died in raid 19/2/42'. It was a bureaucratic nightmare, and the people of Darwin were not impressed. They blamed the administration, and the Administrator.

Some of Administrator Abbott's personal style is caught in his account of the row over the legal status of the air-raid wardens. In the report quoted above, Abbott gives his version of how he first heard that there might be a problem. He chooses to ignore the wardens' delegations on 10 and 12 December and instead cites an approach from the hated trade unions. 'This was first brought up to me by a Committee of what was then known as the "People's Party",' he wrote. He is vague about the date, putting his meeting with them 'between the 12th and the 21st December, 1941'. The actual delegation was made up of 'a Mr Ward, a local solicitor, Mr Ryan, the Secretary of the North Australian Workers' Union, Mr Ming Ket, a local Chinese and another whose name I am unable to remember'.

The committee he refers to was the worthy-sounding Citizens' War Effort Committee, which had been set up by the trade unions in an attempt to shore up their weakening authority in what was increasingly a military town. The fact that Abbott could not remember either the date of the meeting or the names of the delegates is a fair indication of the seriousness with which he treated their submission. This high-handed approach was shortly to cost him dearly. His report continues: 'The Committee stated that there was no legal authority to remove people from Darwin and that there was no legal authority for the A.R.P. organisation to function. I told the Committee that I had a direct and definite instruction from the Prime Minister and the War Cabinet to evacuate women and children from Darwin.' This was not the point, and the delegation retreated, unsatisfied.

The Japanese continued their push south. They streamed down the eastern and western coasts of the narrow Malay peninsula, brushing aside any resistance. They quickly occupied the whole of Thailand. On 16 December they captured Miri in Sarawak, part of the island of Borneo. Brunei's and Borneo's vital oilfields were now within their grasp. The Pacific War was a mere eight days old.

Admiral Nagumo's carrier task force met with a rapturous reception when it returned from Pearl Harbor to the Japanese mainland on 23 December. The failure to knock out the American aircraft carriers was forgotten in the general back-slapping and congratulations. The war was going well on every front, and Nagumo Force had led the way. Mitsuo Fuchida recalled: 'Both the Naval General Staff and Combined Fleet were fully satisfied with the results achieved at Pearl Harbor and saw no need for further neutralising action against the US Pacific Fleet.' Instead they ordered Nagumo's force, now reduced by the Wake Island attack from six to four carriers, to support the impending invasions of Rabaul and Kavieng, on large islands north-east of New Guinea. Nagumo Force left Kure Naval Base on 5 January 1942 and headed south for the staging post of Truk Lagoon and the next phase of the war.

Chapter 6

The judge sums up

There is a noisy orthodoxy that says the Japanese never had any intention of invading Australia in 1941, 1942 or any other time. Whoever proclaims this usually follows up with a paragraph or two mocking the large number of Australians, mostly of older generations, who are convinced a Japanese invasion was once imminent.

These historians are, of course, correct. The Japanese never seriously set about an invasion of Australia. However, this orthodoxy leaves out two important facts. First, Australians didn't know it at the time. And second, the decision not to invade Australia was closer run than many historians care to admit.

By the end of December 1941, with the Pacific War only three weeks old, Darwin was increasingly a military town. Civilian women and children had moved out in large numbers. The military had moved in to take their place. Ships of the American Asiatic Fleet retreated from the Philippines to Darwin. By 23 January, Port Darwin was briefly home to eight submarines, three cruisers and eight destroyers, all from the Asiatic Fleet. Kittyhawk fighters and Douglas A24 dive-bombers of the US

Army Air Force staged through Darwin on their way to the Dutch East Indies. RAAF Hudson bombers flew back to Darwin from Ambon and Timor for refitting and repair. Australian, British, Dutch and American ships used Darwin as a fuelling and supply stop.

On 11 January 1942, the Japanese began their long-awaited attack on the Dutch East Indies. Rather than tackle Java first, they struck at Tarakan Island, off the north-east coast of Borneo, near the town of Tanjungselor. Tarakan was a major oilfield. The Dutch defenders were quickly overwhelmed—and brutally massacred. Given that oil was Japan's principal goal of the war, this was an important victory for them. However, Java remained the ultimate prize, and Japanese forces were now closing on it in a pincer movement. Their surging army swept down the Malay peninsula towards Singapore, threatening Java from the north-west, while their victory at Tarakan gave them an important base to the north-east of the target island.

On 20 January, Nagumo Force took up station off Rabaul, on the northern tip of New Britain. Again Mitsuo Fuchida led the way. With a force of 90 bombers and fighters, he swept in to attack Rabaul harbour and the defending airfields at Vanakanau and Lakunai. To his disappointment, his fliers found little worthy of their attention. 'I saw just two enemy planes,' Fuchida recalled. 'They were attempting to take off from one of the two airfields and were promptly disposed of by our fighters. The second airfield was empty.'

Fuchida's Val dive-bombers sank a lone cargo ship in the harbour while his Kate bombers, 'for lack of any more worthwhile target', dropped their 800-kg high-explosive bombs on the coastal guns at the harbour entrance. To Fuchida the whole sorry affair was a waste of the superb talents of Nagumo Force. 'If ever a sledgehammer had been used to crack an egg, this was the time,' he wrote afterwards.

The despair felt by Allied forces as the Japanese inexorably closed in on them is caught in a cable sent by Wing Commander J.M. Lerew from the RAAF base at Vanakanau, one of the two airfields defending Rabaul. Lerew had sent up the two aircraft so quickly dispatched by Fuchida's fighters. The Wing Commander was originally told to use his discretion in deciding whether to withdraw his forces if Rabaul came under attack. On 21 January, the day after Fuchida's bombers struck, he was ordered to hold on rather than withdraw. RAAF Command in Australia cabled him: 'Begins. Rabaul not yet fallen. Assist Army in keeping aerodrome open. Maintain communications as long as possible. Ends.' The cipher staff in Melbourne at first had trouble with Lerew's reply, which they unscrambled as: *'Nos morituri te salutamus.'* It took them a while to realise it was in Latin, and even longer to translate it. Lerew had replied with the Roman gladiator's traditional nod to the emperor before mortal combat began: 'We who are about to die salute you.'

Fuchida's bombers returned to Rabaul on 22 January, but their attack was hardly worth the trouble. Next day the Japanese captured Rabaul without a struggle.

The various RAAF and Dutch forward bases, in such places as Ambon in the Moluccas and Koepang in south-west Timor, became increasingly untenable. Japanese raiders attacked them with land-based bombers and fighters. The Japanese methodically destroyed aircraft on the ground and shot them down in the air. As the British, Australian, Dutch and American forces withdrew or were captured, the airfields at Darwin and Batchelor assumed new importance. They were a safe haven for the retreating troops. And they were a base from which the Allies could counter-attack the new Japanese positions. Such was the speed of the Japanese advance that, far from being remote from the war, by the end of January 1942 Darwin was on the front line. In eight short weeks the Japanese had redrawn the map of Asia and the Pacific.

◆ ◆ ◆

There can be little doubt that the speed of their advance took even the Japanese by surprise. Their first objective was to capture oilfields, and in less than five weeks from the start of the war they had taken Tarakan and had the major prize of Java in their sights. Where to next?

The Imperial Japanese Navy, anxious to dominate the strategic planning of the war, considered three major new policy directions. It came down to a choice of three targets. They could go for Australia.

They could go for India. Or they could go for the Hawaiian Islands. Whichever they chose, they would need to move quickly. The one luxury they could not afford was to give the Americans time to regroup and rearm.

The argument for invasion of Australia was straightforward. The Allies, particularly the Americans, were bound to counter-attack at some point. American mass-production methods would soon generate a formidable bomber force, so the counter-attack would probably be delivered from the air. Australia was the logical land base from which to mount it. So Australia would have to be placed under Japanese control or, at the very least, cut off from the United States.

Thus the Navy reasoned. However, the Japanese Army would have none of it. Its commanders judged that the occupation of even part of Australia would require ten of their best combat divisions, and they could not spare them. The Navy suspected that the Army had another, unstated reason for rejecting the Australian option. The Army had not lost sight of Russia as a major target. It believed that Germany would attack in the Caucasus in the Northern Hemisphere spring of 1942. If that happened, Japan might profitably attack Russia from the east. The Army preferred to keep that juicy possibility on the table. Australia could wait.

The Army had similar reservations about India. Any attack in this direction would need to be coordinated with the Germans, and Hitler was not as forthcoming as he might have been in cooperating with his Japanese ally. Best not to rely on the Germans but instead focus on Japan's immediate Pacific neighbourhood. That meant looking east, rather than west or south, for new fields to conquer. The ultimate target would have to be the Hawaiian Islands, probably after an invasion of Midway.

Nevertheless Australia could not be ignored. If a land invasion of that vast country was out, the question remained: What could the Japanese do to seal off and neutralise an increasingly dangerous Allied sanctuary?

◆　◆　◆

Thomas Alexander Wells, Judge of the Northern Territory, was something of a maverick. He particularly enjoyed ruling against the government, usually in the person of the Administrator. Mr Justice Wells had little time for the Territory's Aboriginal people, either. Whenever they appeared before him, he was inclined to dismiss their evidence as worthless. The death sentence he imposed on an Aboriginal man named Dhakiyarr, after accepting the very flimsy case against him, made world headlines. It was overturned on appeal.

On 22 December 1941 Wells put aside his judicial robes and waded into the row over air-raid precautions in Darwin. In a five-page letter to the Chief Air Raid Warden Arthur Miller, he quietly demolished the plans already in place to protect the town's citizens in the event of an air raid. His letter makes total sense: in short, he was right.

The printed instructions issued to householders advised them that in the event of an air raid they should 'leave the house or building immediately and proceed without delay to your slit trench or refuge area'. The judge dispatched this with a single sentence: 'As everyone is well aware, there are no "slit trenches"—or "refuge areas" either, in the proper sense of the term—available anywhere in Darwin.' There were slit trenches aplenty for the military, of course. But Darwin's householders would have to take their chances.

As had happened on the night of 11 December, when the air-raid sirens sounded, Darwin's citizens understood that their best option was to leave their houses and proceed to any open spaces in the neighbourhood. This was bad advice, the judge argued. It meant people would take to the roads, where they would be 'in very serious danger of being run down by military vehicles and ambulances which must continue to use the roads without lights, or with dimmed lights'. The judge's advice, heavily underlined in the typewritten letter, required less of Darwin's civilians: 'The proper course for people to follow is to simply turn out all lights and remain quietly in their homes. Let them get into bed, or, if they wish, under the bed.' The judge noted that the houses of Darwin were not packed tightly together but spread out. By remaining in their homes, he said, people would automatically disperse themselves, reducing the risk of mass casualties from a single direct hit.

The judge warmed to his theme.

I notice that in the last issue of the *Northern Standard* volunteers have been asked to come forward for the purpose of digging refuge trenches. It has apparently been completely overlooked that it is quite impossible to dig trenches without extensive blasting in most places in Darwin—including the places particularly mentioned in the advertisement; it has also apparently been overlooked that in the wet season, due to commence any moment now, refuge trenches would be not only useless but definitely dangerous—unless in rare cases where drainage could be arranged.

Last but not least, the judge dismissed as irrelevant the preparations made by the civil defence forces. They had put too much effort into fire-fighting, he said, when it was very unlikely that the Japanese would use incendiary bombs. 'The purpose of a bombing raid on Darwin would be the destruction of the oil fuel tanks, aerodromes, wharf, ammunition dumps and other similar objectives,' Wells wrote. 'All these can be dealt with much more effectively with high explosive bombs, either delayed action or percussion, than with incendiary bombs. The latter are effective against large city buildings and factories, and large congested areas of buildings—none of which exist in Darwin.'

The judge had his own simple plan. Like most tropical towns in Australia, Darwin's houses were often built on pillars to allow air to flow freely beneath them. People should be encouraged to build sand-bag shelters, where possible under their houses, he wrote. After all, there was no shortage of sand, or bags.

Having dealt with the practical details, Wells moved on to the legal status of the air-raid wardens. As things stood, the wardens had none, the judge opined. If they issued an order, the citizens of Darwin were under no legal obligation to obey it. Furthermore, the wardens risked criminal prosecution if they damaged property or caused injury while trying to enforce their orders. The judge cited the breaking of the shop window at C.J. Cashman & Co., the smashing of electrical fittings at Soldiers' Hall and the break-in at Young's Garage during the last air-raid alert. All three acts were criminal. Judge Wells concluded: 'Steps should be taken by A.R.P. officials to ensure that there is no recurrence of such unreasonable officiousness, which is not at all likely to secure the cooperation of the public.'

The letter, far from disturbing the wardens, was music to their ears. Here was confirmation from no less a person than the Judge of the Northern Territory that their lack of any legal framework left them dangerously exposed. Two days later, on 24 December, a delegation of four wardens, led by Arthur Miller and Edgar Harrison, descended on Wells. Three of the four were the same men who had confronted Administrator Abbott in his office 12 days earlier. Essentially, they told Wells they were fed up with lack of support from the Administrator. How could the judge help?

The trade unions, who also had no love for Abbott, had their Citizens' War Effort Committee. On 27 December the judge sent a copy of his letter to the committee. He left its members in no doubt whom to blame for the debacle. The final sentence of Wells's covering letter to the committee read: 'If the information given to me by the A.R.P. officials is correct, it would appear to be quite useless to approach the local Administration authorities.' The trade unions owned the only newspaper, the *Northern Standard*. On 30 December the *Standard* gleefully published on its front page the parts of the letter that set out the inadequacies of the present civil defence arrangements, under the headline 'Judge Attacks A.R.P. Lack.' It also published the judge's confirmation of the wardens' lack of legal status.

The cat was now out of the bag. Darwin's citizens had been told, on no less authority than that of the Judge of the Northern Territory, that they were not being properly protected against Japanese attack. Furthermore, they were under no obligation to obey any order issued by an air-raid warden. If they were told to leave their homes and evacuate to Adelaide or Sydney or Alice Springs or anywhere, they could say no. The evacuation was never popular, so there was a real possibility people would rebel. Even if all they were told was to put out a light, they could still say no if the order came from a civilian air-raid warden. Not only that, they now had confirmation of what was obvious to one and all, that the air-raid precautions for Darwin were seriously misconceived and largely ineffectual.

The Citizens' War Effort Committee called a public meeting on 7 January 1942. There is no record of how many of Darwin's citizens turned up—it may have been as few as seven or eight—but they were certainly of one mind. The meeting voted unanimously for the Administrator to be sacked. The motion passed read:

> This meeting of the people of Darwin demands the removal of Mr Abbott from the post of Administrator in view of:—
> 1. Reports received from the wives of the people of Darwin of despicable treatment accorded to them and their children during evacuation, for the arrangements for which the Administrator admits full responsibility.
> 2. General handling by the Administrator of the war effort in Darwin.
> 3. The complete neglect of the welfare of the town and territory during his administration.

The *Northern Standard* splashed the story across its front page on 9 January 1942, under the headline 'Abbott's Removal Urged: Public Meeting Alleges Bungling of Evacuation, War Effort'. The *Standard* shyly failed to mention how many had actually attended the mutinous meeting, but it published the full text of the motion and noted that it had passed unanimously. Administrator Abbott was now publicly on the rack.

After the judge's comments became public knowledge, the wardens found their job difficult, if not impossible, to carry out. They responded in the only way they could, by staging a mutiny of their own. First to depart was Brough Newell, the Director of First Aid. On 22 January he wrote to Chief Warden Miller, saying he was resigning with effect from noon next day, and quoting public apathy as the reason. He concluded his resignation letter: 'I therefore recommend that . . . the public of Darwin be advised through the press that in the event of their being wounded in an air (or other) attack, they must either walk to the New Civil Hospital or die on the spot.' On 23 January the wardens held a meeting and informed Administrator Abbott that unless they were granted proper legal authority within three days, they would resign in a body. When the 26 January deadline passed without the grant, or indeed any move at all by His Honour, they resigned. Officially, Darwin now had no air-raid wardens. (In fact the wardens did a secret deal with the Army, promising to turn out if needed. They kept their word.)

◆ ◆ ◆

With Rabaul in Japanese hands, Nagumo Force's four giant aircraft carriers, together with their escorting ships, returned to the Japanese naval base at Truk, in the Caroline Islands north of New Guinea. Here they were told to prepare to support 'south-west operations', meaning the conquest of the Dutch East Indies and the Portuguese colony of East Timor. The Navy calculated that the only obstacle to Japanese plans would be a counter-attack by American and other Allied forces operating from bases in northern Australia.

Yamamoto's Combined Fleet headquarters proposed an amphibious invasion of Port Darwin to forestall any problems from that direction. Both the Naval General Staff and the Army responded with a flat 'no'. Combined Fleet then decided there was only one solution to the problem of Darwin. Nagumo Force had proven its ability to strike effectively with its Pearl Harbor attack, followed by its effortless humbling of Rabaul. So Nagumo Force would settle this problem too: on 15 February 1942 the aircraft carriers *Akagi*, *Kaga*, *Sôryu* and *Hiryu* left Palau and headed south for the Banda Sea and Darwin. They were escorted by the battleships *Hiei* and *Kirishima*, two heavy cruisers, *Tone* and *Chikuma*, the light cruiser *Abukuma*, and nine destroyers. This was essentially the same force that had attacked Pearl Harbor, reduced only by the absence of two of the aircraft carriers, *Zuikaku* and *Shokaku*. Nevertheless it was a formidable battle group, capable of doing formidable damage. It proposed to do just that.

Chapter 7

Convoy for Koepang to
return to Darwin

On 20 January 1942, the Japanese mine-laying submarine I-124 attacked three US Navy ships off Cape Fourcroy on Bathurst Island, about 110 kilometres north-west of Darwin. The I-124's torpedoes missed USS *Trinity* and its two destroyer escorts, USS *Alden* and USS *Edsell*. *Alden* replied with depth charges. Three Australian corvettes, HMAS *Deloraine*, *Katoomba* and *Lithgow*, raced to join the fray. The hunt lasted two days. At the end, I-124 and her 46 crew lay at the bottom of the Timor Sea in 45 metres of water. *Deloraine* received most of the credit for the kill. It was a rare victory, but it highlighted the fact that the waters around Darwin were now a Japanese hunting ground.

On 10 February 1942, a Japanese spy plane from the 3rd Reconnaissance Squadron, based on Ambon, flew high over Darwin. The crew counted about 30 aircraft on the ground at the two airfields. They photographed an 'aircraft carrier' and five destroyers in Port Darwin, together with 21 merchant ships. Given that American aircraft carriers remained the Imperial Japanese Navy's highest priority target, the discovery of the USS *Langley* must have caused a frisson of excitement in the Japanese high command.

The *Langley* was an old collier, converted to an aircraft carrier in 1922 by plating a flight deck above the collier superstructure. She was the first ever aircraft carrier in the US Navy, and was known affectionately as the 'Covered Wagon'. By 1937 she had been well superseded by newer, larger carriers, and the US Navy decided to convert her to a seaplane tender. Some of the plating of the forward flight deck was removed, leaving slightly more than half the flight deck in place. The surviving portion was used to transport fully assembled aircraft by sea. *Langley's* flight deck could not be used for take-off or landing, but from a high-flying Japanese reconnaissance plane she must still have looked for all the world like a slightly peculiar aircraft carrier.

Ironically, the *Langley* was the last ship of the American Asiatic Fleet to leave Darwin. She sailed next day, 11 February, for Fremantle in Western Australia, to pick up a load of Kittyhawks. That left the seaplane tender USS *William B. Preston* as Darwin's only remaining warship from the Asiatic Fleet. The *Willy B* stayed in Darwin to support her clutch of PBY Catalina aircraft operating reconnaissance missions from Port Darwin.

♦ ♦ ♦

The evacuation of Darwin's women and children continued apace. On 10 January, 187 sailed south on the *Montoro*. A further 173 left on 26 January aboard the *Koolama*. On 15 February, the final shipload of 77 left on the *Koolinda*.

Not everybody left by sea. The planes that brought the 'Flying Wharfies' to Darwin returned south with women and children evacuees on board. Others left by train for Birdum and Larrimah, then rode in Army trucks to Alice Springs. Some of the Alice Springs contingent then caught the Ghan train south to Adelaide. Others chose to stay in Alice Springs, to the fury of the local administration. As early as 23 December 1941 Police Superintendent A.V. Stretton, the Acting District Officer in Alice Springs, wrote to Administrator Abbott to say: 'A large number of additional troops are likely to be stationed here which will considerably tax our services, particularly water and sanitary. Might I respectfully suggest that public attention be directed to the fact that evacuees will not be permitted to remain at Alice Springs.' He was told firmly that he could not force them to move on. Anybody who arrived from Darwin to Alice Springs had every right to stay there.

Nor was everybody who left Darwin a woman or a child. Audrey Kennon worked as a clerk for the State Shipping Company. She drew up the passenger lists. 'At holiday time,' she remembers, 'there were a lot of men on the ship and it was my job to take them off and book women and children on.' Not all of them accepted Audrey's ruling. 'There was one man in particular who threw a wad of notes on the counter and said: "You get me on the ship." I said: "Don't you think the women and children should go first?" He said: "I've made my money here and I don't want to lose it here." I had to say to him: "I'm sorry." '

Men paid for seats on commercial flights, to the disapproval of those who thought their places should have been occupied by women and children. There was a strong suggestion that those who fled were foreigners, not regular Aussies. Lieutenant Commander McManus, the senior Naval Intelligence officer in Darwin, set out the widespread suspicion when he reported: 'A few Australians, many Italians and Greeks are distinctly "windy", the Italians and Greeks are besieging the Airlines for accommodation on south-bound planes and many have gone by rail to Larrimah and Birdum in the hope that they will be given passages on the military convoys proceeding to Alice Springs.'

◆ ◆ ◆

Aircraft continued to stage through Darwin on their way to reinforce the Dutch East Indies, particularly Java. The fate of the 3rd Pursuit Squadron illustrates the perils of the journey.[1] Eleven Kittyhawks flew into Darwin, with Timor as their next stop. Two of the planes, flown by Lieutenant Robert Oestreicher and Lieutenant Robert Buel, stayed grounded in Darwin with engine trouble. The remaining nine set off on 9 February 1942 for Koepang. One turned back; the rest became lost in poor weather trying to find Penfoie airstrip in Timor and ran low on fuel. The pilots either bailed out or crash-landed on the Timor coast. Seven were rescued by the RAAF, but the eighth was killed. That left Darwin with just two fighter aircraft, both unserviceable.

The military situation to the town's north and west grew increasingly tense. At the beginning of 1942 the Allies had formed the short-lived and ill-fated joint command ABDA (American, British, Dutch and Australian forces), led by the British General Sir Archibald Wavell. On 15 February 1942 the unimaginable happened: Singapore fell. It remains the worst military disaster in Australian history. The Australians lost 1789 dead and 1306 wounded in a vain defence of the 'impregnable' British base. Worse, the Japanese captured 15,395 Australian troops, the Australian Imperial Forces' entire 8th Division. The catastrophe numbed the Australian population at home. What more terrible news would the future hold? Would Australia itself be next, put to the sword by the all-conquering Japanese?

As the British, Australians and Indians crumbled in Malaya and Singapore, Wavell became increasingly desperate for reinforcements and supplies to keep some sort of grip on the Dutch prize of Java. With no air cover and no control of the sea, Java was probably a lost cause from day one, but Wavell piled on pressure. The Australian War Cabinet relented on 5 February 1942.

Port Darwin was giving shelter to three American transports—*Meigs*, *Mauna Loa* and *Port Mar*—and the Australian transport *Tulagi*. Fighting ships in Darwin included the Australian sloops HMAS *Swan* and *Warrego*. The American heavy cruiser USS *Houston* and the destroyer USS *Peary* were not far away and could be diverted to Darwin for escort duty. It was agreed that they should form up as a convoy to carry troops and military equipment to reinforce the Dutch East Indies. The transports loaded the Australian 2/4th Pioneers and an Australian anti-tank troop, together with the 148th US Field Artillery Regiment, and all their equipment. On 15 February 1942, the day Singapore fell, the convoy, escorted by *Houston*, *Peary*, *Swan* and *Warrego*, set off for Koepang.

By 10.30 a.m. on the first day, the convoy was in trouble. The ships were spotted by a patrolling Japanese Kawanishi H6K 'Mavis' flying boat, probably based at Ambon. *Houston* sent an urgent radio call to Darwin for fighter support. The two Kittyhawks, now repaired and serviceable, were the only fighters available. When the call for fighter support came in, Oestreicher was already in the air and could not be reached, so Buel set off alone to tackle the intruding flying boat. What happened next is one of those extraordinary stories of war. As the two aircraft met over the Timor Sea, each managed to shoot the other down in flames. Buel died alone, his fate a mystery to his comrades for more than 40 years. Five of the nine Japanese crew of the Mavis survived. They drifted for five days in a life-raft before reaching shore on Melville Island, where local people handed them over to the Australian Army. The Japanese prisoners succeeded in persuading everyone that they were survivors of a wrecked fishing boat, and stuck to their story throughout the war, which they spent in Cowra prisoner-of-war camp. (One of the repatriated prisoners, Marekuni Takahara, eventually broke silence in 1985 and told the true story. Only then did Buel's fate become known.) Oestreicher returned to Darwin, refuelled, and flew out to look for his buddy. He found nothing: no convoy, and no trace of Buel. He returned alone.

That evening more Kittyhawks arrived in Darwin. Major Floyd Pell's 33rd Pursuit Squadron had intended to fly from Amberley near Brisbane to Port Pirie in South Australia, then on to Perth in Western Australia to meet the USS *Langley*, which would have transported the aircraft as deck cargo to Java. However, ABDA needed fighter cover urgently for the Darwin convoy, so Pell's squadron was ordered directly north from Port Pirie. Again, the perils of the journey are well illustrated by the planes' fate. Twenty-five Kittyhawks had left Amberley air base. Only 15 reached Port Pirie. Of the 15, only ten made it to Darwin. One Kittyhawk crashed at Port Pirie, killing the pilot. Four others experienced engine trouble. The exhausted survivors arrived at the RAAF base on the afternoon of 15 February. Despite the long journey, Pell took off in the late afternoon with five other Kittyhawks and flew over the convoy.

With no enemy in sight, the planes returned to Darwin. All now needed servicing before the long flight to Timor and Java.

◆ ◆ ◆

After the convoy had been spotted by the Mavis, Area Combined Head-quarters in Darwin felt it was unsafe for them to continue. At 17.18 p.m. Darwin time on 15 February, they cabled ABDA Command, with copies to South West Pacific Command in Melbourne: 'In view of enemy knowledge of convoy return to Darwin appears advisable.' They were quickly proved right. Next morning a force of 35 Japanese land-based bombers and nine flying boats struck the convoy. The cruiser USS *Houston* led the counter-attack with a furious anti-aircraft barrage, which proved highly effective. According to an Australian eyewitness on one of the troop ships: 'She spun on her heel, every gun was blazing. She kept the Japs right up in the sky and they could not get down to bomb us.' The Japanese were beaten off, more or less single-handedly by *Houston*. The Japanese claimed afterwards that three transports had been badly damaged, but in fact the convoy suffered not a single direct hit and emerged largely unscathed. Nevertheless, ABDA Command agreed that it was too dangerous for the convoy to continue and on the afternoon of 16 February it cabled Area Command Headquarters in Darwin with a simple message: 'On review of situation today have ordered convoy for Koepang to return to Darwin.' The ships arrived back in Port Darwin on 18 February.

The two American escorts returning with the convoy, *Houston* and *Peary*, did not hang about. They refuelled, then set off the same day to link up with the Allied fleet at Tjilatjap (now usually referred to as Cilacap) on the south coast of Java. They had barely left Darwin when *Peary* broke off to chase a submarine contact, while *Houston* continued towards Java. *Peary* burned up a huge amount of fuel racing after the submarine, and her captain decided it would be prudent to return to Darwin to refuel. She anchored in Port Darwin at about 2.30 a.m. on the morning of 19 February.

The harbour was now packed with ships. As well as the usual clutter of merchantmen and transports waiting to load or unload, there were fighting ships from the Royal Australian Navy and the US Navy. The grand total came to 45 ships. They were anchored in a comparatively confined part of the harbour, with two tied up at the wharf for unloading. The fighting ships were corvettes HMAS *Deloraine* and *Katoomba*, sloop HMAS *Swan*, auxiliary minesweeper HMAS *Tolga*, patrol boat HMAS *Coongoola*, destroyer USS *Peary*, and seaplane tender USS *William B. Preston*. *Katoomba* was trapped inside the floating dock and incapable of manoeuvring, though she could still use her machine guns. The rest could fight. Other Australian Navy ships in the harbour were boom-net ships HMAS *Karangi*, *Kara Kara*, *Koala* and *Kangaroo*, auxiliary minesweeper HMAS *Gunbar*, depot ship HMAS *Platypus*, lugger HMAS *Mavie*, and examination steamer HMAS *Southern Cross*.

The two merchant ships waiting at the wharf to unload were MV *Neptuna* on the outer berth and SS *Barossa* on the inner berth. *Neptuna* was packed with depth charges and other explosives. HMAS *Swan* tied up alongside her, hoping to transfer *Neptuna*'s explosives directly from ship to ship. Out in the harbour stood the troop-ship SS *Zealandia*, the hospital ship SS *Manunda*, the three American transports from the convoy, USS *Port Mar*, *Meigs* and *Mauna Loa*, the American freighter USS *Admiral Halstead*, the transport MV *Tulagi* (also from the convoy), the British oil tanker *British Motorist*, the Norwegian oil tanker *Benjamin Franklin* and the coal hulk *Kelat*. There were 19 other small ships. In addition to the ships in Port Darwin, two US supply ships, *Don Isidro* and *Florence D*, were en route to the Philippines. On the morning of 19 February they were off Bathurst Island, not far away.

Darwin was now an ideal target. The reconnaissance flight on 10 February told the Japanese they could expect to find as many as 30 aircraft on the ground, while the harbour very likely contained ships from the convoy as well as the usual complement of warships and transports. With luck they might even find an aircraft carrier. There was a clinching argument, unknown to Darwin's defenders. The Japanese planned to invade Timor the next day, 20 February. Timor was only 700 kilometres from Darwin, so any counter-attack would very likely come from Darwin. To protect the Timor invasion, Darwin would have to be taken out of the war.

The Darwin defenders may not have known about the Timor attack, but they were very clear about the threat posed by the convoy's presence in the harbour. Captain Penry Thomas, the Naval Officer in Charge, Darwin, told the Royal Commission: 'As soon as ABDACOM [ABDA Command] ordered the return of the convoy I spoke to Group Captain Scherger and told him I thought we should have visitors the following day, and he quite agreed. It is very obvious, is it not?'

That night Arthur Wellington, a postal worker, wrote to his wife and daughter, who had been evacuated south:

My Dear Nin and Aldyth,

It is after midnight, and have been on the paysheets, but hope to get them cleaned up tomorrow with a bit of luck. A hammering with the overtime, as usual.

Our blackout is OK. People are not worrying overmuch about it. The blue paint they put on the light globes soon burns off, and then there is as much light as before.

Sent down three parcels last night, and they should be there Saturday week with a bit of luck. I sent down all the cutlery and silverware and your cottons that you had to leave behind.

Today I insured all our belongings against war risk for 150 pounds, and it cost twelve shillings, so that is not too bad. There is always a chance that we will have to clear out and leave the rest of the furniture behind, and 150 pounds would help us re-furnish.

You asked me to send you down some blue for the washing. There is plenty up here, even if you can't get it in Adelaide. Jolly's are on the short side, but I got some from Yam Yeans, some from Fong Yuen Kee, and nine nobs of it from Fang Chong Loong.

Things are not getting any easier. Business and work is increasing all the time, and there is no doubt the Darwin post office is paying its way.

Mr. Bald hasn't been too good the last few days, and I have been trying to give him a bit of extra help with the trench at the back of his house. It is going to be a very substantial job. It's 13 feet long and about 3 feet wide, with two railway irons the full length for reinforcement for the sand bags. The depth is about 5 ft. We have galvanised iron across the top and hope to get another three layers of sand bags. Everyone says it will be safe from anything but a direct hit. It's where I'll be going if there is a raid.

You mustn't worry about that possibility. A lot of ships came into the harbour late today, they were the same ones that sailed a few days ago. They were bound for Timor. The talk all around town is that the Japs forced them to turn back. If that's right, the enemy can't be far from here, but I can't see that any of the higher ups seem to be too concerned about it.

Sorry that Aldyth is having trouble with her teeth. They are a worry for grownups, let alone nippers. Do hope the worst is soon over.

Now, my dear, it is one a.m. and have just had a ring from the airways mob, Qantas, to say that all their plane arrangements have been altered and we have got to get the mails out early.

Sweet dreams my sweethearts, and loads and loads of kisses and hugs to you both,

From your loving husband and Daddy,

Arthur.

It is worth standing back at this point and looking at the overall picture of Darwin's defences. Darwin could and did expect an attack from land, sea or air, or a combination of any or all of them. In general, a well-organised defence would consist of a hard front line backed up by supplies, support and reinforcement kept well to the south and out of reach of the initial onslaught. Darwin, as we have seen, had the opposite. The hospitals were right on the front line, offering no sanctuary to the inevitable influx of military and civilian wounded in the event of an attack.

Port Darwin is large. Its deep water, huge tides and dodgy sea bed make anchoring difficult in some parts. Nevertheless, scattering the ships in the harbour would seem an elementary precaution against air and sea attack. Instead, the 45 ships packed into a comparatively small area in the centre. Sitting ducks generally display more common sense and more instinct for self-preservation.

The RAAF cannot be held responsible for the lack of fighter aircraft. There were none to be had. However, putting the new RAAF airfield so close to the coast, with no working radar to give advance warning, meant an attacking enemy would be on top of the base before anybody had time to call 'Scramble!'

As a result of internal tensions and poor administration, an official civil defence was nonexistent. The air-raid wardens had resigned *en masse*. They had made a secret pact with the Army to turn out if needed, but they would not be operating at full efficiency when they did, and the citizens of Darwin could expect to pay the price for any shortfall.

Around dawn on 19 February Nagumo Force reached 9°S, 129°E, the prearranged launch point in the Timor Sea south of Maluku Island. The ever-cautious Nagumo sent off a weather-watch plane to check that Darwin was clear of cloud. It reached Darwin just after dawn, at about 7.30 a.m., but the crew's radio failed, and no message came back. Nagumo decided not to wait. They were now about 350 kilometres north-west of Darwin. The four aircraft carriers turned away from the town and into the north-west wind. The flight decks became a turmoil of blue smoke and bellowing engines as 36 Zero fighters, 71 Val dive-bombers and 81 Kate horizontal bombers manoeuvred onto the launch catapults. A total of 188 aircraft took to the skies, five more than in the first wave that attacked Pearl Harbor, and more than twice the force that had attacked Rabaul. The Pearl Harbor force included 43 Zeroes but only 51 Vals. The Japanese could afford to cut down on fighters this time and concentrate on bombers. If Darwin proved to be as poorly defended as Rabaul, fighters would hardly be needed, while a few extra bombers might come in handy. By 8.45 a.m. the entire force was in the air and in prearranged formation. The planes set a course of 148 degrees, a track that would take them a little to the east of Darwin. Mitsuo Fuchida led the way.

Chapter 8

'Zeroes! Zeroes! Zeroes!'

As day dawned on 19 February 1942, the skies above Darwin were far from empty. At that time of year, the sun rises at about 6.45 a.m. At 3.30 a.m. six Hudsons from RAAF 2 Squadron took off from Penfoie on Timor, evacuating all but 23 RAAF men (who had volunteered to stay behind) from the last vestiges of their base. The Japanese had been dropping leaflets all over the island warning the native population against helping the Dutch or taking part in demolition operations. Clearly an invasion was imminent. The Hudsons set course for Darwin, estimating they would arrive at about 8 a.m.

The Hudsons, as we have seen, enjoyed the distinction of being the first to be shot at, in this case by their own side. Instead of arriving via the 'friendly' corridor and flashing the correct light signal, they chose to track in over Fannie Bay without the benefit of a signal and without lowering their wheels, the other way of indicating that they were 'friendly'. The Fannie Bay AA guns fired a single warning shot, leading to all-round recriminations over trigger-happy Army gunners who couldn't tell the difference between a Hudson and a hand-moulded sushi, and RAAF pilots who could not be bothered to follow proper procedures. The day was off to a bad start.

At about 8 a.m. two of the five Catalinas of the US Navy's 22nd Patrol Squadron took off from Port Darwin and headed north on their separate ways to check the seas and skies for intruders. They were particularly on the lookout for enemy submarines. One of the US Navy's best pilots, Lieutenant Thomas Moorer, flew the Catalina assigned to patrol off the coast of Bathurst Island. Moorer had been one of the first pilots to take off from Pearl Harbor on 7 December 1941. He was no stranger to combat or to Japanese attack. However, his main job now was to check the sea below. If he had looked up, he might have seen the nine Zero fighters detach themselves from Fuchida's inbound flight and swoop down on him.

The slow-flying twin-engined Catalina didn't stand a chance against a single Zero, let alone nine of them. Moorer recalled the Zeroes 'setting my plane afire, destroying the port engine and shooting large holes in the fuel tanks and fuselage'. Before anyone had time to radio an alarm, the Catalina and its crew of eight crash-landed on the sea. Four of the crew were wounded in the attack, but the rest escaped unscathed. They piled into the Catalina's rubber dinghy and were picked up about half an hour later, not far from Bathurst Island, by the freighter *Florence D*. Darwin had missed its first chance of an early warning of inbound raiders. The Japanese had been too quick.

◆ ◆ ◆

By 18 February 1942 there were 252 wharfies registered in Darwin. They were broken up into 18 gangs of 14 men apiece. The gangs regularly worked around the clock in three eight-hour shifts of six gangs each. For no clear reason, when the roster was posted on 18 February for work next day, only five gangs were called for the first day shift. They were 1, 2, 3, 17 and 18, a total of 70 men. No. 4 gang was told it would not be required until the next shift. The postings listed only the gang number, not the names of the men.

When the wharfies clocked on, the most urgent task was to unload *Neptuna*, on the outer berth, with her hold full of depth charges and explosives. *Barossa*, on the inner berth, was not quite such a high priority.

She was carrying mostly wooden piles to repair and improve the wharf. The wharfies began the weary task of dragging railway trucks out to the berths and started unloading.

◆ ◆ ◆

The Wirraway fighters of RAAF 12 Squadron had split up as part of an entirely sensible dispersal plan. Most were at Batchelor. Five Wirraways remained in Darwin, but on 19 February all were on the ground and unserviceable, awaiting mechanical work. Darwin's only serviceable fighter aircraft were ten Kittyhawks of the US Army Air Corps' 33rd Pursuit Squadron, and they were due to take off at dawn for Timor, on their way to Java. As it happened, engine trouble delayed the take-off. At 9.15 a.m. they were finally on their way, escorted by a B17 Flying Fortress giving them navigation support. Led by Major Floyd 'Slugger' Pell, but this time including the experienced Lieutenant Robert Oestreicher, the flight set off for their first Timor staging point of Koepang on the long and dangerous route to Java. The Japanese were already attacking all over the Dutch East Indies, and there was no certainty that the landing fields would be safe or even under Allied control. Most of the pilots were raw beginners with fewer than 20 hours at the controls of a fighter. None had ever fired their guns in anger. It was a desperate situation.

The timing could not have been worse. At about 9.35 a.m., US Army Air Corps Operations in Darwin called the flight by radio. Captain Connelly told Pell that Koepang reported low cloud down to 600 feet with scattered heavy rainstorms. He advised Pell to return to Darwin. Conscious of his pilots' inexperience, Pell ordered the flight to turn back. He wanted no repetition of the fate of the 3rd Pursuit Squadron ten days earlier, when all eight aircraft were lost in bad weather. Reluctantly the P40s wheeled around and headed towards Darwin, while the B17 continued to Timor.

◆ ◆ ◆

The Royal Australian Navy stationed two coastwatchers on the Tiwi Islands to guard the approaches to Darwin. Father John McGrath kept watch from the mission station at Nguiu on the south-east corner of Bathurst Island. At Garden Point, on the northern tip of Melville Island, John Gribble, a Navy officer, also maintained a lookout, supported by Tiwi Islanders. Given the direction from which Fuchida's raiding party was arriving, the Japanese planes must have come into Gribble's view first.

We will never know with certainty what happened next. Both Douglas Lockwood and Professor Alan Powell report that at 9.15 a.m. Gribble radioed a warning of 'a large number of aircraft' sighted. Both Powell and Lockwood agree that the message was received at the shore-based naval communication station HMAS *Coonawarra*. Lockwood names the signal officer from *Coonawarra*—Warrant Officer Bill Phaup —who telephoned Lieutenant Commander J.C.B. McManus, Naval Intelligence Staff Officer, in Darwin, to pass on the message. Gribble had given no details of the planes' identification or direction. McManus telephoned his counterpart at RAAF Intelligence and passed on the warning. The RAAF officer told him the planes were probably the ten Kittyhawks en route to Timor (which a glance at a map would have told him was impossible). McManus, as reported by Lockwood, was unconvinced. He told Lockwood later: 'I was confident that Gribble must have seen something unusual. I wanted to sound the alarm at once but was overruled. There had been a series of earlier false alarms which it was undesirable to repeat.' Both Lockwood and Powell then remark on the fact that this first warning is nowhere mentioned in the Lowe Commission report, although McManus gave detailed evidence to Lowe less than two weeks after the event. In particular, McManus gave a detailed account of how the coastwatcher system worked.

There is another version of this story, which did not emerge until 2001. In 2000, two Northern Territory historians, Peter and Sheila Forrest, interviewed Brother Edward Bennett as part of the research for their book *Federation Frontline: A people's history of World War II in the Northern Territory*. Bennett had been with Gribble on the day. In his version, he urged Gribble to radio a warning but Gribble refused.

He said the message would have to be sent in code, and he didn't have the necessary code books. Bennett told the Forrests no message was sent.

Readers will have to make up their own mind about which story to believe. My instinct is to trust Bennett. Phaup makes no mention of the Gribble sighting in his written report of 25 February 1942, submitted to the Naval Board. I have combed through the evidence given under oath to the Lowe Commission by both McManus and Captain Penry Thomas. If the Gribble warning had come through to McManus, who was with Thomas at Navy Headquarters at the relevant time, then failure to disclose it to Lowe would have gone pretty close to perjury by both men. They both had every opportunity to reveal the message, and every reason to do so. The Gribble warning does not appear in any log book or record. There is no mention of it in the Official History, nor in the Lowe Report, nor anywhere in the verbal or written evidence on which Lowe based his findings. Only two things are reasonably certain: Gribble saw the Japanese aircraft on their way south, and at some point the warning process broke down. Darwin had missed its second chance. It is no more than a cliché to say that the memory sometimes plays strange tricks. It seems to have worked its magic pretty heavily on Gribble's sighting.

Gribble's alert may not have got through. Father John McGrath's certainly did. As we have seen, his terse call, 'Eight SE to VID. Big flight of planes passed over going south. Very high. Over,' was received loud and clear by civilian aeradio station VID in Darwin, which telephoned the message to RAAF Operations at 9.37 a.m. By 9.37 Darwin's defenders had their third and best chance to go to action stations.

Pilot Officer Saxton at RAAF Operations passed the VID message on to the Operations Controller, Flight Lieutenant C.G. Fenton. 'I went downstairs and spoke to the Commanding Officer,' Fenton recalled:

I discussed the matter with him because I had other information which did not confirm that any enemy was approaching. I was aware that a formation of P40s and a B24 [in fact it was a B17] had taken off for Koepang, and shortly after they left I was aware they had got a meteorological report when they left. I was told they were ordered to return. As soon as I got the message I plotted the position where they would have been, and it more or less corresponded with the report received from Bathurst.

This, frankly, is tosh. The outbound track from Darwin to Koepang is about 280 degrees magnetic, ten degrees north of west. An aircraft flying low along this track would pass 35 kilometres south of Bathurst Island, well out of sight of McGrath. When the ten Kittyhawks turned back, their inbound track would still have kept them 35 kilometres from the island, flying more or less due east. McGrath's message referred to a large formation flying south. To suggest that a 'big flight of planes' heading south and very high over Bathurst Island could plausibly match the plotted position of ten Kittyhawks flying east and low over the ocean 35 kilometres away stretches credulity too far.

In Fenton's version of events, Wing Commander Sturt Griffith, the Commanding Officer at the RAAF station, accepted Fenton's analysis and declined to order the air-raid sirens to sound.[1] About the only relevant fact that emerges from all this nonsense is that Pell's ten Kittyhawks were returning to Darwin from the west at about the same time as Fuchida's 188 Zeroes, Kates and Vals were arriving from the north.

◆ ◆ ◆

The nine Zeroes that had broken off from Fuchida's group to tackle Moorer's Catalina did not simply rejoin the main formation, which, as far as they were concerned, was now way ahead of them. Instead they continued separately towards Darwin. However, Fuchida led his flight off to the east in preparation for his huge clockwise circle around the town, so the nine Zeroes actually got to Darwin first. They arrived from the north, over the harbour.

Floyd Pell, commanding the flight of ten Kittyhawks, was no beginner. He was an experienced pilot who had once worked on the staff of General Brereton's US Far East Air Force in the Philippines, so he was familiar with Japanese surprise attacks. Instead of simply leading his entire formation back to the airfield, he ordered Oestreicher and four others to climb to 15,000 feet and mount a protective patrol overhead while the remaining five planes landed.

Oestreicher, the most experienced pilot, took the role of 'weaver'. He climbed above his four companions and rolled his aircraft from side to side, checking above and below as well as all around him. As they clawed their way through 8000 feet, Oestreicher's throat suddenly went dry. In his eight o'clock position (just behind his left shoulder) and 2000 feet above him he saw what was obviously a Zero on an attack dive towards the formation. He just had time to shout 'Zeroes! Zeroes! Zeroes!' into his microphone before the first Zero barged through the formation, breaking it up. Oestreicher dropped his belly tank to give his Kittyhawk more speed. Let him continue the story: 'Climbing into the sun I was able to get a small burst into one Zero, who rolled in his climb and shot me. I spun out, regaining control at 4000 feet. I again climbed and around 12,000 feet I counted 18 more enemy planes in a lazy circle at what I would judge to be 20,000 feet. I called 'B' Flight [Oestreicher's own flight] on the radio and advised heading for the clouds about five miles south of Darwin that were at an altitude of 2000 to 2500 feet.' Oestreicher wasted no time taking his own advice, and buried himself in the nearest cloud.

His warning shout and his excellent advice to hide in the clouds came too late for Lieutenant Jack Peres, part of Oestreicher's group of five Kittyhawks. Peres was shot down and killed over Gunn Point, 15 kilometres north of Darwin, becoming the first airman to die in Australian skies as a result of enemy action.

Yamamoto had insisted that Nagumo Force should include the best and most experienced pilots available. Most had fought in the war with China and were aerial combat veterans. The five patrolling Kittyhawk pilots, with the exception of Oestreicher, were absolute beginners. It was about as even a contest as a boxing match between four Muhammed Alis and a lone schoolboy flyweight champion.

Lieutenant Elton Perry's Kittyhawk followed Peres. He was shot down and killed. Lieutenant William Walker was attacked and badly wounded in the left shoulder. Landing a plane one-handed is no mean feat, but Walker managed it. He put his Kittyhawk down safely at the RAAF field, scrambled clear, and watched as his plane was strafed and burned by the wheeling Zeroes. Lieutenant Max Wiecks had his plane badly shot up, and parachuted to safety. He landed in the harbour, was swept out to sea by the huge Darwin tide, and did not reach land until after dark—a feat in itself. That left Oestreicher's Kittyhawk alone to face 36 Zeroes, 71 Vals and 81 Kates.

◆ ◆ ◆

The 14th Anti-Aircraft battery in Darwin consisted of twelve 3.7-inch guns grouped in sections at the Oval, Fannie Bay and McMillans. The battery also had two 3-inch guns at Elliott Point and a section of Lewis guns on top of the oil tanks on the foreshores of Port Darwin. There was a fourth section of four 3.7-inch guns of the 2nd AA battery at Berrimah. Each 3.7-inch section's four guns were arranged in a U shape, with a command post at the centre of the U.

Getting a group of heavy anti-aircraft guns into action is far from simple, but it nevertheless has to be done in a tearing hurry. Once the alarm is raised, the Gun Position Officer in the command post races for the Toc I telescope identification and confirms the presence of enemy aircraft. He then calls a bearing. Next, the three-man crew of the height finder, technical name UB7, use the bearing supplied by telescope identification to lock onto the target. The UB7 operator can see two images of the target through his viewfinder, one of them upside down, and he twiddles his knobs and dials until the images line up opposite each other. He then calls: 'Read'. This gives the plane's height. This number—on the day it was 14,000 feet—is called out to the predictor unit inside the command post, who call: '14,000 set.'

The predictor is a kind of mechanical calculator, about a metre square, standing on metal legs. It has telescopes and adjusting wheels for calculating the bearing, elevation and fuse setting for the guns. This information is relayed electrically to the four guns. On each gun, two gun layers sit with their backs to the target. They each turn their handles until the pointer on their dials matches the bearing and elevation information fed in electrically by the predictor. Meanwhile, the shell to be fired is first passed through a fuse setter, also using information fed in from the predictor. This sets the time—and therefore the height—at which the shell will detonate. The shell can then be locked into the breech of the gun. If all has gone according to plan, the gun is now pointing in the direction and at the angle ordered by the predictor unit, and the shell fuse has been set separately to detonate at the height supplied by the height finder. The gun is now ready to fire. As the target changes height or bearing, new information is fed to the predictor unit and then to the gunners, who adjust accordingly.

Heavy anti-aircraft shells are not looking for a direct hit. The idea is to fill the air around the planes with lethal explosions and thereby disrupt them from attacking their target. It goes without saying, however, that the most effective disruption is to shoot them down. So the gunners aim to have their shells explode as close as possible to a target plane or formation, and have the blast and flying shrapnel do the damage, ideally destroying a couple of bombers with a single well-placed shot. With a skilful predictor crew working closely with a radar unit, the 3.7-inch AA guns could be very effective against high-flying 'horizontal' bombers. On 19 February 1942, Darwin had no functioning radar unit.

Jack Mulholland, part of the Oval group, remembers an ordinary start to the day. The crews serviced the guns at 'dawn manning', then stood down for breakfast. ('Powdered eggs, most likely,' Mulholland remembers gloomily.) The gunners could still hear the engine noise of the patrolling Kittyhawks overhead. This masked any sound of Fuchida's bombers, still miles away to the south. However, there were other eyes watching and other ears listening. As we have seen, the telephonist in the command post at the Oval was casually eavesdropping on the town chatter when he heard an urgent voice refer to a 'dogfight' out to sea. This was almost certainly a reference to the shooting down of Wiecks'

Kittyhawk. The telephonist quickly alerted his Gun Position Officer, who ordered his Oval gun crews to action stations. At this point there was still no official alert. Mulholland grabbed a pack of Craven 'A' cigarettes left over from Christmas, and a cowboy novel, *Gun Whipped*, and headed for his gun. A book and a fag would relieve the boredom during the inevitable false alarm.

As they listened and watched, the gunners gradually became aware of a new, deeper, more menacing sound, bearing down on them from an unexpected direction, the south-east. On one of the gun positions—not Mulholland's—the crews were training by using the five patrolling Kitty-hawks as an imaginary target. As the noise of Fuchida's approaching bombers grew louder, the instructor decided to switch the training drill to the new source of aircraft noise. A gunner swung his telescope to the new target, then yelled: 'Hell, they've got bloody red spots on their wings!'

At the Oval, the Gun Position Officer saw Fuchida's Kate bombers bearing down on the town. His gunners were already alert. He set the predictor process into motion, shouting as he did: 'This is not a false alarm! This is for real! This is for real!'

At the RAAF airfield, Floyd Pell was standing near his aircraft, where he could still hear the radio. He heard Robert Oestreicher's shout of 'Zeroes! Zeroes! Zeroes!' and ordered his five Kittyhawks to ditch their belly tanks and get back into the air. Pell was first to take off. At about 80 feet above the runway, he was attacked by three Zeroes who instantly crippled his plane. He bailed out and miraculously survived the parachute descent. A Zero casually machine-gunned and killed him on the ground as he attempted to crawl to safety.

Next to scramble was his No. 2, Lieutenant Charles Hughes. He was almost certainly dead before his wheels had left the ground, killed on his take-off run by a strafing Zero. Hughes's plane continued into the air, now with a dead man at the controls. Next to take off was Lieutenant Robert McMahon, whose first sight as he lifted off was a fireball on the ground some 2000 yards ahead of him, undoubtedly Hughes' aircraft crashing and exploding on impact.[2]

McMahon escaped Hughes's fate. As he clawed his way into the air he managed to get onto the tail of a Zero. He then fell for the oldest sucker punch in the fighter pilot's handbook: at about 600 feet the Zero he was chasing pulled up hard into a loop, which reversed their positions, putting the Japanese pilot on McMahon's tail. The Zero calmly poured machine-gun fire into the exposed Kittyhawk. Although his plane was heavily shot up, McMahon managed to stay in the fight until he ran out of ammunition. He parachuted into the mangroves surrounding Port Darwin and found his way to the water's edge, where a launch picked him up.

Next to take off was Lieutenant Burt Rice, quickly followed by Lieutenant John Glover. Rice climbed to 5000 feet before three Zeroes pounced. Eyewitnesses saw him diving and zooming and actually outrunning his pursuers, who continued to fire at him. From a position ahead of the three Zeroes, Rice slammed his plane into what he hoped would be a steep left turn, wheeling him around behind his attackers. He was too late. His plane had already taken too much damage: as he tried to enter the turn, the controls stopped responding and Rice bailed out, knocking himself unconscious as he left the cockpit.

By whatever instinct, Rice pulled the rip cord and was floating down inert while the Japanese pilots set about finishing him off with their machine guns. Glover stormed into the fray, firing at and hitting one of the Zeroes. With staggering courage Glover then broke through the ring of attacking Zeroes and put his Kittyhawk into a tight spiralling dive, circling the dangling figure of Rice as they both descended. The Zeroes continued to machine-gun Glover's already damaged aircraft until at 3000 feet his dive threatened to become uncontrollable. Glover fought to get his Kittyhawk level, managing to do so just before he hit the ground. The plane cartwheeled and disintegrated, some of the wreckage flying as far as 100 metres from the crash site. Miraculously, Glover crawled clear of the wreckage. An Australian ran and grabbed him, dragging him to a slit trench before the Japanese could machine-gun him, too. Meanwhile Rice's parachute lowered him safely into a swamp, where he was rescued a few hours later.

With all the Wirraways on the ground and unserviceable, and nine of the ten Kittyhawks blown out of the sky, Darwin's defences against Fuchida's 188-aircraft armada were now reduced to the Army's 16 3.7-inch heavy AA guns and their untested gunners, some largely useless Lewis guns tied to saplings, the AA guns on the small handful of fighting ships in the harbour, a few makeshift machine guns at the RAAF base, and Robert Oestreicher's lone Kittyhawk, lurking in the clouds five miles south of the town.

As the sound of the first explosions rocked Darwin, the ever-meticulous Lou Curnock, at aeradio station VID, noted the time in his log book. It was 9.58 a.m.

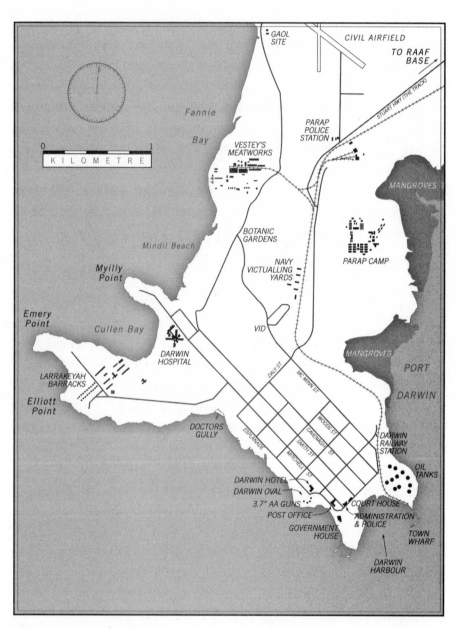

The city of Darwin on 19 February 1942, showing the principal targets.

Chapter 9

QQQ QQQ QQQ de VZDN

M itsuo Fuchida's attack plan was nothing if not methodical. The 81 Kate high-flying 'horizontal' bombers divided into two groups, one to attack the port while the other set about the RAAF airfield. 'I led the main strength of my level bombers in an attack on the harbour installations and a nearby cluster of oil tanks,' Fuchida recalled. 'The rest of the bombers went to destroy the airfield hangars. While the fighter group went after the enemy planes, I detailed the dive bombers to attack ships in the harbour.'

The terror and devastation these matter-of-fact words conceal are almost beyond description. Herb Kriloff, whom we first met as officer of the deck on the USS *William B. Preston* when it was under attack from Japanese aircraft in Davao Gulf, and who went on to serve on escort convoys in the Battle of the Atlantic, wrote: 'No single incident in my life has affected me more than that raid, a disaster of a magnitude and ferocity that is hard to describe. When it was over, had anyone told me that the war was to last another three and a half years, I would never have expected to see it end.'

Fuchida's Kate bombers arrived in tight formation, worthy of an air display fly-past. They flew in carefully calculated giant V formations. The three leading aircraft arranged themselves in the first V; two more Vs, each of three aircraft, formed up close behind them to produce a compact group of nine aircraft. This group of nine then became the apex of a bigger V, with two more groups of nine flying behind them, one on their left and the other on their right. The 27 aircraft were now in a perfect position to pattern bomb a broad swathe of the target area. The first group arrived on an attack line that began at the port, passed over the town, and led on to the Larrakeyah military barracks and the nearby civil hospital.

There is universal agreement that the first bombs from Fuchida's opening salvo fell into the harbour, missing the wharf by 20 or 30 metres. But the next ones slammed into the wharf, ripping out a huge section, cutting off the wharfies unloading *Neptuna* and *Barossa*, and damaging both ships. A bomb fell on the recreation shed near the wharf elbow, blasting it out of existence and killing instantly a group of wharfies who had knocked off for a smoko a few minutes earlier.

The first explosion flicked a locomotive and six railway trucks into the harbour, together with some bystanders on the wharf. Surviving wharfies and ships' crew dived into the harbour, reckoning they would be safer in the water away from the obvious targets.

The first blasts fractured and scattered oil lines running along the wharf. The flowing oil pumped into the harbour and soon caught fire. Oil enveloped the men struggling in the water, blackening them all over and making breathing difficult. Those attempting to swim had to pick their way through the flames. The ebbing tide swept up some of the pools of burning oil and dragged them towards the centre of the harbour and the main anchorage full of ships.

◆ ◆ ◆

Edgar Harrison, the permanent air-raid warden officer, had just left the Post Office when the first bomb fell. He had covered about 150 yards on his way back to his office in the Native Affairs Department. The first blast mingled with the opening wail of the first air-raid siren, sited on a water tower in the town. The big occasion turned out to be more than the siren could handle. It wheezed and died before it could complete its two-minute warning.

Harrison's first instinct was to drop to the ground. Then he realised he had work to do. Although the wardens had in theory disbanded on 26 January, they had made a pact with the Army to do their jobs if the need arose. Clearly it had just arisen. Harrison recalled: 'I picked myself up on [sic] the road and galloped down to my own office a couple of hundred yards away and started the air raid siren. At the time the Army telephone was ringing.'

Harrison's office was understandably deserted: officially, there were no air-raid wardens to staff it, and in any case the wardens were all at their day-job desks. It did not take them long to work out that the long-awaited raid had begun. They could hear bombs falling and Harrison's siren howling its confirmation. Around the town the sirens took up the call.

♦ ♦ ♦

Darwin town lay just beyond the port, on the extended line of Fuchida's opening attack run. There is no proof that the Japanese bombers set out deliberately to attack civilian targets in the town—Fuchida denied it in postwar interviews—but any bomb that failed to find the port would inevitably strike the civilian buildings beyond it. There is universal agreement that accuracy was a hallmark of the bombing attack that day. It is hard to avoid the conclusion, when so many bombs hit civilian targets, that at least some of the Kates deliberately went for the town, concentrating on the administration buildings along The Esplanade.

Darwin's communications centre was on the southern edge of the town, close to the harbour. It occupied a whole block between The Esplanade and Mitchell Street, and housed the Post Office, telephone exchange and cable office—virtually the town's entire civilian communications system. Of the 67 women still in Darwin after the evacuation, six worked in this building, in the telephone exchange and at the Post Office.

Two minutes after the alarm sounded, the staff packed into the shelter in postmaster Hurtle Bald's garden. As we have seen, it was regarded as one of the safest in Darwin, vulnerable only to a direct hit. That was exactly what it took—a direct hit from a 250-kg high-explosive bomb dropped from a Kate. It instantly killed Bald, his wife Alice, his daughter Iris, sisters Eileen and Jean Mullen, Emily Young, Freda Stasinowsky, Archie Halls and Arthur Wellington (the writer of the late-night letter to his wife and daughter quoted in Chapter 7). Police later ripped down curtains from the Balds' living room to cover the women's bodies: the blast had stripped off all their clothing. One of the more horrific sights of the day was the bloodied body of one of the postal staff hanging a metre and a half above the ground in the fork of a nearby tree. He had clearly been thrown high in the air before crashing to his final resting place.

The same salvo wrecked the telephone exchange and cable office, effectively destroying all civilian and most military commun-ication in the town. Four kilometres above the carnage, Fuchida's Kate bombers continued on their serene way. The raid was now perhaps four minutes old.

◆ ◆ ◆

There can be no doubt that Administrator Abbott suffered one of the worst and most terrifying experiences of those who survived the day, but His Honour was an experienced soldier and knew what it was like to be under bombardment. The same could not be said for his wife and his staff.

Government House stood on sloping land near the harbour, right in the main line of the attack. The building, including the Administrator's office, had a concrete floor supported by reinforced-concrete pillars. Below Abbott's office was a concrete strongroom with a heavy iron door, tough enough to hold out against anything but a direct hit. Abbott, his wife Hilda, and their staff piled into the strongroom shelter as soon as the sirens sounded.

Government House took the feared direct hit. A bomb of at least

250 kg landed in the grounds about 15 metres from the shelter. The blast smashed in the iron door and the shock wave lifted the concrete ceiling as the wind might lift a sail. The ceiling crashed back down, snapping the reinforced-concrete pillars. Everybody in the shelter might have been killed on the spot by falling concrete but for the caved-in iron door, which proved strong enough to support parts of the roof. Dust and tons of masonry showered into the strongroom, wrecking half of it.

Abbott's account of this is modest and understated. He set out his version of events in a six-page report, tendered as evidence to the Royal Commission and entitled *Japanese Air Raid, Darwin, 19th February 1942—Movements and Actions of the Administrator Upon That and Following Days.* He wrote:

The raid by Japanese bombers commenced about 10 a.m. on the 19th February. I took shelter under the Office which sustained an almost direct hit and collapsed, killing a half-caste servant girl, and almost burying another half-caste girl and an aboriginal boy.

With the help of Kamper, my driver and messenger, we procured crowbars, which were with other garden tools near by and freed these two people. As the raid went on, we again took shelter until about 11.15.

The girl killed by the falling roof was 18-year-old Daisy Martin. Abbott says she died instantly, crushed under tons of falling masonry, and that is almost certainly the truth. However, as we shall see in Chapter 11, an altogether more terrible version of this event soon began circulating in Darwin, supported by the police. It is a measure of Abbott's unpopularity with the people of Darwin that the counter-story was widely believed. It did nothing to improve Abbott's standing with them in the aftermath of the raid.

The bomb that crashed into Abbot's garden left a crater ten metres wide and six metres deep. The raid was now five minutes old.

♦　♦　♦

Constable Leo Law was in the police barracks in town when the raid began. 'I was in the bathroom. I'd had a shave and was about to have a shower,' he later recalled. 'I was under the shower when the alert went. I immediately ran outside with nothing but a towel on. I dived into a slit trench a foot deep and approximately 18 inches wide. The next thing I looked up—almost simultaneously this happened—and I saw these planes. I didn't count them, but I should say there would be 18 that I saw. Very shortly afterwards—a matter of a minute—there was a terrific explosion. I was covered with three feet of clay. There was a Government Office official in the trench ahead of me. His body was entirely covered. We had to dig him out.'

Constable Robert 'Bob' Darken was standing at the rear of the police station when the raid began. He heard no sirens. 'The first thing I knew of the air raid was when I heard the drone of the planes,' he recalled. 'I looked over the roof of the Police Station and saw a formation of nine bombers. I ran across to the barracks to wake up Constable Mofflin, who was asleep in bed.'

Dave Mofflin had worked the night shift and was dead to the world. Darken waited impatiently as his notoriously slow-waking mate dragged his boots on. The barracks was no place to be. As the two policemen reached the back door, a bomb tore into the ground immediately in front of the barracks, throwing Darken and Mofflin off their feet and hurling them under a concrete water tank. 'There was no shelter for us to take,' Darken explained later. 'There were trenches in the yard but they were all occupied.' They crawled under a car.

The first wave of Kates continued past the town towards the military barracks at Larrakeyah. The barracks had been partly camouflaged with paint and might have been hard to identify from 14,000 feet. The same could not be said for the new civil hospital at Cullen Bay, only a few hundred metres away. It had been painted white and clearly marked with a red cross. It is generally accepted that the Japanese did not deliberately target it, and it may be that the high-flying Kates mistook it for the barracks. Hospitals and barracks can look alike from the air. All that can be said with certainty is that six bombs landed close to the hospital and none went near the barracks.

The hospital had a well-planned air-raid drill. Patients who were reasonably mobile abandoned their beds and headed for shelter under the nearby cliffs at Cullen Bay. Less mobile patients who could nevertheless fend for themselves slid under their beds, with the mattress as their only protection. The staff lifted the least mobile patients and placed them under their beds before heading off to find shelter for themselves. Some doctors and nurses dived into the few available trenches in the grounds, others simply hid among the rocks.

Although none of the bombs hit the hospital directly, the six massive blasts showered the buildings with rocks, glass and other heavy debris. Rocks smashed through the thin roof, crashing onto beds and mattresses vacated only minutes earlier. Three wards and some outbuildings were damaged, and one naval ward was totally wrecked. Incredibly, no one was killed.

♦　♦　♦

At the Oval, Jack Mulholland's 3.7-inch anti-aircraft guns began firing even before the first bombs struck. The thunder of their own artillery was almost as devastating for the gunners as anything delivered by the Japanese. The dozen 3.7-inch guns of the 14th Heavy AA Battery had between them fired a total of *two* live rounds in their entire 14 months' training in Darwin. Both were warning shots fired across the path of 'friendly' bombers. The gunners had no experience of the full fury of an anti-aircraft barrage, when between 40 and 80 deafening rounds a minute are fired by the four-gun section.

An anti-aircraft section fires its first salvo from all guns simultaneously, aiming for maximum surprise. After that each gun fires independently, as fast as it can. To the inexperienced gunners, the first shattering roar of four guns firing at once might have heralded Armageddon. No one had prepared them for this. Gunners could not look up as they worked, so it was impossible to know what was going on around them. All they could do was keep firing. As the barrage continued, the roar of the guns was every bit as intimidating as the thunder of exploding bombs. At times it was hard to tell which was which. 'There was the ever-present wonder as to whether the adjoining gun had fired or a bomb had burst nearby,' Jack Mulholland wrote later.

The spent shells from each round were ejected automatically from the breech of the gun. They were heavy enough to break the leg of an unwary gunner. They were also blisteringly hot and had to be heaved over the revetment wall with gloved hands. There was a real risk the hot shell cases might set fire to the camouflage netting over the guns. The combination of gun noise, smoke, hot shell casings, deafening bomb explosions, Lewis machine-gun fire, plus swarming dive-bombers and fighters screaming low overhead must have seemed to the gunners like a vision of the apocalypse.

In the face of this onslaught, the gunners kept firing. However, lack of practice with live rounds sabotaged their disciplined efforts. Until 19 February 1942 nobody had a chance to discover that tropical heat plays tricks with fuse timers on anti-aircraft shells. As the command post crew watched in impotent fury, the shells burst below and behind the bombers.

◆　◆　◆

There are as many accounts of the tactics of Fuchida's 81 Kates as there were eyewitnesses. No two match exactly. However, there are some common threads, of which the most widely repeated is the grouping of the bombers in three waves. From the dozens of fragmentary eyewitness reports, the most likely scenario is that two waves of 27 Kates attacked the port, the town and the military barracks, while a third wave peeled off and headed for the civil airfield and RAAF base to the north and north-east of the town respectively.

The planes passed over the civil airfield first. As they did, the staff heard the anti-aircraft batteries open up. This was the first indication they had that the aircraft were hostile. Bruce Acland, one of the operations staff, raced to his radio and broadcast the coded message: 'QQQ QQQ QQQ de VZDN', telling the world Darwin was under air attack. Acland waited for confirmation that the message had been received by Daly Waters and other centres before cutting off all electric power, locking the code books in the safe, and heading for a slit trench.

At the RAAF field, the officers and men in the RAAF Operations Room could see the smoke and hear the thud of bombs already blasting the town. Many sprinted for slit trenches and shelters, while others manned the makeshift anti-aircraft machine-gun posts. Group Captain Sturt Griffith, the station commander, noted the time the first bomb struck his base. It was 10.08, ten minutes after the first salvo hit the harbour.

The machine guns could not reach the Kates. With no fighter aircraft to challenge them, the Japanese continued on their leisurely path of destruction. Bombs poured down on the hangars and workshops at the RAAF base, wrecking them all, together with any aircraft inside. Fires broke out at the ammunition dump and stores. When the high-flying bombers had finished their work, the dive-bombers moved in.

Zeroes and Vals flashed across the airfield, strafing and bombing. They flew low enough for the defenders to see the faces of the pilots. The machine guns did their best, but there was no stopping the smiling pilots as they roared effortlessly overhead.

At one of the machine-gun posts, Wing Commander Archie Tindal sat exposed on the lip of a trench, firing his Vickers gun at the swarming attackers. A single bullet, very likely from a cannon, passed through his throat, killing him instantly. He was the first Australian airman to die in combat on Australian soil.[1]

The Vals and Zeroes now spread the attack to the civil airfield, using incendiaries and anti-personnel 'daisy-cutter' bombs as well as high explosives. The daisy-cutters blasted lethal shrapnel in a flat pattern close to the ground, designed to kill and maim anybody caught in the open. The Japanese machine-gunned buildings, set the oil store on fire, and destroyed a light plane owned by a Flying Doctor pilot. They smashed vital radio sets in the administration building, and the emergency power generator. The fire-fighting tender caught fire and was rendered unusable. An ammunition store was soon ablaze, exploding hundreds of .303 machine-gun rounds. The noise of wind, fires and explosions was so great that people could hardly make themselves heard when they spoke.

◆　◆　◆

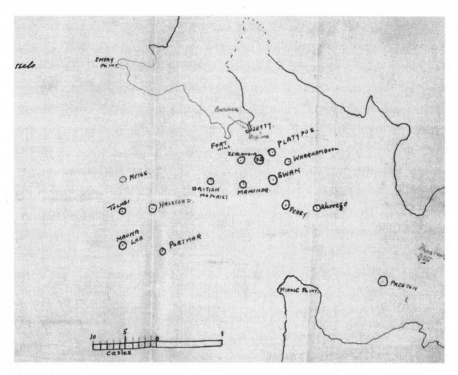

Original sketch map of Port Darwin showing key ships' positions at the beginning of the raid. The map was drawn by Lieutenant John S. Bell RAN, Darwin's harbourmaster on the day.

Over Port Darwin, the dive-bombers worked in pairs.

Darwin may have been packed with ships, but its defenders had no battle plan, no prearranged strategy, no inkling of who should do what in the event of an attack. It was simply every man for himself.

Six fighting ships in the harbour carried anti-aircraft guns: the destroyer USS *Peary*, the seaplane tender USS *William B. Preston*, the corvettes HMAS *Deloraine* and *Katoomba*, the sloop HMAS *Swan*, and the depot ship HMAS *Platypus*. Some others, such as the auxiliary minesweeper HMAS *Gunbar*, carried a single Lewis gun.

Gunbar was the first to come under attack, from the nine Zeroes fresh from dispatching the Catalina and the Kittyhawks. At 9.57 a.m., one minute before the first bombs fell, *Gunbar* was just passing through the boom gate guarding the harbour entrance when the Zeroes swooped.

Lieutenant D.H. Davies, aboard the minesweeper, described what happened. 'Nine fighter aircraft attacked giving in all 18 separate attacks from ahead, astern, port, starboard and the four quarters,' he wrote in his report. 'The attackers used a mixture of armour piercing, tracer and common ammunition of about .303 calibre. The first run hit our single Lewis gun in the magazine, rendering the ship defenceless. Including the Captain, nine men were injured, one of whom, Able Seaman Sheppard F.3384, has since died of wounds received during the attack.' The crew still had a few single-shot Lee-Enfield .303 rifles and the captain's Webley revolver to hand, and they fired away to no effect. The captain, Lieutenant Norman Muzzell, later described the defence of his ship as 'like throwing peanuts at a tiger'.

Even as the first bombs hit the wharf, ships in the harbour struggled to get under way. HMAS *Swan*, tied up alongside *Neptuna*, quickly cast off and headed for more open water. USS *Peary* and *William B. Preston* slipped, followed by HMAS *Warrego*. The depot ship HMAS *Platypus*, which had been one of the first to see the bombers, sounded the alarm and began a furious anti-aircraft barrage. HMAS *Katoomba*, trapped in the floating dock but nevertheless able to use her guns, joined the fray. Between them the ships did not have anything like enough anti-aircraft firepower to beat off the Vals and Zeroes, but they now erupted in a roar of smoke, flame and high explosives.

For the Japanese dive-bombers surveying the target area, the most valuable prize was the *Peary*. She was no stranger to Japanese aircraft. With the Pacific war only three days old, Japanese bombers had attacked the destroyer in a raid on Cavite Navy Yard, in the Philippines. In that raid, a direct hit killed eight of *Peary*'s crew and set her on fire. The Japanese attacked her again on 26 December, this time at sea. On 28 December she was bombed and damaged by 'friendly' aircraft. Next day the Japanese resumed where the friendlies had left off, attacking with bombs and torpedoes. By the time *Peary* limped into Darwin on 3 January 1942, she had already had a tough war.

Peary returned to Port Darwin in the early hours of 19 February to pick up fuel. When the bombers arrived, her skipper, Lieutenant

Commander John Bermingham, was pacing the bridge, desperate to collect his fuel and get away. He ordered engines started and anchor up, and was barely under way when the planes struck. The first direct hit from a dive-bomber caught *Peary*'s stern and destroyed her steering-gear engine. An incendiary ripped into the galley and started the first of several fires. A third bomb failed to explode. *Peary* kept fighting. All over her decks, anti-aircraft guns poured fire in the direction of the swarming dive-bombers, until the ship was almost enveloped in the smoke of her own guns. It was too late. A fourth bomb sliced its way into the ammunition store, triggering a catastrophic explosion that utterly wrecked the destroyer. A fifth incendiary exploded in the engine-room, but it needn't have bothered.

Herb Kriloff, on the bridge of the seaplane tender USS *William B. Preston*, watched from about 300 metres away. He recalled: 'The explosion was blindingly bright. When you opened your eyes, it took time to adjust so you could see again. We were dressed in shorts with short-sleeved shirts. The *Peary* blast made us feel as if every uncovered part of our bodies was on fire.'

Peary was now like a dying animal, dragging painfully along, with her stern gradually sinking. Her guns kept firing to the bitter end. More than one eyewitness reported that the forward guns were still firing as she slid under the burning waters of Port Darwin.

◆ ◆ ◆

The *William B Preston* got under way at about the same time as the *Peary*. *Willy B* had anchored in splendid isolation at the eastern end of Port Darwin, well clear of other ships. That left her dangerously exposed and furthest from the comparative safety of the open sea. Her captain, Lieutenant Commander Etheridge 'Jimmy' Grant, had gone ashore at 8 a.m. to chase up a delivery of aviation fuel and some desperately needed food. The ship's executive officer, Lieutenant Lester Wood, realising he had no time to lose, took command. *Willy B* always kept one boiler going, so the engines were immediately usable. Wood ordered her under way, and she was on the move within five minutes of the first alarm.

Willy B was a converted destroyer with a good turn of speed. She rapidly built up to 20 knots. Suddenly Wood heard a shout of 'Bombers overhead!' He heeled *Willy B* hard right to put the bombers off their aim. No bombs fell, but this new course was taking him straight for the shoals outside Port Darwin's East Arm. Wood slewed *Willy B* hard left. Now he was headed for a buoy marking a second set of shoals. Hard right again. This put him on what looked like a collision course with *Peary*, just under way and yet to be hit by the bombers. Wood judged that, with enough speed, he would just clear *Peary*. He left *Willy B* on full ahead, and scraped past.

While all this violent manoeuvring was taking place, the crew had cause to be grateful for some casual 'souveniring' over previous weeks. Whenever one of *Willy B*'s Catalinas had to be scrapped, the crew made sure they kept any serviceable machine guns or cannons. They improvised mounts on railings, on decks, wherever they could. As a result, *Willy B* was fairly bristling. She had nine .50 and five .30 medium-calibre anti-aircraft machine guns, and she now set about pouring this wholly unexpected fire at the startled Japanese dive-bombers, who responded by treating her with caution.

The luck could not last. After a series of near misses, and at about the same time as *Peary* came under attack, *Willy B* took a direct hit. The bomb triggered a deadly secondary explosion. In his action report, Les Wood wrote: 'At 1010 the ship was struck by probably a one hundred pound bomb [given that it came from a Val, it was probably 60 kg] a few inches aft of frame 137 main deck port. This bomb detonated fourteen 4-inch projectiles stored within four to five feet in an ammunition rack for the after gun. Fire immediately broke out and steering control was lost.'

The scene on *Willy B*'s deck was appalling. Herb Kriloff recalled: 'Aft of the deckhouse lay several bodies, in pieces. One man had been cut in half at the waist, and the area was covered with blood, so much that it was difficult to keep one's footing.'

Willy B was still going flat out. She was now on fire, her steering gear crippled, and desperately difficult to control. She threatened to collide

with the Australian hospital ship MV *Manunda*, about 500 metres ahead.
Wood needed to come left. 'With no steering control (the fire was so
strong aft men could not reach the steering engine room) this was
achieved by using the engines,' Wood wrote in his action report. He
was now steering by altering the thrust on his two propellers, all the
time trying to avoid the bombs and other ships twisting and turning in
the harbour.

At about 10.15, in the midst of all this mayhem, *Willy B*'s second
patrolling Catalina radioed in with an urgent message. The first Catalina,
piloted by Thomas Moorer, had been shot down by nine Zeroes before
it had time to broadcast a warning. The second Catalina's crew told
Willy B they could see one aircraft carrier, four cruisers and three
destroyers about 150 miles north of Bathurst Island. This vital message
did not reach the RAAF (which, at this point, had three serviceable
Hudson bombers at its disposal and might have used them to launch
a counter-strike) until the next day. The collapse of military
communications in Darwin saw to that.

Willy B's crew had pressing problems of their own. They assessed the
damage: no steering control; flooding aft; large fires not under control;
large holes below the waterline aft; heavy casualties killed and wounded.
They could still manoeuvre using the engines, and they continued
towards the harbour entrance. As they tried to escape, they faced a threat
even deadlier than secondary explosions of stacked shells. *Willy B* was
still carrying fifty 500-lb bombs and 30,000 gallons of aviation fuel for
its Catalinas. Kriloff again: 'Should a strafing aircraft pierce our side, we
might go up in one puff, making *Peary*'s loss look like a minor incident.'

There was, however, a far worse explosion threatening. *Neptuna*, tied
up on the outside berth at the wharf, had taken only light damage from
the first wave of Kates. After the first blasts, the crew moved to the
forward saloon for shelter. When the Val dive-bombers moved in, a bomb
sliced through *Neptuna*'s bridge and exploded in the saloon, killing
as many as 45 of the sheltering crew. A second bomb slammed into
the timber-filled No. 1 hold, setting it on fire. Captain William
Michie quickly ordered any wharfies and crew still alive to abandon ship.

Michie knew two of *Neptuna*'s other holds were filled with TNT and 200 tons of depth charges, all of which could go up at any moment.

✦   ✦   ✦

Everywhere there were remarkable escapes. The crew of the sloop HMAS *Katoomba*, trapped immobile in the floating dock, watched transfixed as a Val roared towards their port side. The crew opened fire with rifles and a Vickers machine gun. The pilot pressed on, taking a hail of bullets, until he was within 300 metres of the ship. Then he thought better of it, swerved off the attack line, and dropped his bomb in the harbour.

The second Val now attacked from starboard. *Katoomba* had a 12-pound anti-aircraft gun, not something to be challenged lightly. Captain Cousin ordered the gun crew to use a short fuse. As the plane pulled out of its dive and began its final horizontal run towards them, with no chance of missing, the gun crew fired a single shell that burst in front of the Val. The panicked pilot pulled into a vertical climb and disappeared, never to return.

The Lewis gunners stationed on top of the oil tanks around the harbour's edge kept pouring fire at any Zero or Val with the temerity to come within range. Despite their puny weapons, they managed to disrupt the bombers sufficiently to save the tanks. At the end of the raid the tanks had taken some damage but no direct hits.

Nevertheless, no amount of courage and tenacity from the gunners could prevail against the overwhelming force of Fuchida's attack. The harbour was now a howling, screaming, smoke-filled tumult of dive-bombers, swooping, strafing Zero fighters, exploding bombs, bursting shrapnel, spreading oil (some of it on fire), crippled or sinking ships, and men trying to stay afloat in the oily water.

For those still alive in the wharf area, there was an ominous new development. It began as a low rumbling sound that grew steadily more insistent. It came from the direction of *Neptuna*. The fire lit by the dive-bombers was spreading through the ship towards the TNT and the depth charges.

◆ ◆ ◆

Of the three services, the RAAF emerges from the Darwin raid least well. The Army gunners put up a spirited fight. The ships of the US Navy and the Royal Australian Navy did their best with limited resources. The RAAF had next to nothing to fight with, and it showed.

Although the RAAF base was technically home to the Hudson bombers of 13 Squadron, these planes had spent most of their time at Ambon, in the Molucca Islands. Darwin was not an air base at all in the usual sense of the word: no aircraft were kept there permanently. Instead it was a maintenance facility, a fuel and ammunition store, and a staging point on the route to the besieged Dutch East Indies.

That might not have mattered were it not for a further handicap. The RAAF personnel permanently stationed at the base were mostly technicians and maintenance crew, and did not see themselves as front-line fighters. They had not drilled with even the handful of old Lee-Enfield rifles at their disposal. They had set up a few makeshift machine-gun posts, using guns cannibalised from unserviceable aircraft, but they had no serious anti-aircraft batteries. In the event of an attack they could do little more than jump into slit trenches and hope to survive whatever was thrown at them. To compound the problem, the RAAF usually promoted people for technical competence rather than managerial and leadership skills. The most senior officer in the maintenance section, for instance, would invariably be the best mechanic and not necessarily the best officer.

On 19 February 1942, Group Captain Frederick Scherger, an experienced pilot and natural leader (later, as Air Marshal Sir Frederick Scherger, he became head of the RAAF) was the most senior air-force officer at Area Combined Headquarters at the RAAF base. As the Japanese bombers arrived, he was on his way into town by car to meet the former Chief of Air Staff, Air Marshall Sir Richard Williams, who happened to be staging through Darwin on his way back to Melbourne from London. Scherger recalled: 'When I reached the corner of the main road to Darwin and The Esplanade I heard AA guns firing. I stopped the car, looked out, and saw they were firing at a formation of 27 aircraft which appeared flying at a height of approximately 20,000 feet.'

Scherger quickly judged that the bombers were about to deliver 'a pattern of bombs commencing, as I thought, about the oil tanks and spreading right through to Larrakeyah'. This had one serious implication: the bombs would fall about where he was standing. He jumped back into the car and raced towards the civil airfield. He could hear the thud of bombs exploding behind him, catching up with him as he drove.

At the airfield he stepped out of the car, looked around, and saw smoke rising from the direction of the RAAF base. He jumped back into the car and headed there. 'As I approached I could see it was being dive-bombed and machine gunned, and I realised that anything moving on the station would immediately be fired at,' Scherger remembered. 'I stopped about 300 yards outside the main gate and when there was a lull in the attack I drew onto the station.

'Unfortunately I was only about 150 yards inside the gate when a fighter shooting at a machine gun post nearly hit the car, or his machine gun fire nearly hit the car. I stopped the car, got out, and as there was no shelter trench in the immediate vicinity I lay down in the long grass and remained there until the attack was over.'

In Port Darwin, the carnage mounted. *Peary* suffered worst: 91 dead. After that came *Willy B*: 15 dead. The sloop HMAS *Swan*, having detached herself from the ominously rumbling *Neptuna*, was caught in the harbour and brutally attacked, with three killed. The depot ship HMAS *Platypus* took only moderate damage. Nevertheless, two men died. The lugger HMAS *Marie*, tied up alongside *Platypus*, was sunk by a dive-bomber. *Platypus*'s crew were close enough to see the pilot smile and wave at them as he swept past. Dive-bombers sank the oil tanker *British Motorist*: two dead. The troop transport USS *Port Mar* was towed off her mooring and beached, not before she took heavy damage and one man was killed. *Mauna Loa*, *Port Mar*'s fellow transport from the ill-fated convoy, was sunk: five dead. The biggest transport of all, USS *Meigs*, was bombed and machine-gunned: two dead. The troopship MV *Tulagi* was beached. The boom-net vessels HMAS *Kangaroo*, *Kara Kara*, *Karangi* and *Koala* were all machine-gunned. On *Kara Kara*: two dead. On

Kangaroo: one dead. The *Zealandia*, which had given the women and children evacuees such an uncomfortable trip south two months earlier, would trouble them no more. It was sunk: three dead. The coal hulk *Kelat* was also sunk. Two of *Willy B*'s Catalina aircraft were sunk at anchor.

Of all the destruction, the most bitterly resented involved the hospital ship MV *Manunda*. She was anchored in mid-harbour about 1500 metres due south of the wharf, with the oil tanker *British Motorist* about a kilometre to her west and the destroyer USS *Peary* a similar distance to the south-east. Other ships were not far away, including *Zealandia*, *Katoomba* (trapped inside the floating dock) and *Platypus*. So *Manunda* was certainly surrounded by legitimate targets. She was painted white, with three large red crosses on each side of her hull and large red crosses on her funnel to indicate her status as a hospital ship.

Peary, with her steering-gear engine destroyed, was both under way and out of control in the first few minutes of the attack. Some eye-witnesses said *Peary* passed close to *Manunda* and the hospital ship was hit by accident by aircraft attacking *Peary*. Others say no, *Peary* was already burning and sinking, and was not even close to *Manunda* when the bombers struck the hospital ship. For these witnesses, it was a deliberate and unforgivable assault on a sacrosanct target.

Charles Stewart was Third Officer on the *Zealandia*. When the *Peary* was hit, some of her crew dived overboard. Stewart volunteered to man one of *Zealandia*'s lifeboats to try to rescue *Peary* crew members struggling in the harbour. He was emphatic that *Peary* was never close to *Manunda*. He recalled: 'When we were returning from picking up men from the oily water, one of the dive-bombers made an attack on the *Manunda*. From my position in the boat I do not think that she [*Peary*] was that close. It did not appear to me to be very close. We were close to the *Manunda*.'

So was the attack on the *Manunda* deliberate? 'Yes, because the same plane came back and machine-gunned when over our boat.' Stewart was about 150 metres from *Manunda* at the time of the attack and, having just rescued some of *Peary*'s crew, was in a good position to judge her distance from *Peary*. If he says the attack was deliberate, his view deserves respect.

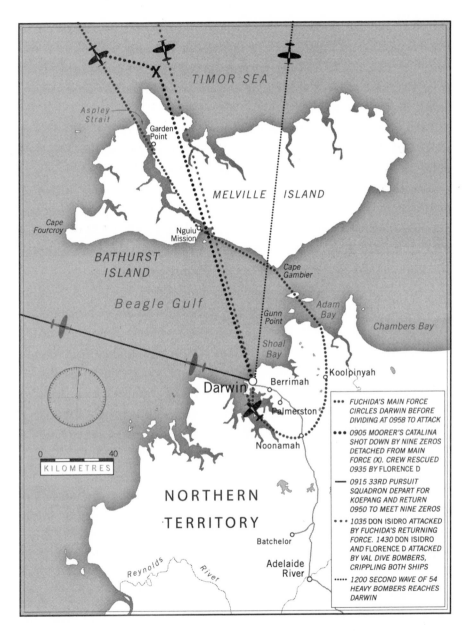

Chronology of the attack, beginning at 0905 with the shooting down of Moorer's Catalina and ending at 1200 with the arrival of the heavy bombers in the second wave. Note the wide gap between Pell's Kittyhawks on their track to Koepang and Fuchida's inbound attackers overflying Nguiu Mission.

Now take the evidence of Lieutenant John Bell, harbourmaster on the day of the raid. Bell had been responsible for assigning berths in the harbour. His sketch of the various ships' positions, reproduced on page 104, was accepted as accurate by one and all. He also witnessed the attack on the *Manunda*.

Had the *Peary* come close to the *Manunda*? 'Yes, it was almost touching. Within a few feet of her.' Was the attack on the *Manunda* deliberate? 'I am strongly of the opinion that it was accidental.'

Whatever the motive for the attack, the outcome is beyond challenge. First *Manunda* rocked from a near miss that spattered shrapnel across her exposed decks. This bomb 'killed four on board and cut 76 holes and over a hundred deep scores in our plating and played hell with our rear and upper decks,' according to Captain Thomas Minto.

> We had just got our wind back and carried on when we heard the same thing again. There was a terrific roar and debris flying around everywhere. The bomb had missed the bridge and pierced the music room skylight. It exploded at B and C decks, doing terrific damage and causing many casualties. The hit and near miss between them killed nine of the crew and three military personnel, including one nurse. It seriously injured seven and caused about 40 minor injuries.

After the war, Mitsuo Fuchida heatedly denied that the attack on *Manunda* was planned. He told the author Douglas Lockwood: 'I was surprised when I heard what had happened. It was the fault of the dive-bomber crews. I questioned them and they said they did not see the Red Cross, though I did.'

Perhaps the most thoughtful and accurate explanation came from Lieutenant Colonel J.R. Donaldson, the Army officer commanding troops aboard *Manunda*. He wrote afterwards: 'The bomb which hit us was apparently deliberate but though one or two dive bomber pilots may have lost their heads during the excitement the remainder left us well alone and if it had been the enemy's intention to destroy us he could easily have done so as the bombing was extremely accurate.'

Tragedy struck again at the new military hospital at Berrimah. As we have seen, the hospital was about 1500 metres from the end of runway 29 at the RAAF base. A machine-gun post close to the hospital had been exchanging fire with the strafing Zeroes. Whether by accident or design, the low-flying Zeroes raked the hospital with machine-gun fire, damaging four wards. As at the civilian hospital, immobile patients had been placed under beds. The mattresses might have given some protection against the odd piece of falling timber, but they were no shield against machine-gun bullets. One patient died from his wounds.

Tokyo radio's English-language broadcast later apologised for the damage to *Manunda*, and for damage to the hospitals at Cullen Bay and Berrimah. Ironically, Major General D.V. Blake, the military commandant in Darwin, saw a glimmer of light in this tragedy. In a secret report to Lieutenant General Vernon Sturdee, the Australian Chief of General Staff, he wrote: 'This attack on Australian soil, combined with its ferocity in attacking hospitals, both military, civil and waterborne, has had much to do with the stiffening of morale of the Forces.' The morale of Army troops in Darwin needed no stiffening. However, as we shall see, the Australian government, under pressure from the military Chiefs of Staff, failed to take this opportunity to do a bit of civilian morale-stiffening instead.

◆　◆　◆

Although the death and destruction inflicted on both civilian and military targets was by now horrific, the Japanese did not have it all their own way. A Lewis gunner in 2nd AA Battery, 'Darky' Hudson, brought down the first enemy aircraft ever destroyed on Australian soil, a Zero fighter. It crashed near HMAS *Coonawarra*, the Navy shore base about ten kilometres west of the town. Hudson was awarded a Military Medal.

Robert Oestreicher's Kittyhawk had been threading in and out of clouds ever since the first attacking Zero had broken up his formation. 'After flying among the clouds for about half an hour,' he recalled, 'I spotted two Series 97 [Val] dive bombers with fixed landing gear on a course for Batchelor Field. Intercepting them at about fifteen hundred feet I fired and saw one definitely burst into flame and go down. The other was smoking slightly as he headed for the clouds.' Oestreicher chased the second Val but lost him before he could witness the result. The next day a coastal battery found both Japanese aircraft crashed within a mile of each other. They were the first confirmed aerial victories in the skies over Australia.

Four Zeroes had been duelling with four machine-gun posts at the Army camp at Winnellie, just to the east of the RAAF field. The Zeroes raked the area with strafing fire while the gunners replied with their Hotchkiss light machine guns, producing not much result either way. The Japanese pilots flew close enough for the gunners to see 'rude finger gestures' delivered from the cockpit, doubling their fury. Then one of the Zeroes swooped over a gun manned by Trooper Max Grant, who managed to track it through 180 degrees as it swept overhead. As the Zero roared away, Grant's fellow gunner Allan Weidner yelled: 'Up his arse! Up his arse!' Grant did as he was bid. To the delight of the gunners, a thick cloud of smoke poured from the Zero. It crashed in flames about a mile away, killing the pilot.

Jack Mulholland's 3.7-inch anti-aircraft section on the Oval had a clear view of the harbour. The big guns employed a different tactic when dealing with low-flying planes. Instead of the complicated predictor unit giving target information, each of the four guns was assigned a 90-degree sector and left to do its own aiming and firing using open sights. Mulholland's sector faced the harbour.

The gunners had a delicate decision to make. If they fired low at the swarming dive-bombers, they risked pouring shrapnel onto their own ships. If they did nothing, the Japanese pilots would have the skies to themselves. In the end, the balance of advantage seemed to be to fire away and try to disrupt the attacking Vals by placing a shield of bursting shells over the ships.

Mulholland's gunners set their fuses to the highly unconventional one and a half seconds (regulations said two seconds was the safe minimum) and began pouring fire low over the harbour. They had their reward as a Val pulled out of its dive. A shell burst near the aircraft's nose.

Mulholland recounted, with his usual modesty: 'It was not a matter of accurate shooting. To be fair it would be more likely the plane ran into the shell. I saw the plane crash into the sea.'

◆ ◆ ◆

The Japanese pilots were not content merely to bomb Government House. The Zero fighters took offence at the Australian flag still fluttering in the grounds, and set about machine-gunning it with furious enthusiasm. The flag held out gamely, though one of the stars and bits of the Union Jack were blown away. The battered flag can be seen today in the Australian War Memorial in Canberra.

◆ ◆ ◆

At the height of the raid, Police Sergeant William McKinnon found himself taking shelter with a Chinese man in a trench at the police barracks. 'During the whole of the time he was there,' Sergeant McKinnon recalled, 'he was saying: "What for aeroplanes? What way our planes? What for not at 'em? Shoot 'em down Japanese planes."' He might have spoken for the whole of Darwin.

After 42 minutes, at about 10.40 a.m., the last Japanese plane from Fuchida's aircraft-carrier group had left the skies over Darwin. The all-clear sounded.

Chapter 10

Between the raids: Can anyone drive?

Darwin was now a smoking shambles. Some 15 heavy bombs had destroyed civilian targets in the town's administration area, smashing buildings and killing and maiming people. The remaining bombs found targets in a huge killing zone extending over 40 square kilometres. The path of destruction began at the port, steamrollered over the town as far as the civil hospital, swung north-east to the two airfields, and then spread its remaining fury over the 45 ships. Black smoke billowed from burning ships, buildings, oil stores, wrecked aircraft and oil floating on the harbour. The air was foul with the smell of oil, smoke, cordite, burnt flesh and charred wooden wreckage. Darwin's dazed citizens, grateful and mildly surprised to find themselves still alive, crawled from their shelters and basements and hiding places and surveyed the ruins of their homes, shops and workplaces.

◆ ◆ ◆

There had been no shortage of heroism during the attack. Apart from the Army, Navy and Air Force anti-aircraft gunners who stood their ground in the face of overwhelming odds, the rescue workers set a standard of selfless courage of which any nation might be proud. As the dive-bombers sank ships, the burning, oil-smeared waters of Port Darwin filled with sailors forced to abandon their vessels and swim for it. A makeshift armada of lifeboats, boom-net vessels, tugs and larger ships now set about rescuing them.

As we have seen, when the USS *Peary* took five direct hits from the dive-bombers, the hospital ship *Manunda* lowered lifeboats that headed straight into the danger zone around the burning destroyer. The 298-ton examination vessel HMAS *Southern Cross* unhesitatingly joined in, lowering her own lifeboats to pick up sailors from *Peary* who were struggling in the oily water. The boom-net vessels *Kangaroo*, *Kara Kara*, *Karangi*, *Kiara* and *Kookaburra* hurled themselves into the turmoil, scooping up sailors, first from *Peary*, then from *British Motorist*. Approaching a blazing oil tanker, which might have exploded at any moment, took more than ordinary courage.

The Department of Civil Aviation maintained a small flotilla of launches on the harbour to ferry passengers to and from the Qantas flying boats. The tender CA22, manned by a civilian, John Waldie, is credited with rescuing more than 100 sailors from the harbour. A second flying-boat tender, CA2, commandeered by Naval Reserve officer Lieutenant Ian McRoberts and a volunteer crew, saved the lives of dozens of struggling seamen.

The most unlikely rescuers took to the water. At Talc Point, on the far side of Port Darwin, a section of four men from the Army's 54th Searchlight battery watched as a rowboat pulled into shore, clearly manned by crew from one of the stricken ships. The crewmen jumped out and fled, abandoning the boat. Phillip Herring and his three mates, Vince Highland, Tommy Reynolds and Sam Langwich, got in the abandoned rowboat and put to sea. They picked up eight swimmers. While their courage was undoubted, their rowing skills left a lot to be desired. One of the rescued, thought to be the purser of the *Tulagi*, spent his journey to shore standing up in the boat calling 'row, row, row' in an attempt to synchronise the landlubbers' efforts with the oars. The searchlighters made repeated trips into the harbour until they were worn out. Seamen from *Tulagi* and *Port Mar* can thank them for their lives.

The Japanese were not in the business of chivalrously standing back to allow the rescue of drowning sailors. Bombs continued to rain down throughout the rescue operation, while the dive-bombers and fighters kept up a murderous hail of machine-gun fire, targeting anything that moved in the port. Ivan Sinclair, who later cleared many of the bodies from the beaches and the mangroves, reported that most had been killed by machine-gun fire in the back. In the midst of this non-stop bombing and machine-gunning, the rescue boats threaded their way through patches of blazing oil to gather desperate sailors from the water. The oil left faces and bodies blackened, to the point where close friends who had been working together for months and even years failed to recognise each other when they met in the water. The oil temporarily blinded some of the victims. For weeks after the raid, the foul taste of oily seawater lingered in the throat and haunted those unfortunate enough to have swallowed some.

Oil and the Japanese were not the only threats. Shrapnel from friendly anti-aircraft shells exploding overhead could be equally deadly. Even when the planes finally departed, the burning oil and dangerously unstable burning ships combined with the regular hazards of Darwin harbour—raging tides, sharks, crocodiles and deadly box jellyfish—to make the rescue operation almost as dangerous after the all-clear as it had been during the attack.[1]

On a day when good fortune was not much in evidence, both rescuers and rescued took comfort from the presence of the hospital ship *Manunda* in mid-harbour. *Manunda* had taken a fearful beating from the bombers, with 12 dead and more wounded, one of the worst casualty lists of the day. Her crew found themselves fighting seven separate fires on board, one of which kept burning for an hour. Nevertheless *Manunda* stood ready and able to accept casualties, with doctors and nurses on the spot to offer treatment to the injured and comfort to the dying. On the day of the raid *Manunda* took aboard 76 patients, and would take on another 190 the next day.

◆ ◆ ◆

At the RAAF base, Group Captain Scherger gingerly got to his feet amidst the long grass near the airfield entrance and set out to assess the damage. There was instant good news. As Scherger recounted: 'Immediately the raid was over I got back into the car, drove round the buildings and the aerodrome, found that three Hudsons were undamaged, and realising that some of the aircraft must have come off an aircraft carrier I ordered these Hudsons on a preliminary search to northward.' Ground crews were told to prepare the aircraft for an extensive search mission.

Scherger did not stop there. 'I also ordered all Wirraways and A24s [American Douglas A24 dive-bombers] to be bombed up, in the case of the Wirraways with two 500-lb semi-armour piercing bombs. The A24s were already bombed up.'[2] The Hudsons' job would be to find the aircraft carriers. The dive-bombers would then sink them. Now the Japanese might get a taste of their own medicine.

It was not to be. The Wirraways were all at Batchelor airfield, 75 kilometres to the south. With the Darwin telephone exchange and cable office wrecked in the first few minutes of the raid, there was no way to pass the order to Batchelor except by sending a dispatch rider on a two-hour ride on a motorbike. Nor was there any ground-to-air radio operating at the RAAF base. Even the Hudsons on the base had to receive their orders by dispatch rider. Without ground-to-air the Hudsons would be useless: they would have no way of sending target locations back to the dive-bombers once they had located the carriers. Scherger fumed while he tried to get some ground-to-air communications working. Meanwhile, the Hudsons sat impotent in their camouflaged dispersal bays.

◆ ◆ ◆

The two ships still tied up at the wharf represented a special problem. *Neptuna* and *Barossa* were both on fire within minutes of the start of the raid and surrounded by burning oil from the burst oil pipes on the wharf. *Neptuna*, carrying 200 tons of depth charges and additional TNT below her decks, might explode at any moment. With luck, *Barossa* could be saved.

Barossa was tied up on the inner side of the wharf and hemmed in by an oil lighter whose hoses had fractured and whose oil was feeding the spreading fire. The Navy tug HMAS *Wato* managed to get a line onto the lighter and drag her out of the way, leaving a path clear to pull *Barossa* to safety. Although the rumbling from *Neptuna*'s fires was now ominously loud, *Wato*'s commander, Warrant Officer Andrew Gibson, and his crew, with extraordinary courage, returned to the wharf and managed to get a line onto *Barossa*. They had just managed to pull her clear of the wharf when their worst fears were realised.

Of all the terrible memories of Darwin that morning, the most terrible for those who saw and heard it was the death of *Neptuna*. No sooner had *Wato*'s lifeline begun to pull *Barossa* clear than the biggest explosion of the day rocked Darwin. Author Douglas Lockwood wrote graphically afterwards:

> I was driving my car along The Esplanade half a mile away and believed the explosion meant another raid had begun. I stopped and ran for the gutter but while doing so saw the column of smoke and flames dwarfing all the other smouldering fires from burning ships and buildings that were blacking out the town. I will never forget that on top of it all, rolling slowly over and over as though it were a dumb-bell tossed by a giant juggler, there was what I took to be, and now know to have been, *Neptuna*'s main mast.

The blast could be heard beyond the RAAF airfield seven kilometres away. A gigantic mushroom cloud blossomed over the ship, which promptly rolled over and sank. It is simply impossible to know how many crew, wharfies and rescuers died in the blast. By now the waters around the wharf were littered with injured, dead and dying from the earlier bombs, and the precise cause and timing of their final agony cannot be stated with certainty.

Incredibly, *Wato* and *Barossa* survived the blast. With *Barossa* well and truly on fire, the auxiliary minesweeper HMAS *Tolga* took over the towing job from *Wato*. *Tolga*'s crew put out *Barossa*'s fires, then dragged her to a nearby beach. *Wato* meanwhile nosed her way back into Port Darwin to look for sailors in need of rescue.

♦ ♦ ♦

When the raid began, John Wilkshire and Don Bergin had been loading sand into Wilkshire's truck at Mindil Beach, north-west of Darwin and outside the target area. As the bombs started falling, they both realised sand might be needed to fight fires. Heedless of their own safety, they drove straight for the danger zone, towards the oil tanks on the edge of the port. The bombing was still going on when they arrived at the wharf. Wharfies and sailors, some wounded, were struggling to get ashore while others remained in the water, cut off by the burning oil.

Wilkshire sized up the situation quickly. He called: 'Can anyone here drive a truck?' A wharfie volunteered. Okay, Wilkshire told him, use the truck as an ambulance to get the wounded to hospital. Meanwhile, Wilkshire plunged into the harbour and started dragging the wounded to shore, then handing them over to Bergin. He could see the splashes of the machine-gun bullets crawling towards him as the Japanese pilots kept up their strafing attack. When Wilkshire and Bergin had finished hauling the wounded to safety, the two civilians heard a naval officer ask for volunteers to man a launch. They agreed at once. Gathering up Lieutenant Jimmy Grant, the captain of the USS *William B. Preston*, they formed the volunteer crew for Lieutenant Ian McRoberts on the Qantas shuttle tender CA2.

♦ ♦ ♦

Major General David Blake was commander of the 7th Military District, which included Darwin. He was also the most senior military officer in Darwin. During the raid he had been sheltering in his 'sanger', a slit trench surrounded by a low mound, at Larrakeyah Barracks. As soon as the all-clear sounded he hot-footed it into town. 'My first job was to see how my batteries had fared,' he recalled. 'I went to Emery [a shore battery on Emery Point near Larrakeyah], and from there to town and the Administration, which had been heavily bombed, and then proceeded to the other battery at East Point to see how they had fared.' This was an eccentric choice of inspection sites. The Emery Point and East Point batteries were heavy guns pointing out to sea, designed to repel a naval attack. So far as I am aware, they didn't fire a single shot on 19 February 1942. Why the general chose to inspect them instead of chatting to the AA gunners, who might have done with a word or two of encouragement, is obscure.

On his tour, Major General Blake saw no evidence of panic. 'Those I saw were mostly Air Raid Precautions workers, and they were doing their job in getting the dead and wounded and that sort of thing.'

◆　◆　◆

Mick Ryan, secretary of the North Australia Workers' Union, which spoke for the wharfies among others, had been sheltering in a gully near the school during the raid. The school backed onto Woods Street, just outside the town centre. He recalled:

> Before the all-clear siren sounded, as it appeared to me to be clear enough to come out, I came out and I called to the men around me to come with me to the wharf in case we could be of some assistance there. I then got into the utility truck, which was standing outside our [Union] office. Then, along with several other men, we drove round through the streets proceeding toward the jetty. We called out to quite a number of men along the street, and the truck very quickly became overcrowded with men.

Then, as they got close to the wharf, they heard shouting: 'Here they are. They are coming again.' Ryan had been too quick in deciding it was safe to move out. Fuchida's planes were returning for another sweep. Ryan's group headed back to the gully near Woods Street and waited for the all-clear.

As soon as it sounded, Ryan and the crowded utility once more headed for the wharf. 'We got down near the bond store,' he recalled, 'and we were turned back by a military guard, who said that nobody would be permitted to go down to the jetty because of the danger that might arise from the likelihood of the munition boat exploding, that was on fire.' The motley group of would-be Samaritans climbed back into the utility and headed for possible rescue work at the Navy Victualling Yard, where, they were quickly told, there had been no damage. Undaunted, they pointed the utility back towards the school and the town.

Here, at last, was useful work. 'We found several men who had been on the wharf during the bombing,' Ryan remembered. 'One man was in a very bad state, and some of the men got a stretcher out of the school, laid him on it, put him in the truck and drove him to the hospital. Whilst this man was being taken to hospital, I assisted in carrying others in, who were arriving in military ambulances.'

Given that there were, officially, no air-raid wardens, the ARP operation in Darwin performed creditably. Edgar Harrison, the Permanent Officer, takes up the story again. After he raced to his headquarters in Mitchell Street to sound the alarm, 'Within half a minute Warden Foster reported to me and I got him to take his post outside the office and stop any people running along the road and to check them and get them to lie down in the grass. It was absolutely impossible to look for shelters because there were no shelters. In the paddock alongside my headquarters in Mitchell Street, at one stage we had anything from 80 to 90 people lying in the grass and did not have a casualty.'

The wardens also had responsibility for sounding the all-clear. Harrison again: 'We received instruction from Larrakeyah [Army headquarters] to sound the "All Clear". I sounded my siren, and then wardens who had been held up during the raid began to report. I gathered up 100 strangers, got the wardens going and sent them up to the spots I knew had been bombed heavily, and rescue work started.'

Harrison then set out to check how much of Darwin's administration had survived the raid. He was not much comforted by what he found. 'The whole Administration broke down entirely,' he said later.

> Administration offices were badly cracked. Mr Giles [the Government Secretary] received a wound in the arm. The accountant, sub-accountant and others were badly upset by the blast, and the whole place became disorganised. I proceeded immediately after the 'All Clear' on a tour of inspection, and endeavoured to see what damage had been caused and how many casualties there had been. I went to the Administrator's office. He was obviously in a very dazed condition. He had received a very bad shaking—Mrs Abbott also, but she recovered her self-possession very quickly, and I must pay tribute to her bravery. She just looked at me and said: 'I am awfully sorry I am so dirty, Mr Harrison. Is there anything I can do for you?' I said: 'Yes, I would like to see you and the few remaining women out of town as soon as possible.' She said: 'Very well, I will pack my bags.' Later I saw the Administrator and he had pulled himself together, but he had received a very bad shaking.

When the all-clear sounded, Constable Bob Darken climbed out from under the car that had sheltered him. He had a fair idea of where help might be needed most. 'I went straight to the Post Office,' he recalled.

> I noticed Mr Bald—I have always known him as that—was almost in a sitting position on top, partly covered by dirt. He was in a terribly battered condition. Most of the bones—his arms and legs—seemed to be broken.
>
> I also recognised his daughter. She had part of her head blown away. I also recognised Mrs Young. The top of Mrs Young's head was blown off. I also saw another man whom Constables Hook and Withnall found lying over the fork of a tree. I saw him when he was being carried in on a stretcher.

Constable Darken and Constable McNab were clear about their first priority. They set about removing the bodies, planning to take them to the hospital morgue.

Brough Newell, the resigned Director of First Aid from the ARP, joined the two policemen at the Post Office. He began identifying the bodies, though their condition made this difficult. 'In one case I made a mistake about identification,' Newell recalled. 'I saw the man some minutes later—the worst shock I had that day, I think.'

The all-clear sounded at about 10.40 but Administrator Abbott, by his own account, stayed in his shelter until 11.15. He then came out to survey the damage. He wrote in his report: 'Although a bomb had fallen between two Government cars which were in Government House grounds at the time, one in a garage and one near the office, making a crater at least 15 feet deep, the two cars escaped with superficial damage, and were got out on the road.' His Honour's two surviving cars, and the use to which he put them, were to lead to some searching questions at the Royal Commission a few weeks later.

For the AA gunners at the Oval, the sudden quiet was eerie after the bedlam of the preceding 42 minutes. Jack Mulholland had 'an uncanny feeling that it was all unreal'. He recalled: 'We came out of the gun pits somewhat "Zombie-like", with dry mouths, glad to be alive. Our main concerns were to see what damage had occurred and to check the safety of the other crews. To our great relief we did not suffer one casualty at the Oval.'

The gunners had used just about every anti-aircraft shell available to them, so their first job was to restock the ammunition recesses from the main storeroom under the Oval's grandstand. Mulholland remembers there was little talk as the gunners struggled with the heavy boxes. Mostly they were anxious to save their breath for the lifting work. But there would have been little point in talking anyway—the gunners were all deaf from the noise of firing. The guns would need cleaning, too. There was plenty to do.

◆ ◆ ◆

Stan Kennon gives an interesting perspective on the state of Darwin immediately after the raid. He was a carpenter on a building site in Smith Street in the centre of the town. He had been boiling a billy for smoko when the planes came.

> I stepped back and looked up and there was this magnificent formation coming straight towards us. I thought hello, the Yanks are here. The next thing I saw two white explosions in the sky [the first salvo from the AA battery]. That woke me up that they weren't Yanks.
>
> We had started an air raid shelter at the company's house, over a six foot chain wire fence. Somehow that six foot high wire fence disappeared—I found myself on the other side of it. I crawled into this ruddy air raid shelter that was about two feet high, concrete blocks just laid around, with sheets of flat iron and bits of timber on top for a roof. It was quite a stupid place to be if bullets came or anything—it was no shelter at all. So I backed out and stood by a tree.

Kennon spent the next 40 minutes shuffling around the tree, keeping it between him and any attacking aircraft.

When the all-clear sounded, he jumped on his bike and went for a tour around the town. His first impression was that damage was 'hardly noticeable'. He rode his bicycle home and grabbed an old movie camera. When he returned to the town he was able to capture moving pictures of the turmoil in the harbour, including shots of the *Manunda*. Then, as is the way of all temperamental machines at vital moments, the camera jammed. Kennon had to open the case and pull out yards of film, which was instantly spoiled. Some film survived, and for years afterwards Kennon showed it to his friends. Then the film was lost, and did not reappear until late 2007. It is now with the Australian War Memorial in Canberra, where experts are trying to salvage it.

◆ ◆ ◆

When the last Japanese plane left, Lieutenant Robert Oestreicher gratefully set his Kittyhawk down at the RAAF base. He landed with a flat tyre and some bullet holes in his wings, but was otherwise in fair shape. Oestreicher, ever the savvy veteran, parked his aircraft in a dispersal area well away from the main hangars.

♦ ♦ ♦

Judge Wells was standing in the back yard of his house on The Esplanade when he heard the first bombs fall. He heard no sirens. Following his own advice, he had built an air-raid shelter under his house, and he now set out to test his theories. They worked well. He remained unscathed, staying out of sight until the anti-aircraft batteries stopped firing. He recalled:

> Immediately after that I left my house and walked down The Esplanade to see what damage had been done. I was anxious about my own staff.
>
> I walked past the anti-aircraft battery and stopped and spoke to some of the men. I wanted to see how they were taking it. They were full of beans. They took it exceedingly well. They did a wonderfully good job. They were ragged at first but they put up a wonderfully good show. I spoke to them probably for a minute or so and walked along toward the Post Office and met the junior officer at the Post Office. He was in a very shaken state and said to me: 'Everybody in the Post Office is killed and I cannot find anybody in authority and I don't know what to do.' I said: 'You had better pull yourself together and see what you can do yourself.' I spoke to him for a couple of minutes and then he said: 'I will, I will go back.'
>
> I then went on past the Post Office and passed the Administrator's residence. Mr and Mrs Abbott were out on the drive and the official car was apparently getting ready to leave. General Blake was also there, I think.
>
> I then turned down to the left past the Administrator's

residence and met a man named McDonald who was formerly secretary of the North Australia Workers' Union. He had recently been working and supervising on the wharf. He told me there had been a number of people killed on the wharf and quite a lot thrown into the water.

I then went round to the Court House and found that none of my staff had been injured although they were badly shaken up. My staff had been in the slit trench and that probably saved them from injury. I then went to the Police Station and saw certain disorganisation there. I spoke to them for a minute or two and then went back to the Court House.

Judge Wells leaves out of this account one of his more imaginative actions immediately after the first raid. Fannie Bay gaol sat on the edge of the civil airfield, which had been heavily strafed and hit with daisy-cutter anti-personnel bombs. One of the strafing Japanese pilots attacking the airfield switched his attention to the gaol, raking it with cannon fire.

Prisons Superintendent Jock Reid ordered all the prisoners released from their cells, and all internal gates and doors opened so the prisoners could take cover inside. When the all-clear sounded, Judge Wells went further. He authorised the release of all prisoners. Twenty Aboriginal prisoners and ten whites streaked through the prison gates and away.

One of the prisoners, Ivan Sinclair, did not simply head into the bush. He was serving a hefty sentence after a shooting incident, but he had previously led a blameless life. A trained ambulance man, he went straight to the hospital and offered his services, but was told they were closing down that night. He then went to the ARP office and was instantly accepted. He is credited with treating 113 victims of the raid, with remarkable dedication and skill. In recognition of this, the Governor-General granted him a full pardon. It was the first free pardon granted by any governor-general since the inception of the Commonwealth of Australia.

◆ ◆ ◆

Judge Wells's tour of inspection of the town establishes an important point. So far Darwin had acquitted itself well. The civilian population might have been shaken but they had not panicked. In general they found the best shelter they could and sat out the raid. The Army anti-aircraft gunners, despite their inexperience, fought doggedly and well, even scoring the odd victory. Ships on the harbour returned fire and managed to disrupt the attack even if they did not succeed in holding it off. The machine-gunners at the RAAF base could make a similar claim. A lone Kittyhawk had shot down two attackers. Volunteer rescuers on the harbour performed heroically in the face of strafing, bombing, exploding ships and burning oil. So far, so good. However, in both Edgar Harrison's and Judge Wells's accounts are the seeds of the problem that was about to engulf Darwin. In the first eerie calm of the all-clear, nobody took charge.

Then the Japanese came back.

Chapter 11

The second raid: Chinese whispers

The Vals and Kates that attacked Darwin in the first raid were one thing. The heavy bombers that now struck were an entirely different proposition. In all, 54 aircraft took part in the second attack: 27 G4M Betty bombers from Kendari, in the Celebes Islands, and 27 G3M Nells from the newly captured base on Ambon.[1] These were big, twin-engined bombers and each carried a payload of 1000 kg of bombs, more than three times the capacity of a Val and 250 kg more than a Kate. They carried heavier machine guns and cannons, and had a longer range than the carrier-based bombers.

This time the warning system worked a little better. The depot ship HMAS *Platypus* sounded her siren as the two bomber groups loomed into view. Army Headquarters informed RAAF Operations that a formation of enemy planes had passed over Larrakeyah and appeared to be headed for the RAAF base. Operations turned on the air-raid sirens and fired a red Very signal, both at 11.58 a.m. The base braced itself. Amidst all the anxiety, there was a degree of curiosity over what might tumble from the bellies of the planes. Paratroops? Or more bombs?

Once again, the Japanese tactics were worthy of an air show. A formation of 27 bombers attacked the airfield from the south-west, another formation of 27 from the north-east. They flew straight at each other at 18,000 feet in an immaculate V, more or less crossing over the RAAF airfield. As they crossed they released their first salvo of bombs. This massive load of explosives from 54 aircraft struck the entire area of the airfield simultaneously and with terrifying force.

For 20 minutes the disciplined waves of bombers wheeled and turned, rearranged themselves in tidy formations, and swept back over the RAAF base for another simultaneous release of up to 13,000 kg of high explosive. Airmen in trenches and shelters could feel the searing heat, deafening roar and violent pressure wave as each pattern of bombs threatened to engulf them. Concrete, metal and wooden debris showered all around them from smashed buildings, ruined workshops, wrecked aircraft and devastated parking aprons. A direct hit was fatal. A near miss could leave a man half buried in his slit trench.

For the weary gunners at the Oval, a second air raid within two hours seemed like cruel and unusual punishment. As the gunners scrambled to their positions, Jack Mulholland found a rude rhyme going round and round in his head:

> Bugger me, said the Queen of Spain,
> Three minutes' pleasure and nine months' pain,
> Three months' rest and I'm at it again.

At the Oval section, the sergeant who called the firing orders had lost his voice during the first raid. Mulholland now found himself bellowing through a megaphone against the overwhelming din of the guns. This time the pain was brief: the second raid lasted only 20 minutes. The Japanese were so confident they would meet no resistance that they brought no escort of Zero fighters, so there was no strafing and no dive-bombing.

The second raid confined itself to the RAAF aerodrome. The people of the town, the ships on the harbour and anybody not immediately involved could watch the spectacle in comparative safety. As each pattern of bombs struck, with a gigantic flash of yellow flame followed by dense clouds of black smoke and thunderous rumbling, the eye-witnesses had only one thought for the men at the RAAF base: surely nobody can live through that.

To the bitter disappointment of the anti-aircraft batteries, the morning's problems with the fuse timers persisted. The shells continued to burst below and behind the bombers. At 18,000 feet the bombers were well beyond the range of the machine guns, so there was nothing to be gained from firing them. So far as is known, no Japanese plane received so much as a scratch in the second raid. The attackers had the skies to themselves.

◆   ◆   ◆

Although the air over Darwin was clear by 12.20, Mitsuo Fuchida's carrier-borne dive-bombers had not finished with the local shipping. Two freighters, *Florence D* and *Don Isidro*, were under way off the coast of Bathurst and Melville Islands. Both freighters had set off to run the Japanese blockade of the Philippines, bringing desperately needed ammunition to General Douglas MacArthur's besieged forces there. The entire Japanese wave would have passed over the two ships on their return journey to the carriers and noted their position. Early in the afternoon, a small task force of Vals took off with orders to mop up the two stragglers. *Don Isidro*, 40 kilometres north of Melville Island, was first to come under attack. She radioed for help, but it was too late. The Vals made short work of her. She rapidly caught fire and drifted helplessly until she beached on Melville Island. Eleven men were dead, 73 rescued.

The Vals now switched the attack to *Florence D*, off Bathurst Island. As we have seen, the *Florence D* had paused to gather up Thomas Moorer and the Catalina crew shot down earlier by the inbound Zeroes. The unfortunate Moorer and his men now found themselves under attack again, by the same force and with the same result. *Florence D* sank with four dead, including J.C. Schuler from the Catalina crew. Moorer and his surviving crew, together with survivors from the crew of *Florence D*, piled into two lifeboats. The wind blew them onto the coast of Bathurst Island, where they remained for two days without food or water before a passing RAAF plane spotted them and organised a supply drop and subsequent rescue. The Vals returned untroubled to the carriers. The carrier-borne assault on Darwin and its shipping was now over. Afterwards Fuchida wrote dismissively of the Darwin raid: 'As at Rabaul, the job to be done seemed hardly worthy of the Nagumo Force.'

◆ ◆ ◆

The Japanese did not escape entirely unscathed. There is still some uncertainty over Japanese losses. The Deputy Director of Japanese Naval History, Hitoshi Tsunoda, told Douglas Lockwood only two Japanese aircraft were lost. This is transparently false. Air Commodore Wilson told the Lowe Commission that Tokyo radio had announced the loss of 23 planes. I can find no record of that particular broadcast. In any case, Wilson's figure seems wildly high. Fuchida told Lockwood that the true figure was seven, and this seems likely to be correct.

We know of the two Vals shot down by Robert Oestreicher's Kittyhawk. Jack Mulholland's 3.7-inch gun at the Oval accounted for one Val, 'Darky' Hudson's machine gun accounted for one Zero, and Max Grant's Hotchkiss accounted for a second. A third Zero fell victim to its lack of armour. It was almost certainly brought down by a single .303 bullet, fired either from a single-shot Lee-Enfield rifle or from a Vickers or Lewis machine gun. There is no way of knowing who fired the fatal shot, but the bullet holed the Zero's oil tank and it drained, causing the engine to seize. The pilot, Petty Officer Hajime Toyoshima, glided his doomed plane into a lightly wooded valley on Melville Island and survived the subsequent crash. He was taken prisoner by a single Tiwi Islander, who told him: 'You come longa me, all same Hopalong Cassidy.'[2] Toyoshima was sent to the main Japanese prisoner-of-war camp, at Cowra in south-western New South Wales. He was one of the leaders of the Cowra uprising in August 1944 and died by his own hand on that terrible night. Toyoshima's wrecked aircraft is on display today in Darwin's excellent Australian Aviation Heritage Centre.

What of the other plane acknowledged by Fuchida as lost? The probability is that it met a fate similar to Toyoshima's Zero. All Japanese aircraft were notoriously under-protected by armour and self-sealing tanks, and would succumb to very light damage. The G4M Betty bomber came to be known derisively among Allied fighter pilots as the 'flying Zippo' or the 'one-shot lighter' when they discovered that a single bullet strike to the fuel tank was enough to produce a very satisfying fireball. The Vals in particular must have taken some battle damage from the likes of *Peary*, *William B. Preston*, *Platypus*, *Swan* and *Katoomba*. It would not come as a surprise if one or two of them failed to make it back to the carriers as a result.

◆ ◆ ◆

The second air raid by the heavy bombers produced nothing like the spread of devastation of Fuchida's mixed assault. Nevertheless it marked a turning point in Darwin's fortunes. So far there had been no panic and no disarray. Morale stood up well, both civilian and military. But the pitilessly brief break between the two raids, the brutal power of the second bombing, the absence of any Allied fighter aircraft mounting a counter-attack, and the inability of the AA guns to destroy or even seriously inconvenience the raiders led to a change of mood in the town.

Among the civilians there was a powerful feeling that there was now only one sensible course of action: get out. There should be no surprise at this. It is the common reaction of civilians of all countries and all centuries when wars take over their streets. Anyone who doubts it might like to take a look at news film shot in New York in the immediate aftermath of the attack on the World Trade Centre. The Big Apple's broad avenues were crammed with wild-eyed civilians screaming and running away. And why not? The civilians of Darwin did not scream, and none of them has been accused of breaking into a jog, let alone a run. But they were very clear what they wanted: out.

On the military side in Darwin, the worst affected were those at the RAAF airfield. They had just gone through one of the most terrifying experiences any human being could be asked to endure. The Zeroes, Kates and Vals of the first raid left a trail of damage. The Bettys and Nells of the second raid simply wrecked the rest of the base. Almost nothing was left standing. In the understated words of the *Official History*: 'The station had lost its two hangars which, with the central store, had been burned out, and the transport section and the recreation hut had been wrecked beyond repair. Four blocks of airmen's quarters and the hospital had been severely damaged, and the officers' quarters and mess had been hit.' Six Hudson bombers were a total write-off, as were two Kittyhawks and a B24 Liberator bomber belonging to the Americans. A Wirraway and a Hudson were badly damaged. The first raid had led to only one death: that of Wing Commander Tindal. The second raid killed at least six, four felled by a single bomb that scored a direct hit on a trench. One of the dead was never identified. His body was found in the bush near the airfield. 'A bomb hit him and cut him to ribbons,' Group Captain Scherger said afterwards. 'He was wrapped around a tree. There was no article of clothing and he could not be identified. Nothing could be found. He was assumed to be an Air Force man because he had blue equipment on.'

Miraculously, Robert Oestreicher's Kittyhawk and the three Hudsons, all dispersed well away from the devastated hangars, survived the second raid too.

At this point it is worth standing back a little and asking what exactly Darwin did need at 12.20 p.m. on 19 February 1942. All around were confusion and destruction. Nevertheless, the priorities were obvious enough. The military needed to assess the damage and get whatever weapons had survived the raid ready to fight again—the Japanese might come back at any time. With three serviceable Hudsons in hand, and a reserve of nine Wirraways not far away at Batchelor, some sort of counter-attack was still possible.

Meanwhile, people trapped in wreckage, both soldiers and civilians, needed to be located and freed. The wounded had to be given medical attention at either a first-aid post or a hospital. The dead needed to be removed to mortuaries or otherwise cleared from the streets, wrecked buildings and ships. Fires had to be put out, whether on land or in the harbour. Sailors who had abandoned sunk and beached ships needed to be picked up from the water or the mangroves. Above all, the first requirement after any disaster is for someone to get the tightest possible grip on the situation. Orders and advice need to be broadcast clearly and quickly, before rumours take hold. People need to be prevented from endangering themselves by entering risky areas. Human nature being what it is, those who seek to profit from the disaster by looting need to be stopped. The immediate aftermath requires public announcements that reach everybody. Areas must be sealed, and people stationed to guard them. Men and women are remarkably willing to brave dangers to help others, often displaying selfless and exemplary courage in the process. But they need to see clearly what to do, and they often need to be told to do it, and where to do it first. Like the dazed Post Office worker, the unionists in the utility truck and the policemen at the station, more than anything else Darwin needed someone to step forward and take charge.

All the town's police had been told to assemble at the Police Station in the event of an air raid. After helping to deal with the carnage at the Post Office, Constable Bob Darken set out to walk back to the station. His route took him past Administrator Abbott's Residency, where he saw His Honour and Sergeant Bill Littlejohn bringing liquor out of Government House and loading it on to a truck. Darken continued on to the station, where he worked for some time collecting bodies and taking them to the hospital.

Darken's version of what happened next is perhaps the most furiously contested story of the entire Darwin saga. In particular, Administrator Abbott saw himself as the victim of perjury when it was put to him under cross-examination at the Royal Commission. When he heard the accusations, he asked Commissioner Lowe if he could be represented by counsel. Lowe refused, leading most writers to sympathise with Abbott.

But no other witness at the Royal Commission was represented by counsel, so Lowe was merely keeping Abbott on the same footing as everybody else. Lowe's principal objective was to save time. The key accusation came from Darken, and the reader will have to decide whom to believe, him or Abbott.

Darken said he arrived at the Residency after the all-clear sounded. There Littlejohn instructed him to remove the crested government crockery and load it onto Littlejohn's truck—presumably the same truck that had been used to remove the liquor. Two policemen were detailed to this work, Darken and Constable Hook. Abbott joined in, bringing out some of the crockery himself. It was bad enough that three desperately needed policemen plus the man who above all others should have been tightening a grip on the town instead busied themselves loading crockery. Worse was to follow.

DARKEN: People at the Residence at the time knew that the half-caste girl was still crying out for someone to take her out of the wreckage, and that carried on for half an hour or twenty minutes.

COMMISSIONER LOWE: Do you mean to tell me that the bystanders saw you leaving that woman there?

DARKEN: Yes. That is the position.

LOWE: That is the position? You understand the seriousness of the position, that you might have given help to this woman and saved a life but you were diverted from that to remove the china and crockery?

DARKEN: Yes.

LOWE: You appreciate the seriousness of that?

DARKEN: Yes.

LOWE: You have no doubt it was true?

DARKEN: It is true.

Administrator Abbott angrily denied this story in his own evidence. He said the whimpering had come from the Aboriginal boy, not Daisy

Martin. Of Martin, Abbott said: 'I was certain she was dead. There were two tons of masonry over her.' Why was he certain? 'The appearance of her limbs, and she had that pallor attributable to death, and she had not moved from the time she had been uncovered, and only her lower limbs were showing.'

John V. Barry, counsel assisting the Commissioner, was not satisfied. Darken had given evidence that when he helped to remove Daisy Martin's body next day, it was unmarked except for 'a little scratch on the lip'.

BARRY: Under those circumstances, there being two tons of masonry over her, you would be astounded to learn that her body was unmarked?

ABBOTT: The information I received was that she was badly crushed from the chest upwards. That was the information given to me before she was taken out.

BARRY: Who informed you of that?

ABBOTT: A Chinese, See Kee, who was my typist.

BARRY: Do you know when that was?

ABBOTT: Next day, I fancy. I had to ask the Superintendent of Police to get a demolition squad to endeavour to remove the masonry so she could be got out.

Bob Darken said extracting the body was comparatively simple and took half an hour using crowbars.

His Honour was unabashed about having ordered the removal of the crockery to safe keeping. He devotes a bit over a page of his five-and-a-half-page written report *Japanese Air Raid, Darwin, 19th February 1942—Movements and Actions of the Administrator Upon That and Following Days* to his solicitude towards the cups and saucers. He wrote:

I told General Blake that I thought I ought to save as much valuable Government property as possible and he agreed. I then saw Superintendent Stretton and Sergeant Littlejohn about getting material away. It was decided that we would endeavour to get two trucks away to the Adelaide River and then onto the railway and afterwards use these trucks between Larrimah, the railhead and Alice Springs. We knew that the Army transport would be far too busy to assist us and that we would have to do this ourselves.

I then mentioned what a terrible pity it was about all the glass and china in Government House which was of a high quality and quite valuable. Sergeant Littlejohn, a most resourceful Police Officer, then asked why I did not get it away. I said it would be impossible to pack it so that it would survive the road journey. He then said that he had transported china and glass many miles during his transfers and that the best way was not to pack them but to lay them separately upon a mattress and pack them with clothing. He said he was sure he could do this. I then agreed and told him to take what he could, but only to take the valuable china and glass which was marked with a crest. Sergeant Littlejohn did this early on Saturday morning, the 21st and I did not see the packing until it was practically completed.

His Honour is claiming that the packing took place two days after the raid and not on the same afternoon, as Darken alleged. For the record, Darwin's most senior policeman, Superintendent Alfred Stretton, confirms that the crockery packing began on the day of the raid and was completed next day. He told Commissioner Lowe that Abbott contacted him about 3 p.m. on 19 February, asking him to send over Sergeant Littlejohn and two Constables 'for the purpose of removing valuable government property from Government House'. Abbott himself said as much in one of his later reports when he wrote that on the first afternoon he had ordered the policemen to collect 'silver tea and coffee pots belonging to the Government and some pyjamas and clothes for myself'.

On the other hand Stretton, who had been at the Residency very soon after the raid, strongly refuted the Daisy Martin story. I believe the Daisy Martin story is untrue. Darken's evidence is hearsay, and he recanted it in an interview in 1999 with the historians Peter and Sheila Forrest. I have included it only because the story spread around Darwin immediately after the raid and added to the general public disillusionment with Abbott.

However, the balance of probabilities favours Darken's and Stretton's (and Abbott's) evidence that the movement of the crockery began on the afternoon of the raid. Littlejohn stated in writing on 6 April 1942 that he had packed only liquor on the 19th. He packed the disputed 'glass and chinaware, silverware, code books, confidential papers (official) and the flag' on the 21st. It is likely that Littlejohn wrote this memorandum under persuasion. His wording leaves open the possibility that Darken and Hook had packed the silverware and china on the 19th, and that Littlejohn finished the job on the 21st.

Eventually he delivered the following articles belonging to the Government to the Residency at Alice Springs:

Glass, including tumblers, wine glasses of all kind,— 415 pieces
China, including plates and dishes,— 351 pieces
Silver, including forks, spoons, fruit knives, etc,— 122 pieces
Cutlery, knives etc,— 33 pieces

Whether the infamous glass, china and cutlery moved on the afternoon of the raid or two days later, Abbott remains indicted on his own evidence of wasting a fair bit of police time as well as his own on a trivial matter. At the time Darwin had only 15 policemen. In general, a day shift consisted of only four men, so to pull three away from front-line policing was a serious decision. Superintendent Stretton told the Royal Commission that the three policemen involved in moving the crockery were not on duty but merely spare policemen who happened to be around at the time. Nevertheless, it beggars belief that three of them should, on the Administrator's orders, be whipped away from the emergency policing of the town and assigned instead to packing the Residency's cups and saucers. It is indeed hard to like Charles Lydiard Aubrey Abbott.

◆ ◆ ◆

Nobody has accepted credit for starting the Adelaide River Stakes, as the mass exodus from Darwin came to be known. The dunny truck is, however, a serious claimant for line honours. In 1942 Darwin had no sewerage, and very few houses had septic tanks. Instead sanitary carts toured the town twice a week and emptied the back-yard lavatories. Each dunny cart began its run with a load of empty lavatory pans, and worked its way around the houses removing the full pan and replacing it with an empty. It was not exactly a glamour job.

One cart had arrived in Smith Street, in the heart of town, when the first bombs fell. The driver, Ludo Dalby, sensibly dumped the pan he was carrying and dived into a trench in a back yard. When the first raid ended, both Dalby and the truck had moved on. History does not record the exact progress of the stately vehicle, but a few facts are known. By the time it left Darwin, it was under the command of a junior government official and had acquired a passenger load of eight prominent Darwin citizens, seated on the roof. It then set off down 'the Track' south towards Adelaide River township, about 120 kilometres away. According to legend, on its way it failed to negotiate a particularly tricky bend and shed its entire load of full and empty lavatory pans. This may be true, or it may just be part of a good story. Nevertheless, the sanitary cart is generally credited with being the first vehicle to arrive that afternoon in Adelaide River from Darwin. It was far from the last.[3] The Adelaide River Stakes had begun.

It gathered momentum with remarkable speed. The all-clear sounded at 12.20 p.m., lunch-time. Relieved citizens scrambled out of their shelters and headed for the refrigerator. In the absence of any clear direction from above, the rumour machine took over. The dominant rumour was stark and simple: civilians had been ordered to leave the town. In houses and pubs and hotels and cafés all over Darwin, people hastily decided to forgo lunch and flee, leaving behind half-eaten plates of food, even half-drunk glasses of precious beer.

The Administrator's wife Hilda was among the first to leave. In his written report, His Honour records that after the first raid he discussed the position with General Blake 'and received reports from the

Government Secretary, Mr Giles, the Superintendent of Police, and the Permanent Air Raids Precautions Officer, Mr Harrison'.

Understandably, Abbott wanted to get his badly shaken wife out of harm's way. His report continues:

> I then decided to send my wife and her household staff off in the two cars, and they left about 12 noon. As Kamper, my messenger, had only just learned to drive a car, Superintendent Stretton detailed a Police Officer, Constable Bowie, to drive one car and Mrs Abbott drove the other. She took the injured half-caste girl and the aboriginal in the car with her. This party took whatever they could hastily get hold of in the way of clothes and some blankets. No other personal effects were taken except a small portable typewriter which belonged to me and which had escaped damage.

Four of Darwin's 15 policemen were now engaged on domestic work for the Abbotts. Littlejohn, Darken and Hall worked on the liquor and the cups and saucers. Bowie drove the household staff. On Darken's evidence, His Honour did not simply leave them to get on with it. He selflessly and democratically abandoned his other work and gave a hand.

◆ ◆ ◆

From the beginning, the Army had been responsible for the evacuation of Darwin's civilians. Having organised his wife's safe exit in a convoy of two government cars, Abbott now went to Army Headquarters at Larrakeyah Barracks 'to see what could be done about getting the few remaining females out of the town'. The Army already had a plan. It hoped to get an evacuation train away about 2.30 that afternoon. Abbott returned to the town. Since his own offices had been wrecked, he set up headquarters in the Police Station. He asked the police to round up the surviving women and children and get them to the railway station at Parap by 2.30.

All of this no doubt laudable activity fell well short of getting a real grip on the crisis. In the absence of clarity, rumours spread. There was a well-justified fear that the air raid was a 'softening-up' operation, the usual preliminary to an invasion. Anybody who stayed could expect to be slaughtered next day when the bestial Japanese hit the beaches. The rumour mill ran hot. Every civilian was to evacuate at once. The police, who seem never to have been properly briefed either by the Administrator or by Superintendent Stretton, added to the confusion by giving contradictory advice and instructions. So did the air-raid wardens. So did the Army.

The result was inevitable. The road south filled with every kind of vehicle—cars, trucks, utilities, a road grader, horses, bicycles (including an ice-cream seller's bike, complete with cool box but no ice-cream), people on foot. Anything that could move did. The road jammed as drivers groped their way blindly in the choking red dust of the Track. Some cars and trucks carried food and personal effects. Other just drove, anything to get away from the bombers and the slaughter that would inevitably follow the arrival of the Japs.

◆ ◆ ◆

Mick Ryan, secretary of the North Australian Workers' Union, sat out the second raid in a culvert behind the union office. When the all-clear sounded, he took a walk around the town, looking for other members of his union executive to discuss what to do. During his wanderings he bumped into Brough Newell, erstwhile Director of First Aid in the ARP unit. Newell was a former Army officer and had, only two days earlier, been appointed Captain of the Volunteer Defence Corps. Ryan was a member of the VDC and he asked Newell what he should do. The VDC had been told they would automatically be taken into the Army in the event of enemy action. 'The Captain was unable to give me any information whatsoever,' Ryan recalled.

At this point Ryan set off again in the utility towards the Darwin Hotel, where some of his union executive were billeted. He went on:

I was in the vicinity of the Darwin Hotel together with some other men, and a police car passed by, and the police constable called out: 'All civil cars to proceed to the PWD [Public Works Department] depot to fill up with petrol. They have been commandeered for evacuation purposes.' We proceeded then to the PWD depot and lined up with the other cars. About an hour later the Administrator, Mr Abbott, came on the scene and gave instructions that no civil vehicles were to be given petrol unless they were on some special duty.

We then pulled out of the line of cars and went back down the town, to our union office and the office of the *Northern Standard*. We picked up some records and things, and decided we would go out of town a little way and then wait to find out what the position would be.

In his report to his superiors in the Department of the Interior in Canberra, and again in his evidence to the Royal Commission, Abbott set out to blame Ryan for triggering the Adelaide River Stakes. He wrote: 'Immediately after the raid the morale of the civilians was good, but it rapidly deteriorated, mainly, in my opinion, through the Secretary of the N.A.W.U. and other prominent union officials leaving the town by car as quickly as they could.' Given that Mrs Abbott was well up with the front runners when the civilian exodus began, departing some four hours ahead of what proved to be the temporary exit of Mick Ryan, this seems unfair, to put it mildly. And, Ryan pointed out in his evidence to the Royal Commission, they left in a utility truck, not a car.

◆ ◆ ◆

At 3.30 p.m. the military police stepped in to try to stem the Adelaide River tide. Lieutenant David Watson, the most senior Provost, gathered up four NCOs in a car and headed down the road. He placed two of them outside the Parap Police Station, close to the railway station, with orders to stop any civilians passing that point. Watson then continued 60 kilometres down the road, turning back any civilians he encountered. It was too late. The horse had well and truly bolted.

◆ ◆ ◆

While Group Captain Scherger fumed and raged over his inability to use the surviving fighting aircraft to launch a counter-strike, Wing Commander Sturt Griffith, the station commander at the RAAF base, was having trouble deciding what to do first. Incredibly, he chose not to organise any sort of salvage operation, leaving vital equipment and material to fend for itself in the damaged hangars, workshops and storerooms. Instead he chose as his first priority getting the water going after a water main had burst. Water and electricity supplies had survived the first air raid. The second raid cut off both. Without power the warning sirens would not work, exposing everyone still on the base to danger if the Japanese came back. There was an emergency generator, but this needed water to function, so until water could be restored there could be no electricity. There was also an emergency water supply, but the tank was secured by a Yale lock and nobody could find the key. Griffith ordered maintenance teams to get to work on the burst water main as the best way of getting the base going again.

There is nothing quite like 20–20 hindsight for clarity of vision, and it is a matter of judgement whether Griffith had his priorities right. What can be said with certainty is that while restoring power was undoubtedly important, there were plenty of other jobs that could be done at the same time. In particular, there was a desperate need to salvage anything serviceable to give surviving aircraft a fighting chance if the Japanese came back. With luck, the salvage teams might even get some sort of ground-to-air radio working. Without it, the three undamaged Hudsons could not be used. The Hudsons were the key to any counter-attack, but they needed to be launched quickly to give them a chance to find the Japanese aircraft carriers. In the course of the afternoon Scherger pleaded six times for someone to get the ground-to-air working, to no avail. Other jobs came first.

With no salvage operation, there was very little else for the rest of the men to do. There were as many as 2000 men linked to the base, of whom only a handful could work on the water and electricity supply. The rest were left hanging about, exposed to danger if the Japanese returned.

Confronted with a large body of men under threat and with nothing to do, Griffith issued the order that led to the biggest fiasco of the entire sorry saga. Most people are familiar with the old game of Chinese Whispers, in which a dozen or so volunteers sit in a line. The maestro whispers something in the ear of the first volunteer, who is told to whisper it to the next person, and so on. The idea is to see how much the message has been distorted by the time it reaches the other end of the line. The most famous military example, supposedly from the First World War, tells of a commander who asked for the message 'Going to advance, send reinforcements' to be relayed verbally to headquarters by a series of runners. By the time it reached HQ, the vital message had become: 'Going to a dance. Send three and fourpence.'

The road to hell is said to be paved with good intentions. The farce that followed resulted from a well-intentioned plan to move those lads with nothing to do to a safer place and fix them up with a spot of lunch. Griffith recounted:

> Group Captain Scherger and I discussed the matter and he agreed that it would be safer to remove the personnel from the aerodrome pending the rehabilitation of the water system. I suggested all the personnel including not only the station personnel but the Area Headquarters personnel should assemble at a point half a mile down the Batchelor Road and half a mile in the timber. The instruction was to Squadron Leader Swan [the station adjutant] that all ranks were to be assembled at this point. He was to move the men to the position indicated, feed them, and I would come over and address them.

There were two problems with this otherwise admirable proposal. Some of the men had already set off down the road, so it was too late to give them the correct order anyway. And those still at the base were scattered in sections over a huge area. Instead of calling them all together and marching them down the road in a body, which might have avoided confusion but would have exposed them to more danger, Swan allowed each section to pass the order to the next. Having received their orders and passed them on, the sections then moved off independently. Griffith spelled out what the reader has probably guessed.

> There seem to have been varying orders transmitted. Some men appear to have been told—though by whom I cannot track down—that they were to go to Batchelor [90 kilometres away]; some men that they had to go five miles down the road; some men that they had to go half a mile down the road; some that they had to go to the 22 mile. The men were prepared to listen to rumour, and if they saw a body of men moving down the road—for instance to the half-mile position—the rumour might have been: 'We are evacuating the aerodrome' or 'We are getting out into the bush,' which may have spread from section to section. Men started off without orders and to seek transport down the road, because there was any amount of civilian and Army transport, and I think the men merely took it into their heads, rightly or wrongly, that they were getting out of the aerodrome.

The result was a shambles on a gigantic scale, compounded by the fact that Swan and a colleague stopped trucks on the road and asked the drivers to give the men a lift. The airmen now had wheels, and they headed south with renewed enthusiasm and much-improved mobility. The mess officer set up a kitchen at the 13-mile point, and a few of the men actually made it there. The rest simply evaporated. One man, showing exemplary zeal and ingenuity, turned up in Melbourne 13 days later. Others reached Batchelor, Adelaide River, Katherine, Daly Waters, wherever they could hitch a ride.

✦   ✦   ✦

Those in authority hotly denied afterwards that there was panic in Darwin that day—the P word was never to be admitted in polite society. The dictionary defines panic as a sudden, overwhelming feeling of terror or anxiety, especially one affecting a group of people. Any distinction between what happened in Darwin and overwhelming anxiety affecting a group of people seems more semantic than real. The ex-ambulance man Ivan Sinclair, who had been freed from Fannie Bay prison under Judge Wells's orders, in evidence to the Royal Commission at first rejected the notion that Darwin had panicked. However, he offered the common-sense view that if someone had given a firm lead, the whole sorry business could have been avoided. It is hard to disagree with his simple summing up: 'My honest opinion is that if a man had been at the 2½-mile road where people were going out in such a panic, and had impressed on the general public that there was no necessity to leave Darwin as there was no immediate danger, I do not think one per cent of the population would have left. I think they would all have stopped here.'

Whatever word anyone chooses to describe what was happening in Darwin that day, worse was to follow. As the civilians abandoned their homes and workplaces and joined the swelling Adelaide River exodus, Darwin's houses, hotels, shops and offices were left empty, wide open and temptingly unprotected.

Chapter 12

Things go badly wrong

It is not possible to determine the exact time on the afternoon of 19 February 1942 when Darwin tipped from mild confusion and chaos into serious ugliness, but a single event probably marked the watershed. Sergeant MacArthur-Onslow of the Provost Corps, well drunk as usual, marched into the Police Station some time in the early afternoon, after the second raid.[1] Brandishing a revolver, he announced that Darwin was now under martial law. Constable Bob Darken, who was at the station at the time, remembers him bellowing: 'We are tops and you will take orders from us.' The tragedy is that the lower-ranking police officers believed him. Darwin was not then, or indeed ever, under martial law. But the police took MacArthur-Onslow's word that the town was now under military control, and they listened faithfully to the deluge of ill-informed, groundless and contradictory instructions arriving from all sides and purporting to emanate from the Army. Only one common thread ran through it all—civilians were under orders to get out of Darwin.

Just as there is no exact time for MacArthur-Onslow's outburst, so is there none for when the looting began. Administrator Abbott suspected that it started almost immediately. Constable Leo Law recalled:

After the second raid the Administrator sent for me. I went along and met him outside his residence near a bomb crater. He said to me: 'There has been some looting going on in my house already I suspect. I want you to go over for a while. I will be there presently.' I went over to his house. He followed me. He said to me: 'I want you to go down into my cellar and tell me what you can see there.' He supplied me with a torch. I went down into the cellar. All I could see there was a large quantity of liquor. I came up and informed him of the approximate numbers of bottles of liquor there. He said to me: 'All right, get a police car and we will take these to the Commandant.' I returned to the Superintendent of Police, and he said there was no car available.

Against His Honour's belief that the looting started with persons unknown at Government House, Gunner Jack Mulholland is willing to declare that he started it himself. His motives were of the highest. 'I don't think we had time to clean the guns properly after the first raid,' he recalled.

After the second raid, we started. The Army had given us a certain amount of rags to clean them. Well, the rags weren't enough. After all the firing, the guns were chopping the rags to smithereens. That's when we had the bright idea that the Darwin Hotel had plenty of serviettes, sheets and God knows what. That's what started the looting.

We were first into the Darwin Hotel. It was eerie. There were half cups of tea with a cigarette beside them. All the humans had disappeared. There was nothing—the hotel was empty. We could walk into the Qantas office, and there were parcels there. We didn't touch them. I don't know why not, but we didn't. We had a look in the fridges and found there was some good food there, which we ate.

The raiding party retreated, well fed and armed with enough white linen to give the guns the clean-up of a lifetime.

By the middle of the afternoon, the looting was in full swing. As Administrator Abbott wrote deferentially in his report to the Department of the Interior:

I regret very much to inform the Minister that looting became very prevalent in the town. I am afraid that I must state definitely that the main pillaging must be attributed to men of the three services in Darwin and officers must be included in it. I also do not except officers and men from the United States Army from this charge. The thefts include a great deal of valuable government property, including electric fans, kelvinators [refrigerators], and articles which could only be taken when transport and parties of men were available.

What Abbott is saying, in a nutshell, is that the looting was carried out by the military, and they took the stuff away in truckloads. This was confirmed by Police Sergeant Bill McKinnon: 'My idea is it was military. I know some was done by civilians. I do believe that some of the military police, although they were supposed to be in charge of the town, some members actually took part in the looting.' Note that McKinnon accepts that the military police were in charge of the town.

Constable Bob Darken agreed:

From what I have heard, the military police would go on to the shops and business premises with their own trucks and loaded materials and goods—they were taken away from the houses by the military police themselves. Sergeant McKinnon and I saw the back door open at the shop of Lorna Lim. We went round the back and an MP [Military Policeman] by the name of Stevens was inside the shop. I said to Stevens: 'Who is responsible for all this destruction?' At the time there was a great deal of goods trodden into the floor. I said jokingly: 'I suppose you Military Police have got most of the stuff?' He said: 'Oh, yes. When we were here someone was looting the place. We heard of it. We came down and everyone just took what they wanted.' Meaning, of course, every member of the military police.

Jack Mulholland concurs. 'As far as I can understand, they [the military police] split the town up among themselves, and you daren't go near any of their property.'

Edgar Harrison, the Permanent ARP Officer, confirmed Abbott's view that Americans were as much to blame as Australians: 'On the Sunday after the raid I went down to the Administrator's house in the course of inspection of the town, and there were a number of Americans coming out of the property with all sorts of articles, clothing etc.'

Some stories betray an almost breathtaking *chutzpah*. In his evidence to the Lowe Commission, Edgar Harrison gave this account of his personal involvement:

Last Sunday morning [1 March, ten days after the raid] I went to my own house to see what I could pick up. It was the first time I had any time to attend to my own personal matters. I found two military officers in the house. [Not junior officers, either. Harrison named them as Major Willshire and Captain Meiklejohn.] I asked them what they were doing in the house. Willshire said he was having a look round to see if there was anything that might be of value to him, and Meiklejohn said he was looking for a kerosene refrigerator. I then acquainted them with the fact that I was the tenant of the house, showed them the state of my personal possessions, and they expressed regret and went out. They did not take anything with them. I immediately gave a written report to His Honour, the Administrator. One of our junior officers who was with me counter-signed it as a witness.

Both Willshire and Meiklejohn appeared before the Lowe Commission, specifically to explain themselves. Both largely conceded that what Harrison had said about them was true. However, they offered an explanation. Willshire said he was looking for anything of military value, not of value to him. Meiklejohn, a medical supply officer, said he had indeed been looking for a kerosene refrigerator—several had been stolen from the Cullen Bay hospital and he had been told they had been seen disappearing on a lorry. The refrigerators were needed to preserve serums and other medical supplies. He had gone into Harrison's house, which appeared to be damaged, remarking to Major Willshire as he walked in: 'I wonder whether I might locate kerosene refrigerators here?'

To be fair, Meiklejohn had made a serious point, one to match Jack Mulholland's. One person's looting can often be another person's resourcefulness. In the immediate aftermath of the raid, Darwin faced a desperate situation. There was a real threat of shortages of food and other resources. In the circumstances, if people chose to leave their homes and flee, why not move in and make good use of whatever they left behind? Among other things, with the electricity supply disrupted, food would quickly rot in refrigerators. That argument is sound. But few could doubt that the 'borrowing' in Darwin went beyond resourcefulness and crossed the line that separates commendable initiative from outright theft. Removing and consuming perishable food from hotels and houses, especially when food might be hard to find elsewhere, is one thing. Stripping houses of tables and chairs, stoves and refrigerators, pianos and radios, bedding and blankets, china and glasses, is looting however you look at it.

Over the next few days, Darwin was picked bare. Officers' messes, which had been hot, bleak and uncomfortable the day before the raid, suddenly and mysteriously acquired electric fans, refrigerators, radios, carpets, cups and glasses, pleasant cane furniture, cushions, curtains and all the comforts of home. Somebody else's home.

The civilian police, who might have put a stop to it, were hampered from the beginning by the belief that the town was under military control, and that military authority trumped their civil jurisdiction. Constable Bob Darken told the Lowe Commission: 'It appeared to me that *if we had been in charge* [emphasis added] immediately after the raid, most of the looting could have been stopped.' The tragedy is that for four days after the raid they *were* in charge but didn't know it.

Captain Bernard Colman, who controlled the Provost Corps in Darwin, told the Lowe Commission he had been powerless to prevent this sorry state of affairs. 'The looting, I am told, started during the second raid, some in Wharf Street and Cavenagh Street, some near the Commonwealth Bank, and some near the Darwin Hotel. I had a limited number of men in town and they could not stop looting. They could stop it when they saw it.' The plain fact is that if Colman's men could stop looting when they saw it, they did not have far to look. They were doing it themselves.

◆ ◆ ◆

The legitimate evacuation of Darwin's remaining women and older men was scheduled to begin at 2.30 from the main railway station at Parap. It would be an uncomfortable journey. The Army had laid on a train, but the best it could find was a collection of cattle trucks and flat-top goods cars. That would have to do. The air-raid wardens scoured the town, telling women and old men to head for the station. There were even one or two children who'd been kept hidden at home after the earlier mass evacuation. Those heading for the station were mostly people who had actively resisted the earlier order to leave. Now they needed no urging. They were told they would travel by rail to Larrimah, then by road to Alice Springs. The 1500-kilometre journey would take five days.

There were scenes at Parap station to outdo even the unseemly scramble down the Adelaide River road. The train had been laid on for women and old men. Young men turned up and became abusive when they were told they could not go aboard. Arthur Miller, the chief air-raid warden, commanded the operation. As more people pressed into Parap, he sensed he was in danger of losing control. At his request, Army Headquarters at Larrakeyah sent two soldiers with sub-machine guns to back him up. According to Douglas Lockwood, Miller told them: 'A live burst at the feet of any young man who tries to get on this train. But don't kill anyone.' Miller had no trouble after that.

Every passenger's name was noted, and by 4 p.m. the train was ready to roll. In *Australia Under Attack*, Lockwood recounts an extraordinary last-minute drama. Just as the train was about to leave, Miller was told an unexploded bomb had been found buried in the middle of the railway line just near the RAAF airfield. Even if it was a dud, it might still be unstable. Worse, it might have a delayed-action fuse. Miller had to weigh the risk of sending his train to pass directly over the unexploded bomb with the very real possibility of setting it off. Otherwise, he could wait until the bomb was defused and removed, delaying the train by several hours. In the end he decided to chance it. 'Go now,' he said, 'but tell the driver to take it quietly past the aerodrome.' The train and its 71 passengers passed uneventfully over the bomb.

♦ ♦ ♦

Administrator Abbott's priorities are a never-ending source of wonder. After falsely blaming Mick Ryan for starting the stampede down the Adelaide River road, His Honour now discovered a new problem requiring his immediate and personal attention. 'The Chinese community joined in the rush and this resulted in cafés and restaurants being without cooks,' he wrote. 'The main objective [after organising the evacuation train] was to get kitchens going so that men who had stayed could be fed and I concentrated on this. Volunteer cooks were obtained and continuous meals (stew, bread and tea) were served from the Eastern Café.' With the town being looted, with civilians fleeing in droves, and with chaos all around him, the highest authority in the Northern Territory saw as his first priority rounding up cooks for the Eastern Café.

Abbott and Ryan could agree on one point: the Administrator went in person to the Public Works Depot some time in the afternoon to see if he could stem the tide of civilians pouring out of the town. 'I found a considerable amount of confusion,' he wrote afterwards. 'There were a line [sic] of civilian cars drawn up, all demanding petrol so that they could get away. I placed Sergeant Littlejohn in charge of the pump and told him that nobody could get petrol without an order from myself or the Superintendent of Police. I also instructed him to tell everyone that there was no order to leave the town and that I wanted everyone to carry on until they received definite instructions.' This last request fell on predictably deaf ears.

Abbott now turned his attention to the looting of his wine cellar. Constable Vic Hall had been at the police barracks when a bomb demolished it. He had been slightly injured. Abbott asked Superintendent Stretton if he could spare a policeman to guard the wine. Stretton nominated Hall. Abbott wrote: 'I asked Constable Hall, if he felt up to it to go down the cellar and bring all the wine up. He did this and later on Sergeant Littlejohn brought a car over and a large quantity of port, sherry and other wines were put in the car. I had this sent out to the Commandant's House where I was going to sleep and later on I asked Major General Blake if he would arrange to have this wine distributed among the various military messes.' Interestingly, considering he was to deny doing anything about the other 'valuable government property' that afternoon, Abbott goes on: 'I also sent out silver tea and coffee pots belonging to the Government and some pyjamas and clothes for myself.' You can't fault Abbott's priorities.

His Honour next went on a tour of the town. 'I had previously arranged to keep the Eastern Café open,' he wrote. 'With the assistance of one of the townsmen, Captain Gregory, volunteer cooks had been obtained and continuous meals were being served. I visited this Café and spoke to all the men there and told them to cheer up and settle down. I also visited the Darwin Civil Hospital and spoke to the patients and nurses.'

Last but not least, there was some serious business to attend to. In the event of an enemy attack, by longstanding plan the bank managers would collect money, securities and ledgers and head down the road to the safety of Alice Springs. At 7.30 p.m., Abbott sent out a summons to the four bank managers. When they dutifully turned up, Abbott was nowhere to be found. Police Superintendent Stretton told them to come back at 9.30 p.m. This time Abbott was there. He told them to be ready for evacuation in two hours, with cash and essential records. The bankers eventually left at 1 a.m. and arrived at Adelaide River seven hours later. They did not travel alone. There were other key citizens to move to safety. In Abbott's words: 'The Deputy Commissioner of Taxation accompanied them.'

♦ ♦ ♦

As night fell, the Provosts turned violent. They were by now largely drunk and well out of control. A second train had been organised to take remaining civilians south. Judge Wells recalled:

About 8.30 p.m. I was told by Mr Abbott that there was some trouble at the 2½-mile, that the Provost Corps had stopped people and there was trouble. I went out there and saw the trouble. MacArthur-Onslow was there. He was even drunker than usual. He was pretty bad, and most of the Provost Corps, as far as I could see, were all in a pretty bad state.

There was a train leaving shortly afterwards and at the time the army decided that no men should leave Darwin, so Jackson and I drafted them out. There were the old men and some who had been slightly wounded and some were sick. We picked out a number of men and told the others they would not be allowed to go. During this time the Provost Corps were firing over the heads of the crowd. The crowd were not giving any trouble at all. The Provost Corps said that if a man stepped forward, they would shoot him. They fired over the heads of the people. Then, if cars came along with lights on, they would stop the car and shoot at the light. It was a disgraceful matter.

Lieutenant David Watson, Deputy Assistant Provost Marshal and therefore the most senior MP in Darwin at the time, was not immune to trouble from his own men. On 20 February he wrote a frank and personal account of the events of the night before:

At 2110 hours I returned to the camp by van which was showing regulation lights. On arrival at the camp Lieutenant Pye [second-in-command of the Provost Company] stepped on the road and instructed the driver to extinguish the lights. The Lieutenant had then just arrived from supervising the loading of the train, which had departed at 2100 hours.

I asked Lieutenant Pye the reason for his instruction to the driver, and he replied that all lights in the town of Darwin were blacked out and that lights on m/vehicles were forbidden. He was unable to tell me who had issued this instruction, and had taken it for granted in view of the air raids during the day. I then asked Captain Colman if he had issued any instruction to that effect and he had not. Lieutenant Pye then stated that he and Sergeant MacArthur-Onslow had shot the lights out on several vehicles belonging to the American Armed Forces.

Administrator Abbott now summoned Watson to the police station in the town to explain all the shooting. Watson continues:

The Administrator was then out and I waited at the Station until 2200 hours. Mr Abbott then complimented the Provost Co^y for excellent work in the town during the Air Raids during the day and in the subsequent control of civilians and prevention of looting, but added that it had been reported to him that members of the Company in the vicinity of Parap had fired several shots and appeared to be excitable. He asked that these men be cautioned. Mr Abbott then drove off in his car without using his lights.

Watson returned to the camp and witnessed the arrest of Pye and MacArthur-Onslow by the Deputy Assistant Adjutant General. That calmed things down a little.

◆ ◆ ◆

The remaining population of Darwin took to their beds on the night of 19 February 1942 in a state of considerable disarray. They also faced something of an information vacuum. Civilians and airmen were camped out along the Adelaide River road, out of touch with civil and military authorities. Others made it to Adelaide River, where there was nothing like enough food or accommodation for them, and nobody to tell them what to do or where to go. Merchant seamen from the sunken ships set up a temporary camp in Doctor's Gully, at the site of the old Darwin Hospital, awaiting word on how they were to be evacuated. Until evacuation came, they could choose between joining the Adelaide River Stakes or indulging in a little light looting for food, blankets and shelter for the night.

Essential services had broken down. Electricity and water came back on in the afternoon, but the sanitary services had decamped south. Surviving ships desperately needed unloading, yet the wharfies had by evening joined the general exodus. The banks had gone. Shops were shut and deserted. So were hotels. Looting was rife. The civil police felt sidelined. The military police were out of control. The Administrator's port, sherry and other fine wines were in safe hands. Otherwise, Darwin was a mess.

Chapter 13

The military takes over

At the end of the first day the authorities in Darwin, military and civil, were all agreed on one thing: they had not seen the last of the Japanese. The Japs would surely be back within 48 hours, and the next attack would be far more destructive than the first. Indeed, it might very well be followed by an invasion. On the military side there was work to be done preparing positions. On the civil side, the town was incapable of functioning. All the bankers and at least half of the shopkeepers, businessmen, hotel keepers, café proprietors, cooks and garbage collectors had fled south with the wharfies and some merchant seamen. Ships in the harbour were stuck with no crews to move them, and often with their full cargoes still trapped in holds.

Having spent what little was left of the night of the raid at the home of Major General Blake, Administrator Abbott began the new day by calling in his Works Director, E.W. Stoddart, to his temporary headquarters at the Lands Office. Stoddart had already done sterling work on the afternoon of the raid restoring the town's water and electricity, and had begun the dispiriting job of clearing the wrecked civilian areas of the town. In Abbott's words:

It seemed to us at that time that steps would be taken to repair the damage at the wharf and that essential defence works would be continued. I visited the Eastern Café again and made sure that food was available and that the cooks were all on the job. Everything there was satisfactory. I then went to the remains of my Office and destroyed all the confidential papers by fire. My reason for doing this was that there had been practically a direct hit upon my confidential cabinet and files, very mutilated, were scattered everywhere. I was able to save the confidential code and cipher book with the exception of one cipher book which was badly damaged. This was also personally destroyed by me.

That took care of the morning. Abbott then met General Blake for lunch. Blake had taken a decision: it would be madness to try to defend Darwin from the Army's present position strung out along the shoreline. He would move his troops well back from the town and await the worst, meeting any Japanese attack with some kind of defence in depth. This was all very well and undoubtedly sensible, though overdue. However, it meant that Darwin became, in Abbott's phrase, 'a kind of no man's land'. The rampaging Japanese could have the town and its few remaining civilians to themselves, and the Army would not strike back until the invaders had rolled over the civilian population and moved inland.

The anti-aircraft gunners, who had performed so well the day before, were particularly miffed. They were not included in the withdrawal, and nobody told them it was happening. The first they knew of it was the sudden discovery that they had no food. The main body of the Army had taken all the stores. Help arrived in the form of tins of ham and rice, floating in boxes on the harbour and washed ashore by the tide. For days the gunners lived on nothing but the washed-up tins, three meals a day of ham and rice. Meanwhile, they faced the disquieting prospect of a Japanese invasion with no Army alongside them to resist it. If the Japanese came, as everybody expected they would, the gunners' reward for their courageous services on 19 February would be to be massacred in the first ten minutes.

Jack Mulholland recalls: 'We were just left up there—mainly search-lights, anti-aircraft and coastal artillery. We were ordered to put all our gear except one pair of boots and a couple of pairs of pants in kit bags with our names on them. They were going to take them down south and put them in a big dump where they would either burn them or give them back to us. We were practising spiking the guns and preparing to burn out. We had 44-gallon drums of petrol and oil.' If the Japs came, scorched earth would be the order of the day, with Mulholland and his gunners as the scorchers.

◆ ◆ ◆

At their lunch meeting, General Blake and Administrator Abbott discussed control of the town. Blake offered to appoint a Town Major to assist His Honour, and the Administrator agreed. Although the civil authorities remained in charge, Darwin moved one step closer to military control.

The General and the Administrator now turned their attention to the mounting chaos at the Adelaide River. 'We both agreed,' Abbott wrote, 'that I should go down there and with the assistance of Army Officers endeavour to clean it up.' Abbott left some time on Saturday, 21 February, in Police Sergeant Littlejohn's truck, together with the famous cups and saucers. They camped out overnight by the roadside and arrived at Adelaide River next morning, three days after the raid. His Honour wrote later:

With the ready assistance of the Army Officers at the Adelaide River Camp, organisation was set in motion, the evacuees there were collected and rationed and the Area Officer compiled a list of eligibles for the Army. These were medically examined, and older men were sent back to Darwin or in the case of the old and infirm, evacuated down the line to Alice Springs and Adelaide.

This took practically the whole day. I spent the night at Mount Bundy near the Adelaide [River] and returned to Darwin the following day.

On 23 February, the government in Canberra gave notice under National Security (Emergency Control) Regulations that the area of the Northern Territory north of Larrimah was under Army control. This amounted to about one-third of the Northern Territory and included Darwin. On his way back to town, Abbott met Blake, who had by now taken up his new battle positions well outside the town, and told him what had been achieved at Adelaide River: some 250 able-bodied men had been drafted into the Army and would shortly return to Darwin. The rest had been packed off south. Abbott presented a picture of Adelaide River and Darwin quickly being restored to order under his firm guidance. Others' experiences do not quite match this version of events.

♦ ♦ ♦

The word 'muster' is often used in military circles to describe calling the troops together for a parade or roll-call. The activities at the RAAF station in the days after the raid had more in common with a cattle muster. Officers headed off into the bush to round up stragglers. Just about everybody from the base had disappeared immediately after the second raid in the mistaken belief that they were under orders to get away. Some returned to the base on the evening of the raid. The rest had to be tracked down and brought back by truck or car from as far afield as Daly Waters.

Squadron Leader Swan, the station adjutant, kept a personal diary of the round-up. He wasn't counting on 19 or 20 February, when he was busiest, but he started to record numbers from the 21st. On that day he found 15 men on the road near the 20-mile point. Another 12 turned up on a truck at the 25-mile point, and 12 more on a similar truck at the 28-mile point, giving Swan a personal tally of 39 for the day. He had less to show for his efforts next day: a mere three men. At the end of the second raid on 19 February the RAAF station's strength stood at 1104 men. On the 23rd, four days after the raid, 826 men had returned to the station, leaving 278 still missing. From that point onwards, they were classed as deserters.

At the base itself, the atmosphere remained jittery for days. Wing Commander Scherger recalled:

Two days after the raid an alarm was sounded. All the staff in Area Combined Headquarters immediately ran at top speed to the nearest shelter trench. By the time the remaining officer and myself had ascertained the reason for the alarm being sounded and waited sufficiently long to ensure that it was a false alarm, we were unable to find any of the staff who had left the building. We looked in all the adjacent shelter trenches, and it was not until approximately 10 minutes after the all clear had been sounded that the staff returned.

It transpired they had taken shelter in the nearest sheltered trench and, as no attack eventuated immediately, they decided the trench was unsafe because it was near the building, so they retired to a sheltered trench further away where they thought they were practically safe. They got into the bush on the far side of the railway line.

♦ ♦ ♦

While the seamen's union in Australia in 1942 could not fully match the wharfies for 24/7 militancy and bloody-mindedness, they were not far behind. The merchant seamen brought ashore from wrecked ships had set up camp in Doctor's Gully, on the harbour foreshore. There was still plenty of work to be done on the surviving ships, with unloading the most immediate and urgent task. Some of the ships were capable of moving, and they needed crews to move them. The seamen would have none of it.

Lieutenant Commander James McManus, the senior Naval Intelligence Officer in Darwin, recalled: 'We wanted men to unload the ships. Our men were working day and night. We were being assisted by Army personnel and we wanted these merchant seamen to assist us.'

McManus went down to the camp and addressed the men. He was met with a blank refusal. 'They wanted to know how they stood,' he told the Lowe Commission. 'They were shipwrecked seamen and they were entitled to pay and return to their own port. One of their Articles is that they must not accept other work, otherwise they would lose all the benefits under the award.'

McManus was not the only speaker to plead with the men. Their own officers spoke to them, as did Navy Lieutenant Commander L.E. Tozer. In the end a few relented, but the rest simply sat. More than two weeks after the raid, 300 merchant seamen were still camping at Doctor's Gully. They turned ugly. Judge Wells told the Lowe Commission on 8 March:

> This morning we had a lot of trouble. The officer who has been more or less in charge of them—I think second or third mate or something—came and said he did not think he could keep them in control much longer. The cook refused duty this morning.
>
> Captain Thomas will probably tell you he offered to take them south on the *Tulagi*, and they refused to go on board. There is also a proposal which Captain Thomas made to take them by another ship. I do not know the name of the ship. I know that these seamen have said they will absolutely refuse to go on that boat. General Blake expressed the view to me that if they did not go on board he would make them. However that is going to be carried out I do not know. They are very definitely determined that they won't go by that boat, and they demand to be evacuated by road.

The recalcitrant sailors had their way. A few were persuaded to go south by sea. The Army eventually shouldered the burden and evacuated the rest by road and rail.

♦ ♦ ♦

The question of who controlled Darwin, civil administration or military, continued to cause confusion. When Administrator Abbott returned from Adelaide River, he complained: 'This [confusion] was greatly accentuated by various wireless broadcasting statements that Darwin was under martial law.' Why Abbott did not grab the microphone and make his own broadcast setting out the facts is hard to understand. I have been unable to trace any of the offending broadcasts, but this is not to doubt that they happened. The probability is that they emanated from the Australian Broadcasting Commission's mobile recording unit in Darwin. Those manning the unit were very likely as confused and misled as everybody else. Abbott clearly did not see it as part of his job to put them straight. As a result, the broadcasts were believed. After all, if the ABC said Darwin was under martial law, who would dare say otherwise?

As soon as Abbott returned to Darwin, he and General Blake agreed on a five-point plan for the future of civilians in Darwin. Abbott set it out in his 27 February report to the Department of the Interior.

1. Men for essential services such as sanitary, electric light and water services would be retained in Darwin and would carry on. If it became necessary these men would be organised into a military unit under Army control.
2. Non-essential civilians, aged persons, merchant seamen, hospital patients etc would be evacuated by the Army authorities as opportunity and transport offered, in order of priority. This priority would be determined by the Army.
3. The Commonwealth Bank staff, with their records, would be sent to Alice Springs as soon as possible so that the Commonwealth Bank could function with the least possible delay.
4. Essential Government property would be salvaged and sent south as transport becomes available.
5. All eligible men to be taken into the Army forthwith and men with technical and other training would be recruited into an Army organisation for work in Darwin or elsewhere.

Abbott wrote:

I estimate that the number of civilians in Darwin, exclusive of seamen who will be returned south as soon as possible, to be slightly under 500. This number is liable to increase as there are about 800 men between the Adelaide River and Katharine [*sic*] and some of them, realising that they cannot get further south, are drifting back to Darwin. These men, as they return, are rationed by the Administration which receives rations in bulk from the Army. In addition, the Administration is feeding all destitute sailors and has arranged supplies of clothing and food and boots.

So far as the future of Darwin is concerned, it would appear to be wise to base the Northern Territory Administration upon Alice Springs and maintain a small staff in Darwin to look after the town. As soon as the situation in Darwin is more or less static I shall go down to Alice Springs and get the Administration functioning smoothly there.

♦ ♦ ♦

Administrator Abbott was not the only Darwin resident to set his sights on Alice Springs. His and Blake's plan allowed for the departure of non-essential civilians. The Army would be responsible for their evacuation and would decide on priorities. Stan Kennon, who hid behind a tree during the first air raid, had been a member of the Volunteer Defence Corps. Like Mick Ryan, he expected to be taken straight into the Army if ever an emergency arose. 'A rumour started that we would be sent around the coastline as observers, but nothing happened,' Kennon recalled. After four days of cooling his heels, Kennon decided he would be more use elsewhere. Some time around 23 February, he chucked his bike in the back of the company ute and headed south with some mates. The mates aimed for Alice Springs. Kennon had more ambitious plans: he would ride his bike to Queensland.

The group made it as far as Adelaide River, and Kennon set up a fire beside the railway line to boil a billy of tea. A train stopped alongside and the driver leaned out and asked: 'What are you doing here?' Kennon knew the driver—they had been having dinner together every night for a year. Though places for able-bodied men on trains south were hard to come by, 'You'd better get on,' the driver told him. Kennon threw his bike on a flat-top truck and rode the train to Birdum, 350 kilometres south and the end of the line.

There was now nothing for it but to jump on the bike and start pedalling for Queensland. Kennon knew it could be done: a few years earlier he had driven from Brisbane to Darwin, leaving the roads behind at Camooweal and picking his way to Tennant Creek along rough tracks between cattle stations. If it could be done by car, it could also be done by bike. Kennon set Tennant Creek, about 450 kilometres south, as his next stopping point. His luck held. A truck took pity on him and gave him a lift all the way to the Creek, turning what might have been a five-day journey into a bumpy eight-hour ride. That still left the problem of getting to Queensland.

In Tennant Creek, Kennon had a word with the man from the mail delivery truck. 'If I start off on my pushbike across from Tennant to Mount Isa, will you give me a lift if you come along, when you've used up a bit of fuel?' he asked. Yes, the man said. 'So I headed off. That night I lay down by the road and got a bit of sleep. I was still there when they came along in the ute. They stopped the ute and threw me and the bike in the back.' A long day later Kennon was in Mount Isa.

He sold the bike and, with a bit of money cabled by his wife Audrey* to top up the proceeds, caught a train to Brisbane, to be reunited with her. His journey was more adventurous than most, but it was not untypical.

◆ ◆ ◆

The government in Canberra now extended the Army's area of control. At midnight on 27–28 February the whole of the Northern Territory was placed under Army rule. The proclamation set out three specific areas of Army responsibility: '(a) persons evacuated from Darwin as regards their destination; (b) enforcement of their return to Darwin, or to such other places as may be necessary; (c) power to enforce evacuation from Alice Springs of any civilians whom it is considered not essential.'

---

*Audrey Kennon appeared in Chapter 7 as the hard-pressed shipping clerk deciding who should stay and who should go in the evacuation ships.

Administrator Abbott was clearly deemed essential. He left Darwin for Alice Springs on Monday, 2 March, 12 days after the raid. Abbott faced his fair share of criticism over his handling of the Darwin air raid, including the repeated allegation that he had fled town on the afternoon of the raid with the rest of the Adelaide River refugees. This particular calumny is in print today in a semi-official diary of the raid, part of a display in Darwin's Air Raid Arcade. The note says: '20th February. Administrator and Superintendent of Police left Darwin and the Military Barracks empty.' It is simply untrue. Abbott has a fair bit to answer for over his failure to impose order on Darwin after the raid, but the charge that he deserted will not stick.

Chapter 14

Telling the world

Lou Curnock, surely one of the quiet heroes of the Darwin saga, stayed on duty at VID aeradio station throughout the two raids. The station was a little outside the centre of the town and therefore not on the main line of attack. Nevertheless, he was close enough to hear the bombs exploding and could even feel the earth shake when they hit. As he tended to his microphones, Morse keys and meticulous signal logs, Curnock was certainly at serious risk if the bombers broadened their target area and VID took a direct hit.

In his methodical way, he set about telling his superiors in Melbourne that all was not well in Darwin. In the gap between the two raids, Curnock transmitted a brief message in Morse to his bosses at the Department of Civil Aviation: 'Devastating air raid. Staff and station intact.' Darwin was not then connected by telephone to the rest of Australia. Not that it mattered. With the telephone exchange and cable station in ruins, VID at this point may have been the only working line of communication between Darwin and the outside world. So far as I can trace, Curnock's terse seven-word message, delivered to the Department of Civil Aviation in Melbourne, gave the first inkling outside Darwin of the seriousness of the raid.

Within minutes of Curnock's message, Darwin opened up a second line to the outside world. The engineers at the cable station had already prepared for the kind of emergency Darwin now faced, setting up a branch cable that terminated at the Lands Office in Cavenagh Street. Two engineers from the cable office, Harry Hawke and William Duke, rescued an undamaged Morse key and associated equipment from the wreckage of the Post Office and carried it all to the Cavenagh Street emergency base. At 11.25 a.m., 45 minutes after the first raid ended, they had hooked up their Morse keys and were ready to transmit. Understandably, their long report concentrated on the effect of the raid on postal and cable links. But they began by telling their Adelaide office: 'We have just had bombing raid which appeared centred on and near postal buildings causing much damage. Several officers lives lost many injured.'

This new line of communication did not last. The second raid on the RAAF base cut the cable. Hawke, the senior engineer, sized up the situation. Their new office was in a frail wooden building that would not withstand another attack. It was also too small to accommodate the cable station crew. Hawke realised he would have to shift base again. He chose a makeshift camp site near an abandoned railway hut 16 kilometres from the town. Some 50 engineers and technicians grabbed what equipment they could, plus some essential belongings, crammed themselves and their kit into some severely battered engineers' vans, and moved. By 3 p.m. they had the line working again. Messages travelled by a tortuous route, first to Batavia, then to Cocos Island, then to a relay station in the Perth suburb of Cottesloe before being sent on to Melbourne.

Meanwhile, Lou Curnock found himself under pressure. At the civil aerodrome, some radio transmitters and receivers had survived the raid. However, the main electricity supply from Darwin had been cut, so the airfield's two-way radio remained useless. It was vitally important to warn civil aircraft to stay away from Darwin. By a great stroke of luck, the direct telephone link between the airfield and VID survived the raid. One of the airfield staff, Ted Betts, established that VID was still on the air. He borrowed a truck and raced across to the VID station. He and

Curnock managed to get a message through to the Department of Civil Aviation in Melbourne telling them to keep all civil aircraft away from Darwin. Curnock and Betts also gave some rudimentary information about the raid.

Curnock stayed on duty continuously for two days following the raid. For the next five days all communication with civilian flights passed through VID. The station was also the sole contact with merchant navy ships at sea and with the civilian coastwatchers. VID also had to cope with armies of Darwin citizens wanting to send reassuring messages to friends and relatives in the south.

Although VID was very likely the first to send details of the raid, it was not the only long-range radio transmitter functioning in Darwin. The Royal Australian Navy maintained a shore-based signal station, HMAS *Coonawarra*, to relay messages to and from ships at sea and Naval Headquarters in Melbourne. Although *Coonawarra* took some minor damage, it functioned perfectly well after the raid. It seems to have been slow to get going on the day of the raid, but by the evening it was busily sending damage reports to the Naval Board.

Finally, the Australian Broadcasting Commission had set up a mobile recording unit in Darwin in December 1941 to transmit news for re-broadcast by the main radio stations in the capital cities. (The ABC had earlier set up a similar unit in Gaza, Egypt, and subsequently established a mobile field unit in Papua New Guinea.) The Brisbane *Courier-Mail* reported that the first the outside world knew of the Darwin attack came from the ABC mobile unit. The Deputy Postal Director in Darwin, a Mr Fanning, had radioed at 10.05 a.m., when the first raid was a mere seven minutes old, to say that the town was being raided and the broadcasting station was closing down.

◆ ◆ ◆

The Australian government directed the war from two councils: the War Cabinet, which was an inner circle of the full Cabinet and therefore drew its membership from the government alone; and the War Advisory Council, which included Opposition representatives and other senior political figures as well as the government members of the War Cabinet. The War Advisory Council's next meeting happened to be in Sydney on the morning of 19 February, with the Chiefs of Staff of the three services in attendance. The Prime Minister, John Curtin, had been in St Vincent's Hospital, Sydney, since 17 February, suffering from exhaustion. He did not attend this meeting or the subsequent meeting of the War Cabinet. Both were chaired in his absence by the Deputy Prime Minister, Frank Forde.

On Darwin's big day Curtin was in the middle of a furious cable row with Churchill and Roosevelt. Curtin wanted to pull two divisions of Australian troops from the Middle East to defend Australia. The War Advisory Council spent most of the meeting discussing this very matter, concentrating on the return of the Australian 9th Division. Government members were firmly committed to bringing the boys home. Opposition members argued for diverting them to Burma, as Churchill had requested. One wonders if they would have continued to pursue this line had they known what was happening on their own soil at that very moment. The Council even found time to discuss the advisability of stocking up on rubber shoes, which the soldiers of the 8th Division had found useful in the jungles of Malaya. Darwin did not get a mention. Nobody knew about it. The full War Cabinet met later the same morning, again in Sydney. Still no mention.

One of the enduring controversies of the Darwin air raid is the extent to which the government lied about it. In general, historians have castigated Curtin and his ministers for wildly understating the extent of the damage, the numbers of dead and injured, and the level of anarchy that was already engulfing Darwin. It has to be said, in the government's defence, that on the afternoon and evening of 19 February 1942 it did not set out to lie. It simply didn't know.

Before dealing with the government's version of events, it is necessary to sketch in a little background. On 4 January 1942, almost seven weeks before the real Darwin raid, the Sydney *Sunday Telegraph* and the Brisbane *Truth* had published false stories of a bombing attack on Darwin. They got their information from enemy propaganda broadcasts. The government was understandably horrified: the evacuation of Darwin was then well under way, and the last thing the government needed was untrue scare stories about air raids devastating those left behind.

The Chief Publicity Censor moved quickly, issuing an instruction on 5 January 'forbidding publication of sensational reports from enemy sources'. Later that day he amplified this with the following instruction: 'Reports from enemy sources claiming successes in any Australian territory, including mandated territories, whether such reports are received in Australia by cable from Empire points or by other means except through the BBC, must not be published without official comment by the Defence Ministry or Service Chief concerned. If no such comment be forthcoming, the item may not be used. BBC statements if used must be quoted accurately without embellishment or comment.' The Newspaper Proprietors' Association discussed the Censor's ruling informally and happily agreed to go along with it.

A week later, at the War Advisory Council meeting on 12 January, former Prime Minister Billy Hughes took the ruling a stage further. He asked that 'reports of this nature are not to be published or referred to on Press posters unless they are sanctioned by a responsible authority of the Commonwealth Government'. On 20 January the War Advisory Council noted 'the instruction by the Chief Publicity Censor, Department of Information, forbidding publication of sensational reports of enemy operations, unless officially confirmed'. Thus in the space of two weeks the Censor's instructions to the media moved from a fairly respectable clampdown on repeating bad news from enemy sources, and became a block on 'sensational reports of enemy operations, unless officially confirmed'. I can find no trace of any specific censorship ruling dealing with the 19 February attack on Darwin, but from 12 January onwards both sides—media and government—accepted that the government or the service chiefs were to be the only source of information on the war, particularly when the story affected Australia. War correspondents had their stories cleared by the Censor's office. As for the rest, the government's version of events would be the first, final and only word.

♦ ♦ ♦

The first public announcement of the raid came from Prime Minister Curtin. Some time early in the afternoon of 19 February he issued a brief statement from his hospital bed. In part it said:

I have been advised by the Department of the Air that a number of bombs were dropped on Darwin this morning. Australia has now experienced physical contact of war within Australia. The extent of the raid and the results of the attack are not yet known. As the head of the Australian Government I know there is no need to say anything other than these words—total mobilisation is the Government's policy for Australia. Until the time elapses when all necessary machinery can be put into effect, all Australians must voluntarily answer the Government's call for complete giving of everything to the nation.

So the first announcement was very short on detail, and came from the Air Ministry, suggesting that Lou Curnock was the original source. Curtin concluded with a warning: 'I make it clear that the statement that has been made is official and authoritative. Nothing has been hidden. There is no ground for rumour. If rumours circulate, take no notice of them, and deal sharply with any person who circulates them. The Government has told you the truth. Face it as Australians.'

Arthur Drakeford, Minister for Air, went into more detail. He issued a statement shortly afterwards saying: 'Japanese bombers raided Darwin this morning. Preliminary reports from Darwin indicate that the attack was concentrated on the township. Shipping in the harbour was also bombed. There were some casualties and some damage was done to service installations, details of which are not yet known. The raid lasted about one hour.' This was followed by an announcement from Deputy Prime Minister Forde that there were communication difficulties with Darwin and no information regarding details of the raid or damage could be obtained. Later the Postmaster General and Information Minister, Senator William Ashley, announced that cable communication had been reestablished. From the fact that the most detailed information came from the Minister for Air, we can deduce that Curnock's messages rather than Harry Hawke's gave the government what little information it had.

Up to this point, the government played it pretty straight. However, it is notable that no newspaper carried reports direct from Darwin. There were three correspondents in Darwin on the day of the raid, including Douglas Lockwood, one of Australia's finest journalists. Each took his story to the makeshift cable office just outside Darwin, where he was told that military traffic had priority and the cable office was unable to file his news stories. Nevertheless, and despite the sketchiness of the information they had, all Australian newspapers understandably reached for their blackest headline type to report the first external attack on Australian soil since the arrival of Europeans in 1788. 'DARWIN BOMBED HEAVILY IN TWO DAY RAIDS: 93 Enemy Planes In First Swoop: 4 Brought Down,' said *The Courier-Mail*. 'DARWIN BOMBED BY JAPANESE PLANES: "Face It!"—Curtin Tells Australians,' said the less restrained Sydney *Daily Mirror*.

◆ ◆ ◆

On the morning of 20 February, the day after the raid, Arthur Drakeford issued a detailed communique giving the casualties in Darwin: 15 killed, 24 hurt. His announcement read:

There were two separate raids. The first, about 10 a.m., was made by a force of 72 twin-engined aircraft, with a fighter escort of Zero type aircraft. This force split into two parts, one of which concentrated on the town, wharves and shipping, while the other flew inland. Several ships were hit and damage was done to wharves and buildings. No vital service installations were destroyed. During the attack on the town, civilian buildings were hit, and some Commonwealth employees were killed. So far as is known, the total killed in the town numbered nine women and two men. About noon a second raid was made and directed

mainly at RAAF installations by a force of 21 bombers
unaccompanied by fighters. Service buildings and aerodromes
were bombed and machine-gunned and some damage was caused.
There were four confirmed casualties to service personnel.
Damage to the aerodrome was not serious.

During the raid several hospitals, both service and civilian, were
bombed and machine-gunned. Some patients were wounded and
one is known to have been killed. Of other casualties not
mentioned above, there are known to have been three killed and
20 injured. Some of our aircraft were damaged on the ground. At
least six enemy aircraft were shot down, but it is not clear whether
by our fighters or anti-aircraft guns. Some of the enemy aircraft
involved are presumed to have come from an aircraft carrier
standing off the North Australian coast.

Although this statement is riddled with errors, it is hardly a cover-up.
The 72 twin-engined bombers in the first raid were, in fact, 152 single-
engined bombers. The 21 bombers in the second raid were, in fact, 54.
However, this reflected inaccurate information coming out of Darwin
rather than an attempt to hide the facts. Some of the misinformation was
probably deliberate: 'No vital service installations were destroyed';
'Damage to the aerodrome was not serious.' All governments do this in
war. But in general the statement told the truth as best the government
knew it at the time while not giving the enemy valuable information
about the extent of the damage.

Next day the government raised the death toll to 19. The Melbourne
Herald on 21 February carried this report, datelined Canberra: 'It was
stated officially today that 19 people were killed during the Japanese air
raids on Darwin on Thursday. The original official announcement said
that 15 were killed—11 civilians and four defence personnel. Later last
night it was disclosed that eight service personnel were killed, making
the death toll 19.' The same day, the *Herald* carried a first-person report
from Douglas Lockwood, cabled from Katherine, giving an account of
the raid but revealing no details of casualties or damage. No doubt the

censors saw to that. It appeared under the nicely ambiguous headline: 'AA Gunners Gave Jap Raiders All They Had'.

Again, the 21 February statement was far from a cover-up. Consider this cable, sent on the 19th, on the evening of the raids, from the Naval section of Area Combined Headquarters in Darwin. The cable is timed at 1321 Greenwich Mean Time—10.51 p.m. Darwin time—and addressed to ABDACOM, the American, British, Dutch and Australian joint command, which included Darwin.

1. PRINCIPAL DAMAGE AND CASUALTIES TO FOLLOWING SHIPS AND ESTABLISHMENTS. SWAN MINOR DAMAGE. A/S [anti-submarine] GEAR OUT OF ACTION. 3 KILLED 14 SERIOUSLY INJURED. PLATYPUS GUNBAR COONGOOLA MINOR DAMAGE. B.W.V'S [boom-working vessels] 6 INJURED. U.S. DESTROYER PEARY SUNK. MAVIE SUNK. MERCHANT SHIPS ZEALANDIA BRITISH MOTORIST MOANA LOA [sic] NEPTUNA MEIGS SUNK. PORT MAR AND BAROSSA EXTENSIVELY DAMAGED. MANUNDA MINOR DAMAGE. COONAWARRA W/T [wireless telegraph] STATION MINOR DAMAGE EFFICIENCY UNIMPAIRED. OIL FUEL INSTALLATION NO 5 TANK CONTAINING ONLY SMALL QUANTITY FUEL SERIOUSLY DAMAGED. NO 6 TANK HOLED ABOUT 6 FEET FROM THE TOP.
2. STOCK OF FRESH AND DRY PROVISIONS VICTUALLING YARD SUFFICIENT ONLY FOR 7 DAYS NORMAL RATIONS.
3. DAMAGE TO MAIN JETTY PRECLUDES USE BY SHIPS AND FUELLING AND WATERING CAN BE CARRIED OUT BY LIGHTER ONLY.

The cable lists only three dead, from HMAS *Swan*. In fact the numbers killed on the named ships were: HMAS *Swan* 3; *Gunbar* 1; boom-working vessels *Kara Kara* 2, *Kangaroo* 1; USS *Peary* 91; *Zealandia* 3; *British Motorist* 2; *Mauna Loa* 5; *Neptuna* 45; *Meigs* 2; and *Port Mar* 1. The number dead was not three. It was 156. The point is that when the government first announced low casualties on the morning after the raid, it was acting on the best information it had at the time.

It continued to receive misinformation for at least four more days. The Chief of Air Staff, Sir Charles Burnett, flew in to Darwin on 22 February to investigate on the spot. Next day he submitted a report to the War Advisory Council and War Cabinet that fell woefully short of any realistic numbers. Marked Most Secret, the report is 'based on information received up to 1200 hours 23rd February'. It concludes by setting out the casualties to service personnel 'reported to date'. These were:

6 injured on the naval boom working vessel
3 Australian RAAF personnel including W/C Tindal
   at RAAF Station
1 American at RAAF Station
1 killed Berrima Hospital
1 injured Berrima Hospital
3 killed on HMAS Swan
14 injured on HMAS Swan
4 pilots missing believed killed

Burnett's report acknowledged 12 service personnel dead, including the four missing pilots, and 21 injured. It made no reference to civilian casualties, and no reference to chaos, looting or the civilian exodus. More dishonestly, it made no reference to the RAAF's evaporation in the wake of the second raid. So the government, still defending the announcement of 19 dead and 24 injured, could hardly be accused of deliberately lying. This was the very best information it could get, from a senior officer sent specifically to find out the facts. However, government ministers must have begun to get a whiff of the real story, and the need to keep it to themselves: at the same War Cabinet meeting that received Burnett's report, 'it was approved that credentials should not be given by Ministers to newspaper representatives proceeding to Northern Australia'.

The government's version, not many dead and not much damage, was reinforced by a series of mendacious cables from Administrator Abbott to the Ministry for the Interior in Canberra. On 24 February, five days after the raid, Abbott cabled, in full: 'DARWIN NOW NORMAL AND ESSENTIAL SERVICES IN HAND STOP SHOPS CAN REOPEN STOP PLEASE ARRANGE URGENTLY FOR COMMON-WEALTH BANK TO FUNCTION UPON TEMPORARY BASIS IN DARWIN SO THAT PAYS CAN BE MADE WORKMEN AND OTHERS.' Next day, 25 February, in full: 'DARWIN QUITE NORMAL STOP SHOPS OPEN STOP GLAD TO RECEIVE ADVICE REGARDING COMMONWEALTH BANK FUNC-TIONING AGAIN.' In part, on 26 February: 'EVERYTHING NORMAL STOP CONSIDER DISTRESSED MERCANTILE MARINE SHOULD BE RETURNED AT ONCE BY SPECIAL CONVOY.'

This picture of Darwin back to normal was nonsense, and well Abbott knew it. The only possible explanation for these cables is his wish to conceal from Canberra the extent to which he had allowed the town to fall into chaos.

Now consider a cable sent from Darwin on 1 March, ten days after the raid. This went to the Australian Navy Board in Melbourne from Captain Penry Thomas, the Naval Officer in Charge, Darwin. Thomas told the Navy Board:

Merchant seaman casualties not yet complete. Known casualties to date, killed 15 Europeans, 10 Asiatics. Missing believed killed 6 Europeans, 25 Asiatics. Missing believed en route Katherine 4 Europeans 16 Asiatics. Injured 12 Europeans 24 Asiatics. A.R.P. estimate of civil casualties is killed 40 mostly Europeans. Injured 250. Estimate of injured considered high. U.S. destroyer Peary casualties estimated 82 killed, 10 injured. Injured from Peary believed evacuated by Manunda. Greatest difficulty experienced in obtaining names.

This second cable gives a total of 178 dead,[1] still well short of the final official figure of 243 (of which more later). The point here is that ten days after the raid the figures were rising sharply, though they were still incorrect and still too low. The bigger point is that, for better or worse, the authorities decided to keep the higher numbers to themselves, at least for the time being. They now knew for certain that casualty numbers went way beyond the original 19 killed and 24 hurt. If they said nothing, then the Censor's ruling blocking publication of 'sensational reports of enemy operations' unless confirmed by the Commonwealth government or service sources would carry on the job. Nothing could be published unless the government offered it, so silence was golden. At the risk of introducing an inappropriate note of levity into what is unquestionably a tragic story, the Australian government chose to follow a trail blazed by sub-editors of *The Times* of London. On quiet news days the subs regularly ran a competition among themselves to invent the world's most boring headline. One of the winners was SMALL EARTHQUAKE IN CHILE: Not Many Dead. The parallel message AIR RAID IN DARWIN: Not Many Dead, together with an assurance that everything had quickly settled back to normal, would keep the story off the front pages for the time being. The censors could do the rest.

♦ ♦ ♦

The government's final announcement of the numbers killed was issued on 30 March 1942, immediately after Curtin received the secret report of the Lowe Commission. Although this statement gave dramatically larger numbers, it was played down by the newspapers, clearly under guidance from the censors. Newspapers printed the story in two or three paragraphs on inside pages. The Melbourne *Herald*'s report appeared on page three under the headline: '240 killed in First Raid on Darwin— Shipping Losses Given in Report'. It would have taken a keen-eyed reader to spot the three-paragraph story. Curtin's statement began: 'The number killed on land, sea and in the air during the first Japanese attack on Darwin on February 19 did not exceed 240.' Curtin then suggested that even this number might be reduced when missing wharfies communicated with the Railways Commissioner or the shipping agents. He concluded apologetically: 'The interests of security prevented me from stating previously the number who were killed or drowned at the harbour and on the wharves. That information, together with the shipping losses, constituted information which the enemy would have valued had it been made public immediately.' This was the last word on the subject from the government until October 1945.

Curtin and his government have been pilloried from that day to this for covering up the facts of the Darwin raid. Professor Alan Powell, in his excellent book *The Shadow's Edge*, wrote that one reason the raid had so little impact on the Australian people at the time was that 'their government would not trust them with the truth'. However, the government did set out to tell the truth in the first 24 hours, and for several days afterwards. Its crime—and major error—was to allow the military authorities to bully it into withholding the full story.

There is good evidence that Curtin himself saw the folly of holding back information. On 4 March 1942, the day after Japanese bombers struck at Broome and Wyndham in the north of Western Australia, Mr McLaughlin of the Department of Defence Co-Ordination sent a teleprinter message to Mr Farrands of the same department: 'In view of the stories being circulated by evacuees from Darwin, which suggest very large death toll, the Prime Minister desires to release an official and authoritative statement showing numbers killed and injured, both services and civilian.' Would Mr Farrands please ask the service Chiefs of Staff if they had any objection, asked Mr McLaughlin, making it plain that the PM was in a tearing hurry. The teleprinter message is timed at 3.57 p.m. The Prime Minister wanted an answer on his desk by 5.30 p.m. that day. Mr Farrands missed the deadline by ten minutes but obliged with the following message: 'The Chiefs of Staff consider that it would not be in the national interest to make any statement giving the details of casualties at any particular place, as to do so would give the enemy valuable information. They also consider that to make a statement in relation to the raids at Darwin, Broome and Wyndham would establish a precedent which would require a similar statement to be made in the case of all future raids.' However reluctantly, Curtin accepted their advice. There would be no statement. And without a statement, there would be no newspaper stories. It is hard to avoid the suspicion that the 'national interest'—does that phrase not have a familiar ring today?—that the Chiefs of Staff were so assiduously defending was in fact their own interest. The full story might have raised some uncomfortable questions about inadequate defences and lack of preparation.

From the *Herald*'s tiny '240 killed' story on 30 March until the end of the war, Darwin's story simply disappeared from public gaze. It was left to the rumour mill to keep Australians informed. The only breach in this wall of silence came, oddly enough, from the Army itself. Throughout the war the Australian War Memorial in Canberra, in conjunction with the Army, published a series of annuals containing articles, poems, cartoons and stories about Australians at war. Authorship was attributed to 'Some of the Boys'. The War Memorial distributed the annuals among the troops and subsequently made them available to the general public, all in an effort to boost morale. Each edition had a different title: *Jungle Warfare*, *Khaki and Green*, and so on. The 1942 volume was called *Soldiering On*. It contained a long article about the bombing of Darwin, signed by 'XV115', under the headline 'WAR CAME TO AUST-RALIA'. XV115 was a *nom de plume* for the Darwin representative of Defence's public relations director. The anonymous public servant wrote a graphic and dramatic account of the raid, painting a much more lurid picture of its scale and intensity than the bland statements issued by the government. A description of the Kittyhawks' tragic challenge to the bombers ended with the statement: 'Four of the American pilots lost their lives in a vain attempt to get into the air and fight.' Then: 'The first bomb to fall on Australia—a 1000-pounder—scored a direct hit on the wharf, killing 20 labourers.' Then: 'Burning oil from an oil tanker spread over the water of the harbour, adding to the holocaust. Men drowned because they could not swim in the heavy oil. Men burnt because they could not escape the flames.' And: 'The *Peary* sank with two-thirds of her complement.' However, XV115 carefully avoided any mention of chaos, looting or the civilian exodus. Those facts were still not for public consumption.

Nevertheless, the *Soldiering On* story was the first insight into what had really happened in Darwin. On 9 December, newspapers around Australia picked it up. The *Sydney Morning Herald* summarised it under the bland headline 'Darwin Air Raid Story—Disclosures in Army Book'. The Melbourne *Herald* was less restrained. 'FIRST OFFICIAL STORY OF RAIN OF DEATH ON DARWIN—BRAVERY OF GUNNERS', it shouted. The *Herald*'s story began: 'A thrilling story of the first raid on Darwin by the Japanese last February, giving many remarkable details not previously released, is contained in "Soldiering On," a new Christmas book for the Australian Army.' Again the government was asked to make a clear statement. On 28 January 1943 Senator Collett tabled a parliamentary question: 'To ask the minister representing the Minister for Defence—As the story of the enemy attack on Broome has been given to the press, will the Government now make available to the public a full account of the bombardment by the Japanese of the Port of Darwin?' The reply to the senator repeated the words of the Chiefs of Staff. It would not be in the national interest to make a statement, so best say nothing.

The military line was seriously counterproductive, as censorship usually is. Curtin had realised that those who left Darwin after the raids were under no obligation to conceal from their friends what they had seen—or heard. As survivors fled south, the rest of Australia rapidly filled with wild rumours about the fate of Darwin. Thousands had died. Looters had been shot. So had deserters. Darwin had been wiped out. Everyone had panicked. The government was covering it up. The Japs would be here soon. After Darwin, Sydney would be next. Or Perth. Or Brisbane. A sharp dose of the truth might have done more to settle nerves than provocative silence in the face of spreading rumours.

To be fair, those left behind in Darwin generally supported the government's silence. Lou Curnock told the Lowe Commission he preferred not to worry friends and relatives outside Darwin. However, the government line created a problem for those left behind. Fed with bland information, people down south simply didn't appreciate the massive problems these stalwarts faced. Lou Curnock told Commissioner Lowe: 'They probably thought it was a picnic—a few planes came across and, after dropping a few bombs, went away.'

Surely the clinching argument for telling the truth is the American experience in the wake of Pearl Harbor. Roosevelt had spared his public nothing when telling the story of the raid, including a clear account of the numbers killed and the extent of the damage. American public indignation over the 'day of infamy' did more than anything else to spur a reluctant and isolationist country into enthusiastically supporting total war. There is no reason to suppose the Australian public would have reacted differently. The most likely consequence of a truthful account of the Darwin raid would have been a surge of national fury, followed by an angry determination to fight back. The Australian government railed endlessly against public indifference to the war effort. The full horror of the attack on Darwin was its best chance to jolt Australians out of their apathy. Unwisely, it chose not to take it.

Chapter 15

Not many dead

The question of how many died in Darwin as a result of the two raids is still controversial. Jack Burton, a former mayor who was in the town on 19 February 1942, estimated the number killed at 'about 900'. Some have put the number as high as 1100—echoing a rumoured early estimate by Army Intelligence. An anonymous contributor to the compilation *Darwin's Battle for Australia*, published by Darwin Defenders 1942–45 Inc., submitted this graphic account: 'I have spoken to four soldiers who were among those detailed to deal with the problem. One said that they were told to collect the bodies and take them down to Mindil Beach. He said: "We stacked them two deep on the back of the trucks." Another said they dug down to the water level and stacked them in. Another said he counted over 300 into one mass grave, he didn't look in the other one. Padre Richards said: "243? I buried more than that myself." These men had no reason to lie, and I believe the Army Intelligence number [1100] to be substantially correct.' So the Darwin Defenders supported the idea that the true toll was anything up to four or five times the official one.

We can make a clean start by demolishing the figure of 243, which is still the 'official' count established by the Lowe Commission. This number is simply wrong. It is made up as follows:

Neptuna	45
Zealandia	3
British Motorist	2
Manunda	12
Swan	4
Karakara	5
Gunbower (presumably *Gunbar*)	1
Peary	80
Meigs	2
Port Mar	1
Mauna Loa	5
Don Isidro	11
Florence D	4
The Army	2
The Air Force	6
US Army and Air Force	7
Civilians in the town	14
Civilians on the wharf	39

The list leaves out the 15 dead from the USS *William B. Preston* and puts *Peary*'s number too low, at 80. The correct figure of 91 for *Peary* was known by 6 March 1942, the date of an action report filed by Lieutenant William Catlatt, a *Peary* officer. Catlatt's report gives not just the number of dead but includes the names of those who died, and can be taken as accurate. The Lowe Commission began sitting in Darwin on 5 March, so the correct figure was both known and available at the time it was collecting evidence. The figure for the Air Force should be at least seven, not six. (It might be eight—the evidence is confusing.) On the other side of the ledger, the figure for *Swan* should be three, not four.

The task of collecting and burying the dead could be carried out only by police or soldiers. It was a gruesome and dispiriting business, made no easier by the fact that tropical heat could play havoc with a body. Speed was important. So was the need to identify the bodies. The dead were congregated in four main areas: in the harbour; around the wharf; in the town, particularly the area around the Post Office; and at the RAAF station. Because the tide was ebbing at the time of the raid, bodies from sunken or damaged ships were first dragged out to sea. When the tide turned, bodies washed up on the beaches or drifted into the mangroves, where they were hard to find and even harder to extract.

Surely Edgar Harrison, the Permanent ARP Officer, was right when he said: 'I am afraid the actual figures will never be known. We do not know whether there are five, 50 or 500 in the swamp. With the sharks and other vermin, I think quite a number of bodies have gone.'

Police Sergeant William McKinnon told the Lowe Commission: 'As far as I know, when the bodies were found they were either buried where they lay or conveyed to suitable places for burial without any documentary authorisation.' The police dug the graves themselves. If the ground was too hard to dig deep, the bodies were moved elsewhere. The police tried to keep a record of the numbers they buried, but the urgency of the work and the general confusion meant the records were far from perfect.

On the beach, police laid out in rows the oil-covered and burnt bodies of seamen and asked surviving crew members to identify them where possible. It was a hopeless task. The bodies were simply unrecognisable. Civilian dead generally went to the hospital morgue, where friends and workmates did their best to say who they were. After the first day, the heat made this task impossible. From the second day onwards, decomposed and unrecognisable bodies were buried on the spot. The police did their best to identify them, but the need to bury them quickly overrode all other considerations.

There was no time for ceremony. Henry Hunter, the mess manager at the East Point shore battery, had been at the hospital as an out-patient on the day of the raid. He said later: 'To my way of thinking it was quite disgusting. There was no service. Whether it was read afterwards, or before they went down, I do not know. Women and men were placed in a common grave.'

Much later, bodies were exhumed and moved to graves in the Adelaide River War Cemetery, the largest group of war graves on Australian soil. Row upon row of crosses mark their final resting place. Some graves carry the name of the victim. Others mark the final rest of unidentified seamen 'known unto God'. To one side of the cemetery lies a group of graves for civilians. A special section, with its own group headstone, guards the bodies of the ten postal workers.

♦ ♦ ♦

So how many died? I can only agree with Edgar Harrison that the final total will never be known. While the official figure of 243 can be proved to be low, numbers such as 1100 are fancifully high. If so many died, who were they? Any claim that large numbers of people died but were not counted rests on the fact that bodies may have drifted out to sea, got lost in the mangroves, or been taken by sharks or crocodiles. If so, the victims must have come from the ships or the wharf. Survivors from ships in the harbour, particularly military ships, had a pretty fair idea of how many were aboard when the raid took place. They would be unlikely to underestimate the death toll by hundreds. And if 900 or 1100 died, why were the numbers of injured so low? The count of the injured is more accurate, because they were treated in hospital or shipped out aboard the *Manunda*. The hospitals and *Manunda* noted names and numbers of those they treated. The Lowe Commission put the number of injured 'between 300 and 400', and there is no reason to doubt that figure. It is implausible that the number killed would be three or four times greater than the number injured. Some wharfies remained unaccounted for, but they are more likely to have disappeared down the Adelaide River road than died on the wharf and drifted away on the harbour.

And what of the mass graves on Mindil Beach, and bodies piled two deep on trucks and tipped into mass graves? Nobody has ever come forward and said they drove the truck or dug the grave. Darwin could stake a fair claim to being the rumour capital of the world in the aftermath of the raid, and these stories are no more than second- or third-hand hearsay.

The most accurate 'official' figure to date appears on a plaque unveiled in 2001 on The Esplanade, near Government House. Placed by the Northern Territory's Administration to mark the centenary of Federation, it amends the *Peary*'s death toll to the correct 91 and lists *William B. Preston*'s fatalities as 10, rather than the correct 15. The plaque increases the RAAF number to seven, the Australian Army number to three, and the *Don Isidro* figure to 14. It then adds 19 who died of wounds on the *Manunda*, and 22 further fatalities among 'various seamen and civilians—circumstances unclear'. Its final total is 292 dead:

Killed on Darwin Wharf	22
Killed in the town area	17
MV *Neptuna*	45
USS *Peary*	91
SS *Zealandia*	3
SS *British Motorist*	2
SS *Mauna Loa*	5
USAT *Meigs*	1
AHS *Manunda*	12
HMAS *Swan*	3
HMAS *Kangaroo*	1
HMAS *Kara Kara*	2
HMAS *Gunbar*	1
SS *Port Mar*	1
USS *William B. Preston*	10
MV *Don Isidro*	14
MV *Florence D*	3
PATWING 10 Catalina	1
Royal Australian Air Force personnel	7
Australian Army personnel	3
US Army personnel	3
US Army Air Force personnel	4
Died of wounds aboard *Manunda*	19
Various civilians and seamen	22
TOTAL	292

With the *William B. Preston* toll corrected to 15, a figure of 297 known dead is the best count anyone is likely to achieve.* If we then accept Edgar Harrison's view that an unknown number of bodies drifted out to sea or were caught up in the mangroves or taken by sharks or crocodiles, and temper that view by saying the number unaccounted for is bound to be low, the full death toll is likely to be a little over 300, perhaps as many as 310 or 320.

Does this make the Darwin raid Australia's worst disaster? The only challenge comes from Cyclone Mahina, which struck Bathurst Bay, near Cape Melville on the far north-east coast of Queensland, on 22 March 1899. Mahina wrecked a pearling fleet. The death toll is unverifiable, and most authorities settle for a figure of 'over 300', with some putting the number dead as high as 400. A minimum figure of 297 for the Darwin raid is provable from records. Mahina's death count is simply an estimate, based on a rough count of the number of ships sunk. In the absence of accurate figures from Bathurst Bay, Darwin's claim is strong.

Prime Minister Curtin said later: 'The results of the raid were not such as to give any satisfaction to the enemy.' Tom Minto, the First Officer of the *Manunda*, responded: 'Well, the enemy must have been very hard to please.'

---

* My certainty on the higher figure for that ship is based on the action reports filed by Les Wood and Jimmy Grant, the ship's First Officer and Captain respectively, which name 15 dead.

Chapter 16

Post mortem

To understand the Australian government's reaction to the events in Darwin, it is necessary to look at them in historical context. Quite simply, 1942 was the worst year of the Second World War for Australia. And in that terrible year, the week beginning 15 February 1942 was the worst week.

The Curtin government was comparatively new. On 28 August 1941, the long-serving conservative Prime Minister, Robert Menzies, bowed to pressure from within his party to resign. He handed over to his deputy, Arthur Fadden, whose government fell five weeks later, when two independent members voted down Fadden's Budget. Curtin's Labor Party took over from Fadden on 3 October 1941. So Curtin became Prime Minister not because the Australian public had voted for him at an election but because the conservatives had lost the confidence of the House of Representatives. The Governor-General, Lord Gowrie, simply sent for the Labor leader and asked him to take over.

On 27 December, with his government a mere 12 weeks old, Curtin stood Australian foreign policy on its head by declaring that the country now 'looked to America' for protection from the Japanese. Until this ringing pronouncement, Australia, in truth, barely had a foreign policy.

As a British Dominion and part of the Empire, its foreign policy amounted to little more than adding a squeaky 'me, too' to whatever Britain decided.

Australians had always been uneasy about threats from the north, whether from China, Japan or Russia. Against this threat stood the mighty British bastion of Singapore. Let no enemy contemplate a southward thrust towards Australia: the invincible Royal Navy and its impregnable Singapore base would rapidly put a stop to that.

As Japanese forces swept unstoppably through Indo-China, Burma, Malaya, Singapore and the Dutch East Indies, the Curtin government could see Australia falling while most of its Army was fighting at Britain's side in the Middle East.

On 15 February 1942, two events of shattering importance dominated the councils of the Australian government. Singapore fell. And Curtin cabled Churchill asking for the return of two Australian divisions from the Middle East. For the next five days, furious cables flew between Curtin, Churchill and Roosevelt. Churchill was willing to see the Australians pull out of the Middle East, but he wanted them to go to Rangoon to defend Burma and therefore India. Curtin wanted them back in Java to block the Japanese advance or, better still, back in Australia to defend the homeland. The strain of these two events—Australia's worst military disaster in Singapore, and a bitter row with Australia's two most important allies—was enough to put an exhausted Curtin in hospital on 17 February.

Then, two days later, came news of the Darwin raid. Invasion appeared imminent. No Australian government or prime minister has ever faced such a quick succession of terrible events. So if, with the benefit of 20–20 hindsight, we can see that not every decision taken over Darwin was wise or sure-footed, it is surely right to point out that Curtin and his ministers had a lot to think about at the time.

✦　✦　✦

Nothing in the minutes of the War Cabinet or War Advisory Council in February or March 1942 gives a clue as to when the government began to grasp the appalling implications of the Darwin raid. The minutes barely refer to the attack. The full horror began to dawn after receipt of a report from Administrator Abbott to the Department of the Interior, dated 27 February. Of all the documents His Honour produced in the aftermath of the raid, this is his best. It is honest, clear-headed and direct. It pulls no punches in describing the looting and the anarchy that swept through Darwin. He wrote:

> The psychological effect of a bombing raid upon civilians is one which should be deeply considered by the government. The confusion which followed the raid was very bad and was greatly accentuated by unauthorised actions by various service sections, including the Provost Corps. Discipline there was very bad, men were drunk, and salutary action including the arrest of an Officer and a Non-Commissioned Officer had to be taken. The worst feature was that soldiers, entirely without orders, kept advising civilians to leave the town. This resulted in a stream of cars, cyclists and pedestrians making down the road as far and even past the Adelaide River. Had it been necessary to fight an action the confusion might have been most disastrous. No official instruction was ever issued by me for male civilians to evacuate.
>
> *A similar type of raid in a large town might have very serious panic results.* [emphasis added]
>
> In regard to casualties and particularly fatalities, I have been endeavouring to get a complete list but this is exceedingly difficult on account of the confusion which extended after the raid. A reasonable estimate is about 300 killed, which includes the personnel of ships attacked and sunk.

This was the first clear indication the government had of just how serious were the results of the raid. Only four days earlier the Chief of Air Staff, Sir Charles Burnett, had come up with a figure of 12 servicemen dead. Now the Administrator was talking about 300. It was also the first full account the government had of the flight of civilian refugees. The Adelaide River Stakes spooked the government as no other aspect of the Darwin raid had done. Did it reveal some previously hidden character flaw in Australians? Might the same sort of thing happen if the Japanese attacked the much larger cities in the south? The thought of hundreds of thousands of people from Sydney or Melbourne taking to the roads in flight was too terrible to contemplate.

The government made two decisions. First, it agreed to accept the advice of the Defence Chiefs of Staff and reveal nothing to the wider public of the extent of the calamity. Possibly it reasoned that the fall of Singapore and the consequent loss of an entire Australian division was enough bad news for the public to digest in a single week. Second, it resolved to find out independently and impartially exactly what had happened. On 3 March 1942, 12 days after the raid, the government appointed Charles Lowe, a Supreme Court judge in the state of Victoria, to head a Royal Commission. His brief was to inquire into and report on all the circumstances connected with the attack, including the preparedness of 'naval, military, air and civil authorities'; the damage and casualties sustained; the degree of cooperation existing between the various services; the steps taken to meet the attack or minimise its effects; whether the Commanders or other officers of the naval, military and air forces or any civil authority failed to discharge the responsibilities entrusted to them; and to recommend what changes in defence measures might be considered necessary to meet a second attack.

There was no delay. After accepting the appointment, Lowe flew out of Melbourne at 1.30 a.m. on 4 March, accompanied by two assistants, John V. Barry, King's Counsel, and Basil Murphy, who fell ill on the plane and was replaced by an Adelaide lawyer, H.G. Alderman. The inquiry began hearing evidence at the Darwin Hotel at 10 a.m. on 5 March. A few days later, it moved to the Parap Hotel, where facilities were better and it was less exposed to constant interruption from air-raid warnings. All evidence was heard in camera. Witnesses were encouraged to be frank, knowing that anything they said would remain secret.

◆　◆　◆

The Lowe Commission deserves a place in the legal history books as an example of what can be done in a short time without serious compromise to good legal practice. Lowe submitted his first report on 6 March—a cable to the Prime Minister stressing the urgent need to station fighter aircraft in Darwin: 'In its existing condition Darwin could not be successfully defended against a major enemy attack. Immediately necessary to have the air defences of four fighter squadrons and recce aircraft, and two additional radar installations.' Lowe was off to a good start.

Between 5 and 10 March, he heard some 70 witnesses. The hearings continued late into the night, stopping only for meals and sleep. Teams of stenographers laboured into the early hours transcribing evidence. On the 12th Lowe and his team returned to Melbourne, where stenographers continued the overwhelming task of typing up the witnesses' words. Lowe resumed the hearings in Melbourne on the 19th, and continued to take evidence until the 25th, examining another 30 witnesses. Incredibly, he submitted his first report, of more than 10,000 words, on 27 March. He then reviewed the entire transcript of evidence (which runs to some 917 pages) and the hefty folders of exhibits, including log books, reports and cables. In the light of this additional reading, Lowe submitted a much briefer, 2600-word supplementary report on 9 April. The whole process, from Lowe's appointment to his final report, was completed in 38 days.

Key passages of Lowe's two reports are reproduced in Appendix II. In essence, his criticisms were simple and unchallengeable. Darwin suffered from a lack of leadership, military and civil. And its defences were inadequate, particularly in the area of fighter aircraft and radar to direct them.

Lowe singled out two clearly identifiable individuals as culpable: Administrator Abbott and the RAAF station commander, Sturt Griffith. In particular Lowe focused on Abbott's failure to get a grip on the town, thereby opening the gate to civilian disorder. 'Had there been effective leadership [immediately following the raids],' he wrote, 'I think that normal conditions might very rapidly have been attained, but leadership was conspicuously lacking.' The row between Abbott and the air-raid wardens was a further blight on civilian order. 'I am clear that this difference prevented the police being aided by officers of the A.R.P. in preserving law and order after the raid,' Lowe added.

He was particularly harsh on the failure of RAAF Operations to raise the alarm after receiving Father McGrath's warning. 'The failure by Royal Australian Air Force Operations to communicate with A.R.P. Headquarters is inexplicable,' he wrote, adding: 'The delay in giving a general warning was fraught with disaster. It is impossible to say with certainty what would have happened if the warning had been promptly given when received by the Royal Australian Air Force Operations at 9.37 a.m., but it is at least probable that a number of men who lost their lives while working on ships at the pier might have escaped to a place of safety.'

He singled out Griffith for blame over the disorderly exodus of RAAF personnel from the air base. 'I am convinced [that] with competent leadership the personnel would rapidly have resumed their duties,' Lowe wrote. 'An order, however, was given by the Station Commander, which I think was extremely unfortunate.' Lowe went on to describe the emptying of the base, and the 278 men still missing four days after the raid. 'As the casualties were small, the result can only be regarded as deplorable,' he concluded.

In the light of subsequent events, it is also worth quoting Lowe's verdict on Group Captain Scherger. 'He was present in Darwin on the day of the raid and acted, in my opinion, with great courage and energy,' Lowe wrote. 'I desire to record the view that, on all the evidence before me, his conduct in connection with the raid was deserving of the highest praise.'

The reader might wonder, at this point, whether heads rolled in the wake of the damning verdicts. The government certainly looked at the possibility of sacking Abbott but decided against it. Only one head rolled. There is a laconic account of what happened in the oral history files of the Northern Territory Archives service in Darwin. The voice is Scherger's: 'The Chiefs of Staff in Melbourne had decided that there must be scapegoats. Now the one man who could not have been criticised under any conditions was Captain Penry Thomas [Naval Officer in Charge, Darwin], who'd been a retired RN bloke called back to the colours. I could find nothing, nothing at all, to throw at him.' Moving to the Army, Scherger continued: 'Now no one ever landed or tried to land so nothing was wrong with Blake [Major General and Army Commandant].' That left the RAAF to take the fall. In April 1942, two months after the raid, Scherger was relieved of his command. It did his RAAF career no permanent harm. As Air Marshall Sir Frederick Scherger, he went on to become a worthy and much admired head of the RAAF.

◆ ◆ ◆

The Darwin raid was by no means Australia's national day of shame, as Paul Hasluck declared. Yet there is no getting away from the fact that Australia did not exactly cover itself in glory on 19 February 1942.

The talk of shame usually flows from accounts of the Adelaide River Stakes. The truth, of course, is that the citizens of Darwin behaved as civilians usually do when bombs start falling. What shocked Australians was the discovery that they were no more stoic or heroic than anybody else. They had seen newsreel films of pathetic lines of refugees fleeing the violence of war in Europe. They called these people 'reffos', a term of mild derision. Reffos who turned up in Australia were foreigners: poor, sad, defeated people in ragged clothes, accompanied by ragged children and clutching at ragged possessions. Australians would never act like that.

With the publication of the Lowe Commission report and the revelation of the Adelaide River Stakes, Australians were confronted with a picture of their fellow countrymen behaving just like reffos. Their self-image as a strong and independent people, cool under fire, brave and resourceful, was shattered. Could these be the sons and daughters of men who had fought in Gallipoli, in Flanders, in Palestine? Worse, since 1940 Australians had been fed endless newspaper and newsreel stories of plucky East Enders smiling stoically through the London Blitz. Surely the Poms were not braver in the face of bombing than the bronzed heroes of God's own country? (The truth, of course, is different. Anyone who has read transcripts of the excellent Mass Observation oral histories of the Blitz knows that the plucky East Enders whinged and complained like nobody's business, and would have cheerfully moved out if there was anywhere else to go.)

If the civilian exodus was not a source of shame, what about the looting? After allowing for the understandable grabbing of survival rations, the plain fact is that the looting became an organised rort using Army trucks and other vehicles to strip Darwin bare. Looting in the wake of military defeat—for the Battle of Darwin was nothing if not a military defeat for Australian and American forces—is a dishonourable tradition dating back to ancient history. However, there was a difference in Darwin: looting is usually carried out by the winners. In Darwin, the losers took all.

What of the lack of military preparation? Certainly there was a shortage of available resources. No doubt Darwin could have used four squadrons of fighter aircraft and some reconnaissance planes to scour the seaward approaches. The ships and the RAAF base could have used some pom-pom anti-aircraft guns to tackle the fighters and dive-bombers. The Army could have done with more 3.7-inch anti-aircraft guns. There were none to be had.

It has been argued that Pell's squadron should never have flown out and left Darwin with no fighter cover. But this is hindsight. Pell's Kittyhawks were always destined for Java. Pure luck brought them to Darwin to give temporary fighter protection to the ill-fated convoy. When there was no convoy to protect, they simply reverted to their original orders and continued their journey to the Dutch East Indies.

Should not the military authorities, particularly the RAAF, have glanced at a map and realised that Darwin was suddenly on the front line? And having seen that, should they have sent more fighter aircraft to protect it? Yes, but which fighter aircraft? There were few available. With the Pacific war only ten weeks old, a lot of the RAAF's fighter strength was still in the Middle East. Should it have reduced the threadbare fighter defences of Sydney, Melbourne and Brisbane still further to shore up Darwin? Maybe. But the political consequences would have been unbearable if the Japanese had chosen one of Australia's major cities as their first target, and the government had meanwhile sent the scarce southern fighters north to defend the tiny town of Darwin.

Specifically, should the nine Wirraways at Batchelor not have mounted an air combat patrol over Darwin that day to protect the port and the RAAF field? With hindsight, yes, of course. But mounting such a patrol would almost certainly have led to nine Wirraways shot down and nine Australian pilots dead, with very little impression made on the Japanese attacking force. The absence of a combat patrol probably counts more as a lucky escape than as evidence of incompetence on the part of the RAAF.

The real failures of Darwin are three. As we have seen, an air attack on the town was widely expected. So although Darwin anticipated an air attack, it did not prepare for it. The civilian air-raid precautions in particular were pitifully thin. Administrator Abbott's failure to give anything like proper backing to the ARP wardens meant that there was no coherent plan for dealing with the consequences of an attack. To be fair, the government endlessly complained that Australians in general were not taking the war seriously. So it may seem harsh to blame Abbott for failing to persuade Darwin residents to show more willingness than southerners. Nevertheless, failure to prepare became one of the town's deadliest killers.

The second failure might be forgiven. While both the military and civilians anticipated a Japanese attack, nobody expected an attack of the scale or ferocity of the one that came. It is notable that everybody in the town underestimated the number of aircraft taking part. The first headlines talked about 93. Lowe accepted estimates of 27 high-level bombers and a total of fewer than 50 dive-bombers and fighters in the first raid, and 27 heavy bombers in the second raid. The true numbers, unknown until after the war, were 81 high-level bombers, not 27, 94 dive-bombers and fighters, not 50, and 54 heavy bombers in the second raid, not 27. The true numbers would have seemed incredible to the stunned defenders. What had Darwin done to deserve an attack on this scale? The anti-aircraft gunners, backed by Pell's ten Kittyhawks, might have disrupted 30 or 40 attacking planes. They did not stand a chance against 242. So Darwin's second failure was in neglecting to anticipate and prepare for what was then one of the biggest air raids of the war.

The final failure was the deadliest: a massive failure of leadership. If readers feel I have been harsh in singling out Administrator Abbott, let me put a question in response. Who else was there who could have shown the leadership needed? Abbott was chairman of the Darwin Defence Committee, which brought together the heads of the Army, Navy and Air Force to coordinate the defence of the town. He was also Commissioner of Police. He was unquestionably the man in charge. It is perhaps unfair to compare the way Mayor Rudolph Giuliani took command in New York in the wake of 9/11 and the way Abbott failed to get a grip in Darwin. He was undoubtedly and understandably shaken by the bombing of his office and his narrow escape from death, but his focus on his wine cellar and his cups and saucers in the immediate aftermath of the raid, when there was a civilian population to be calmed and returned to order, widespread looting to be stopped, an evacuation to be organised, damage to be repaired, and the wounded and dying to be attended to and comforted, indicates a man who was not up to the job.

Wing Commander Griffith's failure to maintain discipline at the RAAF base was surely culpable, as was Major General Blake's failure to keep order among his troops, particularly the Provost Corps. Griffith's sense of priorities is open to challenge. There were more useful things to do at the base than mend the water pipe and move the men down the road. Lowe quoted evidence from 'a very senior officer'—in fact it was Scherger—that Griffith 'was rattled and did not know which were the first things and which were the second things'. His failure of leadership led to the fiasco of the desertion of the base. Restoring morale and confidence must have been a painful task.

Nevertheless, this was no day of shame. The doggedness of the Army and Navy gunners, the heroism of the Kittyhawk pilots, the selfless bravery of the harbour rescuers, the dutiful response of the disbanded

ARP wardens, the parallel response of the hard-pressed police, all add up
to something Australians can look on with pride. But that must be put
alongside a recognition of failures: of preparation, of leadership, and of
discipline. Forget about the Adelaide River Stakes. That was normal
civilian behaviour, made all the more forgivable by the fact that the
fleeing citizens believed they were under orders from the military to
leave town. Look instead at the looting, the leaderless chaos, the
undisciplined shooting-out of car headlights, the unseemly scramble
to shove women and children aside at Parap railway station, and the
bloody-mindedness of the merchant seamen and wharfies when it was
clearly time to forget about the rule book and pitch in. If Australians
wish to hang their collective heads, it should be over those lapses.

♦ ♦ ♦

The raid on Darwin is often described as Australia's Pearl Harbor. The
parallels are obvious. But there were differences. Pearl Harbor came as a
complete surprise. The Darwin attack was widely anticipated. America's
leaders used Pearl Harbor to galvanise a wary and isolationist nation into
willing mobilisation. Australia's leaders chose to play down the bombing
of Darwin for fear of its impact on national morale.

The numbers are striking. More bombs fell on Darwin than on Pearl
Harbor. More aircraft attacked Darwin in the first wave than attacked
Pearl Harbor in the first wave. In Darwin eight ships were sunk. In Pearl
Harbor four went to the bottom, with two more capsized. The Japanese
attacked civilian targets in the town of Darwin, killing 61 civilians. They
left Honolulu alone—the 68 civilians who died there were killed by
fallout from American guns. Of course, the tonnage of shipping sunk in
Darwin was far less than in Pearl Harbor for the obvious reason that the
Japanese were attacking bigger ships in Pearl Harbor. The death toll in
Darwin was very much smaller than in Pearl Harbor, because the larger
ships in Pearl Harbor had bigger crews. And the bombs used in Darwin
were lighter anti-personnel bombs rather than the 800-kg torpedoes
used against the battleships. So while more bombs fell on Darwin, the
weight of bombs was greater at Pearl Harbor.

The Japanese assault on Darwin did not end with the two raids of 19 February. Over the next 21 months, the town faced no fewer than 64 attacks by Japanese bombers. The onslaught ended with a final raid on 12 November 1943. None of the subsequent raids matched the scale or ferocity of the first. The attacks were part of a largely forgotten air war in northern Australia that involved no fewer than 97 attacks on Darwin, Broome, Wyndham, Derby, Katherine, Horn Island, Townsville, Mossman, Port Hedland, Noonamah, Exmouth Gulf, Onslow, Drysdale River Mission and Coomalie Creek.

The attacks grew less frequent as time wore on. The Australian and American fighter pilots and anti-aircraft gunners gradually got the upper hand. Jack Mulholland remembers one raid of nine bombers arriving over Darwin. By then the gunners on the ground were hardened by experience, and problems with fuse setting had been overcome. The gun sections' routine first salvo of four rounds certainly worked this time. It sent four of the nine bombers to the ground in flames. The fighter pilots then radioed to ask the gunners to hold fire while they attacked. They quickly saw off the remaining five bombers. With such losses as this, the Japanese were paying too high a price for attacking Darwin, and they backed off.

The town's fighter defences, both Australian and American, steadily improved in strength and skill. Kittyhawks remained the backbone of the air defence. In January 1943, much-admired Spitfires joined the fray. Although they had proved highly effective in the Battle of Britain, they were less useful in tropical Darwin.

The tide of war began to turn in May 1942, when the Japanese invasion of Port Moresby was blocked by American, Australian and British forces in the Battle of the Coral Sea. Japan never again won a major strategic battle. The tide turned decisively in June 1942, at the Battle of Midway. Darwin's tormentors, the four aircraft carriers of Nagumo force, were all sunk. Japanese sea power never recovered. With control of the sea and sky gradually passing to Allied ships and aircraft, Japan's long retreat to defeat and humiliation had begun.

Darwin continued to play a major part, this time as a base for Allied offensives against Japanese positions in the Dutch East Indies. It was now the turn of the Japanese to dive into slit trenches as waves of Allied bombers from Darwin and other northern bases harried and hammered them.

◆ ◆ ◆

Within a month of the first Japanese air raid, Darwin became a de facto military camp. Most civilians moved out and did not return until well after the end of the war. Administrator Abbott moved his headquarters to Alice Springs, away from the sound of gunfire. He has been criticised for this. One highly respected Northern Territorian confided to me that this was the part of Abbott's performance that most stuck in his throat. 'The King and Queen of England stayed in London right through the bombing,' he said. 'I think Abbott should have set an example and done the same.' Well, maybe. Abbott certainly paid a price for his retreat south. Judge Wells stayed in Darwin throughout the war. Abbott did not. Wells is remembered to this day with affection. Abbott is not.

◆ ◆ ◆

When the Lowe Commission report was published, in October 1945, the public reacted with shock. The Melbourne *Herald* headlined its story: 'JUDGE ON DARWIN RAID PANIC—LEADERSHIP AND DELAYED WARNING BLAMED'. Subheads scattered through the story give the flavour: 'Alien stampede', 'Warning delayed', 'Rush from town', 'Lessons unlearnt', and 'Malicious lying'. It did not make for pretty reading. The reporting concentrated on the Adelaide River Stakes while making room for the inadequate preparations and the poor leadership. The bravery of the gunners and the heroism of the harbour rescuers somehow seemed less important than the disastrous picture of The Town That Ran Away. The legend of Australia's national 'day of shame' sprung from these reports. Darwin is still trying to live it down.

◆ ◆ ◆

I went to Darwin in February 2008 to attend the anniversary ceremony. It is held at the Cenotaph in Bicentennial Park, more or less on the site of the old Oval and Jack Mulholland's guns. In fact there are several ceremonies. The Australian American Association held a 'meet and greet' on the evening of 18 February at the Trailer Boat Club, attended by the American Consul General to Melbourne, Earl Irving. There was a cash bar and finger food provided by the Association. Dress was smart casual. It was a subdued affair. About 20 people turned up.

Next day was typical Darwin weather. The rain drizzled down lightly at first, barely damping the 50 or 60 who turned up for a wreath-laying ceremony at the USS *Peary* memorial on The Esplanade. Dress was Territory rig: men—long-sleeve shirt and tie, long trousers; women—day dress. There was a brief speech by Earl Irving.

We all then traipsed the 500 metres or so from the *Peary* memorial to the Cenotaph, in increasing rain. By the time we were seated in the large marquee, about 1000 of us, the rain was pelting down in drowning tropical bucketloads. Before the speeches, at exactly 9.58 a.m., the air-raid sirens sounded and the Army fired blank rounds with highly coloured smoke from some field guns on the harbour's edge. The noise was shocking, as it was meant to be. I particularly felt for the Army machine-gunners, in their camouflage, who had to lie prone on the waterlogged ground and fire a belt or two of machine-gun blanks. They could comfort themselves with the thought that their soaking in the mud and slush was less lethal than the hail of bombs and bullets their counterparts faced 66 years earlier.

The Navy had stationed some small ships in the harbour, and they fired their guns too. It was impossible to see them in the blinding rain, but they added to the cacophony. An old DC3 flew over us, followed by a couple of FA-18 fighters from Tindal Air Base. I didn't envy the pilots. I would guess that the cloud base was no more than 400 feet, and Darwin has its share of tall buildings. Flying low enough for us to see them took skill and courage. I couldn't help thinking how lucky the Japanese had been with the weather on 19 February 1942. If we are looking for failures, we might add a sour note of condemnation for the weather gods who failed to deliver a normal wet day on 19 February a lifetime ago. They might have saved the town.

There was a recurring theme in the speeches. The rest of Australia is still ignorant about what happened in Darwin, not just in the first two raids but in the 62 that followed. The defenders of northern Australia feel neglected and forgotten. The government decision to conceal the full horror of the raids reverberates to this day. I can only agree with the speakers. While researching this book, I was astonished by how little Australians know of the succession of bloody battles fought under their skies.

After the Cenotaph ceremony, there was a reception in the lobby of the Northern Territory Assembly building, and I chatted briefly to the engaging Chief Minister, Paul Henderson. He was a former Education Minister, and he thought Australian history books needed to be rewritten to give proper space to Australia's northern war. Again, I can only agree. The Australian War Memorial in Canberra gives it a cursory few metres of glass case while devoting huge floor space to single actions such as the sinking of the *Emden*. Darwin could contribute a bit of self-help of its own. The excellent Northern Territory Museum and Art Gallery, near Mindil Beach, devotes huge space and energy to recreating the devastating noise and damage from Cyclone Tracy. It might like to do the same for the bombing of Darwin.

One of the more notable aspects of the commemoration is that the numbers attending have been swelling over the years. The 1000 or so people who watched at the Cenotaph in 2008 formed one of the largest crowds ever. Two days later the *Northern Territory News* ran an editorial under the headline 'Military past an attraction'. The leader writer noted that tourism is a cut-throat business and operators must forever look for new ways to attract visitors. He continued: 'The Territory has one under-exploited attraction—its military history. It has been suggested that a military heritage trail be marked out for visitors. This is a good idea.'

At first I was irked by the editorial, which seemed to me to trivialise what is, after all, the worst disaster on Australian soil. But then I softened. Australians spend large sums to visit remote battlefields such as Gallipoli and to walk the Kokoda Trail. If more of them felt like a trip to Darwin, to walk around the gun sites, the oil tunnels, the makeshift airfields, and to visit the Aviation Heritage Centre, they might be as surprised as I was at what they find.

Whatever happened to . . .?

THE CITY

Darwin remained a military camp for the rest of the Second World War. The ships sunk during the first raid stayed as hazards in Port Darwin until long after the war. (See The Sunken Ships, below.) Many of the wrecked civil buildings went unrepaired until the return of the civilian population, which did not get under way until 1946. Tragedy struck on Christmas Eve, 1974, when Cyclone Tracy flattened the town once more, killing 71 people. Darwin was patiently rebuilt, this time on more storm-proof foundations.

Today Darwin is surely one of Australia's most attractive cities. The lush green tropical landscape, wide streets, busy shops and excellent restaurants make it entirely liveable. While it is now in every sense a modern city, Darwin retains an attractively louche character, a charming reminder of its frontier past. It thrives on tourism. Grey nomads stream through in their camper vans and four-wheel-drives, or fly in to catch the Ghan train south for the two-day journey via Alice Springs through the red heart of Australia to Adelaide. Young backpackers, mostly Australian and European, treat Darwin as a staging post on whatever epic journey has taken their fancy. It is the trading centre for the booming mining, agricultural, fisheries and forestry industries of the Northern Territory. Ironically, the military today is a major contributor to the

Northern Territory's GDP, with some 13,000 Army and Air Force personnel and their families based there. The lessons of 1942 and 1943 have been well learned: Australian governments now regard a strong northern line of defence as essential for Australia's protection.

THE MEN

Aubrey Abbott remained in his post of Administrator of the Northern Territory until 26 May 1946, when he left the Territory on sick leave. He was replaced the next day. In Sydney he wrote a much-admired book on the Northern Territory, *Australia's Frontier Province*, published in 1950. He retired to Bowral in New South Wales and continued with occasional writing. Whatever his failings, there can be no doubt that Abbott's affection for the Northern Territory was profound. He died in Sydney on 30 April 1975, and was accorded a state funeral at St Mark's Church, Darling Point.

Captain Mitsuo Fuchida survived the war. He was struck down by appendicitis on 27 May 1942, a week before the Battle of Midway, and took no part in that decisive action. (See Nagumo Force, below.) He was rescued from the sinking *Akagi* during the battle, and returned to Japan on the hospital ship *Hikawa Maru*. Back in Japan, he and others who knew the truth of Midway were kept isolated from their fellow countrymen while their government tried to conceal the immensity of the Midway disaster. He spent the rest of the war at a desk, or teaching at the Naval War College. His subsequent story is both unexpected and exotic. In 1950 General MacArthur, still governing Japan in the wake of that country's defeat, asked to meet the destroyer of Pearl Harbor. On his way to the meeting, Fuchida was handed a pamphlet in the street by an American Christian missionary. He underwent a profound conversion, and became a zealous promoter of Christianity in Japan, and later in the United States. He died in Japan on 30 May 1976. Before his death he earned a modest supplementary income from books and articles, and as an advisor to makers of Hollywood films featuring the Pearl Harbor attack. The quick-eyed will find his name buried in the small print of the credits on many of them.

Wing Commander Sturt Griffith survived the criticism of the Lowe Report. In civilian life he was an engineer and patent attorney, and in June 1942 he transferred to No. 5 Maintenance Group in Sydney. In December 1943 he was promoted to Group Captain and assumed command of No. 1 Aircraft Depot in Laverton, Victoria. After the war he took to testing and writing about cars as the *Sydney Morning Herald*'s motoring correspondent. He famously tested cars to their limits, hurling them around a course he had designed, near Leura, in the Blue Mountains west of Sydney, while junior *Herald* staff sat in terror in the front passenger seat. Car manufacturers were equally terrified: a Sturt Griffith report could make or break a new model. He died on 14 December 1979.

Commander Herb Kriloff survived the war, something he still looks on with awe and surprise. He transferred from USS *William B. Preston* to command a destroyer in the bitter submarine war in the North Atlantic. After the war he worked as a research engineer in the US. He then moved to the Portuguese island of Madeira, where he lived for 25 years. He now lives in Melbourne, Australia, with his remarkable English wife Dagmar, whom he met in Sydney in 1942 and married in Perth a year later. Readers who keep back issues of Australian *Vogue* might like to look at page 52 of the July 2007 issue, where the vivacious and stylish Dagmar models a few of her favourite outfits and dispenses some worldly and excellent fashion advice. She turned 100 in January 2009.

Charles Lowe, later Sir Charles Lowe, became one of the most respected Australian judges of the 20th century. He enjoyed an enviable reputation for having his decisions upheld on appeal, even when the appeal went as far as the Privy Council. He presided over two further Royal Commissions, including the high-profile Royal Commission into the allegation that the Menzies government had adopted a 'defeatist' plan to abandon the defence of northern and western Australia and retreat behind a 'Brisbane Line'. In addition to his legal career, Lowe became a much-admired chancellor of the University of Melbourne. He died in 1969.

Gunner Jack Mulholland survived the war. He returned to his old civilian job in banking, and continued as a banker until his retirement in 1981. Now a widower well into his eighties, he lives in Wyoming, a suburb of Gosford, north of Sydney, and stays in contact with survivors of the 1942 air raid. His book *Darwin Bombed: An A/A Gunner's Reflections* is a vivid and attractively modest account of the gunners' roles from 1940 to the end of the war. Jack is a very tall man, and his role firing the 3.7-inch gun required him to stand on a platform beside the gun with his whole body exposed well above the protecting revetment. During an air raid, the Japanese had the better part of two and a half metres of Jack and his platform as a target. Happily, they consistently missed both.

2nd Lieutenant Robert Oestreicher was awarded the Distinguished Service Cross for his part in the defence of Darwin. However the citation credited him with shooting down only one enemy aircraft, not two. On 27 February 1942 he was ordered to join the US Army Air Corp's 49th Pursuit Group based in Bankstown, Sydney. On his way south his Kittyhawk, the only fighter to survive the Darwin raid, crashed in Cloncurry, and was wrecked. Oestreicher emerged from the crash, in his own words, 'without a scratch'. He continued flying to the end of the war, including a posting in Darwin with the 49th. On 19 February 1982 he returned to the Northern Territory to accept a small plaque presented by the grateful people of the Cox Peninsula.

Group Captain Frederick Scherger was the only senior official, military or civilian, to face disciplinary action over the Darwin raid. He had been the highest-ranking Air Force officer at Area Command Headquarters on the day of the raid, and therefore the most senior officer of the most conspicuously unsuccessful service. He was relieved of his command two months later. Scherger understandably felt hard done by, and chose the high-risk strategy of appealing against the decision to Arthur Drakeford, the Minister for the Air, over the heads of the RAAF Chiefs of Staff. He was supported in his appeal by, among others, Commissioner Lowe. In service ethos, going to a politician rather than keeping the matter inside the RAAF family would have cost him dearly had he lost the appeal. In the event, he won the day. His career was unchecked, and he went on to attain the rank of Air Chief Marshal and become head of the RAAF and later Chairman of the Chiefs of Staff Committee—in effect the head of all Australian defence forces. He died in 1984.

Judge Wells remained in Darwin throughout the war. At a time when Administrator Abbott had moved with most of the public service to Alice Springs, Wells became de facto administrator of Darwin, and the handful of remaining civilians looked to him for leadership and advice. Circumstances were often difficult: at one point he conducted court hearings outdoors, under a tree. Wells continued as Judge of the Supreme Court of the Northern Territory after the war. He had a stroke in February 1951 and retired in 1952. He died in Darwin on 13 September 1954. His most notorious judgment, the death sentence imposed on an Aboriginal man named Dhakiyarr in 1934, is remembered in Darwin today. Inside the Supreme Court building, a monument of traditional Aboriginal artefacts commemorates an act of reconciliation between Dhakiyarr's family and the family of the policeman he killed.

THE SHIPS

USS *Houston*, the heavy cruiser that almost single-handedly held off the Japanese air attack on the ill-fated convoy for Koepang, was one of three Allied cruisers and five destroyers sunk 12 days later at the Battle of the Java Sea, on 27 February 1942. The battle marked the beginning of the end for ABDA, the ill-considered joint command of American, British, Dutch and Australian forces. The Japanese lost no fighting ships, though four loaded troop transports were sunk and an unrecorded number of men killed. The Allies suffered 2300 dead. It was one of the worst Allied naval defeats of the Pacific War.

HMAS *Platypus*, the base ship that fought back so bravely during the first raid, survived the war. She remained in Darwin until 1 January 1943, then moved to Cairns and later to New Guinea, operating in the Madang, Hollandia and Morotai areas until November 1945. On

20 February 1958 she was sold for scrap to Mitsubishi Shoji Kaisha Ltd of Tokyo, and shipped in pieces to Japan aboard the salvage vessel *Tukoshima Maru*.

MV *Manunda* survived the war. She was returned to civilian service in 1947 and operated as a passenger and cruise ship between Melbourne and Cairns until 1956. She was then sold for scrap, to a Japanese ship breaker.

Nagumo Force, the formidable aircraft-carrier fleet that rewrote the rules of modern naval warfare with its attack on Pearl Harbor, had one more success after the Darwin raid. Mitsuo Fuchida again led a force of 36 Zero fighters, 54 Val dive-bombers and 90 Kate bombers in an attack on Colombo, Ceylon (now Sri Lanka). They were followed by a second force of 80 Vals. The British lost four ships sunk and 27 aircraft destroyed, with 424 dead. The Japanese lost five aircraft. Nagumo Force then returned to the Pacific as the spearhead of what was to prove the decisive naval battle of the Pacific War. It attacked the American base at Midway, intending to invade and hold it as a staging post to the Hawaiian Islands and Pearl Harbor. American code-breakers gave accurate advance warning, and Admiral Chester Nimitz was able to make good use of American aircraft, both land and carrier based. Luck also favoured the Americans. The result was a horrendous defeat for the Imperial Japanese Navy, with all four of their key aircraft carriers sent to the bottom along with a heavy cruiser, and severe damage to other ships in the force. While the Japanese hung on tenaciously for more than three years after the Battle of Midway, the tide of the war had turned. Nagumo Force had been a decisive element in the Imperial Japanese Navy's run of successes, and its destruction proved equally decisive in ending Japanese command of the Pacific seas and skies.

The Sunken Ships *British Motorist, Kelat, Mauna Loa, Mavie, Meigs, Neptuna, Peary* and *Zealandia* remained on the bottom of Port Darwin for the rest of the war and long after. Amid some controversy, the job of removing them was finally handed over to the Japanese salvage company Fujita. In conditions of tight security, the salvage work began in 1959.

The US government refused permission for the Japanese to remove any of the lost cargo, and the bottom of Port Darwin still plays host to a collection of trucks, jeeps, motorcycles, Bren-gun carriers, ammunition and some lengths of railway line scattered from the holds and decks of the ships. The Fujita salvage team cut up most of the wrecks for scrap but refloated *British Motorist* and used her for storage and as crew quarters. Three sunken Catalina seaplanes also remain on the bottom of Port Darwin, ignored by the Japanese salvage team. 'A good dive for small groups,' the Darwin Dive Centre advises on its website.

MV *Tulagi*, used as a troop transport and civilian evacuation ship and beached after damage in the first raid, was quickly refloated and continued to supply Australian and US forces in the Pacific area until 1944. On 27 March 1944, *Tulagi* was attacked by the German submarine U532 en route from Sydney to Colombo. She was hit by a single torpedo and sank within 20 seconds, killing 39 aboard. Then began one of the epic survival stories of the Second World War. The survivors drifted on two rafts tied together by a rope. After more than a month, the rope snapped. One raft with eight survivors was never seen again. The second raft, with seven on board, drifted to the island of Bijoutier in the Seychelles, where the survivors were found and moved first to the island of Alphonse, then on to Bombay and safety.

USS *William B. Preston* left Darwin immediately after the raid and headed down the west coast of Australia looking for a suitable dockyard to repair the very substantial damage she suffered. *Willy B* stopped at Broome and Fremantle but, unable to find a yard, continued to Sydney. There, she completed repairs at the Cockatoo Island naval dockyard on 31 May 1942. Maintaining her impressive record for being in the right place at dangerous moments, *Willy B* returned to anchor in Sydney Harbour a few hours ahead of the midget submarine attack that evening. She survived unmolested and continued to operate in Australian waters until 1944, before moving on to New Guinea and later the US. On 6 November 1946 she was sold to the Northern Metals Company of Philadelphia for scrap.

Appendix I

Evacuation notice

In a leaflet distributed to every Darwin household on 15 December 1941, the two most senior air-raid wardens, Arthur Miller and Edgar Harrison, set out the rules for the evacuation of the civilian population. The initial notice gave no clue as to when this might take place or who would be evacuated. It left the strong impression that the evacuation would apply to the whole civilian population, not just the women and children. This certainly made more credible the Chinese whispers on the day of the raid to the effect that all civilians were to leave by order of the military authorities.

The notice is amateurishly written and shows every sign of haste and wishful thinking. Its author also had a terrible Weakness for Capital Letters.

NATIONAL EMERGENCY SERVICES
Civil Defence—Darwin, N.T.

SPECIAL—Notice to all householders, and occupiers of dwelling houses or any other habitation.

In the event of Enemy Raid or other form of Attack upon or in the vicinity of Darwin, it may become necessary for the Authorities to Issue an Order for the Evacuation of the Civil Population to some other place or places of safety.

Such Order to Evacuate will not be issued until after the Proper Authority or Authorities has or have issued a Proclamation declaring a State of Emergency.

The Civil Population will, after such State of emergency has been declared, receive from the Senior Air-raid Warden a Notice to Prepare for Evacuation.

Such Notice will be issued by one or all of the following methods:

1. Written Notice issued to every Householder or Occupier of a Dwelling House or other habitation.
2. Verbal Notice issued to every householder or Occupier of a Dwelling House or other habitation.
3. A GENERAL ASSEMBLY of the Civil Population at their respective Zone Headquarters.
4. Special Notice in the Northern Standard Newspaper, and/or Notices posted in prominent places throughout the area.

Immediately such Notice of Intention to Evacuate has been issued, each and every person warned to Evacuate will make all necessary preparations to do so.

Each and every Evacuee will be entitled to take the following articles, as personal belongings:

(a) One small Calico Bag containing Hair and Tooth Brushes, Toilet Soap, Towel, etc. (personal only)
(b) One Suit Case or Bag containing Clothing, and such shall not exceed 35 lbs. gross weight.
(c) A Maximum of two Blankets per person.
(d) Eating and Drinking Utensils.

(e) One 2 gal. Water Bag filled for each family.

NOTE: Officers in charge of Evacuation have the power to examine luggage and determine what constitutes personal luggage.

The Senior Warden of the Group will communicate, through his Wardens, full instructions to every Evacuee as to method of Evacuation and time and place of Assembly.

Every Evacuee will be provided with IDENTIFICATION CARDS in duplicate, one of which will be handed to the Evacuation Officer on DEMAND, and the other KEPT ON THE PERSON.

EVACUEES WILL BE DIVIDED INTO SECTIONS OF FOURTEEN (14) PERSONS, ONE OF WHOM WILL BE DETAILED AS SECTION LEADER AND RESPONSIBLE FOR THE CONDUCT OF THE GROUP OR SECTION.

RATIONS WILL BE PROVIDED BY THE AUTHORITIES AND ISSUED TO THE SECTION LEADERS FOR DISTRIBUTION.

PERSONS OTHER THAN THOSE TO BE EVACUATED WILL REMAIN IN DARWIN, AND OBEY THE INSTRUCTIONS ISSUED BY THE CHIEF AIR RAID WARDEN.

No Evacuee shall take, or attempt to take, with him or her, any domestic pet, either animal or bird, and any such pets owned by the Evacuees should be destroyed prior to the Evacuation.

No facilities will exist for feeding of these pets after the Evacuation.

Domestic Poultry would be an Auxiliary Food Supply for those remaining in Darwin, and as such will not be destroyed under any circumstances.

No person or persons will be entitled or allowed to use any privately owned vehicle, or vehicle plying for Public Hire, for the purpose of Evacuation from Darwin, and no method other than that ordered by The Commandant 7th Military District, and affected by the A.R.P. Authorities under such jurisdiction will be permitted in any circumstance.

N.B.—Any Person or Persons acting contrary to these Instructions or additional instructions issued by the A.R.P. Authorities may cause serious upset to the Evacuation Scheme, thereby endangering the lives of themselves and others.

Any Breach of the said Instructions will therefore be dealt with under the National Security Act, and the Offender or Offenders severely punished.

A.R. MILLER, Chief Warden, A.R.P.

EDGAR T. HARRISON, Permanent Officer Civil Defence

DARWIN, N.T.

December, 1941

Appendix II

Report of the Lowe Commission

By any standards, the Lowe Commission investigation into the 19 February 1942 air raids was a remarkable piece of work. As we have seen, Mr Justice Lowe accepted the commission on 3 March, flew to Darwin in the early hours of the next morning, and began hearing witnesses the day after that. He sent a first cabled report on 6 March urging the government to station fighter aircraft in Darwin. By 25 March he had heard 102 witnesses, at sittings in Darwin and Melbourne. On the 27th he handed over his first, 10,271-word report, highlights of which are reproduced below. He then read through all 917 pages of the transcript of evidence, together with two fat folders of exhibits, including diaries, log books, written reports, copies of cables, intelligence reports, action reports and diagrams, and on 9 April produced a 2608-word addendum. The report and its afterthought are models of clarity and commonsense.

What follows is an edited version of the full report, concentrating on its most important findings. Anyone wishing to read the report uncut can find it online at www.naa.gov.au, under reference A431 and titled *Bombing of Darwin—Report by Mr Justice Lowe*. The original is held by the Canberra office of the NAA, and is available for reading there.

Readers may raise an eyebrow over the sub-section on page 231 dealing with fifth-column activity and wonder why I did not mention it in the main narrative. The evidence Lowe refers to came from Wing Commander Gerald Packer, the RAAF's Director of Air Intelligence. While Packer had hard intelligence of local Japanese releasing meteorological balloons to assist in the high-level bombing of Port Moresby, the evidence of local Japanese support for the Darwin air raid is somewhere between thin and nonexistent. Packer gave no dates or physical evidence for the alleged discovery of the balloons, nor did he have any logs giving times, dates and contents of alleged intercepted radio transmissions. Packer himself did not assert the truth of the story, nor did it form part of his first evidence to the Commission. Quite correctly, when he heard the rumours a few days later, he asked to appear again before Commissioner Lowe and pass on what he had been told. Lowe seems not to have believed it, and nor do I.

COMMONWEALTH OF AUSTRALIA
COMMISSION OF INQUIRY
UNDER THE NATIONAL SECURITY (INQUIRIES)
REGULATIONS
IN THE MATTER OF AN INQUIRY CONCERNING
THE CIRCUMSTANCES CONNECTED WITH THE
ATTACK MADE BY ENEMY AIRCRAFT AT DARWIN ON
19TH FEBRUARY 1942
BEFORE HIS HONOUR MR JUSTICE LOWE,
COMMISSIONER
FIRST REPORT OF COMMISSIONER
To The Hon. The Minister of State for Defence
Co-ordination:

I have restricted my consideration to matters which throw light upon the raid itself, the damage arising from it, and the measures to be taken to prevent a like result following from a similar raid. But there are many indications in the evidence of this historical background affecting opinions expressed either in documents sent to the Services or the Government, or in evidence given before me, and exaggerated statements have been made which the evidence does not support. Specific illustrations appear in—

(a) The suggestion that shipping in the harbour at the time of the raid was unduly large because of labour troubles at Darwin. With the possible exception of the *Zealandia* and the *Port Mar* there is no foundation in any evidence given before me for this allegation. Delays undoubtedly occurred and the performance of labour was often unsatisfactory, but these results seem to have been mainly due to lack of facilities in the port equipment, defects of management, and the fact that climatic conditions affected the output of labour as compared with Southern ports.

(b) One official report refers to an exodus of workmen from the town preceded by the Secretary of the North Australia's Workers' Union, Mr. Mick Ryan, and another states, 'Every wharf labourer left the town immediately after the raids and most of them were understood

to have mobbed the train which departed Thursday evening.' These statements are only true in the sense that Mr. Ryan and the wharf labourers acted as the mass of civilian population did in leaving the town, and I shall have to refer later to the lack of leadership which, in my opinion, was responsible for this conduct.

(c) A further statement refers to the probable refusal of train crews to perform their duties and to desert. There is no truth in this statement and it was afterwards withdrawn by the person making it.

The evidence also disclosed the existence in some sections of the population of a lack of confidence in and resentment towards the Administrator. It so happened that most of the witnesses who gave evidence before me on this matter were of this section, and I feel that it is at least dangerous to draw an inference on partial evidence against the Administrator when an examination of all the relevant evidence which may well cover a lengthy period might lead to a different conclusion.

An allegation was made that the Administrator on the day of the raids and after the second raid had removed liquor and crockery and clothing from Government House by the use of police officers when the condition of affairs in the town urgently required the attendance of those police officers for the duties of preserving order. That the Administrator did order the removal of liquor is, I think, plain and indeed not disputed, but I can find no reason for criticizing his action in that respect.

Had action been taken in regard to liquor stocks in hotels in the same way or by effectively picketing it some of the disorder which followed might have been avoided. The allegation against the Administrator in regard to moving crockery on the day of the raid was emphatically denied by him and the Police Superintendent, and has not I think, been established, although the next day or the day following that the crockery, which was Government property, was removed to Alice Springs. The only clothing which I think was removed on the 19th February was contained in certain suit-cases which were taken by Mrs. Abbott, on departing after the raid for Alice Springs.

THE RAIDS.

The first raid commenced just before 10 a.m. I have accepted the evidence of a witness who fixes the time as 9.58 a.m., as he particularly noted it and as he was the person to receive the first warning of the enemy approach. A number of high altitude bombers came in from the south-east of the town, flying in a 'V' formation and at a height which was variously estimated by witnesses but was probably not less than 15,000 feet. One formation consisted of 27 bombers. The bombing was that which is known as pattern bombing in which the individual machines drop their bombs at a signal from the Squadron Leader.

The first bombs fell over the harbour. Having completed their run this group of bombers after a circuit returned and dropped bombs again in pattern over the town. Much difference of opinion was expressed by witnesses as to the number of machines engaged in this attack. I am inclined to think that the view of Air Marshal Williams is correct and that the number of high altitude bombers did not much (if at all) exceed 27.

After the high altitude bombers there came a number of dive bombers escorted by fighters, and these attacked the shipping in the harbour. The number of dive bombers and fighters is uncertain, but I think it probable that Air Marshal Williams is correct in his view that the total number of high altitude dive bombers and fighters did not exceed 50. The cause of confusion lies I think in the impression conveyed to witnesses that the same squadron returning for another run was an added group of enemy planes. An attack was also made about the same time by enemy machines on the Royal Australian Air Force aerodrome and on the civil aerodrome, and by machine-gun fire on the hospital at Berrima [sic] some 9 miles from the town, and in each case a good deal of damage was done which I shall presently particularize. The "All-clear" was sounded about 10.40 a.m.

THE DAMAGE.

(a) On Water.—The attack upon the harbour caused great damage to installations and shipping. The seaward limb of the pier was struck, part of the decking was destroyed, and the metal attachments (rails, &c.) completely distorted. Alongside the inner limb of the pier when the raid started were berthed the *Neptuna* and the *Barossa*. The *Neptuna* had among her cargo a quantity of explosives. She was set on fire by enemy bombs, as was also the *Barossa* on the opposite side of the pier. After the enemy planes had departed the *Neptuna* blew up and caused the destruction of a large section of the inner limb of the pier, and it is probable, too, that the *Barossa* was injured by this explosion. The damage to the pier is thus seen to be very extensive. The outer limb cannot be used and repair to the inner limb will take some months to effect.

Other ships lost in addition to the *Neptuna* were the *Zealandia*, the *Meigs*, the *Maunaloa* [*sic*], the *British Motorist* and the U.S.S. destroyer *Peary*. Ships damaged were the *Barossa*, the *Port Mar* (U.S.) and the hospital ship *Manunda*. In addition, two Catalina flying boats were destroyed. All these losses were in the Darwin Harbour. I have not attempted to determine in what order the enemy inflicted the damage suffered by these ships.

In addition, the enemy planes on their way to or returning from Darwin destroyed another Catalina flying boat and two American vessels, the *Don Isidro* and the *Florence Dee* [*sic*].

(b) *Oil Tanks*.—The oil tanks suffered very little damage and relatively little oil was lost. The damage done to the tanks probably occurred from shrapnel or portions of shell casings or by fragments thrown up by the explosion of the *Neptuna*.

(c) *On Land*.—On land the Administrator's office was hit by an enemy bomb and is a total loss. The front part of Government House had been affected by bomb blast, but the rear portion appears not to have been injured. The Police Barracks are a total loss, together with the Police Station and the Government Offices attached. The Post Office, the Telegraph Office, the Cable Office and the Postmaster's residence all suffered either by a direct hit or blast and are a complete loss. The Civil Hospital was much damaged and it is estimated that the cost of repairs will be in the neighbourhood of £25,000. There was some damage done to two or three private residences, which are probably also to be counted a complete loss. Some huge craters are said to have been caused by bombs of 1,050 lb. weight.

A second raid occurred about 11.55 a.m. and lasted for about 20 to 25 minutes. This raid was by upwards of 27 heavy bombers which flew at a great height and indulged in pattern bombing, more than 200 bombs being dropped according to one observer. These bombers were unescorted by fighters. This raid caused much damage to the surface of the Royal Australian Air Force Station and to the Hospital thereon. No attempt was made in the second raid to bomb the town or the port.

(d) *The Aerodrome.*—I have not sought to discriminate between the damage done on the Royal Australian Air Force Station by these two raids. The hangars and repairs shops were destroyed, the hospital damaged, and damage was also done to the hutments. The losses in aircraft were as follows:—

Australian—

6 Hudsons destroyed on the ground.

1 Hudson in hangar badly damaged.

1 Wirraway badly damaged.

American—

8 P.40's destroyed in the air.

2 P.40's destroyed on the ground.

1 B.24 destroyed on the ground.

1 P.40 damaged in the air.

(e) *Railways.*—The railway line at a point 4 miles out of Darwin was damaged by the dropping of one 250-lb. G.P. [general purpose] bomb close to the permanent way. This was repaired in a few hours, when traffic resumed in a normal fashion. When the pier was bombed a railway engine was blown into the water and remains there. The railway lines on the pier were extensively damaged.

(f) *Other Utilities.*—No damage was done to the water supply of the town generally, though the destruction of portion of the pier destroyed with it the water and oil pipes which were attached, and water pipes on the Royal Australian Air Force aerodrome were also put out of use. The destruction of the Post Office staff put out of action the telephone system of the town, and the electric lighting system was also affected.

LOSS OF LIFE.

The extent of the casualties incurred in the raids has been investigated for me with great thoroughness by Mr Alderman, and I adopt the conclusions which he has arrived at in his inquiry. It is impossible to speak with certainty of the number of people who lost their lives but I am satisfied that the number is approximately 250, and I doubt whether any further investigation will result in ascertaining a more precise figure. [. . .]

INJURED.

Mr. Alderman satisfied himself that it was not possible to compile a complete list of those injured in the raid. The evidence before me also suggests that no accurate estimate of the injured can be obtained, but various suggestions were made, and I think that the number of 400 is probably in excess of those who sustained any substantial injury. An estimate of between 300 and 400 is probably as accurate as any that can be made.

WARNING OF THE RAID.

[. . .] The delay in giving the general warning was fraught with disaster. It is impossible to say with certainty what would have happened if the warning had been promptly given when received by Royal Australian Air Force Operations at 9.37 a.m., but it is at least probable that a number of men who lost their lives while working on ships at the pier might have escaped to a place of safety.

There is other evidence to indicate that this particular Service was conducted with some laxity. No log book was kept before 6th February, 1942, and the log book kept after that date discloses a gap in the entries between 16th and 20th February, 1942.

MEANS OF DEFENCE TO THE ENEMY RAID.

The only defence to the enemy raid over the harbour and over the town was by means of anti-aircraft guns and such defence as the ships in the harbour possessed. There was no defence by air. The evidence before me was all to the effect that the anti-aircraft batteries operated efficiently and that the personnel of the A.M.F. performed very creditably in their baptism of fire. Their earlier shooting seemed somewhat short of the planes at which they were firing, but later their range was better and the defence became effective. The ships in the harbour defended themselves vigorously but with little success in most cases. At the Royal Australian Air Force Station the American P.40's which were grounded attempted to take off and to attack the Japanese planes. They were, without exception, shot down. Thereafter the only defence offered was by means of anti-aircraft fire.

DAMAGE TO THE ENEMY.

There is no very clear evidence as to the damage sustained by the enemy. The best estimate I can make is that the enemy lost five planes certainly and probably five others. It was stated by Air Commodore Wilson that the Tokyo Radio Station had broadcast that the Japanese had lost 23 planes in the attack. Apart from this I do not know the origin of such a statement, and I am far from satisfied that the Japanese loss was so high.

CONDITIONS WHICH DEVELOPED AFTER THE RAIDS.

(a) *The Town.*—Immediately following the raids, the morale of the townspeople was not noticeably affected, and there is evidence to show that nothing in the nature of panic then developed. Had there been effective leadership at that stage I think that normal conditions might very rapidly have been attained. But leadership was conspicuously lacking. Houses were abandoned in haste. I myself observed in the Darwin Hotel tables upon which drinks remained half-consumed, letters started but not finished, papers strewn about, beds unmade in bedrooms, and other signs of a very hasty exit.

On the night of the 19th looting broke out in some of the business premises and sporadic looting occurred thereafter even to the time when the Commission was sitting in Darwin. This looting was indulged in both by civilians and members of the Military Forces. It is hard to believe that, if proper supervision had been exercised throughout, such looting could have gone on.

I am satisfied that the Administrator was not fully acquainted with the conditions which were developing and the telegrams which he sent to the Minister for the Interior failed to give any adequate idea of those conditions. In my opinion, this condition of affairs was largely due to the fact that there had been no adequate foresight of what might result after an enemy raid, and consequently no plans made for the rapid resumption of normal conditions when the raid ceased. There had been an unfortunate difference between the Administrator and the A.R.P. organization in January. I am clear that this difference prevented the police being aided by officers of the A.R.P in preserving law and order after the raid.

(b) *The Air Station.*—The effects of the raid at the Air Station were extremely serious. Much damage had been done, and the personnel, most of whom were experiencing enemy attack for the first time, were shaken by the attack. But at that stage (I am convinced) with competent leadership the personnel would rapidly have resumed their duties.

An order, however, was given by the Station Commander, which I think was extremely unfortunate. He directed that the men should gather in order to be fed at a point half a mile down the road from the aerodrome and half a mile into the bush. The order was completely distorted and by repetition ultimately reached the men in various forms. Some men stated that they were ordered to go 3 miles, others 7 miles, and others 11 miles. Many of the men simply took to the bush. Some were found as far afield as Batchelor, some at Adelaide River, one was found at Daly Waters, and another, by an extreme feat, reached Melbourne in thirteen days.

The Air Station itself was practically deserted. For several days afterwards men were straggling back to the Station, and at a parade on 23rd February, the muster showed 278 men missing. As the casualties were very small, the result can only be regarded as deplorable.

FIFTH COLUMN ACTIVITY.

One matter to which I was asked to direct my attention was whether there was reason to believe that the raids had in any way been assisted by enemy action within Australia itself. Up to almost the last day of the sittings, I should have had to answer this question with a plain negative, because all the witnesses to whom that question was put agreed that there was no foundation for such a suggestion. On the last day but one of the sittings in Melbourne, however, evidence was given which I think cannot be disregarded though it may still leave unchanged a negative answer as to these raids. I was told that meteorological balloons had been found in the vicinity of the aerodrome at Darwin. Similar balloons had been noted at Port Moresby concurrently with a raid upon that town. Their purpose is to indicate air currents in the upper air so as to guide the pilot of a bomber in the operation of his bomb release.

At Port Moresby the matter was immediately investigated, and the release was found to be almost certainly due to the presence of Japanese. The discovery of similar balloons at Darwin led to observation being made, the result of which was that messages in Japanese Morse were detected both outwardly and after a lapse of 40 minutes inwardly towards a point in the direction of Daly Waters. These facts, coupled with the disappearance from Darwin on the outbreak of war of Japanese then residing there, who have not since been traced, furnishes at least a suspicion that there is activity in the neighbourhood of Darwin which may be not unconnected with the raids which took place.

INSTALLATIONS AVOIDED BY THE JAPANESE.

It may not be inappropriate here to remark that there was a large body of opinion expressed before me that the Japanese had deliberately refrained from attacking the oil tanks, the floating dock and the water supply and that, had they wished to destroy any of these installations, they could in the absence of air opposition—which existed on that day—have easily effected their purpose. It is unnecessary to dilate upon the inference that is to be drawn from this abstention on the part of the Japanese. It will be appreciated no doubt that if the opinion of these witnesses is sound, such abstention holds a grave threat of later enemy action against Darwin.[1]

PREPAREDNESS OF THE SERVICES IN RELATION TO THE RAID.

(a) *The Navy.*—The Navy, in my opinion, had taken all proper steps in preparation for an attack. [. . .]

(b) *The Military Forces.*—The only part of the Military Forces required for action in the raid itself were the anti-aircraft equipment and personnel; as I have already indicated in an earlier part of this report, the conduct of the personnel is to be highly commended. [. . .]

(c) *The Air Force.*—Group Captain Scherger acted in command of the north-west area. He was present in Darwin on the day of the raid and acted, in my opinion, with great courage and energy. I desire to record the view that, on all the evidence before me, his conduct in connexion with the raid was deserving of the highest praise. Another officer whose conduct during and after the raid merits commendation is Squadron Leader Swan.

The officer in command of the Darwin Station was Wing-Commander Griffith. He also has had but a short period of service at Darwin, coming there about the beginning of February. [. . .]

It is probably unfair to attribute blame for this lack of organization and dispersal wholly to the Commander of the Station whose service there had been so short, but, in my opinion, the condition of the Station was a prime factor in the extent of the losses which followed.

(d) *The Civil Authorities.*—What I have already said indicates that I feel the Civil Authorities were lacking in foresight in not envisaging the possible conditions which would follow upon the raid. The result was that no plan had been formed to deal with conditions such as those which arose. If the Civil Authorities found themselves insufficiently equipped to meet the situation, I think the

Administrator should have, at an earlier stage than he did, sought the aid of the Military Authorities. [. . .]

(Sgd.) CHARLES J. LOWE
Commissioner.
27th March, 1942

FULL AND FINAL REPORT OF COMMISSIONER
TO THE RIGHT HON. THE MINISTER FOR DEFENCE
CO-ORDINATION:

Having now perused the transcript of the evidence taken at Darwin, I have the honour to make this supplementary and final report upon the attacks made by enemy aircraft at Darwin on the 19th February, 1942. [. . .]

FURTHER DETAILS OF MATTERS REPORTED UPON

(a) *Naval Installations and Equipment.*—H.M.A.S. *Platypus* is a repair ship. Acting-Commander Tonkin gave evidence that there was not sufficient equipment on the ship to enable the full complement of the vessel to get safely away if the ship were sunk. In addition he said that the ship required further guns to give it adequate protection. He suggested that six of the Oerlikon type and also Breda guns were required to attain that object. In his view, unless the ship were adequately armed there was grave danger that she would be destroyed and not be able to discharge her function of repair ship. No other repair ship is available at Darwin.

(b) *Pier.*—Much evidence was given that the pier before its destruction was quite insufficient for the handling of shipping under war-time conditions. The main report has indicated the damage which was done to this pier and an indication was given of the time requisite for the repair of the pier.

(c) *Oil Pipes.*—I drew attention in my Report to the destruction of the oil pipes which were attached to the pier. There was evidence before me that it would be better to adopt the practice which is in existence in many parts of the world of taking the oil pipe under the water to a buoy in the harbour and there supplying ships.

(d) *Minesweeping Equipment.*—The Naval Commandant at Darwin drew my attention to the danger of destruction to minesweeping equipment from the lack of aircraft at Darwin. I quote from his evidence as the most effective way of emphasizing the point he made. He said: On the 5th March—

. . . I received a report from the *Deloraine* to the effect that she was being bombed by enemy aircraft and required assistance. Application was made to A.C.H. (Area Combined Head-quarters) in the normal manner for this assistance within five minutes of the attack commencing. There were enemy fighter aircraft in the air. I was informed by A.C.H. that no fighter aircraft were available in Darwin to render assistance to the *Deloraine* and she got none. She was not damaged by a hit but there were some very near misses which were sufficiently close to put out of action the anti-submarine detection apparatus. It was purely accidental that the ship was not either sunk or severely damaged and put out of action until replacement parts were obtained from the south. This ship happened to be the only ship in northern or north-western Australian waters fitted with the necessary apparatus for sweeping the magnetic and acoustic mine.

(e) *Royal Australian Air Force.*—In my Report I drew attention to the disorganization which occurred on the Darwin Station after the raids. It is important, I think, also to call attention to some of the results which, as the evidence disclosed, followed from this disorganization. I have mentioned that certain Hudson machines were not damaged in the raid.

(f) *Effects of Disorganization.*—(1) *Inability to Use Aircraft.*—A senior officer gave evidence that six times during the afternoon he endeavoured to get these Hudsons into the air in order to search out the whereabouts of the enemy aircraft carrier and to attack it. Owing to the disorganization existing, he was completely unable to get a communication to the necessary quarter. This was largely due to the fact that the Station Commander was unable to organize a ground-to-air wireless link at a time when the organizing of such communication was vital.

The same officer expressed the opinion that at that time the Station Commander was rattled and did not know which were the first things and which were the second things.

(2) *Salvage Not Attempted.*—Moreover, no attempt was made

to salvage equipment and material from the hangars or to salvage stores although in the opinion of competent witnesses such salvage was possible.

(3) *Emergency Water Supply Not Used.*—The water main laid on to the station was damaged in the raid, but to meet such a contingency an emergency water service was in existence from an elevated tank with the necessary reticulation. When it was attempted to use this during the raid, it was found to be chained and locked with a Yale lock, and in the result it proved impossible in the time to make use of this emergency service. [. . .]

(q) *Slit Trenches.*—Much evidence was given before me of the effectiveness of slit trenches to protect those who took shelter in them. The only instances in which they did not prevent injury to those sheltering were the cases of the Post Office and of one trench on the Royal Australian Air Force Station. At the Post Office there was a direct hit upon the trench and the occupants were killed. At the Royal Australian Air Force Station one officer was shot through the throat and killed.

(r) *Commendation.*—I should like to draw attention to the work done by Constable McNabb. All those who spoke of his conduct agreed in the view that his actions on the day of the raid were worthy of the highest praise.

ADDITIONAL MATTERS REPORTED ON.

(cc)*Natives of Melville Island.*—Evidence was given before me that the natives of Melville Island were in all probability more favourably disposed towards the Japanese than towards ourselves. The matter was not fully investigated by me, and a contrary opinion in relation to the majority of natives was expressed by Brother McCarthy, of the Catholic Mission on Bathurst Island.

I draw the Government's attention to these opinions in order that the matter may be more fully investigated if it is thought necessary.

This Report completes my survey of the evidence and of the matters upon which I have been asked to report, and I return herewith my commission.

(Sgd.) CHARLES J. LOWE,
Commissioner.
9th April, 1942

Acknowledgements

So many people have freely given time and trouble to help with the writing of this book that it is hard to know where to start. I owe a particular debt to my cousin Penny Cook, former Director of the National Trust of the Northern Territory, whose affection for Darwin and subtle understanding of Territory social history saved me from many an error of fact or judgement. Some of the buildings mentioned in this narrative are still standing, most notably the mission church on Bathurst Island, thanks in no small part to Penny's energy, charm and persistence.

My lively veterans Herb Kriloff and Jack Mulholland gave me invaluable first-hand accounts of the Darwin raid and its aftermath. They were endlessly patient with my barrage of email and telephone questions, and finally in face-to-face interviews. Jack's book *Darwin Bombed* is a wonderfully evocative account of an ordinary soldier's experience of the war. Herb's book *Officer of the Deck* is an equally graphic account of the extraordinary adventures of USS *William B. Preston*.

Jack Mulholland introduced me to Austin Asche, former Administrator of the Northern Territory. His Honour generously undertook to look after me when I visited Darwin in February 2008 to complete my research. Austin and his wife Val shepherded me through a series of commemorations and reunions where I had a chance to meet and talk to survivors of the 19 February raids. Austin's own sympathetic knowledge of the Northern Territory and its history provided me with an invaluable bridge to that colourful past.

Gordon 'Gordy' Birkett's encyclopaedic knowledge of Kittyhawk history in Australia, including some remarkable detective work on serial numbers and individual aircraft, allowed me to present the pilots' stories in detail, often in their own words. His files include signals traffic and other contemporary records, and they brought a directness and authority to what might otherwise have been no more than the usual mishmash of myth and legend. His group Adf Serials works entirely voluntarily. Anyone interested in more information can go to its website, www.adf-serials.com.

Brian Manning, former secretary of the Waterside Workers Union in Darwin, was unsparingly helpful with descriptions of the workings of the wharf, and with insights into the complex political history of trade unions in the Territory. He is a wonderful raconteur, and his stories of his time in office in Darwin, when his house was known as The Kremlin, would fill a book. I would not expect him to agree with my judgements on the role of the unions in the Second World War, and I hope he will forgive me for them. The wharfies, who suffered horrifically in the first few minutes of the raid, showed more fortitude during and after it than most of their critics. They deserve a fair hearing.

Peter Forrest and his wife Sheila are the Northern Territory's premier historians. I went to school with Peter and, on that flimsy excuse, sought him out. He gave me the touching Arthur Wellington letter reproduced in Chapter 7, and a lot of sound advice. Peter had long thought of writing a book about the Darwin raid, and my arrival on the scene cannot have been good news for him. Nevertheless, he gave generously and freely of his time, for which I am deeply grateful. My equal thanks to Arthur Wellington's daughter Aldyth, who gave me permission to quote the letter in full.

Warrant Officer Gnaire Foster put me in contact with Ian Ward, of the Darwin Defenders' Association, and Ian led me to other local veterans who gave invaluable firsthand accounts of the raid.

A remarkable chain of luck led me to Susan Holland in the tiny French village of Mortagne-sur-Gironde (population 967) in June 2008, just as I was finishing the book. Her father Robert Holland lived in Darwin from 1936, before joining the Australian Army in 1941 (and finishing the war as a guest of the Japanese government in Thailand, after being captured in Timor). She kindly gave me permission to use some of her father's Darwin photographs, particularly the aerial picture of Darwin which vividly brought to life the layout of the town and harbour at the time of the raid. Her father is second from the left in the group picture on the front cover.

The Lowe Commission examined its last witness on 25 March 1942, less than five weeks after the raid. So while the witnesses may not all have told the truth, the whole truth and nothing but the truth, what they did tell was certainly fresh in their memory. I have often used the transcript of the Lowe Commission evidence to allow my cast to tell their story in their own words. The evidence was quietly made public in 1972 when it was deposited with the Federal Parliamentary Library in Canberra, but it was not until 1997 that it became available, again with no fanfare, in the National Archive. All 918 pages are now available at its website, www.naa.gov.au. Two fat manila folders of exhibits are available in the National Archive in Melbourne. Some of the subsidiary documents had not been made public when I began writing this book, and some were released at my request. While no one could accuse successive Australian governments of covering up this material, it is fair to say that none went out of their way to lead the public to it.

All authors owe a debt to those who have tackled their subject beforehand. Douglas Lockwood's book *Australia Under Attack: The Bombing of Darwin 1942* (first published in 1966 as *Australia's Pearl Harbour*) is a first-class account of the raid, as anyone would expect from that great journalist. Lockwood had the advantage over me of being in Darwin on the day of the raid. On the other hand, he was denied access to the transcript of evidence given to the Lowe Commission and was even refused a request for a list of witnesses. As a result, he was forced to rely on his own and other people's memories 25 years after the event.

Sometimes individual accounts altered between Lowe and Lockwood, and whether the tellers' memories improved or faded in the interim is a matter for conjecture. Throughout the book, unless indicated in the text, I have used the Lowe rather than the Lockwood version.

Alan Powell's *The Shadow's Edge: Australia's Northern War* combines those rarest of qualities in history writing: authority and good humour. Professor Powell chose to write little about the events of 19 February 1942, saying modestly that 'the tale of the raids on Darwin that day has been twice told at length, by [Douglas] Lockwood with acumen, by [Timothy] Hall with hyperbole, and needs no general retelling'. I have taken the liberty of going against his advice and embarking on a general retelling. Meanwhile, I happily acknowledge the importance of Powell's research in giving me an authoritative time frame and, particularly, a detailed account of military movements before the raid.

Mitsuo Fuchida's book *Midway: The Battle That Doomed Japan, The Japanese Navy's Story*, written with Masatake Okumiya and published in English in 1955 by the Naval Institute Press in Washington, is a remarkably unapologetic and revealing account of the Imperial Japanese Navy's thinking and day-to-day tactics in 1941–42. Fuchida helped to plan both the Pearl Harbor and Darwin raids, and he was privy to his Navy's strategic calculations from 1941 to the middle years of the war. His book, and my old boss Charles 'Hank' Bateson's *The War With Japan, A Concise History*, enabled me to piece together the Japanese side of the story.

Sir Max Hastings' spellbinding book *Nemesis: The Battle For Japan, 1944–45* tells the story of Japan's descent in the final years of the Pacific War from the cocksure triumphs of the preceding pages to the starving, cornered and ultimately overwhelmed military nation it became. By 1945 the Japanese were surviving on little more than blind tenacity and denial in the face of certain defeat. Max's book—I presume to call him by his first name on the basis of a brief working connection many years ago—was badly received by some in Australia because it deals, however sympathetically, with the sidelining of Australian land forces towards the end of the Pacific War. Australians would do well to grow up and accept the reality of their history, as I have tried to do in this book.

The staff of the Northern Territory Archives Service were endlessly helpful with both research and photocopying. My particular thanks to Cathy Flint and Françoise Barr. The staff of the National Archives of Australia in Darwin, Canberra and Melbourne were equally forthcoming, as were the staff of the Australian War Memorial in Canberra. The Northern Territory Library, housed in the Legislative Assembly building, provided excellent background material, including contemporary newspapers.

The Sea Power Centre in Canberra is a gold mine of information on ships' histories, much of it available online. It proved particularly helpful in providing accurate casualty figures. My particular thanks to John Perryman, the Senior Naval Historical Officer there.

The National Archives and Records Administration in Maryland, USA, were tirelessly helpful in producing action reports. These reports, written within a few days of 19 February 1942 by the officers of the US Navy ships in Darwin during the raid, are matchless in their immediacy and authority. My particular thanks to Jodi Foor, who went to great trouble to dig out original documents that proved, among other things, that the official body count for the raid is nonsense.

Penny Cook, Austin Asche, Jack Mulholland, Herb Kriloff and Helen Young all bowed to my bullying and read the manuscript, subsequently saving me from my many sins. As always, all errors are entirely mine. I am grateful to Penny, Austin, Jack, Herb and Hellie for steering me away from the worst of them.

Mary McCune volunteered to type the Lowe report (Appendix II), thereby sparing me hours of drudgery. Mary has developed something of an addiction to low flying, and accompanied me on the Kittyhawk trail in Foxtrot Juliet Foxtrot (see p. 246, Chapter 5, n. 2). She showed great promise as an air navigator. The Kittyhawk pilots of 1942 might have made a better fist of Outback flying if they had been lucky enough to have Mary in the cockpit and in charge of the map.

My publishers Allen & Unwin remain a powerhouse of flair and good humour, qualities not often in evidence in the accountant-driven book industry of the twenty-first century. My particular thanks to managing editor Rebecca Kaiser for untiring support, and for her patience while we agonised over book titles. (I'm still fond of Bloody Darwin, but that's just me.) My editor Angela Handley did her customary stylish job of converting my words into a book, while Liz Keenan's sharp eye for the most economical way to shape a sentence trimmed away any loose ends I'd carelessly left behind.

Finally, my heartfelt thanks to those who gave me a home while I was researching this book: in Sydney, Karma Abraham and Lenore Nicklin, Mary and Van McCune, and Paul and Debbie Dykzeul; in Melbourne, Robert Foster and Jack Bell.

Notes

Chapter 1: 'Big flight of planes . . . Very high'

1   McManus recalled afterwards: 'We worked it out a long while ago. We based it on 140 knots and the distance from Bathurst Island to Darwin: I think it is 43 miles or 47 miles by air. We allowed four miles a minute to be on the safe side.' In fact the distance between Nguiu on Bathurst Island and Darwin airfield is 42 nautical miles, which an aeroplane flying at 140 knots would cover in 18 minutes. Despite McManus's dodgy arithmetic, his figure of 12 minutes proved remarkably accurate.

Chapter 2: A very sinful people

1   It is only fair to point out that some of the creation stories of the Northern Territory Aboriginal people involve places as far off as Port Augusta in South Australia. Aboriginal trade routes linked northern and southern Australia thousands of years before John McDouall Stuart.

2   It is important to distinguish between Darwin, meaning the town itself, Port Darwin, the large stretch of water enclosed by the East Arm on one side and the town of Darwin on the other, and Darwin Harbour, the tiny enclosed wharf area on the western side of the port and next to the town centre.

3   When the wharf was rebuilt after the Japanese air raid, the new design followed a single curve from ship to shore, eliminating the need for turntables, donkey engines and manhandled railway cars.

Chapter 3: Horribly strained relations

1   The Allies gave Japanese bombers girls' names, and Japanese fighters boys' names. Under this system, the Zero was called a Zeke. However, this proved less easy to remember than Zero, and the Japanese aircraft-type number stuck.

2   Given that the Japanese had no shortage of diplomats and spies in Honolulu at the time, this was an unusually faulty piece of intelligence. Only two carriers were then available to the American Pacific Fleet, USS *Lexington* and USS *Enterprise*. USS *Yorktown* was still operating in the Atlantic. On 7 December 1941 *Enterprise* was on its way from Pearl Harbor to Wake Island, ferrying aircraft, while *Lexington* was on a similar delivery run to Midway. The third Pacific Fleet carrier USS *Saratoga* (not the *Hornet,* which was never involved) was still in San Diego on the American west coast, after completing a refit.

3   As a bizarre footnote to history, all 68 civilians killed at Pearl Harbor died from 'friendly fire', mostly anti-aircraft shells dropping back into the city of Honolulu. The Japanese lost 55 killed to the same guns. Not a single civilian death could be laid at the feet of the attacking Japanese. At Pearl Harbor, defending US forces killed more of their own countrymen than they did their supposed target, the enemy attackers.

Chapter 4: One suitcase, one small calico bag

1   In 1942 Cullen Bay was more commonly known as Kahlin Bay, after the old Aboriginal 'compound' at Kahlin near Larrakeyah. Throughout the text I have preferred the current usage. The name Kahlin survives in the city's most important cricket field, Kahlin Oval, on Cullen Bay.

2   The RAAF airfield, much expanded and improved, is now Darwin International Airport. The civil airfield is no more: the runway has

become Ross Smith Avenue, Parap. Its only surviving artefact is the old Qantas hangar, now owned by the Museum and Art Gallery of the Northern Territory and used as a workshop and vintage car display area by the Motor Vehicle Enthusiasts' Club.

Chapter 5: No place and no time for argument

1   The Kittyhawk looked a bit like the Zero, leading to the famous 1942 training film *The Identification of the Japanese Zero.* In the film, a young Ronald Reagan almost shoots down his buddy's P40 before learning to tell the difference and go on (of course) to shoot down a real Zero.

2   I can sympathise with their problems. As part of the research for this book, in July 2007 I flew the route myself, starting from Camden, west of Sydney, and finishing at the smart new Darwin International Airport. I was piloting a single-engine Beech Debonair, call sign VH–FJF. Foxtrot Juliet Foxtrot and I had the benefit of a GPS and a lot of other 21st-century electronic wizardry. The Kittyhawk pilots had not much more than a rudimentary map, a compass and a stopwatch. I flew up via Walgett, Charleville, Winton, Mt Isa, and Borroloola to Darwin, and back to Camden via Tennant Creek, Birdsville and Bourke. (Someone must have been along with a dustpan and brush after the war, because I saw no sign of crashed planes along the way.)

Elements of the journey were pretty alarming. Pilots navigating 'visually' (as opposed to following radio beacons or other electronic aids) generally draw a line on a map and mark 'waypoints' every 30 or 40 kilometres—a river fork here, a town with a racecourse there, a railway bridge across a highway somewhere else—and fly from waypoint to waypoint. The Kittyhawk pilots were all navigating visually. In central Australia there are no waypoints. On my flight from Tennant Creek to Birdsville, there was a stretch of 173 nautical miles (320 kilometres) across the Simpson Desert without a single ground feature I could use. For more than an hour all I could do was point the aircraft in what I hoped was the right direction and pray that Birdsville would appear ahead of me.

Without the GPS I seriously doubt that I would ever have found it. The Kittyhawk pilots had no GPS and little or nothing else to help them. They navigated by following roads, railways and telegraph lines. For huge stretches of the journey there were none. Their planes regularly overheated and developed engine problems en route. Others got lost and ran out of fuel, crash-landing in the desert before they had a chance to engage the enemy.

3   The citizens of the Northern Territory have good reason to this day to thank 'coloured labour units' from America. Black American troops were the main labour force building what is now called the Barkly Highway road link between western Queensland and the Northern Territory.

4   Author's note: the correct number of children was 969. Harrison, in his evidence to the Royal Commission, said there was a discrepancy of about 500 between the police survey and the wardens' survey, with the error on the police side. V.G. Carrington, the Acting Government Secretary, confirmed to the Commission that there were discrepancies, but said the errors were on the wardens' side. Clearly, this was not a happy ship.

Chapter 7: Convoy to Koepang to return to Darwin

1   In the early days of the Pacific War, the US Army Air Corps used the word 'Pursuit' in squadron names in the way most other air forces used 'Fighter'. The 3rd Pursuit Squadron would now be called 3rd Fighter Squadron. The terms are interchangeable, but I have stuck to the original.

Chapter 8: 'Zeroes! Zeroes! Zeroes!'

1   Griffith told a different and even less credible story to the Lowe Commission. In Griffith's version: 'At a little after 10 a.m. on the 19th the station Operations Room phoned me that there was a report of enemy aircraft approaching. I went immediately to the Operations Room, which is directly above my own office, and was informed by the controller that a message had been telephoned through from Bathurst Island that a large force of unidentified

aircraft was approaching from the north. I remained on the verandah of the Operations Room and ordered the air raid alarm to be sounded. I saw some aircraft attacking the town of Darwin, and then, with the Operations staff that remained, took shelter in a trench.'

2   There is a bizarre footnote to Lieutenant Hughes's tragic story. Although McMahon was able to give a fair idea of the crash site, neither the wrecked plane nor Hughes's body was ever found. He is officially listed as 'MIA', Missing In Action, rather than 'KIA', Killed In Action.

Chapter 9: QQQ QQQ QQQ de VZDN

1   Tindal's name lives on today. The RAAF base near Katherine, 280 kilometres south-east of Darwin, and at the time of writing home to 75 Squadron's FA-18 fighters, was named RAAF Tindal in his memory.

Chapter 10: Between the raids: Can anyone drive?

1   To be fair, it would have taken a shark or crocodile of more than usual coolness under fire to loiter in Port Darwin that day. There is no record of any crocodile or shark attack during the rescue operations. Even the ubiquitous box jellyfish seem to have thought better of it.

2   I can find no trace of the A24s Scherger refers to. There were none in Darwin that day. They were not at Batchelor, nor at Daly Waters further south. The only other aircraft within reach were eight Hudsons at Daly Waters, but they had no crews.

Chapter 11: The second raid: Chinese whispers

1   There is some doubt over their airfields of origin. The official Australian Navy history says Kendari only. The official Army history says Ambon only. The official RAAF history says nothing. Douglas Lockwood says both Kendari and Ambon. The official Japanese history supports Lockwood.

2   A popular star of B-movie Westerns of the day.

3   For the record, Darwin's entire contingent of sanitary carts disappeared in similar fashion down 'the Track'. A Mr Monks was

eventually dispatched to Adelaide River to retrieve the errant vehicles, and returned them to service three days later. Darwin had no sanitary collection for five days after the raid. Some houses waited ten days for their next collection.

Chapter 12: Things go badly wrong

1   James Arthur MacArthur-Onslow's service record was sealed until 2012, and parts of it are still inaccessible. It's a weird story. He was the son of Major General James MacArthur-Onslow, of the great Australian grazier dynasty. He joined the Australian Army on 13 May 1940 under an assumed name—James Vernon. On 30 January 1942, three weeks before the Darwin raid, he was promoted to sergeant (under his real name) but on 19 April 1942 he was demoted to corporal and then to private. Two months later he was discharged. The Wikipedia entry for his father notes that the major general had three children. Of James Arthur it says: 'disinherited and bankrupted by his father'. He died on 17 June 1959.

Chapter 14: Telling the world

1   In files held at the Australian National Archive in Darwin is an undated handwritten note from Flight Lieutenant Colin Bell addressed to Group Captain Scherger setting out the numbers killed and injured. Bell's memorandum comes up with the same figure of 178 dead. His calculation uses almost identical figures to those given in the Navy cable of 1 March, suggesting that the two writers had conferred, and that the two documents were prepared at about the same time. Thomas's figures may even have been based on Bell's. Both documents illustrate the fact that the true numbers were still unclear more than a week after the raid.

Appendix II: Report of the Lowe Commission

1   Lowe is referring elliptically to the widespread belief in Darwin that the Japanese left the oil tanks alone because they wanted the oil for their own use after an invasion. We now know that this was false: they did not set out to preserve the oil tanks, they simply failed to hit them.

Bibliography

Alford, Bob, *Darwin's Air War 1942–1945: An Illustrated History,* Aviation Historical Society of the Northern Territory, Darwin, 1991

Bateson, Charles, *The War With Japan: A Concise History*, Ure Smith, Sydney; Barrie and Jenkins, London; Michigan State University Press, East Lansing, 1968

Calvocoressi, Peter, Guy Wint and John Pritchard, *Total War: The Causes and Courses of the Second World War*, Viking, London, 1972, revised 1989

Edmonds, Walter D., *They Fought With What They Had: The Story of the Army Air Forces in the South West Pacific, 1941–42*, Little, Brown and Company, Boston, 1951

Edwards, John, *Curtin's Gift*, Allen & Unwin, Sydney, 2005

Forrest, Peter and Sheila Forrest, *Federation Frontline: A People's History of World War II in the Northern Territory*, Centenary of Federation Northern Territory, Darwin, 2001

Fuchida, Mitsuo and Masatake Okumiya, *Midway: The Battle That Doomed Japan, The Japanese Navy Story*, Naval Institute Press, Annapolis, 1955

Hall, Timothy, *Darwin 1942: Australia's Darkest Hour*, Methuen Australia, 1980

Hastings, Max, *Nemesis: The Battle for Japan, 1944–45*, Harper Press, London, 2007

James, Barbara, *No Man's Land: Women of the Northern Territory*, Collins Australia, Sydney, 1989

Kriloff, Herbert, *Officer of the Deck: A Memoir of the Pacific War and the Sea*, Pacifica Press, Pacifica, 2000

—— *Proceed Orange: Assume Command*, Detseleg Enterprises, Calgary, 2002

Lockwood, Douglas, *Australia Under Attack: The Bombing of Darwin 1942*, New Holland Publishers (Australia), 2005. First published as *Australia's Pearl Harbour*, Cassell Australia, 1966

Mulholland, Jack, *Darwin Bombed: An A/A Gunner's Reflections*, Bookbound Publishing, Ourimbah, 2006

Pearce, Howard and Bob Alford, *A Wartime Journey: Stuart Highway Heritage Guide*, Northern Territory Tourist Commission, 2006

Powell, Alan, *The Shadow's Edge: Australia's Northern War*, Melbourne University Press, Melbourne, 1988, revised and reprinted NT University Press, Darwin, 2007

Ruwoldt, Rex, *Darwin's Battle for Australia*, Darwin Defenders 1942–45 Inc., Clifton Springs, 2005

Some Of The Boys, *Soldiering On*, Australian War Memorial, Canberra, 1942

Williamson, Kristin, *The Last Battalion*, Lansdowne Press, Melbourne, 1984

A VERY RUDE AWAKENING

For my wife Roslyn, whose mother hid her under the kitchen table while all this was going on. And with special thanks to my publisher and lifelong friend Richard Walsh, whose mother threw him into the umbrella cupboard instead.

Contents

Introduction

The Japanese midget submarine raid on Sydney Harbour is one of those events, like the assassination of President Kennedy or the death of Princess Diana, where everybody seems to remember what they were doing at the time. It is hard to find a Sydneysider who can't tell you where they were, or what their neighbours or parents or grandparents were doing, on the night their harbour became a battlefield.

The raid has been the subject of endless magazine articles, radio and television documentaries, and has featured in many books. Yet one story has remained largely untold: how did Sydney respond to the attack? The focus has always been on the Japanese raiders. Where did they come from? What exactly did they do?

The Japanese were not the only heroes that night. From the civilian nightwatchman in his rowboat who first raised the alarm, to the young Australian Navy lieutenant on his first night of command who fired the first effective depth charge (and crippled his own ship in the process), there were heroes aplenty among the defenders.

There were failures as well. The defences were slapdash, the command was erratic, and there was a lot of undisciplined gunfire, which happily did little damage beyond blasting chunks out of the venerable stonework of Fort Denison in mid-harbour. Some of the command decisions, like the order to commercial traffic on the harbour to keep moving as normal and fully lit, were plain barmy.

By the end of the night 27 men had died—19 Australian and two British sailors, and the six Japanese crew of the three midget submarines. All three submarines were sunk, only one by hostile action. The *Kuttabul*, a converted ferry used as a dormitory for junior seamen, lay partially submerged against the harbour wall, smashed by the torpedo which exploded beneath her.

There can be no doubting the courage of the Japanese sailors. But courage was not in short supply that night. Nor was incompetence, confusion and indecision. Luck, too, played its part, mostly favouring the defence.

I hope the reader will bear with me as I give the political and historical background, both Australian and Japanese, to the raid. In the 21st century we complain of the speed of change, as we adapt to a high-tech global village. Yet at the time of the midget submarine raid, the world must have appeared to the people of Australia to be spinning out of control. The certainties of white supremacy evaporated in the humiliation of Singapore's fall; the invincible British Empire suddenly looked frail and vulnerable; 160 years of Australian foreign policy were overturned in three weeks—a change that has lasted to this day, putting Australian soldiers on the streets of Iraq. It is impossible to understand the actions and reactions in Sydney on the night of 31 May and 1 June 1942, without first delving into this background.

Peter Grose,
March 2007

Part I

PREPARATION

Chapter I

There's a war on

Sydney was suffering an uncharacteristically foul night on Sunday, 31 May 1942. Winter would begin next day, and the golden beaches had long been abandoned. Throughout the day the south-west wind brought squally rain and biting cold to city and suburbs. The rain died back by evening, but the sky stayed thick with cloud, masking the full moon. In town the soldiers, sailors and airmen made the best of their leave at Sydney's traditionally boisterous theatres, nightclubs, restaurants, illegal gambling dens, and brothels. In 1942 entertainment was a seven-days-a-week affair. After all, there was a war on.

Sydney in 1942 would be unrecognisable to the citizens of that gleaming Emerald City today. The iconic Harbour Bridge was a mere 10 years old, and still something of a novelty. Men wore hats. Nice women wore gloves. Divorce was a source of shame. The tallest building in Sydney was the 13-storey AWA tower in York Street, whose art deco walls are today jostled to oblivion by the surrounding forest of skyscrapers stretching up to 300 metres. Sydney's civic architecture in 1942 was still low-rise colonial conventional, a triumphalist embodiment of British Empire solidity and bourgeois virtue rather than the soaring celebration of the imagination which is the Sydney Opera House today.

Australia's rich then were not stock-market wizards or property developers. They were the sheep and cattle barons, the so-called 'squattocracy' made up from old families of the colony. They owned huge tracts of land in the outback, overseen from graceful homesteads, and grew rich from the insatiable worldwide demand for Australian wool and beef. They kept splendid second homes in Sydney and Melbourne, and sent their sons and daughters to expensive boarding schools in the capital cities. Meanwhile, the wrought-iron balconied terrace houses of Sydney's Paddington and Surry Hills had to wait another 25 years to become fashionable. In 1942 they were slums.

It was a city of hypocrites. Pubs closed their bars at 6 pm. Sly grog shops flourished thereafter. The police were quick to ferret out obscene books and bawdy art exhibitions. Yet the city's vice squad seemed unable to pinpoint the location of brothels in Palmer Street and Chapel Street, near Kings Cross. Gambling other than via an on-course bookmaker was illegal. The classic Australian game of two-up, involving the tossing of two coins while punters bet on two heads or two tails, could be found in suburban backyards and bushland clearings everywhere. Thommo's Two-up School, which prudently shifted location every so often including a brief stint on a ferry, had been a household name for over 20 years. It managed to stay several steps ahead of a none-too-zealous police force throughout the war. The notorious Tilly Divine and Kate Lee ruled an underworld of prostitution, illegal drinking and illegal betting. Police demands were very reasonable. No doubt there were some honest vice squad coppers, but the rest offered blind-eye service at affordable prices.

Chicken was expensive. Men drank beer. Few families could afford a car. Luxury was a night out in the gilded splendour of the Hotel Australia in central Sydney where, so it was rumoured, *continental* food was served as well as the traditional steak, roast beef and lamb. Romano's nightclub nearby offered even more sophistication, with live entertainment to accompany a menu which could be navigated only with a smattering of French. Strip clubs had not yet been invented, but at the Tivoli Theatre showgirls appeared topless on stage, on the strict understanding that they stayed rigid and motionless in pursuit of their art.

Nevertheless, in 1942 Sydney was ever more visibly a city at war. Military uniforms were everywhere. The harbour was packed with warships. Newspapers reported the daily progress of the war in anxious detail—while reporting the horseracing news in even greater detail. Increasing numbers of husbands, sons, fathers and boyfriends left home in white, blue and khaki uniforms, while mothers, wives, daughters and girlfriends fretted for their safety. Women joined all three services and donned uniforms, too. Those who didn't were constantly reminded that there was plenty they could do for their country. In a striking phrase, Prime Minister Curtin told the women of Australia: 'The knitting needle is a weapon of war.'

The evidence of war went beyond the profusion of military uniforms. Bondi beach was festooned with barbed wire. Zigzag slit trenches gouged suburban back lawns, ready to provide shelter when the inevitable air raids came. Anthony Hordern's department store in Sydney advertised: 'Now is the time to prepare. Send for your A.R.P. [Air Raid Precautions] equipment.' Among indispensable items for surviving the coming onslaught, Hordern's offered 'new and improved indestructible lampshades, all metal, double purpose, detachable caps for brownouts'. The price was a very reasonable one shilling and a penny ha'penny per lampshade.

Sydney remained a party town. The stuffy Australian Club opened its doors to visiting American officers—though not to Australian officers nor to American other ranks. To the soldiers, sailors and airmen from America, Britain, Holland, India and France, as well as to the Australian troops stationed there or passing through, Sydney was above all a safe city. The lethal jungles of Malaya and the Dutch East Indies were thousands of miles away to the north. So were the howling Zero aircraft and Long Lance torpedoes of the Imperial Japanese Navy, both of which had done so much to give the lie to the name Pacific Ocean. Even when Darwin, Broome and other Australian cities suffered Japanese bombing, it all seemed a long way away. In Sydney, nobody needed to think further afield than Kings Cross, Randwick Racecourse, and the next cold beer.

♦   ♦   ♦

Sydney Harbour was better protected than many. There were shore-based gun batteries facing the sea, anti-aircraft batteries on headlands, searchlight teams to check the skies, armed and unarmed patrol boats scouring the harbour, and a very modest force of fighter aircraft to repel an attack from the air. Outside the harbour entrance, six indicator loops lay on the ocean bed in deep water in a huge arc from the cliffs of Dover Heights in the south to the beach suburb of Dee Why in the north. The loops registered the passage over them of any metal ship. On the night of 31 May 1942, a battleship could have crossed the outer ring without raising the alarm. Two of these six outer loops had failed, so all six were left unmanned.

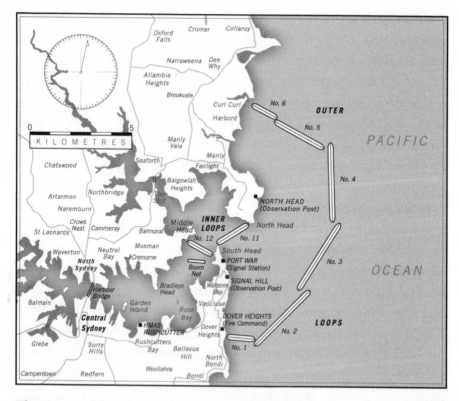

The position of the eight indicator loops protecting Sydney Harbour. Two of the outer loops were not working on the night of 31 May 1942. Of the two inner loops, Inner Loop 12 proved to be the most effective, detecting all three submarines as they entered the harbour.

The next line of defence was a pair of similar indicator loops, this time inside the harbour itself. Inner Loop No. 11 stretched across the entrance of the harbour from North Head to South Head. Further into the harbour lay Inner Loop No. 12, stretching from just inside South Head at Lady Bay (now a celebrated nudist beach), across the inner harbour to Middle Head near Obelisk Bay. The peculiar geography of Sydney Harbour meant that water traffic to the busy and popular harbour suburb of Manly had to cross Inner Loop 12 while still remaining inside the harbour. As well, Inner Loop 12 lay in shallower water than any of its counterparts, at 6 fathoms (11 metres), so smaller and lighter vessels like harbour ferries, tugs and even large launches set off a trace. Inner Loop 12 always had plenty to say for itself.

Watching over all this was the Port War Signal Station on South Head. PWSS checked every vessel approaching the harbour. Any unknown or unexpected vessel would be ordered to halt by Port War until it had been cleared by an examination vessel standing off Sydney Heads. The indicator loops 'tailed' into Port War. As well, PWSS had a secret ASDIC anti-submarine detection system, and a photoelectric beam to detect surface vessels. If Sydney faced a threat from the sea, it was the task of PWSS to raise the alarm and call for help.

The final line of defence was a boom net stretching from the southern shore of the harbour at Laings Point, near Watsons Bay (a short walk today from the famous Doyle's Restaurant), to Georges Head, near the genteel northern harbour suburb of Clifton Gardens. The workings of Sydney Harbour have scarcely altered between 1942 and now: there are two major channels leading from the harbour to the open ocean, the Western and the Eastern. The Western Channel, over on the Clifton Gardens side, is deeper and straighter and is used by larger ships. The Eastern Channel, near Watsons Bay and Camp Cove, is shallower and trickier, and is used by smaller more manoeuvrable ships.

Construction of the boom net began in January 1942. When complete, the net would be 1480 metres long with two gate openings, a 121-metre gate at the western end, and a 91-metre gate at the eastern end. By May 1942 the large centre section of the net and some of the harbour-edge work had been completed, but there were still big gaps facing the channels near each end. Floating boom gates were to be built into these openings, blocking the Eastern and Western channels and completing the defensive line. The gates would be opened and closed by specialist boom vessels. There were no gates, however, and no boom vessels, on the night of 31 May 1942, just two big gaps—275 metres on the eastern side and 293 metres on the western side.

Although the Sydney net was incomplete, in some respects it was superior to nets at other major Allied bases. The central and western section of Sydney's net was strung along 49 clusters of four piles driven into the harbour bed. The eastern end was suspended from floating buoys at the surface. However, the Sydney net was unusual in that it was securely anchored to the harbour bed. Other nets, including the net across Pearl Harbor, simply dangled from the surface to somewhere near the seabed, allowing the possibility that a small submarine might dive under them. Shortly before the bombers struck Pearl Harbor on 7 December 1941, a Japanese midget submarine may have slipped into the harbour past the net defences, possibly taking advantage of the loose net. No submarine could duck under the Sydney net.

◆　◆　◆

On that cold and windy night, Jimmy Cargill had one of the loneliest and least enviable jobs in Sydney. He was employed as a nightwatchman by the Maritime Services Board, the civilian authority in charge of all harbours and navigable waterways in the state of New South Wales. His job was to guard two floating crane punts near the western end of the Sydney boom net, part of the net construction effort. Amid the shortages of war, pilfering of building materials, tools, even wood, was a perennial problem, so Jimmy stayed vigilant. He was an ex-merchant seaman, in his mid-50s, with a no-nonsense style. He died in 1986, but he left behind some remarkable audio tapes, recorded in his soft Scottish brogue. He comes across as the kind of man you would want at your side in a crisis.

The southerly wind creates special dangers on Sydney Harbour. Out to sea that night, it was whipping up 2-metre waves and setting the spray flying. Inside the harbour it produced an uncomfortably choppy surface. Spray and rain combined to soak through the most reliable waterproof. Nevertheless, around 7 pm, Jimmy Cargill knew he had no choice but to go out onto the harbour. The guy ropes on one of the crane derricks were swinging dangerously in the wind. They would have to be tightened, even if that meant an uncomfortable and straining journey by rowboat from his shore base. He clambered into his 14-foot skiff and heaved his way across the rough water to the offending punt.

By 7.30 pm the guy ropes were secure. Jimmy Cargill was now out on the harbour, so he rowed across to the floating pile-driver nearby to chat with his fellow nightwatchman Bill Nangle. They were still chatting at 7.55 pm as the Manly ferry crossed Inner Loop 12 on its outbound route to Manly. The ferry, brightly lit and slow moving, could be seen easily by the Royal Australian Navy watchers at the Port War Signal Station. It left a good trace, and the Loop Station watchers could match the trace to its passage.

Four minutes later, at 7.59 pm, an inbound Manly ferry crossed Inner Loop 12 on its way back to the central ferry wharf at Circular Quay. Again, it was brightly lit and again the Loop Station crew had no trouble matching it to the trace.

Two minutes later, at 8.01 pm, there was a smaller blip on the trace paper. Nobody saw anything, and nobody bothered with it.

Some time around 8.15 pm, while Jimmy Cargill and Bill Nangle were still chatting on the floating pile-driver, they noticed what in the darkness looked like a fishing boat near the net. The boat was showing no lights and clearly shouldn't have been there. Cargill decided to row over and investigate.

When he drew closer, he could see that it was no fishing boat. A strange, metallic object stood in the water close to the net. It had two large, protruding tubes, both with capped rounded ends, reminding him of oxyacetylene bottles. With not a little courage he rowed closer, to within a paddle's length of the object. He still didn't know what it was, but by now the likeliest explanation was that it was a mine.

Every night the navy stationed two patrol boats to guard the net, one at each gate. The Channel Patrol boats were converted harbour pleasure launches bought by the Royal Australian Navy and converted to military use. The boats were given limited weaponry, never more than a few depth charges and a World War I machine-gun. It was scarcely suitable armament to stare down the Imperial Japanese Navy.

That night the duty vessels at the net were HMAS *Yarroma* at the western end and HMAS *Lolita* at the eastern end. Cargill thought he should report his findings, and rowed over to the nearest patrol boat, the *Yarroma*. The captain was sceptical: surely it was just a bit of old naval

Trace left by Chuman (I-27's midget) on Inner Loop 12 as he enters the harbour at 8.01 pm.

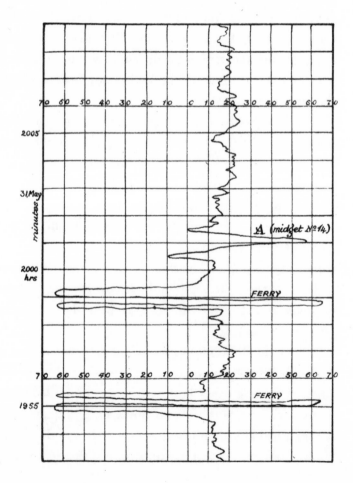

junk that had floated up and got caught in the net. Cargill was adamant. Whatever was stuck there was shiny and brand new, never junk. Cargill asked *Yarroma* to follow him, and rowed off in the direction of the object. *Yarroma* didn't move.

By now angry, Cargill rowed back. *Yarroma*'s skipper explained that he was repairing his searchlight, and invited Cargill aboard. Still reluctant to close in on what was very likely a mine, *Yarroma* instead offered the services of their stoker to row over with Cargill to investigate. Cargill accepted.

The two set off at a leisurely pace to cover the 80 metres or so between *Yarroma* and the mystery object. Again, they closed to within a paddle's length. The stoker shone his torch on the object, which was clearly stuck in the net and thrashing its engines to free itself. By now they could see into the water. In the torchlight were a conning tower, a bow cutting line, and a periscope. The two 'oxyacetylene bottles' were torpedo tubes. The stoker needed no second opinion. 'It's a submarine all right.'

Chapter 2

England expects

Until 1942 Australians lived with a comfortable certainty. Wars took place in that mythic hinterland called 'overseas'. Australia was proud to call itself part of the British Empire, and with that comforting knowledge came an obligation to join with Britain when either home-land or Empire was under threat. Nelson's famous signal at Trafalgar, 'England expects that every man will do his duty', could be heard loud and clear across the oceans to Australia. Before 1942 that invariably meant shipping Australian soldiers and sailors off to some distant land to risk their lives on Britain's behalf. The payoff was obvious enough: if ever Australia came under threat, the invincible British Empire would spring to its defence and crush its enemies with a mighty blow.

Even before 1901, when federation joined the six Australian colonies into a single nation, Australians plunged willingly into Britain's colonial wars. A contingent of 758 soldiers from New South Wales took part in the relief of Khartoum in 1885. A much stronger contingent, totalling 16,175 men, fought in the Boer War from 1899 to 1902. Some 300 Australians, again mostly from New South Wales, fought with British forces putting down the Boxer Rebellion in China in 1900. However, the biggest contribution came in 1914 with the outbreak of World

The composite submarine, assembled from Matsuo's bow and the mid and stern sections of Chuman's midget, is the centrepiece of the most popular display in the Australian War Memorial in Canberra. It is just possible to see the denting of Matsuo's bow caused by the steel cable used to haul it up from the bottom of Sydney Harbour. Although much of the exterior of the submarine has been restored, the War Memorial has left the centre section as it was found, ripped open by the force of Chuman's scuttling charges.

The stern section of Matsuo's midget. This section broke away from the main body when the submarine was being dragged along the harbour bed to shallower water in Taylors Bay.

The bow of Matsuo's submarine, part of the special display at the Australian War Memorial. The bow cage has been straightened and the bow caps have been repaired and locked back into place.

This contemporary photograph, taken just off Bradleys Head on Sydney Harbour, shows Garden Island as it might have looked through Ban's periscope. The *Kuttabul* was moored in front of the low pink building on the centre left. The buoys' positions have changed since 1942, but the large white buoy on the extreme left of the picture is not far from the position of No. 4 buoy, where the USS *Perkins* was tied up on the night of 31 May 1942. From this position, Ban would have faced *Perkins'* stern.

Ban's midget at rest on the seabed off Newport Reef, Sydney. A diver's light illuminates a shoal of fish below the wrecked conning tower. The large hole in the hull is caused by corrosion after 64 years under water, and indicates the fragility of the wreck. Two lines can be seen on either side of the conning tower, both left behind by commercial fishing boats snagging their fishing lines and nets over the years. *(Photograph courtesy* 60 Minutes *and No Frills Divers).*

The graceful 'Tresco' still adorns Sydney Harbour's foreshore at Elizabeth Bay. Rear Admiral Muirhead-Gould could walk down the cliff path to a small wharf, where his barge would deliver him to his headquarters on Garden Island, a few hundred metres away.

Margaret Coote (*née* Hamilton) peers intently at the conning tower of Matsuo's submarine, on display at the Naval Heritage Centre on Garden Island, Sydney. This picture, taken in October 2006, records her first sighting of the submarine for more than 60 years: it last appeared in her life in June 1942, when she watched it being dragged to the surface in Taylors Bay. Previously she had seen its periscope gliding into Taylors Bay, and had watched the depth charge attack that led to its destruction.

This photograph of the western Pile Light was taken from the deck of the Manly ferry on its regular route via the Western Channel from Manly to Circular Quay shortly before its collapse at 4.30 pm on 12 December 2006. Its role in the Battle of Sydney Harbour—Chuman reversed into the boom net while submerged, almost certainly after colliding with the Pile Light—has never been given proper recognition. The old light, rebuilt in 1947, was at least as effective as the newfangled net in foiling Chuman's attack.

Sydney is packed with reminders of its World War II past. This concrete slab on Laings Point, an easy walk from the Watsons Bay ferry wharf and Doyle's Restaurant, was the anchor for the eastern end of a boom net that stretched across the harbour to Georges Head. Today it is marked by a small plaque, including a brief description of the net's role in the Battle of Sydney Harbour.

War I. Some 300,000 Australians enlisted, of whom 60,000 were killed and 156,000 wounded, gassed or taken prisoner. It was a staggering contribution from a nation with a population of less than five million.

Despite the carnage, there was no shortage of volunteers. Each party of Australian troops went off to war in a fanfare of goodwill. They paraded through the cities, watched by cheering crowds. More crowds lined the harbours to wave the troopships off. World War I, and particularly Gallipoli, came to be seen as the birth of the Australian nation. War somehow bound the people of Australia into a single identity. And wars could be relied on to obey three infallible rules: they were fought elsewhere; Britain took the lead; and Britain and her allies won.

Australia, along with Canada, South Africa and New Zealand, enjoyed a high status in the British Empire. The four 'white' countries were dominions, as opposed to British-ruled colonies like India. Each, in theory, was an independent nation owing allegiance to the British crown but self-governing in every other respect, and equal in status to the British motherland.

Reality was far different. Before World War II Australia barely maintained its own diplomatic service. External Affairs consisted of little more than liaison with the Foreign Office in London, there to be kept up to date with the latest British relationships and policies towards the rest of the world. Australian and British interests were identical and inseparable. The dominions had the right to argue and even advise, but ultimately they were expected to fall into line with whatever Britain had in mind.

The way Australia entered World War II graphically illustrates Australian subservience to British foreign policy. The anglophile Australian Prime Minister Robert Menzies, a lawyer, believed Australia was legally at war as a direct consequence of the British declaration of war on Germany. In his speech to the nation announcing Australia's participation, Menzies said: 'Fellow Australians, it is my melancholy duty to inform you officially, that in consequence of a persistence by Germany in her invasion of Poland, Great Britain has declared war upon her and that, *as a result* [author's italics], Australia is also at war.'

Whatever the niceties of dominion status, Australia's independence was immediately thrown out the window. As had happened in World War I, the Royal Australian Navy was simply merged with Britain's Royal Navy into a single force under British command. Australian fighting ships set off for the Mediterranean, the Red Sea and the Atlantic. Australian airmen were shipped to Britain to join the air war against Germany. They fought in Royal Air Force (RAF) squadrons rather than as separate Royal Australian Air Force (RAAF) units. Two entire Australian infantry divisions and part of a third left for the Middle East, where they retained their Australian identity but fought under the overall British command of General Sir Archibald Wavell. When the autocratic Churchill took over as British Prime Minister in May 1940, he made it very clear that conduct of the entire war rested with Britain, and Churchill personally would call the shots. It was business as usual: the war obligingly stayed overseas, and Australians stayed under British control. The only rule which appeared not to be holding was the certainty of British victory.

Poland fell within weeks to an attack first by Germany and two weeks later by the USSR, then Germany's ally. The British and French watched impotently. Seven months of quiet followed—the so-called 'phoney war'—in which little happened beyond the invasion of Finland by the USSR on 30 November 1939. However, during this lull there was one major incident which was to have a curious resonance in Sydney 18 months later.

The Royal Navy used the harbour at Scapa Flow, in the Orkney Islands off Scotland's north coast, as one of their principal bases. The Luftwaffe had flown aerial reconnaissance missions over the harbour, and came back with a good picture of the defences. The commander of the German submarine fleet, Admiral Dönitz, approached one of his best submariners, Günther Prien, with the photographs and a simple question: did Prien think he could sneak into Scapa Flow? Prien said yes.

The German submarine U-47, under Prien's command, arrived off Scapa Flow on the night of 13 October 1939, only six weeks after the declaration of war. Fortunately for the British, the fleet had sailed a few days earlier, leaving only one capital ship, the battleship *Royal Oak*, at anchor in the harbour. If more British ships had been there, the resulting devastation might have had a major impact on the Atlantic war.

The harbour at Scapa Flow is served by four channels between islands. As protection the British had sunk block ships in the channels. Entry to the harbour was via a boom gate. However, the aerial photographs showed that there was sufficient space for a skilful commander to dodge around the block ships, and Prien certainly possessed the skill. He slipped into Scapa Flow via the Kirk Channel shortly after midnight.

Prien fired his first salvo of torpedoes at the *Royal Oak* a few minutes before 1 am on 14 October. One scored a minor hit on the bow of the battleship. The rest missed. The British were so confident that the harbour was impenetrable that they gave no thought to the idea that the blast was caused by an enemy submarine attack. They thought there had been an internal explosion on board the ship, probably in a paint store.

Twenty minutes later Prien fired a second fan of torpedoes. This time there was no escape. All three hit home, tearing huge holes in the hull of the *Royal Oak*. The 29,000-ton battleship rolled over and sank within 10 minutes, killing 833 of the crew in the process. Prien slipped out of the harbour unnoticed and returned safely to Germany and a hero's welcome. Each crew member was awarded an Iron Cross, pinned on personally by Hitler in Berlin. The fanfare of celebration in Germany gave the British the first full explanation of what had happened to the *Royal Oak*.

This was the second-worst naval disaster of World War II for Britain, and the Royal Navy took it very seriously. They set up a Board of Inquiry to investigate how it had happened, and what precautions needed to be taken to prevent a recurrence. Three senior Royal Navy commanders sat on the Board. One was Commander Gerard Muirhead-Gould, an experienced World War I sailor with some knowledge of submarines. Muirhead-Gould was well thought of by the navy, but he suffered from heart problems and was deemed unfit for active service. Shortly after completing the Board of Inquiry, he was appointed Naval

Officer in Command, Sydney, and later promoted to Rear Admiral. He was in control of Sydney Harbour on the night of 31 May 1942. Muirhead-Gould was in a better position than most to know how submarines can sneak into harbours and cause havoc.

◆　◆　◆

The war resumed in earnest in April 1940, and the first fury of *blitzkrieg* sent Europe reeling. On 9 April Germany invaded Denmark and Norway. Holland and Belgium were next to fall. Within six weeks, on 20 May, the Germans reached the English Channel. On 27 May British forces began retreating from the European mainland via Dunkirk. By 4 June the evacuation was complete. Britain and her Empire allies passed it off as a miracle. In fact it was a massive defeat and a humiliation.

The German advance continued. On 22 June France surrendered. Most of Western Europe was now under German control and the simple, brutal truth was that in the space of three violent months Britain and her Empire found themselves alone and losing the war.

Worse was to follow. Britain itself came under attack from the air. Streams of German bombers arrived by day and night, and newspapers around the world carried front-page pictures of British cities in flames. Tens of thousands of tons of explosives rained down on British homes and factories.

Meanwhile, German submarines began attacking shipping convoys in the Atlantic. Vital supplies of food, oil and military equipment from the United States and elsewhere ran a gauntlet of U-boats, with terrible loss of life and tonnage of shipping. Everywhere the news was bad, and no amount of Churchillian rhetoric about finest hours and fighting on the beaches and the hills could disguise the facts.

Australians watched this with a mixture of horror and disbelief. This wasn't how it was meant to happen. Didn't Britain always win? Lines formed outside recruiting offices as young men rushed to enlist, ready to do their bit to turn the tide. The story of my own family was typical. My father was the third of four siblings. The oldest was Molly, then came Jim, my father Fred, and Tom. The brothers discussed what to do. My father was the only one married, so it was agreed that the two unmarried brothers would be sufficient contribution to the war effort from the Grose family. Uncle Tom was first. He joined the army on 20 May 1940, aged 20 years. Uncle Jim enlisted in the army a fortnight later, on 6 June, aged 30 years. Both named my Nan as their next of kin. They were sent off separately in slouch hats and khaki to the Middle East.

Royal Australian Navy ships were soon in action in the Mediterranean and the Atlantic, and Australian airmen fought in the skies over Britain and Europe. However, Australian soldiers had yet to come under serious fire. This respite came to a swift end in September 1940. Mussolini wanted to recapture the glorious Roman Empire for modern Italy. He launched his campaign on 14 September with an attack on Egypt, following this up with an attack on Greece, launched on 28 October. The restoration of the Roman Empire got off to a shaky start. The Greeks took only three weeks to throw the Italians out, and by 7 February 1941, the British, with strong support from Australian troops, had rolled the Italians back to Benghazi in Libya, taking thousands of prisoners in the process. Uncle Jim was there to help. Uncle Tom was busy elsewhere, fighting the Vichy French in Syria. The rout of Mussolini's troops was a rare victory for Britain and Empire, and for a brief few weeks the war looked winnable. Hitler swiftly silenced the optimists.

The German Army commanded by Rommel counterattacked in North Africa on 31 March 1941, and rolled the British and Australians back from Benghazi almost to Cairo, leaving an enclave of mostly Australian soldiers holding Tobruk. The German invasion of Greece and Yugoslavia, launched a week later on 6 April, was equally brutal and swiftly effective. It was followed by the capture of Crete on 2 June. Both Greece and Crete led to heavy British and Australian losses. The war was now 21 months old and going very badly indeed. Australian troops felt they were endlessly let down by poor air support. Only Britain could put this right.

Throughout this period Australia, under the prime ministership of Robert Menzies, played the part of Britain's compliant and uncomplaining supporter. Menzies travelled to London in 1941 and stayed there for months, holding lengthy discussions with Churchill and taking part in some British War Cabinet meetings. On 10 March 1941, he made a statement to the War Cabinet setting out Australia's contribution to the war effort. It is a masterpiece of obsequiousness. In Menzies' own words: 'On the outbreak of war the Royal Australian Navy had been placed at the disposal of the Admiralty.' Australia had one heavy cruiser stationed in the United Kingdom, a second cruiser and four destroyers stationed in the Mediterranean, and two sloops stationed in the Red Sea. 'All, or virtually all these ships', said Menzies, 'have distinguished themselves in action'.

In his War Cabinet statement, Menzies listed the full strength of the RAN: two heavy cruisers, four light cruisers, two armed merchant cruisers, five destroyers, five sloops, one fast auxiliary minesweeping vessel, 19 minesweepers, seven anti-submarine vessels, one depot ship, three boom defence vessels, five patrol and examination vessels and one fleet oiler. By the beginning of 1942 the Australians expected to complete construction of three Tribal class destroyers, one boom vessel, 48 anti-submarine and minesweeping vessels (of which 20 were for the Royal Navy and four for the Royal Indian Navy), plus one oil lighter and one floating dock.

The Australian Army had some 130,000 men in uniform, of which about half were stationed outside Australia. The 6th, 7th and part of the 9th Australian Divisions were in the Middle East. Part of the 8th Division was in Malaya. The rest were in camps in Australia.

The Royal Australian Air Force numbered 8311 men and 223 aircraft, including 96 Hudson bombers and 85 Wirraway fighters. Eight Sunderland flying boats from the RAAF were stationed in the United Kingdom, while 36 RAAF Hudsons and 18 Wirraways were stationed in the Middle East.

The cost of the war to Australians was substantial. In the year before the outbreak of war, Australia's defence budget stood at £14 million. By 1941 annual expenditure had risen to £200 million. Menzies wanted the British War Cabinet to know that Australia was making a major contribution to the war, far beyond what might reasonably be expected of a young country with a population now risen to a mere seven million.

However, Menzies' grandstanding revealed an appalling lack of preparation for the defence of Australia itself. Saloon bar wisdom, which can still be heard today, says that Australia cannot be defended successfully. The long coastline and vast distances make the job impossible. This is far from true. Australia can be defended, but only from the air. Aircraft shrink distances.

Australia's air defence, on Menzies' numbers, was pitiful. The Australian-built Wirraway fighter was slow, under-armed and clumsy. It was no match for a German Me 109 or a Focke Wulfe 190. In any serious dogfight it could expect to be blown out of the sky. The entire fighter force of 85 Wirraways was little more than a day's supply in a serious air war. The Hudson bomber was, if anything, worse. Known to pilots as the Hudswine, it was a converted passenger plane with a formidable record for crashing. It had limited range, limited bomb load, and limited ability to defend itself. In 1941 Australia had none of the best British aircraft—no Spitfires, no Hurricanes, no Wellingtons, no Halifaxes, no Beauforts—and no plans to acquire any.

The RAN might have boasted an impressive number of fighting ships for a small country, but they were geared to supporting a Mediterranean and Atlantic war rather than defending the Australian homeland. Australia had no aircraft carriers, and no submarines. So the RAN lacked the right weapons to harass enemy supply lines, or to meet an invasion force head-on.

There was a further problem: Japan. On 27 September 1940 Japan had signed a Tripartite Pact with Germany and Italy, which effectively placed Japan on side with Hitler and Mussolini. It was a convoluted agreement, but the essence of it was that if any country not already involved in the conflict declared war on Germany or Italy, then Japan would immediately join the war on the German and Italian side. Although the treaty was phrased to apply to any country, the target was obvious. The only way Churchill could hope to turn the tide of war in his favour was to have the United States join the fray. So Japan issued a clear warning to Roosevelt, the US President: join with Britain at your peril. If you do, we will attack.

Back in Australia, the unease was palpable. Newspapers began to publish increasingly sceptical articles about the British direction of the war. The Battle of Britain, fought between July and September 1940, had been a magnificent achievement, holding off the threat of an invasion of Britain itself. But everywhere else the war was being lost. Hitler's ill-judged attack on the USSR, launched on 22 June 1941, had yet to come unstuck. The triumphant German Army swept towards Moscow. Leningrad was surrounded. It looked as though Hitler might succeed where Napoleon had failed. The whole of Europe might soon be in German and Italian hands.

In Australia, Menzies' position was increasingly untenable. His own party saw him as aloof and arrogant. His long absence in London allowed colleagues back home to plot against him. They accused him of spending too much time hobnobbing with Churchill when he should have been back in Australia looking after his own people. He had nailed his colours uncritically to Britain's mast, and this was now beginning to look like a mistake. Australian lives were being lost in badly conducted campaigns in Greece and Crete, as well as the Middle East. Churchill had sacked his Middle East commander, Wavell, and replaced him first with Auchinleck and later with Alexander and the more effective Montgomery. He shifted Wavell to India and the Far East, where he would command British and Australian forces in the event of a Japanese attack. None of this inspired confidence in Australia.

On his return to Australia, Menzies made an attempt to shore up his position by offering a coalition with John Curtin's Labor Party, even offering to stand down as Prime Minister as part of the bargain. Curtin refused. On 28 August 1941 Menzies bowed to the inevitable and resigned, handing over power to his deputy Arthur Fadden.

On his first day in office Fadden pressed Churchill for a stronger voice for Australia in the war. Could Australia have a permanent seat in the British War Cabinet, he asked? Churchill cabled back, on 29 August 1941, on a Prime Minister to Prime Minister basis, saying no. Fadden returned to the attack on 5 September, adopting a rather tetchier tone. 'The views of the Prime Ministers of Canada and South Africa are noted with interest but not with surprise,' Fadden wrote. 'As you are well aware, their attitude is determined by local problems peculiar to each Dominion.' He warmed to his theme:

> We, too, have a special viewpoint based on the closest possible degree of Empire co-operation which, speaking with that frankness permitted within the family circle, is evident by comparison of our all round war effort on land, sea and in the air. The Australian people feel, however, that this effort warrants the right to be heard when vital decisions affecting their interests are being taken.

Churchill said no, again.

The Fadden government lasted five weeks. Two independent members of the House of Representatives held the balance of power and on 1 October 1941 they switched sides and voted against the government's budget. Fadden resigned. On 3 October the Governor-General sent for John Curtin, and Australia had its third Prime Minister in five weeks, a Labor government, and a new outlook on the war.

◆　　◆　　◆

Curtin and Menzies could hardly have been more different. Menzies was an urbane, cosmopolitan lawyer with unshakeable self-belief and an approach to colleagues that was both condescending and high-handed. Curtin had left school at 14. He had never been a minister before he became Prime Minister. His most responsible job had been as secretary of a small trade union and he left that job, so it was said, because he was an alcoholic. (He gave up drink by the time he became Leader of the Opposition, and he stayed teetotal from then on.) He was a tireless political agitator and polemicist, but he was both inexperienced in office and diffident in personal style. Menzies had told the British government Curtin was not up to the job of Prime Minister, and Curtin himself was said to have harboured similar doubts. Nevertheless, he turned himself into a more than adequate wartime leader.

The new cabinet's review of the war situation did not make pretty reading. On the European mainland Hitler's Germany was lord of all it surveyed. Spain, Portugal, Switzerland, Sweden and Ireland were neutral, but every other major European country was now occupied by German and Italian forces, giving them access to the best of Europe's ports and airfields, industry and resources. Russia looked set to fall. In North Africa Rommel was currently on the retreat but regrouping, and far from defeated. German submarines were sinking Atlantic convoys bound for Britain faster than replacement ships could be built or crews trained. The war was at best a stalemate and at worst in danger of being lost. The only way Hitler could be beaten would be for the United States to join forces with Britain. But however close the personal ties between Roosevelt and Churchill, and however much Roosevelt might have wanted to join the war and put a stop to Nazism, the American President was forced by isolationists at home to keep clear. America would not readily join the war.

John Curtin's new government now looked at the disposition of Australian forces. There were three Australian divisions facing the Germans and Italians in the Middle East, and only one division in Malaya to withstand any Japanese attack. Curtin had recognised the importance of air power earlier than others, and knew full well that Australia's lack of any serious air cover was a terrible mistake. But as 1941 drew to a close there was hardly the time, let alone the resources, to put this right.

After only nine weeks in office, as the Australian cabinet retired to their beds on the night of Sunday, 7 December 1941, they must have thought the world looked a dangerous and unpredictable place.

Chapter 3

Running wild

Japan fought alongside Britain and her allies in World War I. The Japanese Navy in particular was pro-Western, and modelled itself on the British Navy. From the beginning of the century, Japanese foreign policy could be reduced to a simple proposition: an Asian nation could and should join the ranks of great powers and, as there were only two Asian nations capable of major power status, Japan and China, Japan should do its utmost to make sure that it and not China prevailed.

Three European powers had colonised East Asia. The French controlled Indo-China (Vietnam, Laos and Cambodia) and a scattering of Pacific islands, the Dutch controlled the East Indies (now Indonesia), and the British controlled Burma, Malaya, Singapore and Hong Kong. The Americans held the Philippines, and the Hawaiian islands, plus a further scattering of smaller islands dotted around the Pacific. The colonies were strategically important in different ways. Malaya had rubber and tin. The Dutch East Indies had oil. Singapore was a major naval base.

The main plank of Japanese foreign policy was the creation of the harmless-sounding if grandiosely named Greater East Asia Co-Prosperity Sphere. This amounted to ending European colonisation of

Asia and replacing it with Asia-for-the-Asians, dominated by Japan. They would be happy to include Australia and New Zealand in this grand scheme, a proposition scorned by both countries. The Japanese plan did not suit the European colonial powers either, nor did it suit the Americans. America's strategic interests would not be best served by the sudden arrival of an Asian superpower as a next-door neighbour. So Japanese ambitions were confronted with hostility all round.

The Japanese were not easily scared off. In 1931 they attacked Manchuria and set up a puppet state there, which they called Manchukuo. In 1933 they withdrew from the League of Nations. Next they withdrew from agreements entered into in Washington in 1922 and London in 1930 which limited their naval strength. They began a furious programme of shipbuilding, while doing their best to conceal its nature and strength.

In July 1937 they attacked China. By December they had taken Nanking, but the war with China remained a scrappy affair. The Chinese government of Chiang Kai-shek offered ill-organised resistance, but the Japanese never seemed able to take advantage of their opponent's feeble performance. By the end of 1938 the Chinese government had withdrawn to Chungking, and Canton and Hankow had fallen, but the war remained in an inconclusive state.

The Japanese fought a couple of battles with the USSR, at Changkufeng in 1938 and Nomonhan in 1939, but these did not add up to a war.

However tentative in its belligerence, the Japanese behaviour could not be ignored. The Americans in particular felt obliged to take action. In 1940 the United States ended its commercial treaty with Japan and imposed sanctions. President Roosevelt stopped the export of scrap iron, aviation fuel, machine tools and other war materials to Japan, and stepped up aid to China.

The Japanese responded by signing their Tripartite Pact with Germany and Italy, and followed it up with a Neutrality Pact with the Soviet Union, signed on 13 April 1941. By getting the USSR safely out of the way, Japan had eliminated the risk of war on two fronts.

They now turned their attention to the European colonies. With France and Holland defeated, and Britain fully occupied with the war against Germany, it must have seemed to the Japanese that it was now or never for the Greater East Asia Co-Prosperity Sphere. Thailand obligingly eased the way by invading French Indo-China, quickly capturing Laos from Vichy French forces. The Japanese mediated the conflict, which amounted to little more than bullying the French into handing over the disputed territories. In July 1941 the Japanese 'stationed' some 120,000 troops in Thailand and northern Indo-China. The difference between this and invasion and occupation by Japanese forces was not readily visible to the naked eye.

This was too much for Britain, America and the Dutch government in exile. They froze all Japanese assets, imposed an oil and steel embargo, and closed the Panama Canal to Japanese shipping. Japan was now cornered. It obtained 80 per cent of its oil from the United States. It had two years of oil reserves in hand, but little more than a year's oil if it had to fight a war. At some point it would have to either capitulate or find a new source. To the south lay Dutch oil and British tin and rubber. Either the Japanese went to war to seize these resources for themselves, or they withdrew and abandoned their dreams of grandeur. War looked inevitable.

Japan's strategic calculation was simple. The French had already demonstrated that they would offer no resistance. The Dutch were relatively powerless. The British, with their Singapore base and their Australian and New Zealand allies, were a more formidable problem. But to fight effectively in Asia would involve diverting resources from a war with Germany which the British were currently losing. The only serious problem was the United States, and in particular the powerful US Navy. Unless the US Pacific Fleet could be taken out of the war quickly, Japan could not hope to win.

The Commander-in-Chief of the combined Japanese fleet, Admiral Isoroku Yamamoto, was a sophisticated and cosmopolitan man. He had studied at Harvard and had a good grasp of America's strengths. He thought Japan could not win a prolonged war with America. The industrial might of the United States would inevitably prevail. He told his political masters: 'If I'm told to fight regardless of consequences, I'll run wild for the first six months or a year. I have no confidence in the second or third years.' Yamamoto therefore proposed to grab everything Japan wanted in the space of a year. After the year, the Japanese could try to reach a peace agreement with the United States which would allow them to hold on to their conquests. But the US Pacific Fleet would need to be knocked out in the first days of the war if any of this was to happen.

The Japanese set a military timetable, dictated by Yamamoto's naval requirements. The campaign would need to start before the north-east monsoon season in the South China Sea, and before the winter gales in the north Pacific. It had to be completed before the end of the Manchurian winter. So early December looked like the ideal starting date. The Japanese estimated they would need 50 days to capture the Philippines, 100 days to conquer Malaya, and 150 days to take the Dutch East Indies. The long Pacific distances would mean doubling the tonnage of shipping needed.

The Washington Naval Treaty of 1922, signed by the United States, Britain,* France, Italy and Japan, limited the build-up of naval power, but was very much confined to World War I priorities. It focused on battleships and cruisers, and to a lesser extent aircraft carriers, while saying nothing about submarines. The 1930 London Naval Treaty added submarines to the restricted list. However, the Japanese pulled out of both treaties in 1936.

The Imperial Japanese Navy was ahead of most strategic thinkers in seeing the importance of air power in future naval warfare. Its leaders set about building up a major carrier-based strike force. As well, the Japanese launched a programme of submarine-building, which included a brand-new weapon, the midget submarine, designed to penetrate

---

* It is a fair measure of Australia's subservience to Britain at this time that the Royal Australian Navy (and the Royal Canadian Navy, for that matter) was simply counted as part of the British Navy. When Britain signed the Washington Treaty and the later London Treaty, she signed on behalf of all the dominions as well as herself.

enemy harbour defences and sink ships while they lay at anchor. The navy went to great pains to keep the existence of the midget submarine force secret.

The decisive knocking-out of the American Pacific Fleet, planned for Pearl Harbor, would involve two attack forces. Carrier-based planes would strike from the air, and a small group of midget submarines would swarm around the harbour and attack from below the surface.

♦ ♦ ♦

The Japanese midget submarine force at Pearl Harbor has an almost forgotten distinction in World War II history: the first shots fired by Americans at Japanese forces on 7 December 1941 were directed at a midget submarine, and they were fired with deadly effect. Just after six in the morning on the fateful day, the target-towing ship *Antares* spotted a Japanese midget sub on its way into Pearl Harbor. The sighting was picked up by a Catalina seaplane on coastal patrol, which dropped a smoke marker, then confirmed by the destroyer USS *Ward*. At 6.45 am the destroyer opened fire with its no. 1 gun. The first shot missed. A few seconds later the *Ward* fired again with its no. 3 gun from a range of 500 metres, hitting the base of the sub's conning tower and sending it reeling. The shot sliced through the conning tower at precisely the spot where the commander, Ensign Akira Hiro-o, would have been standing. He is almost certainly the first Japanese casualty of World War II.

Ward followed up with a pattern of four depth charges, but the sub was already doomed and on its way to the bottom. The first encounter between the US Navy and the Imperial Japanese Navy at Pearl Harbor was a clear win for the Americans.

The *Ward* made frantic efforts to report the encounter to the higher command and raise a general alert. But a combination of poor communications and ill-judged scepticism meant *Ward's* messages were not taken seriously. It is doubtful if the message would have made a difference to subsequent events. However, it provided history with a nice chance to repeat itself in Sydney six months later.

Forty minutes after the *Ward's* opening shot, the planes arrived.

The devastation was terrible. Four American battleships were sunk and another four damaged. Three cruisers were damaged, and two destroyers sunk along with two other ships. A total of 188 aircraft were destroyed, mostly on the ground, and another 155 damaged. Military deaths stood at 2335, while civilian deaths totalled 68. Injuries were 1143 military and 35 civilian. Japanese losses were light: 29 planes shot down, and 55 airmen killed. No Japanese surface ships were attacked, let alone sunk.

Appalling though these losses were, Pearl Harbor was not the knockout blow Yamamoto needed. The American aircraft carrier force escaped entirely. Two were at sea on delivery runs to Midway and Wake islands, while the third had just completed a refit and was still tied up at San Diego on the American mainland. As well, an astonishing number of US ships survived unscathed in Pearl Harbor itself—five cruisers, 26 destroyers, nine submarines and 48 other ships were left undamaged, as were 47 aircraft. Not only ships and aircraft survived: the vital oil tank farms remained largely intact, as did the submarine pens, the machine shops and the port and dock facilities. The US Pacific Fleet might be in trouble, but it still had plenty of fight left in it.

The midget submarine element of the raid was a total failure. Five midgets took part, and all were lost. There was so much confusion and false alarm in the harbour that it is hard to work out, even after all this time, exactly what happened to all of them. One was certainly sunk by gunfire from USS *Ward*. One, commanded by Kazuo Sakamaki and with Kiyoshi Inagaki as crew, never made it to the battle at all. Just before their launch from the mother submarine they found their midget had an unserviceable gyro compass, essential for navigation while submerged. The crew decided to set off anyway, planning to navigate visually either on the surface or at periscope depth. This failed, and the two men repeatedly became disoriented, sometimes heading in hopelessly wrong directions. They finally made it to the entrance channel to Pearl Harbor.

By the time Sakamaki and Inagaki arrived at the harbour entrance, the Japanese air attack was in full swing, and ships in the harbour were alert and had begun to respond. The baby sub was repeatedly shot at and depth-charged, to the point where it was almost totally out of control. Sakamaki ran aground on a reef, damaging one of his two torpedoes. Pinned on the reef, he was shot at by the destroyer USS *Helm*. It may be that the *Helm*'s shells actually helped Sakamaki to break free, because he backed off the reef and submerged.

The sub now began to fill with poisonous fumes. The two men repeatedly passed out. They battled all morning, long after the bombers had departed, to bring the submarine under control. They struck another reef, and damaged their second and final torpedo. All this time they slipped in and out of consciousness. The sub drifted off the reef, still out of control. Near dawn on 8 December and over 24 hours after they launched, the tiny sub struck its final reef. With its batteries near exhaustion, there was no escape. The two crew set their demolition charge fuse burning and leapt into the sea. The fuse failed and the submarine remained intact, stranded on the reef. Inagaki drowned. His body was recovered several days later. Sakamaki made it to shore, where he found himself staring into the muzzle of a pistol held by the Japanese-American corporal David Akui, one of a five-man patrol from the nearby Bellows Field Army Air Base. Sakamaki became America's first prisoner of war in World War II.

At 8.35 am on 7 December, with the air attack 40 minutes under way, the destroyer USS *Monaghan* was on its way out of Pearl Harbor via the North Channel when it saw the seaplane tender USS *Curtiss* firing at close range at something in the water. *Monaghan* quickly identified it as a submarine. The destroyer joined the attack, firing at the sub with its no. 2 gun from a range of 1200 yards (about 1000 metres). The shot missed and instead started a fire on a derrick barge. *Monaghan* now decided a ramming attack might be less threatening to the surrounding scenery and set off at flank speed to run down the midget.

At this point the submarine counterattacked, firing a torpedo. It is not clear whether the torpedo was aimed at *Monaghan* or *Curtiss*, but it passed between them both, missing *Monaghan* by an uncomfortably narrow margin. It then exploded against Ford Island, doing no significant damage. The destroyer continued undeterred on its ramming

course while the Executive Officer, Lieutenant H.J. Verhoye ordered:
'Stand by depth charges, set on 30 feet.'

Monaghan finally closed the gap and caught the sub a glancing blow.
As the midget slid along *Monaghan's* starboard side Chief Torpedoman
G. Hardon, without waiting for orders, dropped a depth charge. Now
under orders, he dropped a second charge and prepared a third. As he
was about to drop the third charge, *Monaghan's* flank speed charge took
a disastrous turn and she ran aground on a mudbank. Thinking quickly,
Hardon abandoned the release of the third charge, knowing it would
very likely destroy his own stranded ship. Seconds later there were two
tremendous explosions off *Monaghan's* stern, followed by a massive oil
slick. The US Navy had sunk its second submarine. *Monaghan* gingerly
eased herself off the mudbank and continued towards the open sea.

The exact fate of the remaining submarines is still a mystery. Shortly
after the USS *Ward's* first shots, the destroyer USS *Chew* dropped no
fewer than 28 depth charges on submarine contacts, and claimed to
have sunk two. A navy plane claimed to have sunk another at 7 am.
At 9.50 am the destroyer USS *Blue* made three separate attacks on
submarine contacts, dropping eight depth charges, and believed it had
sunk at least one submarine. The light cruiser USS *St Louis* saw
two torpedoes racing towards it, took evading action, and saw the two
torpedoes explode on a nearby shoal, again doing no damage. The
cruiser fired at what it thought was a conning tower but recorded no
hits. Nevertheless, there were four or five claimed sinkings of two
submarines.

The submarine sunk by *Monaghan* was recovered from the harbour
bottom a few days after the attack. In 1960 US Navy divers found the
remains of a small submarine in shallow water at Keehi Lagoon, near
Pearl Harbor. It had been holed, apparently by a depth charge. The find
was mysterious in that there was no trace of the crew, who appeared to
have escaped. In 2002 the hulk of a midget was found outside the
harbour in 400 metres of water. It had a shell hole passing through
the conning tower, but was otherwise undamaged. It was almost
certainly *Ward's* submarine. The fifth submarine has never been found.

The submarine element of the Pearl Harbor raid was a catastrophe for the Japanese. All five submarines were lost, and none of their crew found their way back to the mother submarines. Worse, Japan's most secret weapon, the midget submarine, had fallen intact into American hands on the first day of the war. Sakamaki's wrecked submarine, together with the recovered submarine sunk by *Monaghan*, was an invaluable source of intelligence on this new weapon. However the Americans chose not to share this intelligence fully with their Allies, to Sydney's cost six months later.

What followed in Japan was bizarre, even by the usual standards of truth as the first casualty of war. On the evening of the raid, the Japanese mother submarine I-69 sat outside the entrance to Pearl Harbor hoping to pick off any American ships on the way out. At 9.01 pm, the captain reported that he had seen a huge fire inside the harbour, followed by heavy anti-aircraft fire. In fact what he witnessed was the shooting down of some American planes by over-zealous anti-aircraft gunners from their own side. The submarine captain interpreted it differently: he believed he had witnessed an American battleship being sunk by a midget submarine.

Meanwhile, one of the midgets, probably from the mother ship I-16, sent a message at 10.41 pm on the night of the raid using the phrase: 'Tora, tora, tora [Tiger, tiger, tiger].' This was the agreed code to notify the Japanese fleet that the raid had succeeded. The midget's message was sent almost 15 hours after the planes had first struck, and was probably intended to do no more than confirm that the air attack had indeed gone well. However it was taken as confirmation of I-69's surmise: the midget must have sunk a battleship. The midget stayed in radio contact for a further hour before lapsing into silence. Just after midnight the crew sent a final message: 'We are unable to navigate.' They were never heard from again.

The Japanese propaganda machine seized on these two garbled reports, and spun them into a gigantic myth. It began with the official Japanese communiqué describing the raid, which declared: 'Our special attacking force consisting of special submarines broke through the well-guarded entrance of Pearl Harbor. Together with our air forces they attacked the main enemy forces. The special submarines sank at least one of the *Arizona*-class battleships besides inflicting a severe blow on the enemy fleet.'*

This was the first the Japanese public knew of the Special Attack Force of midget submarines. The propaganda machine now set about converting the midget submariners into superheroes. Captain Hideo Hiraide, chief of the Imperial Japanese Navy's information department, broadcast to the whole Japanese nation: 'The unprecedented, peerless, sacrificial spirit of the attack thoroughly demonstrated the tradition of the Imperial Navy, and should be recognised as one of the greatest achievements of the outbreak of this war.' Hiraide then abandoned fact and switched to pure fiction, imagining scenes inside the submarines as the ice-cool crews lay in wait on the bottom of the harbour. The men spent the waiting hours with jigsaw puzzles, said Hiraide. They had packed lunchboxes with chocolates and soft drinks. 'It was just like going on a picnic,' he reported one as saying. Another submariner recited a poem as he lay in wait, including the line: 'I heard Roosevelt whimpering before the King of Hell.' This was all nonsense, and the Japanese navy well knew it, but it worked.

The nine sailors who had died were deified as war gods, the highest level of acclaim available to Japanese warriors. They became the subjects of endless newspaper articles; professors of literature called for books to

---

* In 1998 the US Naval Institute's magazine *Naval History* published an elaborate article arguing that one of the submarines had successfully fired torpedoes at the USS *Oklahoma* and the USS *West Virginia*. The evidence for this came from a digitally enhanced photograph taken by one of the crew of a Japanese Kate bomber flying over the harbour. However, the case for this is thin: the image itself was built from a newspaper print, with all the dubious quality this implies. The 'conning tower' in the photograph might just as easily be a piece of lint, or an ink smudge. There were hundreds of eyewitnesses to the original attack, and none reported seeing this submarine. The photograph purports to show evidence that the sub's propellers had broached the surface, but the 'rooster tail' effect could just as easily come from the propellers of air-launched torpedoes. The highest probability is that no torpedoes were fired successfully by the midget submarines taking part in the Pearl Harbor attack.

be written honouring their deeds, and had their prayers answered with a novel turned into a film; they were likened to cherry blossoms, the spirit of Japan. The myth-making got so out of hand that newspers began to imply that the midget submarines and not the planes had been the spearhead of the attack. The sinking of the *Arizona* by the submarines became an unchallengeable fact, to the point where one Japanese newspaper felt able to write: 'The Navy Eagles [i.e. the pilots of the raiding aircraft] saw the *Arizona* go down and knew at once that the daring underwater attack by the death-defying corps had borne fruit. They held death at bay until they fulfilled the task that went a long way towards changing the map of the Pacific.'

This particular nonsense was too much for the pilots. They knew exactly what had happened to the *Arizona*. It had been sunk by high-flying 'horizontal'—in other words, not dive—bombers, and there were plenty of witnesses to this fact. More woundingly, the nine dead submariners had been posthumously promoted two ranks and raised to the status of war gods. The 55 airmen who died had been promoted only one rank, and none was considered a war god. Lieutenant-Commander Mitsuo Fuchida, who led the first wave of planes over Pearl Harbor, complained bitterly about this injustice and issued an ultimatum: 'The air force cannot co-operate in future operations under this one-sided treatment.' Fuchida got his way. The 55 were belatedly promoted two ranks instead of one. However, they were never elevated to war gods.

The midget submarine raid on Pearl Harbor also led to one of the oddest stories of the war. Kazuo Sakamaki, the submariner who swam to shore after his submarine was wrecked, felt abjectly ashamed of his surrender. While a prisoner of war he repeatedly asked to be allowed to commit suicide, the proper destiny for a Japanese warrior. He was, of course, refused. When he was repatriated to Japan in 1946, he was vilified. He received hate mail, including the repeated suggestion that it was not too late for him now to take the honourable course and end his life. Instead he married and moved to Sao Paulo in Brazil, where he lived for 42 years. He became president of the Brazilian branch of the Toyota motor company. In 1983 he returned to Japan and a more sympathetic reception.

♦ ♦ ♦

The Pearl Harbor attack was the start of Australia's worst nightmare. For the first time in 160 years of European settlement, Australia was directly threatened. The fury of the Japanese follow-up was devastating. Australia's entire defensive strategy depended on the merged British and Australian navies retaining control of the seas around Australia. Even before Pearl Harbor, Churchill had agreed to meet the Japanese threat by reinforcing Singapore with two of Britain's most up-to-date battle cruisers, the *Prince of Wales* and the *Repulse*. Japanese planes sank them both on 10 December 1941, two days after Pearl Harbor. (The International Dateline's position in mid-Pacific meant that the Pearl Harbor raid took place on 8 December, Singapore time, not 7 December.)

On 8 December, Japan attacked the Philippines, Hong Kong and Malaya. By 10 December they had captured Guam. On 11 December they attacked Burma. Hong Kong surrendered on 18 December. Wake Island fell on 23 December.

The new Australian government watched this with horror and incredulity. Their attitudes and Churchill's could not have been further apart. Churchill made no secret of his delight with Pearl Harbor. Now America had joined the war and would tip the balance. Roosevelt and Churchill had already agreed on a policy, should Japan enter the war, which was popularly rendered as 'beat Hitler first'. Churchill later wrote of the American entry into the war: 'Hitler's fate was sealed. Mussolini's fate was sealed. As for the Japanese, they would be ground to powder.' But later, of course.

From Australia's point of view, a beat-Hitler-first policy amounted to a half-hearted holding operation in the Pacific while the two great powers focused their attention on the Atlantic. Australia welcomed America's entry into the war, but for entirely different reasons. It was increasingly apparent that Britain could not, never mind would not, defend Australia against the Japanese. Only America could. On 27 December Curtin published an historic article in the Melbourne *Herald*. The article was mostly directed at telling Australians that beating Japan would require immense effort and sacrifice from every Australian. However, it contained some historic declarations, and it is worth quoting from it more fully than usual. Curtin wrote:

> We refuse to accept the dictum that the Pacific struggle must be treated as a subordinate segment of the general conflict. By that it is not meant that any one of the other theatres of war is of less importance than the Pacific, but that Australia asks for a concerted plan evoking the greatest strength at the Democracies' disposal, determined upon hurling Japan back.
>
> The Australian Government regards the Pacific struggle as primarily one in which the United States and Australia must have the fullest say in the direction of the democracies' fighting plan.
>
> Without any inhibitions of any kind, I make it quite clear that Australia looks to America, free of any pangs as to our traditional links or kinship with the United Kingdom.
>
> We know the problems that the United Kingdom faces. We know the constant threat of invasion. We know the dangers of dispersal of strength, but we know too, that Australia can go and Britain can still hold on.
>
> Summed up, Australian external policy will be shaped toward obtaining Russian aid, and working out, with the United States, as the major factor, a plan of Pacific strategy, along with British, Chinese and Dutch forces.

This brought something akin to an audible gasp from the entire Australian population. The *Sydney Morning Herald* called the article 'deplorable' (while republishing it in full). Curtin's assertion that Australia looks to America is the most quoted line. But the whole thrust of the article was remarkably radical. Japan was not merely to be contained but to be hurled back. Australia and America, not Britain and

America, would direct the Pacific war. The British, the Chinese and the Dutch could tag along if they liked, but Australia and America would be the major players.

The implications were enormous. No longer would the Australian Navy, in Menzies' phrase, be placed at the disposal of the British Admiralty. Australian ships would fight where the American and Australian governments wanted them, and if that meant in Pacific seas rather than the Mediterranean, so be it. Australian soldiers would be deployed in defence of the homeland if their government required it. Australian and American airmen, equipped with modern aircraft, would take the air war to Japan.

It was a bold strategy, but if the intention was to send a warning to the Japanese that life would be different from now on, the Japanese showed no signs of taking notice. Their relentless advance continued unchecked. On 11 January 1942 they attacked the Dutch East Indies. They swarmed through Malaya, rolling back the Australian 8th Division as well as the Indian and British armies. Nothing and nobody seemed able to stop them. The military situation in Asia went from tranquil to desperate in the space of five weeks.

The Allies had always underestimated Japanese capabilities. The briefings given to Allied troops on the Japanese threat were a mixture of infantile racism and groundless optimism. They were told the Japanese were puny, myopic, afraid of the dark and badly armed. All of this was not only wrong, but dangerously wrong. The Japanese understood the use of air power better than their enemies, and capped this with better equipment. The Zero fighter made mincemeat of the outdated aircraft trying to block its path.

The Japanese on the ground employed superior tactics. They improvised, using small tanks and even bicycles. The statistics of the campaign were simply horrific. The normal military calculation is that, to be confident of success, an invading force needs to outnumber the defence by about three to one. In Malaya and Singapore, 60,000 Japanese defeated 130,000 British, Indian and Australian troops. Not just defeated: routed. Far from being afraid of the dark, the Japanese used darkness to encircle the Allied defence positions, racing confidently through the jungle. The writer and journalist Russell Braddon, then a 21-year-old gunner with the Australians in Malaya, noted bitterly after the war: 'We would have done much better had we been armed as the Japanese were armed, supported in the air as they were supported, led as they were led, and motivated as they were motivated.'

Not only that, the local Asian populations did not exactly rush to take the side of their colonial masters. The Japanese promised a Greater East Asia Co-Prosperity Sphere, with a bonus of Asia-for-the-Asians. Well, why not? Large sections of the local populations watched the war with impartial interest, in the spirit of the polite stranger beside you in the bar who offers to hold your coat while you join in the bar brawl.

By 24 January the Australian government saw the situation as out of control. Worse, they had been told by Earl Page, their representative in London, that the British were considering abandoning Singapore. This went beyond heresy. Singapore was the most potent symbol of British power and presence in the Far East. Curtin cabled Churchill: 'After all the reassurances we have been given, the evacuation of Singapore would be regarded here and elsewhere as an inexcusable betrayal.'

Curtin asked for immediate transfer to the RAAF of '250 aircraft of the Tomahawk, Hurricane II or similar type'. His exasperated tone was plain. 'It is impossible to expect us to give effective resistance with the inadequate aircraft at our disposal,' he cabled.

Within Australia, invasion fever mounted, stoked by the government. They produced a propaganda poster showing an ugly and terrifying Japanese soldier, bayonet at the ready, trampling the world underfoot. Above him was the caption: 'HE'S COMING SOUTH.' Advertisements appeared in Australian newspapers with a mass of black arrows thrusting down a map of Asia, and a headline 'The spearhead reaches SOUTH, ALWAYS SOUTH.' The advertisement urged Australians to end strikes and lockouts, avoid wasting money, food or precious petrol, and generally to give their all to the war.

Men who had hesitated to volunteer while the war was being fought in the Middle East now rushed to join up. Again, the story of my own family is typical. My father's two unmarried brothers had urged him, as a married man with family responsibilities, to stay home. In January 1942 he decided that Sydney was too close to the invading Japanese for my mother and five-months-old me. The three of us travelled by train to my Nan's house in Adelaide, where my mother and I were told to stay put until the war ended. My father enlisted in the army on 3 February 1942 at Collinswood in South Australia, naming my mother as next of kin. He was then 30 years old, and I had a long wait ahead of me for my first birthday.

◆   ◆   ◆

The author James Leasor's excellent book on the fall of Singapore is sub-titled: *The Battle that Changed the World*. It was no exaggeration. The fall of Singapore marked the end of white supremacy in Asia, the end of British naval power in the Far East, and the end of British superpower status south of the Equator. The *Sydney Morning Herald* editorial, headed 'Singapore and Australia' was graphic: 'Singapore has been to this country what the Maginot Line was in France—and in the hour of crisis it has no less tragically failed us.'

For a battle with such far-reaching consequences, it has attracted its fair share of myths, of which the most enduring is that Singapore fell because the guns were facing the wrong way. The truth is simpler. The guns that mattered were not the south-facing shore batteries but those mounted on British ships. And the British ships that mattered were at the bottom of the ocean, sunk by Japanese aircraft on the second day of the Pacific war. Singapore was never intended to be defended from land attack: the plan was to have the all-powerful Royal Navy prevent any landing. With the navy shattered, Singapore became indefensible. Churchill knew this, hence his weighing up of the possibility of with-drawing from Singapore with minimum losses.

With hindsight, Curtin would have been better advised to accept Churchill's proposal. To the Australian government, however, this would have been a grotesque betrayal of a solemn British promise made only weeks earlier. On 7 December 1941, the day before Pearl Harbor, the

British Minister in the Far East, Duff Cooper, had told the Australian War Cabinet: 'It has always been the intention of the United Kingdom government to reinforce the Far East, and they are prepared to abandon the Mediterranean altogether if this is necessary to hold Singapore.' The Australians insisted that the British keep their promise and defend Singapore to the end, and Churchill reluctantly agreed.

Singapore fell on 15 February 1942. For Australia this was the worst news yet in a war which brought no shortage of bad news. Apart from the 1789 Australian dead and 1306 wounded in the defence of Singapore, some 15,395 troops from Australia's 8th Division were taken prisoner. The Japanese had a well-deserved reputation for treating prisoners harshly. What fate awaited these men? They were the main land force intended to block Japan's southward thrust, and now they were gone. It seemed as though nobody and nothing stood between the Japanese and invasion of Australia.

Three days later, the Japanese confirmed these worst fears. They bombed Darwin twice. This was the first time since European colonisation that Australia itself had been attacked. Wars, it seemed, were no longer fought overseas. Contemporary newsreels did their best to conceal the extent of the carnage and the inadequacy of the defences. The commentary talked of Japanese planes being handed no end of a lesson by the anti-aircraft batteries. But the footage which accompanied this travesty showed burning docks, airfields and buildings, and no burning or crashing Japanese aircraft. The public were not fooled. The newspapers were heavily censored, so Australians were unable to read the full story of the numbers of dead and wounded, nor were they told of looting, desertion and near anarchy immediately after the attack. It was a shameful episode in Australia's history. The lurid rumours which spread south did nothing to boost the already sagging morale of the civilian population.

How was Australia to be defended now? The answer from the grand strategists in London and Washington was that two divisions of US combat troops were on their way to Australia, and that should be sufficient. This did not satisfy Curtin. As far back as 15 December

Churchill had put it to his chiefs of staff that one of the two and a half Australian divisions in the Middle East should be switched to the defence of Singapore. On 3 January the British formally requested the Australian government to allow two Australian divisions to be transferred from the Middle East to the new Far East command ABDA (standing for American, British, Dutch and Australian forces). The Australians quickly agreed. Both divisions would go to Java in the Dutch East Indies. In all 64,000 Australian troops would be moved, between January and April 1942.

The first eight ships had already sailed when the Australian cabinet began to have second thoughts. Australia's generals advised that, without control of either air or sea, the Dutch territory could not be held. Better to bring the boys home.

What followed is now the stuff of legend. On 15 February, the day Singapore fell, Curtin cabled Churchill requesting that the troops be diverted to Australia. Churchill replied with a request that they be diverted to Rangoon. He did not tell Curtin that he had already ordered some of the ships to Rangoon. Simultaneously, Churchill cabled Roosevelt asking him to put pressure on Curtin to switch the troops to the defence of Burma. To the fury of both Churchill and Roosevelt, Curtin stood his ground. For five days blistering cables flew backwards and forwards between Churchill, Roosevelt and Curtin. In the end, Curtin had his way. The ships turned back from Rangoon. The boys could come home.*

◆　　◆　　◆

The rampaging Japanese continued their drive south and east. They attacked the Dutch East Indies. The newly formed ABDA determined to

---

* In fact they largely stayed overseas. Some went to Java, as originally planned, where they were promptly captured by the Japanese. Others remained in Ceylon, ready to defend India if the need arose. The 9th Division, including my Uncle Jim, remained in Syria until 1943. By the end of June 1942, half of Australia's land forces were still deployed west of Singapore. Nevertheless, Curtin had made his point.

stop them before they seized Java, the last remaining Allied stronghold. A large naval force, under Dutch command and incorporating Dutch, British, American and Australian ships, set off to intercept the Japanese troopships. On 27 February the two navies clashed in the Java Sea. It was a catastrophe for ABDA. They lost five cruisers and five destroyers sunk, with 2300 sailors killed. The Japanese lost four troop transports, but their fighting ships emerged almost totally unscathed. It was the biggest naval engagement since the Battle of Jutland in World War I, and the Allies had lost it badly. With its defeat at the Battle of the Java Sea, ABDA lost all credibility. However, the Americans had lost only three ships, the cruiser USS *Houston* and two destroyers. It was a dreadful loss, but it was not the decisive defeat of the US Pacific Fleet which Yamamoto needed.

On the home front in Australia, invasion fever was now endemic. The Japanese kept it well stoked by continuing their air assault on northern Australian towns. They bombed Broome and Wyndham on 3 March, and Katherine on 22 March. In the major cities there were air-raid drills. Blackouts were enforced. Brown paper covered windows. Festoons of barbed wire appeared on beaches. Gun emplacements sprang up on headlands and hills. Sirens were tested. Searchlights roamed the night sky. Newspapers carried 'Know Your Japanese Planes' features.

The reality of war began to hit home. At school assemblies, head-masters read out the names of past pupils killed in action. Shocked schoolboys listened numbly while the cricket captain of only two years ago, someone they had idolised, joined the ranks of the dead or missing. They itched to join the war and wreak revenge. Meanwhile, potatoes were scarce. Petrol was rationed. So was tea.

Jim Macken was a 14-year-old schoolboy at Sydney's St Ignatius College, popularly known as Riverview. He remembers:

All of us were in the cadets. We had a full armoury underneath the school. We had live ammunition and all the rifles. Everybody lived for the cadets. School holidays were spent in army camps. Nobody expected anything other than that the Japanese would sooner or later arrive.

Old boys who were already in the army would come back to the school and on cadet parade they'd give us some idea of military training. They were looked on as local heroes. They were in the real thing.

The relentless Japanese advance continued unabated. Batavia fell on 2 March. The Japanese penetrated the Indian Ocean, bombing Ceylon on 4 April. On 9 April the Americans surrendered in Bataan. Mandalay fell on 1 May. Corregidor followed on 6 May, with 12,000 Americans taken prisoner.

American troops poured into Australia. Their guns, planes and ships were welcome. So were their bulging pay packets and gifts of nylon stockings. Australian women found them polite, even gallant, a sharp contrast with rough Australian male manners. With touching enthusiasm though little regard for political correctness, the Americans returned the warm feelings. Private George Huffman from the US Army told the Sydney *Daily Telegraph:* 'I come from God's own country and I arrived in this burg expecting to find niggers and kangaroos. I found a bunch of fine people instead.'

Churchill and Roosevelt agreed that Britain would control the European war, while America controlled the Pacific war. This suited Curtin. In March 1942 he asked that the politically well-connected General Douglas MacArthur, recently escaped from the Philippines, be appointed Supreme Commander of Allied Forces in the South-West Pacific, and based in Australia. Roosevelt agreed. Australian troops would be placed under MacArthur's command. Australia now unambiguously 'looked to America'.

MacArthur arrived in Darwin on 17 March and travelled by train to a hero's welcome at Flinders Street station in Melbourne. Australia's war role was now taking shape. It would be a barracks, a farm, a harbour and an airfield. Essentially it would be a secure base from which the Americans could mount a counterattack on Japanese positions.

This did not suit the Japanese. In truth the Japanese had no plans to invade Australia. In MacArthur's less than flattering appraisal, 'spoils here are not sufficient to warrant the risk'. However, Yamamoto still needed to finish off the American Pacific Fleet. He could not allow it a secure base in Australia, within striking distance of Japan's fresh conquests. Japan continued to have naval and air superiority, and he was spoiling for a fight.

Yamamoto agreed that the next Japanese move would be an invasion of Port Moresby. With New Guinea secured, Australia would be isolated. The Japanese could use the New Guinea base to block American supply routes, in effect forcing them back from their safe base in the south. Australia would be forced out of the war. Yamamoto assembled his invasion fleet. If this lured the American Pacific Fleet into battle, so much the better.

That part of Yamamoto's plan succeeded. Armed with intelligence warnings of the Japanese fleet movements, a combined fleet of American, Australian and British ships raced north to block the invaders. Between 6 and 8 May, the two fleets clashed in the Coral Sea. It was a battle unique in all naval history: neither fleet saw the other. It was fought entirely by carrier-based aircraft. For two days carrier planes flew strike and counterstrike. At the end, the Japanese withdrew, abandoning their invasion of Port Moresby.

Both sides thought they had won. Captain Hiraide, of Pearl Harbor and midget submarine fame, took to the airwaves again in Japan. He told the populace that America and her allies had suffered a crushing defeat. Such were the losses that the United States was now a third-rate power. General MacArthur was a nervous wreck. The *Japan Times and Advertiser* added: 'The effect of the terrible setback in the Coral Sea is indeed beyond description. A state of mania is prevalent in the American munitions fields.' General Tojo, the Prime Minister, weighed in by telling the Japanese parliament that Australia was now 'the orphan of the Pacific'.

The Americans were equally vocal in claiming victory. The *New York Times* headlined its report: 'Japanese Repulsed in Great Pacific Battle'. In Sydney, the *Sunday Sun* crowed on 10 May: 'Jap Fleet Beaten Off— Invasion Armada Smashed in Coral Sea Battle'. The *Sunday Sun's* war correspondent Norman Stockton began his story: 'A full-scale attempt to invade Australia has been turned aside.' This was nonsense, of course, since the Japanese target was Port Moresby, not Australia. However Stockton's report fitted in with the anxieties of the times. On page 2, the *Sun* continued its crowing under the headline: 'America Throbs with Excitement Over Naval Victory'.

The truth was, as usual, different. The Battle of the Coral Sea ended, to use a sporting metaphor, as a score draw. The Americans lost the aircraft carrier USS *Lexington*, a destroyer and an oiler, as well as taking some damage to their second aircraft carrier USS *Yorktown*. The Japanese lost a light carrier, a destroyer and some smaller ships. The aircraft carrier *Shokaku* received serious bomb damage and her sister carrier *Zuikaku*'s air group was badly depleted. The Japanese sank a greater tonnage of American ships than they lost themselves. However, the Japanese lost more aircraft and took more casualties. Strategically, they lost the battle: Port Moresby was not invaded, the American Pacific Fleet had been brought to battle and not crushed. For the first time since the Pacific war began five months earlier, the Imperial Japanese Navy did not run wild.

The battle-scarred ships of America and Australia steamed back to port. The American cruiser USS *Chicago* and its destroyer escort USS *Perkins* headed for Sydney, along with the Australian cruiser HMAS *Canberra*. They returned to a heroes' welcome. Both ships and their crews would rest up and refit, before returning to the fray. They could reassure themselves with the knowledge that there was no safer place in the Pacific to rest up than Sydney Harbour.

Chapter 4

Rather peculiar instruction

Reg Andrew came from a long line of sea captains—eight generations, in fact. But he had chosen not to follow the family tradition: at the time he enlisted in the Royal Australian Navy he was the shore-based manager of a Woolworths store in the Sydney suburb of Mosman.

He might easily have chosen the Royal Australian Air Force ahead of the navy. He was an experienced and talented pilot, and had worked as a flying instructor in the aviation business set up by the legendary Charles Kingsford-Smith. The call of the sea proved too strong, however, and on 23 March 1942 he volunteered for the navy.

Despite the flying and the shore job, he had not cut himself off entirely from the sea. With his two brothers he had formed the Manly Sailing Club, which specialised in 16-foot skiffs. At one stage Reg had been state secretary of the 16-foot Skiff Association of New South Wales. Like all keen sailors, he got to know Sydney Harbour well. However, he had no naval experience, and no experience with motor launches, on the day he volunteered. He was 32 years old, and he intended to apply for torpedo patrol boats, which operated in the North Sea, Atlantic and Mediterranean. This would involve a training course at Flinders Naval College in Victoria, then further training in England.

In long taped interviews, recorded in 1977 and 1978, he described the initial training at Flinders as 'rather peculiar instruction'. The entire course lasted only six weeks. Great slabs of precious time were taken up with the navy's biggest 6-inch guns—how to lay them, how to fire them, and how to call the numbers. By the end of six weeks Reg could have pulled a 6-inch gun apart and put it back together again like a seasoned professional. This might have been useful to an officer on a 30,000-ton battleship, but it had no relevance for anyone on a 42-day crash course leading to command of an armed motor launch.

Signal training was a particularly sore point. 'We were supposed to spend a week in signal class at Flinders,' he recalled. 'On the Monday morning the Chief Petty Officer got up in front of the class and he said: "I can't teach you anything. A rating has to be here for 18 months before we allow him to go on the bridge of a warship. You've only got a week. Don't make a noise. I'll be in the next room if you want me. Knock on the wall." The whole week was spent doing our own thing. We signalled to ourselves, and we carried on our own class.'

They were taught about torpedoes. By the end of the course they could recite the number of links on a chain to drop a mine. They learned about all the pistols in the navy since Nelson's day. None of it was remotely relevant. Reg Andrew could expect his first command to be a patrol boat armed with a .303 Vickers machine-gun and anti-submarine depth charges.

The Vickers was not exactly a state-of-the-art weapon. It first went into service with the British Army in 1912. It so happens that I trained on a Vickers in the school cadet corps back in the 1950s. I remember it as a bad-tempered beast, with 13 different ways to jam. We beginners had to learn to strip the complicated lock and reassemble it quickly, as well as learning to work out how and why it jammed. At our annual training camps we were each allowed to fire a 250-round belt of live ammunition, which was great fun though it can't have contributed much to Australia's future defence. Reg Andrew's training consisted of walking past a stand with a Vickers mounted on it and being told: that's a Vickers machine-gun. At the end of his six weeks at Flinders he had no instruction on handling depth charges. He had never even seen a depth charge fired, except in the movies. For someone about to take command of a fighting ship in a shooting war, he could have had better weapon training with me in the Barker College cadets.

♦   ♦   ♦

The defences of Sydney Harbour concentrated, perfectly sensibly, on keeping an enemy out. Nevertheless, the navy had not entirely overlooked the possibility of an enemy getting into the harbour itself. Large warships would be unsuitable to counter this threat—they need plenty of room to manoeuvre. So the navy relied on a fleet of 12 converted luxury launches, mostly built by the Halvorsen yard in Sydney. The conversion involved mounting a Vickers on the deck, and strapping depth charges to the stern. Some of the boats were fitted with ASDIC anti-submarine detection gear. These were known as Channel Patrol boats. They were crewed by full-time Royal Australian Navy sailors, often men who had seen action overseas and were sent back to Australia for rest and recuperation. Some, like the motor mechanics, were newly trained and did a spell on the Channel Patrol boats before moving on to larger fighting ships. The commanding officer was often fresh out of Flinders Naval College. The navy viewed the Channel Patrol boats as a safe enough place for a newly graduated officer to build up experience.

The navy had a second group of converted motor launches at its command inside Sydney Harbour. These were not requisitioned: they were offered up freely by their owners for navy use. The owner usually continued as skipper, and the crew were volunteers. *Lauriana* was typical. It was owned and skippered by Harold Arnott of Arnott's Biscuits fame.

This second group was known collectively as the Naval Auxiliary Patrol, contemptuously dismissed as 'Nap-Naps' or 'Nappies'. As their official name implied, they were patrol vessels rather than fighting ships. In May 1942 they were all unarmed. The whole collection of small boats, with their crisp-uniformed crews and vaguely effete luxury launch aura, were known derisively as the 'Hollywood Fleet'. The regular navy regarded them all as weekend sailors, not to be taken seriously.

The formation of the Hollywood Fleet led to endless rows over money. The story of *Sea Mist* is typical. She was one of the larger boats, 60 feet (18 metres) long and weighing 35 tons, built in 1939 by Lars Halvorsen and Sons in Sydney. *Sea Mist* was requisitioned by the navy on 17 June 1941. She was owned by the racing-car driver Hope Bartlett, who valued her at £5500. Lloyds valued her at £4000. The navy would not budge from £4000. After months of wrangling Bartlett and the legal owner of the boat, a hire-purchase company called Automobile and General Finance, had to back down. Bartlett claimed for the cost of petrol bringing *Sea Mist* from Huskisson, on the New South Wales South Coast, to Garden Island in Sydney—166 gallons at two shillings and seven pence a gallon, a total of £21.8.10. The navy painstakingly calculated that the boat would have used 48 gallons at 8 knots or roughly 80 gallons at 10 knots. In the laborious, handwritten Register of Requisitioned Motor Patrol Boats and Miscellaneous Examination Vessels and Harbour Craft, an anonymous Royal Australian Naval hand opined: '80 gallons appears to be a fairly generous allowance for the trip.' That particular row rumbled on for 10 months. The navy eventually paid £10.6.8—the cost of 80 gallons of petrol at 1941 prices.

Money raised different issues at the Naval Auxiliary Patrol. They were crewed by volunteers, who actually paid for the privilege of serving. They handed over ten shillings to enrol in the NAP, and paid a subscription of a shilling a week. The navy paid for any alterations to the boats when converting them to military use, and paid for fuel and oil while on duty, but no more. The volunteer crews were expected to dip into their own pockets for the rest. Crews were required to pay for their own uniforms, for instance. Service in the Naval Auxiliary Patrol was open to men who met three conditions: they should not be of military age; they should know something of the ways of the sea; and they should be prepared to give up their spare time to patrol activities. They were a Dad's Navy, but they would be right in the front line if the war ever found its way into Sydney Harbour.

When Reg Andrew graduated from Flinders Naval College as a fully fledged Lieutenant in the Royal Australian Navy, he returned to Sydney to await a posting. After a few weeks of nothing to do, he was told his first command would be the Channel Patrol boat *Sea Mist*.

♦   ♦   ♦

Even before Pearl Harbor, Yamamoto had ordered his Special Attack Force of midget submariners to study charts of Singapore, Sydney and Suva harbours. At the time of Pearl Harbor, the crews were told Singapore would be next. However, the speed of the Japanese advance dictated a change of plan. By early February 1942, it was clear Singapore would fall soon. The Imperial Japanese Navy looked around for new places to strike.

The Japanese had beaten the world with the creation of a remarkable weapon: a reconnaissance aircraft which could be launched from a submarine. The British, French and Italian navies had all dabbled with the idea. The Japanese made it work. The two-seater, single-engined Yokosuka E14Y Glen seaplane and its launching system were major technical achievements. The Japanese adapted some of their large 'I' class submarines by extending the conning tower forward, to create a watertight hangar space for a folded Glen. They then built an aircraft catapult which could be mounted on the foredeck of the submarine. A Glen could be dragged out of its hangar and assembled in as little as 10 minutes. It could be ready for launch in under an hour.

Take off was every pilot's worst nightmare, particularly at night. Unlike an aircraft carrier, even a large submarine's deck is only 2 or 3 metres above sea level. So every launch began with the aircraft perilously close to the water, giving the pilot little or no time to get himself out of trouble if anything went wrong. Worse, there was a delay between the pilot's order to fire the catapult and the moment when the aircraft actually took to the air. An aircraft fired from a catapult cannot be pointed up at too steep an angle or gravity will eat into the airspeed, and the plane will stall and crash. On the other hand, if the angle is too shallow then the aircraft will fire straight into the water at full catapult speed, with disastrous results. So the pilots had to time the order to launch to perfection: sit on the catapult with the engine roaring at full throttle, wait until the bow was plunging down towards its lowest point, then call; in the second or so delay before they were airborne, hope that the next wave would swing the bow up from the water but not too far. Then go. Get it right and bingo, they were flying. Get it wrong and they were in the water with 2500 tons of submarine charging down on them from behind.

The search for profitable new targets for midget submarine attack began in early February 1942. The Japanese mother submarine I-25 with a Glen stowed aboard arrived off Sydney on Saturday, 14 February, the day before Singapore fell. The captain, Lieutenant Commander Tagami, brought his sub close enough to Sydney to see the searchlights in the distance. But seas were too rough to launch the Glen, so he retreated 160 kilometres east and waited for better weather.

By Monday night the seas had calmed down, and Tagami agreed to a reconnaissance flight. Just after sunset on 16 February he brought the I-25 back closer to Sydney, and checked by periscope that all was clear. The submarine surfaced in darkness, recharged its batteries and refreshed its air supply. The Glen was assembled after midnight and at about 4.30 am on 17 February, with Warrant Flying Officer Nobuo Fujita at the controls and Petty Officer Second Class Shoji Okuda as observer, it took off. They timed the flight to bring them back to the submarine just after sunrise.

The Glen was not an ideal observation plane. Its wings were low rather than high, blocking large areas of view from the cockpit. Allied reconnaissance seaplanes like the Catalina had high wings, giving the pilot and observer a better look down. The Glen cruised at 90 knots— about the same speed as the slower training aircraft used at flying clubs today. So it was a sitting duck for any anti-aircraft battery. It carried a light machine-gun, operated from the rear cockpit by the observer, but this would have been close to useless against even a Wirraway fighter.

Neither anti-aircraft fire nor enemy fighters presented Fujita with any problems that morning. The two airmen crossed the Australian coast at

La Perouse on the southern outskirts of Sydney, flying comparatively high at 8000 feet. They dropped down to 3000 feet to avoid some cloud, heading west across Botany Bay past Sydney's main airport at Mascot. After crossing the bay they turned north-west in the direction of Parramatta, still with no response from the Sydney defences. Fujita's track must have taken him close to Bankstown, which at this stage was a military airfield. For the last two days this had been the home of the Kittyhawk fighters of the US Army Air Forces' 7th Pursuit Squadron, the 'Screamin' Demons'. Nobody screamed. Nobody even stirred.*

Fujita now turned north towards the Sydney suburb of Ryde then tracked back east over Artarmon and Northbridge, with a clear view of the harbour on his right. Okuda, the observer, counted 23 ships in the harbour, including a large three-funnel warship, two destroyers and five submarines. Sydney was clearly a worthy target. Fujita continued east, still unmolested, and crossed the coast at North Head. He had some trouble finding the mother submarine, but eventually succeeded. The Glen landed safely on the water and was hoisted onto the I-25 and stowed.

Tagami now took the I-25 south. He cruised down the east coast of Tasmania and back up the west coast, fighting bad weather most of the way. He prowled around in Bass Strait, waiting for the right moment for a Glen flight over Melbourne. On 26 February conditions were right and Fujita and Okuda took off again. They followed the coastline to the Point Lonsdale lighthouse at the entrance to Port Phillip Bay and then at 5000 feet turned north-east towards Melbourne. Thick cloud now blocked Okuda's view, so Fujita dropped down through the murk, unsure of his position. He broke cloud at 1000 feet, plumb above Laverton air base, home to Melbourne's fighter defences. This time he

---

* As a footnote to history, the 7th Pursuit Squadron is still active today. It went through a succession of name changes, and is now known as the 7th Combat Training Squadron. It specialises in training pilots for the F-117A 'Stealth' fighter programme. It could fairly claim to have been one of the earliest USAF squadrons to see stealth tactics up close.

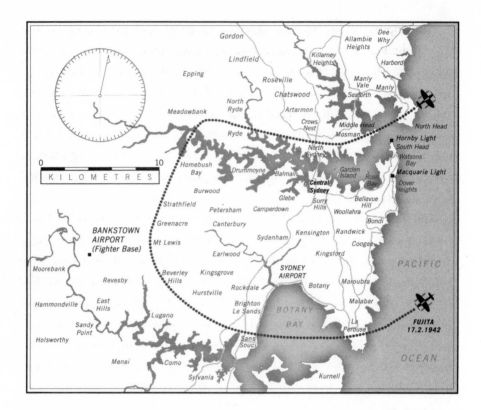

Fujita's track reconnoitring Sydney is fairly well established. He crossed the Australian coast at La Perouse, flying at about 8000 feet, then descended to 3000 feet with Sydney Airport on his right. He crossed the Botany Bay coast near Brighton le Sands, and shortly afterwards turned north-west in the direction of Parramatta. He may or may not have known that this track took him close to Bankstown fighter air base. He then turned right, towards Ryde, before turning back towards the main area of interest— Sydney Harbour. He flew along the north shore of the harbour, passing over Artarmon and Middle Head while getting a good sight of 23 ships in the harbour, before crossing the Australian coast again at North Head.

was spotted. Two fighter aircraft scrambled, but Fujita climbed into the cloud and disappeared.

Fujita now kept popping down into clear air to take a look around, then climbing back into the cloud to hide. One of his sorties below cloud took him into the open over the Williamstown anti-aircraft battery. Again, he was spotted. Instead of opening fire, the Lieutenant in charge responded by telephoning headquarters for permission. By the time he had an answer, Fujita had disappeared back into the cloud again. The Glen flew over the suburbs of St Kilda, Brighton and Frankston, with a clear view of Melbourne's port. Okuda counted 19 ships. More significantly, he counted six warships in single file heading in to Port Melbourne. So Melbourne had possibilities, too. Fujita and Okuda landed safely at the rendezvous point near Cape Wickham lighthouse, hoisted their aircraft back aboard the submarine, and I–25 headed south again.

On 1 March Fujita and Okuda flew over Hobart. They saw five merchant ships but no warships. This time the Glen damaged a wingtip while being hoisted back onto the submarine, but the crew managed to repair it, if roughly. I–25 crossed the Tasman Sea to New Zealand. On 8 March Fujita and Okuda flew over Wellington Harbour. On 13 March they flew over Auckland Harbour. I–25 now turned its attention to Fiji. On 18 March the Glen reconnoitered Suva Harbour. Throughout the entire odyssey not a single shot was fired at it. His mission complete, Tagami turned the I–25 north for home and to report.

♦   ♦   ♦

In April 1942, with the disaster at Pearl Harbor five months behind them, crews from the Special Attack Force of midget submariners intensified their training at home in Japan, readying themselves for the next operation. Submariners always believe they are the elite in any navy, and these were the elite of the elite. They were what we would now call special forces in the tradition of the SAS, Special Boat Squadron, Delta Force, Spetznaz. In Japanese they were known as *Tokubetsu Ko-geki-tai*, reduced to *Toku-tai*. All were graduates of the three-year course at the Imperial Naval Academy, on the island of Eta Jima in the Inland Sea. They were selected for the midget submarine programme on the basis of courage, discipline and skill. They needed to be lightly built yet supremely fit, with plenty of stamina. They were unlikely to be chosen if they were married, or the eldest son: their chances of returning from a mission were slight. They were sworn to secrecy. Not even their immediate family could be told of the special weapon.

Midget submarine training began in April 1941 at the Kure Naval Arsenal. First the crews were taught weapon handling and tactics. In May they moved to the seaplane tender *Chiyoda*, where they trained in the release of submarines from a mother ship. In June they switched to Mitsukue Bay, still in Japan, where they learned to handle torpedoes.

At this stage the men paired off into crews, and each crew stayed together for the rest of the training period, and into battle. The two-man crew consisted of a senior officer, who gave helm and firing orders, operated the periscope and decided course, speed and depth, and a petty officer who operated the helm, the valves for diving and surfacing, the sliding weights for balancing and trimming the submarine, and the torpedo firing trigger.

The men were now introduced to their submarines. It was a shock. The crews found them cramped and uncomfortable, and smaller than they expected. Worse, they were difficult to manage in the water. The midgets were given to sudden and unpredictable rushes to the surface, followed by equally unpredictable plummets to the bottom. If this happened, the crew had to work frantically with a clumsy system of moveable weights to bring the submarine back under control. The controls themselves needed constant attention. A slight lapse of concentration and the sub would roll through a sideways somersault.

Nevertheless, the midgets were potent weapons. They were powered by a single 600-horsepower electric motor fuelled by 224 two-volt batteries, giving them a top speed of 23 knots on the surface and 19 knots submerged. This was faster than most conventional submarines. The batteries had an endurance of 25 hours at low speed, but not much more than an hour at top speed. Their effective range was about 200 kilometres, provided they travelled slowly. The two torpedoes each packed 350 kilos of high explosive, more than most other torpedoes then in use. The torpedoes travelled through the water at 44 knots, and could outrun any ship in any navy. They were driven by a revolutionary internal combustion engine fuelled by a mixture of kerosene, oxygen and sea water, instead of the compressed air and alcohol used in other nations' torpedoes. This gave them a range of 5500 metres, up to three times the range of their Allied counterparts. The fuel system also reduced their wake, making the torpedoes harder to see and avoid.

Given the limited range of the midget submarines themselves, they had to be delivered to the target zone by a mother ship. At first the Japanese experimented with surface ships, often converted seaplane carriers. But these were too easily spotted by the enemy. So even before Pearl Harbor they switched to an ingenious 'piggyback' arrangement, whereby the midget was transported to the target zone strapped on the afterdeck of a large 'I' class mother submarine. The mother submarine and its midget passenger could submerge during the day and surface at night to charge batteries and refresh air supplies, maximising the chances of surprise.

The midgets were emphatically not suicide vessels. Indeed, Yamamoto had made it a condition of approving the midget submarine programme that the crew should be recovered afterwards. However, the midgets were one-mission vehicles. Each sub carried scuttling charges. After each mission the midget crew were to rendezvous with the mother sub and be taken aboard. Then they would scuttle their midget and send it to the bottom, returning to base aboard the mother submarine.

American press reports on the salvage and inspection of the midget submarines from Pearl Harbor gave the Japanese valuable intelligence on the problems the submarine crews faced. They were particularly interested in the reported damage to Sakamaki's submarine. They also had reports from the commanders of the mother submarines on the problems the midgets faced in a real war situation. They began a number of much-needed improvements to the design. Before Pearl Harbor, the crew could enter their midget only while the mother submarine was on the surface. This meant that any servicing of the midget, or launching it for a mission, involved exposing both midget and mother sub to the attentions of enemy ships and planes.

After Pearl Harbor, a special hatch was cut in the bottom of the midget's hull. This formed a seal with a matching hatch on the deck of the mother submarine. The crew could now move between the mother sub and the midget even when both were submerged. The ties holding the two submarines together could be released from inside the submarines. With the crew on board and the hatches re-sealed, the baby sub could be detached from the mother sub while both submarines were below the surface, making both subs much less vulnerable to attack during launch.

The designers responded to complaints from the crews about comfort. Seats were added, and the conning tower rearranged to give the crews a bit more room. The designers added a 'sled' cage to the bow of the midget, so that it would slide over obstacles underwater. They built another cage around the propeller to prevent fouling. A saw-toothed net-cutting line now ran from the bow to the top of the conning tower, giving the submarine a reasonable chance of hacking its way through harbour net defences. Four small saw-toothed blades were fitted to the noses of the torpedoes. With their ferocious speed and jagged blades, the torpedoes would pass unchecked through most nets.

When the five midgets set off for Pearl Harbor in December 1941, the crews had the benefit of three or four years of intensive training at the Imperial Naval College, plus seven months of specialist midget training at other locations around Japan. After Pearl Harbor, the crews for the next mission could add a further four months of intensive midget submarine training, this time on their improved subs. They were a formidable fighting unit, armed with a formidable fighting machine. All that remained was the choice of target.

Chapter 5

Date of attack will be notified

At home in Australia, the government fretted over the population's refusal to take the war seriously. Newspapers carried pages of war news every day. However, they continued to carry even more pages of horseracing results, tips and forecasts. On 1 January the *Sydney Morning Herald*, in a sombre leading article, warned: 'Never before has a year dawned on us with the menace of direct attack.' Next day's regular 'On The Land' feature could find nothing more menacing than the warning: 'Blowflies may be bad.'

There were endless strikes, particularly in the coal mines and on the wharves. The wharfies, the Australian nickname for America's stevedores or Britain's dockers, were particularly militant. They frequently refused to load ships even when they were due to depart next day with troops aboard. The troops were regularly forced to do their own loading and unloading. The wharfies preferred not to work in the rain. The Americans in particular were appalled. John Curtin's Labor government pleaded repeatedly with the trade unions to cooperate with the war effort and keep Australia working. The strikes continued.

In early May 1942 there was a major fiasco over clothing supplies. John Dedman, the Australian Minister for War Organisation, announced that clothing rationing would be introduced in mid-June. People downed tools, deserted their workplaces and headed for the shops, determined to buy all the clothing they could before rationing took over. The shops simply emptied. Within days there was no clothing left to sell. Big stores like David Jones in Sydney and Myer in Melbourne witnessed fights over their fast-disappearing stocks. For two weeks the clothing wars took up almost as much space in the newspapers as the war with Japan. The *Sunday Sun*'s 10 May headline on page 2, 'America Throbs with Excitement Over Naval Victory' (over a report on American reaction to the Battle of the Coral Sea), was matched by an even larger headline on page 3: 'Panic Rush to Purchase Clothes—Many City Stores Are Stripped Bare'. An embarrassed government blamed it all on Mother's Day.

Brown paper covered windows—the so-called 'brown out'. People who lit cigarettes in the open at night were booed. Air-raid drills were stepped up. People were showered with bizarre advice. The best place to shelter inside a house is under the kitchen table after covering the table with a mattress. Shove the table into a corner for even better protection. In the event of an air raid, fill the bathtub with water. Make sure you turn off the gas at the mains. Schoolkids, bite on a ruler during an air raid. Or bite a clothes peg. This will save biting your tongue, and will keep the passages to the ears open and reduce the risk of blast-ruptured ear drums. Wear a name tag on a string around your neck. Carry a drinking cup on another string. It was surreal.

Throughout this period, the government, the military and the civilian population all agreed on two major dreads: air raids, and a land invasion. They braced themselves for both.

◆　◆　◆

As early as March 1942, Yamamoto agreed to give the midget submarines a second and final chance to prove themselves after the fiasco at Pearl Harbor. By late April the targets were known. There would be simultaneous strikes by two attack forces: a Western Attack Group, under the command of Rear Admiral Noboru Ishizaki, would sail from Penang and head for the Indian Ocean in search of British warships; the Eastern Attack Group, commanded by Captain Hanku Sasaki, would sail from Truk Lagoon in the Caroline Islands, north of New Guinea, and head south-east. Its final target would be one of the ports nominated as the most promising by the I-25's Glen in February: Suva, Auckland and Sydney.

Sasaki had commanded the submarine force at Pearl Harbor. This time he was determined to get it right. His Eastern Attack Group would consist of six mother submarines, four carrying midgets and two carrying Glen floatplanes. The four midgets and their crews were ferried to Truk, to await collection by their mother subs.

We know from Japanese postwar records that the purpose of the attack was threefold. It would send a signal that nowhere was safe from the attentions of the all-conquering Imperial Japanese Navy. The Eastern Attack Group would make the Americans think twice about Australia as a secure base from which to counterattack in the Pacific, while the Western Attack Group would threaten the Indian Ocean sea route, blocking the flow of supplies and men between Britain and Australia. Finally, the sinking of American capital ships by the Eastern Attack Group would be another nail in the coffin of the US Pacific Fleet. In its postwar review, the Japanese Navy Ministry summed it up in the following words: 'Our offensive operations proceeded smoothly and our strategic situation had been strengthened and expanded. Nevertheless the enemy fleet still survived. Surprise attacks with midget submarines were planned to wipe it out.'

The Eastern Attack Group consisted of six 2500-ton I-class mother submarines: I-21, I-22, I-24, I-27, I-28 and I-29. Two of the mother subs—I-21 and I-29—were designed to carry Glen floatplanes. The remaining four would carry midget submarines. The two Glen-carrying subs left first. Captain Sasaki slipped out of Truk on 27 April 1942 on the I-21, with its floatplane stowed aboard. He arrived off Noumea on 4 May, and prowled around for ten days looking fruitlessly for Allied warships. However the I-21's journey was not entirely wasted: on 5 May it sank a 7000-ton American 'Liberty' ship, *John Adams*, with its precious cargo of 2000 tons of gasoline. On 7 May it sank a smaller Greek freighter, *Chloe*. After this last sinking, the Japanese gallantly handed out biscuits and tinned food to the survivors in the lifeboats, and pointed them in the direction of Noumea.

Sasaki left Noumean waters for Fiji on 14 May, arriving off Fiji some time around 18 May. Now the Glen could be assembled. On 19 May it took off with Warrant Flying Officer Susumo Ito at the controls and Ordinary Seaman Iwasaki as observer. Their unmarked plane flew over Suva Harbour, where they counted one light cruiser and seven submarine chasers. They flew close enough to the ships to see individual sailors on the decks. Some sailors on the cruiser spotted the Glen. Iwasaki asked Ito if he should open fire with the machine-gun. Ito had a better idea. He ordered Iwasaki to wave. The sailors waved back. The flight continued unchallenged, and Ito landed safely beside the I-21. Suva looked none too promising, he told Captain Sasaki, who reported this by radio to Japanese Sixth Fleet Headquarters at Kwajalein atoll in the Marshall Islands.

Meanwhile, the second seaplane-carrying mother submarine from the Eastern Attack Group left Truk Lagoon on 30 April. The commander, Captain Juichi Izu, headed the I-29 south for Sydney, arriving off Sydney on 13 May. On 14 May there was a flurry of excitement. Izu saw two warships heading for Sydney Harbour—a destroyer, and a large warship which he wrongly identified as the British battleship HMS *Warspite*. The I-29 set off in hot pursuit of this highly prized target. However, Izu never managed to get into the right firing position with his torpedoes, and in the end gave up the chase. Never mind, he might have reassured himself. *Warspite* would make a perfect target for the midgets when they got into Sydney Harbour.

On 16 May off the New South Wales coast near Newcastle, Izu fired two torpedoes at the Russian merchant ship *Wellen*. Both missed. He then surfaced and attacked the *Wellen* from close range with his deck gun. The *Wellen* turned out to be armed, and fired back. Izu chose to retreat. This attack was a serious mistake on Izu's part: the

Russian merchant ship was not worth the trouble, and he had now alerted the Australian defences to the presence of a hostile submarine off the New South Wales coast. Sydney had its first serious warning.

♦ ♦ ♦

The four midget-carrying I-class Japanese submarines, fresh from escorting the ill-fated invasion fleet for Port Moresby, were ordered on 11 May to return to the submarine base at Truk Lagoon to collect their midgets. Three came from escort work during the Battle of the Coral Sea, the fourth from patrol further north.

The Eastern Attack Group suffered two major setbacks before it could get fully under way. On 17 May the American submarine USS *Tautog* spotted the I-28 on the surface and on its way to Truk. The *Tautog* made no mistake. Three torpedoes later the I-28 was on its way to the bottom, taking its entire crew of 88 with it. Only three midgets could now be ferried south. The Japanese had lost a quarter of their attacking force even before setting out for the target zone. The fourth midget, scheduled to be carried south on the I-28, would have to stay behind at Truk instead. After the war, Sub-Lieutenant Teiji Yamaki, the commander of the midget due to sail on the I-24, remembered the crew of the fourth midget, Sub-Lieutenant Ban and Petty Officer Ashibe, making no secret of their bitter disappointment.

The next victim was Yamaki's own midget. On their first day out of Truk, the crew were servicing their submarine while the mother sub, the I-24, ran on the surface. Gas leaked inside the midget and exploded, with both crew on board. The explosion blasted Petty Officer Matsumoto, who had been working in the conning tower, out through the hatch and into the ocean where he was never found. The explosion also seriously injured Yamaki, who had been working inside. The midget was unusable, and was abandoned. The mother sub turned back quickly to Truk, unloaded the wounded Yamaki, and collected a jubilant Ban and Ashibe together with their intact submarine. The I-24 then raced south to catch up with the rest of the fleet.

Meanwhile, the skirmish with the *Wellen* stirred the Australian defences into action. Rear Admiral Muirhead-Gould, Naval Officer in Command, Sydney, ordered all merchant ships to remain in Sydney and Newcastle harbours. He then mounted an air and sea search for the aggressive submarine. After 24 hours, with no trace of the sub, he reopened the harbours. The search continued for several days. The Allied ships and planes found nothing.

It was now time for both Glens to come out from their covers. On 23 May Izu took the I-29 from wherever he had been hiding after the *Wellen* attack and moved to within range of Sydney. There he launched his Glen. Very little has been written about this flight. Many accounts of the midget submarine raid leave it out altogether or confuse it with Ito's subsequent flight over Sydney on 29 May. Yet this was arguably the most important flight of all: it settled Sydney's fate.

The crew of the Glen were not new to the task: Warrant Flying Officer Nobuo Fujita and Petty Officer Second Class Shoji Okuda had already reconnoitred Sydney Harbour once in the early hours of 17 February from the I-25. This time they were even more audacious: the flight took place in broad daylight. The risks involved in a daylight flight were massive. The mother submarine had to sit on the surface for an hour or more, exposed and vulnerable, while the Glen was assembled and launched. Then the mother ship had to return to the surface at the agreed rendezvous place and time to recover the aircraft and crew. This would mean another 30 to 45 minutes on the surface. If the flight was detected and the defences followed the spy plane back to the rendezvous point, then both plane and mother submarine would almost certainly be lost. However the quality of information from a daylight flight would be so much better than that gleaned from a night flight. Izu must have judged it worth the risk.

There is no record of this flight in any of the official Australian accounts of the Sydney midget submarine raid. But we have two remarkable eyewitnesses. Signalman Arthur ('Darby') Munro was on duty at the Port War Signal Station on South Head as Fujita flew down the harbour. And army Gunner Don Caldwell Smith was manning a mobile radar station parked at Iron Cove, 5 kilometres south-west of the Harbour Bridge.

Darby Munro was the first to see Fujita. He had just come on watch, which sets the time as just after midday. Darby was a visual signaller, and worked on the top floor of the Port War Signal Station. The top floor had a 360-degree view both out to sea and up the harbour. Darby first saw a 'white' floatplane approaching the entrance to Sydney Harbour from the north, flying at about 500 feet.* He followed the plane's progress up the harbour as far as the Harbour Bridge. At this point he reported the sighting to Naval Headquarters at Garden Island. Darby recalls Garden Island's response: 'He didn't know what to do. He told me to put it on to Richmond.' Richmond was then the base for the Wirraway fighters of the RAAF. Richmond proved even less helpful. The voice on the end of the telephone told Darby: 'It's no use telling us. By the time we sent someone, he'd be gone.'

Don Caldwell Smith, at the mobile radar station at Iron Cove, now takes over the story. The existence of a radar unit in Sydney was still highly secret, and the brand-new operators had spent their training time attempting to track a Tiger Moth which the RAAF sent up to fly around Sydney as a practice target. The wood-and-fabric biplane was hopeless. Its flimsy frame barely returned an echo on their radar screen. Now, to the delight of the radar crew, they had an unexpected and strong return. The all-metal Glen was a much better quarry. They tracked it enthusiastically down the harbour, with no thought that it might be an enemy aircraft, only that at last they could get in a bit of genuine practice with their secret weapon. The radar unit was linked to a nearby anti-aircraft gun, so the radar crew gave the gunners instructions on the range and bearing of the convenient intruder. Everyone was pleased.

At this point the regulations called for the radar unit to report the intruder to Combined Defence Headquarters near Circular Quay. Don's unit grabbed the telephone. 'The next thing, headquarters came back

---

* A Glen was usually painted grey underneath and green above. As Darby was looking at the underside of the aircraft, white is a fair description.

and they said: Stop! We've just been in touch with the Air Force and they have no aircraft in the air at the moment. So you'd better get that machine of yours tested by an artificer [radar technician] tomorrow.' Combined Defence Headquarters had clearly weighed up the possibilities. If there was a plane over Sydney it had to be one of theirs. So if none of their planes were over Sydney that left only one explanation: the radar must be on the blink again.

Fujita's flight continued undisturbed. At the Harbour Bridge he turned left, still watched by Darby Munro, and headed south-east across the heart of Sydney towards Bondi. He re-crossed the Sydney coast a little south of Bondi, over Waverley cemetery, and turned left along the famous surfing beaches of Bronte, Tamarama and Bondi. He continued north along the coast towards South Head before turning right to head east for the open ocean and a rendezvous with the mother submarine.

We know nothing more of this flight beyond the fact that the Glen must have crashed on landing. It was not available to Sasaki and the Eastern Attack Group when it was badly needed nine days later. However, Fujita and Okuda survived, to bring their precious sketches and reports of promising targets back to the I-29 for transmission to the whole attack group. The spy flight was Sydney's second serious warning in the space of seven days. Not a single alarm bell rang.

♦   ♦   ♦

While Izu's I-29 checked out Sydney, Sasaki's floatplane-carrying I-21 had sailed from Fiji to New Zealand and arrived off Auckland. On the morning of 24 May the regular team of Ito and Iwasaki launched their Glen. Fog blanketed Auckland Harbour, and they could not see anything. However, their reception in New Zealand was nothing if not courteous. As they groped their way in the skies over Auckland, they must have sounded to experienced ears in the control tower at Auckland airport like a lost aircraft trying to find the airfield in the fog. The controllers obligingly turned on the runway lights. Ito declined this well-intentioned offer. He returned to the I-21 to report that he had not been able to see which ships, if any, lay in the harbour.

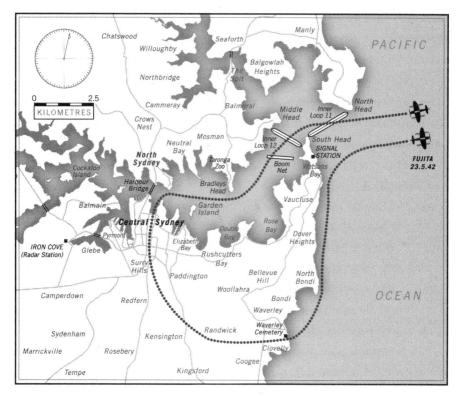

Fujita's second flight over Sydney is not as well documented as his 17 February flight. However, based on eyewitness accounts, he arrived from the north-east, tracked down the centre of the harbour as far as the Harbour Bridge, giving him a good view of fighting ships in the harbour. He then turned south, with a view of Sydney Airport, before crossing the coast a little south of Bondi. He then followed the coast back as far as South Head before heading out to sea for a rendezvous with the mother submarine.

Nevertheless, the brass at the Japanese Sixth Fleet Headquarters at Kwajalein now felt they had enough information to make a decision. Noumea and Suva were out. Auckland was an unknown quantity. But from Fujita's and Okuda's report Sydney appeared to be full of ships, including the possible major prize of the battleship HMS *Warspite*. On 24 May Vice-Admiral the Marquis Teruhisa Komatsu radioed the necessary orders to Sasaki. Sydney was to be the target. The mother subs headed for Sydney.

♦　　♦　　♦

The airwaves now began to crackle with traffic. On the evening of 26 May, from somewhere in the Tasman Sea, Sasaki sent out his order to the Eastern Attack Group.

> Telegraphic order No 3
> 1. Date of attack will be notified.
> 2. Order of dispatching the sheaths [the Japanese term for the midget submarines] will be I-27, I-22 then I-24. The order for the sheaths entering Sydney Harbour will be: I-27, 20 minutes after moonrise, then I-22 and I-24 following at 20 minute intervals.
> 3. Targets for the attack will be at the discretion of sheath commanders, who should concentrate on the following:
>   (a) If there is a battleship or large cruiser beyond the Harbour Bridge then I-22 is to attack the battleship and I-24 the cruiser. If there are two cruisers then I-22 and I-24 will attack them and I-27 will attack the battleship.
>   (b) If there is a battleship or aircraft carrier before the Harbour Bridge then attack it.
>   (c) If there are no suitable targets before the Harbour Bridge then try as much as possible to attack the battleship and large cruiser beyond the Harbour Bridge.
> 4. After completion of the attack, the recovery position will be: Day 1—No 4 recovery rendezvous off Broken Bay; Day 2—No 2 recovery rendezvous off Port Hacking.

There is no evidence that this message was ever decoded by either the Australians or the Americans. However, it did not pass unnoticed. Naval Intelligence officers in New Zealand locked onto it with direction-finding equipment. They placed the Japanese unit which had sent it, probably a submarine, some 700 nautical miles east of Sydney. This wasn't a bad fix.

Appendix II deals in some detail with the activities of the American and Australian code-breakers. At this point it is sufficient to say that by May 1942 the Allies had made substantial progress in breaking the Japanese Navy's JN-25 code. The code-breaking process was still slow and far from complete. We can gain a pretty good insight into just how slow from a declassified US Navy intelligence report, available in the Australian War Memorial in Canberra. The report is signed A.H. McCollum. Arthur McCollum worked on the Far East Desk of the Office of Naval Intelligence in Washington and prepared daily intelligence summaries for the White House. The first page ends with this melodramatic instruction: 'It is requested that this document be burned as soon as it has served its purpose and that in the mean-time it not be placed in any general file.' Only seven copies were made, of which the War Memorial's is number three, marked for 'NAVAL AIDE'. The naval aide in this case was Captain John R. Beardall, who reported directly to Roosevelt. Beardall clearly didn't do as he was told and burn the document, for which we must all be grateful. The surviving copy is headed 'Summary of Japanese Naval Activities of June 2, 1942'.

Item 4 on the first page deals with Japanese submarine activities. It begins:

At various times in the past it has been reported that the principal source from which the Japanese gain intelligence of the movements of Allied forces in the South Pacific appears to be submarines reconnoitring close inshore. At least one such sub-marine spent several days reconnoitring the vicinity of Sydney around the middle of May, and reported details of naval ship movements which in general appeared to exaggerate the actual facts. This particular boat is the one which unsuccessfully attacked the SS *Wellen*.

Another boat, or possibly the same one, spent the period May 19–23 in the vicinity of Suva, Fiji, and reported a number of ship movements.

This intelligence summary reveals a great deal. First, it is clear that messages from the I-29 off Sydney and the I-21 off Suva had been intercepted *and decrypted,* because McCollum appears to know the contents of each message in some detail. His amused reference to the fact that the I-29's report 'appeared to exaggerate the actual facts' is a response to Izu's rather wild estimate of the size and number of warships in Sydney Harbour at the time. McCollum's uncertainty over whether the Sydney report and the Suva report came from the same submarine or from two different submarines suggests that the decrypt was only partially successful. That was correct, as we shall now see.

The Australian government has not released the contents of intelligence reports gathered by FRUMEL (Fleet Radio Unit Melbourne), the joint Australian–American code-breaking unit which was one of a chain of stations around the Pacific at the forefront of the attack on JN-25. However, the American government is not nearly so secretive. Any Australian who wants to read the original documents should get in touch with the Naval Historical Foundation in Washington, which will be happy to oblige. The digest of 30 May decrypts is dated 31 May and the first page, second paragraph, reads as follows. The long dashes indicate undecipherable passages.

0 SB 8 (Jaluit radio (conceals for Comsubfor))—25 May—partly readable 'Reconnaissance report of Sydney Harbour.' 'On the 15th saw one destroyer, and on the 19th one patrol boat patrolling off Port Kembla. On the 16th at 1800 fired 2 torpedoes at 5000 ton merchantman off Newcastle but both missed. Following that fired several rounds of gunfire but she evaded any hits —— (COIC report No 246 indicates USSR vessel 'Wellen' received this attack).' The report then indicates that at 25 miles north of Shark Island saw one BB [US Naval code for battleship] or CA [heavy

cruiser]. In —— of Garden Island were two medium class destroyers (or second class cruisers) and three CA. On patrol to the south of Clark Island were 3 CA. There was a great deal of merchant shipping in the —— (specified anchorages at Harbour Bridge). —— 3 airport hangars at Mascot ——.

This is obviously Izu's report. It is pretty wild stuff. Shark Island is just off Rose Bay in the heart of Sydney Harbour, so 25 miles north would put Izu's battleship or heavy cruiser in the hills to the west of Gosford, where it would certainly have stood out but might have been hard to attack by submarine. The three heavy cruisers patrolling to the south of Clark Island would have found manoeuvring a little tight in the less than 350 metres of harbour which separate this tiny island from the Sydney suburb of Darling Point. Either Izu's geography was weak, or the FRUMEL code-breakers still had a way to go.

The decrypted version of Izu's report hugely exaggerates the size and number of warships in the harbour at the time. This is not wholly surprising. It is not the first time, nor will it be the last, that an intelligence report overstates the enemy's strength (think of Iraq). Whether Izu, or Fujita and Okuda, stretched the facts or whether the FRUMEL code-breakers simply got it wrong, is simply unknown.

Nevertheless, the circumstances of this decrypt provide a gold mine of information. The original message was intercepted on 25 May. It was decrypted on 30 May. So we know that messages were taking up to five days to decrypt. The digest itself was distributed on 31 May, the day of the attack, and does not require years of training in intelligence to interpret. Clearly the Japanese were weighing up targets in Sydney Harbour. The wide geographic spread of nominated targets as well as the reference to airport hangars at Mascot suggests that the report was based on aerial reconnaissance. On the basis of this decrypt, Sydney could expect anything from an isolated submarine attack on ships leaving the harbour to a full-on Pearl Harbor-style mass air assault on the city itself.

◆　　◆　　◆

There was a peculiar protocol for passing on FRUMEL decrypts. The commanding officer at FRUMEL, Lieutenant Rudolph Fabian of the US Navy, passed the decrypts to Vice-Admiral H.F. Leary USN, Commander of Allied Naval Forces, South-West Pacific Area, also based in Melbourne. Leary passed them on to Washington and, at his discretion, to anyone else he felt might benefit from them and was cleared to see them. Leary was notoriously tight with this distribution. Not even General Douglas MacArthur, the Supreme Commander of Allied Forces in the South-West Pacific, received them automatically. This failure led a frustrated MacArthur shortly afterwards to set up his own independent signals intelligence operation.

It beggars belief that this message was not highlighted by whoever decrypted it on 30 May and passed it on to Leary. In the FRUMEL digest it is not even the first item—pride of place is given to the news that 15 Zero fighters had arrived in Rabaul from Truk on 25 May. However Leary appears to have missed its significance, too. He did nothing to alert the Sydney defences to what might have been very serious danger indeed. Given that three US Navy ships were at risk along with dozens of ships from five other Allied navies, Leary's failure might have cost his own navy dear along with those of his allies. Leary was later to complain about the state of Sydney Harbour's defences. He can certainly be credited with one of the major failures in the Battle of Sydney Harbour. Sydney had its third serious warning, in plenty of time to put the defences on notice that one or more enemy submarines were poised off Sydney. Nobody passed it on. Nobody did anything. After all, it was the weekend.

Chapter 6

Day of attack shall be May 31

Susumo Ito is one of the most engaging characters in this entire story. He is still alive at the time of writing, probably the only living Japanese survivor of the raid on Sydney. He has given endless interviews over the years to newspapers and magazines, to television documentary makers and to authors. He invariably comes across as modest, humorous, brave and skilful.

Born in Hyogo province on the largest Japanese island of Honshu, Ito went straight from junior high school to naval flying school at the age of 16. In one of his television interviews he recalls how friends warned him against it—in those days planes were particularly prone to crashing. However, he turned out to be a born flier, and was quickly singled out as one of the Imperial Japanese Navy's outstanding pilots. He flew reconnaissance and attack-directing missions during the war with China. Then he was transferred, like so many skilled pilots, to flying instructing. He returned to active service in September 1941, assigned to the I-21's Glen. He was 27 years old and a seasoned veteran when he strapped himself in to his cockpit in the early-morning darkness of 29 May 1942. The plane had had its Rising Sun red insignia painted out so it could not be readily recognised as Japanese.

Pilots have an expression to describe a bad flying day: 'Even the birds are walking.' May 29 was certainly a day for perambulating birds, especially seagulls. Visibility was fair below a cloud base of about 2000 feet. But there was a strong wind whipping up the sea and making—for reasons already discussed—any catapult launch from a submarine deck a particularly hazardous affair. Ito was equal to the task and, with his regular observer Iwasaki, he clawed his way into the air some time around 3.45 am. The launch point was 35 nautical miles north-east of Sydney, roughly off the New South Wales coast at Terrigal.

Flying time from the launch point to the entrance to Sydney Harbour was about 25 minutes. A little after 4 am Ito crossed the Australian coast at 1500 feet. There are huge discrepancies between the various published accounts of Ito's flight. For instance most accounts, including Muirhead-Gould's official report, describe him circling *Chicago*. However Ito's own sketches show him doing no such thing, but instead circling Cockatoo Island on the other side of the Harbour Bridge and well down the harbour. It seems safest to trust Ito's own version of the flight. It is also a reasonable guess that he used South Head's Hornby Light and Macquarie Light, both of which had been thoughtfully left burning, to guide him in. His sketched track takes him about halfway between them, directly over the Port War Signal Station on South Head, then on to the easterly end of the boom net. He appears to have decided to leave close inspection of the net for later, and instead dropped down to 1000 feet and continued into the harbour.

The boom net stretched from Laings Point on the eastern side of the inner harbour to Georges Head on the western side. Georges Heights, above Georges Head, commanded a good, clear view of the harbour from the entrance right around to the Harbour Bridge and beyond. The Sydney defences knew what they were doing when they placed an army artillery battery there.

In a television interview, Phil Dulhunty, then an 18-year-old serving with the battery, described what happened next:

This particular night I was on guard duty and I caught the 4 till 6 morning period ... the graveyard shift, which was pretty nasty. I was there half asleep and playing around with a couple of possums in a tree. Then suddenly I heard this big truck coming up the hill from down in the artillery battery.

I thought: he's getting an early start. As the noise got closer and closer I saw it was an aeroplane going by, a seaplane. I just thought: it's off the *Chicago* or one of the American warships. You didn't worry about it, nobody worried about it. Everybody thought it was American.

To be fair to the Georges Heights battery, this was not an unreasonable conclusion. When the *Chicago* arrived in Sydney from the Coral Sea a couple of weeks earlier, her spotter planes had flown down the harbour with her. So American cruiser-launched seaplanes were a familiar sight in Sydney. And, as Dulhunty said later, how could a Japanese plane come all this way? It was impossible.

Nevertheless, this was a serious miss, even on a dark night. All servicemen had to study aircraft recognition, and know the difference between Allied and Japanese types. The men at the battery believed the plane to be an American Falcon. Apart from the non-existent American markings—Ito's plane had all its markings painted out—anyone wanting to distinguish a Falcon from a Glen could make a good start by counting the wings: the Falcon was a biplane; the Glen was a monoplane. Furthermore, the Falcon was a land plane. The floatplane version of the Falcon used by US Navy cruisers was the Curtiss Seagull.

The battery crew felt they couldn't simply ignore the aircraft, however harmless. The commander telephoned Garden Island naval base to report it. The duty officer, Lieutenant Percy Wilson, took the call. Wilson was both an able and alert intelligence officer. The report he now received, far from reassuring him, made him very nervous indeed. The battery commander told Wilson the plane was an American Curtiss Falcon float-plane, and that the crew had seen its American markings. On the face of it, the battery commander's report meant there was no problem. Wilson knew differently. He had received an intelligence report that the Japanese had captured a Curtiss Seagull observation plane and therefore might use it for clandestine operations. This particular aircraft type was used only on American cruisers, and Wilson knew from his intelligence plot that, apart from the *Chicago* moored a few hundred metres away, there was no American cruiser anywhere near Sydney Harbour. He asked the security officer at Garden Island, Commander C.F. Mills, if he could go over to the *Chicago* and ask if they knew anything about it.

Meanwhile, Ito's track took him past Rose Bay and Shark Island on his left, and over a fully lit Garden Island and the main concentration of Allied warships. Again he appears to have decided to leave the detailed inspection for later. He continued across Sydney's Central Business District, across Darling Harbour and Birchgrove, to the naval dockyard at Cockatoo Island and the second possible concentration of Allied warships. He made a couple of circuits around Cockatoo Island, noting flashes from the welders' torches, and headed back towards the main harbour.

His flight could not pass unnoticed forever. The searchlights now began to stir. Three times Ito was caught in their beams. Each time he simply climbed into the cloud and disappeared. Nobody fired a shot. A Japanese plane over Sydney Harbour? Impossible.

Ito's track next took him across North Sydney, over the northern harbour suburbs of Neutral Bay, Cremorne and Mosman, behind the battery at Georges Head, across the Royal Australian Navy shore base at HMAS *Penguin* (in Mosman, near the harbour beach of Balmoral) and on to Middle Head. His sketch map shows him at 2300 feet for most of this part of the flight. Clearly he chose to stay close to the cloud base so he could climb for cover if the need arose. He appears to have climbed as high as 3300 feet by the time he reached Middle Head.

At Middle Head Ito turned back towards the inner harbour and began a sharp descent, giving Iwasaki a second chance to sketch the layout of the boom net. He levelled off at a seriously dangerous 160 feet. Harbours, particularly in wartime, are prone to have cables strung across them and to be strewn with various towers and other high obstructions, none of them lit. However at 160 feet Ito could give his observer Iwasaki a chance to identify as well as locate the target ships. So there was no choice. The Glen skimmed towards Point Piper, below the mast height of some big ships, taking a look at the military flying boat base at Rose Bay on its way.

Ito now turned right towards Garden Island. At this low altitude, the low wing design of the Glen was a serious handicap. It blanked out a lot of the view from the cockpit. Ito was forced to bank the plane continually to let Iwasaki see what was below them. They crossed Garden Island at low level, noting a large warship at anchor (the *Chicago*), which Ito doubted was HMS *Warspite,* the battleship he had been told to expect. However here was a cruiser at the very least, with another cruiser (HMAS *Canberra*) further down the harbour. The entire anchorage was littered with juicy targets—destroyers, armed merchant ships, even a submarine.

Ito's mission should have ended now, as he flew past *Chicago.* The cruiser's gunnery officer, William Floyd, had issued instructions that the anti-aircraft guns stay manned even when the ship was at anchor. He recalled later: 'All of the time, day and night, while in the dockyard and later in Sydney Harbour, two anti-aircraft guns, one anti-aircraft director and the associated control party and lookouts were manned.'

However the anti-aircraft crew completely missed the Glen. 'In the *Chicago* not one of the anti-aircraft personnel noted it,' Floyd remembered. 'The Officer of the Deck was the only person who saw it. He was an aviator and identified it as an enemy plane. But it was then too late to take action and it escaped. Obviously during the approximately two weeks in port the watch standing on the anti-aircraft battery had become slack and lackadaisical.'

It is truly incredible that an anti-aircraft crew could fail to notice an unidentified aircraft flying within 200 feet of them. Yet they did. When he heard what had happened, Floyd was furious. He ordered the gun crews to go to a high state of alert. From now on, all hands on watch on the battery would be standing, except the pointers, trainers and rangefinder operators, whose battle duties required them to stay seated. If any more Japanese aircraft appeared, *Chicago* would be ready for them. None did.

Some 20 to 30 minutes had now passed between the Georges Heights sighting of the Glen and the *Chicago* sighting. It is not clear whether Lieutenant Wilson made contact with the officer of the deck on *Chicago,* but it seems unlikely. He returned to Garden Island from *Chicago,* having confirmed that the cruiser's Seagulls were still firmly tied down on the deck. The mystery plane was not *Chicago*'s. Wilson telephoned Fighter Sector Headquarters, then based in a tunnel near Circular Quay in the centre of Sydney. His report relied entirely on the Georges Heights sighting. An unidentified aircraft had been sighted flying in the prohibited area over Sydney Harbour, but Wilson did not specify that it was an enemy aircraft. At 5.07 am fighter headquarters issued an alert and scrambled two Wirraway fighters from Richmond air base, 15 minutes flying time away on the far north-west fringes of Sydney.

None of this troubled Ito and Iwasaki. As they passed over the *Chicago* at Garden Island, Ito's next problem would be the Harbour Bridge, now towering over them. He set the engine roaring at full power and put the Glen into a climbing right turn, giving Iwasaki a lingering chance to look back at Garden Island and the proliferation of targets. The Glen climbed over Kirribilli and followed the northern harbour shore over Cremorne Point and Bradleys Head. The crew had a third and final look at the boom net, then headed out to sea at 3300 feet. The Wirraways never even came close.

This was Sydney's fourth and most serious warning of all. A Japanese reconnaissance plane had flown over the city and been recognised. Yet the *Chicago*'s positive identification of the Glen as a Japanese aircraft does not seem to have been passed on to Rear Admiral Muirhead-Gould or to anyone else in the defence setup. No extra state of readiness was ordered. No defences were stepped up. Instead, Sydney did what it usually did on a Friday: thought about the weekend, perhaps with a lingering look at the racing pages in the papers to see if there was a horse out there somewhere that could make the bookies squirm.

◆   ◆   ◆

The final moments of Ito's flight posed a serious problem—landing the Glen. Strong winds blowing over the sea create large waves, and the

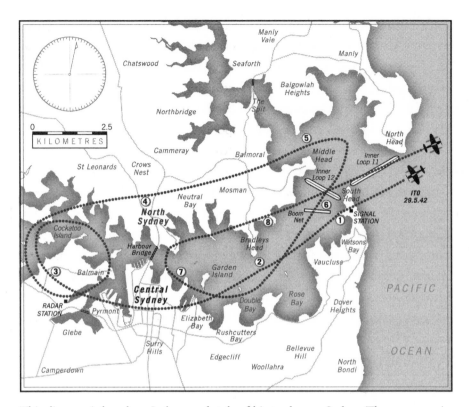

This diagram is based on Ito's own sketch of his track over Sydney. The sequence is:
(1) crosses South Head at about 1600 feet, with a good view of the Boom Net;
(2) descends to 1000 feet for his first pass over Garden Island and USS *Chicago,*
anchored 400 metres east of Garden Island; (3) continues at 1000 feet over central
Sydney to Cockatoo Island, where he circles; (4) climbs to 2300 feet as searchlights pick
him up; (5) climbs to 3300 feet, probably entering cloud; (6) descends to 160 feet,
below the mast level of some ships in the harbour, for a close look at Rose Bay flying
boat base and a second intimate inspection of USS *Chicago*; (7) climbs to 500 feet and
turns right to avoid Harbour Bridge; (8) continues to climb to 3300 feet while passing
over warships anchored in Athol Bay, north-west of Bradleys Head, before crossing the
Australian coast at North Head.

waves move in the same direction as the wind. So a seaplane pilot faces
an impossible choice in a high wind. If he tries to land into wind, and
thereby touch down at the lowest speed, he will inevitably be facing the
oncoming waves. The most likely outcome will be for his dangling floats

to dig into the crest of an approaching wave and force the plane in a forward somersault onto its back. On the other hand, if he tries to land parallel to the waves, he faces a tricky night crosswind splashdown at higher speed, with the combined wind and waves trying to lift a wing and flip his aircraft sideways onto its back. Either way, he loses. The general rule is: *never* land on water in a strong wind. Ito had no choice.

He appears to have opted to land into wind, and accept the inevitable. His float structure collapsed as the float pontoons bit into an oncoming wave, and the plane flipped onto its back. The two crew were now upside down in cold water, and weighed down with heavy equipment like binoculars. Both kicked their way free and found themselves barely supported by their lifejackets. Ito began swallowing water. In the rough seas, he lost contact with Iwasaki. The next few minutes were taken up with confusion and struggle. Then the mother sub appeared. A line was thrown. Ito hauled himself aboard where, to his relief, he found Iwasaki.

Ito later recalled his emotions as he was being hauled aboard. He thought: 'I must look a mess. What a disgrace!' When he was safely on deck, there was a further, vital duty to be carried out. 'I had to apologise to the commander', he recalled, 'for wrecking the Emperor's aeroplane.'

After the drama of Ito's rescue, the submarine's crew faced an unexpected and comic problem. The Glen refused to sink. They tried firing at the floats with pistols and rifles, but the little aeroplane stubbornly refused to give in. They could not use the sub's big deck gun: the noise and flash would have brought the defences racing to the scene. With sunrise already upon them and the near certainty of patrolling ships and aircraft arriving imminently, the problem became desperate. Eventually the crew attacked the floats with sledgehammers, and the Glen had to admit defeat. It slid under the water, shortly to be followed by a grateful and much relieved submarine and crew.

This story has one final and rather touching episode. Phil Dulhunty, the young soldier who first heard the Glen from his Georges Point guard post, later became a qualified seaplane pilot. He rose to become president of the Seaplane Pilots Association of Australia. He devoted a lot of time and trouble to tracking down Susumo Ito in Japan. He then invited him to become an honorary member of the Australian Seaplane Pilots Association. Ito was delighted to accept.

♦　　♦　　♦

On the evening of 29 May and armed with Ito's detailed report, Sasaki sent his final orders to the Eastern Attack Group:

Telegraph order No 4
1. Day of attack shall be May 31.
2. The enemy situation in Sydney Harbour is:
   (a) One US battleship 400 metres east of Garden Island. One large US transport ship 900 metres north of Garden Island. Several destroyers tied up on the west side of Garden Island. These have anchor lights on. Cockatoo Island has no enemy vessels around it. However there are two light cruisers and a destroyer inside the dockyard.
   (b) No special harbour defences other than a boom net, which must be opened frequently to allow the passage of enemy vessels. There are no enemy patrol boats at the entrances.
   (c) There are no control lights inside the harbour. The lights are on at Barrenjoey lighthouse.
   (d) Merchant ships move in and out of the harbour frequently, with lights on. However some vessels may show anchor lights as a decoy.
3. The following alterations are made to telegraphic order No 3:
   (e) Day 1—No 2 recovery rendezvous off Port Hacking. Pickup point will be 180° 20 nautical miles from Sydney harbour entrance, bearing 100° and 4 nautical miles from Hacking Point, four vessels: I-29, I-27, I-22 and I-24 four kilometres apart. One vessel I-21 to stand 6 kilometres 190° from centre point.

(f)   During daytime standby and night withdrawal, set submerged course of 190° and 10°.

(g)   Depending on the situation, some submarines may be ordered to search the foreshores on Day 2.

4.   For your information: I-21 reconnaissance aircraft overturned on landing, no casualties.

Again the New Zealanders intercepted the message. This time their direction-finding unit placed the sender as a single submarine 40 nautical miles east-south-east of Sydney. Again, it wasn't a bad fix. And again, there is no evidence that the message was ever decrypted. Nor is there any evidence that Sydney stepped up its defences, despite the New Zealanders' warning that there was an enemy sub close off the heads. Sydney had missed its fifth chance.

◆   ◆   ◆

There was one more chance to come. On the evening of 30 May, the day after Ito's flight and with almost 24 hours still to go before the Sydney attack, the midget submarines of the Western Attack Group struck in the Indian Ocean. In early May the British had successfully invaded the island of Madagascar, off the east coast of Africa, capturing it from the Vichy French. This did not suit the Japanese, who almost certainly wanted it for themselves, particularly the port facilities at Diégo Suarez on the northern tip of the island. This would have given them a good command of the Indian Ocean and a chance to disrupt supply routes between Britain and Australia.

The usual Glen reconnaissance flight was spotted by the British over Diégo Suarez harbour at 10.30 pm on 29 May. The Royal Navy was quick to act. The largest ship in the harbour, the elderly battleship HMS *Ramillies*, darkened its lights, upped anchor and began moving around the harbour before anchoring at a new site. All next day it steamed in circles in the harbour, with its crew on full alert.

Around dusk on 30 May the Western Attack Group launched two midgets, at least one of which made it into Diégo Suarez harbour.

At 8.15 pm the baby sub fired its first torpedo, which blasted a massive 9-metre square hole in *Ramillies'* plates. The battleship began taking on water and threatened to sink. However, the crew managed to seal off the damaged area and save their ship. An hour later a second torpedo might have finished the job. But the motor tanker *British Loyalty* manoeuvred itself inadvertently into the torpedo's path and paid the price: it sank with the loss of six crew.

The British did not immediately alert their allies around the world. For a start, they were unsure whether the raiders were Japanese or Vichy French. Secondly, they thought it might help the enemy if they were too forthcoming about the success of the raid. So, for the next couple of days, nobody told Sydney that Japanese midget submarines were currently on the prowl, and sneaking into Allied harbours.

Chapter 7

Somehow come back alive

The very new Lieutenant Reg Andrew RAN was due to take command of the Channel Patrol boat HMAS *Sea Mist* at midnight on 31 May. He decided, however, to take his first look at his new ship in daylight, and arrived at Farm Cove around 4 pm on the Sunday afternoon. The handover was about as thorough as the training he had received at Flinders Naval Depot.

'The officer I took over from took the *Sea Mist* away from the moorings in Farm Cove,' Andrew recalled. 'He did a circle around Farm Cove and he brought her back ready to go alongside one of the other ships there. He said to me: "You take over the controls and bring her in alongside." All I had to do was slow reverse and put the line on board, and that was it. He said: "You're okay. You're the commanding officer from now on."'

Sea Mist was not due to go out on patrol that night, so Reg Andrew simply stowed his gear on board and set about getting to know his crew. Each Channel Patrol boat had a crew of around eight. They usually worked a four-on, four-off shift system so that the entire crew seldom sailed together. The rule was simple: each boat should carry a minimum crew of three at all times. The rest was up to the skipper and the roster.

On the night of 31 May, *Sea Mist* had on board a coxswain, Potter; a signalman, Hunter; a stoker, Williams; and a motor mechanic, Winstanley.

Reg Andrew approved of his crew. Coxswain Potter he described as 'a short man with a balding head who was very proud of his ship. I was informed he nearly cried when I managed to put green seas over his beloved fo'c'sle.' Potter was an experienced seaman. Unlike the skipper, he knew how to set depth charges.

Signalman Hunter 'was dark in complexion and used to stutter. He was a good, all-round able seaman.' Stoker Williams was 'a wiry man in his forties, older than Hunter but like a teenager with his practical jokes'. Mechanic Winstanley was 'fair, tall and young and gave the impression of being a GPS graduate. He was a good motor mechanic and did an excellent job.' In Sydney, GPS stands for Greater Public School and refers to the city's eight most prestigious fee-paying schools. Branding Winstanley as being like a GPS graduate but a good mechanic was Reg Andrew's way of saying that, despite his polished accent and manners, Winstanley was a good bloke.

As the weather was foul and *Sea Mist* was not on duty that night, there was no incentive to hang around on the deck. Around nine o'clock, while one man kept watch, the new skipper and crew opted to go below and get a good night's sleep.

◆　　◆　　◆

Roy Cooté was one of the Australian Navy's most skilled and experienced divers. In 1942 the scuba (self-contained underwater breathing apparatus) diving system had yet to be invented. Divers instead dressed in heavy and clumsy watertight suits weighed down with lead-lined boots and topped with a brass helmet. Underwater they could see out through three small glass windows built into the helmet. A tender on the surface pumped air at high pressure down to the diver below. As well as the airline, the diver was connected to the surface by a telephone line and a lifeline, so he was able to communicate and perhaps be rescued if something went wrong. The work was difficult and dangerous. On top of the regular diving hazard of the 'bends', the diver's vital airlines and lifelines to the surface were vulnerable to jagged edges underwater, particularly on the hulls of damaged or wrecked ships. The suit was also vulnerable to puncture, and to leaks.

In wartime, the work was particularly demanding and Roy Cooté often worked weekends. However, he had one piece of good fortune: he lived in Mosman, a northern harbourside suburb of Sydney which was home to HMAS *Penguin*, the shore base for navy divers. He was able to go home to his family when not on duty.

His son Kevin remembers the weekend of 30 and 31 May as like any other. The two Cooté boys, Kevin and Jeff, regularly spent their weekends with the Sea Scouts. They would go to the clubhouse in Mosman Bay on Friday evening and sleep there on Friday and Saturday night, spending the daytime on Saturday and Sunday sailing on the harbour. While they were safely with the scouts, their parents invariably set off on a trip somewhere, perhaps to Newcastle or to the Blue Mountains. The family reassembled at home on Sunday evening about six or seven o'clock.

That weekend Roy Cooté finished work at 1 pm on Saturday, so he still had most of the weekend to himself. The previous week had been busy, ending with a particularly tough Friday. His dive log for the fourth week of May 1942 records:

Monday 25: Dived HMIS Madras, had cable round screws and rudder.
Thursday 28: Dived on boom net.
Friday 29: Dived telephone cable No 1 Buoy and for stores at Garden Island. Dived for damage to Battle Practice Target.

Given the problem of absorption of nitrogen into the blood during prolonged dives—the cause of the 'bends'—three dives in a single Friday was a lot to undertake. As the Cooté family went to bed in Mosman on Sunday night, Roy Cooté probably hoped Monday wouldn't be quite so demanding.

♦   ♦   ♦

An overweight English admiral with a hyphenated name and a reputation for pomposity is about as soft a target as exists. Yet to portray Gerard Charles Muirhead-Gould as some kind of Gilbert and Sullivan caricature would be both unjust and untrue.

He was the son of a British Army officer, and joined the Royal Navy as a cadet in January 1904. He served with distinction in World War I, being awarded a DSC. He was also made a Chevalier of the Legion of Honour by France and a Chevalier of the Order of the Redeemer by Greece. He spoke five languages.

Having spent some time in Naval Intelligence, between 1933 and 1936 he was sent to serve in the British Embassy in Berlin as naval attaché. Here he showed both courage and a clear head. Hitler's massive military build-up was well under way, and Muirhead-Gould set out to raise the alarm. Winston Churchill was in the middle of his 'wilderness years', cast out from mainstream British politics and a lone voice warning against the Nazi threat. Muirhead-Gould agreed with Churchill. He crossed the border from Berlin into Poland to post personal letters to Churchill setting out both his knowledge and his fears. The correspondence can be found in the Churchill archive.

In a letter dated 28 October 1935 Muirhead-Gould wrote to Churchill praising Churchill's speech in the House of Commons on German rearmament. He added that he had to leave Germany before sending the letter as the Germans were so annoyed with Churchill for telling the truth that no letters addressed to him would have got out of the country. Churchill's enemies had to concede that he always appeared remarkably well informed about German affairs: Muirhead-Gould was one of his sources. Given that the British government was in the midst of its appeasement phase, Muirhead-Gould was acting against government policy while still a serving British diplomat. If he had been caught it might have cost him his job. If the Germans had found out what he was up to, they might have taken even more drastic steps.

Despite a reputation for pomposity, Muirhead-Gould was capable of a light touch. In 1944 he wrote an article 'Berlin Memories' for the

Australian War Memorial journal *HMAS Mk III*. In it he recalled how he had met Hitler only once, at a state banquet in Berlin. He was introduced to the *Führer* by Goebbels, who briefly left the two men alone together. Hitler talked about films. He particularly admired a Hollywood film *The Lives of a Bengal Lancer*, a 1935 black-and-white British Raj blood-in-the-dust epic starring the unlikely figure of Gary Cooper in the title role.

'I liked it very much,' said Hitler. 'I have seen it six times. It is a remarkable film, and I have given orders that it is to be shown to every school in Germany. It will show my young men how the pure Aryan races handle the barbarians.' This astonishing piece of social history, with a little film criticism thrown in, certainly falls into the category of little-known facts about Adolf Hitler.

In February 1940 Muirhead-Gould was posted to Australia as Naval Officer in Command, Sydney. It was a prestigious appointment, though usually reserved for an officer headed for retirement. Muirhead-Gould might have gone on to greater things. When he became Prime Minister in May 1940, Churchill was said to have considered recalling him from Sydney to become head of Britain's Secret Intelligence Service, MI6— the role of 'M' in the James Bond books and films. However, Churchill's musings came to nothing, and Muirhead-Gould stayed in Sydney until September 1944.

His was not a popular appointment. Muirhead-Gould came from the more class-ridden traditions of the British Navy, where officers are gentlemen and other ranks know their place. It was a world of servants, fine claret and good silverware, and remote from the more egalitarian Australian Navy, where pomposity could cost an officer a bloody nose as well as loss of his authority. Muirhead-Gould was variously known as 'Manurehead-Gould' and 'Boofhead' (a popular comic strip of the time.)

One of the perks of Muirhead-Gould's appointment was 'Tresco', a magnificent sandstone house on the western shore of the fashionable inner Sydney harbour suburb of Elizabeth Bay. A long set of steps led from the rear of the house down to the water, where the Admiral's barge took less than five minutes to deliver him to his headquarters on Garden

Island, 500 metres away. It offered Sydney Harbour's commander and his wife a gracious life, as befitted a senior naval officer in his final appointment before retirement.

Muirhead-Gould turned 53 on 29 May 1942—the day of Ito's flight over Sydney Harbour. There is no record of how he marked the day. However, we do know how he planned his Sunday evening on 31 May. He had invited Captain Howard Bode (pronounced 'Bow-de'), commander of the USS *Chicago*, and a group of *Chicago's* senior officers to dinner at 'Tresco'. This would have been an all-male affair, with officers turning up in black tie and full-dress naval uniform. As well as the normal courtesy extended to the captain and officers of an important visiting Allied warship, the dinner would be something of a celebration. *Chicago* had just returned scarred but triumphant from the Battle of the Coral Sea.

If things ran according to the usual British invitation-to-dinner pattern, the evening would begin around 7 pm with pre-dinner drinks, followed by a dinner with wine served some time after eight, all of it prepared and brought to the table by Muirhead-Gould's personal stewards. The food and wine we can only guess at. But we do know that Muirhead-Gould regularly offered visiting officers a glass or three of pink gin. For the uninitiated, this is a traditional tipple of British naval officers: swirl a few drops of Angostura bitters in the bottom of a glass, then stir in neat gin, quantity at the discretion of the pourer. No ice. No water. No lemon. No tonic. It is not a drink for the faint-hearted.

♦   ♦   ♦

On the Japanese mother submarines of the Eastern Attack Group, now assembled off Sydney Heads on 31 May, the mood was sombre. The crews were painfully aware that five midget submarines had set off for Pearl Harbor on 7 December, and none had returned. Nine of the 10 Pearl Harbor crews were presumed dead. The Sydney mission would be perilous in the extreme, and there was little chance those remaining behind on the mother submarines would see any of the midget crews again.

The naming and numbering of the midget submarines is endlessly confusing. The Japanese often treated the midgets and their mother submarines as each having the same number. For instance, in Sasaki's third telegraphic order recounted in Chapter 5 he refers to the midgets themselves as I-22, I-24 and I-27, although this was in fact the number of their mother submarines. The most common convention is to number the midgets after their mother subs, but using an 'M' instead of an 'I'. Under this numbering system, the original four midget-carrying 'I' class mother subs I-22, I-24, I-27 and I-28 carried midgets designated M-22, M-24, M-27 and M-28 respectively. I-28 had been sunk by the American submarine *Tautog* before reaching Truk, leaving only I-22, I-24 and I-27 to carry their midgets south. The midget M-24 had been damaged on its first day out of Truk lagoon, so I-24 returned to Truk and collected M-28. Under the conventional numbering system, the final attack group consisted of M-22 aboard I-22, M-27 aboard I-27, and M-28 aboard I-24.

However, the Japanese Navy used a different numbering system, giving each midget a unique designator beginning 'Ha', and this system has been followed in a number of accounts, most importantly in Muirhead-Gould's two reports on the raid. Under this system M-27 is more correctly designated Ha-14, while M-22 becomes Ha-21. To compound the confusion Muirhead-Gould refers to Ha-14 as M-14, and to Ha-21 as M-21. He then adds into his account a Midget 'A' (Ban's midget) and a Midget 'B' (which didn't exist, being Matsuo's midget mistakenly counted twice). To spare the reader (and the author) a lot of unnecessary head-scratching, from now on in this narrative the midgets will be identified by the names of their commanders: Chuman's midget (M-27 or Ha-14 or M-14 or I-27); Matsuo's midget (M-22 or Ha-21 or M-21 or I-22 or Midget 'B'); and Ban's midget (M-28 or Ha-24 or I-24 or Midget 'A'). Whew!

Although the midget commanders had all attended the same naval college and passed through the same training programme, they were very different personalities. The most senior was Lieutenant Keiu Matsuo. His life is also the best documented.

Matsuo was born on 21 July 1917 in Yamaga in the Kumamoto province, the son of an elementary schoolmaster. He had an older brother Jikyo and a younger sister Fujie. He came from a long line of warriors—he could trace his *bushido* ancestry back to the 14th century. He was a black belt judo champion. Matsuo was unusually tall for the midget programme, fair-skinned and softly spoken. He is remembered as gentle, but he could be roused to volcanic anger when things went wrong. He took risks. His fellow students' strongest memory was of his determination: once he had decided on a course of action, he never gave up.

Matsuo's role went well beyond manning the midget which entered Sydney Harbour. He had been one of the principal strategists of the midget submarine programme. In the early days of the midgets, the intention had been to launch the tiny subs from warships in the midst of a battle, and have them wreak havoc on the enemy. Matsuo argued differently: naval warfare would in future not be waged in a series of tumultuous clashes between powerful opposing fleets. So this role for the midgets would be unproductive; war at sea would be decided by air power. The better role for the midgets would be to penetrate enemy harbours and sink warships at anchor.

In October 1941, two months before Japan entered the war, Matsuo was sent to Honolulu aboard the Japanese freighter *Tatsuta Maru* to reconnoitre Pearl Harbor. Quite simply, he was a spy: he travelled under an assumed name, with false papers. During the raid on Pearl Harbor he acted as Captain Sasaki's assistant, briefing the midget crews on the basis of knowledge he had gathered on the spot six weeks earlier.

Much has been made over the years of whether these midget submarine raids were suicide missions. They were not. In the early 21st century the suicide attack is, sadly, a more familiar weapon than it was in 1942. But a suicide bomber boarding a bus in Tel Aviv or a Tube train in London knows that his or her own death is an integral part of the mission. For the attack to work, the bomber must die too. This was never true of the midgets. The crews carried food and water for a week, and were under strict orders to do their utmost to return. It has been said that there was a pact among the midget crews not to meet up with the mother subs, because the rendezvous would expose both mother sub and midget crews to attack. Better for two men to die on the midget than risk 101 lives on the mother sub. But this makes no sense either: the mother subs were all committed to wait at the rendezvous point for three or four days after an attack, and the midget crews knew they would do this. The rendezvous point was necessarily close to the scene of the attack, because the midgets had limited range. So if the midget crew returned as agreed, the mother sub could make a quick getaway. If the midget crew did not return, the mother sub would be condemned to spend three or four days loitering under the noses of an angry and vengeful defence. The mother subs were exposed to much greater risk from the non-return of the crews than they ever would be from a successful rendezvous and a quick departure.

That having been said, everybody involved in the midget programme knew that the chances that a midget crew would survive a raid were close to nil. Nine of the 10 submariners at Pearl Harbor were thought to have perished. And, although they were in no position to know this at the time in Sydney, the crews of the midget submarines which had attacked Diégo Suarez less than 24 hours earlier had also been killed. So there was every reason to be downcast, however glorious the prospects of the attack might be.

Keiu Matsuo certainly seems to have been reconciled to his death. At the end of March, two months before the raid, he had asked his parents and brother and sister to meet him at Kure naval base for dinner. His mother thought he looked pale and stressed. He told his family he would shortly be embarking on a secret mission, of which he could tell them nothing. At the end of dinner he asked his family to tell his fiancée, Toshiko Knoshita, that their engagement must be broken.

After dinner his father presented him with a short, ceremonial sword wrapped in red brocade from his mother's wedding-day *obi* (kimono sash). His sister Fujie presented him with a 1000-stitch *senninbari* (stomach protector). This was a traditional gift to a warrior about to go into battle. As ceremony required, the first stitch was applied by someone close to him, in this case, Fujie. The remaining stitches each came from 999 other women. A lucky five-sen coin had also been sewn into the *senninbari* by Fujie. It would protect Matsuo.

On 27 May, while still on board the mother submarine, he wrote a last letter to his parents. He told them of his love for Toshiko. 'I find it unbearable that I shall not see her again. She knows my feelings for her but I ask you to take care of her.'

Matsuo's crewman aboard the midget was Petty Officer First Class Masao Tsuzuku. He was a farm boy who had left school early, never reaching secondary school. However, he studied hard to enter the navy. He failed his first entrance exam on health grounds, but passed his second with flying colours, overtaking others with full secondary school education. In his final letter to his brother Ichiza he wrote: 'When you receive this letter you will know that I was killed in the Australian area on May 31. I have nothing to regret. Today I will enter —— harbour in order to strike an enemy battleship. Take care of my parents and sisters.' He left 50 yen to his village elementary school.

We know less of the other two crews. The next most senior was Lieutenant Kenshi Chuman. He is remembered as the most conventional and the most unassuming of the three midget commanders. He wrote a last letter to his parents just before the attack, assuring them that he would succeed in his mission. The letter was to be delivered after his death. He gave 500 yen to crewmen on his mother submarine I-27, to be given to relatives of his navigator, Petty Officer First Class Takeshi Omori, in the event of their death in the attack. On the mission, Chuman took with him his short, ceremonial sword. He tucked it into a leather scabbard and tied it up with a brown tasselled cord in a long bag of soft, purple silk. The lining of the bag had Chuman's name inscribed inside it.

Sub-Lieutenant Katsuhisa Ban was the most junior of the three commanders. He was the son of a highly decorated soldier, and could have chosen a career in either the navy or the army—he had passed the entrance exams for both the Naval and Military acadamies. Ban joined the Sydney attack at the last minute, after the explosion aboard I-24's midget. He is remembered as the most dashing, the daredevil of the three midget commanders. His handsome young face stares clear-eyed from his photographs, his jaw firm and his back straight. Ban was the most outspoken in his dismissal of the fear of death. 'Nations that fear death will surely be destroyed,' he wrote just before the attack. 'It is necessary for the youth of Japan to take notice of this. "Sure to die" is the guiding spirit that will bring about the final victory.'

His crewman, Petty Officer First Class Mamoru Ashibe, was the third sibling in a family of eight brothers and sisters. Although Ashibe did not expect to survive the mission, he expected to die gloriously. The midget submarine programme was top secret, and Ashibe said nothing about it to his parents or neighbours. However, he confided to his younger brother Itsuo: 'If the war starts, I will be in a special two-man submarine. It will attack at close range. If war breaks out, I'll be first to perform a feat. Look forward to hearing about me.' Aboard the I-24 mother submarine he wrote a final letter to his mother, asking her not to weep when she heard he had been killed.

As they waited off Sydney Heads, the three crews had practical duties to perform. Based on the briefing from Ito's flight over Sydney, they had to ensure that their torpedoes were correctly set for the task ahead. One of the weaknesses of the Japanese midget design was the sheer difficulty of altering torpedo settings from inside the midget. The torpedoes were 'muzzle loading', which meant they were loaded into their tubes from outside the submarine. They had to be pre-set and fitted into their launching tubes well before an attack (for the Sydney raid, they were probably set and loaded at Truk Lagoon, but they may have been set as far away as Japan). Each torpedo tube then had a bow cap clamped over it, which could be cleared away remotely from inside the midget before firing. In theory the crew could change a torpedo's settings whenever they liked from inside the midget, but in practice this process was slow and complicated, not something to be attempted in the heat of battle. The commander was largely stuck with whatever setting had been programmed into the torpedo before the mission began. As they waited with the mother submarines off the heads on 31 May, the crews had a last chance to choose their torpedo settings.

Torpedoes can generally be set for speed, depth of running, and deflection. There was no need for the midget commanders to worry about speed. Their torpedoes had only one setting: flat-out at 44 knots.

Depth of running would determine which ships could be attacked and which could not. A torpedo set to run deep would pass harmlessly under a small warship but do maximum damage to a battleship or an aircraft carrier. Matsuo and Chuman set their torpedoes to run at 6 metres below the surface—a fairly deep setting even for a battleship or heavy cruiser—while Ban chose the slightly more conservative 5 metres.

The next question was deflection. The Type 97 Special torpedo carried by the Japanese midgets could be set to turn after firing by up to 60 degrees to the left or right, with the deflection angle marked in 5-degree intervals. A submarine commander might choose his deflection with one of two plans in mind. If he thought he would be attacking a moving ship, then deflection could take into account the movement of his target. It is a complicated calculation, though no more complicated than the instinctive judgement of a clay pigeon marksman: aim ahead of the target's movement, so that the target glides into the line of the shot. A commander might line his submarine up pointing directly at a target moving right to left, and fire his torpedo with 30 degrees left deflection. The target would then—he hoped—keep moving left into the torpedo's path.

However, there was a second reason for choosing a deflected shot: it made the whereabouts of an attacking submarine less easy to trace. Torpedoes leave a highly visible wake in the water: follow back along the line of the wake and there's the submarine. If the torpedo is set at 60-degree deflection and the submarine moves off quickly after firing, then the wide angle between the torpedo's wake and the submarine's course makes the sub harder to find and attack. Matsuo and Chuman set their torpedoes at zero deflection. The dashing Ban set his torpedoes at 60 degrees left deflection.*

---

* It is worth noting that Matsuo's and Chuman's midgets were loaded aboard their mother submarines on a different day from Ban's submarine. Matsuo's and Chuman's midgets were loaded onto their mother submarines first. Ban's midget joined the attack a day later, after the explosion at sea aboard I-24's midget. This difference in timing of loading may be a factor in the variation in settings. However, it is more likely that each commander knew what he was doing, and chose the setting which suited him best for the task ahead.

The torpedoes had to be checked to confirm that they would 'arm' correctly. Torpedoes have an abundance of anti-social habits, but two in particular trouble a submarine commander. The sudden jerk when launching can cause an 'armed' torpedo to explode in its tube, destroying its submarine. And a runaway torpedo is capable of turning in a full circle after launch and attacking its own submarine instead of the target. This is particularly true of torpedoes set with a large deflection. To guard against these dangers, each torpedo has to be set to 'arm' well after launch. A small propeller on the outside of the torpedo is made to spin by its movement through the water. After the propeller completes a chosen number of revolutions, it 'arms' the torpedo. Only then is the torpedo capable of exploding. The torpedoes carried on the midgets needed to run some distance underwater before they armed. The actual trigger which then detonates the armed torpedo is an 'inertia pistol'. This is a simple device which sets off the torpedo when it stops suddenly—as it does when it hits the side of a ship, or anything else solid. All three midget commanders carried torpedoes set to arm only when well clear of their submarines.

Finally, the submarines needed to be stocked with provisions for seven days. Each sub took aboard mineral water, wine, whisky and concentrated foods. A typical meal might be 100 grams of soda biscuits, 25 grams of dried bonito, 10 pickled plums, 10 peas, 25 grams of soft chocolate and six caramels. The submarines also carried what were delicately referred to as sanitary utensils.

◆ ◆ ◆

On the afternoon of 31 May, the midget crews began the traditional Japanese warrior's eve-of-battle purification. Each crewman cleansed himself with sake wine, and put on clean clothing, including clean underwear. Their clean uniforms had previously been impregnated with perfumed oil. Some shaved their heads. Each man prayed to his god-emperor at a candlelit Shinto shrine. They drank a little warm sake with the crew of the mother subs, to bring them all health and long life. They ate a farewell meal.

At the end of his meal, Keiu Matsuo asked one of the crew of his mother sub I-22 to cut his hair. While the cutting proceeded, Matsuo was heard to say, almost to himself: 'I wonder what my mother is thinking now?' Sub-Lieutenant Muneaki Fujisawa, the stand-in barber, concluded that Matsuo knew he would not return from his mission. 'Unconsciously, my hand holding the clippers stopped,' Fujisawa recalled. 'I can feel a man's determination hidden in his mind. Lieutenant Matsuo had resolved to die—I felt that intuitively.'

Susumo Ito, whose last-minute flight in the Glen had confirmed the value of Sydney as a target, remembers the mood on board the mother submarines. 'It was heart-rending for those of us who sent them off,' he recalled. 'We knew it was for the sake of our country, but it would cost the lives of six young men. It was so painful to see them go to an almost certain death. We wished they would somehow manage to come back alive.'

Part II

ATTACK

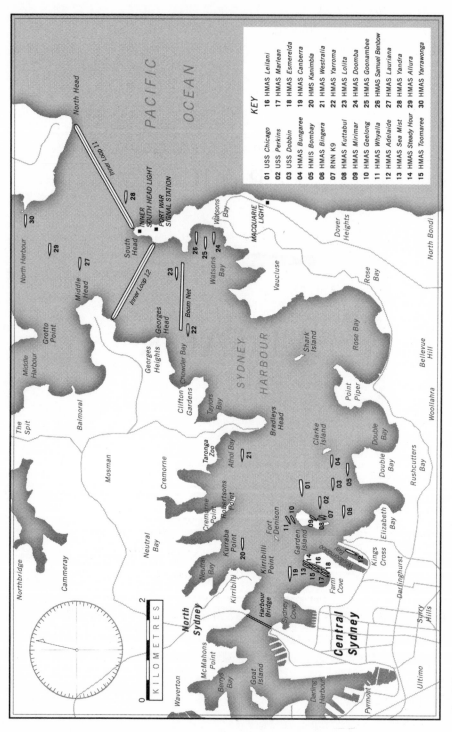

Allied fighting ships in Sydney Harbour on the night of 31 May 1942. These are their positions at 8 pm.

Chapter 8

The net

There was no shortage of fighting ships inside Sydney Harbour on the night of 31 May 1942. There were three US Navy ships: the heavy cruiser USS *Chicago*, the destroyer *Perkins* and the destroyer tender *Dobbin*. The Australian Navy had the heavy cruiser HMAS *Canberra*, the light cruiser *Adelaide*, the armed merchant cruiser *Westralia*, two corvettes *Geelong* and *Whyalla*, two anti-submarine vessels *Bingera* and *Yandra*, three minesweepers *Goonambee*, *Samuel Benbow* and *Doomba*, a minelayer *Bungaree*, 10 Channel Patrol boats *Yarroma*, *Silver Cloud*, *Steady Hour*, *Sea Mist*, *Lolita*, *Toomaree*, *Marlean*, *Miramar*, *Leilani* and *Esmerelda*, three Naval Auxiliary Patrol boats *Lauriana*, *Allura* and *Yarrawonga*, and the converted ferry, now a depot ship, *Kuttabul*. The British Navy had an armed merchant cruiser HMS *Kanimbla*. The Indian Navy had a corvette HMIS *Bombay*. The Dutch Navy had a submarine RNN *K9*. The Free French had a destroyer *Le Triomphant*. It was a fair-sized force to face six men in three midget submarines.

However, most of these ships were off duty and on various levels of notice, from four hours to 12 hours, before they could move. Many of their crews were on shore leave. Inside Sydney Harbour, the final line of defence rested with six duty ships. They were the anti-submarine vessel HMAS *Yandra*, patrolling the area between the boom net and the open ocean, two unarmed Naval Auxiliary Patrol boats *Lauriana* and *Allura* covering the area between North Head, Manly and Middle Head, and the third unarmed NAP launch *Yarrawonga* standing off inner North Head outside the Quarantine Station. Further inside the harbour two Channel Patrol boats HMAS *Yarroma* and *Lolita* with their Vickers machine-guns and depth charges, guarded the boom net and its entrance channels. The Western Channel had been closed to shipping for a fortnight, so ferries and other traffic passed down the Eastern Channel and through the gap at the eastern end of the boom net. *Lolita* covered the busy eastern gate; *Yarroma* could look forward to a quiet night at the western gate.

HMAS *Yandra* was neither new nor particularly well armed or equipped. She was built in Copenhagen in 1928, and had been working for the Coast Steam Ship Company of Adelaide before being requisitioned for the Royal Australian Navy on 27 June 1940. She was commissioned on 22 September 1940, having been converted to anti-submarine warfare by the addition of some detection gear plus a 4-inch gun, a .303 Maxim machine-gun, a .303 Vickers, a two-pounder and two depth charge throwers. She could scarcely be said to be bristling. She was also slow and comparatively heavy at 990 tons.

The *Lauriana* was the most senior duty NAP on the night of 31 May, and put to sea with a crew of nine including her owner and regular skipper Harold Arnott, the biscuit baron. That night she carried the NAP flotilla leader L.H. Winkworth on board, so Winkworth and not Arnott was the most senior officer.

The *Lauriana*'s log for 31 May opens with the usual trivia of a dull night on patrol.

1810: Left moorings. Duty officer requested us place a man on 'Yarrawonga' as crew. Spoke 'Yarrawonga' gave written instructions. Handed 'Allura' instructions. Proceeding. Contacted Channel Boat 1845 E. end of boom. Got very sketchy instructions L.F.B. [Licensed Fishing Boat] list and note that Air Force launch

Vera with Air Force men possibly American returning to port. Put D. Howell aboard Yarrawonga. Proceeding with Patrol. All lights out.

1900: Proceeding O.K. S.E. roll. No moon. Channel Boat on boom. Allura off for tea.

1950: 'Allura' back on patrol. We going to Q'tine for tea.

2008: Moored for Tea, Q'tine.

2050: Proceeding with patrol. Moon up but cloudy, contacted Y'wonga.

◆　　◆　　◆

The five mother submarines of the Eastern Attack Group moved to their initial positions off Sydney Heads some time around the middle of the day on 31 May. They first took up station on a huge arc with a 20-nautical-mile radius from the harbour entrance. The I-27 carrying Chuman's midget waited on the north-east rim of the arc, the I-22 carrying Matsuo's midget stood off to the east, and the I-24 carrying Ban's midget positioned itself to the south-east. A little further outside the arc, the floatplane carrier I-29 waited between the I-27 and the I-22, while the other floatplane carrier I-21 waited between the I-22 and the I-24. The I-21 carried the attack group's commander Hanku Sasaki.

As the afternoon progressed, the three midget-carrying mother ships crept fully submerged in to positions about 7 nautical miles off the heads. It is possible that they had intelligence that the harbour was protected by indicator loops, because they chose their new stations at a point well beyond the six outer loops. Not that it mattered. Two of the six loops were unserviceable, so the whole lot had been left unmanned. The three mother subs were all at their launch points around 4 pm, giving the midget crews an hour to squeeze into their subs and carry out final checks before launching. The sun set at 4.54 pm. The crews waited a little longer for total darkness.

Matsuo launched first. Captain Kiyoi Ageta, who had carried a midget to Pearl Harbor on the same I-22 six months earlier, gave the fateful order, 'Cut the line. Remove the second band. Take off,' some time around 5.20. Ageta heard the midget's propellers begin turning at 5.21. The raid had begun.

Chuman launched next, at 5.28 pm. Ban was last to launch, at 5.40 pm. The full moon would rise at 6.15 pm. The plan called for Chuman to enter the harbour ahead of the others, some time around 6.35 pm, when the moon would give a little light. Matsuo and Ban would follow at 20-minute intervals.

Each submarine carried copies of three British Admiralty charts: Admiralty no. 1021 covering Port Jackson (Sydney Harbour) to Port Stephens north of Sydney; Admiralty no. 1020 covering Jervis Bay south of Sydney to Port Jackson; and Admiralty no. 1069 showing Port Jackson in detail. On Admiralty no. 1020 the crews had pencilled in the rendezvous point off Port Hacking, to the south of Sydney, to which they would return after the raid. The old rendezvous point off Broken Bay had been pencilled in on 1021.

On Admiralty no. 1069 Matsuo had carefully drawn his intended track into Sydney Harbour: the midget would enter the harbour from a position 200 metres south of North Head, then track north-west parallel to the North Head coast; from a position south of the Quarantine Station on North Head he would then turn south-west towards Middle Head; at 150 metres from Middle Head he would turn further south, following the Western Channel through the gap in the boom net and on to a point 1500 metres south of Bradleys Head; then he would turn towards Garden Island and the USS *Chicago*.

The heavy swell outside the harbour made navigation difficult. As well, the strong currents gave the crews some awkward decisions. The prevailing sea current outside Sydney Heads flows from north to south, at 1 to 2 knots. The subs' most economical cruising speed was 3 knots. To fight their way across the current, the commanders would have to set a higher speed. But that would place a strain on their battery reserves. All three subs found the going difficult. They all ran very late.

Navigation as far as the harbour entrance was simplified by the thoughtfulness of the port authorities. The Hornby Light on the tip of

South Head burned brightly, as did its companion Macquarie Light 1500 metres further south on Outer South Head. The Sydney port command, civilian and naval, didn't want any ships to miss their harbour entrance. At 5.25 pm, four minutes after launch, Matsuo fixed his position as 7.2 nautical miles from the Macquarie Light, on a bearing of 260 degrees, putting him directly outside the harbour entrance. He made three more fixes on his way towards the heads: 4.1 nautical miles from the Macquarie Light, on a bearing of 253 degrees; 3.6 miles on 247 degrees; and 1.7 miles on 260 degrees.

Each commander knew that navigation inside the harbour would be fiendishly difficult. The subs would need to travel submerged, or at best at periscope depth. Although the two lighthouses on South Head burned brightly, the lead (navigation) lights inside the harbour had been blacked out. The commanders would be in a strange harbour at night, with strong tides and unpredictable currents, and a boom net to negotiate, all by the weak light of a moon blocked by cloud. It says a great deal for their skill and seamanship that all three made it.

♦   ♦   ♦

Chuman arrived first, as planned. During training the sub crews had devised a simple tactic for entering harbours—follow somebody else. This had everything going for it. Submarines are detected by hydrophones, listening devices which pick up engine and propeller noise, and by sound echoes from anti-submarine detection devices like ASDIC. But if the submarine is close to another ship then there is every chance that any indications given off by the sub will be misread as coming from the other ship. A further and equally important advantage is that the navigation problem is solved: the fully lit ship being followed can be presumed to know what it is doing when it comes to dodging rocks and reefs, not to mention boom nets.

Manly ferries normally use the Western Channel in Sydney Harbour. However, the Western Channel was closed to shipping on 31 May, so the 7.30 pm ferry from Manly to Circular Quay was forced to head across the harbour for the Eastern Channel. Chuman tucked in behind it. The ferry was already running late, and the extended journey across the harbour made it run even later. At 7.59 the ferry crossed Inner Loop 12. At 8.01 so did Chuman. Both, as we have seen, left a good trace. Nobody stirred.

What happened next is a matter for conjecture. We know that Chuman's fellow submariner Matsuo intended to enter the harbour via the Western Channel, and it may be that all three submarine commanders planned to use this wider and simpler way in. We also know that *Lolita* was stationed on the net close to the entrance to the Eastern Channel while *Yarroma* was a fair distance from the Western Channel gap. It may be that Chuman sized this up and decided he stood a better chance of passing through the western gate undetected. For whatever reason, instead of following the ferry through the eastern gate, Chuman headed across the harbour, past the Sow and Pigs reef, to the western end of the boom net and its easier entrance. He slipped gratefully through the gap into the inner harbour and target zone.

At this point it is worth noting that so far Chuman had cleared the ring of six outer indicator loops (not in service), crossed Inner Loop 11 without leaving a trace, evaded the specialist anti-submarine patrol of HMAS *Yandra* guarding the harbour entrance, evaded the three NAP boats *Lauriana, Allura* and *Yarrawonga* watching the area immediately inside the heads, crossed Inner Loop 12 which picked him up but whose human monitors ignored him, then slipped through a 293-metre gap in a net built for the specific purpose of keeping submarines out. All this while evading detection by the Channel Patrol boat *Yarroma* charged with the task of keeping an eye on the very gap he had just used. He deserved a better fate than that which now befell him.

Almost every published account, from G. Hermon Gill's official history of the Royal Australian Navy to the various books, magazine articles and television documentaries about the raid, describes Chuman charging head first into the ocean side of the boom net while trying to find his way into the harbour, and getting stuck in the process. Some accounts go into elaborate detail, describing the sub backing and shoving, trying to use its bow cutters to hack its way in. This is not what happened.

The only account which fits all the known facts comes from Jimmy Cargill, the nightwatchman who first saw the sub. In his own words, and in his delightful Scottish brogue, this is how events unfolded.

> The first Jap that came in, he must have seen me and he dived to get through the gate, like so I wouldn't see him. The gate was open . . . it wasn't finished then. He came through the gate and about 80 feet [around 24 metres] inside the gate he went off his course a little bit and hit the Pile Light. Of course, he was submerged on the bottom then. Well he went astern and he got one of the big rings [of the net] around his propeller.

This account makes total sense. We can ignore the suggestion that Chuman dived after seeing Cargill: he was probably already well submerged when he attempted to pass through the gate. Having found the gap, Chuman would need to turn left, towards the centre of the harbour. Contemporary photographs show the Pile Light as just inside the net opposite the third pile. The midgets were about 24 metres long. If the Pile Light was a bit over 24 metres from the net, and Chuman bumped into it while submerged and in the dark, his first instinct would be to put the sub into reverse and back off the obstruction. He would not need to back far to jam his propellers into the net, and that is certainly what he did—as Roy Cooté's photograph in the photo section illustrates. Chuman was trapped between the second and third piles of the net—directly opposite the Pile Light.* Jimmy Cargill's version matches the facts. No other account could make the same claim.

We can now imagine the state of panic aboard the sub. Continuing to rev the propellers made matters worse. Chuman probably considered

---

* The two Pile Lights, popularly known as the 'Wedding Cakes', marked the entrances to the Western and Eastern channels out of Sydney Harbour. The Western Pile Light survived Chuman's collision and other rigours of war until it was rebuilt in 1947. However it proved to be less than immortal, and at 4.30 pm on 12 December 2006 it comprehensively disintegrated, leaving nothing behind but a swirl of water and some wooden wreckage.

that his best bet was to try to twist the sub free. He had snagged himself about 1.5 metres from the bottom of the net, in around 13½ fathoms (81 feet or 24.7 metres) of water. So whether by accident or design, Chuman swung the bow of the sub sideways and upwards until it was almost vertical, with its hull parallel to the net. The torpedo tubes on the bow protruded from the water, but the rest of the submarine was still below the surface. When he revved his engines the net vibrated, but nothing moved. The sub stayed firmly stuck, tangling itself more deeply in the coils. This commotion is what first attracted the attention of Jimmy Cargill and Bill Nangle, chatting on the deck of the nearby floating crane. Jimmy Cargill rowed over for a closer look at the frantic mystery object.

◆　◆　◆

Accounts differ widely on what happened next. This is hardly a surprise because for the next couple of hours, with the honourable exception of Jimmy Cargill, nobody defending Sydney Harbour exactly covered themselves with glory. Instead they dithered.

Jimmy Cargill saw the sub at around 8.15 pm. He had to row first to the sub, about 50 metres. Then he rowed another 80 metres to *Yarroma* to report his findings. On a blustery night on the harbour this will not have been quick. However, the struggle with the oars turned out to be the least of his problems: *Yarroma's* skipper, Sub-Lieutenant Harold Eyers, wanted nothing to do with Cargill's mystery object. If, as the nightwatchman suggested, it might be a mine then Eyers thought it would be risky to approach it. Among his many concerns, he was carrying the still highly secret ASDIC anti-submarine detection equipment. He did not want to place it at risk at the hands of a mine or submarine. Anyway, he doubted that the object was anything so interesting—more likely it was a piece of naval junk which had got stuck in the net.

It is all too easy to be critical of Eyers. In his 22 June report on the raid, Rear Admiral Muirhead-Gould described his behaviour as 'deplorable and inexplicable'. Muirhead-Gould, who had every personal reason to look for scapegoats, wanted Eyers court-martialled for failing to engage the enemy. He was dissuaded from this by Sir Guy Royle, the Chief of Naval Staff. 'I feel his chief fault was foolishness', Royle wrote to Muirhead-Gould on 16 June 1942, 'and that an admonition by you would meet the case'. The most important thing to say about Eyers is that, although he was a commissioned officer in full and sole command of a Royal Australian Navy ship, he was only 21 years old on the night of the raid. He had enlisted in Melbourne on 4 September 1939, the first day of World War II and a few days short of his 19th birthday. He does not sound like a coward. Before enlisting he worked as a shipping clerk.

Cargill's first proposal to Eyers was that *Yarroma* should follow him while he rowed over to the object. Eyers asked him to describe it. Cargill recalled:

Well, I said, the nearest I could tell there was two great big oxy bottles with bumper bars or guards over them. But, I said, follow me and I'll put you onto it. I went back to it and he didn't follow me. So I went back to him again and told him that it was still there. I said: If it's a mine you'd better hurry up, or you'll have no bloody Navy left.

He then told me to come on board, as something was wrong with the searchlight. Well, I went aboard and I told him to go back to the Pile Light. We were halfway there when he stopped and said: 'It looks like naval wreckage.' I said: Gee, I've been alongside it and I could touch it with my paddle. Everything is shining brand new. Give us one of your men and I'll take him over to it.

So I went down the ladder with this bloke. He was halfway down the ladder when he was pulled up and another man went down to join me. We went over to it, nearly a paddle's distance away from it. It had stopped struggling and we could see the conning tower and the ridge rope and the whole outline of the submarine. The bloke said to me: 'It's a submarine all right. Put me back on board and we'll see what we have to do.'

This whole process seems to have taken an incredible amount of time. Taking Jimmy Cargill's narrative at face value, he spotted the sub at 8.15 pm. First he had to row from the floating crane to the sub. He then rowed over to *Yarroma* and spoke to Eyers. He then rowed back to the sub. When *Yarroma* did not follow him, he rowed back to the patrol boat again. He then waited while Eyers repaired his searchlight. After this Eyers moved *Yarroma* a little closer to the sub before stopping again. More talk. Then the offer to row a crew member over to the object. Then a change of crew member. Then another rowboat journey to the sub, and another rowboat journey back. By the time the process was complete, over an hour and a half had passed. In the course of the 97 minutes, *Yarroma* made increasingly frantic efforts with its signal lamp to alert the Port War Signal Station on South Head that there was a problem. No one responded.

◆　◆　◆

It is worth breaking off the narrative at this point to look at communications on Sydney Harbour that night. In the 21st century, when hordes of schoolchildren communicate with each other remotely by phone or text message from a radio telephone in their pocket or schoolbag, the primitive military communications of May 1942 are hard to imagine. Yet as we shall shortly see, they were a key element in the chaos about to engulf Sydney Harbour.

The navy's main communication centre in Sydney was on Garden Island. Here powerful radio sets could send signals around the world, even as far as the Admiralty in London. In 1942 radio communications came in two forms. The simplest was R/T or radio telephone. This allowed signals by voice. People spoke to each other in the familiar 'over and out' style of World War II movies. However R/T had comparatively limited range. Without going into the arcane issues of skip distances and the reflective properties of the ionosphere, it is sufficient to say that R/T voice signals were 'line of sight'. If hills or headlands or the curvature of the earth blocked the way, the signal would not get through.

The more usual form of radio communication was W/T or wireless telegraphy. This involved a skilled operator sending audible signals by radio in Morse code. W/T signals had longer range than R/T. They could be received and understood 'over the horizon'. W/T was used for long-range communication with ships at sea. R/T was used for short-range ship-to-ship and ship-to-shore messages. Although R/T would be the simplest and best way to communicate with fighting ships inside the harbour, the main communications centre on Garden Island did not have a radio telephone set installed on the night of 31 May 1942.

For short-range traffic around the harbour entrance, the navy's key communications centre was the Port War Signal Station on South Head. PWSS was essentially a lookout and relay station. It occupied a three-storey building with an open platform above. On the ground floor of PWSS the indicator loops guarding the harbour 'tailed' in. There was also an ASDIC submarine-detection device, and a photo-electric beam skimming the water above Inner Loop 12 to detect surface vessels entering the inner harbour. The ground floor staff watched the traces given off by the indicator loops, kept an eye on the ASDIC screen, and waited for any interruption to the photo-electric beam. It was their job to raise the alarm if they came across any strange blips or echoes.

Above them were the radio signallers. Unlike Garden Island, Port War did have R/T as well as W/T. However, the correct R/T set had yet to be fitted, and the improvised set available on the night of the raid failed comprehensively. Not that it mattered. Only the larger and newer warships on the harbour that night were fitted with R/T.

On the top floor and platform were the visual signallers. Their messages could be sent out by something as simple as a string of flags hoisted up a pole. (Nelson's famous signal 'England expects that every man will do his duty' was passed to the rest of his Trafalgar fleet by signal flag.) The lost art of semaphore was also important. A signalman with a flag in each hand could spell out a message by holding the flags in different positions, each position signifying a letter of the alphabet. However, flags and semaphore were largely useless at night.

The most common form of visual signalling involved flashing light beams. The signalman sent his message in Morse code with a series of long and short flashes. This system worked in darkness as well as in daylight. At night the signal light had to be covered by a red or green filter—white light would destroy the night vision of the signaller and the receiver, as well as those around them. To state the totally obvious, all visual signals were also 'line of sight'. Light signals functioned best with two men at each end: at the receiving end, one man 'read' the signal while the other wrote down what he said. A lone signalman could read and transmit, but the system worked much better with two men.

The visual signallers on the top floor or Port War had a 360-degree view of both the harbour and the ocean beyond, so they acted as both lookout and signaller. If someone on the ground floor picked up an ASDIC echo or an unexpected blip from the indicator loop or the photo-electric beam, they would telephone upstairs and ask the top floor to check it out visually.

The signallers at Port War also had telephones to communicate with shore defence centres, including naval headquarters on Garden Island. In 1942, however, telephone capacity was limited by the number of 'lines' available. The system would go into overload very quickly if there was any kind of crisis, and the plaintive cry would go up: 'I can't get a line.' The signallers preferred their trusty signal lights to the unpredictable telephone system, even for messages between Port War and Naval Headquarters 5 kilometres away on Garden Island.

While the Port War Signal Station housed Sydney's most comprehensive set of naval communication equipment, it had no authority to issue orders. These had to come from Naval Headquarters on Garden Island. PWSS simply acted as a relay station. Ships signalled to Port War, who passed the message on to Garden Island, who replied to Port War, who passed the order back to the ship. Generally Port War sent its messages to Garden Island by light signal. Garden Island replied either by telephone or light. It all took time.

Garden Island did not have to send all its signals via Port War. It had its own visual signals section. The signallers operated from a specially constructed tower on high ground overlooking the headquarters buildings below. Despite the tower's height, parts of the harbour were masked from it by surrounding headlands. Garden Island had no way of sending visual messages to significant numbers of the warships under its command. They had a clear 'line of sight' to Port War, but no way of communicating visually with either the Channel Patrol boats on the boom net or with ships further up the harbour and beyond the Harbour Bridge. Finally, because signal lamps are directional, they had to be aimed at a particular ship for it to receive a message. So if a signal needed to pass to all ships, it would in practice have to be sent out a ship at a time. With 30 warships in the harbour, getting even a short message through to all of them by visual signal was a daunting undertaking.

All ships large and small carried visual signalling equipment. All of the larger warships on the harbour carried W/T, and some also carried R/T. However, the Naval Auxiliary Patrol boats and most of the Channel Patrol boats had neither W/T nor R/T on the night of 31 May 1942. They had to rely on light signals to communicate with each other and with Port War and Garden Island. They also had to contend with far from ideal equipment. Their signal lamps were heavy, but were nevertheless hand-held and designed to be operated with one hand. The operating hand had to pull two triggers simultaneously—one trigger turned on the light; the second trigger tilted an internal mirror to make the light 'flash'. The light was directional, and had to be sighted accurately at the recipient for the signal to get through. From a swaying deck on a choppy harbour, it was no mean feat to keep the light pointing at the precise spot occupied by the intended recipient.

On the night of 31 May 1942 only one duty Channel Patrol boat on the harbour carried radio. *Yarroma* was equipped with an FS6, a clunky and primitive piece of kit which nevertheless cost around £1000— $52,000 at today's prices—so the navy felt it could not afford to install them in the whole Channel Patrol boat fleet. An FS6 would simply astonish a 21st-century schoolchild. It weighed a bit over 71 kilos, and needed two men to carry it. (My current mobile phone, which carries about 1000 times the communicating power of an FS6 set, weighs in at

0.1 kilo.) With the flip of a toggling switch, an FS6 could be used either as an R/T voice communications set, or as a Morse code W/T set. However, it was subject to interference from any electrical equipment operating nearby, particularly from spark plugs in an engine. A shipboard FS6 set was next to useless if the ship's motor was running.

There was one other means of communication from ship to ship: audio signals. Each ship carried a loud-hailer and a horn or siren. Messages could be passed by shouting through the loud-hailer, or just by shouting. The horn or siren could be used to raise the alarm.

◆   ◆   ◆

There is no record of the manning level at the Port War Signal Station that night. When ships were expected, a normal Port War watch consisted of a Lieutenant-Commander in overall charge, with a Yeoman or Leading Signalman plus three signalmen on the top floor, a Petty Officer or Leading Seaman Wireless Operator plus three wireless operators on their floor, and a Petty Officer or Leading Seaman ASDIC operator plus three ASDIC operators on the ground floor. The raid took place on a Sunday night, however, and nobody expected anybody of importance to enter Sydney Harbour that night—certainly nobody was expecting a working visit from the Imperial Japanese Navy. 'Darby' Munro, the PWSS signalman who had seen the Glen flight eight days earlier, is of the opinion that when Chuman entered the harbour there might have been only one man on duty on the ground-floor Loop Station and ASDIC centre of PWSS, and one man on the R/T and W/T floor. If Darby is correct, it would go a long way towards explaining why the indicator loop traces from the submarines passed unnoticed.

It also follows that around 9.30 pm there may have been only a single team of two men on the top floor to receive Yarroma's light signals, and a lone R/T watch keeper below to answer the radio. Each would then need to pass the signals on to Garden Island and await instructions. As pressure built up, the signallers no doubt called for help from their sleeping mates in the nearby huts, but it will have taken some time to get the system up to working strength.

Accounts vary on how the message eventually got through. The most likely scenario is that Port War received at least some of *Yarroma*'s light signals but the overstretched light signals crew could not acknowledge them and raise the alarm at Garden Island at the same time. *Yarroma* probably also tried to get through to Port War on the R/T, but this appears to have failed totally, and their radio messages simply vanished into the ether. Finally, somebody on *Yarroma* had the bright idea of toggling the FS6 radio from R/T mode to W/T mode, and sending a Morse signal direct to Garden Island. All that is known with any certainty is that the message finally got through to Naval Headquarters by W/T rather than light signal. At 9.52 pm, 97 minutes after Jimmy Cargill's first sighting, Garden Island received *Yarroma*'s message: 'Suspicious object in net.' Naval Headquarters responded by ordering Eyers: 'Close and investigate.'

♦   ♦   ♦

By now Chuman's midget was not the only Japanese submarine in the harbour. All three midgets had to battle the currents outside the Heads and all arrived late. Next to arrive was Ban. He was due at 7.15 pm. He reached the harbour entrance some time around 9.30, over two hours late. At 9.48 pm, four minutes before *Yarroma*'s first message to Garden Island, Inner Loop 12 recorded an isolated, sharp blip. A second pair of Japanese torpedoes was now in the harbour, past the boom net, and looking for trouble. Again, nobody stirred.

♦   ♦   ♦

At about 10.10 pm Eyers responded to the request from Garden Island to 'close and investigate' with a second message reporting that the mystery object was metal, with a serrated edge on top, and that it was moving with the swell. Although he now had good reason to believe it was a submarine, he chose not to pass on this last fact. Garden Island responded to this latest message by ordering him to give a fuller description. If there is to be criticism of Eyers, then it would be for his next action. He had been ordered to investigate further. He responded

by signalling with his Aldis lamp to his fellow Channel Patrol boat
HMAS *Lolita* to please come over from her station at the other end of
the boom net. Although *Lolita's* skipper Warrant Officer Herbert 'Tubby'
Anderson was almost twice Eyers' age at 38, he was the more junior
officer. At around 10.20 pm Eyers ordered Anderson and *Lolita* to do the
investigating. If anyone was going to tangle with an enemy mine or
submarine, it was not going to be Eyers and his top-secret ASDIC.

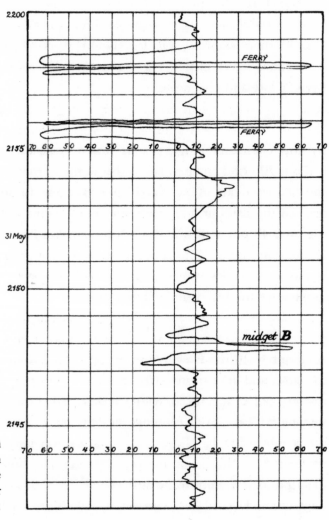

Trace left by Ban
(I-24's midget) on
Inner Loop 12 as he
enters the harbour
at 9.48 pm.

Lolita was on the seaward side of the net. Anderson raced the remaining length of the net and swung *Lolita* through the western boom gate and prepared to take a look. His handwritten draft report takes up the narrative:

> Stood off about 20 feet with stern towards object and machine gun covering same. Inspected object by flashing Aldis Lamp on it, which proved to be a submarine. The bow was pointed approximately south east. She was inside the net, her bow being approximately two feet above water, periscope showing about a foot, and stern entirely submerged. She appeared to be struggling to extricate herself. I realized at once the necessity for immediate action and gave the order to stand by depth charges.

Jim Nelson, *Lolita*'s signalman, recalls flashing a message by light to the Port War Signal Station: 'Have sighted enemy midget submarine and proceeding to attack. Lolita.' The signal was acknowledged.

Lolita dropped its first depth charge and roared off at full throttle to get out of the way of the blast. There was none. Depth charges explode once they reach a pre-set depth. Those aboard the Channel Patrol boats were regularly set to explode at 100 feet (about 30 metres). Without a change of setting, in 81 feet (24 metres) of water they simply tumbled to the bottom of the harbour and sat there in silence.

The bemused crew waited. Nothing. There was no choice but to try again. This time the crew attached some small floats to the depth charge to slow its descent in the hope that this would make it detonate. 'Tubby' Anderson lined up for a second attack run. He roared in towards the net, swung *Lolita* hard to starboard as they came up alongside the submarine and released a second charge. Again he raced off to get out of the way. Another agonising silence. Nothing. Two depth charges now sat on the bottom of the harbour, both 22 feet (6 metres) from detonating.

There is a school of thought which says this was a lucky escape for all concerned. If the depth charges had exploded and set off a sympathetic explosion in the sub's torpedoes and scuttling charges, then

The track followed by Chuman's midget is still the subject of controversy. We know with some certainty that he crossed Inner Loop 12 at 8.01 pm, two minutes behind the Manly ferry. We also know with some certainty that he reversed into the Boom Net close to the Western Gate some time just before 8.15 pm. This diagram shows the track taken by the Manly ferry on the night of the attack, together with the best guess available at Chuman's movements: (1) 8.01 pm, Chuman crosses Inner Loop 12 two minutes behind the Manly Ferry, then heads across harbour, avoiding Sow and Pigs Reef, and enters via Western Gate; (2) 8.10–8.15 pm, reverses into Boom Net. At 10.37 pm, he fires scuttling charges, killing both crew.

a ton of military-grade high explosive would have gone up within a few metres of Sydney's harbour shore. This would have left nothing of the submarine. It would also have spelt the end for *Lolita*, probably *Yarroma*, and every window in Clifton Gardens.

Anderson prepared for his third attack. As *Lolita* headed towards the submarine for the final depth charge run, she was met by a deafening explosion, sending a gigantic column of flame and water towering over the patrol launch. The shock wave lifted *Lolita* out of the water, heeling her over and almost swamping her. As the water settled, a huge oil patch spread on the harbour surface. Realising that their position was hopeless, the midget's crew had fired one of their two sets of 135-kilo scuttling charges, killing themselves in the process. Lieutenant Kenshi Chuman and Petty Officer Takeshi Omori had chosen a warrior's exit. They were the first men to die in the Battle of Sydney Harbour. The time was 10.37 pm.

✦　　✦　　✦

On Garden Island, 18-year-old signalman Ian Mitchell had just worked the 'dog watch' from 4 pm to 8 pm. Instead of returning to his sleeping quarters at Rushcutters Bay after his watch ended, he stayed to eat in the mess. He was still on Garden Island when the excitement began. He was standing in the visual signal tower when a W/T operator from the wireless room below burst in. 'His eyes were sticking out like dog's whatsits,' Ian Mitchell recalls. 'He said: "Subs are in the harbour. We've got a red alert." '

Chapter 9

All hell breaks loose

The blast from Chuman's submarine reverberated around the harbour. Windows were flung open and curtains pulled back as people rushed to see what was going on. The first thought was an air raid. The anti-aircraft batteries woke up with a start. Searchlights snapped on and probed the clouds.

In his report dated 22 June 1942 Rear Admiral Muirhead-Gould lamented: 'Great difficulty has been experienced in making out any sort of chronological plot. A great many ships and boats and, therefore, people were concerned in these operations, and all were so busy that they had no thought for recording actual time of incidents.' It is hard to avoid the suspicion that this blurring of time suited Muirhead-Gould well. His account of his own preparedness does not match the recollection of others.

According to Muirhead-Gould's report, Captain Bode of the USS *Chicago* left the dinner party at 'Tresco' at 10.20 pm 'with suggestion that he should go to sea with *Perkins*'. At 10.27 pm, within a few minutes of *Lolita*'s signal that she was attacking an enemy submarine, Muirhead-Gould issued an order to all ships in Sydney Harbour: 'Take anti-submarine precautions.' He also closed the harbour to outward shipping. At 10.36, one minute before Chuman scuttled, Muirhead-

Gould sent out a general signal: 'Presence of enemy submarine at boom gate is suspected. Ships are to take action against attack.' Muirhead-Gould's orders will have been transmitted from Garden Island by W/T and visual signal, and repeated from the Port War Signal Station by the same means. As we have seen, this left large numbers of ships in the harbour uninformed. Any ship out of sight of both Garden Island and PWSS—the Channel Patrol boats tied up in Farm Cove, for instance—will have seen and heard nothing.

Nevertheless, Muirhead-Gould sets out in his report to present a picture of himself quickly grasping the nature of the threat and responding correctly and effectively. If other accounts are to be believed, it was not quite like that. The lights in the Garden Island construction site stayed burning brightly, outlining ships in the harbour including the *Chicago*. In fairness to Muirhead-Gould, this was not unreasonable. The construction of a massive graving dock at Garden Island was regarded as urgent war work, and it went on 24 hours a day. There were 1000 men on the site at any given time, and the night shift needed light. However, Muirhead-Gould's other orders were less defensible. He specifically ordered that commercial harbour traffic continue as normal, which meant fully lit. He prudently omits this order from his final report, but it appears in his draft report dated 22 June 1942. He wrote: 'Some comment has been made that the ferries were allowed to continue to run. This was done by my direct order as I felt that once there was a submarine, or more than one submarine in the Harbour, the more boats that were moving about at high speed the better chance of keeping the submarines down till daylight.' He could not have been more wrong.

♦   ♦   ♦

By 9.48 pm and the second indicator loop crossing, the anti-submarine specialist HMAS *Yandra* and the three NAP boats *Lauriana*, *Allura* and *Yarrawonga* had allowed two enemy submarines to slip into the harbour unchallenged. The blast from the direction of the boom net, however, alerted all four to the fact that all was not well. *Lauriana*'s log takes up the story.

2237. Large charge exploded Western channel Boom. Orange flash about 20 or 30 feet high followed by charge like depth charge. Water up about 40 feet. Watched searchlights and C.B. [Channel Patrol boat] who were showing on boom for signal. Received no signal from Port War or Channel Patrol boat, thought it was large practice charge.

2248. Proceeding in line towards South Reef from Inner North Head. Visibility fair only, clouds. Noticed flurry on water ahead to port. Thought it may have been paravane* from minesweeper, or shark broaching. Decided to investigate.

2252. Speeded up, put searchlight on at about distance 60 to 80 feet, immediately showed Conning Tower of sub about two points to port. Black in shape about 2′6″ diameter.

This was Matsuo's midget, finally entering the harbour almost four hours late. *Lauriana's* log continues:

Sent flash to Port War (L.L.L.) also Channel Boat and in direction of Minesweeper. Put searchlight on and off and continued to send L's and AA to Port War, to Channel Boat in direction of Boom. No response to our signals.

Lauriana was totally unarmed. The NAP flotilla leader L.H. Winkworth later complained in his official report: 'Had we had our promised depth charges, we could have certainly sent the sub to the bottom. Had we had Verey lights or rockets, we could have immediately illuminated the area for the batteries to open fire.' Instead all *Lauriana* could do was send frantic light signals—'L's' and 'A's' to raise the alarm, 'C's' to attract the attention of the Channel Patrol boat. No one reacted.

---

* Paravanes are large, fish-shaped devices towed by cables extending from the bow of a minesweeper. The cable deflects any mine it comes across and cuts it from its mooring, after which the mine can be destroyed. Paravanes endlessly break away from their towing cables, and the bulk of 'sightings' of midget submarines are in fact sightings of wayward paravanes.

Unlike *Lauriana*, *Yandra* was well armed with depth charges and other anti-submarine weapons. While *Lauriana* was flashing and signalling, *Yandra* was heading back into the harbour from the heads. As she altered course towards the inner harbour, she saw a conning tower about 400 yards (360 metres) ahead and on the same 265-degree course. *Yandra's* commander, Lieutenant James Taplin, estimated the sub's speed at 5 to 6 knots. *Yandra* increased speed to 8½ knots and set off in pursuit.

Matsuo now turned left onto a heading of 186 degrees, which would take him down the Eastern Channel and into the main shipping area of the harbour. Taplin continued to overhaul him. Unlike many of the defenders on Sydney Harbour that night, Taplin was no beginner: he had served 14 years in the navy, and knew what he was doing. He decided that ramming was his best course of action—he was cramped for space, and there were too many other surface vessels nearby to carry out a depth charge attack. (He complained in his official report that surface vessels 'frequently later on prevented an efficient investigation of suspicious objects'.) Let Taplin take up the narrative.

2257. Submarine appeared to be on steady course of approx 186 deg at same speed, hull slightly awash, no periscope visible, trimmed slightly by the stern.

2258. Submarine appearing to submerge a little when hidden from bridge by bow, but was definitely seen to be struck by 'Yandra'. This evidence was given by reliable ratings of foc'sle party. Slight impact felt on bridge. Submarine was seen to break surface on starboard side aft alongside of hull. Submarine was observed by myself and independent witnesses aft to be listed to starboard about 15 deg. and bow out of the water at approx. the same angle. Submarine . . . seen to submerge while turning to starboard when about 100 yards astern.

Yandra had clearly scored a hit with its ramming tactic. However, the sub and its attacker were both on a similar course, so it was a glancing impact. The port side of Matsuo's bow cage almost certainly took the main force of the collision. The only result appeared to be to make the submarine list to starboard. Taplin could see that the damage was not fatal. Depth charges would be needed to finish the job. Having overrun the submarine with his ramming attack, Taplin turned back, facing out towards the harbour entrance, and tried to pinpoint the submarine's position with his ASDIC gear. No contact. But Matsuo solved Taplin's problem for him. Matsuo had also turned back towards the harbour entrance in the hope of evading his tormentor. He surfaced again about 600 yards (550 metres) from *Yandra*, on a bearing 20 degrees to starboard. At this stage the submarine was moving very slowly from left to right across *Yandra*'s bow. *Yandra*'s ASDIC still showed nothing, but Taplin had a visual contact and he set off in furious pursuit, this time at maximum speed. He ordered a full pattern of six depth charges prepared, set to 100 feet (30 metres). The gap narrowed. At 400 yards (360 metres) the ASDIC was now picking up the sub. Taplin hurtled on. At 150 yards (140 metres) the ASDIC signal was very strong. Matsuo tried desperately to submerge while Taplin bore down on him. As *Yandra* passed directly over the disappearing submarine, Taplin dropped his pattern of six depth charges.

The result was not the one Taplin had been hoping for. His official report says simply: 'Submarine was not seen after explosions.' The implication was that it had been sunk. Not so. The main victim of the depth charge attack was the *Yandra* itself. Again, let Taplin take up the narrative.

> The shock of the D.C. [depth charge] explosions resulted in the instantaneous failure of steering gear, A/S [anti-submarine] gear, De-Gaussing gear [used to minimise magnetic interference and thereby foil magnetic mines], phone communication to aft, tunnel bearing covers fractured and partial failure of lighting throughout the ship.

As attacks go, this was not a rip-roaring success. Taplin hand-steered his crippled ship back out of the harbour to a position just off the Heads and set about repairing the damage. Fifteen minutes later he had restored the ASDIC and steering gear and was able to re-enter the harbour. Taplin's report concludes laconically: 'Anti-submarine sweep carried out in the vicinity of the depth charge attack but no contact obtained.'

♦   ♦   ♦

We can only speculate on Matsuo's next move. The standard Japanese instruction for midget submarines under attack after launching was to 'immediately flood tanks and submerge to a depth of 150 to 200 feet [45 to 60 metres] or deeper, and take evasive action on a course which is at right angles to that at the time of launching'. It seems highly likely that Matsuo did exactly that. He submerged into about 12 fathoms (72 feet or 22 metres) of water on a line between Inner North Head and Inner South Head. The highest probability is that he turned right towards the inner harbour, settled his submarine gratefully on the harbour bed, and tried not to make a noise.

♦   ♦   ♦

After crossing Inner Loop 12 at 9.48 pm, Ban made his way cautiously down the harbour towards Garden Island, delicately conserving his batteries. It took him an hour to travel 4 kilometres. By 10.52 pm he had crept to within range of USS *Chicago*, tied up at the no. 2 buoy off Garden Island. The orders governing Japanese midget submarine tactics were quite specific about the timing of an attack. 'If a large ship or transport anchors, a resolute attack should be executed immediately,' the commanders were instructed. 'Attack with the least possible delay. Opportunity to attack is lost if a vessel escapes to sea.'

According to *Chicago*'s action report, the first sighting of Ban's submarine placed him 300 to 500 metres off *Chicago*'s starboard side and at an angle of 45 degrees to *Chicago*'s stern, on a course towards the Harbour Bridge and parallel to *Chicago*'s position at anchor. It has always been assumed that at this point Ban was simply trying to make a positive identification of his target. But that overlooks the fact that Ban's torpedoes had been set to 60 degrees left deflection. Ban's orders were to attack at once, and his present course was taking him into a perfect firing position for his deflected torpedoes, with 183 metres of *Chicago's* starboard side exposed at close range. At this point *Chicago* may have had seconds to live.

There are as many accounts of what happened next as there are people who took part. Taking only from first-person accounts available to the author, including *Chicago's* action report, what followed went something like this.

The anti-aircraft gun crews aboard *Chicago* were doubly alert: William Floyd had read the riot act to them two days previously after they missed Ito's flight; and they had received Muirhead-Gould's 10.27 and 10.36 alerts. They will also have heard Chuman's scuttling charge, indicating that the threat was serious. So they were on the lookout for trouble in the water, particularly submarine trouble.

Floyd takes up the narrative: 'The sky-control personnel began searching to see if they could pick up anything in the harbour. Some little time later they saw what they believed to be a sub. A gun and a searchlight were trained there and the arcs were struck [the searchlight was turned on] so that by opening the shutters they would illuminate this object.' At this point the searchlight was alight but closed, with its beam trapped behind shutters. The crews asked for permission to open the shutters, and to open fire if what they found turned out to be a submarine. While the seconds ticked away, no orders came. After an agony of waiting—and with Ban moving into a perfect firing position, although they were in no position to know this—they decided they could stand it no longer. They opened the shutters. The conning tower of a baby submarine glistened in the searchlight beam.

The officer of the deck, Ensign Bruce Simons, was first to act. His response was not exactly devastating, but it was enterprising. He emptied his .45 automatic pistol at Ban's conning tower, while raising the alarm. All over the ship a gong sounded the general alarm, and the public address system made a difficult-to-understand announcement, something about a submarine.

George Kitteridge was a junior gunnery officer aboard *Chicago*.

I was in the duty section and my recollection of the whole thing was Gong! Gong! Gong! I ran up the ladder to the communications deck. We had a 1.1-inch mount or a Bofors and a quick-firing gun on the bridge there. Jimmy Mecklenberg [the senior officer on board at the time] jumped in the pointer's seat and I jumped into the trainer's seat and he yelled at me: 'Where's the trigger on this thing?' I said: 'Let's switch.' We switched. The trigger was in the foot pedal.

Kitteridge and Mecklenberg blazed away with the anti-aircraft pom-pom at the submarine's conning tower. Eyewitnesses recalled red tracer pouring into the harbour and shots 'falling all around' the submarine, which is a polite way of saying Mecklenberg and Kitteridge missed. They certainly inflicted no known damage.

The *Chicago* now tried some heavier metal. Two 5-inch guns at the stern of the ship joined the battle. However, they could not depress far enough to get Ban in their sights. This did not prevent the gun crews from opening fire anyway. Shells ricocheted across the harbour, miraculously doing no serious harm as they crashed into North Sydney. Chunks were blasted off the venerable stone walls of Fort Denison. Again there were no casualties. A few of the ricochets hit the armed merchant cruiser HMAS *Westralia* anchored in Athol Bay not far from Cremorne Point opposite, again doing no damage.

The searchlight beam and all of this wild firing may not have done Ban's submarine any immediate damage, but it had the effect of distracting him—and very likely temporarily blinding him—making a torpedo attack impossible. Instead, Ban submerged. Three minutes later, he surfaced again about 300 metres off *Chicago*'s starboard bow, having continued on course towards the Harbour Bridge underwater. It is impossible to know whether his disappearance and reappearance were deliberate, or whether the midget was pulling its regular trick of soaring and diving of its own accord. Whatever the explanation, it led to more pandemonium. *Chicago* opened fire again. A ferry pulled out of Circular Quay, to find shots from *Chicago*'s pom-pom falling all around it. The ferry skipper beat a hasty retreat back to the wharf. Red tracer whistled past the Garden Island launch *Nestor*, which had to swerve to avoid a collision with Ban. The sub's new position put it within sight of the Australian corvette HMAS *Geelong*, berthed on the Harbour Bridge side of Garden Island. *Geelong* opened fire on a 'suspicious object' in the direction of Bradleys Head, adding to the bedlam. Somewhere between Garden Island and the Harbour Bridge, Ban submerged again, leading some on the *Chicago* to think they had sunk their target.

Chicago's official action report plays down the amount of gunfire during this episode. Bode's report claims that at the first sighting only one round was fired, from the no. 3 5-inch gun. At the second sighting, according to the report, the 1.1-inch pom-pom fired 20 rounds and the 5-inch deck gun fired another single round. The report was signed by Bode and dated 5 June 1942. As Bode was nowhere to be seen aboard *Chicago* at the time, the first-person accounts from the officers who did the actual shooting, backed up by dozens of eyewitnesses all around the harbour, probably tell a more accurate story.

Meanwhile, plenty else was happening aboard *Chicago*. George Chipley was the duty engineering officer. The ship was on four-hour standby, meaning it had to be ready to sail in four hours. When Chipley heard pistol shots followed by shouting and the alarm gong, he went straight into action. 'I ran for the Main Engine Control in the after engine room, and soon both engine rooms and all four fire rooms reported manned and ready.'

Whatever Muirhead-Gould may have asked us to believe, at 10.52 pm when all the excitement began Captain Bode had not returned to his ship. It was anchored no more than a few hundred metres from 'Tresco', a couple of minutes away in the Captain's gig (launch). So 32 minutes after Muirhead-Gould claimed Bode left 'Tresco' 'with suggestion that he go to sea with *Perkins*', there was still no sign of the *Chicago's* captain.

Lieutenant Commander H.J. Mecklenberg, fresh from his adventures with the anti-aircraft gun, assumed command. He ordered Chipley to do what he was doing already, and prepare the ship to get under way. 'Fires were lighted under the seven cold boilers, and the fire room crews used high rates of oil and air flow to raise steam pressure rapidly,' Chipley remembered. 'I went up on deck to look at the stacks and I could see large volumes of persistent white smoke pouring from both stacks.'

As well as ordering Chipley to get *Chicago* prepared for sea, Mecklenberg signalled his destroyer escort USS *Perkins*, tied up on the next-door no. 4 buoy, to get under way and conduct screening patrols around *Chicago*. At 11.15 pm *Perkins* did as she was bid.

♦　♦　♦

Chicago's guns marked the beginning of a restless night for 17-year-old secretarial student Margaret Hamilton. Her family's home overlooked Taylors Bay, on the northern side of Sydney Harbour. When the wind blew from the south-west, as it did on the night of 31 May 1942, sounds from Garden Island carried clearly across the water to her front balcony. Margaret could hear the distinctive American accents of the loudspeakers on *Chicago* calling orders to the gunners: 'Ready! Aim! FIRE!' She could see what looked like a fireworks display, as the red tracer from George Kitteridge's pom-pom whipped down the harbour. Searchlights reflected on the clouds, bathing the water surface in a pale and eerie white light. She watched for a while, uncertain of what was going on but excited by the whole spectacle. When the sounds of firing and depth charges faded, she went to bed but couldn't sleep.

♦　♦　♦

Sydney Harbour was now in pretty good uproar. Chuman's scuttling charge, fired at 10.37 pm, could be heard all over the harbour, and particularly loudly in the northern suburbs of Clifton Gardens and Mosman. *Yandra*'s six 180-kilo depth charges had detonated at 11.07 pm just off South Head, within good earshot of Vaucluse, Dover Heights and Rose Bay. A few minutes earlier *Chicago* had been blasting away with its 5-inch gun and anti-aircraft gun from just off Garden Island, followed by more firing from *Geelong*. The citizens of Sydney could be in no doubt that something serious was afoot. However an air-raid remained the most likely explanation, with some sort of navy exercise on the harbour as the next best candidate.

The sirens had still not gone off, but people started slipping into their prearranged air-raid countermeasures. It is a common psychological insight that humans reserve their clearest memories for their worst humiliations. Tess van Sommers was a young evening student at Sydney University, working by day for Associated Newspapers and hoping for a journalism cadetship there. She lodged in Double Bay with the formidable Margaret Dalrymple Hay, clerk of the university's Law School. She was within good earshot of the explosions.

'In the event of enemy attack from the air or sea,' she remembers

my role in our household was to nab the two pet dogs, stuff their ears with cotton wool and bind up their heads with scarves to protect their ear-drums from blast.

At the first terrific thump I bounded up, flung on a dressing gown, grabbed the cotton wool and the scarves—of an especially hectic tartan pattern—and stumbled down stairs. In the hall, the dogs' baskets were empty. A faint light showed from a part-open door, where a relative of Miss Dalrymple Hay resided after being evacuated from the Solomons, where she had experienced bombardment.

I dashed in. She was sitting up, a quivering dog under either armpit, smoking a small cigar and tending a large bottle of Gordon's gin. In my haste I had wrapped the lurid scarves over the dressing gown and around my own neck. Our refugee fixed them with a stare and raised eyebrow. 'Well, well, well,' she said, heavily sardonic, '*somebody* got dressed in a hurry.'

It rankled for days afterwards. In my first test in the face of the enemy, I had been suspected of panicking.

At Riverview College, well up the harbour and away from the immediate gunfire, the schoolboys were determined not to miss any of the action. The priests had told them all to go to the air-raid shelters below. They would have none of it. Instead they climbed onto the roof. Jim Macken remembers:

> All we were able to see was searchlights, all over the sky. There were explosions coming from the harbour, which we assumed to be bombs. They were the depth charges. We didn't think there were any bombers there, because we could see in the searchlights that they weren't picking up any planes.
>
> We weren't scared. We were just excited. We wanted to know what was going on. It was the only time during the whole war that we went up on the roof.

Aboard the *Sea Mist*, Reg Andrew could hear firing and explosions up the harbour. He went up on deck to see if he could work out what was going on. 'We could hear firing in the distance,' he recalled. 'But after a while that all disappeared. When there was no more activity, I went back to bed.'

♦   ♦   ♦

At 11.14 pm Muirhead-Gould responded to the increasing tumult on the harbour by issuing his third and, by his account, final order of the night: all ships to be darkened. However, the floodlights remained burning at Garden Island, continuing to silhouette *Chicago* and other ships at anchor nearby.

At this point, things had become relatively calm. There was no actual firing on the harbour, and no depth-charging. The smoke was beginning to clear, as was the cloud, which now began to thin and allow a little moonlight through. Ban's submarine lay submerged in the harbour somewhere near the Harbour Bridge. Matsuo's submarine lay in wait, inert on the bottom of the harbour near the heads. The two submarine commanders will have heard Chuman's scuttling charge explosion (which they probably thought was either a depth charge or, much better, a torpedo attack) and both will have heard *Yandra*'s depth charges. So the submarines knew that the defences were alert, and some of the defences knew there were submarines on the loose. But the full reality was not available to either attackers or defenders. The defence did not know the correct count of submarines still alive in the harbour: Matsuo's submarine, which had gone quiet after *Yandra*'s depth charge attack, was presumed by the defence to be sunk somewhere near the Heads; and Ban's submarine, which had submerged while heading up the harbour near the Harbour Bridge, might have been sunk by *Chicago*'s and *Geelong*'s guns. The midgets' commanders did not know which submarines, other than themselves, had survived the depth-charging and gunfire. Nor did they know that Chuman had scuttled before he could inflict any damage.

At 11.30 the Australian anti-submarine vessel HMAS *Bingera*, which had been tied up near *Chicago*, reported ready to proceed. She was ordered to slip her moorings and carry out an anti-submarine search inside the harbour. In particular, she was asked to follow up a report of a submarine passing her position and proceeding towards the Harbour Bridge—Ban's midget. The two Australian corvettes *Geelong* and *Whyalla*, both tied up alongside each other at the oil wharf on the western side of Garden Island, began searchlight sweeps of the harbour, particularly in the direction of the North Shore from Cremorne Point to Bradleys Head. They all found nothing.

◆　　◆　　◆

It would be interesting to know where and how Rear Admiral Muirhead-Gould and Captain Bode of the *Chicago* spent the time between 10 pm and 11.35 pm that night. The first message suggesting something was amiss was transmitted to Muirhead-Gould's headquarters on Garden Island at 9.52 pm. This reported a suspicious object in the net. The second and stronger report from *Yarroma* was transmitted at 10.10 pm, and talked about a metal object with serrated edge, moving with the swell.

The first message would hardly warrant a phone call to the Admiral. It is credible that the second message, however, was alarming enough for Garden Island to contact Muirhead-Gould by phone at home.

Presumably Muirhead-Gould reacted with as much pleasure to this phone call as anyone else might when being disturbed on a Sunday night towards the end of a pleasant dinner party by a call from the office. From their subsequent behaviour it is apparent that neither Muirhead-Gould nor Bode believed a word of it. As far as Muirhead-Gould was concerned, all this talk about submarines came from a bunch of weekend sailors who wouldn't know a sub if it fell on their heads.

Matters were not improved by the mounting collapse of communications on the harbour. The Port War Signal Station on South Head simply did not cope with the flood of telephone, R/T, W/T and signal lamp messages pouring in from Garden Island, the loop station, Channel Patrol boats, Naval Auxiliary Patrol boats, *Yandra* and myriad others, all trying to pass on information or request it. Given that effective communication and accurate information are the bedrock of modern warfare, Muirhead-Gould was certainly at a disadvantage.

Muirhead-Gould's report paints a picture of the dinner party breaking up the minute the first alert came in, with Bode leaving at 10.20 to take *Chicago* to sea, escorted by *Perkins*. A more likely scenario would have Muirhead-Gould issuing his two precautionary orders, the first at 10.27 to all ships to take anti-submarine precautions, the second at 10.36 to take action against submarine attack, by telephone from 'Tresco' while allowing the dinner party to continue merrily on. Both these orders were issued before the first explosion on the harbour, the 10.37 detonation of Chuman's scuttling charges. Muirhead-Gould may even have issued his third order—at 11.14, to darken all ships—by telephone from 'Tresco' as well.

If this is so, and all the timing points this way, then the dinner party must have come to something of a pause at 10.37 when Chuman scuttled. The explosion could certainly be heard as far away as 'Tresco'. Whatever remaining fun was left in the party would have started to drain away around 10.53 pm when *Chicago*, which was anchored only a few hundred metres away from 'Tresco', opened fire with its pom-pom and 5-inch deck guns. All remaining fun would have evaporated 14 minutes after that with the six thunderous explosions from *Yandra's* depth charges.

Communications on the harbour had by now well and truly broken down. There had been wild firing from nearby heavy guns aboard *Chicago*, and thumping explosions in the distance. It could no longer be ignored. Both Muirhead–Gould and Bode decided, some time around 11.20 pm, that they would have to find out for themselves what was going on.

Chapter 10

Men with black beards

It would be incorrect to say *Chicago*'s officers disliked their captain. Loathed would be the more appropriate word. Reading through their letters and recollections, all written 30 and 40 years after the event, their anger and bitterness towards him remain palpable. One officer likened him to Charles Laughton's Captain Bligh in the 1937 film of *Mutiny on the Bounty*. In 1942, Herman Wouk was still nine years away from publishing his classic novel *The Caine Mutiny*. If he had, *Chicago*'s officers might have found plenty of its unstable central character Lieutenant Commander Philip Queeg in their own Captain Howard Bode.

Bode and his executive officer Commander John Roper returned to *Chicago* from 'Tresco' aboard the Captain's gig some time around 11.30. Bode was in a towering rage. Jimmy Mecklenberg tried to brief him on the events of the night but Bode would not listen. There were no periscopes, he thundered, and no submarines. They were all insubordinate jittery fools. Mecklenberg must at once take the ship off 'general quarters'—its current high state of alert. Preparations to get under way were to cease at once. *Perkins* should come off patrol and return to her mooring. So much for Muirhead-Gould's assertion that Bode left the dinner party at 10.20 with the idea of putting to sea with *Perkins*.

Bode then ordered a message to be sent to Muirhead-Gould, flashed by signal lamp to the Garden Island headquarters. The text has long vanished, but William Floyd recalls that it said, in effect: 'I apologise for the ship opening fire in your harbour. It was done without my permission by some junior officers who mistakenly believed there were enemy midget submarines in the harbour.' Bode then retreated to his cabin, with an order that all officers were to assemble before him on the bridge.

Some time after midnight the officers gathered to meet their captain. According to George Chipley, that night Bode 'rose to new dramatic heights'. He accused all the officers of being drunk. (George Chipley commented: 'Our ships were dry and in two-and-a-half years I never saw alcohol consumed on the *Chicago*.') They were a bunch of incompetents. There were no submarines. They had been firing at shadows. Dire judgements would follow in the morning.

◆   ◆   ◆

Rear Admiral Muirhead-Gould was not the only commander anxious to find out at first hand what was going on in Sydney Harbour. The six Channel Patrol boats not on duty were all required to tie up at Farm Cove, two bays along from Garden Island. This put them out of sight of both Garden Island and Port War Signal Station, so they had no way of receiving visual signals. They carried no R/T or W/T. However, they were close enough to the *Chicago* and *Geelong* for the shooting to be heard loud and clear, never mind the depth-charging and scuttling which had taken place much further down the harbour. Curiosity got the better of *Marlean* and *Toomaree*. Without waiting for orders, they both slipped their moorings and headed off towards the sound of gunfire.

That left *Esmerelda*, *Leilani*, *Sea Mist* and *Steady Hour* as the reserve Channel Patrol boats still tied up in Farm Cove. *Leilani* was unmanned, however, and *Esmerelda* had engine problems. Only *Sea Mist* and *Steady Hour* could offer any additional firepower if required. At the stroke of midnight, with the smoke clearing and the thunder of the first round of explosions now fading, Reg Andrew officially took command of *Sea Mist*. He was asleep at the time.

♦ ♦ ♦

Rear Admiral Muirhead-Gould and his chief staff officer called for the Admiral's barge some time around 11.30 pm. They set off down the harbour at 11.36 in the direction of the boom net. Muirhead-Gould has been criticised for abandoning his headquarters and taking to the water at this juncture, but this criticism seems harsh. The collapse of communications meant that he was starved of reliable information. He was far from convinced that his harbour was under submarine attack. Going out and finding out for himself seems, in the circumstances, to be both an honourable and a defensible action, particularly as he did it during a lull in all the shooting and depth-charging.

According to his own report, Muirhead-Gould arrived at the boom net and boarded *Lolita* at midnight. At this point, accounts of what happened tend to diverge, and the various versions of the story seem to depend on both the diplomatic instincts and discretion of the teller. Were Muirhead-Gould and Bode both drunk? The reader will have to make up his or her own mind.

Muirhead-Gould's manner on board *Lolita* has been variously described as jocular, sarcastic, belligerent, frivolous, sceptical and, in one case, incoherent. 'Tubby' Anderson did his best to describe to him what had happened. Muirhead-Gould simply didn't believe him. Jim Nelson, from *Lolita*'s crew, remembers the Admiral opening the dialogue by asking: 'What are you all playing at, running up and down the harbour dropping depth charges and talking about enemy subs in the harbour? There's not one to be seen.' Nelson continues:

> Muirhead-Gould was very sarcastic about our story. He asked us how we knew we had actually sighted a sub. Tubby told him that Jimmy Crowe [another *Lolita* crew member] had been a First World War submariner. Muirhead-Gould called Crowe over and

asked him: was it a sub? Crowe verified it. Muirhead–Gould asked us if we had seen the captain of the sub. Did he have a black beard?

The grilling of *Lolita*'s crew lasted half an hour. By 12.30 Muirhead-Gould had heard enough. He was still unconvinced. As he was about to leave, he turned to the crew and said: 'If you see another sub, see if the captain has a black beard. I'd like to meet him.'

◆　◆　◆

Ban submerged near the Harbour Bridge some time around 11 pm. It is a matter of guesswork how he spent the next 90 minutes. The highest probability is that his first action was to do what submariners regularly do when under attack—head off underwater in what they hope is an unexpected direction, then make for the seabed and stay still and quiet. All Ban's behaviour up to this point suggests he was conserving battery power, so his every move will have been slow and calculated. The dashing Ban would have to wait his turn: this was a time for cool and calm.

It is worth standing back and trying to see the situation through Ban's eyes (and hear it through his ears, because sound was one of his most important sources of information). He will certainly have heard the thump of Chuman's scuttling charge: Ban was not far away at the time. He probably heard *Yandra*'s six depth charges. Although they were fired several kilometres away, sound carries well under water. The fact that there were six explosions meant they could not be Japanese torpedoes: there were only four other torpedoes in the harbour that night, two each aboard Chuman's and Matsuo's midgets. If the explosions weren't from torpedoes, it was very likely at least one of his fellow submariners was under depth charge attack elsewhere.

Anti-submarine detection gear like ASDIC sends out a sound 'ping', which can be heard by the submarine as it bounces off the sub's hull. The anti-submarine specialist HMAS *Bingera* began patrolling near the Harbour Bridge around 11.30, so from his hiding place nearby Ban will have heard the pinging of her ASDIC. Clearly the harbour was becoming an increasingly dangerous place for submarines. As well, each of the midgets carried a hydrophone to pick up other ship movements through the sounds of their engines and propellers. As well as *Bingera*, the destroyer USS *Perkins* had got under way and was carrying out an anti-submarine patrol near Garden Island to screen *Chicago*. Both *Marlean* and *Toomaree* had slipped their moorings and headed down the harbour. Their propellers will have been less noisy than *Bingera's* or *Perkins'*, but from where Ban sat they will have added to the impression of turmoil all around and above him.

Nevertheless, Ban had a job to carry out. If he went to periscope depth, he could see *Chicago* silhouetted against the Garden Island floodlights. She was still tied to no. 2 buoy, but with smoke belching from her funnels she must be about to get under way. There was no time to lose.

♦   ♦   ♦

G. Hermon Gill's official history of the Royal Australian Navy contains a diagram, drawn by Hugh W. Grosser, depicting Ban's attack. This diagram is universally reproduced in accounts of the raid, whether in books and magazines or on television. It is reproduced here on p. 141. It is simply wrong.* It flies in the face of eyewitness accounts, as well as defying common sense. However, it is fatally tempting for writers and television directors, because it allows everyone to marvel at the fact that Ban had a sitting duck for a target. Almost every account talks about 183 metres of *Chicago's* hull broadside on to Ban's submarine and impossible to miss from 500 metres. That is not how it was.

Chicago's action report records that the cruiser was facing 265 degrees (almost due west) at the time of the attack. She was tied up to no. 2 buoy, which put her about 400 metres due east of the north-east corner of Garden Island. It does not require an elaborate Admiralty nautical chart to work out the firing positions: a Sydney street directory will do the job nicely. The best position to attack would be from north of *Chicago* just off Cremorne Point (or Robertsons Point, to give its less-used but

---

* Alert readers will notice that Grosser also places Chuman's sub on the wrong side of the net. His diagram has much to answer for.

technically correct name). A torpedo fired from Robertsons Point would have as its target the whole 183 metres of *Chicago*'s starboard side. Ban's problem with this ideal firing position was the bristling collection of warships already manoeuvring in the area, plus the armed merchant cruiser HMAS *Westralia* tied up in Athol Bay. If he took up a firing position there, he could expect a hot time from them all, especially *Westralia*.

Instead of stopping at Robertsons Point, Ban opted to move further down the harbour. He looked for a firing position less visible from Athol Bay, which took him to a point south of Bradleys Head. This put him facing *Chicago*'s stern, not her starboard side, and therefore offering a much narrower target. The *Chicago*'s beam (width) was 20 metres. But the hulls of fighting ships are generally 'V' shaped, and 20 metres refers to the ship's beam at its widest point, usually on the main deck. The hull sat 7 metres deep into the water. At 5 of those 7 metres below the surface— the depth at which Ban's torpedo was set to run—the hull will have tapered off to less than 10 metres. *Chicago* lay at a slight angle to Ban's line of fire, presenting a target less than 20 metres wide at a range of 500 metres. To add to the problem, Ban would have to align his submarine to allow for the 60-degree left deflection pre-set on his two torpedoes. Torpedoes do not snap into a turn the instant they leave the tubes: they follow a leisurely curve. It would require fine judgement to position the moving submarine in such a way that the torpedoes would curl into the precise line needed to attack a 20-metres-wide target 500 metres away.

The reader might like to think of it this way. A common way of describing an easy shot is to say it's like hitting a barn door from 10 paces. That would indeed be hard to miss. But if the barn door swings open, so that only the door's edge is almost facing the marksman, then it becomes a lot more difficult. Now add the fact that the rifle is not up to the marksman's shoulder and being aimed directly along the barrel through the sight: instead it is being held at arms length and angled at 60 degrees to the marksman's body, and being sighted through a mirror. It becomes a circus trick shot. That is some measure of Ban's difficulties.

Ban had a further problem. The torpedoes were driven from their tubes by a blast of compressed air. In the instant after firing, the whole trim of the submarine would be lost as the heavy torpedo was replaced by the light air in the torpedo tube, then by water flooding into the tube. The bow of the submarine would rear up sharply, and the crew needed to retrim before the second torpedo could be fired. This job took time— a matter of 30 seconds if the crew were lucky (and skilful), but two or three minutes if the submarine proved obstinate.

Ban took up position off Bradleys Head some time after midnight. There he had a stroke of bad luck followed almost at once by a counter-balancing stroke of good luck. At 12.25 am the lights at Garden Island were doused. *Chicago* was no longer silhouetted against them. The target was now much harder to see. Then Ban's luck bounced straight back: at about the same time as the lights went down, the full moon finally broke through the cloud. His target was now bathed in moonlight.

At 12.29 Ban fired his first torpedo.

Allowing time to accelerate to 44 knots, the torpedo will have taken about 30 seconds to cover the 500 metres or so between Ban's midget and *Chicago*. Even as they struggled to retrim their submarine and fire the second torpedo, each second must have been an eternity for Ban and Ashibe. The 30 seconds passed. No explosion.

Never mind. They fired the second torpedo.

On the USS *Perkins*, now back secured on the no. 4 buoy on Bode's orders, a lookout saw the first torpedo's wake coming from the direction of Bradleys Head. It passed between *Perkins* and *Chicago*, about 25 metres off *Perkins'* starboard bow. Running at 5 metres below the surface, it continued towards Garden Island, passed under the Dutch submarine *K9*, passed under the converted harbour ferry HMAS *Kuttabul*, and slammed into the Garden Island sea wall immediately below *Kuttabul*. Instead of crossing the 500 metres between Ban's midget and *Chicago*, the torpedo had to travel a total of 1100 metres for a full 60 seconds before coming to its jarring halt against the stone wall.

♦ ♦ ♦

On the bridge of the *Chicago*, Bode was still haranguing his officers. He was particularly hard on Jimmy Mecklenberg, but he made it clear they

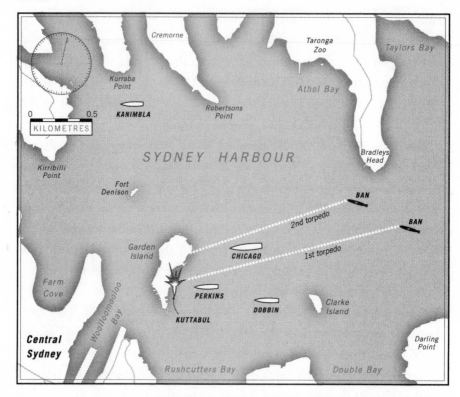

Ban's two torpedoes were fired about 30 seconds apart. The first torpedo passed between USS *Chicago* and USS *Perkins* and exploded against the Garden Island harbour wall, underneath HMAS *Kuttabul*. The second torpedo passed down *Chicago's* starboard side and came to rest unexploded on Garden Island. The two tracks converged slightly, indicating that Ban changed position between firings. Note that the *Chicago's* stern is facing Ban, not her long starboard side.

The diagram on the opposite page, drawn by Hugh W. Grosser for the official history of the Royal Australian Navy, is universally used to describe the midget submarine attack. It is simply wrong. Because the diagram shows USS *Chicago* facing north-west rather than a little south of west, it leaves the impression that Ban was firing at *Chicago's* side, not her stern. As well, it shows Ban's two torpedoes fired on diverging tracks from the same static position, whereas eyewitness accounts make it clear that Ban's two torpedoes were fired on converging tracks. This is possible only if Ban changed position between shots.

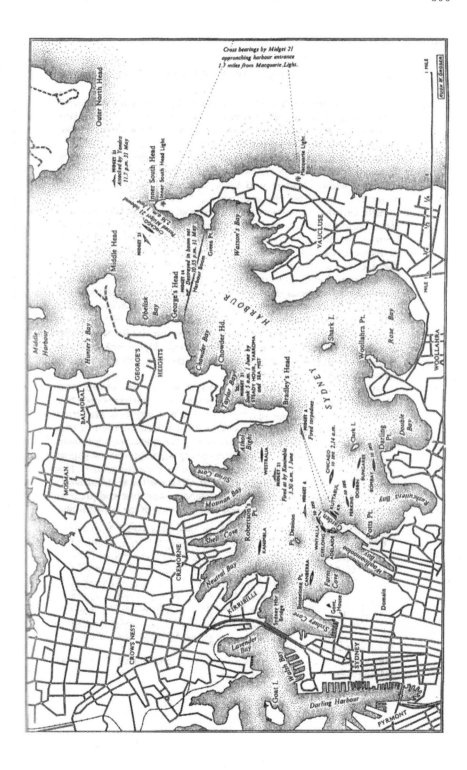

were all to blame. They were young fools. They'd got excited. They had opened fire at something in the water, not a submarine. At this point Ban's second torpedo appeared on *Chicago's* starboard side, running along the surface and crossing *Chicago's* bow from starboard to port. George Kitteridge remembers that it was spotted by several officers on the bridge, who interrupted Bode's tirade. 'It was obviously a torpedo wake and everybody said: look at that, look at that. Bode looked over and said: Hmp! It's just a motor launch going by.

'Just when he said that he faced us again. His back was towards the bow, and boom!'

Bode's next words were drowned by the biggest explosion of the night, only 500 metres away. Ban's first torpedo, containing 350 kilos of high explosive, detonated in the trapped space between the harbour wall, the harbour bed and the steel hull of the *Kuttabul*. The effect was devastating. The old ferry was lifted bodily from the water and brutally smashed. A ball of orange flame billowed from below the surface and lit the surrounding area, while a massive column of water spouted scores of metres in the air. An eyewitness told the *Sydney Morning Herald:* 'I saw the whole ferry lift as though she were on top of an enormous wave and then settle down again, sinking at the stern.'

In the nearby blocks of flats in Potts Point and Elizabeth Bay, crockery crashed from shelves, windows rattled, pictures fell off walls. People rushed to see what had happened. It had to be an air raid. Not a drill, either. The real thing.

◆   ◆   ◆

At the sound of the explosion, Captain Bode hesitated. His officers thought they detected a flicker of doubt as the monstrous roar of the torpedo's blast echoed and rumbled around the harbour. Bode's first response was to return to the attack with a new accusation. 'There you are', he snapped, 'you've got the shore batteries opening up'. However, the doubt must have been real. He turned to Jimmy Mecklenberg and said: 'Commander Mecklenberg, I want you to take my gig and go over to Garden Island. Present my compliments to Rear Admiral Muirhead-

Gould and say there's been an explosion reported and I request the nature of the explosion.'

✦   ✦   ✦

On board *Lolita* near the boom net, Rear Admiral Muirhead-Gould was about to climb back aboard his barge when he heard the explosion. 'What the hell was that?' the Admiral demanded.

Tubby Anderson knew the answer: 'If you proceed up harbour, sir, you might find your Japanese captain with a black beard.'

✦   ✦   ✦

The depth-setting mechanism failed on Ban's second torpedo. It ran along the surface instead of finding its correct depth of 5 metres. As a result, the 'arming' propeller did not spin through the required number of revolutions, and the torpedo failed to arm. It came to rest harmlessly on the shore next to Gun Wharf on Garden Island, spilling its brownish-yellow explosive innards onto the rocks.

For all Ban's undoubted courage and skill, for all his years of training and preparation, for all the meticulous planning which had gone into the raid, his attack had failed. The two torpedoes missed *Chicago* because, at the last minute, Ban's firing position off Bradleys Head made the shot impossibly difficult. The fact that the second torpedo failed to arm was neither here nor there: if it had armed correctly, a few rocks and an old wharf on Garden Island might have been violently rearranged. Yamamoto's dream of the total destruction of the American Pacific Fleet, however, would have remained as distant as ever.

Chapter 11

Sudden death

The *Kuttabul* had a slightly bizarre history. She was one of the first victims of the Harbour Bridge. *Kuttabul* was completed in 1922, destined for big things. She could carry up to 2250 passengers. She shuttled them on one of the busiest routes in the harbour: the short distance between Milsons Point at what became the northern end of the Harbour Bridge and Circular Quay ferry terminal near the southern end. When the bridge opened on 19 March 1932, *Kuttabul* was out of a job. She joined 16 other harbour ferries in the redundancy pool.

When she came off her Milsons Point route, she was used for a time as a concert boat. The concert boats and showboats were a Sydney institution right up until the 1960s. They were invariably big, and offered live entertainment as part of a three-hour cruise on the harbour. The concert boats entertained their packed passenger decks with live music, while the showboats offered a full vaudeville line-up. *Kuttabul's* show-business career came to an abrupt end on 26 February 1941 when she was taken over by the Royal Australian Navy, to be re-born as HMAS *Kuttabul*. The navy tied her up permanently to a mooring at the south-east corner of Garden Island, and used her as a dormitory for sailors who found themselves without a current ship.

Like Sydney ferries to this day, she had two passenger decks. Passengers—or re-housed sailors—entered via a gangplank bridging the shore to the lower deck. They could then climb an internal staircase to the upper deck. There was no exit from the upper deck to shore other than by going back down the stairs. Below the lower deck were the engines. Sailors slung their hammocks on both passenger decks. Their quarters were totally spartan. Cooking and eating facilities were all ashore, as were showers and washrooms. They had card tables and a ping-pong table, but not much else—just a locker, a few lavatories and wash basins, and a place to sling their hammocks.

Kuttabul was fairly loosely controlled, so that it is not possible to say with certainty how many sailors were aboard at any given time, nor who they were. The only certainty from that night is the number of casualties. At 12.30 am on 1 June 1942, *Kuttabul* was home to at least 31 sailors from three navies—Australian, New Zealand and British.

◆　　◆　　◆

The Japanese Type 97 Special torpedo was designed to tear a large hole in the armour-plated steel hull of a battleship or aircraft carrier. Its effect on an unprotected 20-year-old civilian ferry largely built of wood was catastrophic. Ban's torpedo blasted a massive hole in *Kuttabul*'s hull towards the ferry's stern, almost breaking the ferry in two. After being tossed in the air by the initial explosion, *Kuttabul* crashed back into the water and slid straight to the harbour bed. Wintry sea water roared in through the hole in the hull, sinking the ferry instantly by the stern and engulfing the lower passenger deck. The bow remained clear of the water. Any sailors sleeping near the blast on the lower deck were probably dead by the time *Kuttabul* slammed back onto the harbour surface. The force of the blast from 350 kilos of high explosive detonating at unprotected close quarters was simply not survivable. The explosion blacked out all the lights on Garden Island, and cut the telephone cable. It started a small fire on the wharf.

At the Australian National Maritime Museum in Darling Harbour, Sydney, there is a dramatic voice tape from one of the survivors, painting a vivid word picture of the scene on board. He was quartermaster aboard the *Kuttabul* that night, and the tape tells us nothing about him other than that his name was Ed. He was lightly injured in the explosion. Here are his words:

All I can remember was when I was hit I went down on the deck. You couldn't see your hand in front of your face. I just covered up. I'd just come back from the Middle East and I thought: this is an air raid. I heard water running and I said gee, it's time I got out of here.

We all sort of made a move then. I don't know what window we got out of. Three or four of us scrambled through and we pulled ourselves up onto the wharf. Next thing we looked around and the *Kutta* was more or less right on the bottom. So there was nothing much we could do, only turn around and help get the injured.

We took them up to the sick bay on Garden Island. The Petty Officer came and said: 'Ed, you're the quartermaster here. You should know all the chaps on board.' I said: 'I'll give it a go, but they're coming and going like flies. They might be here 24 hours and they get a draft straight away.' He said: 'I'd like you to come up and try to identify some of the bodies up there in the sick bay.'

He took me up there. This will stick in my mind the rest of my life. There was one chap there: all the skin of his face, you could just lift it up, straight off. Embedded itself in my mind, that did.

There were extraordinary acts of courage that night, and extraordinary tales of luck, good and bad.

Bandsman M.N. Cumming was, as his rank implied, not a fighting sailor. He was a musician. He had boarded the *Kuttabul* only five minutes before the explosion. The blast itself caused him a few cuts, but he was otherwise uninjured. He thought the ship had been hit by a bomb. Instead of heading for the safety of shore, then only a metre or so away, he stripped off and dived repeatedly into the bitterly cold, watery wreckage, ignoring shattered glass and jagged woodwork in a frantic search for survivors. He is credited with rescuing three critically injured sailors.

Engineer Captain A.B. Doyle and Commander C.C. Clark had been ashore on Garden Island when they heard the explosion. They raced to the scene and waded straight into the deep water. In pitch darkness they ignored the dangers of splintered decks and other lethal hazards to rescue shocked and dazed sailors, and lead them to safety. Cumming, Doyle and Clark were all singled out for mention by Rear Admiral Muirhead-Gould in his report, with the implication that they all deserved medals. They did.

They had no monopoly on courage. Ordinary Seaman L.T. Combers was below decks when the explosion knocked him off his feet. He smashed through a window to safety outside the ferry. Then he heard a cry for help, and saw a sailor slipping below the surface with the sinking wreckage. Although he was now safely clear, he dived back into the danger area and managed to drag the stricken sailor to the safety of a nearby motor launch.

Petty Officer J. Littleby usually slept aboard the *Kuttabul*. That night he had accepted a friend's invitation to bunk down in a small motor boat tied up nearby. The blast and shock wave almost swamped the tiny boat. However Littleby managed to keep it afloat and bring it up alongside *Kuttabul*. Three injured sailors owe him their lives. Littleby's regular sleeping quarters on the *Kuttabul* were totally demolished in the blast. If he had been asleep in his regular place that night, the death toll might have risen by four.

Others were plain lucky. Able Seaman Neil Roberts had been on sentry duty on land. He was due to be relieved at midnight. When his relief failed to materialise, he went to look for him aboard *Kuttabul*. As a way of apologising for failing to turn up for duty on time, the chastened relief offered Roberts his bunk on the more pleasant upper deck, instead of Roberts' usual bunk on the lower deck. Roberts accepted. And lived.

Able Seaman Charlie Brown had also been on sentry duty. He had heard the gunfire and explosions on the harbour, and wondered what was happening. He went off duty at midnight and by 12.10 was asleep in his bunk on the lower deck near the bow. His next memory is of a gigantic orange ball of fire, and of being blasted between a row of wash basins through the ship's side and into the water. Debris rained down on him, trapping him. He was slipping into unconsciousness when someone saw his hand flailing in the water. He was dragged to safety.

Able Seaman Colin Whitfield, a New Zealander, had one of the most remarkable stories of the night. He was climbing out of his hammock, with his feet on the deck, when the torpedo struck. When he tried to move he found his legs were useless, although he could see no injury. He had to descend the staircase to get to safety, which he managed by bumping down on his backside. At this point he blacked out, and remembers only that somebody helped him to the jetty, then carried him to the sick bay.

His next memory is of waking up in hospital at 3 am, with the surgeon bending over him saying something like: they'll have to come off. The surgeon then told a colleague that the anaesthetist had gone home for the night so they'd have to come off in the morning. In the meantime an orderly was told to make Whitfield comfortable. The orderly took it upon himself to bind up Whitfield's feet. Although the skin was unbroken, every bone inside was smashed. In the morning the surgeon was fulsome in his praise for the orderly. He had done exactly the right thing. Whitfield's feet had been bound in such a way that the bones might re-knit. The surgeon thought the feet might be saved. They were.

Others were less lucky. Petty Officer Leonard Howard, from Penrith west of Sydney, wanted to meet his wife next day. So he swapped duty with another sailor, and stayed aboard *Kuttabul*. He was killed.

Stoker Norman Robson was due to go on leave later that morning. Before going to sleep, he posted a letter to friend, including the words: 'You can never tell with this place. Anything might happen.' The friend received the letter three days after Robson's death.

Ordinary Seaman David Trist had survived the sinking of HMS *Repulse* six months earlier, on the second day of the Pacific war. He did not survive the sinking of the *Kuttabul*.

In all, Ban's torpedo led to the death of 21 sailors aboard the *Kuttabul*, 19 Australian and two British. Of those who died, 19 were killed aboard the ship; one died later in hospital; one sailor was missing. There were 10 injured, some seriously. The death toll in the Battle of Sydney Harbour had now risen sharply, from two to 23.

At about 1 am, half an hour after the torpedo struck, *Kuttabul*'s bow slid under the water, leaving only her wreckage-strewn upper deck slightly exposed.

◆ ◆ ◆

In the wake of the blast, bedlam returned to Sydney Harbour. There was wild shooting from all directions. It was a bad night for floating bits of wood, old packing cases, buoys, broaching fish, and fleeting shadows: all were sent ruthlessly to the bottom in a hail of tracer fire and heavier shells.

Some ships fired aimlessly into the air, believing this was an air raid and they might as well be seen to be doing something. Others felt obliged to sound off with klaxon horns or sirens, adding to the mindless pandemonium. The crew of the Channel Patrol boat HMAS *Marlean*, which had slipped its mooring earlier in the night and moved down the harbour to see what the fuss was all about, sheepishly admitted they had fired at their own shadow in Athol Bay, which they saw projected onto the harbour shore by the roving searchlights. Next day they scoured the papers for any report of casualties among the animals at Taronga Park zoo, which had been right in their line of fire.

This had no effect whatsoever on the two Japanese midget submarines still alive in the harbour. Matsuo continued to hide on the harbour bed just inside the entrance, awaiting his chance. He must have heard the detonation from Ban's attack, but he will not have known whether it was caused by another midget's torpedo or by some other explosive device like a depth charge. If it was a torpedo, he will not have known what damage resulted. He must have hoped that whoever had triggered the explosion had left him some worthy targets to pursue when he could finally get under way.

Meanwhile, Ban continued to creep towards the harbour exit and safety. From his periscope Ban could see the *Chicago* still serenely tied to her moorings. With both torpedoes spent, he had nothing left to fire at her but an 8 mm pistol. Time to say farewell to Sydney Harbour, and head for the open sea.

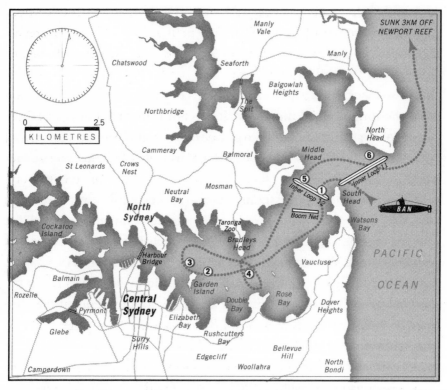

The track followed by Ban's midget is fairly well established. The timings are: (1) 9.48 pm, crosses Inner Loop 12, leaving a clear trace; (2) 10.50 pm, fired on by USS *Chicago*, and submerges; (3) 11.10 pm resurfaces, fired on by USS *Chicago* and HMAS *Geelong*, submerges; (4) 12.29 am fires two torpedoes at USS *Chicago*, both of which miss, but one sinking HMAS *Kuttabul*; (5) 1.58 am crosses Inner Loop 12; (6) 2.04 am crosses Inner Loop 11 and exits Sydney Harbour.

✦   ✦   ✦

The bedlam in the harbour was well mirrored by chaos on land. Radio stations broadcast urgent appeals to sailors to return to their ships. Taxi drivers were asked to scour the streets, cinemas, theatres, pubs, bars, nightclubs and brothels in a hunt for sailors to be rushed back to their stations. Police cars joined in the hunt for roistering crews.

Among the civilians, wild rumours spread at amazing speed. The invasion had started. The Japs were here. Even those who should have known better joined in the madness. A caller to a Sydney radio station remembered a particularly hysterical air-raid warden on his street, knocking on doors and rousing the occupants with an urgent message: 'There's an armada of aircraft. They're coming down. They've flattened Brisbane and they're now over Gosford, and soon they'll be bombing Sydney. Get the children under the table, in the hall, with a mattress on top. Good luck! Good luck!'

The 19-year-old Dorothy Levine had been on duty at the American Service Club in Phillip Street in Sydney's Central Business District. She was trying to make her way home by taxi to Vaucluse. Just as she was passing Rose Bay Police Station she saw tracer fire on the harbour followed by booming explosions.

I said to the taxi driver: my goodness, fireworks in the middle of wartime. I think it's ridiculous.

Then people came running out of all the units along the waterfront. We were told to go immediately to the nearest air raid shelter. We could hear boom, boom, boom, then a huge, loud explosion.

We were very frightened because it just wasn't natural to have all that light. The whole sky was lit up with searchlights. There seemed to be a lot of people. They just came from nowhere. Everyone was running all over the streets, not knowing what was going on.

♦   ♦   ♦

Rahel Cohen, a 23-year-old secretary serving in the Women's Auxiliary Air Force, had come to Sydney from Wagga Wagga on leave. At 12.15 am she caught the last ferry from Circular Quay to Athol Wharf near her parents' home in Mosman. There were only four people on board—

Rahel, an army officer Captain Ross Smith, the ferry captain and the ferry's engineer.

The ferry captain decided to take a slightly longer route this night. The Athol Wharf ferry normally tracked north-east from Circular Quay, passing to the north of the small harbour island of Fort Denison. However, an hour earlier the captain had heard shooting and general uproar from the direction of Garden Island and the USS *Chicago,* so he decided to take his ship south of Fort Denison and close to Garden Island to see what was going on.

The ferry had passed both Garden Island and *Chicago* and was about to turn left towards Athol Wharf. 'I was standing on the lower deck talking to the army man when I said: what's that? It looked like a silver thing, going under our ferry,' Rahel recalls. It was Ban's first torpedo, 5 metres below the surface and well under the ferry's hull, on its way to the *Kuttabul.* 'The Army captain saw it too. He pushed me down on the deck and fell down on top of me to protect me. Then there was a crash, of course. The torpedo had come up on the other side of our ferry and killed all the sailors. I remember the army fellow said to me: don't look.' Within seconds all hell broke loose. Searchlights flashed on all over the harbour. Rahel heard the ferry captain poke his head out of the wheelhouse and say: 'Let's get to hell out of here. Get inside. We're going to try to rush across.'

The ferry raced across the harbour to Athol Wharf. By the time it tied up, the tram which normally met it and carried the ferry passengers up the steep hill to the suburb of Mosman had fled. That night Rahel Cohen walked home, escorted in the darkness by the gallant Captain Smith.

◆　　◆　　◆

Muirhead-Gould left the boom net in his barge and went straight to his headquarters on Garden Island. Clearly his first job was to find out what had happened. This will not have taken long. By now there were plenty of people who knew it was a torpedo attack.

Jimmy Mecklenberg arrived on Garden Island in the *Chicago*'s Captain's gig at about the same time as Muirhead-Gould. His account of his encounter with Muirhead-Gould is a masterpiece of tact. 'The Admiral was well aware that there were submarines in the harbour,' Mecklenberg recalled. 'He suggested that I should tell my commanding officer to take the US forces to sea.' There is another version of this story, which suggests that Muirhead-Gould's words were a great deal more terse and to the point. In this version, his message to Bode was only five words long. 'Get out of my harbour.'

However it was expressed, the order to get under way was repeated around the harbour. The Indian Navy corvette HMIS *Bombay* and the Australian Navy corvette HMAS *Whyalla* were ordered to get moving, while the long-suffering USS *Perkins* once again slipped her mooring and set out to screen *Chicago* while the cruiser built up steam ready to head out to sea. The anti-submarine vessel HMAS *Bingera* was ordered to switch her search from the Harbour Bridge area and sweep the harbour between Garden Island and Bradleys Head, offering further protection to *Chicago*.

None of this was easily achieved. With the general overload of communications, very often there was no way to pass orders to the ships by radio. An officer was dispatched in a speedboat from Garden Island to go around the harbour advising all ships to make ready to go to sea, or to take up anti-submarine duties in the harbour.

At 1.10 am Muirhead-Gould sent out a general message: 'Enemy submarine is present in the harbour and *Kuttabul* has been torpedoed.' It was now five minutes short of five hours since Jimmy Cargill had spotted Chuman's sub in the net. Yet this message from Muirhead-Gould was the first to ships in the harbour giving them any accurate information about what was going on.

♦   ♦   ♦

At 1.58 am Inner Loop 12 recorded its third small, unexplained blip of the night. This was immediately taken to be a third submarine entering the harbour. In fact it was Ban on his way out.

♦   ♦   ♦

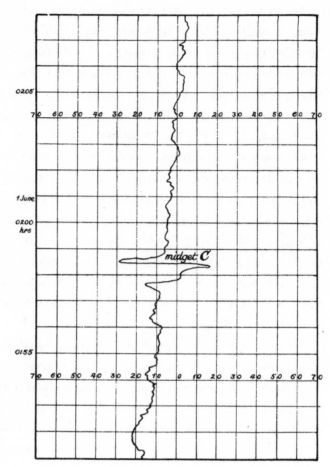

Trace left by Ban
(I-24's midget) on
Inner Loop 12 as he
leaves the harbour
at 1.58 am.

More and more ships got under way. HMAS *Canberra*, on four hours'
notice at no. 1 buoy, was ordered to sea at 1.15 am. The Dutch
submarine *K9*, moored alongside *Kuttabul*, where she had taken a lot of
damage but injured only one sailor, was towed up the harbour and out
of harm's way at 1.20. The Australian minesweeper HMAS *Samuel
Benbow* moored off Watsons Bay reported at 1.25: 'Crew at action
stations. Raising steam.' At 2.14 *Chicago* reported: 'Proceeding to sea.'
The Australian corvette HMAS *Whyalla* informed Garden Island at 2.30:
'Slipped and proceeding to sea.'

It is worth standing back a moment and considering these decisions. Large ships like USS *Chicago* and HMAS *Canberra* are at a massive disadvantage in the tight space of a harbour, particularly a narrow harbour like Sydney's. There were enemy submarines on the loose, so the natural response of both Muirhead-Gould and the respective captains was to take their ships away from the immediate danger and out to sea where they could fight. But that raised a massive question: if there were midget submarines in the harbour, how did they get to Sydney? And if the answer was: on the backs of larger submarines as they had done at Pearl Harbor, then where did that leave the escaping ships? The answer was: in huge trouble. There were five massive 'I' class Japanese submarines, all armed with an arsenal of their justifiably feared Long Lance torpedoes, lurking in the deep water outside Sydney Harbour.

We can only guess at Sasaki's motive in not leaving at least one or two of his mother submarines outside the harbour entrance with orders to pick off any large ships trying to escape. After all, that had been his tactic at Pearl Harbor six months earlier. In his official account of the raid G. Hermon Gill concluded: 'Luck was certainly on the side of the defenders.' Luck was surely with them now. As the ships steamed towards the open ocean, the mother subs had moved off south towards the rendezvous point at Port Hacking. So no Long Lances lay in wait for *Chicago, Perkins, Canberra, Whyalla* and all the other warships racing for the open sea.

Chapter 12

Matsuo's turn

Chicago's departure from the harbour was scarcely dignified. From earlier cancelling Mecklenberg's orders to prepare the ship to get underway, Captain Bode was now in a tearing hurry to get out. Following the torpedo explosion, he had ordered the engine room crews to resume building up steam. The crews responded with frantic efforts. At 2.14 the cruiser was ready, and Bode signalled Garden Island: 'Proceeding to sea.' Crew members had to be sent down to the buoy to unshackle the cruiser from its mooring. *Chicago* slipped with such indecent haste that at least one crew member was left behind, stranded on the buoy and shouting to his ship to wait for him. The telephone line to Garden Island via the buoy was not disconnected, and snapped as the giant cruiser backed off her mooring. Jimmy Mecklenberg, sent to Garden Island on the captain's gig, had to race up the harbour to catch up with his departing ship. *Chicago* paused briefly in mid-harbour to gather him up, then continued her charge towards the open sea and hopes of safety.

At 2.43 am the Port War Signal Station reported: '*Perkins* to sea.' At 2.56 they followed up with: '*Chicago* to sea.' Both American ships had passed through the boom gate, crossed Inner Loop 12 and were on their way out of the harbour.

On the bridge of the *Chicago* Captain Bode was still not convinced by his officers' account of sighting and firing at a midget submarine. As the cruiser steamed up to the harbour entrance Bode turned to Jimmy Mecklenberg and said: 'You wouldn't know what a submarine looks like.' In life it is seldom given to anyone to have a perfect riposte to this kind of remark, but this was Jimmy Mecklenberg's lucky night. 'They looked like that, Captain,' said Mecklenberg, pointing to a midget submarine passing down *Chicago*'s starboard side, too close for the guns to depress and fire at it. The midget was so close that it probably collided with *Chicago*, though nobody aboard *Chicago* felt any impact.

There was now no room for doubt. At 3 am Captain Bode ordered a fresh signal to Garden Island: 'Submarine entering harbour.' At 3.01 Inner Loop 12 recorded its fourth enemy blip of the night. After almost four hours of sitting patiently on the ocean bottom near the Sydney Harbour heads, Matsuo and his two torpedoes were on the move and inside Sydney Harbour.

◆　　◆　　◆

The Lieutenant in the speedboat criss-crossing the harbour with instructions to ships to get under way finally reached the remaining Channel Patrol boats in Farm Cove at around 3 am. His message to Reg Andrew and *Sea Mist* was scarcely a detailed set of orders. 'I think you'd better get under way,' the Lieutenant called out. 'There are subs in the harbour.' That was the first indication Reg Andrew had of what the firing was all about, and what was going on.

At this point Lieutenant Athol Townley appeared on the deck of the Channel Patrol boat *Steady Hour*, tied up behind *Sea Mist*. Townley had officially relinquished his command of *Steady Hour* at midnight (at the same moment that Reg Andrew took over command of *Sea Mist*). However, he had agreed to stay on board to allow the new skipper a night ashore. He was senior to Reg Andrew and the other Channel Patrol boat skippers on the harbour, and he assumed command. Was Reg Andrew ready to move? Yes. Okay, said Townley, go to Bradleys Head. Set your depth charges to 50 feet (15 metres).

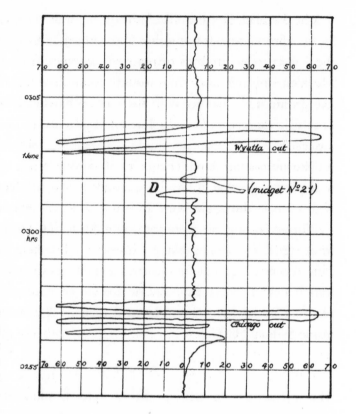

Trace left by Matsuo (I-22's midget) on Inner Loop 12 as he enters the harbour at 3.01 am.

After ordering the motor mechanic Winstanley to start the engines and the coxswain Potter to rouse the crew, Reg Andrew changed into his uniform and collected the vital paper with the code letter of the day on it. Now prepared, he ran to the upper deck and took over the throttles and wheel, ordered the mooring lines cast off, and set off down the harbour. *Sea Mists*'s new skipper was not exactly brimming with confidence. He was not alarmed by the prospect of enemy submarines: he was much more afraid of being mistaken for one of them and shot at by his own side. There had been plenty of wild firing earlier in the night. In the now darkened harbour he threaded his way cautiously through the unlit warships to his allotted station off Bradleys Head.

There was plenty to think about on the way. He had no idea how to fire a depth charge, let alone set it to 50 feet. There was also the Very pistol. Orders required the firing of two red Very flares before launching an attack, to warn other ships to stay clear. There was a Very pistol with red, green and white flares in the darkened wheelhouse. Which were which? The green ones had no serrated edge, and they felt greasy. That was a start.

The order to set depth charges to 50 feet carried serious implications. A depth charge takes about four seconds to drop 50 feet through water. The best *Sea Mist* could hope for was a speed of 10 knots. At that speed, a boat travels 20 metres in four seconds. So *Sea Mist* would have, at most, 20 metres between her and the blast from 180 kilos of military-grade high explosive. It was not a prospect to relish. For a young naval Lieutenant three and a half hours into his first command, working in a boat and with a crew he had met less than 24 hours earlier, carrying weapons he neither knew nor had practised with, going into battle must have been a daunting prospect.

When both *Sea Mist* and *Steady Hour* reached Bradleys Head, Townley ordered *Sea Mist* to patrol between Bradleys Head and the west boom gate. This gave Reg Andrew about 2500 metres of harbour shore to cover, including two bays, Chowder Bay and Taylors Bay. He decided to hold *Sea Mist* on a course following the shape of the shoreline, standing off about 150 metres as he tracked slowly between his two turning points.

It was now 3.35 am and six Channel Patrol boats swarmed around the boom net: *Toomaree* guarded the east boom gate; *Marlean* and *Sea Mist* patrolled the west boom gate and back into the harbour; *Yarroma*, *Steady Hour* and *Lolita* roamed freely throughout the area. *Yarroma* was now a key player: she carried ASDIC, and could look for submerged submarines as well as any sub foolish enough to broach the surface.

✦   ✦   ✦

At 1.05 am Licensed Fishing Boat no. 92 (the trawler *San Michele*) sighted a large submarine off Cronulla, a Sydney beach suburb well south of the harbour entrance. At 3.40 am she reported her sighting, probably to the Port War Signal Station. The mother subs had begun to arrive at the rendezvous point.

✦   ✦   ✦

We can only speculate on Matsuo's progress after entering the harbour. He probably began by picking his way carefully towards the Harbour Bridge. We know that he intended to head for Garden Island and the warships tied up there. By now his principal target USS *Chicago* was well out to sea. That left the cruiser HMAS *Canberra*, still tied up at Bennelong Point, the armed merchant cruiser HMAS *Westralia* moored in Athol Bay off Robertsons Point, and another armed merchant cruiser HMS *Kanimbla* moored at Birts Buoy near Kirribilli Point. All were worthy targets. After that, the harbour was plentifully stocked with smaller warships. If Matsuo made it as far as mid-harbour, and there is evidence that he did, then he will not have wanted for ships to attack.

At 3.50 am *Kanimbla* switched on her searchlight and opened fire on what she thought was a submarine. The anti-submarine vessel HMAS *Bingera*, patrolling between Garden Island and Bradleys Head, raced over towards Kirribilli to join the fray but found nothing. The timing of *Kanimbla*'s sighting—50 minutes after Matsuo crossed Inner Loop 12—suggests that the *Kanimbla*'s lookouts may well have spotted the real thing.

The harbour stayed quiet for the next hour. As Matsuo had something of a track record for lying low, this too is consistent with a genuine sighting. At 4.40 am HMAS *Canberra* sighted what she thought was a torpedo track coming from the direction of Bradleys Head. At 4.50 am the minesweeper HMAS *Doomba* signalled to *Bingera* that they had a submarine contact off Robertsons Point, the next big headland after Bradleys Head on the north side of Sydney Harbour. Again *Bingera* raced to the spot, and again found nothing.

Most accounts of the raid assume that the 'torpedo track' sighted by *Canberra* was a false alarm, in a night when false alarms were in plentiful supply. There is, however, a much more sinister explanation which needs examination. We know from subsequent events that at some time during the night Matsuo fired both his torpedoes, though we have no way of knowing when. Both failed to leave their tubes. The midget's crew had operated the bow cap releases from inside the submarine, but both torpedo tubes remained blocked. The submarine's bow cage had been crushed inwards from both sides as the result of collisions, depth charges or both. This prevented the bow caps from dropping clear. The lower bow cap was damaged as well as blocked. Finally, the lower torpedo tube had been fired while the external adjustment fittings were still engaged, though these sheared off when the torpedo moved inside the tube. The failure of both torpedoes to launch correctly was the result of external damage to the submarine. The question is: when and how was the damage done?

We know for sure that Matsuo's sub was rammed by *Yandra* at 10.58 pm, and that the impact probably was felt in the submarine's bow area. That alone could account for the buckled bow cage, the damaged lower bow cap and the jamming of both caps. *Yandra* then dropped six depth charges from close range, and any one of these might have done the damage, or exacerbated it. There is the possibility that Matsuo collided with *Chicago* on his way into the harbour. This would have been a harsher impact than *Yandra*'s, because Matsuo and *Chicago* were travelling in opposite directions. This impact, if it happened at all, would have been felt mostly by the midget's bow. So it, too, might account for some of the damage. Whatever the reason, it appears certain that Matsuo's torpedoes were unable to launch by the time he made his way down the harbour and prepared to attack. He had no way of knowing this until he tried to fire his weapons.

If he crept down the harbour then went to periscope depth somewhere around Bradleys Head, HMAS *Canberra* would be the sitting duck of legend, tied up to no. 1 buoy in the entrance to Farm Cove off Bennelong Point. Any reader who finds himself or herself in Sydney and who cares to take the attractive bushland drive down to Bradleys Head lookout and ask how easy it would be to fire a shot at the Sydney Opera House from there will know how simple Matsuo's task looked. Matsuo's shot would be from a range of well under 2000 metres aimed at a stationary target, with his torpedo passing between Garden Island and Fort Denison on its way to *Canberra*'s exposed flank.

It is easy to imagine Matsuo lining up his submarine facing *Canberra*, sending his crewman Tsuzuku forward to release the bow caps, then giving Tsuzuku the order to fire. It is even easier to imagine Matsuo's legendarily volcanic temper exploding when the torpedo failed to leave the tube. What had gone wrong? There was no way of knowing from inside the submarine. Okay, let's try the second torpedo. This shot was probably fired in a fury, because the crew forgot to disengage the external adjustment fittings. The problem, however, was the buckled bow cage and the jammed bow caps, not the adjustment fittings. The result was the same—a hiss of compressed air followed by the dismal realisation that the second torpedo also remained firmly stuck in its tube. The long streak of compressed air bubbles released by the two firings might easily account for HMAS *Canberra*'s 'torpedo track'.

If this sequence of events, or something like them, did indeed take place then two things follow. An Allied ship, most likely *Canberra*, just had the escape of a lifetime. And Matsuo's logical next step would be to see if he could fix his problem and still salvage something from the attack. He was in the middle of a hostile harbour so he would need to find somewhere quiet, away from the searchlights and sheltered from the south-westerly wind, where he could risk surfacing and attempt to free the torpedoes. The quietest and darkest parts of the harbour were on the northern side, where bushland rather than houses lines the shore. Taylors Bay, just behind him, would be ideal.

◆   ◆   ◆

Reg Andrew's first impression as he began his patrol was the profusion of ships now active on the harbour. There were minesweepers, corvettes, Channel Patrol boats, Nappies, all swirling around him. Why hadn't the reserve Channel Patrol boats been called in earlier?

Sea Mist cruised her way between the western boom gate and Bradleys Head, scouring the harbour surface for periscopes and other danger signs. She showed no lights, and the crew had only intermittent moonlight to guide them. Sydney Harbour in the early hours of the morning is an eerie place at the best of times. When the wind is up, waves crash on the rocky shores and fling spray high in the air, while the sounds of wind and sea in the darkness can be ominous rather than soothing. The darkened headlands and bays look alike to all but the most experienced. There are reefs and hidden rocks to avoid. In the early hours of 1 June 1942 there was also the small matter of a lethal enemy lurking below the surface, hell bent on inflicting more death and destruction.

◆　　◆　　◆

Margaret Hamilton couldn't get to sleep in her second-floor bedroom overlooking Taylors Bay. She had heard the loudspeakers on *Chicago* barking out orders, and the sounds of *Chicago's* and *Whyalla's* guns, followed 90 minutes later by the blast which sank *Kuttabul*. The events of the night were too exciting for sleep. Some time in the early hours of the morning she left her bed to take a look from her balcony and see if anything new was happening.

Her eyes were already adjusted to the darkness, and she had the help of a little light reflected into the bay from anti-aircraft searchlights shining into clouds over the harbour. In the calm water she saw a submarine periscope making its way gently into Taylors Bay, heading towards the sandy beach 100 metres west of her vantage point.

Beyond the periscope she could see the harbour swarming with patrol boats and larger warships, so clearly the navy had it all in hand. When the periscope disappeared from sight, she went back to bed.

◆　　◆　　◆

Reg Andrew and his crew patrolled their stretch of the harbour without incident for an hour. Then, at 4.30 am the minesweeper HMAS *Goonambee* called to them through a loud-hailer. There was a suspicious object in Taylors Bay. Could *Sea Mist* please investigate and report? *Sea Mist* made a thorough search of the area and found nothing but an old boomerang buoy. This particular design of permanent buoy was prevalent in Sydney Harbour in the 1940s. It was huge and metallic, designed to give a secure mooring to bigger harbour boats, particularly large yachts. A boomerang buoy was big enough for a man to stand on comfortably if he was so minded. *Sea Mist* moved back closer to *Goonambee* and announced through her loud-hailer that Taylors Bay was clear of submarines.

Reg Andrew resumed his patrol. He was now on his second round trip between Bradleys Head and the west boom gate, and he still had nothing to show for it. At around 5 am, with dawn not far away, *Sea Mist* was on a south-westerly heading on the leg from the boom gate to Bradleys Head. She had just passed Chowder Head and was moving across the entrance to Taylors Bay when the skipper spotted a black object in the water about halfway between the patrol boat and the shore. Reg Andrew turned *Sea Mist* to starboard and set off to investigate. As he drew closer, the answer became clear even in the darkness. He was closing in on a submarine, its bow pointing down the harbour towards the boom net, with a metre of its conning tower protruding from the water. It was, in Reg Andrew's own words, 'a shattering experience'.

Andrew brought *Sea Mist* around behind the submarine, still in a right turn. He was now between the submarine and the Taylors Bay shore, about 50 metres from the water's edge, with both vessels pointing north-east towards the boom net. As he circled he called orders. Did anyone know how to set depth charges? Yes, said Coxswain Potter. Okay, prepare charges and set them to 50 feet (15 metres). By rights the depth charges should have had their safety lashings removed on the way from Farm Cove, but nobody had told the coxswain to do this. Potter now worked frantically to free the charges before he could set them to the required depth. Next the Very pistol. Bring me the Very pistol and two red flares, the new skipper demanded. 'Which cartridges are the red ones?' a plaintive voice called from below. More shouting. Andrew continued his circle.

Sea Mist had completed its first circle and returned to its original starting position when Coxswain Potter reported that depth charges were ready. Someone handed Reg Andrew the Very pistol and a single cartridge of unknown colour. This would have to do. At this point Matsuo must have realised he was in deadly danger. His midget submerged, leaving only a swirl of water on the surface. Reg Andrew knew he had to act straightaway or he would lose his quarry. *Sea Mist*'s twin engines bellowed to maximum revolutions. Andrew simultaneously ordered the first depth charge dropped on the spot where the sub had disappeared and fired the Very pistol and its mystery flare. To his relief and mild surprise the flare bathed Taylors Bay in weird red light. This was followed by a tremendous explosion. According to Andrew: '*Sea Mist* rode the resulting wave like a surf boat.' A huge column of water was hurled into the air by the detonation and temporarily blacked out the night sky.

♦ ♦ ♦

Reg Andrew died in July 1984. He went to his grave stubbornly believing the version of events which follows. His refusal to budge from it cost him the sole credit he almost certainly deserved for sinking Matsuo's midget. Andrew's version cannot be correct, and it may be possible after all these years to come up with an explanation which both fits the facts and confirms his place as the hero he surely was.

In Reg Andrew's version, *Sea Mist* continued to circle, once again reaching her original starting point. Andrew could hear splashing coming from the spot where he dropped his first charge. Soon he could see the source of the splashing: Matsuo's twin propellers were rising slowly out of the water, the blades turning in opposite directions inside their metal cage. Andrew called for a second red Very cartridge, and ordered the coxswain to prepare a second depth charge.

Sea Mist continued in a tight circle to starboard. Let Reg Andrew now take over the narrative. He had the unnerving habit of writing about himself in the third person, which did him no good a few days later when he came to submit his action report. These are his words:

The commanding officer of *Sea Mist* now turned his charge to once again come between the midget submarine and the shore.

This time he ventured closer to the hull, which was now clearly visible and upside down. So close was *Sea Mist* that he could have easily stepped off the deck onto the hull of the submarine. At this time *Sea Mist* saw the inverted submarine with its bottom painted red, possibly of red lead origin.

Maximum revolutions were ordered for the engine when there was a shout from the coxswain aft: 'There are two more behind us.'

This amazing sight was probably witnessed as well from the wheelhouse as he remembers confirmation. He took a quick look himself and sure enough there were two more astern with their conning towers clearly outlined not 45 metres away. He had time to note the nearest was in the process of crash diving, but the aspect was peculiar. The submarine was not moving forward and the conning tower was boiling with escaping air. It was slipping below the sea, sinking.

Back to the job in hand, he fired another Verey flare which miraculously turned out to be red. He ordered another depth charge to be dropped. The commander of *Sea Mist* waited with bated breath for the tremendous upheaval from 180 kg of TNT, which was about to explode. Explode it did and *Sea Mist* seemed to receive as much of a shock as the stricken midget. At once its 10 knots were reduced to five knots and the motor mechanic reported one engine had stopped. The attack on this Japanese midget submarine by *Sea Mist* took place at approximately 5.15 am on the 1st of June.

Now we can be absolutely certain of one thing: at no time were there three midget submarines in Taylors Bay that night. Only three submarines took part in the attack. One had long ago scuttled in the net, and one had escaped to sea. That left only Matsuo in Taylors Bay.

The first clue is the red lead. Japanese midget submarines did not have red lead paint on their hulls: boomerang buoys did. On Reg Andrew's own description, we can be fairly certain his second depth charge did nothing to improve the health of the blameless buoy. The tide was low at 5.15 am that morning in Sydney Harbour, so the buoy's chain will have had plenty of slack. The most likely explanation is that *Sea Mist*'s first depth charge, which caught Matsuo squarely, also flipped the buoy on its back. Darkness and disorientation did the rest.

That leaves the question of the 'two' submarines sighted. The propellers which Reg Andrew saw emerge from the water could only be Matsuo's sub in its death throes. Nobody on the Allied side knew that these submarines had cages around their propellers, an alteration made after the Pearl Harbor attack. So the crew of *Sea Mist* could only have known this through a genuine sighting. That leaves two conning towers to be accounted for. From Reg Andrew's description, it is clear that one conning tower was closer to *Sea Mist* and was seen more clearly than the other, so the second conning tower is the problem.

I am indebted to the author Steven Carruthers for an ingenious thought. It came too late for inclusion in his book, *Japanese Submarine Raiders 1942: A Maritime Mystery*, and he generously passed it on.

As we shall see, when salvage operations began on Matsuo's submarine there was an attempt to drag it along the harbour bed to shallower water, away from the main shipping channel. During this process the rear section of the sub, containing the electric motor and propeller shaft, broke off just behind the rear watertight bulkhead. Steven's suggestion is that *Sea Mist*'s first depth charge broke the midget's back, causing a partial separation of the rear section. First the stern appeared above the water, with its propellers turning. Then, as the stern began to fall back to the bottom, the bow and conning tower swung up and broke the surface separately, giving the impression of two more submarines.

This author is inclined to place his trust in a law of science known as Ockham's razor. It is named after the 14th-century philosopher William of Ockham, who spent most of his life denouncing the temporal powers of the papacy. In his spare time William came up with one of science's most fundamental rules, which has stood the test of seven centuries. It states that when there are several possible explanations for something, the simplest explanation is correct.

In this case, the simplest explanation is that Reg Andrew and his coxswain made a mistake. If the great William of Ockham were with us today, he would probably agree that the first depth charge caught Matsuo's sub squarely and blew it out of the water, stern first. The sub then slid back into the water out of sight while *Sea Mist* continued its tight circle. *Sea Mist* then locked onto the boomerang buoy and positioned to attack it. At this moment the submarine resurfaced 45 metres away—they had an impressive track record for doing this sort of thing unasked—showing its conning tower and plenty of bubbles. So in the split second glimpse in poor light, and after the confusion of endless circling, what Reg Andrew and his coxswain saw and correctly identified was the conning tower of Matsuo's submarine, while they prepared to attack the boomerang buoy. And the second conning tower? Very likely a projected shadow of the real thing—after all, Reg Andrew's fellow Channel Patrol boat *Marlean* had fired at her own shadow only a few hours earlier. On a dark night and in the heat of battle, it would be an easy mistake to make.

Whatever the truth, it is clear there was no fight left in Matsuo's submarine after Reg Andrew's first depth charge. First the stern appeared above the water, the propellers thrashing aimlessly, with the submarine clearly out of control. Then a conning tower of a sinking submarine was seen 'bursting with escaping air'. Finally, after the attack divers found a sunken Japanese midget submarine at the precise location of *Sea Mist*'s attack.

◆　　◆　　◆

The scene aboard the submarine after Reg Andrew's first depth charge must have been appalling. Both crewmen would now be deaf, their eardrums ruptured and bleeding from the shock of the blast. The submarine would be taking on water through sprung plates on its hull. The violence of the blast followed by the submarine's contortions in the water will have flung the crew heavily against the hard and jutting metal controls. However, we know from the salvaged wreckage that the waterproof bulkheads appear to have held, so harbour water would not be gushing into the crew area with drowning force just yet.

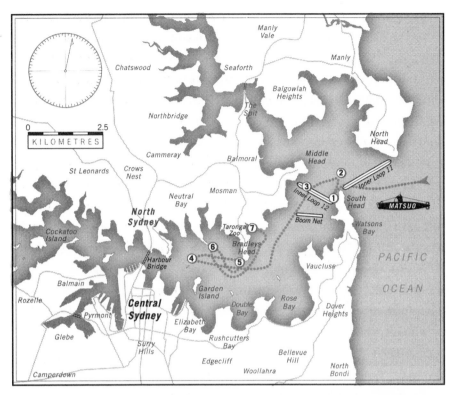

Matsuo's track inside Sydney Harbour remains a matter for conjecture. This diagram assumes that the various sightings and alarms between 3.40 am and 4.50 am were genuine. If they were, then Matsuo followed a complicated path between Bradleys Head and the Harbour Bridge, making two forays into the inner harbour north of Garden Island. His movements were: (1) 10.54 pm seen by HMAS *Lauriana* and HMAS *Yandra* entering the harbour, and subsequently rammed by *Yandra*; (2) 11.07 pm, attacked by *Yandra* with six depth charges at close quarters; (3) 3.01 am crosses Inner Loop 12 and enters harbour via the Western Gate; (4) 3.50 am, HMS *Kanimbla* fires at submarine contact in mid-harbour; (5) 4.40 am, HMAS *Canberra* sees 'torpedo tracks' fired from the direction of Bradleys Head, possibly plume of compressed air from Matsuo's jammed torpedo tubes; (6) 4.50 am HMAS *Doomba* signals to the anti-submarine specialist HMAS *Bingera* submarine contact off Robertsons Point, but nothing found; (7) 5.15 am Matsuo attacked and sunk by HMAS *Sea Mist* in Taylors Bay.

The submarine dived when it heard *Sea Mist* first approaching, so it must have been under the crew's full control up to that moment. At some point the crew attempted to fire both sets of scuttling charges, but the wicks were damp and the charges failed. The most intriguing action involved the access hatch on the bottom of the submarine's hull. It was wide open when the sub was raised from the harbour bed a few days later. There are endless reasons why the hatch might fly open without the help of the crew: one of the depth charges may have forced it, or it could have snagged on the harbour bed and burst open days later when the sub was dragged along the bottom during the salvage operation. But there remains the possibility that one of the crew opened it deliberately with the intention of trying to swim to the surface and survive.

Tsuzuku's body was found in the aft battery compartment of the submarine, with his shoes removed. This gave rise to a suggestion in Muirhead-Gould's report that he might have been planning to escape. If he was, then he was heading the wrong way: the access hatch was in the forward battery compartment, just in front of the conning tower. There was no escape route from the rear of the submarine. He was killed by a single shot to the back of the head, clearly fired by Matsuo. Matsuo then turned the gun on himself. His body was found in the conning tower. As the sun rose on Sydney Harbour on 1 June 1942, the death toll in the Battle of Sydney Harbour also rose—to 25.

The skilful Matsuo did a good job preserving his batteries: his electric motor was still turning gently eight hours later when the divers found the wreckage. The upper torpedo's 10,000-kilometre odyssey from Japan to Truk Island, then on to Sydney and finally into Sydney Harbour itself, ended with a journey of about a metre inside the tube where it had jammed. The lower torpedo fared worse—its entire journey after firing had taken it a mere 45 centimetres.

Chapter 13

Examining the wreckage

One of the more bizarre document folders in the Australian War
Memorial's collection in Canberra is AWM 6945/27. It contains
two letters, one dated 5 October 1948 addressed to the official navy
historian, Commander G. Hermon Gill, from Ric Breydon, the
commander of the Channel Patrol boat flotilla, and a second letter from
Gill replying to Breydon, dated 29 November 1948. It is apparent
from the tone of the correspondence that the row over who sank
Matsuo's submarine still had a good head of steam six and a half years
after the event.

There are two claimants: Reg Andrew and the crew of *Sea Mist*;
and Athol Townley and the crew of *Steady Hour*. It is easy to take
Reg Andrew's side, if only because we have more access to it. He
left behind long taped interviews, several written accounts and
some detailed correspondence. Persistent efforts by the author have
failed to turn up the action reports filed by *Steady Hour* and *Yarroma*,
or their log books, despite thorough searches in all the archives,
libraries and institutions named in the acknowledgements to this book.
Previous researchers on this subject have obviously come to the same
dead end.

Let us therefore begin with Reg Andrew's account. Just to recap: he had dropped two depth charges on what he at first believed was the same submarine (though he would later claim he attacked two different submarines). He had sighted two submarines behind him while attacking the third. One of the two submarines behind him appeared to be sinking, though his first reaction is that it was crash-diving. The long and short of it is that, as far as he was concerned, he had sunk at least one submarine in Taylors Bay, but there were still two enemy submarines alive and kicking in the bay. Both were in urgent need of attention, and his half-powered and crocked boat could do nothing about them.

His first action was to signal with his Aldis light to his fellow Channel Patrol boat *Steady Hour*, standing off the entrance to Taylors Bay about 200 metres away. On board *Steady Hour*, Lieutenant Athol Townley was acting commander of the whole Channel Patrol boat flotilla, as well as acting skipper of *Steady Hour*. He was older than Reg Andrew and had been an officer of the Channel Patrol boat flotilla a great deal longer than Reg Andrew's five hours. Andrew had two urgent messages for Townley: first, there were still two enemy submarines in Taylors Bay; second, *Sea Mist* was crippled and could no longer take part in any attack. Townley needed to get more Channel Patrol boats into the bay before the two submarines escaped.

In Andrew's account, there was no response from *Steady Hour* to *Sea Mist's* Aldis lamp signals. Andrew then set off to crawl on his single surviving engine across the 200 metres separating the two Channel Patrol boats. He called to Townley through a loud-hailer. Townley was more interested in cross-examining the very junior new commander than he was in hunting for submarines.

Had Andrew fired any flares? Had he dropped any depth charges? These were fairly fatuous questions, given that the depth charge detonations could be heard for kilometres around, and the Very flares had lit up the entire neighbourhood. Andrew is happy to admit that he had been feeling pretty pleased with himself up to this point. Now he found himself on the receiving end of a whole lot of sceptical and antagonistic questions. He turned angry. He had explained to Townley that *Sea Mist* was crippled. 'If you don't renew the attack, the subs will get away,' he shouted at Townley through the loud-hailer. Townley's response was dismissive. 'You're no fucking use around here,' he shouted back through his loud-hailer. 'Fuck off to base!'

The crestfallen Reg Andrew retreated a few hundred metres towards the centre of the harbour, but hung around to watch the action. Meanwhile, Townley began a search of Taylors Bay. Having seen and heard nothing, he signalled to *Yarroma*, patrolling the boom net area, to come and join him. *Yarroma* carried both ASDIC and hydrophone, and could hunt for submerged submarines without the need for a visual contact. For 80 minutes the two Channel Patrol boats scoured Taylors Bay, with *Yarroma*'s ASDIC pinging fruitlessly. Then at 6.40 am, an hour and 25 minutes after Reg Andrew's attack, *Steady Hour* had a contact and dropped her first depth charge of the morning.

Eighteen minutes later *Yarroma* picked up an ASDIC contact from the same submarine, and more depth charges tumbled into Taylors Bay. This pattern continued for the next two hours. *Steady Hour* and *Yarroma* scoured the bay, dropping depth charges on contacts. In all, nine depth charges exploded in Taylors Bay that morning. *Yarroma*'s final depth charge, dropped in broad daylight at 8.27 am, was the final shot in the Battle of Sydney Harbour.

♦   ♦   ♦

Reg Andrew's first depth charge detonated about 150 metres from Margaret Hamilton's bedroom overlooking Taylors Bay. The force of the explosion rocked the house—there is still a large crack today in the brickwork of the balcony—and threw her brother Bob out of bed. The whole household rushed to the window to see what was going on. 'There were a lot of searchlights going. They were criss-crossing, flying around the sky. They didn't know where to look,' she recalls.

The bay rapidly filled with patrol boats. 'The whole harbour seemed to be alive. The sea was white froth. They weren't just whizzing round— they were going with a purpose. They were charging, and we could see them rolling the depth charges off the back. Then, of course, they got the hell out of the way as fast as an express train. Then they'd turn, be curious. How did we go?'

Margaret and family watched the unfolding attack while dawn slowly lit the bay. Then she had a ferry to catch. After all, the ferry service and secretarial college had no cause to take a day off just because Sydney Harbour was under attack.

◆　◆　◆

The row over who sank Matsuo's submarine is, in the overall scheme of things, a trivial matter. More than 60 years later, who cares? But insofar as it led to a clash with authority by Reg Andrew and an unjust sidelining of Sea Mist's new commander for most of the war, it is an important illustration of how awkward heroes can often suffer cruelly for their stubbornness.

In fairness to Athol Townley, we need an objective look at his version of the morning's work in Taylors Bay. In the absence of his action report, we can make a start by relying on Breydon's letter to Gill, which is based on Townley's vanished report and which tells Townley's story in good detail. In Townley's recollection, Andrew reported to him that he had attacked one submarine and believed he had sunk it. At the same time, Andrew had also sighted two other submarines about 50 yards (45 metres) away but had not attacked either of them. In the course of the attack on the first submarine, his port engine was put temporarily out of action and he could not carry out another attack for some time. Townley then ordered Sea Mist 'to patrol at a safe distance from the area'.

Townley's Steady Hour now entered Taylors Bay, and called on Yarroma to join the hunt. For 70 minutes the two Channel Patrol boats searched without result. Then, in Breydon's narrative: 'The submarine which Townley attacked was visually sighted (by Yarroma and Steady Hour) as she was surfacing, and was immediately attacked by *Steady Hour*. The C.O. of *Yarroma* did not give any directions regarding the attack.'* Breydon continues: '*Yarroma* did not, in fact, get any ASDIC results until 18 minutes later. Immediately after the attack, and whilst large bubbles, oil, and debris were still rising, Townley dropped a marker buoy on the spot, and subsequently secured his anchor to the submarine until divers descended and fixed wire cables to her hull.' Breydon then describes *Yarroma*'s role. '*Yarroma* did not get any ASDIC contact until 0658, after the submarine had been sunk; he was then ordered by Townley to drop three depth charges as a precaution.'

Breydon now sets out to argue that any submarine sunk by *Sea Mist* and Reg Andrew cannot have been the same as the one attacked by Athol Townley. Reg Andrew had written: 'As I was responsible for . . . finding . . . No 21 [Matsuo's midget] . . . but also in sinking No 21 and another . . .' To this Breydon retorts: 'The weight of evidence is against this claim. There was a lapse of 70 minutes between the attacks by Andrew and Townley. Townley attacked a submarine which was under way and surfacing—it could not therefore have been sunk more than an hour earlier.'

The problem with each story is that both Townley and Andrew accept the completely false premise that two Japanese midget submarines were sunk in Taylors Bay that morning, not one. In Reg Andrew's version, *Sea Mist* sank them both. One was recovered, the second has never been found. In Townley's version, Reg Andrew sank

---

* Breydon says this to support the proposition that *Steady Hour* acted alone and on the basis of her own visual sighting, so that sole credit for the sinking of Matsuo's midget should go to Townley and *Steady Hour*, and should not be shared with Sub-Lieutenant Eyers and *Yarroma*. There is an interesting discrepancy between Breydon's version and Muirhead-Gould's, although both are presumably based on *Steady Hour*'s action report. In his first draft report Muirhead-Gould says *Steady Hour* attacked a definite ASDIC contact. The word 'ASDIC' is crossed out and replaced by the handwritten word 'hydrophone'. The handwriting looks like Muirhead-Gould's. Either way, this meant *Yarroma* and not *Steady Hour* had the contact: only *Yarroma* carried a hydrophone and ASDIC. However, this is not the main point of interest. The important distinction is that *Steady Hour*'s target was not, in Muirhead-Gould's version, sighted visually but instead located below the surface by detection devices.

one submarine and Townley sank the other. Reg Andrew's submarine was never found. Townley's was. Matsuo's midget was his. In fact there was never more than one submarine, so only one skipper deserves the glory. Which?

Townley's claim to have sunk Matsuo's submarine single-handed rests on two propositions: the submarine he attacked was visually sighted, surfacing and under way; and he dropped a marker buoy and secured his anchor chain to the submarine he had successfully attacked. As we have already seen, there is good cause to doubt the first proposition. As we shall shortly see, there is even better cause to doubt the second.

◆　　◆　　◆

To 10- and 12-year-olds Jeff and Kevin Co#oté, their father Roy was already a hero. A certain magic attached to divers, and the boys knew that Dad was one of the best in the Royal Australian Navy. His status in their eyes received a sharp boost around 6.30 am on the morning of Monday, 1 June 1942. There was a thunderous pounding on their front door. When they opened it, a policeman in full uniform from the local Mosman police station was looking agitated on the doorstep. His motorcycle and sidecar were parked outside. Roy Co#oté was needed urgently at Garden Island. He should jump in the sidecar straightaway and the policeman would whisk him there.

Other members of the dive team arrived at Garden Island by more conventional transport. Lance Bullard caught the 7.30 am ferry to work. The dive team which now assembled on Garden Island contained no raw recruits. The diving officer, Lieutenant George Whittle, was 54 years old and had joined the navy in 1927. Lance Bullard, then 40, was the most experienced. He had joined in 1917. Roy Co#oté was also 40, and had joined in 1920. James Munn was the youngest at 34. He had joined in 1929. They were all familiar with wrecks, and with the recovery of bodies. Nothing prepared them for what they now saw. The cosy and familiar HMAS *Kuttabul* lay shattered in front of them, with only her funnel and wheelhouse out of the water. A high-voltage underwater cable had snapped in the blast. Their first task would be to make this cable safe.

Then they could see if, by some miracle, there were any survivors trapped in the wreckage. Their final task would be to find bodies.

They had their own immediate disaster to contend with. The dive team had finished work the previous Saturday at 1 pm. They tied up their dive boat between *Kuttabul* and the stone wall of Garden Island, and removed the woollen gear, helmets, diving suits and telephones to the diving shed. However, the vital heavy gear including two pumps, air hoses, breast lines, boots, weights and ladders remained on the boat. It had taken the full force of Ban's torpedo. All their heavy gear now lay wrecked at the bottom of the harbour.

With some ingenuity and resourcefulness they tracked down a new dive boat, plus pumps and other heavy diving gear. This had to be fitted up and tested before anybody could enter the water. Lance Bullard reported afterwards: 'We were in business again and under water by about 9.15 am, which was fast work.'

Roy Cooté's dive log tends to be pretty terse. His record of this phase of the operation is a miracle of brevity. 'Dived under wreckage of *Kuttabul* examining High Power cables. Dived and recovered 6 bodies from *Kuttabul* wreckage.'

Lance Bullard's account, by contrast, is extraordinarily vivid. He was the senior rating in the dive team that day, and it fell to him to compile a report. 'I will never forget the scene when we arrived on the sleeping deck of the sunken ship,' he wrote.

The sun was shining through a gaping hole in the deck head, giving a green glow to the still water. Blankets and clothing were scattered around the deck. Hammocks were still slung with their occupants as if asleep.

There were two men sitting on a locker leaning towards each other as if they had been having a yarn before turning in. There was not a mark on any of them of any kind. The blast from the explosion must have killed them instantly. I think we passed up seventeen bodies before we were called up and ordered down the harbour to Taylor Bay.

Work on the *Kuttabul* continued with trainee divers. The senior team had a new and vastly more dangerous task: Matsuo's midget. Roy Cooté and Lance Bullard stayed suited up as the launch crossed the harbour from Garden Island to Taylors Bay.

♦   ♦   ♦

The divers were ordered to investigate 'oil slick and bubbles coming to the surface' in Taylors Bay. Neither Bullard nor Roy Cooté gives a time for when this work began. Evidence from Bullard's account and from Roy Cooté's dive log suggests it must have been around midday. Let Lance Bullard continue the narrative:

When we arrived at Taylor Bay, Lieutenant Whittle dropped anchor about 50 yards upstream from the bubbles as the tide was running out. The depth was about 85 feet. Roy Cooté finished dressing and dropped down. He made a complete circular sweep, trailing his lines. He reported nothing and was called up.

Lieutenant Whittle moved the boat further upstream and I dropped down. While descending, I heard a continual throbbing noise in my helmet, but I assumed it was caused by some boat on the surface. On the bottom I walked to the full extent of my lines and started to sweep. The bottom was about six inches of mud on hard sand. Walking and trailing heavy breast rope and air hose was hard going and stirring up the mud made for poor visibility. After about 10 minutes I stopped to let the water clear and have a breather, and as the water cleared I caught a glimpse of a steel wire stay about 20 yards away.

I walked towards it and saw a submarine lying practically on an even keel and apparently undamaged. I put my hand on the hull, which was quite warm. Suddenly, I realized that the sound I had heard from the time I entered the water was coming from the sub and was quite loud.

I thought she might take off at any minute and I hated the thought of tangling up with her if she did. I reported by phone to the boat and Lieutenant Whittle asked me to hang on for a while and he would send Roy Coté down my lines with a buoy rope. While I waited I stepped the length of the sub and made it about 85 feet. I had a good look at the bow and was surprised to see the doors of the two torpedo tubes, one on top of the other, were partly open with the noses of the torpedoes protruding. The top one was out about three feet and the lower about 18 inches.

Soon I felt my lines tighten and heard Roy Coté say over the phone: 'I can hear the motor running and will be getting out of this as soon as this buoy rope is made fast.'

Roy Coté's dive log is, as usual, the soul of brevity: 'Dived off Taylor Bay for Jap sub. Found it still alive and moving.'

There is one addendum to this story which is worth recording, though it is not to be treated as cast-iron fact. There is a standard procedure for divers sent down to find and recover stricken submarines. They tap on the hull. If any of the crew is still alive, they tap back. Both Jeff and Kevin Coté tell the same story. Their father told them more than once that he had tapped on the sub's hull on this dive and got a response from the sub's crew. Coté's reference in his dive log to the sub as 'still alive' may refer to the crew's response, and not merely to the turning engine. However, Lance Bullard's account makes no reference to this highly significant fact, so it may simply be part of a good yarn.

◆　　◆　　◆

The divers' work was far from finished. Having tied a buoy to Matsuo's submarine in Taylors Bay, they then moved on to the boom net to look for Chuman's midget. Lance Bullard continues: 'We went down harbour to the boom defence net at the Watsons Bay end [Bullard is incorrect here—the sub was found at the Clifton Gardens end of the net] and found another sub hopelessly fouled by her propellers in the steel mesh. I inspected the fore end of this sub on the bottom. There was debris scattered everywhere, but both torpedoes were intact.'

Roy Coté's dive log at this point becomes positively garrulous. 'Dived for other sub and found it fouled with boom net tangled in screws.'

Coté's next entry will have the conspiracy theorists leaping to their websites. Still on Monday, 1 June, he records: 'Dived for third sub. Found it off Chowder Bay.'

Matsuo's sub now lay dead in the water in Taylors Bay with a buoy attached, Chuman's sub lay trapped in the boom net, and Ban's sub had been picked up by Inner Loop 12 slipping out of the harbour more than 12 hours ago. Where can this miraculously discovered extra submarine have come from? Reg Andrew and Athol Townley would, of course, have an answer. But the evidence that only three submarines took part in the attack is so overwhelming that we can simply rule out the 'fourth submarine' possibility.

Most false sightings of midget submarines can be traced to paravanes towed by minesweepers. But Roy Coté was too experienced and too skilled to make this elementary mistake. If he says he saw a midget submarine, we would do well to listen.

The following is simply a suggestion by the author but it would seem to fit the facts. Bullard's account of the dive on the net uses the word 'we' to describe finding the stern of the sub tangled in the net. However, his report of finding the bow section is very much in the first person. He had spent a lot more recent time in deep water in Taylors Bay than Roy Coté, so it may be that when he arrived at the net he was close to his time limit for deep-water diving, whereas Roy Coté had dived much earlier and had time to recover. (Coté's second Taylors Bay dive, to bring down the buoy, was very brief.) When Chuman fired his forward scuttling charge, it blew the bow section off the submarine. The bow came to rest about 6 metres from the main body of the sub in the direction of Chowder Bay. The most likely scenario is that the dive boat tied up at the net and Roy Coté dived alone and found the stern of the sub tangled there. The dive boat then left its position on the net and moved in the direction of Chowder Bay, perhaps in response to a metallic contact. Both Coté and Bullard dived again, and found the bow. Coté's first reaction was that this was another submarine.

Roy Coté's dive log is a contemporary record of each day's diving, while Bullard's (undated) account was written some time after the event. Coté never again refers to this Chowder Bay submarine, while there are repeated references later on in the dive log to searches for submarines elsewhere in the harbour, notably near the Heads where *Yandra* claimed a submarine sunk. The most likely explanation, therefore, is that the Chowder Bay submarine was simply the bow of Chuman's sub, and that Roy Coté realised this soon after. However, for years he would tell his two sons Kevin and Jeff, and his grandson Craig, that he knew where the missing third submarine lay. But he wasn't telling.

◆　　◆　　◆

Incredibly, the divers' day was still not over. They now undertook an operation which took more than usual skill and quite incredible courage. They returned to Taylors Bay with orders to secure two 2½-inch (6-cm)-thick steel cables to Matsuo's sub. Picture the scene. They have just come from a dive on a sub which had fired a devastating demolition charge, blowing itself apart and killing its crew in the process. So the Japanese would have no qualms about doing the same with the Taylors Bay sub. As far as the divers could tell, the Taylors Bay sub was still 'alive'—its hull was warm, the engine was still turning, there may even have been a signal from the crew that they were still alive and capable of doing damage. Two torpedoes were hanging out of the bow, very likely armed and lethal if disturbed.

Muirhead-Gould in his 31 August report on the salvage operation sets out the problems in stark detail.

> The preliminary survey by the divers indicated that some form of explosive was attached to the bows. Intelligence reports also indicated that some form of demolition charge might be expected in the tail. The difficulty of divers in ascertaining that the protrusion from the submarine's bow was the warhead of an undischarged torpedo is understandable, considering the operation was in 13½ fathoms [81 feet or 24.7 metres], with the poor light

at that depth in the late afternoon. Divers were instructed to shackle on two 30-fathom [180 feet or 55 metre] lengths of 2-inch wire, and to avoid interference with both the tail section and the inside of the bow protector guard. The state of the live torpedoes was unknown and, as the submarine was lying in a line with bows up harbour, it was considered unwise to pass any strops around the forward section at this stage.

Roy Cooté's dive log is as terse as ever. 'Dived again on first sub,' he reports. 'Attached wires for lifting.' This time there was no response to tapping on the hull.

The two wires were attached to the minesweeper HMAS *Samuel Benbow* on the surface. Matsuo's midget was now securely in the grip of the Royal Australian Navy.

◆   ◆   ◆

So who sank Matsuo's submarine? In his 5 October 1948 letter Ric Breydon wrote, basing his words on Townley's action report: 'Townley dropped a marker buoy on the spot, and subsequently secured his anchor to the submarine until divers descended and fixed wire cable to her hull.' That is not how the divers remembered it. If there had been a marker buoy in Taylors Bay on the site of the wrecked submarine, and a patrol boat with its anchor secured to it, then surely that would be the place to start the search? In the divers' view, they found the submarine themselves from a stream of bubbles. The only buoy they refer to is the one tied to the sub by Roy Cooté.

That leaves the question of Townley's submarine being visually sighted, surfacing and under way. As we have seen, Muirhead-Gould disputes this: in his version, Townley attacked a submarine after picking up its location from *Yarroma*'s hydrophone. The point is important because if the submarine was sighted on the surface then it still had plenty of life in it and Reg Andrew's depth charge did not finish it off. If it was merely picked up by hydrophone then it could have been resting on the bottom with its engine still running but otherwise lifeless, the condition in which it was ultimately found. Without being able to read the action reports, it is impossible to make a considered judgement. Whatever special pleading G. Hermon Gill received from the Townley and Andrew camps, he made his final conclusion clear in the official history. Waxing slightly poetic, he wrote of *Yarroma*'s and *Steady Hour*'s Taylors Bay action: 'Intermittent depth charge attacks were delivered on submarine contacts recorded by detection gear and by visual "sightings" in that deceptive period of twilight and shadow-borne illusion of a growing dawn.' The quote marks around 'sightings' are Gill's. The use of words like 'deceptive' and 'illusion' tell the whole story: when it came to *Yarroma*'s and *Steady Hour*'s sightings, he clearly didn't believe a word of it.

When Matsuo's submarine was hauled to the surface, it had taken a fearful battering from depth charges. The midget had suffered far more damage than could ever be traced back to Reg Andrew's single charge (or even two charges). However, it should be remembered that Matsuo had spent an uncomfortable night in Sydney Harbour: he was rammed at least once, quite probably twice; *Yandra* had dropped six depth charges pretty close to him; Reg Andrew had hit him squarely with at least one charge; and finally *Yarroma* and *Steady Hour* had dropped no fewer than seven depth charges in his immediate area.

In the nightmare world of nuclear warfare theory, the high priests use a particularly macabre phrase. Referring to the fact that the various nuclear and thermonuclear powers have enough weaponry to destroy the planet several times over, they talk about 'making the rubble bounce'. Matsuo's midget seems to have suffered a similar fate. It was almost certainly taken out of the war by Reg Andrew's first charge. The next eight simply made the rubble bounce.

Part III

AFTERMATH

Chapter 14

No reference whatsoever

Sydney woke up on the morning of 1 June 1942 asking itself the regular party-goer's question: what on earth happened last night? Nobody seemed to know. As dawn broke, the smoke and smell of explosives still hung in the air over the harbour. The all-clear had sounded, and people crept out from their shelters and from under their kitchen tables, turned the gas back on, drained the bath, and put the clothes peg they had been chewing back in the peg basket. What was that all about, they asked each other?

The newspapers and radio stations gave no clue. At 3.30 am on Monday morning, just as Reg Andrew was setting off for Taylors Bay in *Sea Mist*, the Federal Censor in Canberra sent an urgent telegram to all newspapers, radio stations, magazines and wire services saying: 'Pending official statement no reference whatsoever to incident in Sydney Harbour last night.' Foreign correspondents had their stories censored to oblivion. Not even the morning radio news bulletins were allowed to explain the thunderous explosions, pyrotechnic gunfire and swarming naval activity seen and heard by thousands of Sydney's harbourside dwellers.

The censor's edict probably made little difference to the morning newspaper coverage. The main action had taken place too late for a full account to appear there anyway. Instead the *Sydney Morning Herald* led off with news of the first 1000-bomber raid on Germany. However, Brian Penton, the legendary editor of the Sydney *Daily Telegraph*, made a rare mistake. A former *Telegraph* reporter worked the switchboard that night at Naval Intelligence. She overheard what was going on and against all the rules rang her old paper in plenty of time to make the early editions, before the censor's edict came into effect. She tipped off the news desk: Japanese submarines are attacking in Sydney Harbour. Penton told her not to be a silly girl, and spiked the story. Instead the *Telegraph* informed its readers breathlessly, in a report from London, that Princess Elizabeth last night gave a private informal dance in the drawing room of her country home. It was, said the report, the first at which she was hostess since her recent coming out. Social historians might like to note the substantial change which has taken place in the use of the phrase 'coming out'.

The strict censorship was not unusual. All military authorities in similar circumstances tend to start by suppressing the story until they can think of some face-saving formula for describing what happened. The authorities broke their silence at 2 pm on Monday afternoon with a brief statement of more than usual duplicity, cabled from General Headquarters in Melbourne. 'In an attempted submarine raid on Sydney three enemy submarines are believed to have been destroyed, one by gunfire, two by depth charges. The enemy's attack was completely unsuccessful. Damage was confined to one small harbour vessel of no military value.'

Let no one think, after reading this, that Goebbels was the sole trader on the Big Lie stand. Apart from the disservice it did to the 21 dead sailors on HMAS *Kuttabul*, omitting them entirely and dismissing with contempt the fate of 'one small harbour vessel of no military value', the statement was dishonest in almost every respect. The authorities well knew that at least one of the submarines had been destroyed by its own hand, not by depth charges or gunfire. The statement's principal aim was to suppress the brutal truth that luck rather than competence had saved Sydney from a far worse fate. For a while, it served its purpose.

♦   ♦   ♦

For the 10-year-old Peter Doyle, later to become famous as the owner of Doyle's Restaurant on Watsons Bay, Monday, 1 June was a great day for a young boy living near Sydney Harbour's shores. He had spent a large part of the night under the kitchen table with a peg in his mouth, wearing a pair of improvised ear muffs made from powder puffs. Now, with the arrival of daylight, the harbour shore was littered with desirable souvenirs: bits of floating wreckage, perhaps even the odd spent shell. He remembers people wading out in to the harbour to pick up stunned fish, victims of the depth charges.

♦   ♦   ♦

There must have been a moment in the course of 1 June 1942 when Rear Admiral Muirhead-Gould realised he was potentially in a lot of trouble. He was in charge of Sydney Harbour's defences, and they had failed badly. No fewer than three enemy submarines had slipped into his harbour, two of them ignored by the indicator loop watch and unmolested by no fewer than six patrol vessels tasked with guarding the harbour entrance. All three submarines had passed effortlessly through the boom defence. It was a miserable performance, suggesting poor discipline and even poorer planning and training. Having further wrong-footed himself by disbelieving the submarine reports when they first reached him, Muirhead-Gould was now in a precarious position. He had publicly made a fool of himself in front of the entire crew of *Lolita*, and there would always remain the suspicion that the dinner party at 'Tresco' was a factor in the Admiral's handling of Sydney's defence. Some kind of inquiry or, worse, a Royal Commission, would be unlikely to leave his career or reputation other than in tatters. The evidence of *Lolita's* crew alone would be enough to destroy him. To avoid this danger he needed to come up quickly with some plausible narrative which would not leave him too exposed, and which would satisfy those who might otherwise press successfully for some sort of inquiry. A few scapegoats would come in handy, too.

The Australian government's first reaction—and also their final decision—was to share Muirhead-Gould's view. They had already set up a judicial inquiry into the humiliating shambles in Darwin in the face of Japanese air attack. The last thing they needed was a second inquiry revealing shaky defences and poor leadership, this time in Australia's most important port. So there was a common interest in coming up with a credible story which didn't delve too deeply into the flaws in the system or the personal failings of those at the top. Muirhead-Gould would have to provide the necessary account, and quickly.

The submarines themselves were a useful distraction. By the afternoon of Monday, 1 June two of the attacking submarines had been located. If they could be raised from the harbour bottom, they would yield all sorts of useful intelligence. There might be code books and charts with clues to future attacks, as well as a host of useful information about weapons, equipment and tactics. As a bonus, if the newspapers could be induced to focus on the submarine raising instead of conducting an embarrassing post mortem into how they got past the defences and inside Sydney Harbour in the first place, that might buy Muirhead-Gould and the government a little time.

The most urgent need was to establish exactly what happened. How many submarines had got into the harbour? Had any escaped? How many were sunk? Who sank them? After any battle, the commanders are required to write an action report summing up what they did, and when and where they did it. There were plenty of ships playing an active role in the Battle of Sydney Harbour that night, and Muirhead-Gould needed their accounts urgently. The most important reports would come from *Yandra*, *Yarroma*, *Lolita*, *Sea Mist* and *Steady Hour*, all of whom had dropped depth charges on credible submarine contacts. *Yandra* had also rammed a submarine. *Kanimbla* and *Geelong* had opened fire on submarine contacts. The unarmed Nappie *Lauriana* had made close visual contact with a submarine. The anti-submarine specialist *Bingera* had chased submarine contacts around Kirribilli and Cremorne Point. All could help to establish what had happened. Better still, all would have stories to tell which would show the defences in a good light.

The two US Navy ships *Chicago* and *Perkins* would also prepare action reports, but these would be submitted to the US Navy's Pacific command in Pearl Harbor rather than to Muirhead-Gould. As we shall see, they would tell a less flattering story.

♦ ♦ ♦

Muirhead-Gould was not the only commander starved of information on 1 June. Off Port Hacking, the five Japanese mother submarines waited for the return of the midgets. They had seen searchlights roaming the Sydney night sky in an agitated way, suggesting that some sort of attack was under way. They had no idea whether or not it had succeeded, or what had happened to the midgets and their crews. All they could do was sit and wait.

♦ ♦ ♦

Although the last shot in the Battle of Sydney Harbour had been fired at 8.27 am (*Yarroma's* last depth charge in Taylors Bay), there was plenty of military activity on 1 June. Nobody knew how the midget submarines had been transported to Sydney. They might have been carried aboard a surface vessel, but the chances were they arrived strapped to the deck of a larger submarine, or larger submarines. Whatever the method, there was a near certainty that one or more mother ships were lurking outside Sydney waiting for the return of the midgets and their crews. Eight aircraft were ordered to search the area, while another six stood by as a striking force to attack anything they found. The various warships which had fled the harbour in the early hours of the morning also joined the hunt. The five mother submarines stayed submerged and silent. Nobody found anything.

♦ ♦ ♦

Monday marked the emergence of one of the consistent heroes of the entire saga, a civilian torpedo fitter at Garden Island, Frank Lingard. His widow Ivy Lingard recalled in a television interview her fears for his safety that day when he set off to work. 'I was a bit worried that morning,' she remembered. 'It was wet and miserable. I had visions of him rushing off down the gangplank at Garden Island and slipping.' She didn't know the half of it. If slipping on a wet gangplank had been the worst danger Frank Lingard faced that day, he could have counted himself a lucky man.

There is no record of whether Ban's second torpedo was still resting on the rocks when Frank Lingard first tackled it, or whether it had been moved to a safer place. It had come to rest not far from a munition store, so the risk of a calamitous explosion was very real. The highest probability is that it was moved away quickly, and disarmed later. A contemporary newsreel shows a close-up of Frank Lingard, face untroubled beyond a look of fierce concentration, in a workshop applying a screwdriver to a torpedo which is still very much alive. Some of the explosive had spilled out, but the pistol and detonator were firmly in place, and the fact that it had been fired meant the mechanism was in its most potentially dangerous state. The detonator alone would be capable of killing a man at close range.

Lingard's first examination told him the design resembled British torpedoes with which he was already familiar. This judgement mercifully proved to be correct. The wires and the charges were more or less where he expected them. Gingerly he removed the pistol and primers. Ban's torpedo was now harmless. All this was done entirely voluntarily.

That night Ivy Lingard reacted as any wife might have done. 'I knew nothing about all this until he came home,' she recalled. 'Of course I was horrified to think that he'd taken such a risk when he had two little sons to think about.'

Lingard's heroism that day alone would have been enough to win him a place in the roll of honour in the Battle of Sydney Harbour. He could not know it at the time, but for him it was only a beginning. There was much more dangerous disarming work ahead.

✦　✦　✦

What of Sub-Lieutenant Ban and Petty Officer Ashibe? Until November 2006 their midget's fate remained a mystery. Japanese radio broadcasts after the raid reported that no midget submarine crew had been recovered, so the defence knew that both sub and crew must have been lost somewhere. The supposed wreck was 'discovered' on no fewer than 40 different occasions over the next 64 years. Award-winning documentary makers mistook a heap of sand in Broken Bay for a buried submarine. Others triumphantly photographed sunken paravanes, boomerang buoys, old pipes and other plausible junk and waved their pictures aloft before an admiring populace. It fell to a group of engaging and happy-go-lucky weekend explorers called No Frills Divers to find the real submarine in late 2006 in a bit over 50 metres of water, about 3 kilometres off Newport Reef on the northern Sydney beaches. The wreck is largely intact—the scuttling charges have not been fired. However it has taken a battering from professional fishermens' lines and nets and from the ravages of its long years underwater.

In the light of this discovery, what do we know with anything approaching certainty of Ban's and Ashibe's intentions and final fate? We know that at 1.58 am on the morning of 1 June something crossed Inner Loop 12 heading for the open sea, and it must surely have been Ban. Six minutes later Inner Loop 11, which stretched between North Head and South Head, recorded a crossing very likely caused by Ban's midget. Ban had made it to the open sea. What happened next?

A bit of speculation first. Everything Ban did that night suggests that he intended to survive if he could. He was, of course, an exponent of the 'sure to die' warrior's code. But everything points to his wish to live to fight another day. His progress through Sydney Harbour is usually portrayed as fast and furious. It was not. He travelled very slowly from his Inner Loop 12 crossing at 9.48 pm to his sighting by *Chicago* near Garden Island at 10.52—he averaged about 3 knots, his best speed for conserving his batteries. He probably had to put on a bit of speed when *Chicago* opened fire on him, but that will have been for no more than a few minutes. He took 90 minutes to travel from his last sighting near the Harbour Bridge to his firing position at Bradleys Head, a distance of about 3 kilometres. He then took another 90 minutes to travel from Bradleys Head to Inner Loop 12, again a distance of about 3 kilometres. So the idea that his batteries were close to exhaustion by the time he crossed the loop outbound will not hold. He still had between 4 and 8 hours useful battery time left.

We are also entitled to attach some significance to the fact that his torpedoes were set to 60-degree left deflection. As discussed earlier, this is a tactic used by a submarine commander who intends to play hard to catch. The torpedoes' wakes told the eyewitnesses on *Perkins* and *Chicago* that they had been fired from the direction of Bradleys Head. But Ban's heading will have taken him quickly away from this firing line and thus improved his chances of survival. All the evidence points to an intention to survive the night.

So what happened? If he intended to return to the agreed rendezvous point with the mother submarines, Ban should have turned right and headed for Port Hacking to the south of Sydney. However, he clearly turned left and headed north. Why?

The most commonly touted theory is that he turned away from the rendezvous point to avoid giving away the position of the mother subs, waited until his batteries were exhausted, then committed suicide. At the time of writing, there has been no attempt to enter the submarine, so we have no idea of the final fate of the two submariners inside—if, indeed, that is where their remains lie. However, we should not rush to judgement. The scuttling charges were not fired, and the crews of *Toku-tai* submarines that took part in earlier raids did not always choose suicide.

At Pearl Harbor, Sakamaki and Inagaki both abandoned their wrecked submarine and attempted to swim to shore. Inagaki drowned, but Sakamaki made it to safety. While Sakamaki later asked to be allowed to commit suicide, it is significant that he did not attempt suicide when his submarine was finally trapped on a reef. He chose instead to swim for it.

Another of the Pearl Harbor submarines was discovered in shallow water in Keehi Lagoon in 1960, damaged by depth charges. The remains of the crew were not aboard. Japanese midget submariners wore a uniform that closely resembled the flying suits worn by Japanese pilots. The most sensible explanation is that the crew escaped successfully from their sinking submarine but subsequently drowned. Their bodies were then mistaken for the bodies of downed Japanese pilots. Scraps of

Japanese naval uniform were found in Pearl Harbor after the raid, lending support to this theory.

At Diégo Suarez the midget submarine that attacked HMS *Ramillies* and sank *British Loyalty* escaped from the harbour. However, the sub had rudder problems and grounded on a reef shortly afterwards. The two submariners escaped from their stricken midget and managed to reach the shore. They set off on foot for the rendezvous area. After a tip-off from a local resident, British forces moved out to capture them. Both Japanese sailors were killed, along with a British soldier, in the ensuing gunfight. The fact remains that both Diégo Suarez sailors made it to shore and attempted to rendezvous with their mother submarines. Suicide does not seem to have entered their calculations.

So a clear pattern emerges from previous midget submarine missions: the crews generally set out to survive. A further argument against a planned and lonely suicide by Ban and Ashibe is the obvious one—they might have done more damage if they had remained inside Sydney Harbour. If they were determined to die, they would have done better to creep underneath *Chicago* or *Canberra* and fire their scuttling charges, in the hope that they could take one of their targets with them.

Finally, Ban and Ashibe were in an entirely different position from their fellow submariners in the Sydney raid. Chuman and Omori suicided while trapped in the boom net and under attack. Matsuo and Tsuzuku were cornered in Taylors Bay with depth charges raining down on them. The crews of both midgets were doomed, and knew it. They chose suicide rather than hand victory to their tormentors. Ban and Ashibe had made it to open water, where they were in no way cornered and were not under attack. Suicide was not an obvious response to their situation.

So what *did* happen? Despite the discovery of the wreck and subsequent examination by the divers who found it and by a Royal Australian Navy remote submersible camera, the midget leaves plenty of unanswered questions. Did Ban's submarine take battle damage? The sunken hull has lost its bow and stern cages, the bow casing above the upper torpedo tube and half of the upper torpedo tube itself, the casing around the conning tower, the net cutter, most of its rear horizontal and vertical rudders, the conning tower hatch and the top half of the periscope. This damage is readily traceable to the various fishing nets and lines snagged on the bow and conning tower of the wreck and wrapped around its hull. Some of the missing parts can be seen amongst the debris on the seabed alongside the wreck, showing that this damage took place long after Ban had left Sydney Harbour.

The hull has been repeatedly holed, but most of the holes are either part of the design of the sub or are the result of corrosion from its 64 years underwater. They do not show the 'dimpling' effect of bullet strikes. Nevertheless it seems unlikely that Ban escaped entirely untouched by the hail of fire from *Chicago* and *Geelong* when he was caught on the surface near Garden Island and again near Fort Denison. It is possible he was hit by one or more bursts from *Geelong*'s Vickers machine-gun or *Chicago*'s anti-aircraft pom-pom. These hits cannot have inflicted major damage or the submarine would have been crippled there and then. However, they may have inflicted minor damage, leading to slow leaks and other gradually developing problems.

Ban must have been under power and under control for at least three hours, from 10.52 pm to 2.04 am, to carry out his attack on *Chicago*, and to make his way out of Sydney Harbour. So if he had problems, they cannot have been critical until the time he was leaving the harbour. His first problem after clearing the Heads would be the weather. The wind had backed around from south-west to south and increased to 20 knots, gusting to 30 knots. If he turned south towards the agreed rendezvous point, he would be running into the teeth of Sydney's notoriously ferocious southerly. At this point his torpedo tubes would be wide open after firing, so the sub's clumsy bow would be almost totally unmanageable facing into the weather. His best hope for survival would have been to turn north and ride with the wind, leaving the rendezvous for another day.

Did Ban and Ashibe attempt to reach land, like their six fellow midget submariners at Pearl Harbor and Diégo Suarez? The conning tower hatch of Ban's midget was open when the wreck was found, suggesting the crew might have tried to escape. However, video footage recorded by No Frills Divers of the interior of the control room shows the sub's conning tower ladder folded and stowed. It seems unlikely that the crew would tidy the ladder away in the frantic moments after abandoning their submarine. So the highest probability is that the ladder was not used at all. The crew had no other way of exiting the submarine. The only conclusion possible is that there was no escape attempt by the crew. As for the open conning tower, the hatch was found resting on the seabed a few metres away from the wreck of the sub, indicating that it was ripped off and dumped by a passing fishing boat's line or trawl net not long before the sub's discovery in November 2006.

We need to look at one possibility, long championed by the historian and retired judge Dr James Macken. Jim made his first appearance in this book as a Riverview schoolboy watching the raid from the school's rooftop. His subsequent theory on the fate of Ban's midget was enthusiastically taken up by the makers of the 2005 television documentary *He's Coming South*. The documentary-makers have continued to defend it even after the discovery of the wreck of Ban's submarine many kilometres away from the place where they claimed to 'find' it in 2005.

Jim Macken's theory was that in the weeks after the raid there were a number of plausible sightings of a midget submarine around Broken Bay, just north of Sydney's fashionable Palm Beach. The entrance to Broken Bay is about 11 kilometres north of where the wreck was actually found. According to this theory, Ban and Ashibe set their sub to neutral buoyancy before committing suicide. Their submarine then drifted out of control for several weeks in the waters around the entrance to Broken Bay. It rose to the surface and submerged of its own accord, probably as a result of changing water temperatures and salinity, before finally coming to rest. Jim Macken's theory ends there: he has never made any claim to have found the submarine, nor to know its exact location.

The documentary-makers, however, have continued to argue that there is no conflict between this theory and the subsequent discovery of the actual submarine. According to this view, the submarine did indeed drift around Broken Bay before being dragged out to sea by the tide and pushed south by the current to its final resting place off Newport Reef. The fatal flaw in this theory is that the submarine simply did not have enough battery power left to make it to Broken Bay in the first place. Cruising economically, it had somewhere between four and eight hours of battery left when it passed through the Sydney Harbour Heads. Taking the current and wind into account, Ban had between 6 and 12 nautical miles of life if he headed north. He came to rest about 9.7 nautical miles from the Heads.

Additionally, setting the sub to neutral buoyancy and leaving it to drift would go against all of Ban's training and instincts. The midget submarines were still regarded as one of Japan's most secret weapons. Leaving the sub to drift would be an invitation to the enemy to seize it intact. Ban's training would tell him that the sub had to be kept safe from enemy hands. As for the 'sightings' by qualified observers in Broken Bay, these can be referred to William of Ockham for judgement: the highest probability is that they made a mistake.

At this point in the narrative, nothing would make the author's day quite so sunny as a simple answer to the question of why Ban headed north, and what he chose to do when he arrived at the midget's final resting place. Both questions are likely to remain permanently unanswerable. If the wreck is raised, or if the contents are sucked out and examined, then it may be possible to discover if the submariners did indeed perish with their boat, and how they died. At the time of writing, the wreck seems destined to remain undisturbed, clinging to its secrets.

Nevertheless, we can make some intelligent guesses. It seems highly likely that Ban was in some sort of difficulty by the time he entered the open ocean. The sub may have sprung a small leak or two, either as a result of *Chicago*'s and *Geelong*'s attack or as a consequence of the violent manoeuvring inside the harbour. Even a very small leak could build into a major problem over the space of three or four hours. The sub may have become difficult to control, as did the Diégo Suarez sub, or it may have developed an engine problem as a result of a leak or battle damage.

Another strong possibility is that Ban found himself facing the same difficulties as Sakamaki at Pearl Harbor. Battery fumes caused both Sakamaki and his crewman Inagaki to pass out repeatedly, and they frequently lost control of their sub. Ban will have submerged around the time he entered Sydney Harbour, some time before 9.48 pm when his midget set off a trace on Inner Loop 12. He will have spent most or all of his time fully submerged or at periscope depth with the conning tower hatch closed until around 10.52 pm when he was sighted by *Chicago*. The hatch will have remained closed throughout his encounter with *Chicago* and *Geelong*, and for all the time he lay underwater before his torpedo attack at 12.29 am. He probably stayed fully submerged, or at periscope depth but still with the hatch closed, until he reached the open ocean around 2.04 am.

Thus he manoeuvred for five hours, from around 9.30 pm until 2.30 am, with his hatch mostly closed and the engine running for much of that time. The build-up of fumes inside the submarine must have been crippling, and it is possible that by the time they reached open sea Ban and Ashibe were finding life inside their craft impossible. Their problems would increase with every minute they remained sealed and under way. In those circumstances, it would be a matter of wonder that Ban and Ashibe managed to control the submarine at all.

If any or all of these problems—bad weather, slow leaks, loss of control and fumes—gained a grip on the submarine, then Ban's best bet would be to remain on or close to the surface and go where the wind took him. He could do this until his batteries ran out. After that? His position would then be hopeless, and suicide might begin to look like the only option. If his scuttling charges refused to fire as a result of water damage or failed batteries, then opening the conning tower hatch and putting the submarine into a dive would keep it out of enemy hands and make for a clean end for its crew.

For now, all these mysteries will remain unsolved. All we can say with certainty is that the submarine is firmly settled a few miles off the

Sydney coast, with its hull unbroken by powerful scuttling charges left unfired by the crew. Until the wreck is raised, or its contents examined, we will be no closer to an answer to the last great question from the Battle of Sydney Harbour: How did Ban and Ashibe die, and is the newly discovered wreck the final resting place of two brave men?

Chapter 15

Has *everybody* seen a submarine?

The newspapers had a field day on Tuesday, 2 June. 'Enemy subs enter Sydney Harbour—three midget raiders destroyed,' proclaimed the *Sydney Morning Herald*'s front page. There followed pages of pictures and news stories, including pictures of midget submarines from the Pearl Harbor raid. However, the censors set very narrow guidelines on what could be written. They were particularly anxious to conceal the fact that the submarine crews had suicided, judging probably rightly that the Australian public would be even more alarmed by the thought of suicide raiders than they already were by the news of enemy submarines in their beloved harbour.

Meanwhile, the government took the line that everything had gone swimmingly on the night, and would everybody please calm down and congratulate the defence forces on an excellent job done. The Minister for the Navy Norman Makin made a statement on the raid to Federal Parliament in Canberra on 2 June. It was a world-beating piece of effrontery. 'This attempt was unsuccessful,' said Makin.

Its failure was due to the preparedness of our defences for such an attempt and to prompt counter attack carried out by harbour defence vessels and other warships in the harbour.

That the attempt by such midget craft to enter Sydney Harbour in the middle of the night was instantly detected, and that the counter measures were so prompt and so effective reflects credit on those responsible for the harbour defences.

The first alarm was given by a patrol vessel at Sydney Heads shortly before 10 o'clock on Sunday night . . . the alarm having been given, patrol vessels and warships in the harbour were on the alert . . . we have good grounds for satisfaction at the results achieved.

So that's all right, then.

Later that day Prime Minister Curtin continued the reassurance while raising the submarine count from three to four. He said in a radio broadcast: 'Vigilant and prompt action of the naval forces guarding our shores has prevented any material success being achieved by the submarines. After careful analysis of all reports of fighting and attacks it is now confirmed that four midget submarines attempted to enter Sydney Harbour on the night of May 31. At least three of these submarines were destroyed.'

The submarine count remained at four for the rest of the war, and was not reduced to three until much later when Japanese naval documents became available. The four were: Midget 'A' (Ban), which fired the torpedoes that sank the *Kuttabul* and which was thought to have escaped; Midget 'B', sunk by *Yandra* near the harbour entrance; M–14 (Chuman), trapped in the net and scuttled; and M–21 (Matsuo), sunk by depth charges in Taylors Bay. In fact *Yandra*'s submarine was not sunk. Midget 'B' and M–21 were the same submarine.

◆　　◆　　◆

Over in Taylors Bay, the minesweeper *Samuel Benbow* attempted to tow Matsuo's midget to a safer position. In particular *Benbow* wanted to swing the hull so that the bow pointed towards the shore rather than up the harbour. If the jammed torpedoes somehow gained a new lease of life, then it would be better if they ran aground rather than ran amok in the main harbour. However, the sub stubbornly refused to move. The stern was well stuck in the harbour mud, and the *Benbow* simply did not have the strength to shift it.

Roy Cooté's dive log is more than usually terse. 'Diving on first sub. Rough weather broke 4-inch wire strops.' Tomorrow they could try again, this time using a crane.

✦　✦　✦

By the morning of Wednesday, 3 June, something akin to submarine fever had taken over Sydney. There was hardly a fisherman who had not seen a submarine, sometimes as early as 48 hours before the attack. Swirls of bubbles suddenly assumed huge significance. Ferry passengers were convinced they had seen periscopes, conning towers, even whole submarines. One man claimed to have held onto the periscope of a submarine trapped in the net, and walked on its hull. He then rowed flat out across the harbour to Naval Headquarters on Garden Island to recount this remarkable tale, and was told to 'take more water with it next time'.

Everybody had a story. What did you see? What did you hear? How did you spend the night? Mary McCune, then two years old, was close to the action at Whiting Beach in Mosman, next door to Taronga Park zoo. This placed her opposite *Chicago*'s and *Geelong*'s gunfire, not far from *Kanimbla*'s guns, and just 1000 metres from Taylors Bay and the depth charges dropped by *Sea Mist*, *Steady Hour* and *Yarroma*. It was a lively night for any toddler. Mary recalls:

I can't remember any sounds or anything else like that. What I remember most was being woken up in the middle of the night, which was unusual. I remember being dressed in a Chinese black silk dressing gown with red dragons on it and taken off to a garage along the street that was built into the cliff. That was the air-raid shelter for the street.

I think it sticks in my memory because of the dressing gown. It was my first vain memory. I really fancied myself in it. I think it's informed the rest of my life. I've been concerned ever since with what to wear for the occasion.

Donald Dunkley's story speaks for most of Sydney. He was 12 years old and living in Chatswood, a northern Sydney suburb kilometres away from the harbour and the main action. The air-raid sirens went off some time around midnight. The family did not have an air-raid shelter, and had been told to get under a bed or a kitchen table instead, or stand in a doorway arch. The entire family—mother, sister, brother and young Donald—opted to get under the main double bed.

Even before they scrambled into their improvised shelter, they knew there was something different this time. Usually the street's air-raid warden came around beforehand and told them a trial air-raid drill would be carried out that night. The warden would then parade up and down the street, knocking on doors to warn that there was a chink of light coming from this or that window. Not this night. There was no warning before the sirens sounded. 'So we thought: this is the real thing,' Donald remembers.

> We were quite concerned about it. But we could hear no guns, no bombs, and we thought this was very strange. We were waiting for the bombs. We were listening and thinking it'll come soon, it'll come soon, it'll come soon. And nothing happened.
>
> We were under the bed a long time, waiting and waiting. Then the all clear came and we got out. We immediately went to the radio, the ABC, to try to find out what it was all about. We were a bit confused, not hearing any sign of warfare or anything.

The radio told them nothing. The censors made sure of that.

Meanwhile, the newspapers continued to accept the government's version of events. Yes, some submarines had managed to enter the harbour. But look what a great job the defences had done. Sydney had been saved by their alert professionalism.

◆　　◆　　◆

Reg Andrew's first attempt at an action report was not a huge success. He wrote it jointly with a fellow Channel Patrol boat skipper who happened to be a solicitor in civilian life. When he handed it over to Ric Breydon, the flotilla commander, it was thrown back at him across the desk. He was told to go back and rewrite it in the first person. No more 'we'. Action reports had to be 'I'.

◆　　◆　　◆

For the five mother submarines waiting in a disciplined line off Port Hacking, this was an agonising time. Japanese standing orders required a reconnaissance flight after any raid, to assess damage. But with both Glens crashed and sunk, Sasaki and the Eastern Attack Group had no way of finding out whether or not the attack had succeeded, or what damage had been done. They simply had to wait for the return of the midgets. They stayed submerged, resting on the seabed during the day, their ears glued to the hydrophones hoping for the sound of a midget submarine approaching. At night they surfaced, charged their batteries, and listened some more. The radio and the hydrophones stubbornly refused to come up with the good news that a surviving midget crew needed picking up.

Meanwhile, the defence's search for the mother ships continued, still with no result. The pilots explained that it was impossible to see a submarine in deep water even in daylight, unless you happened to pass directly overhead. This time luck was with the submarines.

Some time on Wednesday, 3 June, Sasaki decided that they had waited long enough. Three whole days had now passed with no sign of any of the midgets. Like the crews at Pearl Harbor and Diégo Suarez, all must have been lost. Sasaki ordered the mother submarines to disperse, and to switch their attention to sinking any ships they could find, warships or merchant ships.

The first strike took place on the evening of Wednesday, 3 June. It was a total failure. I-24 fired a torpedo from close range at the small Australian freighter, *Age*. It missed. I-24 now manned its deck gun and fired four rounds at the *Age*. All four missed. The freighter had been manoeuvring using standard evasive tactics, and they worked. It arrived unscathed in Newcastle Harbour some four hours later.

The next attack was far more deadly. Ninety minutes after the *Age* incident, I-24 came upon a second coastal freighter, the 4800-ton *Iron Chieftain*, owned by the Australian mining giant BHP. Two torpedoes later the ship was headed for the bottom, taking 12 of the ship's company with her. The ship's wireless operator stayed at his post and managed to send a signal reporting the attack and giving the ship's position. He was lost with the ship. However, 12 of the crew found safety on a raft, and another 25 survived on a lifeboat. The 12 on the raft were picked up five hours later by the anti-submarine ship HMAS *Bingera*. The lifeboat with its 25 survivors made it to the beach at The Entrance.

The defences now went into overdrive. Sydney Harbour was again closed to outbound shipping. RAAF reconnaissance planes scoured the ocean hunting for the attacking submarine. As before, they found nothing.

Next it was the turn of I-27. Around dawn on Thursday, 4 June near Gabo Island off the south-eastern coast of Australia, the submarine fired a torpedo at the freighter *Barwon*. The torpedo mysteriously failed. It passed under the ship and exploded 200 metres away, causing no damage. I-27 now tried its deck gun, but this too failed to inflict any damage.

That evening I-27 spotted the freighter *Iron Crown*. This time there was no mistake. I-27's torpedo sank its target in less than a minute, taking 37 of the ship's 42 crew with it. The submarine was seen by a patrolling RAAF Hudson which attacked with two anti-submarine bombs. Although both bombs went close, the submarine appeared to survive. It submerged and escaped.

In the space of 24 hours the mother submarines had managed to inflict far more damage than was ever achieved by the midgets. The Eastern Attack Group still had plenty of fight left in it, whatever the fate of the Sydney Harbour attack.

◆   ◆   ◆

The divers returned to Taylors Bay on Wednesday. Roy Coóté and Lance Bullard went down together and changed the hemp buoy rope for a steel wire rope which they could use to travel up and down. Lance Bullard recalls: 'The weather was bitterly cold with a southerly wind causing a choppy sea. The riggers at Garden Island had been making slings to bring the sub to the surface. They were made of 3-inch wire rope. The harbour crane *Hawk* was placed in position.' Roy Coóté is his usual loquacious self: 'Dived on first sub again. Attached more wires.'

On Thursday morning the serious business of raising the sub began. For the crane to do its job, the divers had to pass two slings under the submarine's hull, one near the bow and one near the stern. This was both difficult and dangerous. Although three days had passed since the sub was sunk, there was still no certainty that the crew were not still alive and capable of detonating their scuttling charges as soon as they heard activity nearby. The divers had to be stealthy as well as thorough.

A lighter had tied up alongside the crane, and dropped the slings over the side. Let Lance Bullard take up the story:

We left the surface at 1.30 pm, and the first job on the bottom was to find the slings and sort them out. The sub seemed to have sunk deeper in the mud at the stern. We started digging at the bows and after half an hour we met and passed one end of the sling through, leaving half on each side, then hauled the ends up on the sub's deck and passed one end through the eye and laid it on the deck leading aft.

The bow sling had been comparatively easy. The stern was another story. Bullard continues: 'We were using our hands and knives, and seemed to be working a long time, as the hole had to be fairly big to go in head first and leave room to dig and scrape the mud back.' Picture the scene: the divers are 85 feet (26 metres) under water, trying to dig a hole under the buried hull of the submarine using only their bare hands and knives. The hole has to be big enough to allow their huge helmets to pass through. They have to do this while not banging the hull of the sub with their helmets or lead-weighted boots for fear of stirring the sub's crew into violent action. It can't have been easy.

Bullard continues:

Finally, Roy poked his arm through. I backed out and passed one end of the sling through. I walked around to him as he was backing out of his hole. When he stood up I pointed to his breast rope which was still leading into the hole. He pulled but could not clear it. Finally, he had to go back in and clear it. We had the ends of the two slings together and joined them with a big shackle which had to go on the hook of the *Hawk's* lift.

The big block carrying the wires of the lift was a huge affair, and had to be as she could lift 60 or 70 tons. The weather must have got worse, as now the block was jumping up, down and sideways continually. We were both wet and cold and tired. We could not get our shackle onto the block. The block was swinging too much. We had five minutes spell and then decided to have one more try, as the light was getting bad. I grabbed the big shackle and Roy was trying to steady the block. I lifted the shackle at the same time as the *Hawk* dipped, and it was on. Just like that.

We reported finished and left the bottom, knowing we had four steps on the way up: the first at 50 feet only for about seven minutes, and the last at 10 feet where we had over an hour. These stagings were to decompress and the timetable had to be carried out strictly by the book, otherwise diver's paralysis or bends was the result. We finally got back to the boat at approximately 6.45 pm.

They had been underwater for over five hours, cold, wet and in constant danger. It was too late to try lifting the submarine that evening. The commander in charge of salvage operations decided they would simply tighten the slings and wait until the morning. Bullard was unhappy with the arrangements. If the slings were tightened, he warned, the up-and-down movement of the *Hawk* would make them rub against the serrated net cutter of the submarine, seriously weakening them. Lieutenant Whittle, the senior diver, agreed with Bullard. The commander overruled them both.

The salvage team assembled at 7.30 am next morning. The divers were not sent down to check the slings. At 8.15 am the *Hawk* took the strain and began hauling in, watched by a flotilla of launches and small craft on the harbour, and with the shores of Taylors Bay lined with spectators. First the block broke the surface. Everybody tensed. Then the shackle appeared, and the slings. Empty. The sub had cut through both slings and remained firmly on the bottom. Bullard had been proved right. All yesterday's courage and toil had been wasted.

The salvage team now decided the steel buoy rope might be strong enough to do the job. Lance Bullard was sent down to take a look. He arrived on the harbour bed but could not see the sub. Panic stations. Had the sub and its crew somehow escaped? He searched around frantically, then looked up and saw the sub's bows about 12 feet (3.5 metres) off the bottom, swinging backwards and forwards. 'I went up quick smart,' he wrote.

The sub was now dragged along the bottom into shallow water, and lifted using the 3-inch wire rope attached to the bow. More tension. Then the sub's bows broke the surface, followed by the hull, dangling vertically from the wire rope like a big game fish about to be landed. The stern section had broken off during the dragging operation, but the main body of the submarine was clear of the water. Matsuo's midget was now ready for closer examination.

◆　　◆　　◆

First to board the submarine was Lieutenant Percy Wilson, the Garden Island intelligence officer. His most vivid memory is of the seamen's hair. Both Matsuo's and Tsuzuku's hair had turned bright green, the result of leaking battery chemicals.

Now it was the turn of Frank Lingard to display more remarkable courage. His wife Ivy Lingard recalls: 'As the submarines were brought to the surface, Frank went into them and saw that some of the demolition charges had not been used. He took the responsibility of removing them, and the charges from the torpedoes.' As well as the demolition charges, Matsuo's two torpedoes protruded from the bow of the submarine, both in an unknown state of readiness and stability. They might well have both been armed. Lingard had no way of knowing.

Ivy Lingard continues: 'He had to go down into the submarines, but not while they were in the water. They were brought up on land by huge cranes and there were still dead bodies in the submarines.' The bodies of Lieutenant Keiu Matsuo and Petty Officer First Class Masao Tsuzuku, with their neat, single-shot bullet wounds, were removed and transported to the police morgue.

After his experience gained disarming Ban's second torpedo on Garden Island, Lingard had some idea how to tackle the two torpedoes from Matsuo's midget. The demolition charges were a different story. Although the salvaged submarines from Pearl Harbor had given the Allies some idea of where and how to find the charges, the Americans had passed on very little intelligence from their find. So Lingard had little to go on. Nevertheless, he succeeded in disarming both sets of scuttling charges, from the fore and aft ends of Matsuo's midget.

He must have dreaded the thought of Chuman's submarine still to come.

◆　　◆　　◆

The tail of Matsuo's sub was lifted several days later. Roy Cooté was fulsome. 'Dived while crew lifted Sub 1,' he wrote, followed by: 'Dived on Sub No 2 surveying for lifting.'

◆　　◆　　◆

While all this was going on, far more important events were taking place in the Pacific to the north. After the score draw in the Coral Sea, Yamamoto still needed his decisive battle with the US Pacific Fleet. In particular he needed to finish off the aircraft carriers. He had enjoyed a flawless six-month run of successes, stretching from Pearl Harbor to the

Java Sea, and he was confident that one more major attack would finish the job. Over-confident, in fact.

He chose the US fleet's base on Midway Island as his target, and set out to lure the American aircraft carriers there for a final, decisive knockout round. But the code-breakers were now into their stride, and they anticipated him well. In fact luck played a major part, too, this time favouring the Americans. A group of American aircraft had set off in the wrong direction, and chanced on the Japanese carrier force with its planes on the deck refuelling and rearming. The next seven minutes were some of the most extraordinary and dramatic in all military history. Quite simply, they swung the Pacific war in the Allies' favour. The Japanese lost four heavy aircraft carriers, one heavy cruiser, 234 aircraft and 2200 men. In the space of seven minutes, the Imperial Japanese Navy became a broken force. The defeat was so total and so humiliating that the Japanese commanders at Midway at first could not bring themselves to tell Tokyo what had happened. The Japanese government did not pass on the information to the remains of their navy, let alone the Japanese public, for several weeks.

Yamamoto finally had the decisive battle he had been yearning for. And lost it comprehensively.

♦   ♦   ♦

In Sydney the newspapers hardly knew which way to turn. They divided their attention between the events in Midway, the submarine attacks on merchant shipping in Australian waters, and the lifting operation on the midget submarines. They also continued to publish eyewitness accounts of Sunday night's excitements. For once, the news from the north was good. The tide of war might be turning the Allies' way. In Sydney, the government and navy story continued to hold. The harbour defences had done a fine, professional job. Very little harm done.

It could not last. And it didn't.

Chapter 16

Caught napping

Smith's Weekly occupies an odd corner in the history of Australian journalism. It began its life on 1 March 1919 as a weekly newspaper devoted to the cause of ex-servicemen. It was doggedly in favour of the little bloke. It was also jingoistic, racist, bigoted and small-minded. It missed no opportunity to refer to Italians as Dagoes, Chinese as Chinks and Japanese as Japs or Nips. Its major claim to fame is that, together with its offspring the *Daily Guardian*, it introduced the Packer family to Australian journalism and publishing. The Packer fortune started here, though by 1942 the Packers had long since sold their interest in *Smith's Weekly*.

The paper's coverage of the submarine raid got off to a flying start with a remarkably prescient Donaldson cartoon, reproduced below. The cartoon appeared one day *before* the midgets arrived. *Smith's Weekly* kept up this cracking pace the following week. The 6 June issue devoted the whole of its third page to committing the worst crime any journalist can perpetrate. It is guaranteed to drive governments and military establishments into a state of purple-faced apoplexy, and have them reaching for their gags and rattling their gaol keys. The crime? *Smith's Weekly* got the story right.

"It's undersize. Do you think we ought to throw it back?"

This cartoon by Donaldson appeared in *Smith's Weekly* on page 5 of the Saturday, 30 May issue—one day before the midget subs arrived in the harbour.

Under the headline, 'Battle of Port Jackson'—Whose the Responsibility?', it went into self-righteous overdrive. In large type, its sub-headline set out the key demand. 'How submarines entered Sydney Harbour calls for inquiry and sackings. If it's the navy or the coastal defences that neglected safeguarding the great port of Sydney, the responsibility should be sheeted home.'

The story which followed began by recalling: 'Early in the war at Scapa Flow the Nazis sank a battleship under the eyes of the British Navy. That, and what happened at Pearl Harbor, should have been sufficient warning of what to expect in Australia's greatest port.'

The paper then went on to list the failings of the defence. Precautions at Sydney Heads were believed to have been taken. There should be no possible chance of a submarine entering Port Jackson. Where were the detector devices? Why had the government taken so long to announce the facts? The city was alive with rumours. Most people thought Sydney was under attack from the air. Others thought ammunition aboard a ship had exploded. Why did the government not put a stop to the rumours by telling the truth straightaway?

The paper went on to imply that the defences had been caught napping. 'Suddenness of the incident was underlined by the fact that through it all Sydney Ferries and Manly Ferries continued to run. Watchers saw Manly boats, both outward and inward bound, carry on with their trips and pass across the scene of the action as though nothing were happening.'

'Sole cause for satisfaction', Smith's Weekly concluded, 'is that the Japs didn't pull off the trick. But more safeguards and greater vigilance are plainly called for at the entrance to Sydney Harbour.'

The story ended with two provocative declarations. 'After Pearl Harbor, Emperor Hirohito of Japan granted posthumous promotion to the heroes of his suicide squads who manned these pigmy submarines and did not return. They were all named by Tokyo radio. Here's a chance for a few more posthumous promotions. They are brave men without a doubt.'

This was followed by a second declaration, a throwaway line to end the story. 'Incidentally, the part our US allies played in this Port Jackson incident was splendid. We salute them!' As we shall see, this apparently innocuous final pat on the back was delivered with enough force to send a positive horde of unpalatable facts stumbling into the daylight a week later.

This attack lasted 16 minutes, and gave the batteries at Fort Scratchley time to fire four rounds back. None hit the I-21. It too now submerged and slipped out to sea in search of merchant ships.

♦　　♦　　♦

On Monday morning the divers switched their attention to the boom net and the remaining submarine. Lance Bullard recalls: 'I inspected the fore end of the sub on the bottom. There was debris scattered everywhere but both torpedoes were intact.

'We had to cut out the stern with underwater cutting gear, and finally shackled a 10-foot patch in the hole, which will give a good idea of how badly her propellers had fouled up with the net.'

Muirhead-Gould, in his account of the salvage operation, records that the salvage party had learned valuable lessons in Taylors Bay. 'In view of previous experience of passing strops round the hull, and hanging the lifts, the operation of lifting the submarine was carried out without any difficulty.' He is free in his praise for all involved.

> It is considered that in the early stages of securing wires to the submarine 21 [Matsuo's submarine in Taylors Bay], and during the subsequent lifting operation, the Naval divers, diving party, Maritime Services Board officials and plant staff, also Naval Dockyard riggers, carried out an excellent salvage job, as the possibility of booby traps had to be considered and the potential danger from some form of explosion could not in any way be discounted. Furthermore, the danger of wires parting, or gear carrying away, causing a premature explosion, was a practical possibility.

Roy Cooté was, as usual, less wordy. His dive log for Monday, 8 June, reads: 'Dived and lifted No 2 sub.'

The badly mangled bodies of Lieutenant Kenshi Chuman and Petty Officer Takeshi Omori were taken from the submarine and brought to the police morgue, ready for burial next day.

That left the job of disarming the submarine. This time Frank Lingard knew his way around both torpedoes and midget submarine demolition charges. Chuman's forward demolition charge had already detonated, but the rear charge had failed to explode, so only one set of charges needed Lingard's attention. Chuman had made no attempt to fire his torpedoes, and they remained in their tubes unarmed. It was Lingard's simplest task yet. When the last torpedo pistol and detonator had been gently eased from their mountings, he must have heaved a sigh of relief audible around the harbour.

◆   ◆   ◆

With the benefit of 20–20 hindsight, not every action by Rear Admiral Gerard Charles Muirhead-Gould in the course of the Battle of Sydney Harbour was either wise or adroit. But his next action reflected great credit on him. It was innovative, dignified and humane. It may have contained an element of calculation, but if it did then that too reflects well on Muirhead-Gould. The Admiral ordered that the recovered bodies of the four Japanese sailors be buried with full military honours.

The ceremony at Rookwood Crematorium on Tuesday, 9 June, was brief, simple and moving. It lasted only 15 minutes. The bodies of the sailors were brought to the crematorium in coffins draped with the Japanese flag. Inside the chapel, not a word was spoken. When the coffins disappeared from view, a naval party fired three volleys in salute. A bugler sounded the Last Post.

The ashes of the four Japanese sailors were preserved, and sub-sequently returned to Japan via a Swiss diplomatic intermediary. It is said that Muirhead-Gould ordered the burial with full honours in the hope of securing better treatment for Allied prisoners. It was intended to show the Japanese the chivalrous way to treat an enemy. If the intention was to help Allied prisoners, it transparently failed. However, the gesture was genuinely and warmly appreciated in Japan, and did much to pave the way for good relations between Australia and Japan after the war.

Muirhead-Gould defended his decision in a radio broadcast of great dignity and humanity.

I have been criticised for having accorded these men military honours at their cremation, such honours as we hope may be accorded to our own comrades who have died in enemy hands: but, I ask you, should we not accord full honours to such brave men as these? It must take courage of the very highest order to go out in a thing like that steel coffin. I hope I shall not be a coward when my time comes, but I confess that I wonder whether I would have the courage to take one of these things across Sydney Harbour in peacetime. Theirs was a courage which was not the property or the tradition or the heritage of any one nation: it is the courage shared by brave men of our own countries as well as the enemy, and however horrible war and its results may be, it is a courage which is recognised and universally admired. These men were patriots of the highest order. How many of us are prepared to make one thousandth of the sacrifice these men made?

The speech was warmly and widely reported in Japan. It is quoted there to this day.

Muirhead-Gould referred to the fact that he had been criticised for his actions, and some accounts refer to 'widespread criticism'. If there was, it is hard to find. A search of the more jingoistic publications, from *Truth* to *Smith's Weekly* to *The Bulletin* turned up no editorials, no letters to the editor, no snide attacks. The same was true of the mainstream newspapers of the day. The only sour note the author could find appeared in the Sydney *Daily Telegraph* on the morning of the ceremony. Any journalist reading this book will smile knowingly at what follows. It is a common and legitimate tactic for a newspaper to work out who is most likely to be offended by whatever is at issue, and ring them up for a 'quote'. The sub-editors then can justify the headline 'Fury over Jap Funeral' or 'Row over Admiral's Jap Flag', even though there was no such thing until the newspaper got on the case. Thus the news is created by newspapers rather than merely reported.

On the morning of the funeral, the *Daily Telegraph* had clearly spoken to Mr H.R. Reading, general secretary of the Australian Natives'

Association, to get a 'quote'. He was not best pleased with the Admiral's plans. The ANA was a loony bunch of ultra-patriots which spoke for nobody much but itself. Mr Reading opined:

> On behalf of the Association, I enter my emphatic protest at the decision to accord full military honours. Apparently the atrocities committed on British men, women and children in Hong Kong, and the maltreatment of Australian soldiers in islands off Australia are forgotten very quickly. I say Australians should not forget these events or the loss of life on the depot ship in Sydney Harbour or last night's attacks. We want a total war effort. Well, let us have it without cant or hypocrisy.

In general, the Admiral's decision was widely welcomed and seen as both chivalrous and shrewd. Rightly so.

Chapter 17

The nightwatchman's tale

The 6 June story in *Smith's Weekly* put the government and particularly the Minister for the Navy on the back foot. The newspaper had demanded an inquiry. Norman Makin would have none of it. However, he issued a statement on Wednesday, 10 June, which went some way towards acknowledging that all had not been right on the night. 'A thorough investigation has been made into the entry of Japanese midget submarines, and this has proved the defences are up to the mark,' Makin began. He continued disarmingly: 'It must not be forgotten that the defences are not yet complete. It was the first time they had been tried out, and the experience gained of the enemy's methods and of any shortcoming in the defences will be valuable. Steps have already been taken to tighten them up.'

Smith's Weekly pounced. If the powers-that-be were irritated by the paper's first entry into the fray, they went ballistic in the face of the next week's issue, dated 13 June. This was genuinely fine popular journalism, exposing the smug cant of the official version of the story and getting right to the heart of it. The paper blazoned across the top of its front page: 'With War at the Door—Our Navy Must Never Be Caught Napping.' The story below was headlined: 'Conflicting

Statements on Sydney Harbour Raid—There Should Be a Public Inquiry.'

On page three the paper warmed to the subject with a story headlined: 'Submarines Attack in Sydney Harbour—Story of the Night-Watchman.' As we have seen, the official version of events was that a well-trained, highly disciplined and professional defence force sprang instantly and effectively into action, quickly detected the intruders and sank the attacking submarines before much harm resulted. Not so, said *Smith's Weekly*. Far from the navy picking up the submarines using all its high-tech detectors and weapons, the first alert had come from a civilian nightwatchman in a rowboat. Worse, the navy would not believe his story when he tried to warn them.

The *Smith's Weekly* story did not name Jimmy Cargill, and the odd incorrect detail makes it unlikely that he was the source. However, the story was essentially correct, and profoundly embarrassing. 'About 10 o'clock he [the nightwatchman] noticed unusual movement in the water not to be accounted for by tidal or other natural influences,' *Smith's Weekly* wrote. 'He thought he detected a dark object submerged at a point where the disturbance was most evident. He at once rowed to an auxiliary naval vessel on duty not far distant. There he reported what he had seen, and was told he was talking nonsense and had better go home and get to bed, or words to that effect.'

Smith's Weekly had discovered that the nightwatchman was employed by the Maritime Services Board. When they tried to get confirmation of the story from his employers, a Board spokesman told the paper to contact the navy. A reporter duly called the Naval Establishments Office, where a spokesman said: 'We won't make any statement on anything you publish.' When it was pointed out to him that this was serious, he said after some hesitation: 'I will see the admiral's secretary and see what he thinks about it.' Later the spokesman called back. 'The admiral will not make any statement on that. If you wish to make any inquiry on that you must address it to the secretary of the Naval Board.' The newspaper promised to do just that.

But if the story of the nightwatchman irritated the navy, the paper's front-page story sent them apoplectic. According to *Smith's Weekly*, the newspaper had been handed a statement on the sequence of events by 'a Sydney resident, a businessman of standing, a public figure, a man of calm judgement, of unquestionable repute, and of military experience'. To this day we have no idea who this insomniac paragon of truth and excellence might have been, but we do know he had a fine view of the action. 'His residence is on one of the harbour points overlooking the scene of the focal point of the battle,' Smith's Weekly reported. 'From his balcony he had a dress circle view of what happened, and he observed closely.

'He states that it was near 11 o'clock when the first shot was fired. This was from an Allied warship in the harbour.' The term 'Allied warship' is highly significant. In other words, the first shot was not fired by an Australian ship, but by a ship from some other navy. The story continued:

Immediately afterward, tracer bullets were cutting the water, were ricocheting nearby. Pom-poms were firing. In a searchlight beam, about fifty yards from the Allied ship, the conning tower of a submarine was half showing. It travelled on a course parallel with the side of the ship and from the bow towards the stern. One or two shots were fired from the five-inch gun of the warship, the submarine then being slightly astern of the vessel. When the smoke cleared the conning tower was no longer visible.

So far, this was a pretty good account of Chicago's prompt response to sighting Ban's submarine. Smith's Weekly then came to the nub of its story. 'The eye-witness further states that there was also an Australian warship in the harbour and not far distant from that of our ally. But it was fifteen or twenty minutes before our vessel showed any sign of life or before it used a searchlight.'

So the Australian defences, far from springing smartly into action at the first hint of a threat, simply sat with their arms folded while the Americans did all the reacting. More was to follow. 'Again', said the paper, 'if Garden Island batteries fired any shots at all, they must have synchronised perfectly with those from the Allied warship, since no sound from the island was distinguishable.

'Question, did Garden Island fire any shots? If not, why not?'

The paper then pointed out that the torpedo which wrecked the *Kuttabul* was fired 90 minutes later.

This means that for an hour and a half one of the submarines at least had the run of the inner waters of Port Jackson.

The eye-witness further states that in the upper part of the harbour no depth charge was fired until 6 am.

He also declares that two or three nights previously, an aeroplane flew over Sydney. It came from the direction of the sea, with lights showing, and subsequently, with lights out, flew between the Allied warship and Garden Island.

It was supposed to have been identified, but was it? If so, and if it was recognised as one of our own planes, why was it that an alert which took place at that time, at an air force camp, was continued for four hours, with personnel dispersed throughout that time?

The foregoing are statements too well grounded to be dismissed.

This was an astonishingly good piece of reporting. It also committed the unforgivable crime of making the navy look silly, and the navy responded accordingly. The Director of Naval Intelligence, R.B.M. ('Cocky') Long, had an early sight of the article and decided it was time for the full majesty of the law to descend on the impertinent hacks. He drew up a charge sheet of the newspaper's crimes and presented it to the Navy Board on 12 June. His minute paper was accompanied by a draft letter which he suggested the Board should send to the Attorney General's Department, setting out the basis for a prosecution. *Smith's Weekly's* crimes? There were two: (a) under National Security (General) Regulation 42 for endeavouring to influence public opinion in a manner likely to be prejudicial to the defence of the Commonwealth; and (b) under National Security (General) Regulation 17 for publishing—in a manner prejudicial to defence—information with respect to measures for the defence or fortification of a place on behalf of the Commonwealth.

The essence of Cocky Long's complaint, in his own words, was that *Smith's Weekly* had 'deliberately attempted to foster public disquiet by discrediting and belittling counter-submarine measures taken by the Royal Australian Navy, by drawing odious comparisons between the efficiency of Allied ships and ships of the RAN, to the detriment of the latter, and by insinuating that neglect and inefficiency characterised one of the RAN's ships and one of the RAN's shore establishments.' The article had also 'disclosed the alleged presence of fixed defences on Garden Island and the presence of Allied warships and RAN ships in Sydney Harbour, publication of which was forbidden by regulation'. So off to prison, then.

Cocky Long's draft letter and minute paper are addressed to the Chief of Naval Staff, his deputy, and to the Minister for the Navy. The circulated version has been well scribbled on and annotated by no fewer than nine signatures and sets of initials. The scribblers' signatures are mostly impossible to decipher, but one looks very like Norman Makin, the Minister for the Navy. He wrote in longhand: 'I am afraid there is no chance of a conviction under Reg 42, and very little hope of one under Reg 17. Smith's will state that their motive was the highest. All papers referred to warships and shore defences & Smith's has done little more. There is no harm in asking A.-G. [the Attorney General] for an opinion, however.' This note is dated 15 June. A quite heroically indecipherable set of initials has added below it the single word: 'Concur.' Whoever concurred did so on 18 June. The next set of indecipherable initials, dated 22 June, is appended to a scribbled note to the effect: 'C.N.S. [Chief of Naval Staff] has decided that no further action should be taken in this matter.' At the bottom of the page is a final, laconic instruction dated 23 June: 'File.'

The cat was now well and truly out of the bag. The government and the navy could no longer pretend that all had gone well on the night of the submarines. They had already acknowledged that lessons had been learned, and defences had been tightened. *Smith's Weekly* continued to call loudly for an inquiry. The paper pointed out that the American government had instantly set up an inquiry into Pearl Harbor, presided over by a Supreme Court judge. The Australian government had done the same when Darwin was bombed. Surely a submarine attack *inside* Australia's most important port warranted an inquiry, if only to answer public unease. Not necessary, said Makin. The Admiral's report would do.

◆　　◆　　◆

By the week beginning Monday, 15 June, a fortnight after the first submarine attack, the air was positively sulphurous with the smell of serious trouble. The usual government tactic of dismissing newspaper stories as the ill-informed musings of over-excited hacks would not work in this case. Too many people had seen from behind parted curtains that the enemy had managed to evade the defences and wreak havoc inside Sydney Harbour. Any doubts that Sydney's defences were leaky were settled with the shelling of the Eastern Suburbs. The public was now well and truly alarmed.

Then a new and vastly more dangerous critic entered the arena: the United States Navy. As early as 2 June the executive officer of the destroyer USS *Perkins*, G.L. Ketchum, had filed a brief action report to his skipper. The following day *Perkins'* skipper, W.C. Ford, filed a full report, including a sketch showing two torpedo tracks passing either side of and chillingly close to USS *Chicago*. On 5 June, Captain Bode followed up with *Chicago's* action report. Both reports went to the US Navy's Pacific headquarters in Pearl Harbor, Hawaii. Both reports were highly critical of the defences of Sydney Harbour.

Perkins' commanding officer Ford wrote:

The fact that there is no net at the entrance to the harbour and ferries were continually coming through this entrance made it a very simple matter for the submarines to get into Sydney Harbour. The torpedo which sank the ferry passed close aboard CHICAGO's stern and close aboard PERKINS' bow and only had a small chance of missing. It was good fortune rather than good harbour defence which prevented great damage.

The USS *Chicago*'s captain was equally scathing. Bode had a fair bit to hide about the night's proceedings, but that did not prevent him from sticking it to the Sydney defences. 'The necessity for protecting harbours', Bode wrote, 'requires submarine nets, or the new type of torpedo nets, backed by at least two Light Indicator Nets. These must be provided with positively operated gates. All other electrical devices such as electric loops, asdics, sono buoys, mine fields, etc., should be considered ancillary to such positive closure and not substitutes therefore. Until such positive measures are provided, the danger will be great.'

To put it mildly, the US Navy did not like what it saw. The Commander of the US Navy's Destroyer Division Nine, F.X. McInerny, added his own damning assessment when he concluded a report to the Commander of US Naval Forces, South-West Pacific (Admiral Chester Nimitz) with the following words:

From personal observation, entering Sydney during daylight and darkness, the control over entering ships leaves a great deal to be desired. Apparently there are many ships, merchant and naval, that do not have private signals for entering, and still are not prevented from entering until properly inspected. I believe that an enemy surface ship, flying false colors and making false signals, could enter the harbour during daylight or darkness, under present conditions.

The US Navy demanded action. On 12 June the Commander of Allied Naval Forces, South-West Pacific Area, Vice-Admiral H.F. Leary, wrote to Sir Guy Royle, the Chief of Naval Staff of the Royal Australian Navy, enclosing copies of *Perkins*' action report and sketches plus McInerny's scathing assessment. Leary concluded his letter to Sir Guy with a stark demand: 'It is requested that necessary action be taken to provide maximum protection to vessels in Sydney Harbour from enemy submarines.'* The implications for the Australian government and the Australian Navy were horrendous. If Sydney Harbour was not properly protected, then US ships could not safely anchor there. Australia's whole defence strategy of 'looking to America' was under threat. Indeed, given that Japan's objective was to cut off the sea routes between Australia and America and thereby make Australia untenable as a base for an American counterattack, Leary's letter shows that the Sydney raid had taken the Japanese some way towards success. The Naval Board's regular meeting was due to take place on Monday, 15 June. The meeting was delayed a day to make way for the King's Birthday celebrations, and the full Board met on 16 June. It cannot have been a happy meeting.

There was now an urgent need to come up with a narrative which could be defended against the likes of *Smith's Weekly* and which would convince the US Navy that it was safe to tie up ships in Sydney Harbour. Sir Guy Royle wrote in hand on Leary's memorandum: 'I will answer this after I receive NOCS [Naval Officer in Command, Sydney—in other words Muirhead-Gould's] report and his reply to my letter of today 16/6.'

The Chief of Naval Staff then wrote sympathetically, if somewhat elliptically, to Rear Admiral Muirhead-Gould: 'I am afraid you have been having a very hectic time and are competing very ably with the many problems that arise.' He probably meant coping very ably with the many competing problems that arise, but that is only a guess. Sir Guy's letter ranged over a number of topics, from the possible court martial of the skipper of *Yarroma* to the posting of the Free French destroyer *Le Triomphant*. Where it is relevant, it has been quoted in other parts of this narrative. However, the key section amounted to a demand for some kind of explanation from Muirhead-Gould for the failure of Sydney's defences.

---

* This was a nice piece of hypocrisy on Leary's part. His failure to pass on the warning implicit in the 30 May FRUMEL decrypt, discussed in Chapter 5, was at least a contributory factor in the less than maximum protection Sydney Harbour offered its guest vessels.

'Leary and I are still rather disturbed', Sir Guy wrote, 'by thoughts such as the following:-

'Three submarines were able to pass through a gap which was supposed to be under observation by the "YARROMA".

'That the Loop Officer failed to recognise the signatures of the midget submarines. This you have already explained.

'That there is sufficient close liaison between the Loop Officer or X.D.O. [External Defence Officer] and the searchlights and the patrol boats.'

Muirhead-Gould needed to come up with something fast. On 17 June he responded to Sir Guy with a two-page report. It amounted to not much more than a brief account of the action, and fell far short of Sir Guy's need for some way to reassure the Americans. It also gives a fair idea of how much confusion still surrounded the whole story more than two weeks after the event. Muirhead-Gould accepts Reg Andrew's three submarines, and tentatively raises the sub count to five taking part in the raid. He lists them by loop crossing.

2001   Sighted in boom net at 2130 approx by Maritime Services watchman and reported by him to YARROMA. Self destroyed at 2230. (No 1)

2148   Sighted off Garden Island Ferry Wharf at 2252 by CHICAGO and many other craft. Fired two torpedoes from direction of Bradleys Head at 0030 at CHICAGO. Sank KUTTABUL. Other torpedo on rocks near gun wharf steps unexploded. Sighted in Taylor Bay or Chowder Bay 0500 approx. by SEA MIST's crew and possibly sunk. (No 2)

——   2254 sighted by YARROMA and LAURIANA (at inner Heads). Rammed by YANDRA and attacked by six depth charges at 2307, before crossing the loop. Probably destroyed. Not reported till next day. (No 3)

0159   Not sighted until seen with two others in Taylor Bay or Chowder Bay, at 0500 approx. by SEA MIST. (No 4)

0301   sighted by CHICAGO at Heads at 0250 approx. Sighted in Taylor Bay at 0500 approx. by SEA MIST. (No 5)

He then gave the result of the attacks.

No 1)   Self-destroyed. Hull has been recovered.
No 2)   Two of these were probably sunk in Taylor Bay but only one has been found.
No 4)
No 5)
No 3)   Is considered unlikely to have survived YANDRA's attack. If it survived, it could have been identical with No 4 or No 5.

This brief document was hardly going to do the job of satisfying a seriously restless US Navy. Sir Guy needed more, and five days later it was forthcoming. The 22 June report was a different matter. This time Muirhead–Gould set out to address some of the failures of the defence, and to allocate blame for what had gone wrong. All his ire was directed at juniors, of course. The watch keepers at the Loop Station were first in the firing line. There had been a 'regrettable failure' to identify the 2001 and 2148 crossings. 'I consider that the Loop system fully justified itself', wrote Muirhead–Gould, 'though, naturally I must deplore the fact that the human element failed'.

Next in the blame game was Jimmy Cargill. 'A midget submarine was in the harbour for about two hours,' said Muirhead–Gould. 'It was seen by Mr James Cargill of the Maritime Services Board Staff who took some time to collect a friend and to communicate this vital information to the Channel Boat on patrol.' This was simply untrue, and Muirhead–Gould must have known it.

Eyers and *Yarroma* were next. '*Yarroma* did not open fire because he thought it might be a mine,' said the report. 'This is deplorable and inexplicable.' Well, yes. But it might have been more honest to add that *Yarroma* and not Jimmy Cargill was the principal cause of the two-hour delay.

The report credited Townley's *Steady Hour* with sinking the submarine in Taylors Bay, adding: 'Further investigation shows that *Yarroma* and *Sea Mist* were equally concerned in this attack, and *Yarroma* thus to some extent made up for her previous indecision.'

It also accepted Reg Andrew's count of three submarines, going into some detail on the point. 'Although *Sea Mist's* report, at 0500, that she had seen three submarines in Chowder Bay sounded at that time fantastic, it is now considered that this was actually possible,' Muirhead-Gould wrote.

> Examination of the captured charts shows what may have been the position of the submarine in this area. *Sea Mist's* subsequent reports give great promise of a successful attack in Chowder Bay. Members of her crew drew a most convincing sketch of the stern cage of the submarine which they claim to have seen. At this time, no one was aware that these submarines had tail cages. It is unfortunate that all efforts to locate this submarine have failed.

They failed because the submarine did not exist. Reg Andrew and the crew of *Sea Mist* saw the tail cage of Matsuo's submarine, already accounted for in Taylors Bay.

Muirhead-Gould then went on to list the lessons learned. First, the signal chaos had to end. Channel Patrol boats would have proper radio telephone sets as soon as possible. Arrangements were being made to stop ferries immediately at the request of an authorised naval officer. The night movement of tugs and barges would be kept to a minimum to reduce confusion at the Loop Station.

Some actions had already been taken. The Naval Auxiliary Patrol boats had all been armed with depth charges. A new depth charge detonator able to function in less than 42 feet (about 13 metres) of water had been developed and was now being supplied to Channel Patrol boats and Nappies. Garden Island's operations room was being provided with a radio telephone set. No more would the Admiral communicate with his fleet by sending a hapless Lieutenant in a speedboat around the harbour delivering messages.

It was not all bad news. The report concluded by commending 'the general good conduct, zeal and determination of all who took part in a very exciting operation'. Muirhead-Gould recommended to the notice of the board: Mr James Cargill, for his vigilance and initiative and for his personal efforts to report a suspicious circumstance to proper authorities; and to a lesser degree Mr W. Nangle who helped him; Lieutenant A.G. Townley RANVR and the crew of HMAS *Steady Hour*; Sub-Lieutenant J.A. Doyle RANR(S) and crew of HMAS *Sea Mist* (note: not Reg Andrew); Lieutenant J.A. Taplin RANR(S) and the crew of HMAS *Yandra*; Engineer Captain A.B. Doyle CBE RAN, Commander (E) C.C. Clark RAN; and Bandsman M.N. Cumming. The last three were commended for rescue work on *Kuttabul*.

In his 16 June letter to Muirhead-Gould, Sir Guy Royle says in part: 'I am sorry you have been unable to locate the *Sea Mist*'s midget submarine. I will certainly send congratulations to Lieutenant Taplin [note: poor old Reg misses out again—Taplin was the skipper of *Yandra*, not *Sea Mist*], but I propose to wait a little longer as I understand you intend carrying out some sweeping operations in his area. I haven't settled any award yet, but DSC would seem to be about the right standard.'

So it is clear that at this stage the Chief of Naval Staff did not regard the whole affair as a catastrophe, and was of a mind to hand out medals at the comparatively high level of a Distinguished Service Cross to Reg Andrew and presumably to others who had performed well. There is something of an unofficial scale for these awards, and the usual reward for sending a submarine to the bottom was the slightly lesser Distinguished Service Order. Sir Guy intended to be more generous. Yet, as we shall see in the next chapter, somewhere along the line the medal list sank as surely as the submarines.

Chapter 18

The Admiral's report

It is a nice area of speculation to ask why Muirhead-Gould's 22 June report did not satisfy the Naval Board and why the Admiral felt obliged to write further. The chronologies attached to the two reports are identical. The information in the appendices to the 16 July report is more elaborate than the information in the 22 June version, but otherwise the story is much the same. There is no correspondence to be found in any of the archives ordering Muirhead-Gould back to the drawing board, but the Admiral nevertheless felt obliged to pick up his pen again. The most striking difference between the 22 June report and the final 16 July report is that 16 July omits much of the criticism of junior officers contained in the 22 June version. It may be that the Naval Board felt the 22 June report would do little to reassure the Americans. They needed something soothing rather than probing.

As far as reassurance of the public was concerned, a blander report was essential. The Australian government steadfastly refused to set up an inquiry, whether open or behind closed doors, into the midget submarine raid. The Admiral in charge of Sydney Harbour was preparing a report, they said, and that would have to do. After all, Rear Admiral Muirhead-Gould had been judged capable enough to sit on the

Royal Navy's Board of Inquiry into the sinking of HMS *Royal Oak* by a German submarine in Scapa Flow. So who better to look into the sinking of HMAS *Kuttabul* by a Japanese submarine in Sydney Harbour? This really was an appalling decision. If heads were to roll, then the most likely first head on the block would be that of the person in charge of Sydney's harbour defences. To put the entire inquiry into the hands of the man most likely to be its first victim was about as sensible as asking the average working criminal to conduct his own trial single-handed, and decide his own sentence. Muirhead-Gould must have accepted the challenge with relish.

Politically, the report had to fulfil two functions. It had to supply the navy and the Australian government with a defensible narrative, a story they could tell to the public without having it torn apart by the likes of *Smith's Weekly*. It also had to satisfy the US Navy that Australian harbours were now safe places to anchor American ships. Finally, it had to get Muirhead-Gould off the hook. It needed to give the impression that Sydney Harbour's defences had been, in Norman Makin's phrase, 'up to the mark'. Given these objectives, Muirhead-Gould made a fair fist of it with his 16 July account. The report is not marked 'SECRET'. However, it was never intended to be made public, at least not at the time. It contained a lot of military information which the navy, very reasonably, wished to keep to themselves. It was declassified on 2 February 1965.

The report is reproduced in its entirety in Appendix III. At this point in the narrative it is sufficient to look at how Muirhead-Gould put the best spin he could on the story to reassure the government, the Australian public and—most important of all—the US Navy.

The report, addressed to the Secretary, Naval Board, Melbourne, runs to 16 pages and some 4000 words. It begins with a four-page narrative, followed by six appendices. The first appendix is a detailed chronology of events, starting with the first loop crossing, which Muirhead-Gould times at 8 pm, and ending with *Yarroma* dropping her final depth charge at 8.27 am the next morning. The second appendix deals with the documents and maps recovered from Matsuo's sub. Next comes an analysis of the recovered torpedoes, two from Matsuo's submarine, two from Chuman's, and the unexploded torpedo from Ban's midget, which grounded itself on the rocks of Garden Island. The Admiral then deals with the indicator loop crossings and their tell-tale traces. After that come two pages of hand-wringing under the heading: lessons learnt— mistakes made and remedies. However, it was not all bad news. The final appendix is headed: 'Recommendations for recognition of personnel', and offers what is clearly a medals list.

The report puts the midget submarine count at four. 'Of these,' Muirhead-Gould wrote, 'two are known by their actual Japanese numbers (No. 14 and No. 21). The other two unknown midgets are referred to as "Midget A" and "Midget B" respectively.' The Admiral then went on to get the number of mother submarines right. 'It is considered that the force which attacked Sydney consisted of five "I" class submarines, four midget submarines, and one, possibly two, float planes,' he wrote.

However, he began to stray from the straight and narrow when describing Ito's spy flight. 'The attack was possibly preceded by aerial reconnaissance, which may have been carried out on 29th, 30th and 31st May,' the Admiral wrote. 'A reconnaissance of Sydney Harbour, especially the Naval Anchorage area, was carried out by one biplane single float plane at approximately 0420K/30 May.' This is, of course, incorrect. The Glen was not a biplane, it had two floats and not a single float, and Ito's flight took place on 29 May, not 30 May. Otherwise Muirhead-Gould has got everything right.

His inaccurate reporting of Ito's flight did not end there. He continued: 'The plane, which was burning navigation lights, approached the harbour from a northerly direction, flew over the Naval Anchorage, circled USS *Chicago* twice, and departed in a due east direction.' This is not how Ito remembers it. The account given in Chapter 6 is based on Ito's own sketches. Given that Muirhead-Gould got the date and the plane's description comprehensively wrong, it is probably safer to stick to Ito's version. However, the Muirhead-Gould version appears in most accounts of the raid, including the official history.

Next came a really serious whopper. 'Allied warships in Sydney Harbour at the time included the following,' wrote Muirhead-Gould.

'No. 1 Buoy—HMAS *Canberra*; No. 2 Buoy—USS *Chicago*; No. 4 Buoy—USS *Perkins*; No. 5 Buoy—USS *Dobbin*; No. 6 Buoy—HMAS *Bungaree*; Birt's Buoy—HMS *Kanimbla*; Off Robertson Point— HMAS *Australia*.'

This is outrageous. The weasel words 'warships . . . included' allow Muirhead-Gould to slide over the fact that he had many more warships and much more useful firepower at his disposal than he cared to admit. He does not list the two anti-submarine specialists HMAS *Yandra* and HMAS *Bingera*, nor does he list the 10 Channel Patrol Boats, all of which carried anti-submarine depth charges and some of which carried the latest ASDIC submarine detection equipment. Muirhead-Gould's great tactical failure on the night of the raid was his abysmal use of his available resources. By his own account, he issued only three orders, all of them vague and general. Throughout the entire night he failed to direct his forces in any coordinated way. For the record, HMAS *Australia* was not in the harbour at the time, and was therefore not tied up off Robertsons Point. If any ship could be said to be moored off Robertsons Point, it was the armed merchant cruiser HMAS *Westralia*. Most accounts, including the official history, place *Westralia* in Athol Bay. However, she was moored well off the Athol Bay shore, placing her somewhere between the shoreline and Robertsons Point.

Muirhead-Gould's account then moves on to the midgets themselves. 'The first attempt at an entry was made by Midget No. 14 [Chuman], and was unsuccessful', he wrote. 'She crossed the loop at 2001 and, by 2015, was caught in the nets (centre portion, close to the Western gate). She was unable to free herself, and blew herself up at 2235.'

Muirhead-Gould is being a bit economical with the truth here. He describes Chuman's entry as 'unsuccessful', then says he was caught in the net, implying that the net did its job and prevented Chuman's entry. But Chuman did in fact succeed in entering the harbour. After he had made it past the net, he backed into it, tangling himself in the net on the harbour side. This may seem like hair-splitting, but it is part of the general pattern of Muirhead-Gould's report to say things worked well when they didn't.

Muirhead-Gould's next error is scarcely his fault. He accepts that *Yandra* attacked and probably sank a submarine near the Sydney Harbour heads, outside the boom net and indicator loop. He wrote: '"Midget B" made an unsuccessful attempt to enter the harbour but failed to reach the effective loop (No. 12) or, consequently, the boom. She was sighted by *Yandra* (the Duty A/S Vessel on patrol within the Loop Area) and later by *Lauriana* who illuminated her until intercepted between the Heads, at 2254, by *Yandra*. Two separate attacks were carried out by *Yandra* on "Midget B" during a period of 9 minutes, starting from the time she attempted to ram the submarine at 2258 until her second attack—a full pattern of six depth charges—at 2307. It is considered that "Midget B" was destroyed by this second attack, in a position 023° 3.6 cables* from Hornby Light.'

This is, of course, incorrect though that is no fault of Muirhead-Gould's. In fact Midget B (Matsuo's submarine or Midget No. 21), survived *Yandra's* attack. She was eventually sunk by *Sea Mist* in Taylors Bay six hours later. However, this error is part of the general pattern of the report, which repeatedly says the defences worked when they didn't.

The Admiral's narrative now moves to the Taylors Bay attack. He wrote:

> Midget No. 21 entered the harbour at 0301, at which time she crossed No. 12 Loop. She proceeded up harbour unobserved until she reached Bradley's Head vicinity. Here she was sighted by *Kanimbla* and fired on at 0350 and gave rise to the unconfirmed contact made by *Doomba* off Robertson Point at 0450.
>
> She was detected in Taylor Bay and attacked with depth charges, first by *Sea Mist* at 0500, then by *Yarroma* and *Steady Hour* until 0827. The effect of these attacks was clearly shown in the great amount of damage done to Midget No. 21, which was evident in the wreck when it was recovered. It is probable that the

---

* A 'cable' is a regular nautical measure of distance. It is equal to 200 yards or approximately 180 metres.

first attack caused the submarine to run into the bottom, because the lower bow cap was damaged and both caps were jammed, although set to release. The torpedo tubes had both been fired, although the bow caps had jammed on release. The lower tube had been fired with the external adjustment fittings engaged, and these had sheared off when the torpedo moved in the tube. This suggests that an attempt was made to fire in a hurry, and was prompted by, or interrupted by, the depth charge attacks.

Muirhead-Gould's conclusion that Matsuo's submarine damaged its bow cage and torpedo caps while crash diving in Taylors Bay and subsequently failed to launch its torpedoes is reasonable within the logic of the report, but is almost certainly incorrect. Muirhead-Gould's problem is that he believes Matsuo's midget was sunk by *Yandra*, when in fact it survived *Yandra*'s attack and made it into the harbour. However, it is also fair to point out that this version suited Muirhead-Gould nicely. Far better to say the torpedoes failed after Reg Andrew's depth charge attack in Taylors Bay than to admit that an Allied ship like *Canberra* had a lucky escape from a torpedo attack an hour earlier. Again, the defences are portrayed as working when they didn't.

There is a curious little blip in the chronology section. At 10.30 pm, according to Muirhead-Gould, *Yarroma* reported—'Object is submarine. Request permission to open fire.' It is hard to reconcile this with 'Tubby' Anderson's account, supported by Jim Nelson, that it was *Lolita* which initiated the attack, not *Yarroma*. However, *Yarroma* had been the source of all earlier communications, and this may simply be a slip of the pen on Muirhead-Gould's part. Note that there is no record of the order to open fire being given.

The chronology records that at 11.14 pm Muirhead-Gould ordered: 'All ships to be darkened.' However, there is no trace in the 16 July report of his earlier order that ferries and other harbour traffic should continue to run, fully lit. In his 22 June report he defended this by saying: 'The more boats that were moving about at high speed the better chance of keeping the submarines down till daylight.' Sometime between 22 June and 16 July he must have realised that this was not the brightest order he had ever issued, so he air-brushed it out of the final report.

The chronology then comes up with another whopper. At 11.15 pm, according to Muirhead-Gould, 'USS *Perkins* slipped and was ordered back to buoy by *Chicago* securing again at 2340 to No. 4 Buoy.' This account of *Perkins'* movements is a monstrous slur on her blameless crew. Muirhead-Gould is simply covering up for the inadequacies of *Chicago's* Captain Howard Bode, and for the role of the 'Tresco' dinner party in the night's proceedings. The Admiral manages to imply that *Perkins* had somehow taken it upon herself to leave her buoy, and had to be dragged back to it by *Chicago*. As we have seen, *Perkins* slipped under direct orders from Lieutenant Commander Jimmy Mecklenberg, then senior officer aboard *Chicago*. Mecklenberg correctly wanted *Perkins* to screen *Chicago* until the cruiser could get under way. Bode foolishly ordered *Perkins* back to her buoy because he did not believe the submarine story.

However, Muirhead-Gould's 2315 entry does give better insight into the timing of Bode's movements. His mendacious 2220 entry read: 'Captain Bode, *Chicago*, left Tresco with suggestion that he should go to sea with *Perkins*.' Bode cannot have been aboard *Chicago* before 11.15 pm, when *Perkins* slipped. And he must have been aboard before 11.40 pm, when *Perkins* returned to her buoy; 11.30 pm seems about right, not 10.20 pm.

The author has every sympathy with the Admiral by the time the chronology moves to 5 am next morning and the attack on Matsuo's submarine in Taylors Bay. To this day there is no agreement on the exact sequence of events there, and Muirhead-Gould has simply let each skipper have his say. The first entry says: 'Red Verey's Light seen in Taylor Bay by *Yarroma* and depth charge explosion heard. *Yarroma* proceeded to scene at full speed and en route saw 3 more Verey Lights and heard further detonations.' Clearly this is *Yarroma's* version of events.

Muirhead-Gould now moves to Athol Townley's version. '*Steady Hour* sighted suspicious object. Whilst proceeding up West Channel *Sea Mist* attacked and fired Verey Light (red). *Sea Mist* reported 3 submarines.'

Goonambee now takes over. '*Sea Mist*, at request of *Goonambee*, investigated suspicious object in Taylor Bay. Fired 2 depth charges on each occasion firing a Red Verey Light before so doing. Aldis Lamp was used to illuminate target.'

The report does not include a version which exactly matches *Sea Mist*'s account. However, Muirhead-Gould can hardly be blamed for this. Everyone involved in Taylors Bay that morning told a very different version of the same story. Muirhead-Gould has simply picked out three versions and recounted them, albeit briefly. Chapters 12 and 13 of this book attempt to separate fact from fiction, and medal-seeking from honest reporting.

There is one rather odd entry at 5.40 am: 'Rear-Admiral-in-Charge and Chief Staff Officer proceeded down harbour.' This second venture onto the harbour by Muirhead-Gould and his chief staff officer is no-where documented except in this brief sentence in the official report. There is a later reference to the chief staff officer proceeding down the harbour at 7.30 am and to *Winbah*'s arrival at Taylors Bay between 7.30 am and 7.55 am. It would seem that Muirhead-Gould and his CSO commandeered the harbour launch *Winbah* and set off down the harbour together at 5.40 am to check up on proceedings. The Admiral was presumably delivered back to Garden Island at some point, leaving the CSO to head off alone at 7.30 am to Taylors Bay and talk to Townley and *Steady Hour*. As the depth charge attack in Taylors Bay was still under way, it cannot have been helpful to either *Steady Hour* or *Yarroma* to have the CSO prowling about in an unarmed launch while they were busy trying to finish off Matsuo's midget.

The report concludes with 'recommendations for recognition of personnel'. This section is worth quoting in full.

The following are recommended to the notice of the Naval Board for their display of zeal and determination throughout the operation:-
(1) Mr. J. Cargill.   For vigilance and initiative in his personal efforts to report a suspicious circumstance to the proper authorities.

> (It is for consideration whether this man has merited an award under the provisions of A.F.O. 1464(1) of 1941.)

and

(2) <u>Mr W. Nangle</u>   who, to a lesser degree, assisted Mr Cargill.*

(3) <u>Lieutenant A.G. Townley, R.A.N.V.R.</u>

> and the crew of HMAS *Steady Hour.*

(4) <u>Sub-Lieutenant J.A. Doyle, R.A.N.R. (S)</u>

> and the crew of HMAS *Sea Mist.*

(5) <u>Lieutenant J.A. Taplin R.A.N.R. (S)</u>

> and the crew of HMAS *Yandra.*

(6) <u>Engineer Captain A.B. Doyle, C.B.E., R.A.N.</u>

and

(7) <u>Commander (E) G.C. Clark, R.A.N.</u>

> These officers arrived on the scene minutes after the explosion which sank *Kuttabul*, and displayed commendable fortitude in searching the vessel for any man who might be trapped. In doing so, they had to wade in deep water, under hazardous conditions, in darkness, as it was not known at the time which portion of the decks had been rendered dangerous by the explosion. They lent assistance to a number of men who had been shocked by the suddenness and force of the action.

(8) <u>Bandsman M.N. Cumming, Official No. 20501.</u>

> This rating, who was onboard *Kuttabul* at the time of the explosion, showed determination in diving into the water from the vessel, swimming a few yards and assisting a rating on to *Kuttabul*'s deck. He also again dived

---

* The words 'to a lesser degree' have been crossed out in ink.

into the water into *Kuttabul*'s wreckage in order to see whether anyone needed assistance. Although no great courage or endurance was necessary, he displayed considerable initiative.

(9) <u>Mr F.J. Lingard (Torpedo Fitter)</u>.

For the removal of pistols and primers from torpedoes, and demolition charges from submarines, this work being carried out entirely voluntarily.

<u>The Skipper and crew of Naval Auxiliary Patrol Boat, *Lauriana*.</u>

For prompt action in illuminating the submarine.

<u>The Captain and crew of HMAS *Yarroma*.</u>

For their part in the sinking of Midget 21. It is considered that this action redeemed, to some extent, their earlier failure.

<u>All personnel of the Dockyard First Aid Party.</u>

For their efficient handling of casualties.

Muirhead-Gould's final appendix was, of course, a list of recommendations for medals. It differs from the 22 June list only by the very welcome addition of the name of the torpedo fitter Frank Lingard. As we have seen, as early as 16 June the Chief of Naval Staff Sir Guy Royle was of a mind to award medals at the high level of Distinguished Service Cross (DSC). That is not what happened, however.

Dealing with the medals list first, I have no quarrel with any of the names on it. However, I would be inclined to add a few more. 'Tubby' Anderson and the crew of *Lolita* displayed cool and ready aggression when they found Chuman tangled in the net. Their depth charges may not have been effective, but their actions undoubtedly led to the scuttling of the midget submarine. They sank a submarine as surely as Reg Andrew did, and rather more surely than Athol Townley. But Muirhead-Gould had made a fool of himself in front of the whole crew of *Lolita*, and the Admiral must have felt it would be too much of a climb-down to include them now in any awards. The other glaring omission is the divers. Lance Bullard and Roy Cooté displayed astonishing courage in securing Matsuo's submarine in Taylors Bay. As far as they could tell, the submarine was still 'alive' when they tackled it. They knew that the Japanese had explosive charges aboard which would surely have killed them both if they had detonated while the divers were anywhere nearby. Bullard's and Cooté's courage was not brief and furious in the heat of battle: it was cool, unwavering and sustained over more than a week. It has gone unrecognised until the publication of this book.

The Battle of Sydney Harbour is unique in Australian military history in that no medals were awarded to any of the participants. Every other major action dating back to the Boer War brought a crop of medals for those who took part. The consensus among those involved in Sydney is that somewhere along the line the government and the navy decided that the whole battle had been a complete fiasco, and the best bet would be to draw a line under it and move on. No courts martial. And no medals. It is a monstrous injustice, and it is not too late for the Royal Australian Navy and the Australian government to do something about it. (If the United States government wanted to do something for Jimmy Mecklenberg, that would be a further piece of belated justice.)

◆   ◆   ◆

In the National Archive in Melbourne there is an undated letter from the Secretary of the Naval Board addressed to the Naval Officer in Charge, Sydney. From other sources it is possible to date the letter as being sent on 3 October 1942, four months after the attack and 11 weeks after the submission of Muirhead-Gould's 16 July report, to which it refers. The letter is headed 'Midget submarine attack on Sydney Harbour'. It is worth quoting in full.

I am directed by the Naval Board to refer to your letter of 16th July, 1942, No. B.S.1749/201/37, appendix VI, in which you bring to notice the names of certain officers, ratings and civilian personnel for recognition in regard to operations against enemy midget submarines in Sydney on May 31st–June 1st, 1942.

The Board have read with pleasure your report and commendation and have directed that appropriate notations are to be made in the records of the following officers and ratings:-

Engineer Captain A.B. Doyle, C.B.E., R.A.N.
Commander (E) C.C. Clark, R.A.N.
Lieutenant A.C. Townley, R.A.N.V.R.
HMAS *Steady Hour*
Lieutenant J.A. Taplin, R.A.N.R. (S)
HMAS *Yandra*
Sub-Lieutenant J.A. Doyle, R.A.N.R.
HMAS *Sea Mist*
Bandsman M.N. Cumming, O.N. 20501.

They desire also that the thanks and congratulations of the Naval Board be communicated to Mr. F.J. Lingard (Torpedo Fitter) and to the Dockyard First Aid Party.

The Naval Board further request that their congratulations be communicated to the crews of HMA Ships *Steady Hour*, *Sea Mist* and *Yandra*, and to the skipper and crew of the Naval Auxiliary Patrol Boat *Lauriana* for their efficient work, and to the captain and crew of HMAS *Yarroma* for their part in the sinking of Midget 21.

The Naval Board have recommended that a monetary reward of £40 be made to Mr. J. Cargill and £10 to Mr. W. Nangle, and desire to express their appreciation of the vigilance shown and prompt action taken by them.

Signed
Secretary.

In the margin alongside the name of Sub-Lieutenant J.A. Doyle and *Sea Mist*, an anonymous hand has scribbled: 'Should be Lieut. Andrew.'

That was the sum total of all awards and commendations made to Australians for their part in the Battle of Sydney Harbour: 'appropriate notations in the records' of five officers, one of them incorrectly named; a pat on the back for the crews of five ships; thanks and congratulations for Frank Lingard; and 40 quid for Jimmy Cargill and a tenner for his mate Bill Nangle. At least the Imperial Japanese Navy promoted their submariners two ranks. Though their sailors had to die first.

Chapter 19

Final rest

The story of the midget submarines of the Eastern Attack Group was never other than bizarre. Their path to their final rest proved to be every bit as exotic.

Within days of the raid, two submarines had been recovered: Matsuo's from Taylors Bay, and Chuman's from the net. Both had broken in two. Chuman's submarine snapped just forward of the conning tower, with the separated and largely demolished bow section flung towards Chowder Bay by the blast from his scuttling charges. Matsuo's submarine had lost its tail section from just behind the rear battery compartment, broken off while the sub was being dragged to shallow water before being raised. The two sections of each submarine were lifted from the harbour bed. The broken remains were carried to Clarke Island, not far from Garden Island in the middle of Sydney Harbour.

First they were thoroughly searched for any intelligence they might yield. The harvest was good, particularly from Matsuo's submarine. His midget had taken less internal damage than Chuman's scuttled wreck. As we have seen from Muirhead–Gould's report, there were copies of British Admiralty charts, with rendezvous points and entry tracks neatly drawn. And there was more. There were bundles of photographs, mostly aerial pictures of Sydney and Newcastle, together with cuttings from 1938 Australian magazines and newspapers showing the various features of Sydney Harbour, including Garden Island, Cockatoo Island and the Harbour Bridge. The Japanese had cast their net wider than the harbour itself: there were also references to Sydney's Government House, Central Railway Station and the Town Hall. Other cuttings dealt with the city of Wollongong, the Hawkesbury Bridge, Newcastle Harbour and Airfield, the BHP steelworks and the steelworks at Port Kembla. The Japanese had prepared well.

The submarines contained the personal effects of their crew: ceremonial swords, Matsuo's 1000-stitch *senninbari* (stomach protector), even a red umbrella. The navy released very few details of these finds: best not tell your enemy how much you know about him. On 25 June the Navy Office in Sydney sent a teleprinter message to the Department of Naval Intelligence in Melbourne: 'Press have got information that crews of midget S/MS [submarines] were shot in mouth. They also bringing up report of red umbrella. Suggest facts should be released in order to prevent imaginative stories being published.' The Naval Intelligence department would have none of it. They cabled back: 'Your 0231Z/24 [02.31 am Zulu time on 24 June, meaning 12.31 pm on 25 June, Eastern Australian Time] have requested publicity censorship forbid any reference personnel or equipment midget submarines unless officially released Navy Melbourne.' The navy was particularly anxious to suppress any hint that the Japanese had arrived on a suicide mission.

By the end of June the submarines had been thoroughly examined from top to bottom. Engineers drew up detailed plans and diagrams. They were able to estimate the subs' speed and endurance. Intelligence officers concluded from the food supplies and other evidence that these were not suicide missions. The engineers also examined the five dis-armed torpedoes, two from Chuman's submarine, two from Matsuo's, and one unexploded torpedo aground on Garden Island. The Dutch Navy conducted extensive tests on the torpedoes. They were particularly interested in the unexploded torpedo fired by Ban. Why had it missed? Why had it not armed? (Their findings, largely overlooked, have been incorporated into earlier chapters of this book.)

Once the submarines had given up their secrets, there remained the question of what to do with them. The navy had been thinking about this right from the beginning. Sir Guy Royle's 16 June letter to Rear Admiral Muirhead-Gould mostly dealt with the consequences of the attack. However, it contained two revealing paragraphs. 'The charts and other relics you obtained from the midget submarines have been most valuable,' Sir Guy wrote. 'I am looking forward to seeing the ceremonial sword which is on its way to Navy Office. I will have it transferred to the National Museum.' At the end of the letter Sir Guy added a handwritten postscript: 'I should like the midgets to be used eventually to obtain funds for Navy House Sydney i.e. after all official investigations are completed.' The word Sydney had been underlined by Sir Guy. God forbid that any money should find its way to Navy House Melbourne.

Sir Guy had his way. The navy prepared the submarines for a grand tour of Australian cities. Chuman's bow section had been well and truly detached from the rest of the midget by the blast of his scuttling charge. The navy completed the job of shortening the submarine by removing the tail section as well. That left about two-thirds of the submarine, including the conning tower and forward and rear battery compartments, ready to be mounted on a large trailer. The forward battery compartment was a key element. It had taken most of the force of Chuman's scuttling charge, and the navy left the ripped and jagged hull section on display for all to see. The trailer and its battered submarine were then hooked up behind a heavy truck, and began a 4000-kilometre publicity tour. Although this was primarily a fund-raising venture, the tour clearly had a secondary purpose. The navy had a morale-boosting message to sell to the Australian public, and a warning for the Japanese: mess with the Australian Navy and you'll finish up looking like this. The truck drove inland to Canberra, then continued down the Hume Highway to Melbourne, crossed to Adelaide, and finally made its way back to Sydney. It stopped at towns along the way, and hordes of the curious gathered around to marvel at this exotic sight. The crowds were invited to make donations to the Navy Fund, which supported seamen and their widows and families. There is no record of the amount raised, but it was probably substantial.

The navy now set about creating a composite submarine for display. They sliced cleanly through Matsuo's submarine on either side of the conning tower, and detached Matsuo's bow section. This bow, together with its highly visible dent where the steel cable had cut into the hull while the midget was being raised from Taylors Bay, was matched up to the centre section of Chuman's submarine, fresh from its triumphant road tour of all points south. Chuman's tail section, which had been removed to make the submarine fit the touring trailer, was now reunited with the centre. All three sections were moved to Canberra and put on open-air display on the west lawn of the Australian War Memorial. At this point the three sections were supported on blocks but remained separate, with the public able to peer inside the submarine from the gaps between the sections.

Matsuo's sliced-off conning tower remained on Garden Island, awaiting further orders.

◆　　◆　　◆

When war broke out between Japan and Australia, each country still had diplomats in place. They remained there until August 1942, when an exchange was agreed through Swiss intermediaries. On 13 August 1942, over 10 weeks after the attack, Tatsuo Kawai, the Japanese Minister at the Legation of Japan in Melbourne, wrote to the Swiss Consul-General in Sydney to say:

> I have the honour to inform you that the ashes of the four Japanese officers and men, whose bodies were recovered from submarines sunk in Sydney Harbour, were duly delivered to me this morning by the Swiss Consul in Melbourne, Mr Pietzcker, in person.
>
> In acknowledging the receipt of same, I hasten to express to you my sincerest thanks for your whole-hearted assistance given to this matter. I am grateful to the Australian authorities, too, for their handing over to me of the ashes for return to Japan.

Next day Kawai and his mission sailed home, carrying the ashes with them. They followed a convoluted route, via the port of Lourenco Marques in Portuguese East Africa (now Mozambique). When the diplomats and their sad cargo finally arrived in Yokohama, thousands turned out to greet the return of the remains of the four submariners. Matsuo's fiancée Toshiko was in the crowd.

The results of the Sydney attack became known in Japan some time around 4 June 1942, at about the same time that Japanese aircraft carriers and cruisers were sinking in horrific numbers in the Battle of Midway. There had been no inclination to and no opportunity for the crowing and myth-making which followed the midget submarine attack on Pearl Harbor. The Sydney funeral with its full military honours and Rear Admiral Muirhead-Gould's broadcast had been widely reported in Japan immediately after the event, but very few details had been released to the Japanese public of the raid itself. Japanese commentators interpreted the funeral and Muirhead-Gould's defence of it as evidence of Australian admiration for Japan.

However, on 8 December 1942, the first anniversary of Pearl Harbor, Admiral Yamamoto announced a citation for the midget submariners of the Eastern and Western Attack Groups, for 'brilliant results at Sydney Harbour and Diégo Suarez'. Full recognition did not come quickly. It was not until 27 March 1943 that the Japanese Navy gave any details of the raids. They also announced that Yamamoto's citation had been 'brought to the attention of the Emperor'. All submariners who had taken part in the Sydney and Diégo Suarez raids were posthumously promoted two ranks. Unlike their Pearl Harbor colleagues, however, they were not publicly proclaimed as war gods, although they were unofficially worshipped along with other war gods at the Yasukuni shrine. There was a curious parallel in the lack of honours for both the Japanese and the Australian heroes of the Battle of Sydney Harbour.

◆　　◆　　◆

In Australia, a modest little industry now sprang up. The navy sold souvenirs. Even after constructing the composite submarine, the navy had plenty of leftover material. Bits of brass pipe from the submarines, together with a certificate of authenticity confirmed by the printed signature of Muirhead-Gould, went for sixpence each. So did a piece of electrical cable, similarly authenticated. A 25-mm square of copper with an indecipherable Japanese character on it was a much more substantial purchase. That would cost the buyer a shilling. All proceeds went to the Royal Australian Navy Relief Fund.

The navy organised the production of 313 dozen (3756) tiny lead submarines and 25,000 postcards. Some of these were handed over to the Department of Information, which shipped them off to the United States for sale there. Metal from the submarines—very likely from the bow of Chuman's submarine and leftover parts of the centre section of Matsuo's—was melted down or beaten and converted into ashtrays, together with an inscription confirming to the buyer he was stubbing his cigarette in a genuine bit of a Japanese submarine sunk in Sydney Harbour.

The navy now had to consider what to do with whatever had been left behind by the souvenir industry. In August 1944 the Department of Supply informed the navy that it was of a mind to accept a tender of £30 from Kallion Brothers for the scrap metal which hadn't been converted into ashtrays. However, Kallion Brothers withdrew their offer when the navy insisted that the submarines must not be cut up and sold for souvenirs. This was, of course, a nice bit of hypocrisy on the navy's part. But it saved what remained of the submarines for posterity.

Meanwhile, the composite submarine gathered rust and graffiti outside the Australian War Memorial in Canberra. In 1966, in the middle of Beatlemania, a group of university students painted it yellow. They were ordered to pay for the paint's removal.

In 1968 Matsuo's 86-year-old mother accepted an invitation to come to Australia and visit the War Memorial. She climbed into the submarine and sprinkled some *sake* in the conning tower area, a traditional Japanese salute to the dead. Nobody told her that this was Chuman's conning tower, not her son's. She read aloud a poem she had written on the first anniversary of her son's death. Amid some controversy, the War

Memorial presented her with Matsuo's lightly blood-stained 1000-stitch *senninbari*. She was not told her son had died by his own hand. The Australians allowed her to believe he had been killed by depth charges after putting up a hard fight.

The composite submarine remained on the lawn, its condition continuing to deteriorate. By the beginning of the 1980s the War Memorial's trustees were forced to recognise that their prize exhibit's problems went beyond the attentions of pranksters with cans of yellow paint. They decided to send the submarine to the naval dockyard on Cockatoo Island in Sydney for restoration, including the removal of 40 years of graffiti.

The restored submarine is now the centrepiece of the Australian War Memorial's special section devoted to the raid. It remains one of the most popular exhibits in the entire collection. Instead of displaying the submarine in three separated sections, the Cockatoo Island restorers welded it together to create a more convincing replica of the original. The black-painted hull hovers menacingly in a dimly lit room, rippling light playing over it to simulate the movement of water. The brightest light shines inside the devastated sides of Chuman's forward section, still dramatically flayed open by the blast of a scuttling charge fired a lifetime ago. The crushed bow cage and damaged bow caps from Matsuo's submarine have been lovingly repaired and restored. They gleam in the soft light.

The tail of Matsuo's submarine is also kept at the War Memorial, not far from the special exhibit. It can be found in the Pacific War room of the Second World War section.

The sliced off conning tower of Matsuo's submarine was kept for years at Garden Island in Sydney. It was finally restored by students from the Wagga Wagga Technical and Further Education College, who undertook the work as a training exercise. The restored conning tower is now back on Garden Island, mounted on a special plinth in the café of the new and excellent Naval Heritage Centre there. Garden Island is, of course, no longer an island. The graving dock under construction during the raid has filled the gap between the original island and the mainland at the foot of Macleay Street, Kings Cross. The salvaged wheelhouse of the *Kuttabul* for years served as the gatehouse to the still-active naval shore base there, renamed HMAS *Kuttabul* in honour of the old ferry. In November 2000 the wheelhouse moved to the Australian War Memorial in Canberra, where it now sits close to the composite submarine whose fellow midget did it such an injury all those years ago.

◆ ◆ ◆

The ultimate fate of Ban's midget, resting on the seabed in a bit over 50 metres of water off Newport Reef, Sydney, has yet to be decided. It is in water controlled by the Australian state of New South Wales. Both the state and the Commonwealth of Australia have set up overlapping legal protection for the site. No one may enter a zone with a radius of 500 metres around the position 33 degrees, 40' 21" south and 151 degrees 22' 58" east. Fines for disturbing the wreck could reach $1.1 million under New South Wales law, while Commonwealth law provides for further hefty fines plus immediate confiscation of boat and dive equipment.

The wreck is not without its dangers. The Sydney submarines carried two sets of scuttling charges, each of 135 kg of TNT, packed in round canisters fore and aft. There is no record of exactly where these charges were stored on the subs, or of whether the canisters were watertight. Each charge had two detonators, one electric (connected to the batteries) and one non-electric (fired by lighting a 'match' fuse). While the TNT would be hard to set off without a detonator, the state of the detonators themselves remains unknown. They are certainly being given the benefit of the doubt by all divers approaching the wreck.

After proclaiming their legislative controls, the authorities proceeded to set up sophisticated monitoring systems to guard the wreck against intruders. These include a shore-based fixed camera trained permanently on the wreck site, plus camera-mounted buoys with permanent lights stationed over the wreck, and a sonar listening device on the sea bed nearby, all connected directly to and monitored by the New South Wales Water Police. Any unauthorised boat or diver approaching the midget can expect brisk attention from the authorities.

The wreck has settled to about the depth of a metre into the sandy seabed. It has filled inside with sand, again to the depth of about a metre. Although the hull is largely intact, the effect of corrosion over the years has made it fragile and vulnerable. Any attempt to raise it would run the substantial risk of destroying the very object it set out to save.

If Ban and Ashibe died with their boat, then any remains would very likely be found buried in the sand at the bottom of the control room, or in the nearby access areas. It would be technically feasible to place a large pipe through the open conning tower hatch into the control room, suck out the contents and draw them to the surface. However this would be a grotesque and indefensibly brutal approach to a delicate problem. Drawing the hull contents up to the surface would badly disturb the wreck, destroying any archaeological clues the remains might offer. Quite simply, this will not be allowed. Recovery of any human remains will take place only through a complete recovery of the hull. Such an operation would cost tens of millions of dollars as well as risking the destruction of a major heritage site.

At the time of writing, something of a consensus was beginning to emerge between the Japanese and Australian authorities, the families of Ban and Ashibe, and the various heritage offices involved. This is likely to mean that the sub and its contents will be left entirely undisturbed on the seabed, at least in the short term. However, there is some precedent for the idea of constructing a metal cage around the wreck, after which divers will be permitted to dive to visit the cage to view and photograph the submarine inside. Such cages are not cheap to build: the cost could run into millions of dollars. Under this scheme, the cage would need to be maintained and access to it controlled, with permits issued to parties of divers approved to approach the wreck. The cage could include a lockable door, so that authorised entry to the submarine would still be possible.

For the time being, the New South Wales Heritage Office, assisted by other heritage agencies and industry, is carrying out detailed surveys of the site, trying to determine the condition of the structure and to unlock its secrets. This information will be needed before any new steps are taken to protect and manage the wreck, perhaps even to design a cage.

✦   ✦   ✦

There is one other collection of midget submarine memorabilia known to the author. It is a clear plastic bag full of odds and ends, and it lives under the desk of John Perryman, the Senior Naval Historical Officer at the Royal Australian Navy's Sea Power Centre in Fyshwick, Canberra. The Sea Power Centre holds navy archives and conducts research for the navy. John very kindly invited me to help myself to a couple of pieces from the bag and I chose two circular wooden seals, one about 11 cm across and the other about 5 cm across. The larger one was once painted white, but the paint has faded over the years and some of it has been replaced by scorch marks, possibly from the scuttling charges which destroyed Chuman's midget. I had them mounted and framed, together with their certificate of authenticity signed by John. They hang over my desk in London, and they kept an eye on me while I wrote this book.

Epilogue

Whatever happened to . . .?

A remarkable number of the men and ships who took part in the Battle of Sydney Harbour lived to tell their tales. Many of those who emerge well from this story, particularly officers from the US Navy, had their abilities recognised and were promoted. Others fared less well. I hunted high and low for a photograph of Captain Howard Bode, but could not find one anywhere. His tragic story, recounted below, no doubt accounts for the fact that he has been air-brushed from history.

THE MEN

Warrant Officer Herbert 'Tubby' Anderson moved on from the Channel Patrol boats to a shore posting in the port of Darwin. He left the navy on 24 April 1946, and returned to Adelaide, where he rejoined the fire service. For years he was coxswain of *Fire Queen*, the only floating fire-fighting vessel protecting the port of Adelaide. He retired in 1964, but continued his love affair with the sea, building his own 34-foot racing yacht, *Ghost*. He died of a stroke in 1966 at the age of 63. His son Harold, at the time of writing entering his eighth year as mayor of the city of Charles Sturt in Adelaide, recalls that his father often said without bitterness that those Australians who took part in the Battle of Sydney Harbour had never received the recognition they deserved.

Lieutenant Reginald Andrew remained in command of HMAS *Sea Mist* for nine months before transferring to HMAS *Lolita*. He never enjoyed a comfortable relationship with navy authority, and after 18 months with the Channel Patrol boats he was moved to menial and routine shore jobs, first in Cairns in northern Queensland and then to Milne Bay in New Guinea. He left the navy as soon as he could after the war. For a time he worked in the petrol industry, first as Queensland sales manager of the long-disappeared oil company Purpull, then with his own independent petrol station. Reg Andrew died in 1984, survived by his remarkable widow Jean, who celebrated her 100th birthday in April 2006. For the rest of his life Reg clung tenaciously to his story of sinking two submarines in Taylors Bay. In correspondence with the author Steven Carruthers, Steven tried to persuade Reg that only three submarines entered Sydney Harbour that night, and Reg had sunk one of them. Reg would have none of it. He wrote dismissively to Steve: 'If only three midgets came, then I am a bloody hero!' He was.

Captain Howard D. Bode of the USS *Chicago* is ultimately one of the tragic figures of this story. His personal inadequacies caught up with him a few months after the Battle of Sydney Harbour. On 9 August 1942, he was aboard *Chicago* in command of one of two mixed battle groups of British, Australian and American ships escorting troop carriers near Savo Island in the Solomons. Contrary to normal naval practice, Bode chose to lead his battle group from the rear. They were 'jumped' by a more agile Japanese group, and *Chicago* took some serious but far from fatal damage in the early exchange of fire. Although Bode was in command of the group, he decided to withdraw, taking *Chicago*'s long-range guns with him and leaving his group to their fate. Bode then compounded this tragedy by failing to warn the second Allied battle group of the presence of a powerful and aggressive Japanese force in their area. They too were taken by surprise. The resulting carnage was appalling, leading to the sinking of three heavy American cruisers, USS *Vincennes, Quincy* and *Astoria,* and the heavy Australian cruiser HMAS *Canberra.* The Allied death toll was 1024, with a further 709 wounded. The Japanese lost no ships, and confined their casualties to 35 killed and 51 wounded. It was the worst blue-water defeat in the US Navy's history, and they set up an inquiry under Admiral Hepburn into the causes. The report of the inquiry was not intended to be made public at the time, but on the eve of its delivery Bode learned he had been singled out for censure. On 19 April 1943, he shot himself. He died next day.

Lance Bullard left the Australian Navy on 30 January 1946. After the war, he never dived again. He worked on a farm near Muswellbrook in the Hunter Valley of New South Wales, before retiring. He then indulged a passion for sketching. His account of the divers' work raising the two midget submarines, written decades after the event, is sharply observed and fluently written. If he had combined his writing with sketching, he might have produced a classic book. He died in 1978 at the age of 76.

Jimmy Cargill remained with the Maritime Services Board, though not always as a nightwatchman. He became involved with general security on the wharves at a time when militant industrial action made this job no sinecure. He retired from the Maritime Services Board in 1953 and died in 1986, aged 96, largely forgotten despite his key role in the events of 31 May 1942. The only mention of his passing was a single-paragraph story in a free suburban newspaper, the *Wentworth Courier.*

Roy Coote left the navy on 31 March 1946. Like his comrade Lance Bullard, he never dived again after the war. He bought a general store in remote country north of Mildura, and for years lived an amiable life dispensing petrol and general supplies to a handful of surrounding landholders. He eventually sold the store and retired to Melbourne. A combination of heavy smoking and years of wear to his lungs from diving took its toll. He died of emphysema in 1984, aged 83.

William Floyd, *Chicago*'s gunnery officer who read the riot act to his anti-aircraft crews after they missed Ito's flight, was later promoted to Rear Admiral. He survived the war and retired to Coronado, California.

Warrant Officer Susumo Ito survived the war. He did well to do so: by the end of hostilities he had flown over every Australian capital city. He returned to the skies over Sydney on 19 February 1943, where he was fired on by anti-aircraft batteries and chased by fighter aircraft. He managed to evade his attackers. In the last months of the war he had the appalling task of dispatching *kamikaze* pilots to their certain death. The process so sickened him that he would have nothing to do with aviation after the war. In the peace, he set up his own electronic business in the Japanese city of Iwakuni. He was 'discovered' in the most extraordinary way. There were plenty of Australian occupation forces stationed in Iwakuni after the war, and the mayor organised a dinner for visiting Australian journalists. He cast around, desperate for someone local who knew something about Australia. Ito shyly admitted that he had indeed visited Australia several times, though without ever actually making contact with Australian soil. He did subsequently manage a visit to Australia, this time at ground level. He was slightly surprised by how big Australians were, and by the fact that many of the women had moustaches. He is still alive at the time of writing, probably the only Japanese survivor of the Battle of Sydney Harbour.

Jimmy Mecklenberg, the quick-thinking officer whose prompt attack on Ban's submarine saved *Chicago* from early destruction, was later promoted to Captain, USN. He survived the war and returned to civilian life where he worked in the fledgling telecommunications and IT industry in Alexandria, Virginia.

Rear Admiral Gerard Charles Muirhead-Gould remained at his post as Naval Officer in Command, Sydney, for most of the war. However, as the Allies advanced into Germany, his knowledge of that country and his language skills in German meant he could be better employed in Europe.

He was transferred to Wilhelmshaven in September 1944 as Officer in Command of the former German naval base. While serving there, the heart problem that kept him away from active service finally caught up with him. He died of a heart attack in Wilhelmshaven on 26 April 1945, only 11 days before Germany's surrender ended the war in Europe.

Lieutenant Athol G. Townley had the most glittering subsequent career of all the participants in the Battle of Sydney Harbour. On the night itself he had shown commendable leadership skills and a talent for quick thinking, and both these attributes stood him in good stead after the war. He entered Federal Australian politics, and rose to be Minister for Defence in the Menzies government. In 1960 he accepted the job of Australian ambassador to the United States, but died suddenly of a heart attack before he could take up the post. Sadly, it has been impossible to find in any public archive his action report on the events in Taylors Bay on the morning of 1 June 1942. It might have helped settle the question of who did what.

THE SHIPS
USS *Chicago* was damaged during the Battle of Savo Island (see entry for Captain Howard Bode, above). She was sunk by Japanese land-based bombers on 30 January 1943 during the Battle of Rennell Island. Although there were few American casualties from *Chicago* (62 dead while 1049 of her crew were rescued), her sinking was seen as potentially a major blow to American morale. Admiral Chester Nimitz, Commander of US Naval Forces, South-West Pacific, threatened to 'shoot' any of his staff who leaked her loss to the press.

HMAS *Lauriana* went on to greater glory. On 31 May 1942 she was part of the Naval Auxiliary Patrol fleet, and still owned by Harold Arnott. The navy bought her from Arnott on 27 August 1942 and fitted her with a 20-millimetre Oerlikon anti-aircraft gun, a Vickers machine-gun and 10 midget depth charges. She frequently travelled to New Guinea, where she acted as sleeping quarters for General Douglas

MacArthur. *Lauriana* is credited with shooting down two Japanese Zero fighters. She still carries bullet holes from strafing attacks by Japanese aircraft. She was returned to Arnott on 27 November 1945. She then changed hands several times before being bought by her present owner, a Sydney dentist. She is now being refitted in loving detail after coming to grief when a rope fouled her propeller, cracking her engine's gearbox, and forcing a complete re-build of her decking and superstructure. She is expected to re-emerge some time in 2007, and take her rightful place as one of the most beautiful yachts on Sydney Harbour.

HMAS *Lolita* did not make it. The Channel Patrol boats were inclined to accumulate petrol vapour in their bilges, and each boat was equipped with ventilating exhaust fans to remove it before it reached a dangerous build-up. In Madang Harbour on 13 June 1945, with the war almost over, an attempt was made to start *Lolita*'s engine while fumes had been allowed to gather. The immediate explosion led to the death of two crew members and the total destruction of the veteran patrol boat.

USS *Perkins* had the most tragic end of all the ships involved in the Battle of Sydney Harbour. While on convoy escort duty on 29 October 1942, she was involved in a collision with the Australian troopship HMAS *Duntroon* in darkness at sea. The impact cut her in two. She sank immediately, with the loss of four lives. Ian Mitchell, the young signalman who manned Garden Island signal station on the night of the midget submarine raid on Sydney Harbour (see Chapter 8), was a signalman on *Duntroon* on the night of the disaster.

HMAS *Sea Mist* still appears on the register of the Australian Maritime Safety Authority, though without her HMAS label. Immediately after the war she was bought by the Sydney radio station 2GB and made available as a 'perk' to the radio personality Jack Davey. She changed hands several times and underwent major refits. She is said to be in excellent condition today. AMSA lists her home port as Sydney. However, she is believed to be based in Queensland.

HMAS *Steady Hour* did not survive the war. She was destroyed by fire on 3 March 1945, while stationed in Darwin.

HMAS *Yandra* survived the war. She was paid off at Port Adelaide on 25 March 1946 and returned to her original owners, the Coast Steam Ship Company of Adelaide, in July 1946. She does not appear on the current Australian Maritime Safety Authority list of registered ships.

HMAS *Yarroma* also does not appear on the current Australian Maritime Safety Authority list. The last traceable entry in the Royal Australian Navy register of requisitioned ships, dated 18 May 1945, shows that her engines had been condemned and that she was awaiting the arrival of reconditioned engines. According to the Royal Australian Navy's publication *A–Z Ships, Aircraft and Shore Establishments* she was sold on 15 December 1945. The *A–Z* does not name the buyer. After that the trail goes cold.

Appendix I

Genuine seller

One of the great legends of the submarine raid is the crash of house prices which followed it in Sydney's harbourside suburbs. While researching this book, the author was repeatedly told about an uncle/cousin/neighbour/grandparent who knew of a house sold for £25 in Rose Bay in the days immediately after the shelling of that suburb. Urban myth. It never happened. However, there was some genuine if brief impact on house prices, and some genuine action from people who saw the raid as the possible forerunner of an invasion. The reality is that a lot of people had already made plans to get out of the cities and into the country if ever the Japanese arrived, and the shelling of Sydney's suburbs made these plans seem more urgent. In particular, people looked to the Blue Mountains, an hour's drive west of Sydney, for sanctuary. Why they would do this remains a mystery to the author. It hardly seems likely that the Japanese, having taken the trouble to invade Sydney, would lose heart 50 kilometres inland and leave the rest of the country to its own devices. It is fair to acknowledge, however, that the genteel mountain hideaways of Leura and Katoomba would be unlikely to suffer the kind of heavy bombing and shelling which Sydney could expect if the Japanese arrived in serious numbers.

So what actually happened? The classified advertising section of the Saturday edition of the *Sydney Morning Herald* is the traditional bulletin board for Sydneysiders wishing to sell anything, from their car to their house. If there were a property crash, it would be evident here. A host of new properties would appear on the market, average prices would plummet, and the scent of desperation would be strong in the air. An examination of the *Herald's* advertisements for 'Flats, Residential' and 'Houses, Land for Sale' in the weeks before and after the raid tells the story, and punctures the myth.

On Saturday, 30 May, the day before the raid, there were 26 flats advertised in the *Herald* with Rose Bay addresses, and four houses. The rentals for the flats were generally between £2 and £3 a week. The four houses ranged in price from £1050 for a brick cottage with four rooms and a tiled bathroom to £2100 for a modern bungalow with two bedrooms, sunroom, lounge, dining room, hot water service, refrigerator and harbour views. No price was given for a rather more splendid gent's new residence in Wallangra Road, Rose Bay Heights, with four bedrooms, three reception rooms, two bathrooms, three toilets, a ball-room and a double garage. The *Herald* also carried a 'Houses and Land Wanted' advertising section, and Rose Bay appeared there once: a cash buyer was willing to pay up to £3000 for a cottage or bungalow, new or old, in Rose Bay Heights.

So how were house prices two weeks later, on 13 June, when the submarines had been and gone and the shells had fallen all around? The number of Rose Bay flats on offer had fallen slightly from 26 to 21. Rentals stayed between £2 and £3 a week. No houses were offered for sale in Rose Bay. However, in 'Houses and Land Wanted' there was one buyer offering up to £3000 for a four-bedroom modern home in Rose Bay Heights. In other words, no change.

A week later there was some sign of movement. On 20 June the *Herald* listed 25 flats in Rose Bay. This time the cheapest was £1.12.6 a week, down from the £2 lowest price of the week before. There were only two houses for sale, including the gent's residence in Wallangra Road, still unpriced. However, a tone of mild hysteria crept into the wording of the second ad. 'Rose Bay, convenient Tram, Bus and Shops', it began enticingly. 'Commodious bungalow home, 3 reception rooms, 4 bedrooms, all conveniences, Refrigerator, Garage. The OWNER is a GENUINE SELLER and is prepared to SACRIFICE for a QUICK SALE. PRICE £2200 or near offer.'

By the following week, GENUINE SELLER had to face the fact that he was in trouble. His price dropped to £1930 or near offer. There were now six houses for sale in Rose Bay, the largest number yet. The prices were: £1030, £1450, £2330, £2330, £3100 and GENUINE SELLER's £1930. Far from dropping, the average price had actually risen microscopically, whatever the travails of GENUINE SELLER. The only real change was in flat rentals. Flats could now be had for as little as £1.10.0 a week, a 25 per cent drop from the £2 minimum before the attack.

This pattern continued through July and into August. GENUINE SELLER appeared for the final time on 4 July with the price still set at £1930 or near offer. He dropped out of the running on 11 July, presumably because he had genuinely sold. By the end of August it was all over. After the Battle of Midway, the threat of Japanese invasion had evaporated, and the threat of further attacks on Sydney had diminished to vanishing point. Property prices, whether for sale or rental, were emphatically back to pre-attack levels. Instead, the myth of the property crash became part of estate agents' hype. On 8 August the *Herald* carried an ad for a Rose Bay property: 'Pair maisonettes £4350 sacrificed hundreds below cost. Brand new ultra-modern home and investment combined. Beautiful texture brick building, each home contains two reception, 3 b'rooms, beautiful Modern Bathroom, Shower Recess, sep toilet, h.w. service throughout. Garage.' As readers can judge for themselves, it was offered for about the same price as it would have fetched on 30 May, before the subs came. On 15 August the *Herald* carried a similar advertisement for a two-storey home in Rose Bay Heights priced at £2800. The ad was placed by the Laton Smith estate agency and declared: 'It's seldom we are privileged to offer a home of this quality at this price.' Again, the price was no different from the pre-raid price. By 22 August landlords were asking £3.7.6 a week for flats. It was business as usual, if not better than usual.

David Goldstone was a seven-year-old schoolboy living in a block of flats in Old South Head Road near the corner of O'Sullivan Road, Rose Bay. O'Sullivan Road runs parallel to and one block away from Balfour Road, which was hit by two of the I-24's shells. One of the Balfour Road shells exploded, seriously damaging a house and injuring a sleeping woman with flying glass. So the Goldstone family lived pretty much on the front line.

David attended the nearby Scots College, one of Sydney's eight elite GPS schools, as a day boy. Scots had a country campus near the town of Bathurst, about 150 kilometres west of Sydney. In David's words, his parents did 'a minor flip'. They rapidly switched young David from day boy to boarder, and packed him off to the country campus. 'I was pretty upset about it,' he recalls. 'I wanted to know were my friends coming with me. Of course, they weren't.' The whole experience left him scarred to this day: he still can't bear the taste of rhubarb. 'They had fields full of rhubarb,' he recalls. 'They gave it to us for breakfast, lunch and dinner.'

By the end of the year, the Goldstone parents were confident the invasion threat was over. The Australian school year begins in January, not September. When the new school year started in January 1943, David was back to the Sydney campus of Scots College as a day boy, with the menace of both invasion and rhubarb now a thing of the past. To his huge relief, everything in Sydney was as he had left it. The same families lived in the same blocks of flats. His friends hadn't moved. Life could get back to normal.

However, whole families did at least lay plans to move. Donald Dunkley remembers:

A lot of families were ready to go to relatives up in the country. If an invasion actually did take place, we had some relatives living in Harden, the Riverina part of New South Wales. We were advised to contact relatives in the country and see if they were willing to take us if we had to evacuate. They said yes, by all means, we're happy to take you. So, had there been an invasion, I don't know how on earth we would have got there, but we did have this place earmarked that we could have gone to.

I think a lot of other families around the place had relatives in the country, and they were all ready to go if necessary.

Did he have any friends or neighbours who actually moved as a result of the raid? 'I don't know of any.'

The raid did produce one bizarre scramble. Jim Macken's ability to bob up in unexpected places in this narrative will now be apparent from his Riverview and missing submarine contributions. His final appearance in the story flows from the fact that, at the time of the submarine raid, his father managed the fashionable Hydro-Majestic Hotel in the Blue Mountains near Leura, 100 kilometres west of Sydney. He recalls:

I was living at the Hydro with my father and family. He'd been deluged with phone calls from people wanting permanent bookings at the hotel for the duration of the war. He said, we're not doing it because it would preclude ex-servicemen from coming up here. We don't want permanent bookings. We're looking after people who want a holiday. So he knocked them all back with one exception, a man who'd been there before the war, an old colonel who'd been a permanent resident before 1939.

None of this rush for permanent bookings happened before the submarine attack. The submarines and the shelling of Sydney's eastern suburbs triggered it off. Why did people want to move into the Hydro-Majestic?

They all wanted to get out of Sydney. They wanted to rent their houses, or try to sell their houses. But houses were very hard to sell. They wanted to get out of what they saw as the danger area in Sydney. Although they couldn't get to the Hydro, they were buying houses up all over the Blue Mountains.

It petered out after a while. After Midway and the Coral Sea the panic went out, and people stopped buying and went back home. The fear of a Japanese land invasion faded.

So what is the reality of the Great Sydney Harbourside Property Crash? The core truth is that it never happened. Property prices trembled for about eight weeks, and a few people saved 10 shillings a week—$26 a week in today's money—on the rent they might otherwise have paid if the subs had not come. But there was no rush, no widespread panic selling, and certainly nobody bought a house in Rose Bay for £25.

Finally, there is an unpleasant little lie which needs to be held up to the light and then stomped on and consigned permanently to the rubbish bin. A lot of the stories of the property price crash and the subsequent rush for bargains are told by anti-Semites. The eastern suburbs of Sydney have always been attractive to Sydney's Jewish population, just as they are attractive to the *goyim*. It's as nice a place to live as you would find anywhere in the world. The legend would have you believe that jittery gentiles sold their houses off cheap, and the Jews craftily bought them up at bargain prices. That, says the legend, is why there are so many Jews in Sydney's eastern suburbs today.

It is the purest claptrap. Apart from the non-existence of the property crash, so that there were no bargains to be had anyway, there is no evidence that the mix of population in Sydney's Eastern Suburbs altered one jot after the raid. The truth is that most families were in the same houses and flats six months after the raid as they were before the subs and the shells arrived. Ask David Goldstone.

Appendix II

Other gentlemen's mail

One of the enduring controversies of World War II revolves around who knew what, and when. Given that the British at Bletchley Park were reading Germany's most secret diplomatic and military signals, did Churchill know in advance about Pearl Harbor and fail to tip off the Americans because he wanted them in the war? Did Roosevelt know, too, but fail to act for the same reason? Did the Americans know in advance about the midget submarine raid on Sydney Harbour but fail to tell the Australians through carelessness or malice?

These questions still cannot be answered with absolute certainty. However, it is possible to make some reasonable judgements on the basis of what is already known.

Australian Naval Intelligence built a formidable reputation for itself in World War I. It operated as part of British Naval Intelligence, with responsibility for the whole Pacific area. Wireless telegraphy was now an established means of communication, and embassies and armed forces around the world used it to send messages to each other and to their respective governments and headquarters. As these radio broadcasts could be overheard by anybody, messages had to be sent in code.

Cracking the other side's code is a massively time-consuming process, and the intelligence revealed after hundreds or even thousands of hours of analysis often comes too late to be of any practical use. Rather than employ some of the finest brains in the country to go without sleep while trying to crack codes, by far the better tactic is simply to pinch the other side's code books, taking great care to make sure they don't know you have done it (or they will change the code).

In this matter, Australia got off to a flying start in World War I. On the third day of the war an Australian boarding party seized the unsuspecting German ship *Hobart* in Port Phillip Bay, Melbourne. The German captain was caught trying to remove the code books, which the Australians promptly grabbed, along with the captain. The captain was locked up, and the books were sent to the Admiralty in London. They were used throughout the war to decrypt German signals. Intelligence from this source was critical in tipping off the British of the whereabouts of the German Pacific Fleet, leading to its destruction in the Battle of the Falklands on 9 December 1914.

For the rest of World War I, the Australians concentrated on the two forms of intelligence they did best. They set up a chain of informants throughout the Pacific to report on shipping movements. And they set up powerful listening stations to gather what would now be called SIGINT, intelligence gleaned from listening in to the other side's signal traffic. They made several breakthroughs reading German naval codes, and were roundly praised by the British for their efforts.

The end of hostilities in 1918 brought no let-up in the hunt for SIGINT. The Japanese, who had been allies of the British and Americans, proved to be particularly vulnerable. As early as 1919 their codes had been targeted by American cryptanalysts. In 1921 American agents broke into a Japanese consulate, probably New York, and copied the current Japanese Navy codes, producing what came to be known as the 'Red Book'.

The first major intelligence coup followed in the same year. The Washington Naval Conference was set up to agree a limit on peacetime naval strengths. Japan demanded a navy with 70 per cent of the strength of the British and American navies—the so-called 10:10:7 option. The Americans wanted to limit Japan to 60 per cent or 10:10:6.

The American Office of Naval Intelligence, led by Herbert Yardley and known to insiders as the 'Black Chamber', succeeded in cracking the Japanese diplomatic codes. The American Secretary of State Charles Hughes went to the conference chamber knowing from decoded signals that the Japanese were willing to settle for 10:10:6. He simply sat tight until the Japanese capitulated. A treaty was signed in 1922.

Naval intelligence boomed. The Americans set up listening stations in Guam, the Philippines and Shanghai. A stream of cryptanalysts sailed for Japan on three-year language courses, including Lieutenant Joseph Rochefort, the brightest and best of the US Navy code-breakers.

However, back in the US the character flaws of Herbert Yardley, the head of the Black Chamber, led to disaster. Yardley was a brilliant cryptographer but he was not, to put it mildly, an ideal employee. He was a gambler, a drunk, a womaniser and an opportunist. Uncle Sam's interests were allowed to languish while Yardley played poker (he wrote two books on the subject), ran his unsuccessful property business, sold codes commercially, and offered consultancy services on codes to private companies. This left somewhere between little and no time for the job at hand.

It all had to end. In 1929 the Signal Corps began an investigation, and didn't like what it found. At the same time the American Secretary of State Henry Stimson discovered to his horror that Americans were sneakily prying into other people's private communications and issued his famous decree: 'Gentlemen do not read one another's mail.'* The Black Chamber was closed down.

Yardley responded to this indignity by writing a best-selling book, *The American Black Chamber*, published in 1931, which gave chapter and verse of all the American codebreaking efforts, including the coup at the

---

* There is some doubt as to whether Stimson actually said this. It may be apocryphal, rather like the famous Humphrey Bogart line 'Play it again, Sam', which is never actually uttered in *Casablanca*. However, the closure of the Black Chamber was real enough.

Washington Naval Conference. This is about as big a betrayal as any intelligence officer ever committed, making the *Spycatcher* publication rows of the 1980s look small time. The Japanese were furious, accusing the Americans of bad faith. There is evidence, but no proof, that Yardley had earlier sold the same information to the Japanese for $7000, delivering it to them privately before the publication of the book. The facts were bad enough, the Japanese might have reasoned, but to pay $7000 for information which they could have had for $1 by buying a book a few months later was treachery beyond imagination.

Yardley then tried to publish a follow-up book, *Japanese Diplomatic Secrets*, in 1933. Congress passed a special Act banning its publication, the first and only time such action has been taken. Yardley disappeared, working briefly for Chiang Kai-shek while the Japanese planned to invade China, and later for the Canadians, who quickly dumped him.

The upshot was predictable. The Japanese changed their codes.

The SIGINT battle now entered a new phase: the era of the code machine. Enigma, the machine used by the Germans, was largely mechanical, with a series of rotating wheels and drums controlling flashing lights. The wheels were swapped every 24 hours, as were the code keys. The Japanese developed a slightly more sophisticated version, using electrical telephone switching gear in place of the cogs and wheels.

Enigma first saw the light of day in 1919, when it was sold commercially in Holland. The Germans began using it in the 1920s, and continued to develop and improve it until the end of the war. Enigma was first broken by the Polish secret service. They managed to reconstruct an Enigma machine and successfully read German coded traffic between 1932 and 1938. However, the Germans constantly added new twists and variations to Enigma, to the point where the Poles could no longer unscramble the messages. They handed over two of their reconstructed Enigma machines to the British and French secret services, and briefed the British as best they could on how the system worked.

The British were slow to realise the potential of Enigma, and left it to a single cryptographer in 1938. In 1939, the year war broke out, the Enigma team doubled in strength . . . to two cryptographers. But by 1940 the British had seen the light, and a veritable army of cryptographers worked on the German codes. This first proved its mettle in the Battle of Britain, between July and September 1940, giving the British a lot of information about German squadron locations and strengths. The British named their new source of information 'Ultra'.

The Americans continued to lead the way in the attack on Japanese codes. By 1926 navy code-breakers had broken into the main Japanese naval code, and by 1929 they had the entire code in two red buckram binders. This was known as the Red Code. On 1 December 1930 the Japanese switched to a new code, but the Americans broke this quickly too, naming the new model Blue Code.

So far the US Navy had led the way. Now the US Army entered the fray, having taken over the files from Yardley's Black Chamber. They set about tackling the machine-encrypted codes produced by the Japanese version of the German Enigma machine, and by 1937 they were reading Japanese machine-coded messages reasonably easily, using traditional decrypt techniques. They called the Japanese machine Red (no relation to the Red Code).

However, in 1939 the Americans began to intercept messages encrypted on a new and more sophisticated machine, which they called Purple. These turned out to be brutishly difficult to crack. By August 1940 the US Army SIS (Signals Intelligence Service) began to make progress, and in September 1940 they had the breakthrough they needed. The code was solved. Decrypts from this source were known as 'Magic'.

The next step was extraordinary. No one in America had ever seen a Purple machine, nor did anyone have the faintest idea what it looked like. Nevertheless, the Americans built their own version of Purple. They had been using telephone switching gear as a way of speeding up the decryption process, and they now based their Purple machine on the telephone kit. Incredibly, the switching system they chose was the exact same brand and model as the one used by the Japanese in the real Purple. No Purple machine was ever captured during the war, and the first sight of it was some damaged remains found in the Japanese embassy in Berlin in 1945. The real machine looked remarkably like the American cobbled-up version.

Eight Purple machines were built, and they captured a stream of invaluable information throughout the war. There was a major difference between Purple and Enigma. The Japanese version of the Purple machine had two hefty electric typewriters attached to opposite sides of the central machine. An operator typed in the message to be encoded on one typewriter, and the coded version emerged from the other. This made Purple bigger and heavier than Enigma, to the point where it was too bulky and clumsy for operational military use. While the Germans regularly carried Enigma machines on ships, submarines and even tanks, Purple could only be used in embassies and consulates. So it carried diplomatic traffic only, and diplomats did not receive operational military information. In the last days before the outbreak of war Roosevelt and his cabinet had plenty of warning via Magic that war was imminent and that the Japanese were playing for time. However, Magic produced no coded message saying: 'We are attacking Pearl Harbor on 7 December, using planes and midget submarines.' The timing and target for the attack were never revealed to the diplomats.

When the bombs rained down on Pearl Harbor, the urgent need was for operational rather than diplomatic information. There are two ways intelligence services approach intercepts. The simplest, and often the only option, is traffic analysis. How busy are the airwaves? If there is a lot of traffic, something big is brewing. Direction-finding equipment to track the origin of the signal can be equally revealing. Who sent this message? Who replied? Patterns begin to emerge. 'A' in Tokyo sends a message to 'B' in Java about once a week, and 'B' replies straightaway. Every time this happens, a massive air raid is launched from Java next day. So next time 'A' talks to 'B', get ready for an air raid. Knowing the exact content of the message would be nice, but the mere fact that it was sent tells the traffic analyst what he needs to know.

The Holy Grail remains the full decrypt . . . read the enemy's messages and you are reading his mind. So the spies began a double attack on

Japanese naval signals, analysing the traffic and attempting to crack the code.

Highest priority was given to a decrypt of the Japanese naval code known as JN-25. This code was introduced by the Japanese in June 1939 and had been a major target for US Navy code-breakers ever since. It was another brute to decrypt. There were 45,000 characters in the code, each of which could be rendered in 18,000 different ways, giving 810 million possibilities to unscramble.

On 10 December 1941, three days after Pearl Harbor, a team led by an American Navy cryptanalyst, Lieutenant-Commander Joseph John Rochefort, joined the attack on JN-25. There should be a statue in his honour in every Australian town: he and his team at Station HYPO, as the Pearl Harbor spy base was known, played an important part in the Battle of the Coral Sea and a vital part in the Battle of Midway, which finally turned the tide of war against the Japanese.

The cryptographers at Station HYPO were scruffy, eccentric and generally distrusted by the regular navy. Joe Rochefort fought his entire war in carpet slippers and a red smoking jacket. However, their dedication was total. Rochefort worked 20-hour days, and his team pitched in with equal zeal. By February they began making inroads into the code, to the point where they could read between 10 and 15 per cent of an intercepted message. On 16 March 1942 the combined efforts of HYPO and the US Navy spy base on Corregidor (Station CAST) produced the first complete decrypt of a JN-25 message.

Throughout this period, British and Australian code-breakers had not been idle. They had independently made huge inroads into the JN-25 code. Now the two forces were to combine. Corregidor code-breakers were evacuated to Melbourne in February and March 1942, and formed the American contingent at FRUMEL (Fleet Radio Unit Melbourne). FRUMEL was a joint US–Australian SIGINT unit which became a vital link in the intelligence-gathering chain now surrounding Japan.

Nevertheless, the situation was still dire. John Winton, in his 1994 book *Ultra in the Pacific: How Breaking Japanese Codes and Ciphers Affected Naval Operations against Japan, 1941–45* estimates that by 26 May 1942, five days before the midget submarine attack on Sydney, the US Navy was intercepting about 60 per cent of Japanese messages, and reading about 40 per cent. The decrypts were usually incomplete, sometimes as little as 10 per cent of the message. If all you have is five words of a 50-word cable, the result is not usually enlightening.

With a combination of traffic analysis and decrypt, however, Rochefort and his team had managed to piece together a picture of Operation Mo, as the Japanese had rather unenterprisingly called their attack on Port Moresby and its Australian air base. Rochefort even had the dates right. On 3 May the Japanese would attack Tulagi in the Solomon Islands; on 10 May they would attack Port Moresby. If they won, Australia would be cut off and vulnerable. Thus did Rochefort arm Admiral Frank Jack Fletcher, with vital information to fight the Battle of the Coral Sea, on 6 to 8 May 1942.

Within a month Rochefort scored a second triumph, generally recognised as the turning point in the Pacific war. JN–25 traffic analysis and decrypts pointed to a major Japanese attack on a target they called 'AF'. Where was AF? The 'A' indicated an American base. But which one? Pearl Harbor again? The Aleutians? The American mainland? Midway? From traffic analysis and partial decrypts, Rochefort and his team were already convinced that AF was Midway. However, they needed to persuade the top brass of the US Navy before the admirals would commit scarce resources to a major battle at a specific location on a specific date. How could the brass be made to believe that the decrypts were accurate and Midway was the target? Rochefort arranged for the commander on Midway to send an uncoded radio message to the effect that Midway's water-processing plant had been damaged and the island was running out of fresh water. Sure enough, a few days later Rochefort intercepted and decoded a Japanese message saying: 'AF is short of water.' The target was now confirmed, as was the date of the attack—4 June.

Admiral Nimitz had fewer overall resources than the Japanese, but Rochefort's intercept enabled him to position them with devastating effect. The Japanese Navy suffered a crushing defeat, from which it never recovered. Until 4 June the Japanese had never lost a major strategic battle. After 4 June, they never won one. The tide of war had turned.

So if the spies could get good advance warning of the Port Moresby attack and Midway, did they have advance notice of the midget submarine attack on their ships in Sydney Harbour? There is no evidence that they did. The Sydney attack was planned in early March 1942, and the orders to mount it went out to the submarine commanders on 1 April. The first submarine sailed from Truk Lagoon on 27 April. It is very unlikely that much of this was directed by radio, so there would have been little or nothing to intercept up to that point. Nor would Magic intercepts of diplomatic traffic have raised the alarm. The Imperial Japanese Navy was not in the habit of informing its diplomats about where it would strike next.

Direction-finding and traffic analysis from New Zealand did lead to a submarine warning to Sydney, issued on 29 May, two days before the attack. Although the fix was pretty accurate—40 nautical miles from Sydney—the report warned of one submarine, not five, and certainly did not mention midget submarines. The decrypt which should have set the alarm bells ringing was the FRUMEL digest of 30 May, which was only partly decrypted but which was clearly a reconnaissance report identifying targets in Sydney, particularly ships *inside* Sydney Harbour. The biggest 'what if . . .' of the Battle of Sydney Harbour revolves around this message. If, instead of simply passing the FRUMEL decrypt on to Washington, Admiral Leary had also alerted the Australians then things might have turned out differently.

Suppose Leary had sent a message to 'Cocky' Long, the Director of Naval Intelligence, Australia, along the following lines:

Further to New Zealand warning of May 29 reporting submarine presence in vicinity Sydney. Intelligence from a most secret source [the standard cover phrase for intercepted and decoded Japanese signals] indicates Japanese submarine which attacked *Wellen* on May 15 carried out reconnaissance, possibly aerial, of Sydney Harbour and Mascot airfield on or around May 25. Reconnaissance identified naval targets inside Sydney Harbour.

If such a message then led to an anti-submarine alert, Muirhead-Gould might have reacted quite differently to *Yarroma's* and *Lolita's* claims to have located and attacked a submarine in the harbour itself, and Captain Bode might have been less sceptical of his officers' sightings of a midget submarine. The Port War Signal Station might have added a few hands to their watch, and might have responded more effectively to the traces given by Chuman's and Ban's submarines. The end result might still have been the same, but Leary's failure to pass on his intelligence surely diminished Sydney's chance to react promptly and well.

However, even a full decrypt of this signal would not have told much about the exact nature of the Japanese threat. The only messages which might have given a clear warning of the timing and nature of the attack were Sasaki's two signals, reported in Chapters 5 and 6, and there is no evidence that either of these was ever decrypted. This was a time when all SIGINT resources were concentrating on the looming attack on Midway. Summaries of naval intelligence by Arthur McCollum, at the Office of Naval Intelligence in Washington, for the period from 15 May to 4 June 1942, are dominated by decrypts of messages setting out Japanese preparations for this major attack, and the diversionary attack on the Aleutian Islands. All intelligence efforts throughout the Pacific focused on Midway, and rightly so. The Sydney raiders were under orders to keep radio transmissions to a minimum, so there was very little radio traffic to excite even the traffic analysts. Any intercepted signal from a single submarine off Sydney may well have been legitimately passed over as low priority for full decryption. The Midway attack was the main intelligence target.

Nor does it make sense to suggest, as some have, that the Americans knew about the raid but kept the information away from the Australians for fear of revealing they had broken into the Japanese codes. FRUMEL was a joint American–Australian operation and, while there was plenty of tension between the Australian and American contingents, the fact that Japanese codes were being broken was well known to the Australians. The Americans were not remotely squeamish about using signal intelligence to fight the Battle of the Coral Sea, and later the

Battle of Midway, so they would surely have been equally brisk about the Sydney raid.

No, like so many conspiracy theories the suggestion that the raid was known about in advance and that knowledge became the subject of a massive cover-up will not stand examination. When things go wrong the question always arises: conspiracy or cock-up? There can be no doubt about the answer in the case of the midget submarine raid on Sydney Harbour. Cock-up wins.

Appendix III

The Admiral's report

One of the joys of researching this book is the opportunity it gave the author to return to the forgotten world of manual typewriters and carbon paper. Terms like 'top copy' have left the language now that computers and word processors can churn out 20 immaculate and identical copies of a document in under a minute. In the world of 1942, documents were typed on six or seven pages at once, with carbon paper between the pages. The top copy would be easily readable, but anyone so low on the pecking order that they were destined to receive copy seven could expect to wrestle with fuzzy and often unreadable type, laced with barely readable corrections. After a day in an archive ploughing through a succession of seventh copies, any researcher can be forgiven for hoping his next project will be set in a time when the computer has taken over. However, there is a softness and a vulnerability about manually typed documents which the computer can never match, and it gives them a special charm.

Happily, the top copy of Rear Admiral Muirhead-Gould's report is available in the Australian National Archive in Melbourne. I have tried to capture its flavour by setting it out here in a form as close as I could get to the original. The first page of the top copy is littered with initials and dates as it circulated around the Navy Board. The first set of initials, dated 16 July, probably belong to Sir Guy Royle. The last set of entirely indecipherable initials is dated 31 July. Occasionally someone has scribbled a note on the National Archive's top copy, but the identity of the author of these jottings remains a mystery, as does the timing of their musings. Other copies have been more heavily annotated but it is impossible to tell by whom or when. The annotations on the other copies tend to be a bit more sceptical: one anonymous scrutiniser has tried to work out in the margin which submarine did what, clearly not accepting Muirhead-Gould's version at face value.

Royal Australian Navy

From ..... The ~~Commodore~~-in-Charge, H.M.A. Naval Establishments,
Rear-Admiral
       Sydney

To .... The Secretary, Naval Board, Melbourne

Date ...... 16th July, 1942.   No. ...... B.S.   1749/201/37.

Subject ... MIDGET SUBMARINE ATTACK ON SYDNEY HARBOUR
             MAY 31st – JUNE 1st, 1942

1.   Submitted for the information of the Naval Board is
the following report on the Midget Submarine Attack on
Sydney Harbour, May 31st — June 1st, 1942:-

2.   Appendices supporting the narrative are attached:
           Appendix   I — Chronological sequence of
                            events.
           Appendix II — Sources of information.
           Appendix III — Submarine and torpedo
                            particulars (operational only).
           Appendix IV — Loop indications and signatures.
           Appendix V — Lessons learnt.
           Appendix VI — Recommendations for recognition
                            of Personnel.

3.   It is considered that four midget submarines
participated in the raid. Of these, two are known by
their actual Japanese numbers (No. 14 and No. 21). They
are thus referred to in the following narrative. The
other two unknown midgets are referred to as "Midget A"
and "Midget B" respectively.

4.   It is considered that the force which attacked
Sydney consisted of five "I" class submarines, four
midget submarines, and one, possibly two, float planes.
These were:

"I" 21 (Float plane)

"I" 24

"I" 22

"I" 27

"I" 29 (Possibly float plane)

Midget No. 14

Midget No. 21

"Midget A"

"Midget B".

5. The attack was possibly preceded by aerial reconnaissance, which may have been carried out on 29th, 30th and 31st May.

6. A reconnaissance of Sydney Harbour, especially the Naval Anchorage area, was carried out by one biplane single float plane at approximately 0420K/30 May.

7. Allied warships in Sydney Harbour at the time included the following:

No. 1 Buoy	-	H.M.A.S. "CANBERRA"
No. 2 Buoy	-	U.S.S. "CHICAGO"
No. 4 Buoy	-	U.S.S. "PERKINS"
No. 5 Buoy	-	U.S.S. "DOBBIN"
No. 6 Buoy	-	H.M.A.S. "BUNGAREE"
Birt's Buoy	-	H.M.S. "KANIMBLA"
Off Robertson Point	-	H.M.A.S. "AUSTRALIA"

8. The plane, which was burning navigation lights, approached the harbour from a northerly direction, flew over the Naval Anchorage, circled U.S.S. "CHICAGO" twice, and departed in a due east direction.

TACTICS

9. The contents of Midget No. 21 (ample food supplies, first aid kit, charts, lists of call signs etc.) suggest that this was by no means regarded as a "suicide" venture.

10. The establishment of "picking up dispositions", rendezvous at which midgets were to rejoin their parents, had been made. Five of such rendezvous were spaced at fairly regular intervals (an average of 18 miles apart) two to the northward and three to the southward of Sydney.

11. The waiting parent submarines were in each case spread 2 miles apart on a line of bearing at right angles to the coastline.

RECONSTRUCTION OF EVENTS OF MAY 31st/JUNE 1st

12. Weather conditions were reported outside the heads at 1900K as — rough sea, moderate swell, wind S. by W. force 4, dark and overcast. The moon was full and rose at 1813K. Dawn on Monday, 1st June, was at 0545K; high tide 2125K, height 6 feet.

13. Four midget submarines (Midget 14, Midget 21, "Midget A" and "Midget B") were released (from "I" submarines 22, 24, 27 and 29) off Sydney Heads, a short distance to seawards, but outside the Loop area, during the afternoon of Sunday, 31st May.

MIDGET NO. 14

14. The first attempt at an entry was made by Midget No. 14, and was unsuccessful. She crossed the loop at 2001 and, by 2015, was caught in the nets (centre portion, close to the Western gate). She was unable to free herself, and blew herself up at 2235. Her propellers were thickly covered with grease when the wreck was recovered. No food had been touched, neither had any sanitary utensils been used.

"MIDGET A"

15. The second entry was made by "Midget A". She crossed the loop at 2148, and entered the harbour unobserved.

16. "Midget A" was not sighted until 2252. She was then sighted by "CHICAGO" and a ferry in the proximity of Garden Island. She was also sighted by Dockyard Motor Boat "NESTOR" and an officer on Ferry Wharf, Garden Island, at the same time. She was then close to Garden Island (200 yards off) and proceeding towards the Harbour Bridge.

17. "Midget A" was fired on by "CHICAGO" and apparently turned towards North Shore instead of proceeding further up the harbour. She was next sighted at 2310 from the Oil Wharf at Garden Island (by H.M.S.* Vessels "WHYALLA" and "GEELONG") in the direction of Bradley's Head. They fired at her and kept the area under observation for half an hour.

18. "Midget A" fired two torpedoes from the direction of Bradley's Head at 0030. One of these failed to explode, after running ashore at Garden Island. The other passed under the Dutch Submarine K9 which was lying alongside "KUTTABUL" at Garden Island, hit the sea bottom and exploded, sinking "KUTTABUL".

19. It is presumed that these torpedoes were fired at "CHICAGO" at No. 2 Buoy, who was about to slip and proceed. The dock floodlights, which would have silhouetted "CHICAGO", were extinguished just before the torpedo was fired. "Midget A" then escaped, passing over the loop on her exit from the harbour at 0158. ◆

"MIDGET B"

20. "Midget B" made an unsuccessful attempt to enter the harbour but failed to reach the effective loop (No. 12) or, consequently, the boom. She was sighted by "YANDRA" (the Duty A/S Vessel on patrol within the Loop Area) and later by "LAURIANA" who illuminated her until intercepted between the Heads, at 2254, by "YANDRA".

---

* It should have been H.M.A.S.

21. Two separate attacks were carried out by "YANDRA" on "Midget B" during a period of 9 minutes, starting from the time she attempted to ram the submarine at 2258 until her second attack – a full pattern of six depth charges – at 2307.

22. It is considered that "Midget B" was destroyed by this second attack, in a position 023° 3.6 cables from Hornby Light.

MIDGET NO. 21

23. Midget No. 21 entered the harbour at 0301, at which time she crossed No. 12 Loop. She proceeded up harbour unobserved until she reached Bradley's Head vicinity. Here she was sighted by "KANIMBLA" and fired on at 0350 and gave rise to the unconfirmed contact made by "DOOMBA" off Robertson Point at 0450.

24. She was detected in Taylor Bay and attacked with depth charges, first by "SEA MIST" at 0500, then by "YARROMA" and "STEADY HOUR" until 0827. The effect of these attacks was clearly shown in the great amount of damage done to Midget No. 21, which was evident in the wreck when it was recovered. It is probable that the first attack caused the submarine to run into the bottom, because the lower bow cap was damaged and both caps were jammed, although set to release. The torpedo tubes had both been fired, although the bow caps had jammed on release. The lower tube had been fired with the external adjustment fittings engaged, and these had sheared off when the torpedo moved in the tube. This suggests that an attempt was made to fire in a hurry, and was prompted by, or interrupted by, the depth charge attacks. The tubes can be fired only from the Control Room; the release of the bow caps can be carried out only from forward; other operations in the tubes may be carried out from the Control Room or the forward compartment.

25. Both members of the crew were shot through the head; the demolition charges had been fired but the fuzes were drowned. It is possible that the junior member of the crew had attempted to escape, as he was found with his boots off. The Captain was wearing boots. This suggests that an early depth charge attack damaged the midget, and later ones progressively wrecked her.

SUMMARY

26. It is, then, considered that four midget submarines attempted to enter the harbour, of which only two —

      "Midget A"
      Midget 21

succeeded in passing the boom, and of which one —

      "Midget A"

got away again.

27. The other three midget submarines were destroyed:
      Midget 14 in the net at 2235/31.
      "Midget B" between Heads at 2307/31.
      Midget 21 in Taylor Bay between 0500 and 0827/1st June.

                    G.C. Muirhead-Gould
                        Rear-Admiral

JAPANESE MIDGET SUBMARINE ATTACK —
31st MAY — 1st JUNE, 1942
CHRONOLOGICAL NARRATIVE

TIME (K)	EVENTS
2000	Recorded crossing on No. 12 Loop
2015 approx	Watchman sighted suspicious object in nets near Sheerlegs — Western Channel. Watchman and mate proceeded in skiff to investigate.
2130 approx	Watchman proceeded to "YARROMA" and reported suspicious object. ("YARROMA" was duty Channel Patrol Boat at West Gate) "YARROMA" would not approach for fear that object was a magnetic mine.
2148	Recorded crossing on No. 12 Loop.
2152	88"YARROMA" reported "Suspicious object in net" and was told to close and give a full description.
2210	"YARROMA" reported object was metal with serrated edge on top, moving with the swell. "YARROMA" was ordered to give full description.
2220 approx	Stoker from "YARROMA" sent in Maritime Services Board skiff to investigate and reported object as submarine. "LOLITA" closed "YARROMA". Captain Bode, "CHICAGO", left TRESCO with suggestion that he should go to sea with "PERKINS".*
2227	N.O.C.S. to All Ships, Sydney — "Take A/S precautions." Port closed to outward shipping.

* A likely story!

2230   Watchman sent back to work.
        "YARROMA" reported — "Object is submarine.
        Request permission to open fire."

        "GOONAMBEE" ordered to proceed forthwith to
        investigate object at West Gate. 2nd Duty Staff
        Officer proceeded to Channel Patrol Boats not
        duty. ("GOONAMBEE" was duty M/S Vessel in
        Watsons Bay.)

2235   "YARROMA" reported submarine had blown up.

2236   N.O.C.S. TO GENERAL —
        "Presence of enemy submarine at boom gate is
        suspected. Ships are to take action against
        attack."

2252   "LAURIANA" noticed flurry on water ahead to port,
        investigated with searchlight which showed conning
        tower of submarine, distance 60 feet to 80 feet.
        Signalled Port War Signal Station, Channel Patrol
        Boat and Minesweeper entering harbour and Channel
        Patrol Boat at boom. ("LAURIANA" was one of four
        duty Naval Auxiliary Patrol Boats.)*
        No response.
        "CHICAGO" to N.O.C.S. — "Submarine periscope
        sighted about 500 yards off our starboard bow,
        heading up the channel."

2250   U.S.S. "CHICAGO" at No.2 Buoy switched on
to   searchlight and opened fire towards Fort Denison
2253   — red tracers (pom-pom).
approx Dockyard Motor Boat "NESTOR" halfway between
        ferry wharf and No.2 Buoy noticed disturbances
        in water 40 yards ahead. "CHICAGO'S" searchlight
        then illuminated periscope of submarine coming
        towards "NESTOR". Submarine was steering towards

---

*   In fact there were three, not four.

harbour bridge 200 yards off Garden Island.
Officer on Ferry Wharf saw periscope in
"CHICAGO'S" searchlight. Shots falling all round
it.

2254   "YANDRA" sighted conning tower 400 yards away
028° - 3 cables from Hornby Light. ("YANDRA" was
duty A/S Vessel on patrol within Loop Area.)

2255   "YANDRA" approached to attack.

2258   "YANDRA" attempted to ram submarine which
reappeared 100 yards astern, damaged, and slowly
turning to starboard. Position 283° 2.5 cables
from Hornby.

2259   "YANDRA" ordered to carry out A/S Sweep.
Negative result.

2300   "GOONAMBEE" proceeded from Watson's Bay to Gate
in West Channel. Patrolled Bradley's Head to
Gate. "YANDRA" at West Gate.

2303   "YANDRA" sighted conning tower 600 yards away.

2304   A/S contact obtained. "YANDRA" prepared to attack.

2307   "YANDRA" fired pattern of 6 depth charges set to
100 feet. Position 023° 3.6 cables from Hornby
Light. Submarine was not seen after explosions.

2310   "GEELONG" fired at suspicious object in line to
left Bradley's Head and, with "WHYALLA", swept
with searchlights for half an hour. ("GEELONG"
was A.M.S.* refitting alongside oil wharf.
"WHYALLA" was A/S vessel self refitting
alongside "GEELONG")

★ An Australian Mine Sweeper.

2314   N.O.C.S. signal — "All ships to be darkened."

2315   "BINGERA" ordered to immediate notice.
        ("BINGERA" was Stand Off A/S vessel at No.7
        Buoy.)
        U.S.S. "PERKINS" slipped and was ordered back to
        buoy by "CHICAGO" securing again at 2340 to No.4
        Buoy. ("PERKINS" at 4 hours notice at No.4 Buoy)

2330   "BINGERA" to N.O.C.S. — "Ready to proceed."

2334   "BINGERA" ordered to "slip and carry out A/S
        search in harbour. Submarine reported passing —
        proceeding towards harbour bridge."

2336   "BINGERA" reported — "Ready to proceed."
        Rear Admiral and Chief Staff Officer proceeded
        down harbour.

2340   "PERKINS" secured again No.4 Buoy. "BINGERA"
        slipped and proceeded up harbour.

0000   Rear Admiral and Chief Staff Officer boarded
        "LOLITA".

0025   Flood lights new dock extinguished by orders
        N.O.C.S.

0030   "KUTTABUL" hit by torpedo. All lights on Island
        were extinguished by the explosion and the
        telephone went out of order.

0034   Lights and telephone switchboard, Garden Island,
        come into service.

0045   "BOMBAY" "WHYALLA" ordered to raise steam.
        ("BOMBAY" was A.M.S. at 4 hours notice at No.9
        buoy.)
        "PERKINS" slipped.

0103   "BINGERA" ordered to slip between Bradley's Head and Garden Island.

0110   N.O.C.S. — General — "Enemy submarine is present in the harbour and "KUTTABUL" has been torpedoed."

0120   Submarine K.9 slipped and proceeded up harbour in tow. (K.9 was alongside "KUTTABUL")

0121   "ADELE" ready. Told to remain at Buoy. ("ADELE" was Stand Off Examination Vessel at Watson's Bay.)

0125   "SAMUEL BENBOW" reported — "Crew at action stations raising steam." ("SAMUEL BENBOW" was Stand Off M/S Vessel at Watsons Bay.)

0158   Crossing reported on No.12 Loop.

0214   "CHICAGO" to N.O.C.S. — "Proceeding to sea."

0230   "WHYALLA" to N.O.C.S. — "Slipped and proceeding to sea."

0230   Staff Officer, Channel Patrol Boats, received
to   orders to proceed and patrol when ready vicinity
0245   Bradley's Head.
        "TOOMAREE" — East Boom Gate.
        "MARLEAN" — West Boom Gate
        "SEA MIST" -   "   "   "
        "STEADY HOUR" to contact duty C.P.B's at boom —
        "LOLITA" and "YARROMA".
        (Stand off Channel Patrol Boats at Farm Cove.)

0243   "PERKINS" to sea.

0245   "STEADY HOUR" ordered "SEA MIST" to patrol
approx Bradley's Head — Boom.

0256   "'CHICAGO' to sea" reported by P.W.S.S.

0300   "CHICAGO" reported — "Submarine entering harbour."

0301   Crossing reported on No. 12 loop.

0305   "'WHYALLA' to sea" reported by P.W.S.S.

0307   N.O.C.S. ordered "BINGERA" — "Carry out A/S
        patrol in vicinity of 'CANBERRA'."

0320   "BOMBAY" reported — "Ready to proceed."

0335   C.P.B's proceeded on patrol
        Lieutenant Adams embarked in H.M.I.S. "BOMBAY"
        and proceeded to sea on A/S search as per
        N.O.C.S. 1735z/31.*

0340   L.F.B. 92 reported sighting submarine 5 miles
        off Port Hacking at 0105k/1.

0350   "KANIMBLA" switched on searchlight and opened
        fire. "BINGERA" searched area. ("KANIMBLA" was
        12 hours notice at Birts Buoy.)

0450   "DOOMBA" signalled "BINGERA" about submarine
approx   contact off Robertson Point. This was
        investigated without result.
        "CANBERRA" signalled unconfirmed sighting
        torpedo track from Bradley's Head at 0440.
        ("CANBERRA" at 4 hours notice at No 1 Buoy.)‡

---

* It is a bit of a mystery why Muirhead-Gould, with his reference to 1735z/31, should suddenly slip into Zulu time, commonly known as Greenwich Mean Time. Throughout the report he uses Kilo time, usually known as Australian Eastern Standard Time. There is a ten-hour difference between the two. The order referred to was therefore issued at 3.35 am on Monday morning Sydney time, and presumably is the same order as the one which sent the Channel Patrol boats into action.

‡ An anonymous hand has scribbled 'at immediate notice from 0115' below this entry.

0500   "YARROMA" and "SEA MIST" and "STEADY HOUR" all patrolling.

0500
approx Red Verey Light seen in Taylor Bay by "YARROMA" and depth charge explosion heard. "YARROMA" proceeded to scene at full speed and en route saw three more Verey Lights and heard further detonations.

0500
approx "STEADY HOUR" sighted suspicious object. Whilst proceeding up West Channel "SEA MIST" attacked and fired Verey Light (red). "SEA MIST" reported 3 submarines.

0500
approx "SEA MIST", at request of "GOONAMBEE", investigated suspicious object in Taylor Bay. Fired 2 depth charges on each occasion firing a Red Verey Light before so doing. Aldis Lamp was used to illuminate target.

0511   N.O.C.S. stopped all sailings from Newcastle and Port Kembla.

0532   "BOMBAY" to sea.

0540   P.W.S.S. reported 2 Red Flares, apparently from ship anchored on bank.
Rear-Admiral-in-Charge and Chief Staff Officer proceeded down harbour.

0545   "BOMBAY", "WHYALLA", "YANDRA" on patrol outside Heads.

0640   "STEADY HOUR" dropped depth charge ("STEADY HOUR", "SEA MIST" on patrol Chowder Bay — Bradley's Head.)
"STEADY HOUR" dropped second charge and marker buoy in same place.

0658   "YARROMA" picked up A/S contact of submarine —
        confirmed dropped one charge.

0718   "YARROMA" — second attack — one charge. Brown
to   oily tinge in disturbance — oily smear arose.
0721

0725   "STEADY HOUR" reported attacking definite Asdic
        contact — oil and air bubbles.

0730   "WHYALLA" and "BOMBAY" joined company and
        conducted search.
        C.S.O. proceeded down harbour.

"WINBAH'S"   Reported by Commanding Officer, "STEADY
arrival at   HOUR" that his anchor had caught up in
Taylor Bay   submarine and light oil film and large
                bubbles clearly visible.

0755   "YARROMA'S" third attack — same attack
        0718-0721. (Then stationary.)

0827   "YARROMA" — 4th and last attack — Oil and air
        bubbles continued to rise.

APPENDIX II
SOURCES OF INFORMATION

(a) <u>Documents recovered from Midget 21</u> (translated at Navy Office, Melbourne).

These disclosed the existence of an "Advanced Detachment" comprising:

Four Surface Vessels.

Eleven "I" Class submarines:

	I 10
	I 16
	I 18
	I 20
	I 21
	I 22
	I 24
	I 27
	I 28
	I 29
	I 30

Eight "Midgets"

	9
	21
	22
	23
	25
	26
	27
	28

Call signs for aircraft attached to I 10, I 21, I 29, I 30.

It is interesting to note that Midget No. 14 is not mentioned.

(b) <u>Charts recovered from Midget 21.</u>

(i) "Picking up dispositions" apparently placed five "I" class submarines at various rendezvous North and South of Sydney.

These were —
I 21
I 22
I 24
I 27
I 29

Two of the above, I 21 and I 29, were allotted aircraft call signs.

(ii) The courses from Sydney to the rendezvous off Broken Bay (shown on the Photostat portion of Chart attached) led to four "I" class submarines (I 22, I 24, I 27 and I 29), leaving I 21 apparently free to act as leader and possibly with her aircraft in lieu of, and not in addition to, a midget.

(iii) A working chart showing fixes due East of Sydney Heads, the seaward one being marked "1625".

These fixes (marked on attached Photostat of portion of Chart) were :

Outer South Head Light 260° 7.2 miles
Outer South Head Light 253° 4.1 miles
Outer South Head Light 247° 3.6 miles
Outer South Head Light 260° 1.7 miles

(iv) Courses were marked on a Sydney Harbour chart recovered from Midget No. 21.

APPENDIX III
SUBMARINE AND TORPEDO PARTICULARS
(operational only)

	Submarine No. 14	Submarine No. 21	"Midget A"
Depth set on Midget's Depth Gear.	46'		
Maximum depth which can be set on submarine.	30 metres.		
Depth set on torpedoes:			
Metres:	6m./6m.	6m./6m.	5m.
Feet:	19.5'/19.5'	19.5'/19.5'	16.3'
Angle set.	Zero.	Zero.	60° left.
Torpedoes:			
Stop Valves:	Shut.	Open.	
Bow Caps:	On.	Half off, levers moved to "release"	
Air Vessel pressure:	2810 lb/sq.in 2810 lb/sq.in	Nil. Nil.	
Demolition charges:	1 fired. 1 fuze drowned	2 fuzes drowned	

APPENDIX IV
LOOP INDICATIONS AND SIGNATURES

Although two loops were in operation (No. 11, laid in 14/15 fathoms, and No. 12, laid in 6/7 fathoms) signatures were registered on No. 12 only.

Four signatures were observed on this loop, at 2001, 2148, 0158 and 0301.

At first these were all believed to indicate inward crossings.

Subsequently, however, it was decided that the 0158 signature could have recorded a crossing in the opposite direction from the other three.

It has accordingly been taken as an outward crossing.

Prints of signatures are attached.

APPENDIX V
LESSONS LEARNT

MISTAKES MADE AND REMEDIES

(a) Unidentified loop crossings at 2001 and 2148 were
     not recognized. Considerable confusion is caused by
     traffic over loops.

Remedies

(i)   Manly Ferry Service has been curtailed and
       arrangements have been made to stop it at
       short notice.

(ii)   Port will be closed to small boats at night.

(iii) Loop Indicator Signal Apparatus is being
       fitted to Local Defence Vessels.

(iv)   Searchlight illumination of the loop area
       has been improved.

(v)   Maritime Services Board is stopping trips by
       spoil lighters and tugs at night.

(b) "YARROMA" failed to engage the submarine.

Remedy

All officers commanding Channel Patrol Boats have
been given more definite instructions.

(c) Depth charges were not capable of exploding in
     depths under 42 feet.*

Remedy

All depth charge pistols issued to Channel Patrol
Boats and Naval Auxiliary Patrol have been modified
to fire at 25 feet.

---

* An anonymous hand has written below this entry: 'The charges were dropped in greater
depths than 7fm.' Seven fathoms is, of course, 42 feet.

(d) <u>Communications</u> through the Port War Signal Station
were very slow. The correct R/T transmitter at Port
War Signal Station was not fitted as it was not
completed. The improvised set was not satisfactory.
The F.S.6.R/T in the Channel Patrol Boats was
unsuitable and could not be used when engines were
running.

<u>Remedies</u>

A suitable R/T Teleradio Set has been tried out and
is being recommended for fitting in Channel Patrol
Boats and Naval Auxiliary Patrol boats.

It is recommended that R/T Sets be fitted in
Examination Vessels, and the Staff Office, Pott's
Point. This will save personnel in Examination
Vessels and permit control of Channel Patrol Boats
from Staff Office, if required.

It is recommended that W/T Set ex Port War Signal
Station be fitted in Staff Offices, Pott's Point,
for use as Port Wave W/T Station. This will reduce
delay in working Local Defence Vessels and save
overloading telephone lines between Port War Signal
Station and Staff Office. (See also Lt.Cdr Cox's
AC/5?42 on 3rd June, 1942, to D.N.I. & D.S.C.)

(e) Naval Auxiliary Patrol vessels were not armed.

<u>Remedy</u>

Naval Auxiliary Patrol Vessels are being supplied
with depth charges, machine guns, Verey Pistols and
Aldis lamps.

APPENDIX VI
RECOMMENDATIONS FOR RECOGNITION OF PERSONNEL

The following are recommended to the notice of the
Naval Board for their display of zeal and determination
throughout the operation :-

(1) Mr. J. Cargill. For vigilance and initiative in his
personal efforts to report a
suspicious circumstance to the
proper authorities.
(It is for consideration whether
this man has merited an award under
the provisions of A.F.O. 1464(1) of
1941.)

and

(2) Mr W. Nangle   who, to a lesser degree, assisted
Mr Cargill.*

(3) Lieutenant A.G. Townley, R.A.N.V.R.
and the crew of H.M.A.S. "STEADY
HOUR".

(4) Sub-Lieutenant J.A. Doyle, R.A.N.R. (S)
and the crew of H.M.A.S. "SEA
MIST".

(5) Lieutenant J.A. Taplin R.A.N.R. (S)
and the crew of H.M.A.S. "YANDRA".

(6) Engineer Captain A.B. Doyle, C.B.E., R.A.N.
and

(7) Commander (E) G.C. Clark, R.A.N.
These officers arrived on the scene
minutes after the explosion which
sank "KUTTABUL", and displayed

---

* The words 'to a lesser degree' have been crossed out in ink.

commendable fortitude in searching the vessel for any man who might be trapped. In doing so, they had to wade in deep water, under hazardous conditions, in darkness, as it was not known at the time which portion of the decks had been rendered dangerous by the explosion. They lent assistance to a number of men who had been shocked by the suddenness and force of the action.

(8) <u>Bandsman M.N. Cumming, Official No. 20501.</u>

This rating, who was onboard "KUTTABUL" at the time of the explosion, showed determination in diving into the water from the vessel, swimming a few yards and assisting a rating on to "KUTTABUL'S" deck. He also again dived into the water into "KUTTABUL'S" wreckage in order to see whether anyone needed assistance. Although no great courage or endurance was necessary, he displayed considerable initiative.

(9) <u>Mr F.J. Lingard (Torpedo Fitter)</u>.

For the removal of pistols and primers from torpedoes, and demolition charges from submarines, this work being carried out entirely voluntarily.

<u>The Skipper and crew of Naval Auxiliary Patrol Boat, "LAURIANA"</u>.

For prompt action in illuminating the submarine.

<u>The Captain and crew of H.M.A.S. "YARROMA"</u>.

> For their part in the sinking of
> Midget 21. It is considered that
> this action redeemed, to some
> extent, their earlier failure.

<u>All personnel of the Dockyard First Aid Party</u>.

> For their efficient handling of
> casualties.

Acknowledgements

Every author owes a debt to those who have tackled his subject before him, and I am happy to acknowledge the huge debt I owe to others. My old boss Charles ('Hank') Bateson's magisterial work *The War with Japan: A Concise History* remains the definitive account of Japan's role in World War II, and was an invaluable insight into Japanese motives and plans. *Total War: The Causes and Courses of the Second World War* by Peter Calvocoressi, Guy Wint and John Pritchard provided a detailed chronology of the war, and some new perspectives.

Australia Under Siege: Japanese Submarine Raiders 1942 by Steven L. Carruthers is the first full account of the midget submarine raid on Sydney, and challenged the bland reassurances of the official version. Steve did all the hard work of obtaining previously hidden documents, using the Freedom of Information Act. An expanded and revised version of the first book was published in 2006 under the title *Japanese Submarine Raiders 1942: A Maritime Mystery*. My debt to Steve goes deeper than the pleasure of reading his two books: he generously gave me access to all his tapes and files accumulated over 25 years of living with this story. Steve's and my priorities are different, and our accounts are very different in style and emphasis. However, much of the first-hand material in this book about Reg Andrew and the events in Taylors Bay, and also the events aboard the USS *Chicago*, comes from Steve's files, including the taped interviews with Reg Andrew. In some 39 years in the publishing business, I have never known an author to be so uninhibitedly generous to a fellow scribe.

The Coffin Boats: Japanese Midget Submarine Operations in the Second World War by Peggy Warner and Sadao Seno broke new ground by telling the Japanese side of the story in detail. David Jenkins' *Battle Surface! Japan's Submarine War against Australia 1942–44* is a fine work of scholarship and sets a standard against which all subsequent books on this subject will be judged. It is currently out of print. The same author's *Hitting Home: The Japanese Attack on Sydney 1942* is a briefer account, but equally sound, and happily now available again. *Curtin's Gift* by John Edwards is by far the most authoritative account of Curtin's role in the war, and neatly skewers a lot of myths surrounding Curtin's wartime leadership. Dr Steven Bullard's *Blankets on the Wire: The Cowra Breakout and its Aftermath* takes the reader as close as any Westerner can come to understanding the Japanese warrior's acceptance of death, and shame at the thought of surrender. Dr Bullard is the grandson of Lance Bullard, the diver who played so large a part in the raising of the midget submarines. I confess to a soft spot for *Toku Tai: Japanese Submarine Operations in Australian Waters* by Lew Lind. The author and I have often come to very different conclusions from the same set of facts, but his book is distinguished by an entertaining scepticism when confronted with an official account, and I enjoyed every word of it.

The staff at the Public Records Office in Kew, England, were endlessly helpful as I ploughed through war cabinet records. Veteran submariners at the Submarine Museum in Gosport, England, gave valuable advice on the vexed question of how and why torpedoes miss. The staff at the Australian War Memorial in Canberra were unsparing in their help, as were the staff of the State Library of New South Wales in Sydney and the State Library of Victoria in Melbourne. The Australian National Archive collection in Melbourne gave me superb access to original documents. I confess to a hair-prickling moment as I handled the original typed top copy of Rear Admiral Muirhead-Gould's 16 July report on the incident, neatly signed in his blue fountain pen ink.

The staff of the Naval Historical Foundation in Washington and the Modern Military Records Branch of the National Archives and Records Administration in College Park, Maryland, were endlessly and cheerfully helpful. My particular thanks to Laura Waayers and Jodi Foor.

In Sydney, the National Maritime Museum oral history collection gave me some excellent first-hand accounts of the night of 31 May 1942. Dr David Stevens and John Perryman of the Sea Power Centre in Canberra guided me through fascinating day-to-day original documents from cash account books to ships' histories. David's investigation into torpedo tracks, published in the *Australian War Memorial Journal* in April 1995, was the first account I read which made sense of why Ban's torpedoes missed *Chicago* and found *Kuttabul* instead. Commander Shane Moore, director of the Naval Heritage Collection at Spectacle Island in Sydney, was tirelessly patient as I plied him with layman's questions on subjects as diverse as how torpedo engines work to the prevailing sea currents off Sydney Heads. Sue Thompson, deputy curator of the Naval Heritage Collection, went to endless trouble to dig out and scan historic photographs. Tim Smith, Senior Heritage Officer at the New South Wales Heritage Office, patiently explained the niceties of dealing with historic wrecks. John Darroch's encyclopaedic knowledge of Sydney ferry history was patiently offered, and willingly accepted. Rodney Champness gave invaluable help unravelling the mysteries of 1942 military radio sets, especially FS6.

David and Kristin Williamson generously allowed me to share their research for *The Last Bastion*, a television mini-series setting out the political background to Australia's entry into World War II, which David co-wrote with Denis Whitburn. Kristin's book *The Last Bastion* rises well above the television tie-in category, as befits the holder of a first-class honours degree in Australian history.

My French friend Vanessa Pigeon translated original Japanese documents into English from her home in Monterey, Mexico, thereby demonstrating that the global village has well and truly arrived. Roger Doyle used his spectacular talents as a sound engineer to resuscitate Reg Andrew's 30-year-old audio tapes. Without Roger, they might have been lost to posterity.

My special thanks go also to Google and the World Wide Web, whose 24/7 services were particularly helpful in the early stages of my research. There cannot be a single crackpot theory without its web page, and a Google search of some of the key words in this book will take you on a magical mystery tour through irrationality, hysteria, fantasy, paranoia and plain old-fashioned nuttiness, relieved by some wonderfully erudite and helpful material.

Nelson Mews, Steven Carruthers and Helen Young all read the manuscript and saved me from my many sins. All remaining errors are, of course, mine alone. There would have been more of them without Nels, Steve and Hellie.

I cannot find words of praise enough for my publishers Allen & Unwin, who were endlessly encouraging (Rebecca Kaiser, managing editor), then stylish, meticulous, sympathetic and patient (Angela Handley, my editor) throughout the whole process of creating this book. It is a measure of A&U's personal commitment to the project that the cover features a picture of Angela's family preparing for the worst in Sydney in 1942. In an age when the cultures of book publishing and factory farming seem to be converging, A&U is an oasis of flair, good humour and professionalism.

I owe a debt to friends and family who gave me bed and food while I was researching in Sydney: Leigh and Jenny Virtue, Mary and Van McCune, Karma Abraham and Lenore Nicklin, and my brother-in-law Selwyn Owen; elsewhere in New South Wales, Kristin and David Williamson, and Annie and Barry Knight; in Victoria, Sheryl and Craig Cooté, Robert Foster and Jack Bell.

John and Cabby Gunter patiently ferried me around Sydney Harbour in *Delta Skelter*, while I pored over charts trying to find the *exact* location of long-disappeared torpedo tracks, boom nets, indicator loops, and the like. My brother Doug handed over his venerable and dogged Ford

Fairlane, and it shuttled me flawlessly between Sydney and Canberra. Without their generosity, support and good company the task of writing this book would have been much less enjoyable.

Official reports are inclined to skim over unpalatable facts. Their first purpose is often to win medals or to protect the writer's backside, rather than to record the truth. For that reason, in these pages I have often parted company with the accepted version of events. I have also tried hard to stick to primary sources rather than pick my way through the maze of conflicting stories in books, newspapers and magazines, and in radio and television documentaries. With that in mind, my biggest vote of thanks must go to the people who gave unsparingly of their time and memories while I was researching this book. The heroism of the Japanese sailors who mounted the raid on Sydney Harbour has been widely and rightly recognised. My heroes and heroines are the men and women of Sydney: the under-armed, under-trained and often erratically led soldiers, sailors and airmen who found themselves facing a lethal attack where they least expected it, in their own harbour; and the ordinary citizens of Sydney, fearful of an unfamiliar and apparently invincible enemy, who reacted with characteristic good humour to his sudden arrival on their doorsteps.

Bibliography

I have deliberately avoided peppering the text of this book with a profusion of footnotes and references. The publishers and I readily agreed these would achieve little for most readers while slowing the pace of the narrative. Nevertheless, specialist readers and scholars are entitled to know on what authority the author bases his facts.

My primary sources included taped interviews with Jean Andrew, Don Caldwell Smith, Rahel Cohen, Jeff Cooté, Kevin Cooté, Margaret Coote (*née* Hamilton), Donald Dunkley, David Goldstone, Dr James Macken, Ian Mitchell, and 'Darby' Munro. Copies of these interviews will be deposited with the Naval Heritage Centre, Garden Island, where they will be available to researchers. I also drew on taped interviews with Reg Andrew, and log books and other documents, from the author Steven Carruthers. Steve's material included transcripts of research interviews with officers from USS *Chicago* conducted in 1981 and 1982 for the television documentary *Warriors of the Deep*. The interviews were not included in the broadcast version, and only the transcripts survive. Steve intends to deposit this material with the Sea Power Centre in Canberra, where it will be available to scholars.

Roy Cooté's dive log and photographs were supplied by his grandson Craig Cooté. The original log book is now with the Naval Heritage Centre on Garden Island. Other first person accounts came from publicly available documents lodged in the Australian National Archive, most often with its Melbourne centre, and at the Australian War Memorial, in Canberra. I drew on British cabinet minutes and papers from 1939 to 1942, freely available at the Public Records Office in Kew, and on intelligence digests and summaries for April, May and June 1942, lodged with the Naval Historical Foundation in Washington. Contemporary newspapers also provided a host of material. Newspapers are stored on microfilm at the various state libraries around Australia, and I drew heavily from records held at the State Library of New South Wales and the State Library of Victoria.

BOOKS

Bateson, Charles, *The War with Japan: A Concise History*, Ure Smith, Sydney; Barrie and Jenkins, London; Michigan State University Press, East Lansing, 1968.

Bullard, Steven, *Blankets on the Wire: The Cowra Breakout and its Aftermath*, Australian War Memorial, Canberra, 2006.

Burlingame, Burl, *Advance Force Pearl Harbor*, Naval Institute Press, Annapolis, 1992.

Calvocoressi, Peter, Wint, Guy and Pritchard, John, *Total War: The Causes and Courses of the Second World War*, Viking, London, 1972, revised 1989.

Carruthers, Steven L., *Australia Under Siege: Japanese Submarine Raiders 1942*, Solus Books, Sydney, 1982.

—— *Japanese Submarine Raiders 1942: A Maritime Mystery*, Casper Publications, Sydney, 2006.

Edwards, John, *Curtin's Gift*, Allen & Unwin, Sydney, 2005.

Fullford, R.K., *We Stood and Waited: Sydney's Anti-Ship Defences 1939–1945*, Royal Australian Artillery Society, Sydney, 1994.

Gill, G. Hermon, *Royal Australian Navy 1942–1945 Vol. 2*, Australian War Memorial, Canberra, 1968.

Jenkins, David, *Battle Surface! Japan's Submarine War against Australia 1942–44*, Random House, Sydney, 1992.

——*Hitting Home: The Japanese Attack on Sydney 1942*, Random House, Sydney, 1992.

Leasor, James, *Singapore: The Battle that Changed the World*, Hodder & Stoughton, London, 1968.

Lind, Lew, *Toku Tai: Japanese Submarine Operations in Australian Waters*, Kangaroo Press, Sydney, 1992.

Newcomb, Richard F., *The Battle of Savo Island*, Henry Holt and Company, New York, 1961.

Oppenheim, Peter, *The Fragile Forts: The Fixed Defences of Sydney Harbour*, Australian Military History Publications, Loftus, 2005.

Pfenningworth, Ian, *A Man of Intelligence: The Life of Captain Eric Nave, Australia's Codebreaker Extraordinary*, Rosenberg Publishing Pty Ltd, Sydney, 2006.

Reid, Richard, *No Cause for Alarm: Submarine Attacks on Sydney and Newcastle May–June 1942*, Department of Veterans' Affairs, Canberra, 2002.

Royal Australian Navy, *A–Z Ships, Aircraft and Shore Establishments*, Navy Public Affairs, Sydney, 1996.

Stevens, David, *A Critical Vulnerability: The Impact of the Submarine Threat on Australia's Maritime Defence*, Sea Power Centre, Canberra, 2005.

Warner, Peggy and Seno, Sadao, *The Coffin Boats: Japanese Midget Submarine Operations in the Second World War*, Leo Cooper/Secker & Warburg, London, 1986.

Williamson, Kristin, *The Last Bastion*, Lansdowne Press, Melbourne, 1984.

Winton, John, *Ultra in the Pacific: How Breaking Japanese Codes and Ciphers Affected Naval Operations against Japan, 1941–45*, Naval Institute Press, Annapolis, 1994.

KEY DOCUMENT FOLDERS
National Archives of Australia, Melbourne
B6121 Midget Submarine Attack on Sydney Harbour—Signals.

MP138/1 Steady Hour—Sinking of Japanese Midget Submarine.

MP138/1 Japanese Midget Submarine—Sections Stowed at Clark Island.

MP150/1 Naval Auxiliary Patrol.

MP151/1 Awards in Connection with Japanese Midget Submarine Attack.

MP1049/5 Midget Submarine Attack on Sydney Harbour.

MP1185/9 Publicity Contravening Censorship Requests, Midget Submarine Attack.

Australian War Memorial, Canberra

AWM52 Weekly Intelligence Summaries—Submarine Attack Sydney Harbour.

AWM54 Japanese Midget Submarine Attack—Reconstruction of Events.

AWM54 Weekly Intelligence Summaries—Submarine Attack Sydney Harbour, 1942.

AWM54 Plans and Diagrams, Photographs of Midget Submarine.

AWM67 Official History, 1939–45 War: Records of Gavin Long, General Editor.

AWM124 Report of Investigation into Japanese Torpedo.

PR 86/24 Lance Bullard's Account of the Divers' Role.

Sea Power Centre, Canberra

Register of Requisitioned Motor Patrol Boats and Miscellaneous Examination Vessels and Harbour Craft.

Naval Historical Foundation, Washington

SRNS-0001-0078 Summary of Japanese Naval Activities.

SRNS-1517 FRUMEL Daily Digest.

Public Records Office, Kew

Cabinet Minutes and Papers, 1939–1942.

Television documentaries

He's Coming South—Animax Films, 2005.

Sydney at War: The Untold Story—Australian Film Commission, 2004.

Warriors of the Deep—Program Development, 1982.